Economic Analysis of Law in European Legal Scholarship

Volume 21

The purpose of the book series "Economic Analysis of Law in European Legal Scholarship" is to publish high quality volumes in the growing field of law and economics research in Europe, from a comprehensive theoretical and practical vantage point. In particular, the series will place great emphasis on foundational and theoretical aspects of economic analysis of law and on interdisciplinary approaches in European Legal Scholarship. Following Nobel laureate Ronald Coase's famous essay "The Problem of Social Cost" (1960) fifty years ago law and economics has become the lingua franca of American jurisprudence. In recent decades, law and economics has also gained widespread popularity in Europe and its influence on Legal Scholarship is growing significantly.

Therefore, the economic analysis of law in European Legal Scholarship academic book series illustrates how law and economics is developing in Europe and what opportunities and problems – both in general and in specific legal fields – are associated with this approach within the legal traditions of European countries. Rather than further exploring economic analysis as such, the main focus of this series lies on the implementation of economic methods in legislation and legal adjudication from a European perspective. It takes into account the particular challenges the European legal systems face. Volumes will address law and economics research in Europe from a critical and comparative viewpoint. The studies in this series are strong and bold narratives of the development of economic analysis of law in European Legal Scholarship. Some are suitable for a very broad readership.

Contributions in this series primarily come from scholars in Europe. The purpose is to provide the next generation of European lawyers with the models and skills needed to understand and improve the economic analysis of law in their own legal field. The series includes monographs focusing on specific topics as well as collections of essays covering specific themes.

Silvia Zorzetto • Betzabé Marciani Burgos
José Enrique Sotomayor Trelles
Francesco Ferraro
Editors

Developments in Law and Economics in the Italo-Iberoamerican Context

Springer

Editors
Silvia Zorzetto
Department of Law
University Telematica Pegaso
Naples, Italy

José Enrique Sotomayor Trelles
Pontifical Catholic University of Peru
Lima, Peru

Betzabé Marciani Burgos
Pontifical Catholic University of Peru
Lima, Peru

Francesco Ferraro
Department of Law "Cesare Beccaria"
University of Milan
Milano, Italy

ISSN 2512-1294 ISSN 2512-1308 (electronic)
Economic Analysis of Law in European Legal Scholarship
ISBN 978-3-032-03316-1 ISBN 978-3-032-03317-8 (eBook)
https://doi.org/10.1007/978-3-032-03317-8

This Springer imprint is published by the registered company Springer Nature Switzerland AG
The registered company address is: Gewerbestrasse 11, 6330 Cham, Switzerland

Contents

Civil Law as a Common Heritage, Challenges for Law and Economics and for Comparative Law

Hans-Bernd Schäfer

Abstract This chapter reproduces the lecture delivered at the conference of the Italian Law and Economics Association in Brescia in December 2023. The programme itself demonstrates how vibrant and fruitful our discipline remains in Italy—perhaps the only Western country where an institutional approach to economics has deep roots and has never faded. I have often felt that Italian scholars have easier access to the study of institutions than their German counterparts. In the nineteenth century, the latter were influenced by the historical school, which rightly emphasised the role of institutions but was often insufficiently analytical to produce significant general hypotheses or theorems. Subsequently, German economists adopted neoclassical economics, which, while analytical, lacked a comprehensive understanding of institutions. I am also mindful that Italy is both the birthplace and ancestral home of civil law as we know it. In the late medieval period, university scholars in Italy not only revived Roman law but also developed new legal concepts and frameworks. They conceptualised law as a system—a legal order—and placed particular emphasis on the individual. Jim Gordley has recently described this phenomenon as a big bang, while Harold Berman referred to it as a legal revolution. The work of the eminent academic figures of the twelfth and thirteenth centuries had a formative influence on the development of law across much of Western (Latin) Europe for centuries to come. The original lecture, and thus this chapter, offers an opportunity to share reflections on Western European civil law with distinguished Italian scholars. This chapter explores that legacy, viewing it both as an inspiration and a challenge.

H.-B. Schäfer (✉)
Bucerius Law School and University of Hamburg, Hamburg, Germany
e-mail: hans-bernd.schaefer@law-school.de

S. Zorzetto et al. (eds.), *Developments in Law and Economics in the Italo-Iberoamerican Context*, Economic Analysis of Law in European Legal Scholarship 21, https://doi.org/10.1007/978-3-032-03317-8_1

1 Some Critical Voices on Civil Law

First, I want to summarize some views of private law—that is the law of property, contracts, and torts—in civil law countries, and ask how these views influence economic research on civil law. Unlike common law countries, civil law countries have national civil codes. Many of these are heavily influenced by the French Code Civil of 1804, some others by the German BGB of 1900. I would like to comment on several propositions about civil law that can be found partly in the law and economics literature and partly among legal scholars.

1. The fact that the rules of private law are codified and enacted by a legislative body led to the view that law and economics scholars can analyze the consequences of these norms. However, the research results of the scholars cannot influence jurisprudence as a decision-making theory for courts because judges in civil law countries only interpret the law, not create and develop it as they do in common law countries. Normative economic postulates based on welfare and efficiency can only be addressed to the legislature but not to a court.[1] A second and related view on private law of civil law countries is that it follows a top-down approach from the center of the state and is distorted by vested interests and lobby groups. Common law, on the other hand, is a bottom-up approach.[2] Courts in common law countries follow the public interest because they cannot be captured by interest groups. The decentralized structure of their decision-making and their independence guarantee this. This view explicitly or implicitly assumes that the role of judges in civil law countries is fundamentally different and more constrained than in common law countries. Another related criticism claims that civil law rules are sticky and inflexible. Judges cannot correct outdated black letter law if parliaments remain inactive because enacting marginal changes overwhelms their organizational capacity.[3]
2. The national codifications since the end of the eighteenth century put an end to the continental European jus commune, which was common to all Latin European countries, regardless of their polity. This reduced the scientific character of the discipline of law, which was based on reason, teleology, and systemic thinking about a "legal order" and which it had achieved in the late Middle Ages. The study of law thus mutated into a kind of area studies or a national geography of law.[4] This made it more difficult to understand the foundations of civil law.[5]

[1] Eidenmüller (2015).

[2] De Geest (2020).

[3] Ehrlich and Posner (1974), pp. 257–286. For a survey on an extended debate see Parisi (2004), pp. 519–22.

[4] Kötz (1996) Europäisches Vertragsrecht, Mohr Siebeck, European Contract Law (2017), Oxford University Press, VI. 2nd English ed.

[5] Zimmermann (2001), https://doi.org/10.1093/acprof:oso/9780198299134.001.0001.

3. A widespread view among legal scholars is that a more economic approach to law is an external concept alien to law, which has no place in the study of civil legal norms or at least not in the interpretation of the rules of the civil codes.[6]

I shall deal with these three aspects in more detail.

2 Inflexibility of Civil Law Systems?

A civil code may, but need not, lead to rigidity and inflexibility. This view is supported by Montesquieu, who called for a clear division of labour between the judiciary and the legislature. However, this would make the judiciary not one of the three branches of government, but powerless, or in Montesquieu's words: "Dans de tels régimes, en effet, la puissance «de juger est, en quelque façon, nulle»". In such a state, the power to judge is in some way nil.[7] This view that the law is written in black letters that determine all decisions was a rationalist idea of the eighteenth century. Developed in France, it became particularly influential in Prussia, the first European state to enact a comprehensive code, the Prussian State Law of 1794, 10 years before the Code Civil. Initiated by King Frederick II, it became a model of precision and rationalist perfectionism. The king controlled its drafting and was obsessed with eliminating "all the subtlety stuff", replacing it with precise norms, simplifying the law and making "lawyers superfluous", thus resolving all conflicts with a large machine at his service.[8] This perfectionist law, whose authors confused the ideal legislator with the ideal watchmaker and which contained 19,000 articles compared to the 2300 articles of the Code Civil, was insofar a caricature and the result of an idée fixe. No wonder that it never really got off the ground. It did, however, promote the popular view of law in civil law countries. The more successful codifications, such as the Code Civil of 1804, the Austrian Civil Code of 1811, the Italian Codice civile of 1865, and later the German Civil Code of 1900, did not attempt to abolish legal reasoning and the role of judges. They are part of a centuries-old legal tradition that is common to all Latin European countries and that continues to shape legal thought in Western Europe.

3 The Legacy of Jus Commune

That Western Europe has long been a zone of strife, feuds, and wars can easily obscure the fact that it is also a part of the world with a longstanding common legal tradition. Drawing on Roman law and its reception across much of Europe,

[6] Canaris (1993), pp. 377–391, http://www.jstor.org/stable/20820926. See also Eidenmüller (2015).
[7] Montesquieu (1748).
[8] Schäfer and Ott (2022).

introducing canon law, and merging with Germanic legal traditions, a ius commune emerged as a Western European legal order that existed independently of the polities.[9] Scholastic lawyers and clerics laid its foundations in the twelfth and thirteenth centuries, along with groundbreaking legal innovations. Individual will and autonomy became more and more the focus of the law. Judge-made law abolished the classical Roman numerus clausus of enforceable contracts and replaced it with a general freedom of contract based on private autonomy. Scholastic scholars developed a science of law for the content of private (civil) law, mercantile law, urban law, manorial law, and feudal law, which included a systematic and consistent "legal order" with rules of interpretation, the hierarchization of legal norms, the resolution of conflicts of law, the proposition of overarching legal principles, the use of analogy and teleological reasoning, and the preservation of the internal consistency of the legal order.[10] This gave law a new coherence, flexibility, and capacity for innovation. A "legal order" replaced the pre-existing thicket of custom. Reinhard Zimmermann has written of these developments: "A characteristic feature of this tradition is the pursuit of rationality, a scientific character of law, intellectual coherence and system, while ensuring organic capacity for development".[11] Universities, which enjoyed a high degree of autonomy became centers of education, especially legal education. As Joseph Schumpeter points out in his book on the history of economic analysis, a non-clerical intellectual class with university degrees supplanted the traditional clerical elites. Judges were increasingly university-trained "legal experts". The discipline of "learned law" became international and independent of statehood within Latin Europe, with the same curricula, including Roman and canon law, in almost all Western European universities, including Oxford and Cambridge in England. These legal changes in the late middle ages had a long-term positive impact on the economic development of Western Europe.

4 Example, the Removal of the Ban on Interest

Joseph Schumpeter and Elaine Tan,[12] in their writings on the medieval prohibition of interest on loans, showed how far scholastic legal reasoning could go. Legal scholars and judges in the canon courts of the thirteenth century turned this prohibition into an empty shell for commercial loans. It was gradually abolished throughout Europe, first in the ecclesiastical canon courts, which had jurisdiction over the sin of usury, and later in all other courts during the legal revolution of the twelfth and thirteenth centuries. Lawyers had argued that the sale of goods on trade credit at a higher price was a circumvention of the prohibition of taking interest on loans.

[9] Zimmermann (1990).

[10] Berman (1985); Gordley (2013).

[11] Translated from Zimmermann (2016), pp. 321–332.

[12] Tan (2002), pp. 177–195.

The difference between the contract price and the spot market price should be considered interest and therefore usury. The scholastics, on the other hand, argued that the higher price was legitimate. The price difference was not usury because the creditor lost something along the way, such as the opportunity to participate in a trade fair, as long as the price was not paid. Thus, the markup could be claimed as a kind of liquidated damages in the sense of losses (damnum emergens) or lost profits (lucrum cessans) if the debtor refused to pay the higher price. Under these conditions, the scholastics flatly rejected the prohibition of interest because it was not usury. Joseph Schumpeter writes in his History of Economic Analysis that this reasoning of the jurists came close to a general theory of interest, and that between their writings in the thirteenth century and the conceptualization of a general theory of interest in the nineteenth century, especially with the writings of Boehm Bawerk nothing of substance was written on the interest rate. This is an early example of an economic analysis of law with great impact. The explicit rejection of the prohibition of interest placed commercial credit contracts with an interest under the protection of the law and sparked the rise of a financial and banking industry, first in Italy and later in other countries of Latin Europe. In Muslim countries, on the other hand, this teleological reasoning, which led to the rejection of a norm because it did not serve the underlying rationale of prohibiting usury, did not develop. As Oberauer writes in his book on Islamic contract law, there was a substitute institution for an interest-bearing loan, the mudaraba, a silent partnership in which the partner received a fixed profit as a percentage of the amount invested, regardless of whether the company was profitable or not, insofar comparable with a credit.[13] But this was only a stilted workaround. It could not provide the legal protection of an outright teleological rejection of the prohibition of interest as in Western Europe. In Islamic countries, the prohibition of interest (riba) was often neither strictly enforced nor was the practice among merchants always in conformity with the law. However, the ban on riba remained an obstacle to the development of a financial industry because parties could not be sure whether a court would uphold the practice or reject it as an evasion. Although such practices were widespread, they did not have the full support of the legal system. As a result, credit institutions and a financial industry did not develop in Islamic countries until the nineteenth century.[14]

The scholarly and scientific perception of law in Western Europe, which began in the twelfth and thirteenth centuries, did not disappear with the national codifications since the late eighteenth century, but lives on in the reasoning of lawyers and legal practice even in the European Union and its member states. This heritage views the law as a consistent and principled legal order. Independent courts in this European tradition regard statutes and treaties not as mechanical black letter law but as living instruments.

I proceed to show how important Supreme Court decisions are for the development of law in countries that belong to the civil law family and that draw on

[13] Oberauer (2021).

[14] Oberauer (2014), pp. 111–123.

centuries of jus commune. This heritage, in turn, is based on a resurrected Roman law, the concentration of duties and rights at the individual level, the importance of individual choice, and the coherence of the legal order.

5 The Role of Courts in Civil Law Countries, Filling Gaps in Incomplete Laws

When the code civil was drafted, France was an agricultural country. Tort cases were neither complex nor numerous. Shying horses were a main cause of accidents. Accordingly, the authors of the code civil devoted only five sections to tort law. They did not pretend to have the knowledge to structure an undeveloped field of law in detail. Art. 1383, which has not been modified since 1804, is the only and comprehensive general clause of tort law, and it became a model for the civil codes of dozens of other countries. It reads:

> Any act whatever of man that causes damage to another, obliges him by whose fault it occurred to repair it.[15]

These few words are all that French courts have had to interpret a host of subtle legal issues. The question of when a compensation replaces repair, how to calculate damages, how to deal with future damages, with pure economic damages, normative damages, widespread damages, legitimate infliction of damages, emotional damages, mitigating damages, and problems of causation were left to the courts, which built an entire system of tort law on this narrow textual basis.

Law and economics scholars are familiar with the 1942 decision of the French Court of Cassation on the shipwreck of the *Lamoricière*. When a storm came up, the captain sought to reach a safe haven. When he ran out of coal, which was moreover of poor quality, the ship's speed was much reduced and the ship sank. In the ensuing legal proceedings, it was unclear whether the storm or the defendant (the coal dealer) had caused the accident. An expert witness testified that with better coal, the ship would have had a chance of reaching safe harbor. The Court of Cassation overturned the decisions of lower courts that had dismissed the case and awarded compensation. However, it held the defendant liable for only 20% of the damage because the accident was mainly due to external causes for which the defendant was not responsible. The French court assigned a liability amount equal to the damage multiplied by the probability that the ship sank due to an act for which the defendant was responsible.[16] This is just one of many causation rules that have been developed

[15] Code civil, translated by Georges Rouhette and rship's owner Anne Rouhette-Berton, https://www.fd.ulisboa.pt/wp-content/uploads/2014/12/Codigo-Civil-Frances-French-Civil-Code-english-version.pdf.

[16] University of Texas at Austin, Case:D (1951) 717, Case Transports maritimes de l'Etat v. Brossette and Bastard, 19 June 1951. https://law.utexas.edu/transnational/foreign-law-translations/french/case.php?id=1436.

in different countries to deal with this causation problem. Steven Shavell observed that this French judge-made rule, called "perte d'une chance", trumps all others in terms of efficiency.'[17] It is the only rule that guarantees that a wrongdoer's expected compensation is equal to the expected harm he has caused. It provides the right incentives to achieve the efficient level of care, as conceptualized by the Learned Hand test, and therefore leads to neither over—nor under-deterrence, regardless of whether the liability regime is fault—based or strict.

More generally, in civil law countries courts play a crucial role in contouring the law when the black latter law is vague or silent on the legal issue at hand. However, this is not their only role. More importantly, the courts maintain a legal order by using scientific methods to preserve its consistency and keep it related to fundamental principles. This is an important legacy of the scholarly legal revolution of the thirteenth century, which inter alia removed the inconsistent thicket within customary law.

6 Preserving Consistency

Does interpretation end when a legal norm is as precise and clear as possible? This would, of course, contradict a scientific approach to maintaining a consistent legal order, as two examples from German law show. A speed limit of 30 km per hour in a residential area is a crystal-clear legal rule based on a decree that contains no exceptions. However, several courts of appeal and the Supreme Court have ruled on exceptions. A physician rushing to an emergency can break the speed limit without violating the law. Someone driving a woman in labour to the hospital, or speeding to warn a truck driver that his load is about to break loose does not violate the law.[18] These are cases of exceptions, which contradict the wording of the black letter law. One can argue that these exceptions are implied conditions of the legal norm. The norm setter knows that there must be exceptions, but lacks the knowledge to enumerate them. Therefore, the norm of a speed limit contains an implicit delegation norm that allows the judiciary to introduce exceptions based on the principle that the ratio legis of a speed limit is to protect human health and life and that a speed limit without exceptions would violate this rationale. In line with this rationale, a court has ruled that a driver who speeds for the health or life of a pet must pay the

[17] Shavell (1987), pp. 123–126.

[18] Transportation of a pregnant woman after contractions began (Oberlandesgericht Düsseldorf, Beschluss vom 22.02.2015, Az. 5 Ss (OWI) 411/94 - (OWi) 211/94 I); emergency visit of a medical doctor (Oberlandesgericht Hamm, Beschluss vom 03.10.2001, Az. 1 Ss OWi 824/01); warning of a truck driver whose load was unsecured (Oberlandesgericht Köln, Beschluss vom 17.05.1994, Az. Ss 169/94 (B) - 93 B); speeding by a surgeon rushing to an emergency operation. Bayerisches Oberstes Landesgericht, Beschluss vom 01.10.1990, Az. 1 Ob OWi 331/90). Schäfer (2019), pp. 425–455.

administrative fine. Thus, while courts may override black letter law, they must remain loyal to the rationale of the law, which is to protect human life.

Without such interventions into black letter law, a legal order would become inconsistent and chaotic over time. All Western European civil law countries have developed such judicial routines to neglect the wording og black letter law when necessary to maintain consistency. But this is not a universal or necessary feature of civil law but a cultural achievement. Russia imported the civil law system in the nineteenth century, but a tsarist Russian reform commission explicitly rejected the introduction of the legal technique of complementary contract interpretation, which existed for instance in France, Italy, Germany and even in England under the concept of implied term of contract. This meant that Russian courts had less legal leeway in comparison to their colleagues in Western Europe.[19]

7 Removing Intolerable Value Contradictions

Can a court in a civil law country legitimately reject black latter law when it is either explicit or clear from the circumstances that the legislature wants to decide the matter without interference from the courts? It can, and when it does, the decisions are often milestones in legal development. Here is a case from German law: The owner of a brewery in Cologne was a passionate military rider. A photographer took a photo of the horse and the rider jumping over a fence and sold it to a company that used the photo to advertise its products (aphrodisiacs) in a magazine. This violated the rider's privacy, which German tort law protects with an injunctive right, a property rule in the sense of Calabresi & Melamed. Economically, this makes sense because property rules are more efficient than liability rules when transaction costs are low for voluntary transactions. This is clearly the case here, since the advertising firm could have made an offer to the plaintiff. The problem with this and similar cases was, however, that the injunctive right remained ineffective because the victim learns of the violation of his right only after the magazine is on the market, which is too late. The right to an injunction has not the intended effect. Therefore, the only way to protect privacy in such cases is to award damages to the plaintiff. And here is the legal problem: German law only provides for compensation for financial damages—emotional damages cannot be compensated. There are exceptions, but they are clearly stated in the Civil Code itself, namely compensation for pain and suffering in the cases of physical injury and interference with the victim's sexual self-determination, mainly in the case of rape, and some other explicit exceptions. Thus, the legislator clearly preferred a rule with a closed list of exceptions. And according to this rule, the plaintiff's damages were equal to his financial wealth without the violation of his privacy minus his wealth with the violation. This difference was zero as the tortious act did not reduce the plaintiff's brewery's sales. Still, contrary

[19] Avinarius (2014), p. 553.

to the wording of black letter law, the Supreme Court (BGH) awarded a sizeable damage compensation. The defendant appealed to the constitutional court, arguing that the BGH judges had violated Art. 20 (3) of the German constitution, which states that "the judiciary is bound by law and justice", and that the BGH's decision was unconstitutional. The Constitutional Court dismissed the appeal and upheld the award of damages. Essentially, the argument was this: The legal order protects privacy with the sharpest instrument, an injunction, i.e. a property right. Given the special circumstances of the press market, this instrument is of no value to the potential victim. This constellation usually leads to a second-best solution, namely an award of damages. In such cases, however, there is often no financial damage and consequently no legal protection of privacy at all. This leads to an intolerable contradiction with a legal principle of justice that justifies judge-made law, even contra legem, in order to give a protective norm some effectiveness. This landmark decision was not the end of the subsequent development. For some time, damages remained so low that publishers often continued to invade privacy by paying damages instead of honoraria, thus replacing a voluntary transfer of rights with an involuntary one, and still making a profit. This practice only ended when damages were increased to reflect the marginal profit from the invasion of privacy. To estimate the unobservable profit from the invasion of privacy, the courts use the observable price of an advertisement covering the same amount of space in the magazine as the story that violated the plaintiff's right to privacy. Only since then, and since this ruling has become judge-made law, has privacy been effectively protected. It incentivizes the yellow press to prefer negotiated and voluntary transfers of privacy to invasions of privacy and compensating the victim.[20]

We thus learn that legitimate judicial rejection of black letter law can even include contra legem jurisdiction when the consistency of the legal order and its central legal principles are otherwise jeopardized. Such judicial decisions have their roots in a tradition shared by all Western European countries, regardless of their political systems, a tradition that began in the twelfth and thirteenth centuries and that aims to maintain a legal order by defending its consistency and effectiveness. This is what legal historians have called the scientificisation (Verwissenschaftlichung) of legal reasoning.

8 Changing Interpretation of an Unchanged Law

In civil law countries, there are sometimes major changes in the law as the Supreme Court replaces one interpretation of the law with another that it deems superior. In Germany, the USA, and several other countries, damages are compensated only if they result from an injury to property, health, life, or another erga omnes property

[20] For a detailed presentation of the development of privacy protection in German civil liability see Kötz H & Wagner G, 172–74.

right. All other damages are considered pure economic losses for which there is no entitlement to compensation. Often such pure economic losses are socially irrelevant, because the tortious act uno actu causes losses and gains that cancel each other out. They are then comparable to losses that an entrepreneur inflicts on a competitor in fair competition. In this sense, non-compensation of pure economic losses is often economically justified. However, the German rule is clearly overinclusive and often leaves valuable resources legally unprotected.[21] Fishermen who lose income as a result of an oil spill are not compensated because they do not own the fish in the sea. They have no legal claim because their interest is not protected by a property right and is therefore a purel economic loss, even though this damage is not socially irrelevant. This is still the rule in Germany. In Italy, Art. 2043 of the codice civile contains a general clause that does not differentiate between damage to property and pure economic loss. However, until the 1970s, the Italian Supreme Court followed the German legal doctrine and its distinction between pure economic loss and loss resulting from the impairment of a property right under the concept of unlawfulness (un danno ingiusto). The Italian doctrine regarded only damage resulting in a violation of an erga omnes property right as a "danno inguisto".Otherwise the damage was not unlawful and was therefore comparable to damage resulting from the lawful acts of a competitor. However, in the 1970s, the Italian Supreme Court drastically changed the interpretation and case law, and with it Italian tort law.[22] Since then, the judge made law has differed significantly from German tort law, allowing compensation in cases where the losses are not socially irrelevant. This fundamental change occurred by reinterpretation, without one word in the Italian civil code being changed.

9 Responding to Economic Needs by Inventing New Legal Forms

In his book "The Mystery of Capital", Hernando de Soto laments that most developing countries fail to find routines to pledge movable assets like cattle, cars, or machines for better access to credit. He therefore calls these movable assets 'dead capital'.[23] For instance, the ability to pledge movables was drastically different in Tennessee and in Paraguay, two states with large ranching populations. In Tennessee, a valid credit contract requires only that the bank and the rancher agree that all the cattle on a well-defined parcel of land could be seized and sold by the bank if the debtor fails to service the debt. In Paraguay, this was much more complicated. Each head of cattle had to be listed by name or brand number. The list had to be continuously updated. If the entries in the list did not correspond to the individual pieces of

[21] For a survey of the discussion see Schäfer, H-B & Ott C, 278.

[22] Corte di Cassazione, 26.1.1971, Foro it. 1971 I 345. Schäfer and Ott (2022) Op. cit. pp. 279.

[23] De Soto (2000). See also, Cooter and Schäfer (2012), p. 101.

cattle on the designated land, the creditor had no right to seize and sell the cattle. Complying with these legal requirements proved to be so complicated and costly that the cattle were worthless for the purpose of mobilizing credit and, therefore, indeed dead capital for the ranchers. Statistics show that in most Latin American countries, movable property cannot mobilize much credit. All Latin American countries are civil law countries. That movables are often dead capital in South America results however not from an inherent stickiness of civil law but from a stickiness of supreme courts in particular countries, where parliaments remain inactive and supreme courts shy away from improving the existing law and adapting it to economic necessities. A counterexample from another civil law country supports this thesis.

After World War II, German solicitors introduced and the Federal Supreme Court (BGH) endorsed the development of a new form of property, although Germany has a numerus clausus of erga omnes property rights. Companies introduced the extended reservation of title, the current account reservation of title, group reservation of title, downstream reservation of title, forwarded reservation of title, processing reservation of title. In this way, they overcame the traditional rule of pledging movables, which required the creditor to be in possession of the movable. This works well for securities, but not for tangible assets that a company needs for production or in any other department. As a result of various forms of title reservation, the movable assets of companies were mobilized for collateral purposes down to the last item and claim. This bottom-up legal innovation contributed to the rapid reconstruction of Germany after World War II, a country with a bank-based, i.e. credit-based, financial system, in which equity financing through capital markets was relatively undeveloped at the time.

Another example is that German courts had already fully developed the judicial control of standard contracts before parliament enacted a law that did little more than convert established case law into legislation, and before the European Union issued directives. The same is true of producer liability for defective goods, which German courts established long before the national parliament and the EU took action to that effect.

Overall, judge-made law plays an important role in civil law countries. This is achieved by interpreting vague or undeveloped statuses, by doctrinal concepts that ensure consistency when a statute is obviously incomplete, by the outright rejection of black letter law when legislative inaction leads to intolerable encroachments on fundamental legal principles, and even by accepting new forms of property proposed by the business community when this is economically necessary because obedience to black letter law would otherwise prevent the use of movable assets for credit.

The widespread view that civil law is a sticky, top-down system and common law a bottom-up system is a myth. It is most prevalent in the United States, even though the two most illuminating books on the twelfth century legal revolution in Europe that established the discipline of law as we know it were written by American scholars, Berman and Gordley.[24]

10 Empirical Research Should Not Disregard Important Judge-Made Rules in Civil Law Countries

These findings on the importance of jurisdiction and judge-made law in civil law countries have consequences for empirical studies on the effects of civil law. If such studies rely on black letter law without taking into account important Supreme Court decisions, they can easily fail.[25] Here is one example: LaPorta, López-de-Silanes, Shleifer and Vishny have empirically shown that the so-called "widely held corporations", i.e. public limited companies with free float, are the predominant form of enterprise only in the USA and the UK. On the European continent, most companies are controlled by block holders such as families, the state, or other companies like banks. This widely cited and highly influential study also finds that the rights of portfolio investors are generally better protected in common law countries than in civil law countries.[26] This finding is based on the authors' coding of anti-director rights that they collect from the corporate laws of different countries. Implicitly, they regard the black letters of a statute not as a living instrument, but as a legal command that changes only when parliaments change black letter law. This is a mistake. Accordingly, the authors' propositions have not stood up to scrutiny. Much of the German comparative law literature, for example, would deny that the small size of the German stock market compared to the USA can be largely explained by such factors. Critics of a generalization of the propositions of La Porta et al. point out, for example, that in Germany, unlike in the USA, there is no legal obligation to list companies above a certain size on the stock market. Moreover, many anti-director rights in German corporate law are not contained in the company act but rather result from Supreme Court decisions.[27] Spamann, a comparative law scholar and economist, found that the indicators of "anti-director rights" in corporation law compiled by La Porta et al. were based on incomplete coverage of the relevant legal norms and failed to include judge-made anti-director rights. If these additional sources are identified and coded, there is no indication that investors are better protected in common law countries than in civil law countries, or that the indicators of investor protection are positively correlated with the free float of stock corporations or the size of the stock market.[28]

[24] Berman (1985), Gordley (2013), Op. cit.

[25] Schäfer and Ott (2022), p. 579.

[26] LaPorta et al. (2000), pp. 3–27. LaPorta et al. (2002), pp. 1147–1170.

[27] Kuntz (2018), p. 559 et sec.

[28] Spamann (2010), pp. 466–486.

Empirical panel studies of the economic consequences of legislation in civil law countries that ignore judge-made law run the risk of overlooking important developments. It is also worthwhile to analyze landmark decisions of civil courts, as law and economics scholars have done for US law, and to compare different judge-made solutions in different civil law countries.

11 National Codifications and Legal Scholarship and Education

Have national codifications of civil law destroyed the scientific character of civil law in Western Europe? They reinforced the security and power of national law, but as Rudolph von Jhering already argued in the nineteenth century, this was achieved at the cost of reducing legal scholarship to an unscientific "Rechtskunde", a kind of study of legal areas. However, a science of law that aims to preserve the legal order by maintaining its consistency and promoting generally accepted legal principles must, by definition of a scientific approach, transcend national borders and be international. In their writings, Hein Kötz and Reinhard Zimmerman deplore the loss of internationality in the discipline of law.[29] Until the national codifications, all European law schools had the same curriculum, which consisted of the teaching of Roman and canon law. The LL.M. degree—legum legum magister, master of both laws, i.e. Roman and canon law—is a reminder of this tradition. Law professors, mainly from Italy, used to change their positions freely throughout Europe, including England, and nowhere were they aliens. Judges learned local laws and customs on the job. By contrast, the codifications focused legal teaching and writing on the national level, at the expense of overarching and fundamental issues. The general problems of law that had been central during the times of jus commune became peripheral to legal teaching, and what had been peripheral became central. The discipline of comparative civil law is an attempt to counter this development and to provide lawyers with a more comprehensive view of how different legal orders solve similar social and economic problems, maintain consistency, and follow the teleology of the law. This makes comparative lawyers the most obvious counterparts of law and economics scholars. Many comparative lawyers understand the need to open up legal scholarship to economics and other social sciences, as this is the only way to maintain the teleological perspective at a contemporary scientific level.

[29] Kötz (2017); Zimmermann (2004).

12 The Difficult Discussion on a more Economic Approach in Legal Reasoning

In a paper on doctrinal private law and economic analysis, Gerhard Wagner of the Humboldt University, one of the most knowledgeable German legal scholars using law and economics, points to the current problems of law and economics in the EU and its member states. He writes that for more than 15 years, the European Court of Justice has been favouring "a more economic approach" over purely doctrinal reasoning in member states. The ECJ has consistently emphasized that member state laws must punish breaches of European standards of conduct with sanctions that have a "genuine deterrence effect" or are "effective, proportionate and deterrent".[30] The Court argues that this can be achieved in particular by granting claims for damages under private law. With regard to European competition law, in the Courage case, the ECJ recognized the incentive effect of private actions for damages and emphasized that they could "significantly contribute to the maintenance of effective competition in the Community".[31] The EU directive on antitrust damages specifies what this principle means for the design of liability, compensation, and civil procedure. European law thus expressly recognizes the behavioural effect of private law rules. The ECJ acknowledges that the interpretation of the applicable law also includes the evaluation of the consequences for the behaviour of the legal subjects together, with using competing doctrinal solutions. Thus, the law and economics approach is now firmly established at the level of the ECJ.

Yet, as Wagner points out, this is not so much the case at the level of the member states. German legal scholars have criticized this more economic approach of European law as a "relapse into archaic thinking", as "Old Testament style", and as "a screwed-up construct", criticizing the deterrence effect of damage compensation as being "system shattering" and a transformation of civil liability to "a vehicle of sanctions". The lawyers are joined in their criticism by economists of the so-called Freiburg school, who disparage teleological fine-tuning of legal norms, such as an efficiency defense in merger cases, and instead prefer relatively simple norms and per se rules.[32]

But attitudes are also changing in Germany. Legal scholars are increasingly embracing an economic approach that seeks to achieve efficiency directly by using legal norms as instruments. In a vivid debate that has lasted about 40 years, the critical voices have not disappeared, but are becoming less aggressive. The early verdict of Claus-Wilhelm Canaris, one of the most profound contemporary German civil law scholars, that an economic approach to civil law is unlawful, has not been heard for quite some time now.[33] And those who favour a more economic approach to the interpretation of civil law norms have become more numerous. There is also a grow-

---

[30] Wagner (2017), pp. 281–318.

[31] Wagner (2017), p. 287, and ECJ, 20 June 2001, C-453/99 (Courage Ltd./Crehan).

[32] Wagner (2017), p. 288.

[33] Canaris (1993), pp. 377–91.

ing acceptance of the impossibility of a strict separation between the arguments that influence the legislator and those that the courts may take into account. Rather, there is a continuum between the two spheres, with teleological interpretation as the hinge.[34]

In civil law countries, commentaries on statutory laws are an influential body of legal literature. They are handbooks for judges and lawyers on how courts interpret the legal norms, detailing the ruling opinion and alternative opinions on the interpretation of the norms. According to the Beck online database, these commentaries and handbooks currently contain more than a thousand German-language references to "ökonomische Analyse" (economic analysis). This is quite encouraging for law and economics scholars. Unfortunately, I cannot provide a more comprehensive and comparative picture on such developments in other member states of the European Union in this lecture.

13 Consequences for Legal Education and Scholarship

I conclude with an observation about legal scholarship and education in Western European civil law countries. We share a great tradition of legal thinking, arguing and interpretation of the law. It was developed mainly by Italian scholars in the late Middle Ages, who for centuries dominated legal scholarship not only in Italy but also in the newly founded universities in the Holy Roman Empire north of the Alps and in other parts of Europe, including England up to the time of the Tudor monarchy. This tradition of a scientific discipline of law is a precious heritage that did not vanish with the civil codes. It preserves the rule of law and a legal order, which excludes that parliament has unlimited and unrestricted sovereignty and is not bound by any rules in its individual measures.

The continental tradition regards law not as an arbitrary collection of rules, as a thicket of norms, but as a legal order with principles, consistency, a system, and a hierarchy of norms. It has developed ways of thinking that serve to reinterpret preexisting rules, to constrain intolerable arbitrariness of new legislation, or to compensate for the legislator's failure to respond to the needs of society. These methods necessarily include logic, principled systemic thinking, and impact assessment of legal norms. By definition, such a methodological legal science based cannot be local or national, but must be international. For centuries, the legal education of so-called learned lawyers in universities was the same throughout Western Europe, with its multiplicity of polities, statutory and customary law. The Holy Roman Empire consisted of hundreds of different free city republics, kingdoms, counties, and even villages, and each of these polities had its own laws and statutes and answered only to the emperor. These laws, however, were superseded and infiltrated by the jus commune. The national codifications that started in the late eighteenth

[34] Wagner (2017) 304.

century ended this and, as a by-product, brought forth a national focus on law and legal education. While this did not destroy the heritage of continental European legal scholarship, it did have an adverse effect. At present, legal education and even legal scholarship do not nurture and maintain the common foundations of law as much as it should. The study of comparative law, which shows how and why different legal systems solve the same problems with different norms, helps to preserve this heritage. The integration of social sciences, and especially economics, into such studies can serve to highlight the societal consequences of norms. Such courses are rare in the legal curriculum. In Germany, they are not even compulsory. With regard to comparative law, the situation is different in Italy, where every law student must take a course in either comparative civil law or comparative public law.

The narrow national focus of legal education and legal scholarship strains our great tradition. Even prominent law scholars sometimes comment on outstanding legal research results from neighbouring disciplines as if they were tourists. I am not criticizing that law students learn practical routines that have value only in their own country, nor am I advocating a pan-European civil code that disregards national, regional, and local customs and preferences. And although I am convinced that knowledge of only local value has no place in higher education, I do not criticize the teaching of such local knowledge in law schools in order to better prepare students for their profession. But this teaching should not neglect or even reject the teaching of what jurisprudence is today, characterized by the internationalization of questions and answers and by interdisciplinarity. Otherwise, the discipline of scientific jurisprudence in the European tradition will not disappear, but it may emigrate from law schools to Max Planck Institutes and similar organizations, to business schools, and to schools of governance.

References

Avinarius M (2014) Fremde Traditionen des römischen Rechts, Einfluß, Wahrnehmung und Argument des "rimskoe pravo" im russischen Zarenreich des 19. Jahrhunderts (Foreign Traditions of Roman Law, Influence, Perception and Argument of the "rimskoe pravo" in 19th century Tsarist Russia), Wallstein Verlag, Göttingen.

Berman HJ (1985) Law and revolution: the formation of the Western legal tradition. Harvard University Press, Cambridge, MA.

Canaris C-W (1993) Funktion, Struktur und Falsifikation Juristischer Theorien (function, structure, and falsification of legal theories). JuristenZeitung 48(8):377–391. http://www.jstor.org/stable/20820926

Code civil, translated by Georges Rouhette and Anne Rouhette-Berton, https://www.fd.ulisboa.pt/wp-content/uploads/2014/12/Codigo-Civil-Frances-French-Civil-Code-english-version.pdf

Cooter R, Schäfer H-B (2012) Solomons knot, how law can end the poverty of nation. Princeton University Press

De Geest G (2020) American law: a comparative primer. Edward Elgar

De Soto H (2000) The mystery of capital: why capitalism triumphs in the west and fails everywhere else, Internet Archive, open Source. https://archive.org/stream/Hernando_De_Soto_The_Mystery_Of_Capital_Why_Capitalism_TriumphsIn_The_West_And_Fails_Everywhere_Else

Ehrlich I, Posner R (1974) An economic analysis of legal rulemaking. J Leg Stud 3:1

Eidenmüller H (2015) Effizienz als Rechtsprinzip – Möglichkeiten und Grenzen der ökonomischen Analyse des Rechts (Efficiency as a legal principle – the scope and limits of the economic analysis of law), 4th edn
Gordley J (2013) The Jurists, a critical history. Oxford University Press
Kötz H (1996) Europäisches Vertragsrecht, Mohr Siebeck, European Contract Law (2017) VI. 2nd English edn. Oxford University Press
Kötz H (2017) European contract law, 2nd edn. Oxford University Press
Kötz H, Wagner G Deliktsrecht (Tort Law), 13th edn. Vahlen
Kuntz T (2018) Mannesmann. In: Fleischer H, Thiessen J (eds) Gesellschaftsrechts-Geschichten, p 559 et sec
LaPorta R et al (2000) Investor protection and corporate governance. J Financ Econ 58:3–27
LaPorta R et al (2002) Investor protection and corporate valuation. J Financ 57:1147–1170
Montesquieu C (1748) L'esprit des lois, Projekt Gutenberg (2008). https://www.gutenberg.org/cache/epub/27573/pg27573-images.html
Oberauer N (2014) Das islamische riba Verbot (the Islamic riba ban). In: Casper M, Oberauer N, Wittreck F (eds.) Was vom Wucher übrigbleibt. Zinsverbote im historischen und kulturellen Vergleich (What remains from usury. Bans on interest in historical and cultural comparison), Mohr Siebeck, Tübingen, p 111–123
Oberauer N (2021) Islamisches Wirtschafts- und Vertragsrecht: Einführung, Zweite Auflage (Islamic economic and contract law), 2nd edn. Nomos Verlagsgesellschaft, Baden-Baden
Parisi F (2004) The efficiency of the common law hypothesis. In: Rowley C, Schneider F (eds) The Encyclopedia of public choice. Springer, Boston, MA, pp 519–522. https://doi.org/10.1007/978-0-306-47828-4_86
Schäfer H-B (2019) Rules versus standards in developing countries, the case for clear and precise legal norms on eminent domain power. Law Dev Rev 2019(5/27):425–455
Schäfer H-B, Ott C (2022) The economic analysis of civil law, 2nd edn. Edward Elgar Publ
Shavell S (1987) Economic analysis of accident law. Harvard University Press
Spamann H (2010) The "Antidirector rights index" revisited. Rev Financ Stud 23(2):466–486
Tan ES (2002) An empty Shell - rethinking the usury Laws in medieval Europe. J Legal Hist.23(3):177-196
Wagner G (2017) Privatrechtsdogmatik und ökonomische Analyse (Private law doctrine and economic analysis of law). In: Festschrift für Claus-Wilhelm Canaris, pp 281–318.
Zimmermann R (1990) The law of obligations: roman foundations of the civilian tradition. Claremont, Juta and Company Ltd, South Africa.
Zimmermann R (2001) Roman law, contemporary law, European law: the civilian tradition today. Clarendon Law Lectures, Oxford, online edn. Oxford Academic, 1 Jan. 2010. https://doi.org/10.1093/acprof:oso/9780198299134.001.0001
Zimmermann R (2004) Comparative foundations of European law of set-up and prescription. Cambridge University Press
Zimmermann R (2016) Kulturelle Prägung des Erbrechts? JuristenZeitung 71(7):321–332

Perspectives on the Normativity of L&E

Against the Myth of Methodological Neutrality: The Philosophical-Political and Moral Assumptions of Law and Economics

Betzabé Marciani Burgos

Abstract The 1990s were the Golden Age of Economic Analysis of Law (EAL) in Peru and other Latin American countries. It entered law faculties not only through the direct incorporation of law courses but also through the adoption of its teaching methodology in other courses. Simultaneously, EAL gained ground in Public Administration and, especially, in the newly established regulatory, consumer protection, and competition law bodies.

Although the advocacy for EAL has diminished over time and some of its initial proposals have been moderated, its methodology continues to be used without acknowledging the underlying political and moral philosophical assumptions. EAL carries a set of assumptions that should not remain concealed under the guise of methodological neutrality.

The pronounced economism of more traditional EAL trends, its tendency to consider individual preferences as the starting point for welfare valuations, its strong skepticism or ethical subjectivism, and its critical view of the regulatory or promotional role of the State—along with its consequentialist approach—prompt us to examine the theoretical assumptions influencing postulates from utilitarian or libertarian schools. This document aims to uncover and critically analyze these assumptions.

Finally, some EAL theses have been evaluated within the context of a Constitutional State of Law and their potential compatibility with the principles it upholds.

This work is part of a research funded by the Research Support Fund—FAI 2022, promoted by the Direction of Research Promotion of PUCP's Vice-Rectorate of Research.

B. Marciani Burgos (✉)
Pontifical Catholic University of Peru, Lima, Peru
e-mail: marciani.bx@pucp.edu.pe

S. Zorzetto et al. (eds.), *Developments in Law and Economics in the Italo-Iberoamerican Context*, Economic Analysis of Law in European Legal Scholarship 21, https://doi.org/10.1007/978-3-032-03317-8_2

1 Introduction: The Philosophical-Political and Moral-Philosophical Assumptions of the EAL. Between Libertarianism, Utilitarianism, and *Something Else*

In the 1990s, an innovative and compelling approach to law gained ground in the traditional understanding and teaching of law in Peru and other countries in the region. This approach primarily impacted areas that were more receptive to dogmatic and conceptual perspectives. Simultaneously, it spread to public administration and, especially, to the newly established regulatory consumer protection, and antitrust law bodies. The influence of the so-called Economic Analysis of Law (EAL) was part of a global trend that coincided with the implementation of the neoliberal economic model in Latin America and the so-called *Washington Consensus*.

Although the advocacy for EAL has waned over time, its methodology remains widely used—especially in many public institutions that administer justice, as well as in regulatory agencies—often without noticing its philosophical-political, ethical, or even ideological assumptions.

This aspect has not been extensively discussed in Peruvian academic circles. Most works on EAL develop this methodology assuming the acceptance of certain philosophical or even ideological premises, which are treated as inherent to it (or nearly so), or they criticize it for its lack of objectivity, failure to align with reality (for example, the widely criticized *homo economicus* model), or its alleged neoliberal ideological content. It is often unclear whether many of its assumptions are truly as liberal as claimed. Others assert that EAL employs a neutral methodology, as if its approach to law, with its pragmatist and consequentialist perspective and objectives, were not grounded in certain political and/or moral philosophical commitments.

Professor Alfredo Bullard, one of the foremost experts and advocates of EAL in Peru, has suggested that many criticisms of EAL may not be relevant as they stem from a distorted understanding of it. He has humorously referred to some of these criticisms as "schizophrenic reactions" to EAL, in that they either perceive things that do not exist or fail to see the full scope offered by this methodological tool.

It seems to me that the type of criticism he calls "the neoliberal invasion"[1] may, for example, have a certain degree of truth. The EAL "de-ideologization" process in recent years tries to turn it into a useful tool for the jurist.[2] I certainly agree that this is the case, but with the limits imposed by its approach, which is grounded in a consequentialist vision focused on specific goals (such as efficiency) and a

[1] According to Bullard, the "hallucination" of the "neoliberal invasion" is a confusion of the tool with the ideological or perceptual framework that may guide its application (2015, p. 758).

[2] Mercado (2013), p. 89.

particular understanding of the law. Methodologies within the law are not neutral; they presuppose certain theoretical commitments, as I insist.

Authors such as Guido Calabresi (quoted by Bullard) hold center-left ideologies and cannot be considered neoliberals, and, thus, they do not share libertarian and utilitarian philosophical bases. In my opinion, they are far from many of the philosophical and axiological assumptions of EAL—especially over time, as Calabresi has deliberately distanced himself. For example, they do not commit to the idea of efficiency as the ultimate goal, which represents a poor model.[3]

In *The Future of Law & Economics*, Calabresi tries to clearly distinguish Economic Analysis of Law (EAL) from Law and Economics,[4] presenting them as perspectives based on different concepts.

EAL symptomatically begins with Bentham's utilitarianism. Although, as Calabresi notes, it no longer necessarily aligns with Bentham's economic theory, it remains rigid in its resistance to forms of rationality that are not merely economic and often claims to be value-neutral—except, perhaps, regarding the final and singular goal of utilitarianism (the principle of "the greatest happiness of the greatest number," which for utilitarianism justifies any action).

In contrast, Law and Economics, as supported by Calabresi, is rooted in the contributions of John Stuart Mill, who is more sensitive to human experiences that cannot be measured in terms of economic rationality. Mill's framework offers a broader vision of values—values that can be plural and, due to their importance, should not be dismissed as irrational.

In my view, the core utilitarian and libertarian assumptions of many EAL advocates remain intact and continue to law, justice, and influence perspectives on EAL itself.

For instance, Bullard argues that efficiency does not replace justice. The latter concept, for a legal realist like him, is an entirely vague concept, unlike efficiency, which has been clearly specified by economists. However, he contends that efficiency can be considered related to justice, since one of efficiency's goals is "to prevent legal systems from generating waste".[5] I believe it is impossible to support this claim without adopting a philosophical-political or even ideological stance that, for example, defines which rights or interests can be sacrificed, the limits to be set to avoid waste (in fact, what exactly do we mean by waste?), the duties involved (only negative duties as libertarianism claims, or also positive duties?), and who holds these duties (does only the state, or also private individuals due to the horizontal effects they create, bear them?).

Likewise, Gustavo Rodríguez asserts: "Good law has positive effects and is not simply presented as 'aesthetically good' according to certain arbitrary values".[6] He

[3] Calabresi, Ackerman, Bobbit, Mishan, or Polinsky, according to Hierro, could accept "having done 'economic analysis', but not belonging to the school of 'economic analysis'" (1994, p. 945, note 4).

[4] Calabresi (2016), pp. 1–23.

[5] Bullard (2018), p. 34.

[6] Rodríguez García (2019), p. 19.

then mentions examples such as the *inefficient* minimum wage or consumer protection regulations, which bring up the perennial debate on paternalism. This debate extends beyond liberals and conservatives (moralists, for instance) and even divides egalitarian liberals from libertarians. Furthermore, Rodríguez argues that there is a false dilemma between pursuing wealth accumulation and wealth distribution in society. He contends: "Law should not focus on taking wealth from those who obtain it, but on allowing free exchanges that enable the poor to become rich".[7]

The latter is, precisely, the central debate that has divided liberals into libertarians and egalitarians (or equalitarians),[8] leading to discussions on topics such as: entitlement justice derived from natural rights to liberty and property (Nozick); the possibility of redistribution when accepting the arbitrariness of the "lottery" (whether natural, social, or based on luck) that places us in the world with varying advantages and capabilities, and the view that we do not own our talents (Rawls)[9] versus the idea that we are not born in debt to our neighbors[10]; the role of merit in distributive justice; the possibility of limiting transactions between free individuals when social structures of subordination exist; and how the Kantian maxim of non-instrumentalization of the individual should be interpreted.

Garzón[11] has analyzed various ethical justifications that have historically supported the market. I believe his classification is useful for distinguishing the philosophical-political and philosophical-moral assumptions underlying EAL or its various schools of thought. He distinguishes between consequentialist (or pragmatic) and deontological arguments. It is commonly noted that EAL is built on liberal—typically libertarian—principles, with a utilitarian approach, though these concepts can often be at odds. However, not all consequentialism is necessarily utilitarian. As Garzón points out, consequentialist arguments supporting the market may include purposes such as economic and political liberties.

Among the consequentialist justifications for the market, the following are typically offered:

(1) The efficiency argument, often defended by the leading exponents of EAL, such as Posner (who links it to the even more established objective of wealth maximization) and Coase.

[7] Rodríguez García (2019), pp. 109–110.

[8] Libertarians and what Brennan calls left-libertarians (such as Rawls) defend civil rights, but they disagree on the extent of government control in the economy and the scope of the so-called welfare state. The main difference between them lies in their views on economic freedom (Brennan 2012).

[9] Rawls states: "Perhaps some will think that the person with greater natural endowments deserves those assets and the superior character that made their development possible. Because he is more worthy in this sense, he deserves the greater advantages that he could achieve with them. This view, however, is surely incorrect. It seems to be one of the fixed points of our considered judgments that no one deserves his place in the distribution of native endowments, any more than one deserves one's initial starting place in society" (1971, pp. 103–104).

[10] "Libertarians reject the idea that we are born in debt to our neighbors" (Brennan 2012, p. 14).

[11] Garzón (1995).

(2) The argument that the free market is perhaps the best means to guarantee economic and political liberty. This view is championed by, for example, Milton Friedman, who claims that "the bigger the market, the greater the individual liberty". For while the market "represents harmony and consensus", the state "is the sphere of imposition and conflict".[12]
(3) The argument that the market facilitates the coordination of individual interests, which ultimately results in achieving objectives that benefit the community. In this view, "in the end, everyone gets what they wanted and additionally promotes an objective that was not part of their intentions".[13]
(4) The argument that the market provides individuals with freedom of choice (again quoting Friedman), so that when the market allows the exchange of property rights, it contributes to individual choice among different life plans.

Deontological justifications, on the other hand, assume that the market has intrinsic value. It is "not a means to obtain other goals, but the result of the correct practice of fundamental principles, such as those related to the defense of property and freedom".[14]

2 A Deontological Justification from the Perspective of the Libertarianism of Possessive Individualism, and Minimal State Intervention

According to Garzón, the deontological justification of the market presents the following two arguments:

(1) One argument, defended by Buchanan, asserts: "The market is good in itself". Therefore, "the intrinsic goodness of the market is due to the consensus of those who participate in it".[15] This explanation highlights how individuals exercise their autonomy, in contrast to the perfect interventions of the state ("whose primary function is to guarantee the free play of the market rules".[16]
(2) Another argument posits that the "market is good because we can reach it as a consequence of the exercise of unquestionable rights". This thesis stems from Nozick's libertarian position, which establishes freedom and property rights as inseparable values.[17]

[12] Garzón (1995), p. 10.
[13] Garzón (1995), p. 10.
[14] Garzón (1995), p. 12.
[15] Garzón (1995), p. 13.
[16] Garzón (1995), p. 13.
[17] Garzón (1995), p. 14.

Since the market is not mere instrument but a manifestation of the exercise of certain individual rights considered essential and prior, instrumental criteria such as cost-benefit analysis can never prevail over it. Therefore, an economic perspective of law based on a libertarian concept cannot simultaneously be utilitarian, as utilitarianism has no objection to sacrificing the rights of some individuals when doing so benefits the calculation of happiness or global welfare, which presents a significant issue. In its market perspective, libertarianism can entertain a degree of consequentialism, but only as long as the rights to liberty and property, as generators of negative[18] duties, are not in question.

Regarding Rothbard's libertarian thought, for instance, it is necessary to examine a non-utilitarian and rather deontological justification of both the market and the law. Rothbard proposes a model of normative ethics and a political philosophy of liberty grounded in natural rights.[19] He develops his theory during the mid-1970s, a time when ethical relativism (over iusnaturalism) and democratic egalitarianism (as proposed by Rawls) prevailed.[20]

Rothbard's thesis, like Nozick's, critiques the abandonment of the libertarian tradition based on the philosophy of rationalist natural rights in favor of technocratic utilitarianism, a shift that occurred in the first half of the nineteenth century:

> It is the transition from the search for liberty based on the morality of law towards a common good. From the utilitarian perspective, liberty becomes a resource and a means where costs and benefits are calculated.[21]

Rothbard's theory is based on certain foundations common to other libertarian theories:

(a) **A Strong Methodological Individualism**

> Only individuals have goals and can take action to achieve them. There are no aims or actions attributable to "groups", "collectivities" or "states" that cannot be redirected to the actions of specific individuals. [...] Therefore, claiming that "governments" take action is merely a metaphor; [...] only individuals can desire and take action.[22]

(b) **Defending the Right to Property Based on the Iusnaturalism Perspective (Lockean and Neo-Scholasticism)**

---

[18] In the most extreme model: "Nozick does not admit any consequentialist argument. If it were empirically demonstrated that the free market based on the right to property had pernicious consequences, this would not be used as a justification for introducing modifications that could alter inalienable rights" (Barbarosch 2013, p. 56, note 142).

[19] Mazzone (2000), pp. 9–10.

[20] It is important to remember that Rawls' *Theory of Justice* is from 1971, and Nozick's *Anarchy, State, and Utopia* (which receives significant influence from Rothbard) is from 1974. Both are presented as deontological theories (egalitarian liberalism, in Rawls' case, and libertarian liberalism, in Nozick's case) rather than utilitarianism, which was more dominant at the time.

[21] Mazzone (2000), p. 36. I translated the quote.

[22] Mazzone (2000), p. 21, note 13. The quote is a literal translation I did.

The right to property is presented as the original or initial right that each individual has over themselves. According to the concept of Thomas Aquinas, this right derives from the capacity of the human being as a rational individual. Thereafter, it extends to legitimate property titles are obtained through the cultivation and use of land that has not been previously cultivated.[23]

(c) **The Idea of a Minimal State**

Nozick's justification for a minimal state is based on a lack of confidence in the market's ability to guarantee individual rights to property and liberty, as well as to ensure social peace.

Rothbard criticizes Nozick's thesis, arguing that the contract that created the minimal state is illegitimate and results from the alienation of the inalienable rights of the individual.[24] In this regard, Rothbard's perspective can be seen as more extremist and anarcho-capitalist.[25]

(d) **A *negative conception of Liberty***

This is another central thesis of libertarianism, related to the idea that when there are negative liberties, only negative duties are possible. Positive duties are only admitted provided they result from a free agreement between individuals.

Negative liberty can be understood as the absence of obstacles, obligations, or prohibitions that limit the action or decision-making capacity of an individual. On the other hand, positive liberty presupposes certain conditions, such as material resources, which enable an individual to act and make decisions autonomously. Therefore, it is claimed that there is no positive liberty (the capacity to make decisions or take actions autonomously) when an individual is in a precarious, subordinate situation or lacks capacities, etc.

As Farrell explains, libertarians conceive of the neutrality of the state (a principle of political liberalism) as negative neutrality.

> The libertarian state accepts, for instance, the current distribution of property and respects the *status quo*. The state is neutral by omission. [...] The libertarian state relies on the market to satisfy the life plans of its citizens.[26]

In contrast, the egalitarian liberal understands state neutrality as positive neutrality, which, in the eyes of a libertarian, would constitute a violation of the principle of neutrality:

> The liberal [egalitarian] state does not accept the current distribution of resources as untouchable. Its neutrality is evident when all its citizens have the same probability of accomplishing their life plan, and this requires—to some extent—the redistribution of resources. The idea of positive neutrality is associated with the idea of positive liberty [...].

[23] See Mazzone (2000), p. 25.

[24] Mazzone (2000), p. 52.

[25] Mazzone (2000), pp. 53–54.

[26] Farrell (2007), p. 22.

> A liberal [egalitarian] can accept that the market is a suitable instrument for satisfying citizens' life plans, but he will first ensure that all citizens can convert their preferences into demands by having enough resources.[27]

From a radical libertarian viewpoint, every time the state intervenes (sanctioning, redistributing, or even regulating), it affects the (negative) liberty of individuals. Therefore, if we accept the necessity of the state's existence, we must also accept that its actions must be the most elementary and absolutely necessary. In Nozick's model of the minimal state, the state should primarily guarantee security (through the police system, for instance) and the administration of justice (ensuring the execution of free transactions between individuals). Everything else, including all the machinery of the welfare state that involves redistribution mechanisms and is oriented toward guaranteeing positive liberty, would be illegitimate.[28] Thus, Nozick absolutely rejects the redistributive conception of Rawlsian egalitarianism.

As we know, Rawls' second principle establishes that it is possible to determine a certain type of resource distribution when it implies a greater benefit for the less privileged (the global difference principle). Here, redistribution is not aimed at achieving pure equality and even allows the existence of greater differences, provided that these differences contribute to improving the situation of the less privileged. Regarding the idea of mere formal equality (of rules) or even equality of opportunities (initial equality, typical of meritocratic societies and accepted by egalitarian liberalism), Rawls establishes an even more demanding criterion for redistribution. His proposed difference principle offers a way to address, at least partially to some extent, the problem of the moral arbitrariness of the natural lottery.

On the other hand, according to Nozick, with this second principle of justice, Rawls violates Kant's maxim of non-instrumentalization of individuals and privileges a criterion based on envy.[29] Nozick argues that individual rights do not represent collective aims:

> [...] there is no social entity with a good that undergoes some sacrifice for its own Good. There are only individual people, different individual people, with their own individual lives. Using one of these people for the benefit of others uses him and benefits the others. Nothing more.[30]

Thus, for Nozick (and for many libertarians), "[the things] come into the world already owned, by the people who produced them (or by those who have paid for the labor of those who produced them)".[31] It does not matter to analyze how this initial distribution was executed, nor whether the following distributions (left to free exchange between individuals) were carried out by individuals who had the capacity to negotiate or were conditioned by necessity. Nor does it matter, as Rawls

[27] Farrell (2007), p. 23.

[28] Nozick, however, accepts the enforceability of positive duties when they arise from prior injustice that must be rectified, as in the case of the so-called "justice of rectification" (1999, p. 231).

[29] Nozick (1999), pp. 228–229; and, similarly, Hayek (2011), pp. 155–156

[30] Nozick (1999), pp. 32–33.

[31] Swift (2014), p. 61.

indicates, whether good or bad luck contributed to an individual's education, health, intellectual capacity, or even beauty, which might place them in a better or worse position in this world of free transactions. As Swift sarcastically states:

> Those of us who missed out on the initial acquisition stage—who came into the world when everything had already been snaffled up—shouldn't worry too much. We own ourselves and are therefore in a position to lease ourselves to others.[32]

According to Holmes and Sunstein,[33] the libertarian vision of negative liberties and obligations is not real, even when speaking of the sacred right to property, because in reality, the guarantee—and the very existence of this right—requires costly positive duties (such as those related to security and the administration of justice) from the state,[34] which, in addition, implies sacrifices (such as taxation) from everyone, not just its holders. Therefore, the authors argue:

> It, therefore, makes no more sense to associate property rights with "freedom from government", than to associate the right to play chess with freedom from the rules of chess. Property rights exist because possession and use are created and regulated by law.[35]

Holmes' and Sunstein's critique also challenges the illusory idea of the minimal state, with its typical aversion to any kind of legal regulation and its trust in *laissez-faire*, which underpins libertarian thought. As the authors explain, it is not possible to speak of a market without government (without legislation, judges, defense, etc.). And they argue that capitalists know this: "Not free-enterprise but robber capitalism—the rule of the violent and the unscrupulous—thrives in the absence of law and order".[36]

Ultimately, the liberal tradition that underlies the libertarian perspective—ranging from Hobbes through Locke to Nozick and other more recent authors—establishes what Macpherson has called a form of possessive individualism, based on the vision of society as a vast market. In such vas market, individuals who owe nothing to that society—but who are owners of their capacities and everything they have acquired thanks to them—establish exchange relationships.[37] Does the EAL follow that path?

According to Hausman and McPherson:

> [m]ost libertarian economists are less influenced by distinctive philosophical commitments than by specific reasons for doubting the efficacy of government intervention to improve efficiency or redistribute income.[38]

---

[32] Swift (2014), p. 64.

[33] Holmes and Sunstein (2000).

[34] The authors refer to the large figures behind the U.S. Defense budget (2000, p. 62), as well as public investment in the protection of intellectual property rights (2000, p. 65).

[35] Holmes and Sunstein (2000), p. 60.

[36] Holmes and Sunstein (2000), p. 72.

[37] Macpherson (1990), pp. 1–4.

[38] Hausman and McPherson (2006), p. 172.

For instance, Coase has political conclusions that a libertarian philosopher would agree with, but for consequentialist reasons, he would reject.[39]

As for Posner, he shares some points with libertarian ideology but:

> [...] adopts a typically utilitarian skepticism regarding moral rights and argues instead, on basically consequentialist grounds for positive rights and argues instead, on basically consequentialist grounds, for positive rights which, in the event, turn out to be extensionally identical to Nozick's fundamental moral rights.[40]

Finally, the Austrian School is closer to a libertarian approach than the EAL of the Chicago School, which is more aligned with a utilitarian approach.

According to Goldman, the Austrian School's theory of human action shows that individuals pursue an array of objectives that are not necessarily aimed at only one purpose, as proposed by the economistic approach of the EAL. This approach, guided by neoclassical economic theory, is based on a reductionist view of the rational action of *homo economicus*.[41] By acknowledging the diversity of purposes and the variability of individual preferences over time, the Austrian School places the individual at the center again, advancing framework aligned with libertarianism rather than utilitarianism. Thus, for instance, on the basis of a coherently libertarian perspective (albeit debatable), Goldman proposes in his text a sort of privatization of criminal law. This libertarian perspective can be presented as follows:

(1) The most important thing is not the supposed collective aims (welfare, efficiency, peace, etc.) behind criminal prosecution, but the concrete interests of the victims. According to Rojas, quoted by Goldman:

> Considering the prosecution of criminals as a public asset means ignoring the possibility for each person to decide for himself: first, whether he considers himself a victim of a crime or not; second, whether he wants to prosecute the criminal or not; and finally, his concrete complaint against him. Those intimate and fundamental decisions are replaced by the arbitrary and generalized imposition of the government through a law.[42]

(2) There is a bid for privatizing criminal law by removing it from the state and bringing it into voluntary transactions between private individuals. In the minimal state dream, the state would fulfill, in any case, a subsidiary role. In the author's words, we find the following:

> In fact, it is possible to imagine alternative models of criminal law in which the victims would have enough incentives to overcome the functioning of the coercive apparatus. For instance, if instead of only punishing a crime such as theft with a prison sentence, the Criminal Code considers extinguishing the criminal action when the offender returns the stolen goods to the victim, asks for forgiveness, performs work on his behalf for a certain period of time and assumes the payment of the costs of the process. Then private companies

[39] Hausman and McPherson (2006), p. 172.

[40] Campbell (1988), p. 134.

[41] Goldman (2017), pp. 16–32.

[42] Rojas (2000), p. 71; quoted in Goldman (2017), p. 36.

> could start offering the necessary means to clarify this type of event and bring the perpetrators to court, as well as numerous "clients" willing to hire them.[43]

(3) Another element, though not strictly libertarian but often invoked by libertarians, is to complain about the inefficiency of the state apparatus. This inefficiency would arise from the lack of objective parameters for assessing the value of the assets that constitute the good life of individuals, which are instead subject to mere personal preferences. Regarding this issue, Goldman says:

> Assuming that the state monopoly of criminal prosecution is an ideal means for the maximization of social welfare by reaching a point of balance between the harm caused by criminal activity and the cost of its prevention, also implies ignoring the reasons why no centralized planning body possesses (nor can possess) the necessary tools to allocate resources efficiently.[44]

(4) A final element is the marked ethical skepticism that leads to the individual's preferences being the only parameter of moral validity. As the author himself explains:

> […] as in matters of moral ideas there are no objective parameters or revealed truths, I clarify once again that my objections start from a liberal worldview, in which individual autonomy is the supreme value of all balance. The fundamental idea of the liberal value system is that each individual is an aim himself and not a means to achieve other people's aims. The only valid reason for limiting an individual's liberty is to pursue his own life plan, in order to assure identical liberty to his fellows. As Nozick argues, for liberalism "[…] individuals are aims, not merely means […] Individuals are inviolable."[45]

> *The idea of justice refers to a merely subjective evaluation. People classify as "fair" or "unfair" a certain order of things to the extent that it fits or does not fit the set of preferences derived from their scale of values. And this individual scale of values, by definition, cannot have a universal character or any rational justification.*[46]

Contrary to utilitarianism, which can support the objectivity of an ultimate good (the greatest happiness of the majority), libertarianism seems to lead us into the relativism of subjective preferences.

For libertarianism, there are no objective valuations and no way of knowing what is good for the human being. As a result, such decisions are subject to the arbitrariness of personal preferences, which can only be known by the individual agent. Therefore, it is not possible to establish solutions from a centralized body. Instead, it is preferable to rely on transactions between individuals who are presumed to know better than anyone else what they want and what is good for them.

From the libertarian perspective, value assignments made by a legislator are arbitrary, while those made by individuals are seen as supreme, as each person is regarded as the ultimate evaluator of what is best for themselves. However, this view overlooks the fac that individual preferences can also be shaped by various biases or

---

[43] Goldman (2017), p. 40.

[44] Goldman (2017), p. 41.

[45] Goldman (2017), p. 45; the emphasis is mine.

[46] Goldman (2017), p. 56, the emphasis is mine.

preconditions subject to the environment, lack of information (or lack of understanding of it), etc. This is evident in phenomena such as adaptive preferences, for instance.[47]

3 Consequentialist Justifications: The Predominance of the Utilitarian Approach Based on *Efficiency*

According to Bentham's classical model, utilitarianism is guided by a single principle for morally evaluating individual actions. According to this principle, the moral rightness of an act is determined by something that produces the *greatest happiness for the largest number of people*. Happiness results from the sum of the satisfaction of pleasures or interests of individuals. Furthermore, the happiness of a community is the sum of the pleasures or interests of its members. However, in this sum, there is no consideration of the degree of inequality that there might be in the distribution of pleasures.

Utilitarianism is an attractive theory since it appears to address the actual preferences of individuals and treats all individuals equally (their desires or interests are summed up in a single general interest, regardless of the individual's social, racial, economic, etc., status and preferences). Additionally, utilitarianism considers the consequences of our actions, which seems more realistic and in accordance with what can be psychologically demanded of people. As Amartya Sen indicates, it is fundamental when evaluating the outcomes of social institutions (for instance, public policies).[48]

Nevertheless, utilitarianism faces significant objections related to its blindness in terms of the qualification or valuation of preferences, which depends on the individual. This leads to at least three problems: adaptive preferences (discussed in the previous section), offensive tastes (for instance, when an individual's preference involves discriminating against another due to their race), and expensive tastes.[49] Thus, when a person living in extreme poverty has a preference for eating anything once a day, it would be considered equal to the eccentric tastes of a millionaire who can only enjoy eating black truffles harvested in a very exclusive manner.

However, the fiercest criticism against utilitarianism has been developed by neo-Kantian liberalism, as seen in the work of Rawls and Nozick. This criticism refers

[47] An adaptive preference occurs when individuals, placed in a context of persistent deprivation, psychologically adjust their preferences to these deprivations (Sen 2000, p. 67). This does not imply a simple attitude of mediocrity, as is often claimed by certain conservative sectors in our emerging economies, supposedly based on mere personal merit. "The deprived people", says Sen, "tend to come to terms with their deprivation because of the sheer necessity of survival, and they may, as a result, lack the courage to demand any radical change, and may, even adjust their desires and expectations to what they unambitiously see as feasible" (Sen 2000, p. 63).

[48] Sen (2000), pp. 58–63.

[49] Cf. Cohen (1990), pp. 360–361.

to the fact that utilitarianism does not consider the independence and separability of individuals. It tends to treat individuals as mere means to maximize overall welfare, thereby violating the principle of the dignity of the individual, which asserts that each person should be treated as an end in themselves and not as a mere means. As such, it gives rise to what Posner calls the problem of the moral monstrosity of utilitarianism, a concern that can also be linked to the EAL.[50]

The maxim of the greatest happiness for the greatest number of people has evolved through time across different utilitarian approaches until it reached the concept of welfare, which is followed by utilitarian economics and can be related to EAL. Welfare theories can be classified into substantive and formal. Substantive theories, such as hedonism, establish what is good for people, while formal theories do not specify what is good but focus on how to achieve it—such as by satisfying the preferences of individuals.[51] As Hausman and McPherson note, economists tend to prefer formal theory because it supposedly involves fewer philosophical commitments, following the same path of moral skepticism that often underlies many economic conceptions and EAL itself.

> Most economists do not directly address questions concerning welfare, and we have no systematic evidence concerning their views. Among those economists who do talk about welfare, most are attracted to a formal theory, no doubt because formal theories appear to involve less controversial philosophical commitments than substantive theories about what is good or bad for people. By leaving the substantive question of what is good for an individual up to the individual, normative economists aim to show their philosophical modesty. The preference satisfaction view of well-being also appeals to the anti-paternalist values of many economists.[52]

However, the choice of formal theory leads to several problems: the already mentioned adaptive preferences or expensive tastes; those related to the lack of information or preferences based on false and unreasonable beliefs; conflicts between the preferences of different agents[53]; issues when an individual's preferences change over time[54]; the malevolent attitudes individuals sometimes adopt, etc.

Certainly, economists are aware of these objections, but they consider that, given the lack of better indicators and more objective criteria for measurement, preference satisfaction remains the best (or least bad) criterion.[55] On the other hand, a substantive conception of welfare should lead to a certain level of moral objectivism, which

---

[50] Posner (1979), pp. 116–119.

[51] Hausman and McPherson (2006), pp. 119–120.

[52] Hausman and McPherson (2006), pp. 119–120.

[53] Hausman and McPherson (2006), pp. 126–127.

[54] Hausman and McPherson (2006), pp. 123–124. The authors argue: "A second and more plausible explanation for why we give no weight to satisfying preferences that people no longer have is that giving people what they no longer want brings them no "satisfaction." But in giving this reason one has shifted from a preference satisfaction theory to a mental-state theory of welfare. Can someone who holds a preference satisfaction theory of well-being explain why the satisfaction of preferences that people no longer hold is of no moral importance?" (Hausman and McPherson 2006, p. 123).

[55] Hausman and McPherson (2006), pp. 119–122.

is what we will discuss in the next section. Therefore, I agree with Hausman and McPherson when they claim that there is no moral justification for recognizing the preferences of individuals as determinants of public justice, regardless of their content. The fact that something is valuable to one person (because they desire it) does not mean that it must be valuable to everyone else. Therefore, there is no moral duty to care about individual preferences. According to Nagel:

> Others have no reason to satisfy Ellen's preferences unless they can make sense of why she wants is worth wanting, or why her life will be better in some substantive way if she gets what she wants.[56]

In other words: why can there be objective, rather than merely subjective or personal, reasons to comply with Hausman's request? Otherwise, as the authors argue, antisocial preferences (which in the end are preferences!), such as racism and sadism,[57] would also have to be considered.

According to Sen, the deeply skeptical view of moral philosophy held by many economists leads to conflicts when valuing interpersonal preferences, which underpin welfare economics based on the criterion of utilitarian efficiency. Thus, when it became clear that interpersonal comparisons of preferences could have normative or ethical implications, allegedly neutral instruments were proposed to avoid engaging in this kind of discussion.[58]

EAL (or a certain form of EAL) is supported by utilitarian assumptions due to its consequentialist vision and is oriented toward the search for a purpose. This purpose, despite its ethical skepticism regarding other values, is considered to be objective: and therefore efficient. Consequently, the EAL has adopted several strategies used by economists to address the problem of evaluating preferences without considering moral theory. The so-called Pareto optimality or the Kaldor-Hicks criterion, for instance, has attempted to offer a technical solution to this issue. However, these proposals present problems that can be evaluated from a moral point of view.

The Pareto criterion assumes that:

> [...] a situation is more efficient than another one when an individual improves their situation without making any other person worse off. Or, in other words, the world is better off if at least one individual gets better off, and no one gets worse off.[59]

The so-called Pareto optimality (the ideal situation of greater efficiency) occurs "when, with the existing resources, it is not possible for someone to get better off

---

[56] Hausman and McPherson (2006), p. 126.

[57] Hausman and McPherson (2006), p. 127.

[58] Sen (2004), pp. 30–31. The author explains it as follows: "If that position were accepted. Then the statement that person A is happier that B would be nonsensical—*ethical* nonsense just as much as it would be *descriptive* nonsense. I guess it is a reflection of the way ethics tends to be viewed by economists that statements suspected of being 'meaningless' or 'nonsensical' are promptly taken to be 'ethical'. The peculiarly narrow view of 'meaning' championed by logical positivists [...] caused total chaos in welfare economics when it was supplemented by some additional home-grown confusions liberally supplied by economists themselves" (2004, p. 31).

[59] Bullard (2018), p. 28.

without someone else getting worse off".[60] On the other hand, the Kaldor-Hicks's criterion states that:

> [...] a subsequent situation is better than the previous one not only when someone gets better off and no one gets worse off, but also when someone gets better off, another gets worse off, but the one who gets better off, gets much better than the one who gets worse off.[61]

As Bullard states, Kaldor-Hicks is employed when it is not possible or appropriate to resolve a dispute with transactions between the affected parties. In this case, regulation may be necessary.[62]

Calabresi and Bobbit argue that Pareto standards do not address the distributional consequences of political decisions[63] and are useless for assessing measures—or assets—which are (or should be) outside the market for moral reasons.[64]

In turn, Sen has criticized the Pareto criterion, since it can be compatible with the largest differences, as it does not consider distribution:

> A state can be Pareto optimal with some people in extreme misery and others rolling in luxury, so long as the miserable cannot be made better off without cutting into the luxury of the rich.[65]

Furthermore, the kind of compensation that could be created using the Kaldor-Hicks criterion also raises problems. If translated into real compensation (rather than a mere possibility), then it would imply the application of the Pareto criterion ("is a Pareto improvement") and would be superfluous. Moreover, it would show that the Pareto criterion "can scarcely be extended to cover judgments of distribution without actually making an interpersonally comparative distributional judgment".[66]

Faced with the possibility of taking mere individual preferences as an indicator of welfare, Sen reminds us that while utility can be an indicator of individual well-being, it is not the same as well-being itself. Consider, for example, the case of adaptive preferences we mentioned earlier. We must also be aware of how the market itself affects or determines our preferences and how this affects the development of our capabilities. This is why it is relevant to evaluate the level of agency of the individual and consider that agency is not equivalent to a mere choice: "the formula of taking any choice as a reflection of the valuable agency is plainly inadequate".[67] This leads us to an objective, rather than subjectivist, ethical valuation.[68] This is why Sen states the following:

---

[60] Bullard (2018), p. 28.

[61] Bullard (2018), p. 30; cf. Kaldor (1939).

[62] Bullard (2018), pp. 32–33.

[63] Calabresi and Bobbit (1978), pp. 83–86.

[64] Calabresi and Bobbit (1978), pp. 89–90.

[65] Sen (2004), p. 32.

[66] Sen (2004), p. 33, note 4.

[67] Sen (2004), p. 44, note 15.

[68] Sen (2004), pp. 41–42.

> Well-being is ultimately a matter of valuation, and while happiness and the fulfillment of desire may well be valuable for the person's well-being, they cannot—on their own or even together—adequately reflect the value of well-being. "Being happy" is not even a valuational activity, and "desiring" is at best a consequence of valuation.[69]

Since the utilitarian approach does not take the liberty of the individual seriously enough—since it views rights from a merely instrumental perspective[70]—and does not guarantee respect for the agency or the development of individual capabilities, it is not a good theory,[71] which affects the utilitarian aspect of EAL.

4 The Pragmatist Non-Utilitarianism of Posner and Efficiency as a Way of Maximizing Wealth

Posner distinguishes his theory from utilitarianism, arguing that the latter faces numerous issues caused by its lack of clear definitions(especially concerning what constitutes happiness or satisfaction) and, therefore, of practical applications.[72] One of Posner's main goals is to provide clarity regarding the objective that law should pursue from a consequentialist approach. Thus, for EAL, law should not aim to maximize happiness or welfare (as utilitarianism does in its various forms), but rather maximize wealth.[73]

While increasing wealth may be an indicator of increasing happiness, this is not necessarily so, and it is therefore distinct from a utilitarian approach. As Posner remarks, the relationship between wealth and happiness is uncertain.[74] According to Posner, the model of efficiency as wealth maximization, in contrast to happiness, offers the following advantages:

(1) "the pursuit of wealth is more consistent with our intuitions concerning ethical behavior than the pursuit of happiness",
(2) "the wealth principle can more easily be made to yield the formal elements of an ethical theory—including notions of rights and of corrective justice",
(3) "the wealth principle is more defined than the happiness principle. This is important not only in generating specific guidelines for conduct and policy but in setting bounds on governmental intervention in people's lives".[75]

---

[69] Sen (2004), p. 46.

[70] Sen (2004), p. 49.

[71] Sen (2004), pp. 59–60.

[72] Posner (1979), pp. 103–107, 111–119.

[73] "Wealth is the value in dollars or dollar equivalents [...] of everything in society. It is measured by what people are willing to pay for something or, if they already own it, what they demand in money to give it up" (Posner 1979, p. 119).

[74] Posner (1979), pp. 120–121.

[75] Posner (1979), p. 122.

According to Posner, the wealth maximization model even promotes certain protestant virtues such as honesty, fulfillment of promises, and even altruism.[76]

From the aforementioned, we can draw some conclusions about Posner's proposal. First, we see an intuitionist aspect in Posner's view of ethical truths ("the pursuit of wealth is more consistent with our intuitions concerning ethical behavior than the pursuit of happiness"). Second, Posner seems to try to elaborate a moral theory for EAL as an alternative to utilitarianism, which supports it and refutes the criticisms made by some moral philosophers such as Dworkin ("the wealth principle can more easily be made to yield the formal elements of an ethical theory"). However, Posner's approach to this objective is sinuous. Although he develops a moral theory in this document—which he will later abandon in favor of a more instrumental and pragmatic vision[77]—he also makes a point to separate the work of economists from that of philosophers. He does so by clarifying that the relevance of conclusions drawn by economists does not depend on their philosophical choices. For example, he states:

> It is widely believed that before the economist can offer suggestions for legal reform designed to make the legal system more efficient, he must derive and defend the moral foundations of efficiency. This view is incorrect.[78]

For Posner, it seems that morality derives from the economic principle itself. For instance, when discussing the market for newborn children, Posner argues that it could be efficient. Concerning potential moral objections, he states:

> These points have no weight to one who embraces the wealth-maximization principle. He can find no immorality in the idea of a baby market, when morality is derived from the economic principle itself.[79]

This example, however, reveals the absolute perversion of Posner's sense of "morality". But, of course, if all moral values are seen as relative, subjective, intuitive, emotional, or as mere preferences, then any value assigned to morality by any individual, society, or emotion seems valid. If we abandon any attempt to give content to moral values (i.e., any form of moral objectivism), then Posner's response becomes less absurd.

Finally, Posner defends the wealth maximization principle because of its more concrete or tangible nature ("the wealth principle is more definite than the happiness principle").[80]

The wealth maximization principle proposed by Posner can be summarized in terms of its assumptions and effects as follows:

---

[76] Posner (1979), pp. 123–124.

[77] Mercado (2013), p. 89, note 5.

[78] Posner (1979), p. 109.

[79] Posner (1979), p. 139. Similarly, when he claims that "the economic theory of law is a theory of rights as well of exchange. As we shall see, rights can be derived from the theory itself; they do not have to be postulated" (1979, p. 109).

[80] Posner (1979), p. 122.

> To recapitulate, the wealth-maximization principle implies, first, an initial distribution of individual rights (to life, liberty, and labor) to their natural owners[81]; second, free markets to enable those rights to be reassigned from time to time to other uses; third, legal rules that simulate the operations of the market when the costs of market transactions are prohibitive; fourth, a system of legal remedies for deterring and redressing invasions of rights; and fifth, a system of personal morality (the "Protestant virtues") that serves to reduce the costs of market transactions.[82]

The mechanisms of redistribution are clearly not included in Posner's model. Redistribution, according to him, is only possible when it is an effect of the application of the wealth maximization principle itself. For example, when income redistribution helps reduce (or discourage) the commission of certain crimes.[83] In fact, Posner claims that there is no public obligation to support very poor individuals,[84] just as there is no obligation to support disabled individuals who, due to their disability, cannot actively participate in the market. Posner acknowledges that this is an unfortunate consequence, but he argues that there is no way to avoid it.

When addressing Rawls' theory, which, as we have seen, justifies redistributive measures through the second principle of justice (the difference principle), Posner—like Nozick—rejects this option, arguing that it violates individual autonomy.[85]

For Posner:

> An efficient society is one in which goods are in the hands of those who are able and willing to pay the highest price for them, since these are the persons who value them most highly.[86]

However, this thesis is fallacious because it overlooks certain underlying problems. First, it is not sensitive to possible injustices at the starting point, and, in many cases, the outcome is the result of the pure arbitrariness of chance (as Rawls warns). In this sense, it represents a conservative vision that legitimizes the status quo without considering the injustices it may be based upon. Even Nozick considers these issues, speaking of the need for rectification of justice.[87] Moreover, Posner's argument is circular,[88] as demonstrated by Dworkin's example of the slave writer.

---

[81] This refers to the classical libertarian concept of rights, but with an instrumental justification: "The rights derived from economic theory are not, to be sure, bestowed by God or otherwise transcendental; they are 'mere' instruments of wealth maximization" (Posner 1979, p. 127).

[82] Posner (1979), p. 127.

[83] Posner (1979), p. 131.

[84] Posner (1979), p. 128.

[85] Posner (1979), p. 128.

[86] Campbell (1988), p. 135.

[87] Nozick (1999), p. 231.

[88] As Campbell said: "Posner's own proposal—that resources be distributed where they are most productive of wealth—is methodologically as well as morally flawed. Wealth is a matter of the individual's ability to pay and cannot, therefore, without circularity, be used as the standard for determining the proper distribution of wealth" (1988, p. 143). Similarly, Hierro states that "Posner's claim is impossible. And it is impossible because there is no possibility of configuring an efficient initial allocation of rights, since efficiency depends on the initial allocation of rights" (1993, p. 402).

In this example, Agatha is a slave and a brilliant writer. Her owner is an enlightened man who efficiently exploits her writing talent. Agatha could buy her freedom by obtaining a loan, as her liberty is worth more to her than it is to her owner. Any bank could offer her a loan, since her writing skills could generate enough income to repay it. However, Agatha values freedom not for the opportunity to write but for a different kind of happiness, one that would not allow her to repay the loan. In this case, Dworkin concludes: "She will only cease to be his slave by becoming a slave of the First National Bank (of Chicago, of course)".[89] In this case, the starting point—the right to liberty that Agatha lacks—is crucial in evaluating both her desire and her ability to pay for something.

Second, Posner's thesis confuses the ability to pay with valuation, assuming that all goods can be subjected to market metrics (i.e., a price). This is problematic because there are goods that can or should be excluded from the market for good reasons.[90] Posner's approach, which follows Becker's path, assumes that "any ethical preference can be monetizable" and which is based on the phenomenon of economic imperialism and the principle of universal commodification, a hallmark of the original conception of EAL.[91]

It is true that Posner has made his theory more flexible over the years, acknowledging several of these criticisms, such as the view that "EAL analysis makes the 'economic' analysis of human behavior a vacuous and unverifiable hypothesis compatible with any consistent pattern of actual choices".[92] However, as Campbell warns, many of Posner's followers continue to use EAL without fully addressing these objections in their applications.

It turns out that, although Posner tries to reject utilitarianism by all means, he ends up confronting the same problems that utilitarianism faces as a moral theory: skepticism about rights[93]; the problem of moral monstrosity[94]; and the valuation of justice based solely on the subjective preferences of those who have the capacity and desire to pay for something; etc.

The main advantage of Posner's theory of wealth maximization, as opposed to utilitarianism, would be its greater degree of objectivity. "Wealth, it is argued, can be objectively measured by market mechanisms",[95] unlike happiness, which seems

[89] Hierro (1993), pp. 401–403.

[90] Cf. Sandel (2012). Calabresi has also noted that there are goods that should not have a price (2016, p. 144). Instead, he advocates for a shift in perspective in economics, one that incorporates the valuation of moral costs. This broader view embraces a wider array of values that reflect the aims of a society, which, consequently, should also inform the aims of economic and economic-legal analysis. This stands in contrast to the reductionist approach that simplifies everything into a single ultimate value, such as efficiency or efficacy understood as wealth maximization (Calabresi 1994, p. 557).

[91] Mercado (1994), p. 106.

[92] Campbell (1988), p. 143.

[93] Campbell (1988), p. 135.

[94] Posner (1979), pp. 116–119.

[95] Campbell (1988), p. 139.

to depend on subjective states. However, while Posner's theory has this advantage over utilitarianism, it loses its teleological character. For better or for worse, Benthamite utilitarianism aims at an objective (maximization of happiness) that is not instrumental but an end in itself. In contrast, the maximization of wealth cannot avoid being instrumental. Wealth is not valued for its own sake, but for something else (such as happiness), which either brings us back to utilitarianism or presents the problem of determining the ultimate aim that justifies the maximization of wealth.

Dworkin has argued that efficiency understood as wealth maximization is not a value in itself:

> [...] the fact that goods are in the hands of those who would pay more to have them is as morally irrelevant as the book's being in the hands of the alphabetically prior party.
>
> Once social wealth is divorced from utility, at least, it loses all plausibility as a component of value.[96]

Those of us who defend the view that efficiency, understood as wealth maximization, can be an important component of justice—but who do not fully align with it—should embrace a substantive view of justice, and perhaps even a certain level of moral objectivism. As Hausman and McPherson suggest, objective approaches to welfare can be found in proposals such as Rawls' notion of certain primary goods[97] or in Sen's capabilities approach.[98] On the other hand, those who hold a relativistic or skeptical view of the content of values may feel compelled to subordinate them to efficiency or even to identify them with it, as many followers of EAL do.

As Hierro rightly points out, a problem originates from the pretended neutrality pursued by both economists and liberal political philosophers. This leads to merely procedural theories,[99] since, as it is inevitable to assume a certain level of commitment to some substantive values and, therefore, a "certain conception of the good".[100] The idea that certain human needs are objective—in a sense that desires are not—addresses this issue and sets a limit to efficiency.[101]

---

[96] Dworkin (1985), p. 245.

[97] For Rawls, there would be a sort of consensus among rational citizens about the need to acknowledge a list of primary goods for each individual subject, as defined by them (among those are basic rights and liberties, the social bases of self-respect, income, and wealth). This is because "we suppose that all citizens have a rational plan of life that requires for its fulfillment roughly the same kind of primary goods" (Rawls 1996, pp. 180–181, nota 8).

[98] Hausman and McPherson (2006), pp. 130–131.

[99] Beyond the list of primary goods, Rawls suggests a procedural theory of justice aimed at political and not substantive liberalism, leading us to the problem identified by Hierro.

[100] Hierro (1998), p. 133.

[101] Hierro (1998), p. 159.

5 Some Conclusions and a Bid for Minimal Moral Objectivism for EAL

As we have seen, depending on its authors and trends, Economic Analysis of Law (EAL) can be related to the philosophical assumptions of utilitarianism or libertarianism.

In recent decades, some shifts have occurred in the theories or approaches related to EAL, which now follow a path of methodological modesty. These approaches aim to provide tools for studying legal institutions and legislative or public policies while acknowledging the limitations inherent in this framework. However, there are still some conceptions of EAL that remain entrenched in the contributions of neoclassical economics and an economistic approach. These theories are based on a reductionist view of rationality and human behavior, as well as on a conception deeply influenced by scientific positivism. This perspective dismisses the wisdom of other disciplines—such as philosophy and ethics—as purely metaphysical, relative, and impractical, while presenting itself as objective and neutral.

Thus, under the premise of supposed scientific purity, the technical approach to economics has abandoned certain ethical questions such as those related to the meaning of welfare and other valuable objectives.[102] This shift has guided socially relevant discussions into the realm of technocratic imperialism. However, this scientific nature has been built at the expense of naturalizing certain social realities (such as the existence of the market),[103] without addressing the philosophical, political, and ethical assumptions underlying them.

Even though EAL may be associated with the philosophical presuppositions of utilitarianism and libertarianism, many of its proponents do not see these reflections as necessary or even useful for their goals. In the end, there remains strong skepticism at the metaethical level—despite the utilitarian ethical objectivism found in some of its versions—and a preference for solving moral issues based on highly subjective, intuitive, and emotional considerations derived from individual preferences.

This scientific and supposedly superior conception of EAL is clearly present in Posner, an author who has strongly influenced the development of EAL in Latin American countries, such as Peru. Posner's manifest rejection of the need to develop a moral theory to justify EAL, along with his pragmatist approach,[104] exemplifies

---

[102] Sen (2004), pp. 2–5.

[103] For example, Hayek defends the naturalization of the market based on the idea of spontaneous order (cf. Escalante 2016, pp. 42–48).

[104] Posner says: "This book asks whether, when the methods of legal positivism fail to yield a satisfactory resolution of a legal issue, the law should take its bearings from philosophy or from science. And it answers, 'from science'. But this is not a book just for lawyers and others who are interested in law. *I argue not only that moral philosophy has nothing to offer judges or legal scholars so far as either adjudication or the formulation of jurisprudential or legal doctrines is concerned, but also that it has very little to offer anyone engaged in a normative enterprise,* quite without regard to the law" (1999, p. VIII, the emphasis is mine).

this. As Posner himself states, judges emphasize consequences rather than doctrines.[105] Consequently, he adopts a skeptical view of morality, with allusions to emotivism[106] which denies moral objectivism, but not the possibility of speaking about historical and contextual truths. For example, Posner argues that the immorality of slavery or infanticide is not grounded in universal moral principles, but rather is contingent and subject to local circumstances.[107]

I believe that part of this rejection of moral theory stems from a misunderstanding of what minimal moral objectivism is, and how it can be compatible with a certain level of relativism and consequentialism.[108] While an exhaustive analysis of this issue is beyond the scope of this article, it is worth clarifying some key though obscure concepts related to this discussion.

Posner states that there are no universal moral principles, only local and contingent ones. For example, abortion may be considered moral in cultures with liberal attitudes toward sex or that have adopted a gender-inclusive perspective, but immoral in others that restrict sexual freedom or uphold religious beliefs about the sanctity of human life.[109] This is a correct description of moral variability across cultures, but it does not preclude the defense of a minimal form of moral objectivism, which would render Posner's claim incorrect in normative terms.

As Moreso[110] argues, moral objectivism is perfectly compatible with certain forms of relativism, such as vagueness (the idea that moral concepts are vague but some moral statements may be super-false or super-true); relativism as pluralism

---

[105] "Judges who don't insist that a legalistic algorithm will decide every case tend to be 'pragmatists', not in some pretentious philosophical sense (though there are affinities with pragmatic philosophers, such as Charles Sanders Peirce, a friend of Holmes, and John Dewey, an admirer of Holmes) but in the sense of an approach to decision making that emphasizes consequences over doctrine, or, stated otherwise, fits doctrine around consequences. Thayer and his followers were pragmatists" (Posner 2013, p. 168).

[106] "The non-cognitivist (or expressivist) believes that moral claims are expressive rather than referential, and what they express is an attitude or emotion that has no cognitive content. For example, the subset of non-cognitivist known as emotivists believes that a statement such as 'You are unjust!' is an expression of anger no different (from a cognitive standpoint) from slapping the person in the face. […] I think it is false, because insofar as a moral claim, or for that matter a slap in the face, embodies an evaluation of conduct, it has a cognitive content; we can say it is wrong to be angry at the person you slapped because he was not acting contrary to the moral code, as you believed he was. But I agree with the spirit as it were of noncognitivism because many moral claims are just the gift wrapping of theoretically ungrounded and ungroundable preferences and aversions" (Posner 1999, p. 11; see also p. 4).

[107] Posner (1999), p. 20.

[108] Having an objectivist conception of primary goods, needs, or human capabilities does not preclude adopting a consequentialist approach. For example, Dworkin clarified to Posner that his approach is more consequentialist than deontological (2006, p. 61). Similarly, Sen (2000) highlights the importance of the consequentialist approach when we consider public policy.

[109] Posner (1999), p. 23.

[110] Moreso (2003).

(the recognition that people have different life plans and commitments); or benign moral relativism (the idea that our moral norms should be applied with consideration of factual circumstances). Therefore, as Putnam notes:

> [...] holding that ethical inquiry is objective in the sense that some 'value judgments' are definitely true and some are definitely false, and more generally that some value positions (and some 'ideologies') are definitely wrong, and some are definitely inferior to some others, is not the same thing as holding the silly position that there are no indeterminate cases at all.[111]

Minimal moral objectivism does not suppose, strictly speaking, a form of moral realism (understood as the existence of moral properties similar to the objects of the physical world), let alone a form of moral absolutism. It also does not demand dogmatism, as it recognizes a certain level of fallibility in it, like in science.[112] Instead, minimal moral objectivism assumes the possibility of offering reasons instead of mere sensations, beliefs or private preferences. This is what Rawls calls "public reasons" that any rational and reasonable person could understand and accept.[113] From this perspective, moral reasoning would not be merely a matter of personal preference.[114]

Can we avoid moral theory? In the context of State Constitutional Law, I do not think so, especially when dealing with issues related to rights and justice (such as distributive justice).

Today, the State Constitutional Law enables us to use its most important tools (the principles established in constitutional texts) to achieve the ends of justice that we, as a society, want. If we accept Rawls' view that "[j]ustice is the first virtue of social institutions"[115] and that a fair society is one that pursues certain principles of justice, I believe that the aversion to moral theory found in certain strands of EAL undermines this objective. Therefore, EAL should be seen as a useful tool, but not as a set of infallible rules.[116]

---

[111] Putnam (2004), p. 148.

[112] Atienza (2017), pp. 200–212.

[113] Rawls (2001), pp. xvii–xviii.

[114] As Atienza states, "whether we should respect the autonomy of individuals or seek to meet their basic needs for food, shelter, health, etc. is not something we may or may not prefer, it does not depend on our choices. If we were to choose otherwise, we would simply be doing (choosing) the wrong thing" (2017, p. 195).

[115] Rawls (1971), p. 3.

[116] As Mercado states: "Regulatory impact analysis and economic cost-benefit analysis are tools, not rules. They are mechanisms to inform decision-making, but they do not constitute or anticipate the decision itself. The decision itself is and must be an exercise of political judgment by the public authorities" (2013, p. 107).

References

Atienza M (2017) Filosofía del derecho y transformación social. Trotta, Madrid
Barbarosch E (2013) Teorías de la justicia y la metaética contemporánea, 2nd edn. La Ley, Buenos Aires
Brennan J (2012) Libertarianism. What everyone needs to know. Oxford University Press, New York
Bullard A (2015) Análisis económico del derecho. Entre el funcionalismo y la esquizofrenia jurídica. In: Fabra J, Núñez A (eds) Enciclopedia de filosofía y teoría del derecho. UNAM, México D. F, pp 737–766
Bullard A (2018) Análisis económico del derecho. PUCP, Lima
Calabresi G (1994) An exchange—about law and economics: a letter to Ronald Dworkin (1980). Hofstra Law Rev 8:553–562. http://hdl.handle.net/20.500.13051/1274
Calabresi G (2016) The future of law & economics. Yale University Press, New Haven
Calabresi G, Bobbit P (1978) Tragic choices. W. W. Norton & Company, New York
Campbell T (1988) Justice. Macmillan Education, London
Cohen GA (1990) Equality of what? On welfare, goods and capabilities. Louvain Econ Rev 56:357–382
Dworkin R (1985) A matter of principle. Harvard University Press, Massachusetts
Dworkin R (2006) Justice in robes. Harvard University Press, Massachusetts
Escalante F (2016) Historia mínima del neoliberalismo. La Siniestra, Lima
Farrell M (2007) Utilitarismo, liberalismo y democracia, 2nd edn. Fontamara, México D. F
Garzón E (1995) Mercado y justicia. Isonomía 2:7–28
Goldman D (2017) Análisis económico del derecho penal y derecho penal liberal: confluencias y bifurcaciones. Derecho Penal y Criminología 38(104):13–74
Hausman D, McPherson M (2006) Economic analysis, moral philosophy and public policy. Cambridge University Press, Cambridge
Hayek F (2011) The constitution of liberty. The University of Chicago Press, Chicago
Hierro L (1993) Contra el imperio de la riqueza (Dworkin v. Posner). Revista de Ciencias Sociales 38:383–411
Hierro L (1994) La pobreza como injusticia (Dworkin v. Calabresi). Doxa 15–16:945–967
Hierro L (1998) Justicia, igualdad y eficiencia. Isonomía 9:129–171
Holmes S, Sunstein C (2000) The cost of rights. W. W. Norton & Company, New York
Kaldor N (1939) Welfare propositions of economics and interpersonal comparisons of utility. Econ J 49:549–552. https://doi.org/10.2307/2224835
Macpherson CB (1990) The political theory of possessive individualism. Hobbes to Locke. Oxford University Press, Oxford
Mazzone S (2000) Stato e anarchia. Il pensiero politico del libertarismo americano: Murray Newton Rothbard. Università di Catania, Milan
Mercado P (1994) Análisis económico del derecho y utilitarismo. Concordancias y divergencias. Télos 3(2):99–123
Mercado P (2013) Calidad de la ley: evaluación de impacto normativo y argumentos económicos. Anales de la Cátedra Francisco Suárez 47:85–108
Moreso J (2003) El reino de los derechos y la objetividad moral. Cartapacio de Derecho 4:1–46
Nozick R (1999) Anarchy, state, and utopia. Blackwell, Oxford
Posner RA (1979) Utilitarianism, economics, and legal theory. J Leg Stud 8:103–140
Posner RA (1999) The problematics of moral and legal theory. Harvard University Press, Cambridge
Posner RA (2013) Reflections on judging. Harvard University Press, Cambridge
Putnam H (2004) Reason, truth and history. Cambridge University Press, Cambridge
Rawls J (1971) A theory of justice. Belknap Press, Massachusetts
Rawls J (1996) Political liberalism. Columbia University Press, New York
Rawls J (2001) Justice as fairness. A restatement. Belknap Press, Massachusetts

Rodríguez García G (2019) Mucho más que palabras bonitas: economía, instituciones y el impacto del buen derecho en el enriquecimiento de las naciones. Thēmis, Lima
Rojas RM (2000) Las contradicciones del derecho penal. Ad-Hoc, Buenos Aires
Sandel M (2012) What money can't buy. The moral limits of markets. Allen Lane, New York
Sen A (2000) Development as freedom. Alfred A. Knopf, New York
Sen A (2004) On ethics and economics. Blackwell, Malden
Swift A (2014) Political philosophy. A beginners' guide for students and politicians. Polity Press, Cambridge

The Symbolic Aspects of Law Between Expressive Theories and Economic Analysis

Francesco Ferraro

Abstract The symbolic aspects of both law and behaviour under the law are independent of enforcement and depend on the way social norms interact with legal rules and principles. The outcomes of such interaction can be hard to explain from an economic standpoint, and a strand of 'expressivist' thought focusing on these aspects has thus emerged, setting itself in opposition to, and as incompatible with, rational choice theory and the economic analysis of law. But expressive and economic accounts of the law can nonetheless fruitfully cooperate, provided that the former relinquish their typical hostility towards consequentialism and the latter renounce their claim to exclusively rely on monetary measurements of value and show themselves open to alternative methods for measuring and making interpersonal comparisons of utility.

1 Introduction: The Effort to Understand Symbolic Behaviour Under Legal and Social Norms

Legal theorists have almost exclusively been concerned with one specific function of the law, namely, the one consisting in creating duties, rights, powers, and other Hohfeldian 'jural relations'. Courts and agencies are expected to enforce such relations. This function, then, is basically about guiding behaviour, that of lay citizens and officials alike. In what follows, I will focus on functions of a different kind that the law fulfils—what we might call its *symbolic* functions. These are not directly dependent on enforcement of the law, so much so that, sometimes, the mere enactment of a statute, or even the notice of its enactment, can suffice for it to fulfil its symbolic functions (see Gusfield

F. Ferraro (✉)
Department of Law "Cesare Beccaria", University of Milan, Milan, Italy
e-mail: francesco.ferraro@unimi.it

S. Zorzetto et al. (eds.), *Developments in Law and Economics in the Italo-Iberoamerican Context*, Economic Analysis of Law in European Legal Scholarship 21, https://doi.org/10.1007/978-3-032-03317-8_3

1963, p. 177). However, these functions depend on the citizens' attitudes and their disposition to treat the law as symbolically meaningful. Social norms usually shape intersubjective symbolic meanings, including those ascribed to the law and those which can be expressed by the citizens' behaviour under the law. At times, the symbolic relevance of private conduct can interfere with the laws' efficacy and/or effectiveness, and it can therefore hinder the fulfilment of the behaviour-guiding function. This happens when the citizens' behaviour is prompted not by 'instrumental' or 'outcome-oriented' motivation but by 'symbolic' or 'expressive' concerns (see Schuessler 2001, pp. 3–4). Typically, citizens acting (or refraining from acting) on symbolic grounds do not seem to respond, or seem to respond in unpredictable ways, to rewards and punishments, that is, to the incentives (widely understood) that the law usually relies on for compliance.

When the symbolic aspects of the law are involved, then, social norms interact (and at times interfere) with legal rules and principles in ways that can be hard to grasp from the standpoint of an economic approach. A whole strand of 'expressivist' thought focusing on these aspects has emerged, presenting itself as opposed to, and incompatible with, rational choice theory and the economic analysis of law. Here, I will attempt to build a metatheoretical bridge between expressivist and economic approaches to law, offering some suggestions as to how this bridge can be crossed in the analysis of legislation, constitutional law, and criminal law.

In Sect. 2, I will offer an account of the 'second layer' of symbolic meaning that the law can take on, on top of the 'first layer', consisting of duties, rights, and other legal relations. Symbolic meaning is often equated with expressive meaning, in the sense that it conveys attitudes, values, moral judgments, and individual and collective identities. In Sect. 3, I will point to some attempts at explaining compliance with social norms in terms of rational choice theory: ingenuous as they may be, these explanations usually fall short when it comes to accounting for people's purely expressive behaviour, i.e., noninstrumental behaviour merely motivated by a desire to express one's own identity, beliefs, and values. In Sect. 4, I will describe some instances of symbolic and expressive behaviour in the legal system in two different modes: *under* the law, on the part of citizens, and *by means of* the law, on the part of lawmakers who use legislation to send out messages rather than to guide the conduct of citizens and officials. In Sect. 5, I will try to show that expressive and economic accounts of the law can fruitfully cooperate, provided that the former relinquish their typical hostility towards consequentialism, and the latter renounce their claim to rely exclusively on monetary measurements of value and show themselves open to alternative methods for measuring and interpersonal comparisons of utility, like polling for preferences.

2 The Symbolic Mode and Its Expressive Applications

What makes something a *symbol*? This question is perplexing enough to have received a considerable variety of different answers over the course of the history of thought,[1] most of them pointing to the presumptive differences between symbols and *signs*, or else between symbols and *other kinds* of signs (thereby taking the latter to be a more general category inclusive of the former).[2] Symbols *mean* or *stand for* something else, but in a different way than signs do. Despite the indeterminacy of linguistic signs, the relation between signs and their signified is often seen as more straightforward. This view typically proceeds from the observation that signs (such as words in any natural language) are entirely conventional, which somehow limits and guides their interpretation. The relation between *symbols* and what they stand for, by contrast, is seen as somehow shakier, or more indeterminate, as it is often very unclear not only what the symbol refers to but also if whether is a symbol at all (rather than a mere sign). The picture of a lion could be a mere representation of the animal in question, but it could also symbolize wildlife in general, or even one or more qualities that are usually associated with that animal, such as strength, royalty, or courage. We can thus say that symbols connote 'a much more imprecise, open-ended sequence of events and experiences' than (other) signs (Firth 1973, pp. 66). According to Eco ([1984] 1986), symbols convey a 'nebula' of 'underdetermined and vague' content; interpreting something as a symbol is a modality of textual *use*, originating from a *pragmatic decision* which 'produces at the semantic level a new sign-function, by associating new content—so far as it is possible, undetermined and vague—to expression already correlated to a coded content. The main characteristic of the symbolic mode is that the text, when this mode is not realized interpretively, remains endowed with sense—at its literal or figurative level' (ibid., pp. 162–163).

Eco's characterization of the 'symbolic mode' of interpretation could be integrated by noting that any human activity or object, even if it is not originally a sign, can fulfil a *symbolic function*, that is, it can 'work as' a symbol. In this sense, law can be treated as a kind of human activity, or a complex of human activities, made up of acts by officials, legal professionals, and regular citizens. Now, '[a]ctions are expressive: they carry meanings. [...] What can be said for actions can also be said of law' (Sunstein 1996a, pp. 2021–2022). Law fulfils a symbolic function when it 'makes a statement,' that is, when it expresses a certain message which transcends the face-value meaning of legal provisions (like a permission or prohibition to engage in a certain behaviour) and adds a 'second layer' of meaning (van Klink

[1] See Eco ([1984] 1986), pp. 130–131, on the difficulties encountered by thinkers who have attempted a plausible definition of 'symbol'.

[2] This latter approach is quite widespread in semiotics: see, for instance, Morris (1971), pp. 100–102; Peirce (1976), pp. 241–244. However, de Saussure ([1916] 1995), p. 101, does not consider symbols as a species of signs, because in his view symbols retain some 'rational' link to what they refer to, a link that (unlike what is the case with signs) is never entirely arbitrary or conventional.

2016, pp. 20). For instance, a criminal law making a certain behaviour punishable with imprisonment not only prescribes that those found guilty be punished in a certain way (the 'first layer' of meaning) but also *symbolizes* moral condemnation of that behaviour (Kahan 1996, pp. 597–601) and expresses 'attitudes of resentment and indignation' and 'judgments of disapproval and reprobation' (Feinberg 1970, pp. 98).[3] That 'communicative' aspect of criminal punishment has been associated with retributivism and considered an instance of communicative behaviour consistent with the Gricean account of meaning (see Nozick 1981, p. 370).

Accordingly, theories of law which have focused on its symbolic functions have been labelled as 'expressive'.[4] Their main fields of inquiry so far have been criminal law (as hinted at above) and US constitutional law, with a particular focus on the antidiscrimination principle (under the Equal Protection Clause) (see Anonymous 1999). US constitutional doctrines have also resorted to expressive arguments in outstanding cases, not only with regard to racial discrimination but also in interpreting and applying the Endorsement Clause of the First Amendment (as in the well-known concurring opinion by Justice O'Connor in *Lynch v. Donnelly*).[5] Regarding US antidiscrimination law, many have endorsed a 'stigma theory', under which the central concern of antidiscrimination is with prohibiting official action whose social meaning is a message stigmatizing some groups, with an implicit declaration of their inferiority on sexist or racist grounds.[6]

Interesting applications of the expressive approach include the study of social norms, both in themselves and in relation to the law. Cass Sunstein (1996a, p. 2025), for instance, has pointed out that some of the 'statements' the law can make 'may be designed to affect social norms and in that way ultimately to affect both judgments and behavior'. In such cases, the government attempts to influence the normative climate of society, much like private 'norm entrepreneurs' do; if any behavioural changes are actually sought, they are pursued as 'independent effects'

[3] A slightly different terminological choice is proposed by van der Burg (2005), pp. 252–258, who distinguishes between a properly expressive function of law (consisting in the expression of constitutional values and other cherished values of the political community) and a *communicative* function (consisting in the creation of a shared vocabulary and framework for discussion, as a function distinct from that of guiding conduct). These constitute two different senses of the 'symbolic function' of law.

[4] But compare McAdams (2014), p. 13, who identifies 'four categories of expressive claims in the legal literature: (1) that law influences beliefs, emotions, or behavior by what it expresses, an expressive theory of law's effects; (2) that expressive politics determine the content of law, an expressive-politics theory of law; (3) that the normative status of law depends on its meaning, a normative theory of expressive law; and (4) that the normative status of the private behavior the law regulates depends on its meaning, a normative theory of expressive conduct.'

[5] *Lynch v. Donnelly*, 465U.S. 668 (1984) (O'Connor, J., concurring). The first endorsement of an 'expressivist' account of the Equal Protection Clause by the US Supreme Court is usually considered to be *Strauder v. West Virginia*, 100U.S. 303 (1880).

[6] For an extensive discussion of the theory and a review of authors who have endorsed it, see Koppelman (1996), pp. 57–76.

of the laws,[7] namely, effects which do not depend on rule-following on the part of the law's addressees. But social norms also provide in and of themselves a field for application of expressivist theories, in that 'individuals see norms as meaningfully *expressing* their social identities, their relationships to other people, or shared intentions and values' (Anderson 2000, p. 171, emphasis added). At the same time, social norms are required for individuals 'to express their attitudes adequately and intelligibly in action, to express them in ways others can grasp. If a society lacks the social norms needed to adequately express its members' reflectively endorsed valuations, the rational thing to do is to invent and institute such norms' (Anderson 1993, p. 18).

3 Rational Choice Accounts of Social Norms and Expressive Criticisms

It would seem that the expressive approach concerns itself with aspects of the law which fall outside of the scope of the Law & Economics discourse, taken as both a descriptive and a prescriptive intellectual enterprise. Law & Economics focuses on the development of models based on analytical techniques and on the values of economic analysis to account for the law-related phenomena of human activity, i.e., 'the ongoing decisions and actions of such legal institutions as legislative bodies and the judicial process, and such practices as the legally permissible interactions of individuals' (Brion 1999, p. 1042); when it takes a prescriptive stance, it advocates the application of economic principles to public decision-making and 'in shaping the permissible scope of interactions among legal persons' (ibid.). At a first glance, it seems very difficult for this kind of economics-driven approach to give adequate consideration to the purely expressive aspects of the law, and of people's behaviour under the law. Sometimes, actions are carried out only in order to express some value, belief, cultural identity, or the like. This is where individuals do not act with a view to the foreseeable consequences of their actions, but at the same time those actions cannot, properly speaking, be considered irrational: they are instead rationally oriented 'with regard to value' rather than 'with regard to purpose', to use Max Weber's well-known distinction (Weber 1921, pp. 24–25; cf. Schuessler 2001, p. 8). Apparently, individuals acting in this way do not seek their personal utility but rather seek self-expression: '[e]xpressiveness, not utility, is what flows back' (Nozick 1993, p. 28). What holds for individual decisions can also holds for official decision-making, either legislative or judicial (and administrative, one might add).

For these reasons, Pildes (1998, p. 726) observes that

> [m]uch of the emerging literature on social norms takes as its antagonist rational-choice theory. [...] Social norm analysis takes rational-choice theory and economic analysis of law to task for failing to understand the complexities of social interaction—in particular, that

[7] See van Klink (2016); the distinction between direct, indirect, and independent effects is drawn from Griffiths (1979).

> actions of individuals not only bring about certain immediate material consequences but also express an individual's values and attitudes. Because people care about the character they manifest (whether for instrumental or intrinsic reasons), action is motivated by these expressive concerns as well as by more familiar material concerns. Background social norms help determine social understandings about what particular attitudes and values are expressed by certain actions, taken in certain contexts.

For Sunstein (1996b, p. 909), '[s]ometimes people do not behave as economists predict. Many important and well-known anomalies in human behavior are best explained by reference to social norms and to the fact that people feel shame when they violate those norms. Thus when people deviate from economic predictions—when they appear not to maximize their "expected utility"—it is often because of norms.' It has been observed that, among other things, rational choice accounts miss the *first-person* point of view when it comes to compliance with social norms, i.e., the possibility of accounting for the *reasons* that those who participate in a practice would *themselves* offer when asked why they are following the rules governing the practice.[8]

Now, Pildes himself acknowledges that people care about the character they manifest, not only for intrinsic reasons but also for *instrumental* ones. When the expressive potential of the law is consciously exploited to influence (or strengthen) social norms, as in many instances of so-called 'symbolic' legislation, this kind of behaviour is clearly geared towards a definite purpose and can be interpreted in terms of expected utilities. This is the case with individuals Sunstein refers to as 'norm entrepreneurs', i.e., 'people interested in changing social norms'. Lawmakers, as political actors, often try to steer social norms towards a desired direction by using the law as a communicative device. In this sense, legislation can address *attitudes* rather than *actions*.[9]

The symbolic functions of behaviour under social norms can also be exploited (more or less consciously) by individuals in order to maximise their personal utility in a concrete, empirically assessable, and even quantifiable

[8] For Wendel (2002), p. 5, '[w]hen it comes to social norms like the practice of showing gratitude, rational-choice theorists face the challenge of offering an explanation that provides an adequate account of these norms, while remaining faithful to the methodological commitments of law and economics. Expressions of gratitude are no doubt functional, in the sense that they contribute to social cohesion. But functional explanations slight the first-person perspective—that is, the reason that might be given by a person actually embedded in the social practice of expressing gratitude who is concerned with expressing her authentic feelings.'

[9] This has been called the 'law as symbol' (LAS) or 'communicative' approach to legislation, as opposed to the 'law as instrument' approach: see van der Burg (2005); van Klink (2019). A slightly different 'expressive' function of the law in influencing social norms is described in Cooter (1998), pp. 593–596: legislation can solve coordination problems in transitioning from a system of social norms that is stuck in a Pareto-inferior, first-order Nash equilibrium to one that is Pareto-superior. Tushnet and Yackle (1997, pp. 74-76) call '*expressive* statutes' those laws that attempt to change the values and preferences of their targets, thereby indirectly altering the costs and benefits of their courses of action (in contrast with '*instrumental* statutes,' which take those values and preferences as given and only alter costs and benefits of the courses of action, and properly '*symbolic* statutes,' which simply 'make a stand' and lack definite targets).

manner. This is the hunch followed by those who have tried to provide an account of social-norm compliance in terms of rational choice theory. Among them, we find EA Posner (1998), who observes that symbolic behaviour is part of people's everyday life and applies a 'signalling model' to analyse such behaviour and its implications for the legal system. Posner considers that symbolic behaviour is 'intended as a signal that the agent has a characteristic that the agent wants the receiver of the signal to believe that the agent has, but that the receiver cannot directly observe' (EA Posner 1998, p. 767). In other words, '[s]ymbols matter because a person's manifested attitude toward symbols tells others something about that person's character. People rely heavily on this information when deciding whether to engage in cooperative behavior' (ibid.). The model devised by EA Posner to explain the significance that symbolic behaviour has for cooperation is that of a 'cooperation game' in which the participants (the citizens) can be divided into 'cooperators' and 'cheaters'. The former 'care enough about future payoffs that they would want the game to continue', whereas the latter 'value the immediate payoffs more than the (highly discounted) stream of future payoffs' (ibid., p. 768). Normally, in the first round of the game, participants do not know who the cheaters are. Therefore, to secure cooperation, genuine cooperators send signals: that is, costly actions intended to distinguish them from the cheaters, because cooperators can afford these actions, while cheaters cannot. Those who engage in such action are displaying an expectation of high returns on cooperation, which make the costly signalling action both affordable and worthwhile. Of course, signals must have the appropriate cost structure, because if cheaters also find it advantageous to send them (at least in the game's first rounds), they can mimic the cooperators' behaviour and ultimately undermine trust and others' willingness to cooperate.[10] Generally speaking, symbolic acts allow agents to express genuine commitment to internalized values, thereby gaining a competitive advantage in cooperative societies (see Cooter 1998, pp. 606–607).

Behaviours can spontaneously take on symbolic value owing to mere historical contingencies, but symbols can also be fabricated: in the latter case, 'norm entrepreneurs' decide what counts as a signal and participants in the cooperation game decide which symbols to endorse, in order to signal their willingness to cooperate. Some symbols will be 'pure', in the sense that they do not yield any material benefits: think, for instance, of the act of saluting the national flag. Other symbols will be 'impure', because they contribute to the

[10] 'Several kinds of signals have received little attention in the literature but are of great significance. When a person shows respect for the national flag, performs civic obligations like voting and jury duty, and avoids people who are considered enemies of the state but are in fact desirable cooperative partners in the short term, this person engages in actions that are costly. If receivers interpret these actions as a means of revealing one's type, and if the actions are cheap enough that cooperators can recover their costs through payoffs from cooperation, but costly enough that cheaters cannot recover their costs by defecting in the first round, the actions may serve as signals' (EA Posner 1998, p. 769).

public good, benefitting the citizenry at large: falling into this category are acts like voting or discriminating against perceived enemies of the country (as in the McCarthy years in the United States).[11]

Other attempts to apply rational choice theory to social norms include the analysis of coordination conventions and explanations based on social sanctions. Accounts of the first kind have been criticized, among others, by Anderson (2000), who holds that coordination conventions can at best explain only a small range of social norms. These models rely on purely self-interested incentives, which must be sufficient for people to contribute to a groups' collective aims and to motivate them to sanction deviations and reward compliance with norms. However, most of the time incentives to deviate from the norm are too strong, and it is unclear what purely self-interested incentives could actually motivate those who are meant to sanction the deviations: there must be at least some agents who engage in sanctioning for motivating reasons other than pure self-interest (see Anderson 2000, pp. 177–178). Similar objections attach to explanations based on social sanctions. If we apply rational choice theory by holding that people comply with social norms because of the attached sanctions, we must explain why agents actually sanction deviations, since sanctioning is costly. Failure to sanction, in turn, is rarely sanctioned, and people sometimes even observe norms which *forbid sanctioning* others' violations: think of norms against tattling, even when actual violations of other norms are disclosed. Sanction theories, generally speaking, do not account for instances of norm-following where no convincing threat of sanction is actually present, nor do they make room for acceptance of authority or endorsement of the rules' rationale in motivating conduct (see ibid., pp. 181–182). Anderson argues that the traditional *homo oeconomicus* model adopted by rational choice theory should be replaced with the model of the *homo sociologicus*, embodying a different paradigm of practical reasoning, not focused on incentives for action and quantifiable returns. Under this paradigm, '[t]o count as a reason for action, a consideration must appeal to a person's self-understanding, not her self-interest. It must fit in to her understanding of her identity' (ibid., p. 192).

Interestingly, what is difficult to explain in terms of economic rationality, can be accounted for in terms of what we might call 'evolutionary' rationality, i.e., behaviours that make perfect sense if looked at from the perspective of natural selection. As recently highlighted by Kłusek (2024), the early human societies of hunter-gatherers valued cooperation more than anything else as a crucial condition for survival in a hostile environment. Cooperation failures posed a threat to the survival of the entire group, and those who did not share fairly or who stole, cheated, or harmed other members had to be punished. Being subject to punishment meant a loss of status within the group, a diminishment that in turn decreased the chances of procreation. At the same time, the very fact that punishing is costly meant that those who engaged in it would gain in social status: '[i]n short, punitive reactions, through

[11] See EA Posner (1998), p. 775, commenting that Senator Joseph McCarthy was 'a classic norm entrepreneur' who turned avoidance of communists into a powerful signal of loyalty to the national community.

their effect on social standing, influence the process of natural selection. [...] Punishment comes at a cost—one risks the possibility of retaliation. Carrying it out sends a signal to the opposite sex that one is a strong, courageous, valuable potential partner' (Kłusek 2024, p. 299).

Anderson's expressive approach can be fruitfully applied as well to EA Posner's signalling model. We can agree that people often act in pursuit of expressiveness, rather than for more tangible returns: they wish to express their identities while, at the same time, confirming *to themselves* that they are indeed the kind of person they purport to be, before even considering sending out signals to others regarding the values they endorse. Posner points out that, sometimes, if people decide not to send the requested cooperation signal, this is not out of a wish to leave the game after the first rounds because they do not intend to invest in cooperation: sometimes people who do not send signals are not of the cheater type, but rather abstain from signalling on principle. They find the signal too costly for other reasons.

> Thus, the principled communist or liberal might refuse to show respect for the flag, because he or she believes that the true patriotic person is one who points out the deficiencies in the existing political system. The difference between a real cheater and, say, a principled liberal is crucial: the former does not care about the future while the latter cares about the future but believes that the required symbolic behaviour is repugnant. But the two types are lumped together by the cooperator who is persuaded of the value of the signal. (EA Posner 1998, p. 777)

As undoubtedly expedient as it may be to distinguish principled nonsenders from cheaters, Posner's analysis here seems to be lacking in two respects. First, it does not explain at all why principled dissenters should find it especially costly to send the signal when required. After all, if the signal, in and of itself, is not considered by them as deserving special consideration, they could simply choose to go with the flow and send it out just like all the other cooperators. Why should these dissenters regard such an action as too costly? Why should they expose themselves to the risk of being seen as the cheater type? Second, cooperators who are convinced of the value of the signal do not simply lump together the potential cheaters with the principled nonsenders. Usually, cooperators of this kind (call them 'conformist cooperators') deny dissenters their trust even when offered explanations for their refusal to send the expected signal. How can we explain the obstinate distrust of conformist cooperators?

A plausible hypothesis in answer to these questions is that the reasons for principled abstention from sending the signal, as well as for conformist refusal to accept explanations for such abstention, are of the expressive kind. On the one hand, principled dissenters refuse to bow to conformist signals, because doing so would contradict their self-image, or the image of the person *they* want to be. They also want the symbols and signals to change, because they associate them with values they do not endorse or otherwise see them as a distraction from the values they do endorse (and which they think others should endorse, too). On the other hand, conformist cooperators identify with a certain signal because of its symbolic value, that is, because in their view it expresses their identity and what they believe in, and they do not countenance disregard and disrespect for the signal itself, much less criticisms and efforts to change it. What both kinds want to flow back from their actions is expressiveness. If the economic approach neglects to incorporate these considerations into its analysis, it runs the risk of misunderstanding crucial aspects not only of social norms but also of law.

4 Symbolic Legislation and Other Expressive Behaviour in the Legal System

Sending out messages through behaviour becomes particularly relevant in the domain of legislation. Laws are sometimes passed that do not seem intended be complied with (see Atienza 1989, p. 389), or at least—considering how difficult it is to prove this kind of legislative dishonesty—they appear to be crafted in such a way that compliance and enforcement do not seem to be of paramount concern. There are number of clues, both semantic and pragmatic, that hint at this character of the statutes in question. One is the lack of adequate secondary provisions aimed at enforcing the substantive provisions. Another is the vagueness or ambiguity of the language employed, which makes it more difficult for the addressees to comply with the law, and for the authorities to enforce it. While these are semantic clues, pragmatic ones, relative to the lawmaking context, also tell us that a piece of symbolic legislation is probably being issued: these typically include the presence of conflicts between social groups, the politization of such conflicts (i.e., some group considers that a 'moral victory' would be gained by passing a certain law), and an actual or perceived crisis or emergency affecting the community, seemingly calling for immediate legislative action.[12]

Sometimes this kind of legislation answers to some instrumental purpose envisaged by lawmakers. They might be sending out a signal accordant with already existing social norms, thereby strengthening their ideological bonds with the constituents. Or, as discussed, they could be trying to influence social norms, by changing them or by confirming them through the force of the law. They might even be *pretending* to address a perceived social problem, knowing that it cannot actually be solved by statute and yet resorting to statutory enactment even so, in order to signal that they share the concerns of the electorate, and specifically of their constituents, and are doing something to address the issue in question, or they may be using the statutory enactment as a statement of power, in order to show that they are in control of the situation even if, in reality, they lack the power needed to address it. These instrumental uses of symbolic legislation seem to make an easy fit with the methods of rational choice theory and the empirical analyses of political economy.

---

[12] See van Klink (2016), p. 20, who refers to these as 'criteria' for identifying symbolic legislation, but it seems more expedient to interpret them as mere 'semiotic clues' to the fact that the lawmakers may be trying to exploit the law's symbolic connotations (see Ferraro 2022, p. 112).

Nonetheless, other uses of symbolic legislation, which we might label as noninstrumental, seem at a first glance less apt to be analysed in terms of rational choice theory. When legislators use the law to send a message, but the message becomes an end in itself (with no regard for the further effects of sending it out), they are acting expressively. Think, for instance, of politicians who oppose the decriminalisation of cannabis consumption for nonmedicinal (recreational) purposes. They may well hold that, while they recognise that the consequences of criminalisation are not what they would wish for, the law should nonetheless express the message that doing drugs is wrong and harmful and that the best way to convey this communicative content is to criminalise such behaviour.

In such cases, rational choice theory seems less adequate for understanding and explaining the use of the law that is being made: insofar as the stance taken by lawmakers seems genuinely principled (and not, for instance, a pretext to craft a signal or send one to the electorate), it is difficult to empirically assess and quantify the effects of their actions and to link them to a rational choice (as intended consequences of their acts). Note that this is not the familiar objection to the *homo oeconomicus* model, charging that the model is based on the reductionist fiction of a 'rational fool', leaving out of account sympathy, altruistic concerns, and all other interests which are not strictly self-regarding (see Sen 1977). The agents in question could very well be acting out of purely self-centred motivations, utterly unmoved by other-regarding considerations, wishing only to express their own personality, identity, ideology, etc. However, signalling theory and other similar models seem to focus on incentives for symbolic behaviour that could work only when agents are acting instrumentally and with a view to attaining some definite purposes. When symbolic behaviour is not seen by the agent as instrumental to some end, but rather as an end in itself, such models seem ill-suited to explaining and predicting the behaviour in question.

In criminal law, understanding symbolic behaviour is of the utmost importance not only when those involved are acting as makers or 'issuers' of law, but also when they are acting as 'receivers', as the law's addressees. Specific problems arise, for instance, with regard to 'culturally motivated offences', that is, offences incurred because of behaviours that are commonly accepted, or even required, in some specific minority group (such as ethnic groups of recent immigration) but are stigmatized by the cultural majority and criminally prosecuted by the legal system. An example of such a crime is female genital mutilation. Other examples are vindictive violence and duelling. Some could be perfectly aware of the legal consequences of these practices and the harsh punishment they are going to incur if they follow them, but will still be undeterred. The problem does not seem to be that punishments are not severe enough to outweigh the expected utility of the action, this for the simple reason that agents may not be acting out of utility expectations: they may not be pursuing some definite objective as the result of action.

Another area where the symbolic aspects of law take centre stage is constitutional law. As noted, the expressive approach has gained popularity in both constitutional scholarship and constitutional doctrines in the US. In the constitutional field, Pildes and Niemi (1993) have coined the notion of *expressive harm.*

> An expressive harm is one that results from the ideas or attitudes expressed through a governmental action, rather than from the more tangible or material consequences the action brings about. On this view, the meaning of a governmental action is just as important as what that action does. Public policies can violate the Constitution not only because they bring about concrete costs, but because the very meaning they convey demonstrates inappropriate respect for relevant public values. (Pildes and Niemi 1993, pp. 506–507)

Expressive harms are 'social rather than individual. Their primary effect is not as much the tangible burdens they impose on particular individuals, but the way in which they undermine collective understandings' (ibid., p. 507). They bear on the meaning of governmental *actions*, which can be accordingly be taken to mean that constitutional norms and values are being rejected, denied, or disregarded and thereby undermined. If the courts are to apply the notion of expressive harm, they have to interpret not merely legal text but also what meanings a certain governmental action can express in the specific social, political, and historical context. Hellman (2008) has offered an expressive account of wrongful discrimination: discrimination is wrong when the social meaning of the discriminating policy or action is 'morally problematic'. More to the point, actions can be *demeaning*: in a certain context, their social meaning—something Hellman considers to be 'objective'—can be that some people are deemed inferior because of their ethnicity or gender.[13] In these applications of the expressive approach, however, no account is taken of who the senders of a symbolic message are or what their purpose is in sending the message, and their intentions likewise count for little, if at all. For Pildes, Niemi, and Hellman, it is the context that makes the message: the question is not about what the agent (usually a policymaker or lawmaker) had in mind or what her purpose was but rather concerns the social meaning such as it could be reasonably assessed by an external beholder, like a court. For Sunstein, 'the meanings of actions are not fully within the agent's control. Indeed, some agents may not even be aware of the relevant meanings. [...] The social meanings of actions are very much a function of existing social norms' (Sunstein 1996a, p. 2022). Now, if the functioning of social norms is not adequately explained, it will also be hard to explain this very peculiar kind of harm.

5 Can the Symbolic Aspects of Law Be Made Amenable to Economic Analysis?

Despite the concerns just outlined, and some challenges claiming otherwise, the economic analysis of law can fruitfully be brought to bear in understanding the symbolic aspects of law. But some qualifications need to be made in following such

[13] Hellman (2008), pp. 34–58. To clarify Hellman's position, what she describes as conditions for wrongful discrimination involves not only an *expressive* element (an action or policy expresses the idea that a person or group is of lower status) but also an element of *power* (the actor or institution expressing such a message must have sufficient social power for the expression to have force).

an approach. This is only possible if we reject the pristine version of expressivism presented by Anderson (1993)—propounding a theory of value and rational action alternative to, and incompatible with, consequentialism in all its forms—and in its place we substitute an approach that considers the possibility of including expressiveness as part of the very utility of those who engage in symbolic action.[14] Alternatively, expressive and symbolic considerations can be considered as what makes something (part of) someone's utility: in this sense, symbolic value shapes preferences.

Anderson (1993) seems to provide 'an expressive theory of law as a theory that accords foundational or canonical relevance to certain types of sentence meaning possessed by the actions of legal officials' (Adler 2000a, p. 1494). As Adler (2000a) compellingly argues, such a theory—a kind of normative moral theory applied to law—is unconvincing insofar it cuts the connection between the moral significance of the linguistic meaning of actions and the causal impact of that meaning. In a rejoinder to Adler (2000a), Anderson and Pildes (2000) have restated the normative expressive theory they both endorse as one that focuses on the expression of *attitudes* through action: what makes a certain action right (or wrong) is not its linguistic meaning in and of itself but rather the fact that it expresses the right (or wrong) attitude towards other persons. In this way, and as Adler (2000b) himself acknowledges, their theory so restated eschews the kind of criticisms he previously levelled at it (Adler 2000a).

Be that as it may, there is undeniably an anti-consequentialist thrust to this kind of expressivism,[15] as is also evident from Anderson and Pildes's treatment of the abovementioned notion of expressive harm. In their view, proper expressive harm is not causal: individuals suffer this kind of harm when they are treated in ways that express the wrong attitude towards them, while the causal consequences of such treatment (such as psychological and reputational damage and factual diminution of the victim's social status) are labelled 'nonexpressive' harms. The two kinds of harms are not only different but also incommensurable, in the sense that they cannot be measured and added up on the same scale. Thus, governmental action can be right or wrong and (in Anderson and Pildes's view) constitutional or unconstitutional solely on the ground of the kind of attitudes it expresses, irrespective of cultural or material consequences (see Anderson and Pildes 2000, pp. 1529–1531).

[14] See Nozick (1993, p. 28), who speaks of the utility of expressive actions.

[15] According to Anderson and Pildes (2000), pp. 1510–1514, expressive theories do not deny that consequences matter in moral evaluation, but rather provide a foundation for their moral importance, because an appropriate attitude towards people requires that we also consider the way our actions affect their interests. They also make it clear that their normative theory differs from both a 'purely consequentialist approach' (which sees actions as mere means to some desirable ends, capable of justifying them in all cases), as well as from what they call a 'vulgar deontology' (prohibiting certain kinds of actions no matter what). For Anderson (1997), p. 107, 'to grant deliberative priority to the meanings over the consequences of action is neither to assign meanings a larger weight than the consequences nor to deny the consequences any value at all. [...] It is to derive the role the consequences play in deliberation from the principles that express how we ought to value the people concerned with them.'

> Policies adopted out of contempt or hostility toward a racial group, or with the purpose of branding a racial group as inferior, are expressively harmful and therefore unconstitutional regardless of their direct material, social, and psychological consequences. For example, the harm from racial segregation does not lie simply in its material consequences. (Ibid., p. 1542)

However, a more nuanced version of the theory, capable of recognizing the causal significance of symbolic expression, can still be made compatible with the economic analysis of law, as well as with (sophisticated versions of) rational choice theory. In what follows, I will only sketch out some very general suggestions about the way in which such a reconciliation could be accomplished.

In the first place, symbolic legislation understood as instrumental to sending signals or messages to constituents is already amenable to analysis by means of the signalling models. To be sure, symbolic legislation understood as noninstrumental expressive action, seems more puzzling. But one fruitful approach could be to consider this kind of symbolic behaviour as *ideological*. Here, '"[i]deology" refers to political actors' personal definitions of the public interest, pursued as a consumption good that yields satisfactions in the form of moral sentiments' (Kalt and Zupan 1990, p. 104). In other words, while agents may not be driven by a purposive search for some good in their behaviour—including a conscious search for moral satisfaction—nonetheless their symbolic ideological behaviour is neither irrational nor entirely lacking its specific rewards. Such rewards are not sought after as such, by means of instrumental action, but rather attach to the action itself, and from a certain point of view, they are *part* of the action. In a sense, the action becomes an end in itself for the agents. So understood, ideological behaviour can be seen as expressing preferences of a peculiar kind, though not at odds with microtheoretic approaches to the economics of politics. This is why Kalt and Zupan (1990) have suggested seeing ideology as a 'consumption good' and parting with the model under which political agents are only driven by investment motives (that is, by a desire to maximize their own wealth). In this way, they can account for cases such as those in which legislators and regulators push their own ideological preferences in policy decisions even at the expense of the interests of their constituents (ibid., p. 103). If we take ideological preferences to be a consumption good,

> [t]he utility from such a good might derive from a number of sources: (a) entertainment of the popular good-guy/bad-guy variety; (b) the same sorts of satisfactions as motivate altruistic acts (that is, political ideologies are prescriptions about how to make society–other people better off); or (c) the genetic, evolution-based predilection of a mind that requires self-confidence and feelings of moral rectitude, rather than guilt, in order to function well. (Ibid., p. 105)

Despite problems of method and measurement, 'ideological rating scales' can be adopted where an 'ideology residual' can be assigned to individual lawmakers; the residual's explanatory power can then be tested against specific-issue voting, and in each case an assessment is made about the hypothesis of ideological behaviour as a consumption good (by verifying whether the behaviour in question constitutes on-the-job shirking on the lawmakers' part, in a relationship where the lawmakers are considered 'agents' and the constituents their 'principals') (ibid., pp. 106–115).

In criminal law, the application of economic analysis should take into account both (1) the symbolic and expressive value of criminal legislation and (2) the deterrence effect that punishment has on potential 'culturally motivated' offenders. In the first case, the assessment of the utility that the lawmakers and/or their ideologically cognate constituents reap from expressiveness can be extremely difficult. Moreover, translating such utility into a single value scale (typically, a monetary one) could prove even more difficult. The difficulty in question can be illustrated by a study in behavioural Law & Economics on the juries' assessment of punitive damages. In tort law, punitive damages awarded by juries are extremely unpredictable, almost to the point of utter randomness. Sunstein et al. (1998) have shown that, even though there is a remarkably high consensus on the degree of outrage and punishment appropriate for punitive-damage cases—cutting across differences in gender, ethnicity, income, age, and education—the consensus breaks down when the legal system uses money to measure moral outrage. Arbitrariness is further increased when using an unbounded monetary scale. The jurors' outrage towards a transgressor—which is largely governed by social norms—is expressed through punitive damages. The 'punitive intent' is determined by both moral outrage and other factors, such as harm. By conducting experiments with simulated juries, the authors have found that harm (as a factual consequence of the transgression) is somehow taken into account when determining the amount of the punitive damages, but it does not really affect the jurors' outrage. This suggests that, rather than using a monetary scale, some form of opinion polling could yield more predictable outcomes.

As for culturally motivated offences, this is a case where deterrence needs to be achieved by taking account of qualitative differences in punishment. For instance, punishing duelling with imprisonment would prove ineffective with members of minoritarian revenge societies. However, as Lessig (1995, pp. 968–972) has shown, providing for ineligibility for public office as a punishment affects both the expected utility of a potential dueller (since a man of honour is supposed to run for public office) and the *social meaning* of the act of duelling (since refusing confrontation is no longer seen as a mere act of cowardice *by the restricted revenge society itself*).

As concerns the application of economic-analysis approaches to constitutional law, and more specifically to cases where the notion of expressive harm comes into play, Anderson and Pildes's (1993) aforementioned noncausal interpretation of the notion seems to entirely leave out of the picture any possibility of measurement and quantification. The plausibility of this way of interpreting the notion of expressive harm is open to question, but it rests on the general tenability of the kind of normative moral theory put forward by Anderson (1993), and an extensive critique of such a theory obviously falls outside the scope of the present chapter. The possibility of a different *causal* interpretation of expressive harm seems to be left open by Pildes and Niemi (1993), who, as noted, hold that expressive harms undermine collective understandings: this could be taken to mean that governmental action can be impermissible on constitutional grounds because its expressive content causally corrupts society's normative climate. More specifically, it alters and disfigures constitutionally protected values and the ways in which society understands and practices those values.

Against such a consequentialist understanding of expressive harm, the objection could be raised that if this harm is considered a ground for unconstitutionality, then judges are being endowed with the power to act *outside* and *above* the law. That is because, instead of applying constitutionally entrenched values and principles—that is, instead of applying the law—judges would be acting as 'conservative guardians' of those values and principles, in the sense of shielding their understanding by society (their social meanings) from change (see Ferraro 2022, p. 205). Aside from this kind of objection, expressive harms in constitutional law seem very tricky to pin down for the purposes of economic analysis. If we identify them with the less material, less tangible, less individualized negative consequences of governmental action, it becomes extremely difficult to *prove* that such consequences include an undermining of public values and understandings. Even more difficult is any kind of *measurement* of this kind of impact. With that said, considering that public values actually emerge out of the interpretations that citizens give them, here too, opinion polling could support an assessment of the harms in question. While expressive harms could be seen as more intangible than other kinds of harms, there must be some shared, material ground for their assessment: the alternative would be pure arbitrariness on the part of those called on to make such assessments.

More generally, finding a place for the symbolic aspects of law in economic analysis requires rejecting Anderson's contention that the expressive theory of value is set in opposition to consequentialism and stands as an alternative to it.[16] In embracing a pluralistic vision of the irreducible variety of values, based on an expressive account of social choices, Pildes and Anderson (1990) set this vision against the claims of monistic rational choice theory. However, *incommensurability* does not entail *incomparability*: the former involves the impossibility of comparing two things on some cardinal scale of units of value, while the latter consists in the impossibility of any comparison whatsoever (Chang 1997).[17] Roughly speaking, incommensurability only concerns cardinality, while incomparability also encompasses ordinality (Gardbaum 1998, p. 1687). Anderson herself (1997, p. 103) purports to offer an *expressive theory of rational choice* that builds on 'a nonscalar conception of intrinsic value'; in her view, such a theory provides an alternative to optimization as a plausible criterion for choice rationality. In and of itself, however, such an expressive theory would not rule out ordinal rankings.

While Anderson could be right about the incommensurability of different values from a first-person standpoint (as when she rejects the idea of tradeoffs between friendship and money), when official decisions affecting the lives of many individuals are at stake, incommensurability might prove a hindrance to predictability or to rationally justifiable outcomes. Considering that individuals could regard symbolic expression as an incommensurable good, whose value does not translate into money or other single scales, using wealth as the only scale for assessing what is at stake in

---

[16] See, for instance, Anderson (1993), p. 202: '[a] person's attitudes embody conceptions of the significance of her preferences and choices that the economist's bare consequentialist representations of her preferences cannot capture'.

[17] For a different terminological choice, see Andersson and Herlitz (2022), p. 7.

legal interactions could limit the explanatory power of our model. One does not need to assume that humans take expressiveness as an *irreplaceable* good: they might very well be willing to renounce some of it in particular cases, sometimes even in exchange for more wealth; however, the price for such relinquishment is extremely difficult to fix and predict. In this case, it is not monetary scales that would work as the most reliable instrument for aggregating and comparing value but, more likely, the expression of preference rankings, which could be collected by means of polling.

6 Conclusions

Elster (1989, p. 99) observes that

> [o]ne of the most persistent cleavages in the social sciences is the opposition between two lines of thought conveniently associated with Adam Smith and Emile Durkheim, between *homo economicus* and *homo sociologicus*. Of these, the former is supposed to be guided by instrumental rationality, while the behavior of the latter is dictated by social norms.

That may well be so, but it does not thereby make it impossible, at a metatheoretical level, to reconcile those two models of human action. The symbolic meanings of both the law and citizens' behaviours in legal systems are intersubjectively established by social norms. Humans perform symbolically meaningful acts either with instrumental concerns (as through their 'signalling' behaviour) or for noninstrumental (i.e., purely expressive) motivating reasons. Both kinds of symbolic behaviour can be made amenable to an economic analysis of law, as has already been done in political economy (in the analysis of political participation, for example: see, e.g., Schuessler 2001). In the first case, signalling models can be used to explain symbolic behaviour, both on the legislators' part (as in so-called symbolic legislation) and by the law's addressees. In the second case, a more nuanced approach to economic analysis would serve us best, where measurement and interpersonal aggregation of utility could be pursued by means of opinion polling.

The resistance of expressive accounts to economic analysis and interpersonal utility comparisons—and, more generally, to consequentialist thinking—seems to rest on the assumption that the only appropriate point of view is the first-person point of view of individuals who, as often happens, consider it unacceptable to trade some immaterial goods (like friendship or personal integrity) for money. But the analysis of social phenomena like the law needs to integrate the first-person point of view into a wider perspective. The fact that individuals see those goods as incommensurable and unnegotiable does not imply that, from an external point of view, those same individuals cannot be seen as actually trading, for instance, time and money for the opportunity to cherish human relationships or take part in political campaigns. Oftentimes, they can reluctantly give up their symbolic and expressive aims on account of costs they deem excessive. So, even in the realm of symbolic action individuals respond to incentives, and they regard expression as a resource.

Even if they do not see fit to put a price on such a resource *ex ante*, they still treat it as part of their set of interests and pursue it rationally, by balancing it against other goods for which they may want to exchange it. However, because individuals are both reluctant to assign a price to their expressive interests and are simply bad at doing so, the economic analysis of law will often have to resort to metrics other than monetary scales of value for measuring, comparing, and aggregating those interests.

As Schuessler (2001, p. 30) notes

> although existing economic approaches have been very successful in modeling outcome-oriented, or instrumental, human behavior, to date they have been quite unsuccessful in approaching symbolic or expressive behavior. The first realm is that of *Doing*—individuals perform X in order to do Y—and the second is that of identification, attachment, or *Being*—individuals perform X as this is how they become X-performers.

As we have seen, humans sometimes engage in symbolic behaviour for instrumental purposes, while other times they only pursue expression of their identities and the values they cherish, thereby reaffirming their self-image and self-understanding, or the person they want to be. Expressive choice is still rational choice; only, as Schuessler (ibid.) observes, it is governed by the logic of Being rather than by the logic of Doing. For instance, when voters participate in elections they can 'purchase', at the cost of participation, a certain status: that of outcome-producers or, at least, of supporters of the group or ideology they identify with. Were it not so, participation would be irrational, since the costs it imposes on voters cannot be justified by the likelihood (next to zero) of determining the electoral outcome with any single vote they cast.[18]

Once expressive choice is folded into in the domain of rational choice—not in the sense of a radically distinct form of rationality, but as a species within a wider genus, with its differences from other species, but also with its similarities to them—there is in principle no reason why it should be considered an unfit subject for an economic analysis of law. '[E]conomics is the science of rational choice in a world—our world—in which resources are limited in relation to human wants. The task of economics, so defined, is to explore the implications of assuming that man is a rational maximizer of his ends in life, his satisfactions [...]' (R Posner 1986, p. 4). As long as we are not acting on pure instinct or driven by uncontrollable urges, our actions can be made sense of in economic terms, even if they are not intended as instruments for bringing about some state of affairs.

[18] See Schuessler (2001), pp. ix–x, 5–6. In political science, this is known as the paradox of participation.

References

Adler MD (2000a) Expressive theories of law: a skeptical overview. Univ Pa Law Rev 148:1363–1501

Adler MD (2000b) Linguistic meaning, nonlinguistic 'expression', and the multiple variants of expressivism: a reply to professors Anderson and Pildes. Univ Pa Law Rev 148:1577–1594

Anderson ES (1993) Value in ethics and economics. Harvard University Press, Cambridge

Anderson ES (1997) Practical reason and incommensurable goods. In: Chang R (ed) Incommensurability, incomparability, and practical reason. Harvard University Press, Cambridge, pp 90–109

Anderson ES (2000) Beyond homo economicus: new developments in theories of social norms. Philos Public Aff 29:170–200

Anderson ES, Pildes RH (2000) Expressive theories of law: a general restatement. Univ Pa Law Rev 148:1503–1575

Andersson H, Herlitz A (2022) Introduction. In: Andersson H, Herlitz A (eds) Value incommensurability: ethics, risk, and decision-making. Routledge, New York, pp 1–25

Anonymous (1999) Expressive harms and standing. Harv Law Rev 112:1313–1330

Atienza M (1989) Contribución para una teoría de la legislación. Doxa 6:385–403

Brion DJ (1999) Norms and values in law and economics. In: Bouckaert B, de Geest G (eds) Encyclopedia of law and economics, vol 1. Edward Elgar, Cheltenham, pp 1041–1071

Chang R (1997) Introduction. In: Chang R (ed) Incommensurability, incomparability, and practical reason. Harvard University Press, Cambridge, pp 1–34

Cooter R (1998) Expressive law and economics. J Leg Stud 27(S2):585–608

Eco U ([1984] 1986) Semiotics and the philosophy of language. Indiana University Press, Bloomington

Elster J (1989) Social norms and economic theory. J Econ Perspect 3:99–117

Feinberg J (1970) Doing and deserving: essays in the theory of responsibility. Princeton University Press, Princeton, NJ

Ferraro F (2022) The puzzling rationality of symbolic legislation. In: Ferraro F, Zorzetto S (eds) Exploring the province of legislation. Springer, Cham, pp 103–123

Firth R (1973) Symbols: public and private. George Allen & Unwin, London

Gardbaum S (1998) Law, incommensurability, and expression. Univ Pa Law Rev 146:1687–1700

Griffiths J (1979) Is law important? New York Univ Law Rev 54(2):339–374

Gusfield JR (1963) Symbolic crusade: status politics and the American temperance movement. University of Illinois Press, Urbana

Hellman D (2008) When is discrimination wrong? Harvard University Press, Cambridge, MA

Kahan DM (1996) What do alternative sanctions mean? Univ Chicago Law Rev 63(2):591–653

Kalt JP, Zupan MA (1990) The apparent ideological behavior of legislators: testing for principal-agent slack in political institutions. J Law Econ 33(1):103–131

Kłusek M (2024) Punishment and social standing in an evolutionary perspective. In: Załuski W, Bourgeois-Gironde S, Dyrda A (eds) Research handbook on legal evolution. Edward Elgar, Cheltenham, pp 292–306

Koppelman A (1996) Antidiscrimination law and social equality. Yale University Press, New Haven

Lessig L (1995) The regulation of social meaning. Univ Chicago Law Rev 62:943–1046

McAdams RH (2014) The expressive powers of law: theories and limits. Harvard University Press, Cambridge

Morris CW (1971) Writings on the general theory of signs. Mouton, The Hague

Nozick R (1981) Philosophical explanations. The Belknap Press, Cambridge

Nozick R (1993) The nature of rationality. Princeton University Press, Princeton, NJ

Peirce CS (1976) In: Eysele C (ed) The new elements of mathematics, vol 4: Mathematical philosophy. Mouton, The Hague and Paris

Pildes RH (1998) Why rights are not trumps: social meanings, expressive harms, and constitutionalism. J Leg Stud 27:725–763

Pildes RH, Anderson ES (1990) Slinging arrows at democracy: social choice theory, value pluralism, and democratic politics. Colum Law Rev 90:2121–2214

Pildes RH, Niemi RG (1993) Expressive harms, 'bizarre districts', and voting rights: evaluating election-district appearances after *Shaw v. Reno*. Mich Law Rev 92:483–587

Posner EA (1998) Symbols, signals, and social norms in politics and the law. J Leg Stud 27(2):765–797

Posner R (1986) Economic analysis of law. Little, Brown and Company, Boston

Saussure F ([1916] 1995) In: Bally C (ed) Course in general linguistics. Duckworth, London

Schuessler AA (2001) A logic of expressive choice. Princeton University Press, Princeton

Sen A (1977) Rational fools. Philos Public Aff 6:317–344

Sunstein CR (1996a) On the expressive function of law. Univ Pa Law Rev 144:2021–2054

Sunstein CR (1996b) Social norms and social roles. Colum Law Rev 96:903–968

Sunstein CR, Kahneman D, Schkade DA (1998) Assessing punitive damages (with notes on cognition and valuation in law). Yale Law J 107:2071–2153

Tushnet M, Yackle L (1997) Symbolic statutes and real laws: the pathologies of the Antiterrorism and Effective Death Penalty Act and the Prison Litigation Reform Act. Duke LJ 47:1–86

Van der Burg W (2005) The irony of a symbolic crusade: the debate on opening up civil marriage to same-sex couples. In: Zeegers N, Witteween W, van Klink B (eds) Social and symbolic effects of legislation under the rule of law. Edwin Mellen, Lewinston, pp 245–275

Van Klink B (2016) Symbolic legislation: an essentially political concept. In: van Klink B, van Beers B, Poort L (eds) Symbolic legislation theory and developments in biolaw. Springer, Cham, pp 19–35

Van Klink B (2019) Legislation, communication, and authority: how to account for the bindingness of law? In: Oliver-Lalana AD (ed) Conceptions and misconceptions of legislation. Springer, Cham, pp 81–106

Weber M (1921) Wirtschaft und Gesellschaft, vol 1. Mohr, Tübingen

Wendel WB (2002) Mixed signals: rational-choice theories of social norms and the pragmatics of explanation. Ind Law J 77:1–62

The Principle of Social Wealth Maximization and Rule Utilitarianism: Some Considerations

Eduardo Stordeur Jr.

Abstract This article aims to discuss the key aspects of the two main versions of Richard Posner's proposal of maximizing social wealth. The underlying idea is that much of the debate around these versions helps illuminate the challenges of providing a solid moral foundation for the application of economic principles to law. One of Posner's central arguments is that his principle of wealth maximization avoids many of the classic problems associated with traditional utilitarianism. In the final part of the article, I will tentatively suggest that rule-based utilitarianism, at least in principle, overcomes several of the issues identified by Posner, as well as some of the criticisms raised in the specialized literature regarding his proposal. Finally, I will outline a pragmatic-instrumental approach through which rule utilitarianism could be applied, particularly in the context of European continental legal systems.

1 Introduction

Economic theory can be used for both descriptive and normative purposes. In the latter case, economic theory is used for the purpose of suggesting modifications to the legal system or for the purpose of providing an economics-based justification for some legal institution or the legal system.

When that justification assumes that efficiency or some form of utility consistent with efficiency is the foundation of the legal system, Law & Economics ceases to operate as a tool for examining the legal system and becomes a theory of philosophy of law that must compete with alternative philosophical explanations.

The purpose of this article is to comment on the central aspects of the two most important versions of the proposal of the maximizing social wealth by Posner, in the idea that a good part of the discussion allows us to shed light on the eventual

E. Stordeur Jr. (✉)
University of Buenos Aires and Universidad Torcuato Di Tella, Buenos Aires, Argentina
e-mail: estordeur@utdt.edu

S. Zorzetto et al. (eds.), *Developments in Law and Economics in the Italo-Iberoamerican Context*, Economic Analysis of Law in European Legal Scholarship 21, https://doi.org/10.1007/978-3-032-03317-8_4

problems of offering a moral foundation for economics applied to law. One of Posner's fundamental arguments suggests that his principle based on maximizing wealth avoids many of the problems of classical utilitarianism. In the last part of the article, I will suggest, in a very preliminary way, that rule-based utilitarianism surpasses, at least in principle, a significant portion of the problems stated by Posner and even a significant portion of the problems highlighted by specialized literature regarding the principle of maximizing social wealth proposed by Posner.

2 The Wealth Maximization Principle

In the 1970s Richard Posner published his book *Economic Analysis of Law*, that aimed to demonstrate that the legal system could be interpreted as a system focused on maximizing social wealth. However, Posner later suggested something even more ambitious: that the law also should be designed with the explicit goal of maximizing social wealth.[1]

Initially, I am going to comment on the main aspects of his first proposal, which was ambitious, suggesting that all legal decisions should be made with the aim of maximizing his own conception of wealth. Then, later on, I will consider his more sophisticated (yet equally problematic) proposal based on the hypothetical contract, in the idea that people would agree that common law judges make decisions with the goal of maximizing social wealth. In the end, a significant portion of the problems from the first proposal are replicated in the second one (and they are eliminated or mitigated by rule-based utilitarianism).

Posner argued that what he called the principle of social wealth maximization (here in after MSW) had its own attractive normative properties to be the foundation of the legal system. While Posner's views on this matter have evolved over time, it is worth examining his most significant and systematic normative proposals regarding the maximization of social wealth. This controversy can help shed light on the normative plausibility of efficiency as a value in law on the more fundamental level.[2]

In essence, MSW suggests that law should primarily function as a system aimed at maximizing social wealth, defined by the willingness of people to pay for rights. In this view rights are instrumental to the efficient allocation of scarce resources to those who value them most, measured in monetary terms. The basic idea relates to the Coase Theorem, that poses that in a world with no transaction costs and clear definition of property rights, the initial allocation of rights has no impact on the final efficient allocation of resources. Regardless of the initial owner, the resource will end up in the hands of the one who values it the most. This means that without transaction costs, the final allocation of resources will always be the same and efficient,

[1] See, Stordeur (2006), pp. 308–420.

[2] Posner (1979) and Posner (1980). Tullock also believes that efficiency is a very important, almost fundamental, goal of the legal system. See Tullock (1980).

regardless of the initial allocation. In other words, it is irrelevant for efficiency who is entitled to what, under zero of too low transaction cost and well-defined property rights.[3]

The MSW principle is based on the idea that rights should be assigned to the individuals who value them the most. However, in many situations, positive transaction costs can hinder transactions. These costs can include identifying parties, formalizing, and supervising agreements, and executing them. Therefore, efficient allocation of property rights is necessary to minimize these costs and maximize social wealth. The goal is to mimic ideal market conditions with zero transaction costs, to maximize the wealth. This has naturally generated a lot of controversy in the specialized literature of the time.[4]

According to the principle of MSW when facing a positive transaction costs scenario, the judge should assign the right to the party who would have acquired it under these ideal conditions. For instance, in the case of noise-emitting air-conditioning, assigning the right to operate the equipment to neighbours reduces transaction costs and minimizes externalities (assuming the owners would have paid more than non owners).[5]

The efficient allocation of rights is a key concept in the normative economic analysis of law, which seeks to simulate a market without transaction costs and allocate property rights efficiently in order to maximize social wealth. While probably a reasonable defence of "social wealth maximization" would have been to associate it with utilitarianism assuming that such a conception of wealth is a good conduct or maybe a (useful) false target to a reasonable and plausible concept of utility, Instead, Posner suggested that "social wealth maximization" had its own credentials to provide a normative principle to law which faces many problems.

---

[3] In a scenario without transaction costs, if person X values resource A more than their neighbour Y, then regardless of who initially owns it, X will end up with the resource. When the initial right to the resource is assigned to X, it is the most efficient allocation since X value it the most. However, if the initial right is assigned to the neighbour, a surplus can be created for both parties, if the resource goes to X. Ultimately, in the absence of transaction costs, the final allocation of resources will always be both efficient and the same, regardless of the initial allocation of rights. See, Coase, Ronald (1960).

[4] For a critique of Posner's proposal, see especially, the special edition of this subject in *Hofstra Law Review* 8, de 1980. In particular, Coleman (1980), Dworkin (1980a, b), Kornhauser (1980), Rizzo (1980), and Tullock (1980). See also Kronman (1979), Posner (1981a) and Posner (1985), Veljanovski (1981), Allen Leff (1974), Boyd White (1987) and Ellickson (1989). For a different proposal that attempts a moral foundation of the economics applied to law, see Kaplow and Shavell (2001).

[5] I take this example from Demsetz. This case of noise-emitting air-conditioning equipment illustrates the concept of externalities, which occur when the actions of one party impose costs or benefits on others who are not involved in the transaction. In this case, the homeowners who operate the noisy air-conditioning equipment impose costs on their neighbours who are forced to bear the noise.

2.1 *The Moral Foundation of the Principle of Maximization of Social Wealth*

In "Utilitarianism, Economics and Legal Theory" Posner attempts for the first time his moral foundation of the principle of "social wealth maximization" in extremely ambitious terms: it constitutes, he affirms, a moral principle from which it is possible to derive the central aspects of a theory of law, explaining and offering a justification for the most basic institutions of the legal system and basic rights and liberties but also instrumental in shaping a good part of the fundamental values of society that allow the accumulation of wealth, those "protestant values" associated since Max Weber's classic to the birth and development of capitalism.[6]

Posner's proposal is not only ambitious in substance but also in scope: in this initial version, he suggests that all legal decisions, not just those of common law judges, such as those made by legislatures or executive agencies, should aim to maximize social wealth, his version of efficiency.

In the base of the MSW would rest an attractive normative property, one that connects decisions with results: the allocation of wealth is meritocratic, meaning that those who produce the most receive the most. The MSW also requires considering the preferences of others in order to make progress: in fact, in the market, under certain conditions, profits can only be made by satisfying the relative needs of others, as expressed through the demand for goods and services.[7]

The MSW, moreover, always for Posner, draws from the most fundamental virtues of utilitarianism and of what he calls "Kantian theories", avoiding a good part of their respective problems and deficiencies. The MSW principle would be more appealing than these classic traditions in many fundamental aspects (although it later focuses more on the utilitarianism).[8]

Posner argued that common criticisms of the Economic Analysis of Law are often based on a confusion between economics and utilitarianism, which mistakenly ascribes to economics the problems associated with the latter. Utilitarianism is a vast tradition of moral and political philosophy, which dates back at least to the works of Hume and occupies an important place in political and moral thinking but according to Posner, the MSW principle avoid many of its problems while retaining

---

[6] See Posner, "Utilitarianism..." in the revised version of The Economics of Justice, op. cit. p. 66. In fact, from now on I will refer to this book as it includes revised versions of previously published works.

[7] However, at least for many authors, it is clear or could become clear that market outcomes do not solely depend on individual decisions. There is a lot of contexts, luck, and the starting point and innate talents can have a decisive influence. These are issues that Posner does not examine, despite these arguments against the free market being quite common. There is much to be said about this matter, which has at least not been fully examined in the more specialized literature on MSW.

[8] Posner does not define precisely what he understands by "Kantian theories," but he seems to suggest that they correspond to deontological theories, in which justice does not depend on consequences. At times, however, he appears to consider a particularly libertarian version of this vast and varied tradition of normative philosophy.

most of the plausible normative attribute of this tradition. We could say that MSW for Posner, in this work, constitutes a more plausible version of consequentialism than traditional act utilitarianism, which he examines and compares in this work.

Posner distinguished the MSW from the "greatest happiness for the greatest number", emphasising the distinction between wealth and utility. According to Posner, the value that integrates the "maximization of social wealth" is the "exchange value," which has market expression, either explicitly or implicitly.[9] This idea of social wealth derives from the sum of goods and services valued in the market. By focusing on the maximization of social wealth, rather than the maximization of happiness, Posner believes that economics can provide a more accurate and useful framework for analysing and offering a moral foundation of legal the legal system based in economics.

In Posner's view, value is not merely a matter of simple utility, but rather a narrower concept based on what people are willing to pay for a good or service, whether in actual or hypothetical markets. This willingness to pay represents the effective or hypothetical demand for the good or service, and is the basis for determining its value. While value always implies some degree of utility, the reverse is not necessarily true. However, as we will see later, this distinction between value and utility is one of the main challenges of the "wealth maximization" principle.[10] According to this principle, the wealth of society is the sum of individual values or preferences held in monetary demand, whether actual or hypothetical.[11]

The strong influence of Coase on Posner's thinking is evident. He emphasized the need to allocate resources efficiently, considering the positive transaction costs that exist in the real world. When transaction costs are low, private arrangements are often the most efficient solution, but when they are high, the legal system must mimic the market to promote the maximization of wealth (and not utility).[12]

Posner argued that MSW is clearly superior to classical utilitarianism, in the sense that his principle could offer clear solutions to classic problems of the "greatest happiness for the greatest number" tradition. The utilitarianism that Posner considers is classical act-based utilitarianism, which suggests that each decision should be made with the aim of maximizing utility, happiness, or well-being. This version of utilitarianism was strongly criticized at that time, particularly by the critiques of

[9] Posner accuses Epstein and Hart of confusing economics with utilitarianism. The reference can be found in Posner's work "Utilitarianism" in *The Economics of Justice*, on pages 48 and following.

[10] Posner (1981a), pp. 49–50.

[11] See Posner (1981a), p. 66.

[12] However, in Coase's view, it is not clear that even in cases where there are high transaction costs, state intervention is convenient or necessary. Everything depends on the comparison between the alternative costs of market solutions and other institutional solutions and state intervention. In fact, Coase makes strong statements to the effect that the mere presence of externalities does not justify government intervention, and there are sufficient reasons to assume the same regarding transaction costs. It might be possible to offer alternative economic justifications of the law based on Coase's insights that may be different and possibly more attractive than Posner's initial approach.

Rawls and Nozick, who advocated for theories of justice based on principles. Utilitarianism was, at that time, a "defensive" theory, facing significant challenges.[13]

In general, classical utilitarianism has been fundamentally questioned due to (a) the moral monstrosity it entails, which has three fundamental aspects: (a.1) using people as a means to an end, as what matters is total utility or happiness, (a.2) the lack of distinction between types of pleasures, which forces us to consider the satisfaction of a sadist who, for example, tortures animals, on equal footing with the pleasures of reading or poetry, and (a.3) the fact that it could lead us to results where we have to sacrifice innocents if it leads to an outcome that maximizes the utility of the act. For example, torturing a person could be justified as long as the overall happiness or net well-being is greater as a consequence. It also faces, among others, the problem of boundaries, as it is not clear whether the well-being of animals (which also experience pleasure or pain) or of people incapable of experiencing pleasure and pain due to illnesses, future generations, and even the preferences or well-being of foreigners should be considered. Problems associated with the value to maximize, the calculation of how to maximize or compare states of the world to be maximized, are other issues with traditional and simplistic utilitarianism that Posner believes are overcome by his principle of MSW.[14]

In particular, the type of preferences that should be taken into account and how they should be taken into account, problems that could eventually be better addressed by appealing to wealth than to utility. As well as classic problems associated with the instrumentalism of utilitarianism, which in principle allows people to be used as a means to improve others, and possible morally intuitive outcomes, especially due to the fact that preferences or mental states that imply well-being always have the same value.

Classic utilitarianism might face difficulties in determining the kinds of preferences or happiness to be maximized, for example, but the MSW theory would overcomes these problems. In the later, only preferences supported by money are considered, eliminating the classical discussion concerning which kind of preference must be included in the calculus (i.e., hedonistic, informed, external, etc.); also eliminating problem concerning the boundary regarding who counts and how they are counted (i.e., foreigners, minors, insane, animals, etc.). By closing preferences to the concept of value based on effective demand supported by money, MSW offers a practical solution to the limitations of the most common form of utilitarianism, according to Posner. In MSW, only money-supported preferences count, and those who do not support their preferences in this way are included in the calculation as the objects of the preferences of others. Animals, for instance, are considered only

---

[13] Kornhauser argues that the MSW still does not fully escape, or escapes very little, from the well-known problems of classical utilitarianism. However, according to the author, it could lead to an improvement in terms of calculations for comparing effects, given the use of money. See Kornhauser (1980).

[14] For a classic, see Williams (1973). Now I am primarily considering the problems of utilitarianism that Posner discusses in his work.

as objects of the utility function of those who are willing to pay and can actually pay.[15]

MSW Posner considered, could also avoid problems of utilitarianism associated with the content of preferences and certain counterintuitive outcomes inherent to utilitarianism (in its simplest and naive version, worth noting; mainly some very simple form of act utilitarianism).[16] The "utilitarian monster" problem, which counts all preferences equally regardless of their content, poses a moral dilemma. In this view, sadism and philanthropy are considered of equal value, which would be difficult to accept at an intuitive level. However, the MSW principle would avoid this problem in principle because in circumstances where transaction costs are low, individuals must pay for others to carry out any action. Thus, the sadist, for example, should pay their victims, who clearly cease to be victims. The fact that individuals must use contracts eliminates or at least limits some of these problems, always according to Posner.

On the other hand, the very well known problem of calculating utilities or preference satisfaction in utilitarianism would be a minor one in the case of social wealth where money facilitates the calculation. It is challenging to demonstrate a total increase in happiness or welfare, according to Posner, but this would not be a serious issue in the MSW, that would probably only emerge in cases of high transaction costs when hypothetical markets need to be used as an instrument to assign rights.

In this way, he attempts to show that MSW is more appealing than this simple version of act utilitarianism in many fundamental aspects. For example, many argue that instrumentalism presents a problem, as it allows for individuals to be used as means to the greater utility or happiness of others, potentially leading to the utilization of some for the benefit of others. However, for Posner, the MSW principle suggests a strong defence of individual rights, albeit not as fanatical as the "Kantian traditions".[17] According to MSW, if A desires something from B, A must obtain the rights to B's assets in exchange. If A values B's assets more than B does, the exchange increases social wealth. While simply increasing utility could involve taking property from one person and giving it to another, MSW, on the other hand, requires (provided that transaction costs are low) and markets are functioning properly (I would add) that any transfer of rights be carried out based on consent, that is, by using markets.

Posner sees MSW as providing a solid defence of individual rights while classical utilitarianism might tend to prioritizes increasing overall utility without considering people's individuality and rights. As Rawls famously pointed out, utilitarianism

[15] Dworkin has questioned the supposed advantage of the MSW in establishing these limits that Posner claims. See Dworkin (1980b), pp. 28–29.

[16] As mentioned, Lewis Kornhauser, for example, is not very convinced that the MRS actually has so many advantages over utilitarianism. See Kornhauser (1980).

[17] I assume he is referring to deontological traditions, but in this case to those of a libertarian nature, such as Nozick's or Rothbard's, for example. The literature has been critical of Posner's somewhat careless use of this term (for example Dworkin).

is criticized for failing to take people's individuality seriously, thereby leading to the use of some individuals for the practical benefit of others.

For Posner, as mentioned, the efficiency rule provides a solid basis for defending individual rights, without being fanatical like the Kantian theories (I assume in the libertarian tradition). The MSW rule assigns property rights to their most valued uses when transaction costs are low. If an ambulance needs to pass through a neighbouring property under very low transaction costs, it can buy the right from the owner. In cases where transaction costs are very high, such as in emergencies, it is clear that the MSW allows for the use of another's property and then compensation. This ultimately implies a social gain and is the way in which property rights would be assigned under zero transaction costs. However, under a principled and highly libertarian approach to private property rights, for example, it would always be prohibited for an ambulance to pass through someone else's property, leading to highly implausible situations where property rights seem sanctified without regard for consequences. Ultimately, in the example, a minor inconvenience to a neighbour that can be compensated may (for example) save a life, but very strict private property rights based on principles do not permit this intuitive solution, which is allowed by the MSW principle. Posner argues that the "maximization of social wealth" offers a strong foundation of individual rights, without being as fanatical as (what he calls) the "Kantian" theories.

In the utilitarian tradition, individual rights are seen as instrumental to the greater happiness or welfare of society, rather than an end in themselves. Although there are more sophisticated variants of utilitarianism that may address some of the problems associated with the classical version, sacrificing one individual for the sake of others could still be justified under certain circumstances.

Posner finds that the MSW principle minimizes the problems associated with the instrumentalism of private rights, but not to a point where consequences are completely disregarded, as could occur in the libertarian deontological tradition, for which property rights have a justification independent of consequences (or wealth). In this sense, a thief could potentially obtain, in many cases, assuming that they are much poorer than their victims, greater utility than the loss suffered by the victims.

This also relates to the problem of instrumentalism in utilitarianism, since in certain conditions, depending on the type of utilitarianism, people could be used for the benefit of others, treating them as means and not as ends, adding them to the social calculus without taking into account their own identity and personal value. In this sense, while utilitarianism (as considered by Posner) may justify actions that go against our perception of morality, the MSW might avoid some of this problem associated with the aggregation of preferences or hedonistic mental states.

Moreover, should we murder an innocent person to save 10, 100, or even a thousand lives? Is it reasonable to assume that an authoritarian majority, fuelled by racial hatred, would sacrifice the rights of a minority for the sake of "happiness" or "utility"? Despite Hare's claim that objections to utilitarianism usually apply only to extreme cases that are far from our daily moral experience, we need only glance at recent history to realize that both minorities and majorities have wielded arbitrary and despotic power, often in ways that conflict with our most basic moral intuitions and principles. Classical utilitarianism does not seem to provide a sufficiently strong defence of individual rights. In fact, it also does not provide a solid argument for fulfilling our previously agreed-upon obligations: why should I pay a debt if I can allocate that money to poor people who will likely find it more useful?

Posner's approach, which emphasizes the maximization of social wealth, claims to avoid the moral monstrosities associated with traditional utilitarianism. According to Posner, the use of free and voluntary covenants as a mechanism for the transfer of rights would prevent such forms of moral aberration. However, we will later question whether this claim holds up to scrutiny.[18]

In short, Posner argues that the MSW principle justifies the basic institutions of the legal system by avoiding some of the classic problems of utilitarianism and having advantages over "Kantian theories" as well. He also claims that the MSW principle is based on meritocracy, which links results to people's decisions and contributions to wealth creation and promotes some of the classic values associated with Protestantism that are historically linked to the emergence and development of capitalism. His argument based on meritocracy is intuitively sound in moral matters. After all, we want individuals to achieve outcomes in accordance with their choices (even though it is clear that wealth does not solely depend on individuals' decisions). It would justify our most fundamental rights and liberties, as well as the central institutions of the legal system, in a reasonable manner that incorporates principles but also takes into account the consequences.

However, this initial effort by Posner to differentiate his principle of wealth maximization from utility, which he later reiterates in other similar works, comes at a cost that we are going to discuss. While utility does seem to be a goal that could be an end in itself, and there are other goals that have a tradition in political philosophy and theory of justice, such as the protection of certain property rights o some forms of equality or outcomes that we would choose behind an impartial veil of ignorance, it is not entirely clear why we should make legal decisions solely with the exclusive aim of maximizing wealth.

2.2 *Is Wealth a Value?*

If both judges and lawmakers, according to the principle of the MSW, must formulate and apply the law to maximize wealth, it seems evident that this should consist of a special value, to the point that it is consistent not to pursue other classical or more classical goals such as utility or respect for individual rights. After all, the MSW consists of a form of consequentialism, that is, a theory for which institutions

[18] As Posner points out: The perils of instrumentalism are also less acute in a system of wealth maximization than in a utilitarian system. In the wealth maximization approach the only basis for interference with economic and personal liberty is such a serious failure of the market to operate that the wealth of society can be increased by public coercion, which is itself costly". Posner (1981b), p. 80.

are based on consequences, in this case wealth, and it is clear that this must have a determining value in order to plausibly justify the legal system as a whole.[19]

In any case, Posner has not been entirely clear regarding this issue, and this constitutes the most significant problem of his theory. Sometimes he appeared to uphold the notion that wealth is an inherent social value, irrespective of whether it advances other values such as freedom, equality, individual rights, or certain virtues. But at other times, it seems to suggest that wealth allows for the advancement of other values, such as savings, merit, or the value of hard work. Probably, the most reasonable thing to assume is that he has not been explicit about this issue, which poses a problem for his argument, given that if all legal decisions must be made to maximize wealth, an explicit argument about the special value of wealth would be expected.

We could assume that Posner considers wealth, as he defines it, to be a valuable goal in itself, in the sense that its justification does not derive from the achievement of other goals or values, such as greater utility or the protection of certain rights, but simply a state of affairs is preferable because it includes more wealth. Or at least that argument is implicit, but the problem, as Dworkin has plausibly shown, is that the argument is not sufficiently consistent.

Dworkin successfully challenged the underlying idea of Posner's proposal that wealth can plausibly constitute a value in itself, capable of justifying that all legal decisions should aim to maximize it. He gave an example of Derek, who owns a book valued at $2, and Amartya, who is willing to pay up to $3 for it. The negotiation results in a surplus of $1, which is society (1). Now, imagine a situation where an enlightened king, following this normative economic approach to Law, simply takes the book from Derek and gives it to Amartya, with the resulting transaction costs being saved. However, does it make sense to claim that society (2) is better than society (1)?

The MSW principle posits that agreements, rather than theft, are the means by which society achieves long-term wealth creation, and that one society (1) is ultimately preferable to another (2). However, Dworkin's argument, while not disputing this principle, seeks to draw attention to a distinct point: the principle of MSW may result in morally counterintuitive scenarios that shows wealth itself lacks inherent value. Although society (2) is wealthier than society (1), we do not necessarily view it as superior to society (1), since we do not actually consider the value of wealth to be independent of the way in which it has been obtained.

If we assume that rights and agreements are primarily instrumental and possess only indicative value, we can still acknowledge that there may be some societal benefits in society (2) when compared to society (1). If we were to argue that "social wealth" prioritizes agreements, we would be contradicting our original assumption that these agreements hold only instrumental value. In fact, we want to examine

[19] I will mainly follow Dworkin's arguments, See Dworkin (1980b), p. 191, See for the same argument, Coleman (1980), p. 528.

whether society (2) holds any inherent value over society (1), which is less prosperous.

It is possible to argue that option (2) is preferable to option (1). Dworkin suggests that this argument could be based on the criterion of utility, which he considers to be a more reasonable measure than wealth. Some may still contend that option (2) maximizes utility, but this argument fails to hold up under certain circumstances. For instance, consider a scenario in which Derek is destitute and deeply cherishes a book, but is forced to sell it to survive, while Amartya is a casual collector with little interest in the book. In this case, selling the book to Amartya would not maximize utility, as it would provide greater value to the seller than the buyer. Therefore, the argument in favour of option (2) collapses. Dworkin argues that wealth cannot even support the claim that option (2) offers greater utility, which is perhaps its strongest argument.[20]

But, maybe, this argument is not entirely clear and it may be convenient to reformulate it with a decision problem that clearly shows, or could show, that wealth cannot plausibly be considered a value in itself, given that by its very nature it seems instrumental to other ends, such as (at least in many cases) well-being or happiness.

Let us assume, following Dworkin, that an individual is faced with a choice between two lives: (1) a life where they maximize their wealth, and (2) a life where they are happier or where their total utility, even with less wealth, is maximized. Choosing life (1) would simply make no sense because no one would choose more wealth and less total utility. This is because wealth ultimately "dissolves" into utility, as we will explore in more detail later. While wealth may seem like an attractive and sometimes necessary means for achieving other valuable ends, it is complicated to attribute value to it and to assume that everything else must be ordered in terms of its attainment. In fact, no one questions that wealth is important, but its importance should be measured in terms of its contribution to overall well-being (if, I think, some form of utilitarianism is the best possible moral foundation of economics applied to law).[21]

The concept of wealth is intimately tied to utility, and it is difficult to argue that wealth has any intrinsic value independent of the utility it provides. Thus, wealth can be considered an exclusive or principal value for a theory of justice or moral foundation of the legal system unless it can be linked to utility, even it is obvious that it has "some" instrumental value, probably, in many settings, a fundamental one.

The notion of maximizing social wealth as an independent principle is flawed because people do not necessarily maximize wealth itself; rather, they aim to maximize utility, and wealth is simply a means to that end. Instead, a more plausible idea is that people seek to maximize utility, and that rules which maximize wealth can in many cases increase average utility.

---

[20] The conclusion is very intuitive: Aristotle had already affirmed that wealth is instrumental (a means) for the achievement of other ends, which seems appropriate to common sense.

[21] See Dworkin (1980b).

But in the formulation made by Posner, as mentioned, it is not even possible to ensure this, since the efficiency criterion he employs (something I will comment on later in more detail), where efficiency is realized or satisfied when winners can compensate losers (Kaldor Hicks), it is not always the case that greater wealth leads to greater average utility.[22]

Essentially, the problem (which is central since there are several) is that this efficiency criterion must assume that the marginal value of money is equal for all people, which is evidently false. It is possible that people may demand more for a right, but they may not be the ones who value it the most, since the ability to demand is influenced by people's wealth. Additionally, there is a serious problem for the MSW: the ability to make claims depends on prior wealth, which in turn depends on previous distributions of property rights that cannot be justified from wealth or efficiency in an independent way.[23] For example, one person may be willing to pay more for a good than another (imagine a rich person, as the example provided before) value that good less. This depends largely on the initial distribution of wealth.

Later on, I will return to this point, and we will see that this problem arises again in Posner's more sophisticated but ultimately flawed argument based on hypothetical consent. For now, following Dworkin and Coleman, it seems clear that wealth cannot plausibly be considered as an end in itself but rather as a clearly instrumental value.

Certainly, no one denies that a richer society, all being equal, is better or more attractive than a less wealthy society, and no reasonable person would probably say that wealth has no value at all, and for sure many people would suggest that it is a very important value; but it seems evident that (as Aristotle noted) its value is rather of an instrumental type.

The idea is intuitive, after all: a brush seems to have instrumental value, while a painting could have at least some intrinsic values. The type of value that wealth has is more similar to that of a brush than to the value that could be attributed to a beautiful and valuable painting.

2.3 *Wealth as a "Component of Social Value"*

It has been argued, and Calabresi is often attributed with this position, that wealth or efficiency could be an important aspect of social value: this argument is more pluralistic than the previous version, as it acknowledges that social value is not just

[22] This is a very well-known problem that faces Kaldor Hicks. See also Dworkin (1980b). Essentially, the value of money should be the same for all individuals to ensure that an improvement where the winners can hypothetically compensate the losers implies a gain in utility. It is generally assumed that poor individuals should value a dollar more than wealthy individuals. Alternatively, that conclusion implies an unsustainable interpersonal comparison of utility, which is often at least implausible.

[23] In another work, I have thoroughly considered this problem. See Stordeur (2005a, b).

about wealth, but rather a combination of wealth and other factors, such as justice or equity. In this view, wealth is not the only supreme value that overrides everything else, but rather one component of social value among many.[24]

However, this argument has been challenged by Dworkin, who has pointed out that it is inconsistent to disregard something that has value (like justice) for something that does not have intrinsic value. If wealth has no intrinsic value, it cannot be combined with justice as part of a recipe for social value, either as part of justice itself or as part of a negotiation where different aspects of social value are traded off against each other.[25]

Setting aside the issues with this type of analysis, it would not be logical for rational individuals to base their choices solely on wealth, because self-interest would dictate consideration of utility rather than wealth. Therefore, it would be more reasonable to consider a "transaction" between utility and justice rather than one between wealth and justice.[26] Additionally, if the question is asked from the perspective of a "just" society, rather than self-interest, then efficiency loses its significance in that context. This is especially true if we agree that efficiency is not a valuable goal in itself.[27]

If we agree that wealth has no intrinsic value, then it cannot be considered a "value component" when compared to other values. It wouldn't make sense to sacrifice something that has inherent value, like justice, for something that has no value in itself, like wealth.[28] Or at least, that negotiation between justice or equity and efficiency doesn't make sense until it is clear what the value or type of value efficiency has. However, wealth may have instrumental value when it comes to achieving other values, such as equality or freedom. But, in order to pursue wealth for those reasons, one must carefully consider the potential drawbacks and challenges, which I will explore in the next section.

2.4 Maximizing Social Wealth as an Instrumental Value

We must now then explore another possibility: that wealth serves as a means to other values that are valuable in themselves. Maybe wealth causally enhances these outcomes, generates conditions for them, or acts as a suitable "false target" for achieving these objectives. Pursuing efficiency could be seen as a useful "false

---

[24] Calabresi, however, ultimately argues that he does not assume a trade-off between justice and efficiency, but that justice, somehow, involves a "veto" on efficiency. See Calabresi (1980), pp. 552–553. I think this position is potentially more interesting, but I cannot analyse it now. Probably, a problem is the definition of "justice".

[25] Dworkin (1980b).

[26] Once again, Posner incurs high costs due to the divorce of his proposal from the maximization of utility.

[27] See Dworkin (1980b).

[28] I follow Dworkin on this argument.

target" for realizing other values maybe for simplicity. For instance, it may be reasonable to argue that pursuing efficiency leads to greater utility, either on average or in total, in situations where the wealth we're examining serves as a good conduit of utility.[29]

Despite the undeniable instrumental value of wealth in relation to other values, Dworkin warns against considering this relationship as simply "weak." Merely relying on a weak rule cannot justify the extreme normative position that judges must make decisions solely based on maximizing wealth. Instead, a much stronger assertion is required: either wealth operates causally or it serves as a false target that creates the values deemed valuable in themselves, ultimately granting value to the "maximization of social wealth."[30]

But this approach could further complicate the argument. Now, you not only have to demonstrate some causal or other type of relationship between wealth and those values being pursued, but also provide an argument as to why we should make legal decisions with the purpose of obtaining those values. This strategy seems to simply shift the target without fully addressing the issue at hand. It is necessary now to argue that the purpose promoted or facilitated by the MSW is an end in itself. We must carefully examine the causal relationship between these values and the material benefits provided by wealth, ensuring that they are not contradictory or mutually exclusive in the context of social wealth. It is essential to take a holistic approach in assessing the interplay between these values and the role of social wealth in achieving them. But it is not entirely clear why one should pursue wealth to achieve those values instead of directly making legal decisions with the aim of directly obtaining those values. The question arises as to whether seeking wealth is the most effective approach or if making legal decisions that directly align with those values would be a more appropriate course of action.[31]

Posner must demonstrate not only that there is some kind of causal relationship as indicated, but also the reasons why we should pursue those ends or goals and, moreover, the complex order of priority or rate of exchange between other values, given that it is unlikely or impossible to maximize many values simultaneously. All of this poses a tremendous challenge to an instrumental pluralist strategy for the MSW.

Even when the causal relationship is established, we face the challenge of establishing a mechanism to recognize which principles and values are more fundamental. At a theoretical level seems very difficulties identifying these values or outcomes and if identified we still face problems of order, hierarchy, and compatibility. Among others' problems, we might need to carefully consider the trade-offs between these different outcomes and make thoughtful decisions that balance our various goals and objectives. While I prefer not to delve into complex matters, it's worth considering that depending on the context and values or goals at play, a lexicographic

[29] I follow Dworkin on this, in the mentioned work "Is Wealth a Value? See Dworkin (1980b).

[30] I take this argument from Dworkin (1980a, b).

[31] See Coleman (1980). In particular p. 530.

ordering may be necessary rather than relying on a trade-off mechanism, being all this very complex for the MSW.[32]

A simpler strategy, although obviously not easy, is to suggest that the principle of MSW allows for obtaining another value, such as, for example, as Posner suggested for a moment, a defence of private property rights in the libertarian tradition, or, which would be more plausible, achieving well-being in the utilitarian classical tradition. However, we still need to explain why these values and outcomes are more valuable than others that may be set aside by the rule of maximizing social wealth, such as certain notions of positive freedom or income distribution that may be rejected by the MSW principle.

But problems arise as soon as we consider only the causal relationship or the conditions under which the MSW would allow us to achieve these goals, without the need to investigate further. We have already showed the problems for the MSW for being considered a mean for greater utility or wellbeing, so now I will comment briefly on Posner's argument for judges to use "maximizing social wealth" as the decision rule that leads to the protection of classical rights and liberties in the libertarian tradition.

Firstly, it is unclear why "maximizing social wealth" should be preferred over directly protecting negative liberty or absolute rights. Additionally, the relationship between "maximizing social wealth" is not very clear both at the analytical and empirical levels. It seems evident that a strong enough causal relationship does not exists between libertarian property rights and liberty and the MSW principle, as (for example) demonstrated by the Derek and Amartya example.

This example highlights how the principle of MSW can conflict with a solid classical definition of property rights: sometimes it is possible to improve wealth simple taking libertarian classical property for a person, especially (in practice) in high transaction costs scenario. Think of differences when considering regulations of market failures: while clearly, for example, the MSW principle would regulate private property when exercise to exclude rivals in violation of antitrust provisions, the libertarian would, in the Nozick tradition, for example, insist that such a regulation based on efficiency is simply inadmissible. After all, having a right in this tradition does not depend on consequences, but on how it has been obtained and the condition of not violation other people negative rights, and the possible anti-competitive effects of exercising a right should not have an impact.

In general, this divorce between efficiency and private property rights in the libertarian tradition is present in the presence of serious market failures, in which, however, there is no contractual violation or harm to another person's rights, in a

[32] At times, it can be challenging in consequentialism to consistently maximize a single value, and maximizing multiple values simultaneously can be simply impossible. Establishing an optimal trade-off or a lexicographic order among them requires highly complex arguments that Posner has not provided. I find all this too complex. For example, Rizzo argues that the analyst may not even have the correct information to maximize efficiency in Posner's terms. Rizzo (1980). The reader can get an idea of the problems associated with examining how wealth can or cannot maximize various values or goals together.

traditional sense. These cases cover too broad a field to assert that maximizing output causally leads to the protection of private property rights in the classical sense of the term. If the goal is to protect property rights, actually, the most sensible thing is to directly resolve the cases and apply the law accordingly.

But the problems of this principle regarding property rights are even more serious, so serious that in fact the matter requires an examination, even if brief, separately. Simple put, the MSW can not even offer a foundation of the basic rights. A proposal of legal philosophy that cannot provide a foundation for the most basic rights of individuals seems inevitably doomed to fail.

The concept of maximizing social wealth, while it conceptually includes the notion of rights, may not be sufficient to consistently establish them. Posner argues that wealth implies the recognition of fundamental human rights to the "natural" owner, such as the right to the product of one's labour, personal freedom, or freedom of speech. However, Dworkin points out that we can only recognize the instrumental value of social wealth regarding these fundamental values if rights are consistently assigned to their "natural owners" using the principle of maximizing social wealth. This raises the question of whether the "natural owners" could actually acquire their basic rights in an imaginary auction always applying the rule of maximizing social wealth.[33]

Posner has advanced the argument that individuals would be willing to buy their "natural rights" from others, even if they were initially assigned to someone else. However, as Fried has pointed out, the use of the term "natural rights" implies a different meta-criterion than social wealth, which poses a problem in itself. Leaving that issue aside, there are other difficulties with Posner's argument that deserve closer examination.[34]

One major concern is whether people could realistically purchase their "natural rights" from others, given that wealth is often tied up in rights themselves. For instance, if "A" owns property or resources that are essential to "B's" work and productivity, then it may not be feasible for "B" to purchase their freedom from "A." Even if "B" were to become more productive outside of their current situation, it may be difficult to obtain the credit necessary to buy their "natural rights" if they have no other assets to offer as collateral.[35]

Posner's response to these concerns is not entirely satisfactory. Assuming that individuals always act to maximize their wealth, it is likely that "B" would demand compensation from "A" equal to their marginal productivity. However, if "A" has no other assets or means to generate wealth, then it may be unrealistic to expect them

[33] See Posner (1979) and Dworkin (1980b).

[34] Posner (1979).

[35] As Dworkin argues, it is not clear that if Agatha Christie is assigned as property to a utility maximizer, she would be able to buy her natural right to her work. After all, Agatha would be demanded to the limit of her productive capacity and would not have the means to purchase her own work if she only has her labor, as is the case for most people. Additionally, she would not be able to borrow money and pay interest since her owner would demand the maximum from her. See Dworkin (1980b).

to pay the necessary price plus interest. This raises questions about the hypothetical market argument plausibility, crucial to Posner's argument. To sum up, the MAW MSW principle doesn't seem even to offer a plausible justification or our basic rights. It is difficult to plausible suggest that the MSW can seriously be defended as a mean to protect classical rights.

As can be seen, the MSW principle does not allow for the justification of basic property rights, which is also required for any plausible theory of justice, nor does it consistently allow for the argument that wealth is instrumental to the protection of rights, since analytically libertarianism and Posner's consequentialism differ significantly. Although it is evident that solid and well-defined property rights do allow for an increase in wealth, this is not true once we assume high transaction costs and must operate with hypothetical markets. In fact, as we have noted, Posner himself has suggested that his principle allows for a strong, albeit not "fanatic," defence of classical liberal property rights.[36]

A serious problem that Posner's proposal faces, which I cannot examine in depth in this article, is that the willingness to pay, on which his allocation rule depends, is influenced by relative wealth, which in turn depends on a prior distribution of property rights that is unrelated or minimally related to social wealth maximization. Maximizing social wealth would imply maximizing normative distributive properties of the initial state, which are entirely exogenous to wealth maximization. If we apply Pareto to an initial distribution where some are slaves to others, the rule simply maximizes from that state of affairs. It is also not clear what explanation or justification the MSW could offer for inalienable rights.

In conclusion, an instrumental defence of wealth, which may seem attractive at first glance, faces too many problems. It is not only unclear why we should pursue wealth over other values that have intrinsic value, but it is also not always possible to maximize multiple goals, values, or states of affairs simultaneously. Furthermore, one would have to justify why it is morally justified to make decisions that maximize these values. As we have seen, even with two very attractive candidate, such as the property rights of libertarianism and maximizing wealth presents serious problems for the MSW principle.

---

[36] See additionally, Posner (1985). Posner insists that the pursuit of wealth does provide a good foundation for private rights and liberties. However, as we have seen, it is not clear whether the MSW can provide a strong argument, even though a prosperous society may require them. In this regard, as I will suggest later, rule utilitarianism has a more consistent argument available in this regard. See, Posner (1985), pp. 85–104. He analyzes some of the traditional criticisms of the principle of the MSW, taking a more moderate and skeptical position with regard to the moral debate that would become evident in later works. In this paper, the author again explains the MSW principle and acknowledges some problems. In essence, however, many of the problems I am discussing remain. See Posner (1985), pp. 85–104.

3 Posner, the MSW Principle and Contractualism

Contractualism constitutes an old (although also variable, yielding different results) tradition of political philosophy, associated with authors as dissimilar but also classic as Rousseau, Hobbes, Locke, and currently John Rawls. Appealing to the idea of a hypothetical contract allows for many advantages, in particular, claiming the hypothetical consent of individuals to legitimize public decisions and can also function as a mechanism to examine the rationality of certain social decisions or rules. Posner, after the proposal of MSW that I have already examined, moved away from that more intuitive argument to offer a more systematic one based on the idea of a hypothetical contract. The argument now, although more sophisticated, is narrower: only common law judges should make decisions to maximize social wealth.[37]

In essence, Pareto, he points out, can be defended not only on the grounds of consequences, as is usually done, but also from the perspective of consensus and autonomy. Thus, as we will examine, it attempts a defence of the MSW based on the tradition of the hypothetical contract. But as we will see, the same problems and deficiencies of the principle of the MSW make it indefensible also from this approach. In addition, as noted by many authors, there are other problems associated with the deficiencies in the construction of its own contractual theory.

At least in the particular way that Posner constructs the theory, the argument faces many problems. After "Utilitarianism, Economics and Legal Theory," Posner presents this much more sophisticated argument based on the idea of a hypothetical contract. In summary, since Pareto requires unanimity, it also implies consent and, with it, autonomy of the will comes into play. People not only increase wealth (or utility?) when they contractually operate the Pareto rule, but they also fundamentally agree with those distributions and therefore the value of autonomy is implicated.

Consent, according to Posner, is the "operational base" of Pareto and enables a non-utilitarian argument in favour of the principle, but one that—unlike "Kantian theories"—also takes consequences into account. The attractive idea of a theory that allows for plausibly taking into account both consequences while adopting principles. Posner suggests something extremely ambitious from the point of view of moral and political theory: that his rule surpasses both deontologist (meaning "Kantian theories" in the strange jargon of this author) and utilitarianism.

Through the idea of consensus, he attempts to link social wealth to the long tradition of autonomy of the will, and through self-interest, he intends to give the analysis a certain consequentialist element, in the idea that the combination of both promotes a moral principle with the main advantages and without the classic problems and excesses attributed to both traditions of normative moral philosophy. If the rule of efficiency implies consensus, Posner reasons, then it can be supported not only in the efficient consequences of the normative arrangements and solutions that maximizing social wealth promotes but also in the tradition of autonomy of the will

[37] Posner advanced this version of the argument in Posner (1980) and presented a version in a book published in 1981, which I will use in the following discussion.

in the line of authors such as Locke, Kant, or more contemporaneously, libertarian authors such as Nozick or Epstein.

But Posner also appeals to self-interest: it is in people's interest to choose rules that maximize wealth, and—as we will see—in fact, Posner postulates, these are the rules that people would choose in an original situation subject to certain conditions. Posner's argument based on rational choice theory not only supports his—weak—argument regarding the consensual basis of "maximizing social wealth," but also provides another argument based on self-interest.

Posner's reasoning is essentially as follows: he postulates that the Pareto rule can be supported not only from classical utilitarian bases, as it promotes greater utility for the parties involved, but also because the principle requires unanimity in the new distribution, implying consensus and thus linking Pareto with the long tradition of autonomy of the will.

But this approach, based on hypothetical choice, has its own flaws, starting with some that we have already discussed regarding the MSW principle itself: people would not choose to maximize wealth but rather utility. In fact, as we have discussed, Posner does not offer, and probably could not offer, a consistent justification for why people would choose to maximize wealth and not another value, such as freedom or utility or the protection of certain rights or basic constitutive principles of a society that people, in a situation of impartiality (like Rawls' veil of ignorance), would choose.[38]

This argument highlights a prominent problem with "maximizing social wealth": once again, people would not maximize wealth but rather utility. Suppose that in "X," Mr. A has $20 and Mr. B has $20, and in "Y," Mr. A has $17 and Mr. B has $22 (so that not even Kaldor Hicks is satisfied). If Mr. A agrees, for whatever reason, for example, because he is benevolent, Pareto is satisfied since there are no losers, but social wealth has not been maximized, given the very narrow sense that Posner has given to the concept in his argumentation. That is, not only does it not make sense to assume that people ideally would choose to maximize wealth and not utility, but even more serious, Posner cannot even use the Pareto argument in his favour, since it does not always lead to the maximization of social wealth, that is, the allocation that maximizes the product.[39]

All of this represents a complicated problem for the renewed and more sophisticated argument of Posner: the MRS principle doesn't even have a necessary relationship with Pareto—the basis of normative economics in its most frequent version—as it constitutes a very deficient version of efficiency. And since it doesn't have a necessary relationship with Pareto, it can't claim either consensus or utility. Coleman, for example, has pointed out, it is entirely possible for people to reach agreements that do not satisfy MRS: for example, when someone exchanges an

[38] See Dworkin (1980b) and Coleman (1980), p. 527.

[39] See in particular, Coleman (1980), p. 532–3.

orange for an apple, both have clearly increased their utility, but it does not follow that the "dollar value" of things has increased.[40]

Certainly, in this latter case, it is always possible that at least the people would gain in the "hypothetical" market, considering that both would have paid more for their respective orange and apple, an argument that Posner could use in defence of the principle's application. But let's suppose a world with perfect property rights and complete absence of transaction costs, where a group of people consensually arranges the application of non-wealth maximizing rules in some part of their transactions, such as a group of romantic socialists who resolve without affecting the rights of others. In fact, relationships between patients, friends, and even people within the same group in an extended sense often consist of voluntary exchanges or cooperative voluntary actions that are not of the type that captures the maximization of wealth.

There are many arrangements that do not necessarily maximize wealth, although they do, of course, at least ex ante, maximize utility. Such is the case of a marriage, like many, that resolves that one of the spouses will take care of the children even though it would be cheaper to simply hire that service in the market. But if Posner has problems with the simplest and least controversial Pareto rule, from which the idea of consensus and wealth maximization seems easier to extract, such a question becomes extremely complex with respect to the Kaldor Hicks efficiency criterion. If in Pareto it is still possible to admit that the application of the rule implies consent (and its relationship with autonomy, although not with wealth), the same does not happen, on the other hand, with Kaldor Hicks, nor with the rule of adjudication of rights of the greater "social wealth", where there are losers.[41]

How does Posner defend, then, his principle from consent in a rule that by definition implies uncompensated losers? After all, those who lose in the "maximization of social wealth" could reasonably not consent to it, especially considering that there is no real compensation, only hypothetical. Posner appeals to a criterion that has raised serious objections: the ex-ante compensation principle.

In summary, the idea is that even though there are necessarily losers when laws are applied because people differ in their interests and preferences, the point is that an efficient society compensates ex-ante the losers, so that they are potentially compensated, as with the Kaldor Hicks efficiency criterion. Probably, for example, not everyone benefits from the establishment of property rights, but these allow for a level of productivity that compensates non-owners.

In this sense, for example, Posner assumes that Mr. "A" would consent to his loss under a system of presumed consent, since the negligence system is more efficient and benefits society in general in the long term, including Mr., even if that rule is not in his best interest. The judges, he argues, as in a contract where un foreseeability is

[40] See, Coleman (1980) p. 536. As he claims, it is implausible that a rational voter, given the assumptions of Posner's election, would choose Kaldor-Hicks, considering that there are losers. As we will see, the argument of ex-ante compensation is not entirely plausible.

[41] These arguments have been presented by Dworkin (1980b) and Coleman (1980).

not contemplated, must interpret the presumed or implied consent of the parties, since, after all, those are the rules that they would choose from their own interest.

Let's suppose that for car accidents, a strict liability rule is more efficient than a negligence rule, since it minimizes the cost of preventing accidents and the present value of the accidents (their probability multiplied by their expected magnitude). It is clear that a habitual pedestrian is favoured by such a rule, assuming that the rule is applied perfectly, as he has full insurance coverage in case of accidents. He is certainly compensated before any accident occurs. Also, in a world with efficient rules, in general, greater productivity should compensate "ex ante" those who are losers, such as, in this case, car owners or road transport entrepreneurs.

If in Pareto it is still possible to claim consent, the same does not happen under a rule where there are uncompensated "losers" as in Kaldor Hicks. Only a presumed consent derived from a supposed ex-ante compensation can be claimed, an argument that has been widely questioned: after all, can we infer consent from such weak bases? Would an inveterate pedestrian choose a negligence liability system when an objective liability system would be more beneficial to them? Everything depends on the restrictions under which we ask the question. Posner, in fact, attempted to base the argument on self-interest. The question is raised as to what kind of rules individuals would choose in an original position.[42]

This certainly depends on how the foundations of the election are constructed. For example, if, as in Rawls, the rational elector does not know anything that affects their impartiality (such as wealth, talent, social position, etc.), they will be induced to make an impartial choice. And thus, it is possible to consider other scenarios, but it is clear that the usual knowledge rule that people have (as Posner suggested to build his decision scenario) does not constitute an attractive rule for founding the election: rights simply go up for auction and are assigned in a self-interested manner, so there are not even clear incentives for voters to choose even the same rule. Thus, a habitual pedestrian should choose a rule of strict liability, while a transporter should choose a rule of negligence liability. Posner doesn't even construct a hypothetical contract based on which people would choose the same rule, given that with the usual ignorance, people would simply choose what is most convenient for them, probably replicating the results of the worst version of utilitarianism.[43]

In any case, It is clear that people would not choose to maximize wealth, as suggested by Posner. Let's suppose that I have the option (1) where I can choose rules that maximize wealth, and (2) where I can choose to maximize utility. If wealth is a perfect substitute for utility, the question would not make sense. But as, at least in Posner's formulation, wealth is distinguished from utility, the question makes complete sense: does it make sense to choose (1) when I can choose (2)? But if people choose utility, it doesn't seem reasonable to choose a principle that cannot even claim a necessary relationship with Pareto (which guarantees utility) and whose rule of adjudication in conflicting cases (Kaldor Hicks) does not guarantee an increase

[42] See Coleman (1980), pp. 534–539.

[43] See Dworkin (1980a), p. 582.

in utility. But furthermore, if people know their "personal situation", why should they choose the MRS? Or rather, why should everyone choose a rule? With "natural ignorance" and as long as "there are losers"—as Dworkin has pointed out—people simply choose the rule that suits them (and as long as there are losers, Pareto is not possible), which is why we simply have a non-attractive utilitarian argument (one where people simply choose by majority what benefits them).

If people—unlike the "veil of ignorance" of Harsanyi or Rawls or Buchanan's argument—know their situation and the impact that rules have, they are not positioned symmetrically with respect to them. It is difficult to obtain the type of rule appealed to by contractualism. Simply put, under the deficient postulates upon which Posner constructs the contractualist argument, everyone chooses what it is best for them and not those rules that "maximize wealth": an inveterate pedestrian, a rule of strict liability, an accomplished driver, a rule of "negligence," as one might assume. Posner needs an argument that places people in a "symmetrical" position with respect to the rules in order to obtain the type of rules that people would choose to construct a goof argument.

In fact, Posner fails to fully comprehend the plausibility of Rawls', Buchanan's, or Harsanyi's argument in comparison to his own. The veil of ignorance or some form of symmetrical situation with respect to the rules, which implies a complete lack of knowledge about one's own abilities and luck in the market, introduces an element of deeply egalitarian impartiality that many consider to be at the foundation of moral reasoning, a reconstruction of the moral point of view. For Posner, the "more realistic" assumption of "natural" ignorance is precisely the fundamental problem in his argument. Once everyone knows their probabilities of success in the market, they simply choose the rule that favors them if the rule is "maximizing social wealth," and there is no criterion of impartiality but rather a majority criterion that leads directly to the problems of utilitarianism.

Posner should have assumed "symmetry" with respect to the rules, for example, that we are all "pedestrians - drivers" in the same proportion under a rule of civil liability for traffic accidents, or appeal to a principle of ignorance regarding each person's position in order to introduce impartiality and generate an instrument from which it is possible to extract a rule to which a "rational maximizer" would appeal. On these bases, can we think that those who lose would or could, in a hypothetical situation, give their consent for the application of Kaldor Hicks? But even assuming "symmetry" or a "veil" or some restriction that allows for some impartiality and at the same time the choice of a common rule, the argument would face certain problems, according to Coleman. There are two distinguishable theses in the contractual argument, one of which is completely overlooked: (1) that people in an original situation with uncertainty would actually choose wealth over other values, and (2) that once they chose that type of institution, they would also choose Kaldor Hicks and not other institutional arrangements.[44]

---

[44] See Coleman (1980), pp. 536–540.

Posner sets out to demonstrate the second point, that risk-neutral rational individuals would choose Kaldor Hicks over Pareto, but forgets the first thesis: if rational choice under uncertainty indicates that people choose the pursuit of wealth over other values or rules, such as Rawls' maximin or some variant of utilitarianism. For Coleman, Posner does not tackle this task simply because we all know that wealth is not a value in itself, so people would only choose wealth as a means to other things, but then they should choose those other things directly.

However, if Posner chooses—for example—as would be very plausible, utility, he cannot appeal to Kaldor Hicks as he does, since—as we have seen—this principle does not guarantee an increase in utility. If he argues that the MRS is instrumental in defending individual rights, it is not understood why individuals would not choose rules that tend directly to the protection of those rights, especially when, perhaps—as the example of Dworkin illustrates—they can easily collide. As the argument has been developed (I do not want to examine possible alternatives), Posner cannot claim consent or unanimity for the MRS. His attempt to found Kaldor Hicks on the autonomy of the will fails and—always within the limits of his arguments—he is reduced to utilitarianism. But, as we have seen, the MRS is Kaldor Hicks, and this rule does not assure us an increase in utility, and the Pareto rule increases utility but not necessarily wealth.[45]

Probably many of those rules are not strictly chosen, but rather they are simply those that allow acceptable levels of social cooperation and that simply come from social practice, where the contract is the way to prove their rationality and acceptability by an impartial spectator of the type of Smith or Hume or anyone who replicates the minimum conditions of the moral point of view.

Also, of course, the argument of rules and average utility could certainly be used as a typically utilitarian argument, without the need to appeal to the idea of an original contract. In any case, Posner's argument, with its rational "ignorance," not only implies a type of bias that undermines the plausibility of the argument, but also a choice structure that does not necessarily guarantee a "single" choice based on wealth and Kaldor Hicks.

4 Rule Utilitarianism, Efficiency and the Law

In this final part, I just want to show the following: that rule utilitarianism, which seeks to maximize utility not in every individual decision, but by adopting rules that maximize utility even if they don't do so in every particular case the rule applies to. As Hume stated, it is possible that property may not always lead to good outcomes, but it is clear that respecting property as a rule, leads to good outcomes. I don't intend to defend now that this type of utilitarianism is correct or plausible, but simply to initially present some general aspects of the approach and then argue that this

[45] Coleman (1980), p. 539.

type of utilitarianism avoids the problems of both the MSW and classical utilitarianism, according to Posner's argument.[46]

However, I do want to introduce at least two initial assertions. The first is that even though utility or well-being is what holds value, in a complex system like the legal system, thinking about maximizing utility through rules as an operative basis can make perfect sense considering the cognitive limits of individuals, including judges.[47] Most if not all of the most important principles or rules of the legal system leads to plausible consequences, such as the right to a fair trial (which minimizes the probability of errors in judgments) or freedom of expression (which functions as a precondition for the exercise of rights and democracy). It is clear that they can be justified by appealing to their indirect increase of well-being, meaning that they precisely do so not by seeking to increase utility in every application but through a rule that, on balance, leads to good outcomes.

A significant portion of these rules may be the product of social experience, and their existence and functioning, in its basic aspects, could be highly intuitive even for individuals who are not well-versed in philosophy or law or economics. On the other hand, it is true that "not lying" generally leads, with its exceptions, to good outcomes. However, in the case of law, we use rules, which makes sense given the complexity of the system and allows for a reduction in errors in adjudication. Even if judges were good at maximizing outcomes (and there is evidence to suggest they are not), reasons of legal certainty and system consistency could suggest that operating through rules, even at an operational level, is a good strategy for increasing social well-being or utility.

But what I want to show is that rule utilitarianism does not face the problems that classical utilitarianism faces, according to Posner's criticisms, and moreover, it overcomes at least a significant portion of the problems faced by the MSW. This does not imply that rule utilitarianism is morally correct or that it does not encounter problems. It simply means that within the realm of discussion surrounding the plausibility of Posner's proposal, rule utilitarianism fares quite well, and as far as I know, this has not been thoroughly examined.

It could be possible, following Kornhauser, also to show that the MSW does face many of the problems that Posner claims it avoids; and then demonstrate how rule utilitarianism overcomes these problems and also those of the MSW. However, I will limit this last part to the latter and only in a preliminary manner, given the concise nature of this work. Before that, however, I need to address the basic relationship between economics and rule utilitarianism.[48]

The connection between the two is quite close. Economics assumes rational individuals who seek to maximize their utility and are usually modeled as self-interested.

[46] For this classic argument, see Hume (1740), *Teatrise on Human Nature,* Part III.

[47] Following rules could contribute to alleviate or avoid biases and noise in judicial decisions. See, Daniel Khneman et al. (2021), pp. 13 and ss. See also, Lord et al. (1979), pp. 2098–2109; and Rassin et al. (2010), pp. 231–246 and Harley (2007), pp. 48–63. Judges might not use economics properly even in simple cases of unfair competition.

[48] See Kornhauser (1980), pp. 601/602.

Since most legal institutions regulate impersonal situations, this rational model (which can obviously be relaxed when necessary) allows us to explain individuals' responses to changes in the rules that shape the legal system. Economic tools can be employed to explain the rules of the legal system and of course also to help to increase overall welfare improving these rules and their application. It is common for utilitarian philosophers to utilize economic tools, and certainly, the relationship between this discipline and the utilitarian philosophical tradition is close and very well-known.[49]

Regarding its operability, rule utilitarianism would function in a manner quite similar to the MSW in the sense that it would prioritize broad spaces of individual freedom and rights, as long as their exercise does not lead to a high probability of severe and irreversible harm. In such cases, limited and rational paternalism could be justified. Similarly, when markets function correctly or close to competitive markets, the legal system should prioritize free and voluntary contracts, which allow goods to be allocated to their best uses. Of course, there is room for rational and empirical discussion about the extent of distribution and the best way to achieve it in order to improve overall welfare.

When there are high transaction costs or market failures that can be corrected by the legal system or direct state intervention, at lower costs, rules and regulations that usually restrict contractual freedom are justified. Naturally, it is the tools of economics that centrally inform the course of action to adopt rules and institutions that are more likely to lead to an increase in social utility. However, I do not intend to argue for the moral plausibility of rule utilitarianism at this moment; I merely aim to explain its close connection with economics, especially with the field of law and economics.

What I am most interested in proving now is that rule utilitarianism allows us to overcome the problems that Posner refers to when he implausibly divorces his principle from the MSW, a problem that replicates in each alternative argument we have considered.

To begin with, it is undeniable that utility constitutes an end in itself and that many socially desirable goals can be translated into utility, at least conceptually. The discussion about what is meant by utility is not relevant at this point, as this issue is rarely discussed in the literature I am addressing. It is clear that, regardless of other problems that utilitarianism may have, it does not face the problem of wealth, as it constitutes, at least, a historically plausible and persistent candidate that can explain, albeit in a general sense, the most fundamental aspects of institutions without resorting to unnecessarily complex concepts or concepts of dubious existence or argumentative plausibility. Asserting that contract law contains rules that lower transaction costs and make promises more credible, thereby increasing transactions to promote cooperation and social welfare, is not an argument that requires further explanation from a teleological standpoint.

[49] See for example, Little (2002).

In this way, the biggest problem of Posner's argument is resolved, as it becomes clear in the first version of the argument that utility can plausibly be considered a valuable goal, and in the second version, the idea that people would choose rules that maximize utility, for example, on average, is plausible. This idea is found, for example, in the well-known contractual-based arguments of authors such as Harsanyi, Buchanan, or Gauthier.[50] In fact, a contractual-type argument could be used to examine the rationality and impartiality of the rule. I do not mean to say that rule utilitarianism does not have problems, but rather that it does not have the problems faced by the MSW and classical utilitarianism, which Posner disavows.

It is clear that rule utilitarianism allows for the inclusion of fundamental rights and freedoms of individuals.[51] As Posner himself states, it is evident that a randomly chosen group of economists would affirm that granting each person the right to the fruits of their labor is a rule that leads to good results. The same applies to other fundamental rights, such as freedom of movement, freedom of expression, property rights, or the presumption of innocence in a trial. The foundations of a legal system based on rules that promote well-being under conditions of moderate scarcity, limited generosity, and cognitive limitations can be found in the works of Hume, who emphasizes the central importance of individual rights for the proper functioning of society. For example, theft may increase utility in some cases, but it does not function as a rule. The great contribution of economics is that it allows us to go beyond bureaucratic experiences and simple intuitions and identify the type of rules we need for much more subtle situations, such as minimizing the overall cost of environmental damage or its associated processes. However, the analytical operation remains the same.

It is natural to think that when it comes to the legal system, which is constituted by rules, choosing the right rule is a more or less complete or correct description of what should be done. An examination of the interaction between law and economics shows that, rather than focusing on individual cases, the emphasis is often placed on rules, such as the type and extent of civil or accident liability, remedies for contractual breaches, or types of property rights, and the best way to applicate them to concrete cases. The idea of indirect maximization through rules is not foreign to the practice of law, as evidenced by the field of Law and Economics, which offers a rationality that applies to a subset of cases, going beyond the somewhat casuistic analysis of traditional ex post legal analysis. What is examined are the effects and rationality of certain rules in general cases and not how to maximize wealth in concrete cases.

While there is not currently a clear description of how the legal system incorporates efficiency, it is at least clear that many traditional institutions of the legal system can be explained as mechanisms to facilitate cooperation, regardless of whether other rules achieve this goal. However, a system based on the utility of rules has the

[50] See Harsanyi (1977), Buchanan (1962) and Gauthier (1994).

[51] For example, the relationship between property rights enforcement and economic growth is acknowledged in the literature. See, for example, Acemoglu, Johnson, and Robinson (2005), pp. 949–995; North (1997) and North and Paul Thomas (1973).

undeniable advantage, shared with rule utilitarianism, that it cannot only suggest changes but also explain the salient features of institutions, and in some cases quite plausibly, as evidenced by the significant reception of this approach in legal education.[52]

Indeed, in complex societies under normal conditions, it is crucial to prevent the instrumental use of individuals in favour of the majority. There is a precise connection between the rule of law and well-being. If someone wants to use another person instrumentally, they must convince and compensate them. In cases of high transaction costs, any instrumental use must be justified (such as restrictions during a pandemic). It is possible that some residual instrumentalism may still exist, but it is not necessarily undesirable, although it is important to recognize that discretion can be controversial. However, when considering the utility of rules rather than individual acts, the problems associated with aggregating individuals, using them for the benefit of others, and cases of moral monstrosity are greatly limited.

Naturally, establishing boundaries can be problematic, as Posner suggests. However, considering animals not only as valuable objects based on utility functions tied to effective demand in monetary terms, but also as beings capable of pleasure and pain, and perhaps deserving of some form of special respect, may ultimately be plausible. Depending largely on the metaethical and philosophical stance of the analyst, it is always possible to support a fully programmatic utilitarianism of rules and limit the scope to human preferences. The protection afforded to certain animals, minors, foreigners, unborn individuals, and future generations depends on the preferences of decision-makers (and indeed, this is the case in practice). This means that there may be some ambiguity, but such ambiguity can be considered an interesting philosophical perspective (as in Singer's utilitarianism, for example, or in the more classical approach of Bentham). Ambiguity and exploration do not always pose a problem for a philosophical tradition.

I don't believe that measuring utility is as serious a problem when it comes to rules as it is for individual actions. In fact, it is likely to be simpler than the more complex uses of the MSW rule proposed by Posner. The amount of information required to always allocate rights to those who would hypothetically pay the most can be a problem, in addition to a rule that, compared to stable rules shaped by experience, may involve a high degree of indeterminacy in its applicability.[53] In many cases, however, it is possible to use economics to examine effects, and in many subtle applications of economics in law, convincing results can be reached. It

---

[52] There is no clear-cut answer in the literature, although many authors assume that common law, originating from judicial precedent, tends to be more efficient than legislation. Posner's original hypothesis suggested a visible hand process: the judges during the classical period of the development of American common law were liberals. Later, more interesting models of the invisible hand emerged, such as the idea that the legal system acted as a filter for inefficient laws, which were subjected to more litigation. Classic articles on common law include: Rubin (1977) and Priest (1977). For an argument in favor of the efficiency of common law, Mahoney (2001), pp. 503–525. There is a significant variety of literature on this subject. Nevertheless, it seems indisputable that some classical institutions should enable a certain degree of cooperation and social welfare.

[53] See, Rizzo (1980).

is likely that in other cases, more experience is required, but given the limits of human knowledge and the changes in preferences and technology, allowing for some ambiguity for learning and experimentation when there is a method for estimation based on shared observation and tools like those of economics, this should not necessarily be a problem. It would be undesirable and absurd to think of a normative system like law that has all the answers with precision, particularly when they depend on effects.

Unlike the MRS, the allocation is not dependent on previous allocations in a philosophical sense, as it does not matter the allocation based on demand capacity and therefore on previous wealth, which determines the ability to demand. Instead, it is a rule oriented towards the future, in the sense that what matters is the utility of all individuals involved under conditions of equality and therefore a certain impartiality that is not as clear in the MRS as in rules that are intended to maximize utility for all members of the community. Regarding maximizing and the total or the average, it is clear that rules that maximize utility would have more room for redistribution than a rule based solely on increasing output, as Posner suggests. This does not necessarily constitute a problem, as it again shows a high level of compatibility between our intuitions, practices, and the rule of maximizing utility.

Unlike the MSW, there is no need to appeal to a complex double standard where the best of principles and the best of consequences are preserved. In this case, the approach is much clearer and evident: we have principles, rules, and rights precisely because they lead to good consequences. There is no need to delve into complex arguments like the ones Posner introduces in his second version of the argument. Even if we want to frame the argument in contractual terms, the question is clear and straightforward, as we simply need to choose those rules that maximize utility.

It is clear that there are many unanswered questions, and certainly rule utilitarianism, like other positions in theories of justice, faces its own problems. There is no way to prove that it is the correct position, at least in the sense that we can prove a Nash equilibrium or the validity of supply and demand laws. However, in any case, in a very preliminary manner, I have attempted to show that rule utilitarianism, at least in principle, can considerably avoid many of the problems faced by classical utilitarianism and the MSW, a principle that was defended by Posner and sparked much debate in the specialized literature.

5 How It Could Work: Civil Law, Judicial Decision-Making, and Rule Utilitarianism—An Overview

Economic analysis of law is useful for any theory of justice, as even approaches rooted in the natural law tradition consider consequences, albeit less prominently. For instance, the original acquisition of private property in Nozick's theory of rights requires that individuals are not worse off than before the acquisition (e.g., if someone occupies a riverbank or land). Similarly, one of the central principles in Rawls, a notable critic of utilitarianism, demands improving the prospects of the least advantaged members of society.[54]

None of these tests can be conducted properly based on bureaucratic intuition alone. For example, an environmental tax would have vastly different distributive effects depending on whether it applies to essential goods (like electricity) or goods consumed by higher-income groups (such as aviation fuel), as well as on the market structure. Only in trivial or very simple cases can these approaches be applied without recourse to economics. Regulations concerning the initial ownership of watercourses or radio frequencies underscore the importance of economic analysis in understanding the scope and regulation of initial property rights. However, it is unlikely that judges explicitly adopt moral theories or moralized explanations of law, as Posner rightly pointed out. In practice, such theories are too abstract, typically fail to resolve specific cases, and are often too demanding for the concrete problems the legal system must address.[55]

By contrast, rule utilitarianism provides a more intuitive and workable framework in many cases, even within the more rigid, codified legal traditions of Continental Europe. It aligns well with the structure of law and common sense, offering a practical basis for decision-making. At the same time, it integrates economic analysis to refine decisions and ensure their outcomes are consistent with broader social utility. This combination of practicability and analytical rigor makes rule utilitarianism a valuable approach, especially in complex judicial contexts.[56]

An interesting way to integrate economics into law could involve adopting a rule utilitarian approach similar to Posner's pragmatic instrumentalism (advocated after his earlier emphasis on maximizing social wealth) but with a critical distinction: the model would seek to maximize social utility rather than pursue Posner's broader and more ambiguous notion of reasonableness. This focus on utility is more precise and consistent with the core tools of economic analysis.[57]

Rule utilitarianism should not encounter significant obstacles or face major challenges in civil law systems given its greater rigidity compared to common law traditions. A reasonable application of rule utilitarianism in a limited democracy would likely involve adherence to the system's established rules and principles,

[54] See Kymlicka (1990), Chapters 3 and 4.

[55] I think Posner is right, judges are unlikely to employ moral philosophy or theories of justice to resolve cases. That does not mean that they do not make normative judgements or reasoning, certainly but not influenced by the usually abstract theories of the sort. There are other less ambitious approaches within the moralised theories of law, but I do not want now to examine their degree of acceptance. If anything, it is more likely that in difficult cases at least, where the stakes are high, above all, judges will take the consequences seriously. See Posner (1999), pp. 45–90.

[56] Wasserstrom, for example, examined several decision rules and considered, in a classic work, that rule utilitarianism was the most attractive or 'best' criterion.... See Wasserstrom (1961), p. 1. I do not want to say now that it is the 'best' one, only that it is interesting to explore and that it eliminates many problems of other defenses of the use of economics in law.

[57] I believe that Posner's criterion of reasonableness loses normative force and precision. Of course, incorporating utility as a goal incorporates other problems, but I think the gain is well worth it. For this criticism see, Somin (2004).

recognizing the welfare benefits of respecting rights, procedures, and norms that are generally beneficial to society.[58] This would only permit deviations where the marginal benefit of doing so clearly outweighs the systemic costs in terms of legal integrity.[59]

In other words, a judge well-versed in law and economics should not always seek to maximize outcomes directly. Instead, they should aim to maximize them indirectly by respecting the rights, principles, and procedures embedded in the system's rules. This approach indirectly achieves favorable consequences, as pragmatic jurists like Justices Holmes, Cardozo, Frankfurter, and even Posner have demonstrated to varying degrees, often deference to the law and legislative decisions.[60]

Several reasons underlie this deference. Primarily, the separation of powers is a foundational principle of liberal democracies. Maintaining coherence and predictability in legal systems significantly contributes to upholding the rule of law. Following rules also minimizes biases, heuristics, and noise, making the estimation of consequences more reliable. Moreover, courts are not designed to regulate public policy, and judges often lack the necessary training to do so. Executive and legislative agencies are generally better equipped to pursue specific goals.

Many classic legal norms codified in statutes also represent accumulated societal experience, often reflecting rules that are efficient or at least conducive to social cooperation. These codes, rooted in Roman legal traditions and enriched by medieval and modern European developments, offer valuable insights. But of course, a utilitarian judge employing economic reasoning might occasionally enforce inefficient laws if the systemic cost of departing from them exceeds the benefit—particularly when the norms are clear and precise, leaving little room for alternative interpretations.[61]

Pragmatic civil law judges using economics (and other social sciences) as tools can resolve cases by interpreting the legal codes and norms to maximize social welfare indirectly. They can do so by applying the best interpretation allowed by the

---

[58] I now want to show only the salient aspects of how this approach would work, in very general terms, in a codified type of law. But it is undoubtedly true that, at least, rule utilitarianism has some appeal at the level of judicial decision-making. If only as an operational criterion that eliminates the (impossible) need to estimate the effects of particular cases. Even it is not entirely clear that Bentham himself did not at least partially postulate an indirect utilitarianism. See, Ferraro (2010), pp. 1–24.

[59] This is a very common procedure in economics. Posner, for example, has used it on several occasions. In this case I am generalising it to the more general issue of how to make a trade-off between order or integrity of the system and flexibility and change based on decisions that modify the rules.

[60] See Posner (2013), pp. 150–177.

[61] The thesis of the efficiency of law based on precedent is well known. It is likely that inefficient laws are more litigated, that efficient ones are more chosen by the parties, that it is more difficult to obtain distributive benefits from judges than from legislatures, or simply that many of the basic institutions were formed in periods when classical liberalism was more appreciated than in current times. There is no clear or simple explanation for the thesis of the efficiency of law of a judicial nature. But it is clear that many classical rules to some degree favour social co-operation. This is a central part of any book on law and economics.

legal system, one that aligns with welfare maximization. Economic analysis is naturally valuable for this task, even though many cases can be resolved through consistent, well-ordered legal reasoning without economic models.

Judges operating within this framework rely on welfare-oriented interpretations or use discretion to impose sanctions, order evidence, or evaluate it, leveraging economic tools to achieve optimal outcomes. They aim for a balance where the systemic cost of departing from a norm equals the marginal benefit of a better allocation, although such calculations often serve as heuristic guides rather than precise metrics.

The flexibility of legal systems, especially regarding constitutional review, varies significantly across regions like Latin America. For example, codified systems often provide judges, particularly in higher courts, with considerable leeway to employ welfare-maximizing criteria. In many cases, economic tools like game theory and statistics prove far superior to bureaucratic intuition or common sense in addressing complex legal problems.

Since the range of legal solutions is usually finite, judges typically compare marginal changes in costs and benefits among available options—often binary decisions, such as granting or denying a remedy. Economic analysis is particularly fruitful in ambiguous situations, such as legal gaps, rights collisions, or dynamic social changes like technological advances and public emergencies.

Yet, even within the rigid structures of codified systems, economics offers subtle improvements that preserve systemic integrity. In most cases, pragmatic approaches align with traditional methods, as Posner observed. For example, adhering to principles like the presumption of innocence often yields better societal outcomes, even if pragmatic adjustments are theoretically possible. Similarly, many higher-level norms and principles in European legal traditions provide indirect social utility.

The interplay between systemic integrity and decision outcomes often requires balancing costs and benefits using economic reasoning.[62] For instance, rule utilitarian judges weigh the marginal benefits of deviations against the systemic costs they entail. In extreme cases, such as national security crises, judicial decisions may justify overriding explicit laws, as seen in historical examples like Argentina's 1923 Lanteri ruling, a judicial decision that followed the more expansive and regulatory look at police power that was already taking place in the United States in cases such as Home Building.[63] In fact, legal systems, both in the civil and common law tradition, adapt to circumstances, especially when the application of the rule leads to

[62] Probably the most important variables are the ambiguity value of the rule and the usefulness of the case for society. When the ambiguity value of the rule is low, there is more judicial directionality and the legal system is (usually) less affected by a new rule. When the value of a decision is high, especially because it affects many people in an intense or serious way, deviating from an inefficient rule becomes more attractive. The model should match the cost with the marginal benefit.

[63] In Ercolano v. Lanteri de Renshaw the Argentine Court abandons a classic vision of the defence of property and adopts a criterion of broad police power, by limiting contractual freedom in favour of the general welfare in cases of public emergency. In this case the Supreme Court of Argentina considered a law regulating the price of urban rents to be constitutional. Naturally, I do not want to suggest now that this ruling is pragmatically correct; in fact, on the contrary, I think they used very bad economics and few facts. But this is only an example.

dramatic or disastrous results, but also in intermediate situations. This can be explained intuitively by appealing to the idea of maximizing through rules, but extending their interpretation according to changes in costs and benefits to new circumstances when this is welfare-enhancing. Given the importance for the rule utilitarian of the structure and integrity of the legal system in general, it can be applied to systems of continental European tradition where consistency is very important.

Ultimately, the pragmatic rule utilitarian judge seeks to balance systemic integrity with broader social utility, ensuring decisions reflect long-term societal benefits. This approach avoids extremes of activism or deference, offering a realistic framework for judicial decision-making.

6 Conclusion

In summary, I have initially attempted to highlight the problems of the MSW in the two most comprehensive versions presented by Posner. While this matter is not currently under debate, it provides an explanation for the plausibility of a moral foundation for the use of economics in law. In fact, to a large extent following Dworkin's criticism of Posner's initial presentation of the MSW principle, I have discussed the most important variants that the argument can take, pointing out the problems it presents. In the second version, largely following Coleman but also drawing from Dworkin and other authors, I have attempted to show that the more refined argument based on hypothetical contract fails, not only due to Posner's poor technique in constructing the contract, but primarily because the idea that individuals choose to maximize wealth is not a plausible one.

Throughout this analysis, there was always an underlying suggestion that it was a mistake for Posner to so decisively abandon the principle of utility, which has a long tradition in moral thought, especially in the Anglo-Saxon tradition. In the final part of this article, for that reason, after a brief characterization, I attempt to show that rule utilitarianism allows us to overcome many of the problems faced by Posner and also classical utilitarianism, from which Posner sought to distance himself. This does not mean that it is the morally correct position or even a description of what lawyers or judges do or should do, but simply, for more modest purposes, that it helps overcome these problems. In general, given the weight that rule utilitarianism should plausibly confer on the integrity of the law, it should not face too many problems in its application to a codified system of law in the continental European tradition. A more extensive study could further investigate the relationship between rule utilitarianism and the economics of law in greater depth.

References

Acemoglu D, Johnson S, Robinson JA (2005) Unbundling institutions. J Political Econ 113(5):949–995
Allen Leff A (1974) Economic analysis of law: some realism about nominalism. Va Law Rev 60(3):451–482
Boyd White J (1987) Economics and the law: two cultures in tension. Tenn Law Rev 54:161–202
Buchanan JM (1962) The relevance of pareto optimality. J Confl Resolut 6(4):341–354
Coase RH (1960) The problem of social cost. J Law Econ 3:1–44
Coleman J (1980) Efficiency, utility and wealth maximization. Hofstra Law Rev 8(3):512–549
Dworkin R (1980a) Why efficiency? A response to professors Calabresi and Posner. Hofstra Law Rev 8(3):563–590
Dworkin R (1980b) Is wealth a value? J Leg Stud 9(2):191–226
Ellickson R (1989) Bringing culture and human frailty to rational choice actors: a critique of classical law and economic. Chicago- Kent Law Rev 65(1):23
Ferraro F (2010) Direct and indirect utilitarianism in Bentham's theory of adjudication. J Bentham Stud 12(1):1–24
Gauthier D (1994) La Moral por Acuerdo. Gedisa, Barcelona
Harley EM (2007) Hindsight bias in legal decision making. Soc Cogn 25(1):48–63
Harsanyi J (1977) Rational behavior in games and social situations. Cambridge University Press
Hart HLA (1977) American jurisprudence through English eyes: the nightmare and the Noble dream. Ga Law Rev 11(5):969–989
Kaplow L, Shavell S (2001) Any non welfarist method of policy assessment violates the Pareto principle. J Polit Econ 109(2):281–286
Khaneman D, Sibony O, Sunstein C (2021) Noise. A flaw in human judgement. William Collins, London
Kornhauser L (1980) A guide to the perplexed claims of efficiency in the law. Hofstra Law Rev 8(3):591–639
Kronman A (1979) Wealth maximization as a normative principle. J Stud 9(2):227–242
Kymlicka W (1990) Contemporary political philosophy. Oxford University Press, New York
Little I (2002) Ethics, economics & politics. Cambridge University Press
Lord C, Ross L, Lepper M (1979) Biased assimilation and attitude polarization: the effects of prior theories on subsequently considered evidence. J Personal Soc Pscichol 37(1):2098–2109
Mahoney P (2001) The common law and economic growth: Hayek might be right. J Law Stud 30(2):503–525
North DC (1997) The New Institutional Economics and Development. WIDER Annual Lecture No. 1. UNU-WIDER, Helsinki
North DC, Paul Thomas R (1973) The rise of the western world: A new economic history. Cambridge University Press, Cambridge
Nozick R (1974) Anarchy, state and utopia. Basis Books Inc., New York
Posner R (1979) Utilitarianism, economics, and legal theory. J Law Stud 8(1):103–140
Posner R (1980) The ethical and political basis of wealth maximization. Hofstra Law Rev 8(3):487–507
Posner R (1981a) The economics of justice. Harvard University Press
Posner R (1981b) A reply to some recent criticisms of the economic theory of the common law. Hofstra Law Rev 9(3):775–794
Posner R (1985) Wealth maximization revisited. Notre Dame J Law Ethics Public Policy 2:85–105
Posner R (1999) The problematics of moral and legal theory. Harvard University Press
Posner R (2013) Reflections on judging. Harvard University Press, Cambridge
Priest G (1977) The common law process and the selection of efficient rules. J Law Stud 6(1):65–82
Rassin E, Eerland A, Kuijpers I (2010) Let's find the evidence: an analogue study of confirmation bias in criminal investigations. J Investig Psychol Offender Profiling 7(3):231–246
Rizzo M (1980) The mirage of efficiency. Hofstra Law Rev 8(3):641–658

Rubin P (1977) Why is the common law efficient? J Law Stud 6(1):51–63
Somin I (2004) Richard Posner's democratic pragmatism. Crit Rev 16(1):1–22
Stordeur E (2005a) Derechos Iniciales de Propiedad y Eficiencia Económica: un problema para el Análisis Económico del Derecho Normativo. Opinión Jurídica 4:139–154
Stordeur E (2005b) La Eficiencia de Pareto y las Teorías Deontológicas: una respuesta a Kaplow & Shavell. Ideas & Derecho 5:103–141
Stordeur E (2006) La desventuras de la Maximizacion de la Riqueza Social. Libertas 44:327–412
Tullock G (1980) Two kinds of legal efficiency. Hofstra Law Rev 8(3):658–669
Veljanovski C (1981) Wealth Maximización, law and ethics. Int Rev Law Econ 1(1):5–28
Wasserstrom RA (1961) The judicial decision. Stanford University Press, Stanford
Williams B (1973) A critique of utilitarianism. In: Smart JC, Williams B (eds) An outline of a system of utilitarian ethics: for and against. Oxford University Press, Oxford

CALABRESI V. PARETO. Preferences, Harm, and Efficiency

Giovanni Tuzet

Abstract Calabresi has developed a powerful critique of Pareto's efficiency in the field of law and economics. Among other things, he has shown that Pareto improvements require the unanimity of the relevant preferences (because they require, at least, that someone is better off and no one is worse off). The present work aims to defend Pareto's test for efficiency, with an argument built upon Mill's 'Harm Principle' and thanks to the analytical distinction between self-regarding and other-regarding preferences, which, for short, I will call *internal* and *external* preferences. If the core of Calabresi's critique is the unanimity condition required by Pareto's test, this requirement can be better satisfied by counting only internal preferences and justifying this with Mill's Principle. At the same time, the work explores the limits of the redefined Paretian approach.

1 The Question

Pareto efficiency is one of the meanings that is given to the phrase 'economic efficiency'. It is susceptible of some variations depending on how the work of Vilfredo Pareto is read and according to the theoretical framework in which it is placed, if utterly ordinalist or still indebted to the cardinalist conception of utility. Here I will not perform a philological exercise on what Pareto 'really said' or 'really meant to say'. Rather, I will adopt Pareto efficiency in its standard understanding.[1] I will do

[1] See, e.g., Coleman (1980) and Singh (2019). The standard way to address Pareto efficiency is to compare it to other conceptions of economic efficiency, such as the Kaldor-Hicks test (see below, Sect. 4) or Posner's 'wealth maximization'.

G. Tuzet (✉)
Department of Legal Studies, Bocconi University, Milan, Italy
e-mail: giovanni.tuzet@unibocconi.it

S. Zorzetto et al. (eds.), *Developments in Law and Economics in the Italo-Iberoamerican Context*, Economic Analysis of Law in European Legal Scholarship 21, https://doi.org/10.1007/978-3-032-03317-8_5

this in order to analyze Guido Calabresi's criticism of it, and look for a possible defense of the Paretian approach. It must be premised that Calabresi's arguments are much solid and a strategy in defense of Pareto must try to circumvent them. Furthermore, it should be emphasized that the question addressed here concerns not only economic efficiency as such (as many 'technical' approaches seem to assume) but also some moral and political problems that law and economic policies are called to handle and resolve.

The work proceeds as follows: Sect. 2 presents the notion of Pareto efficiency and its critique by Calabresi, focusing especially on the unanimity condition posed by that understanding of economic efficiency; Sect. 3 develops an argument in favor of Pareto efficiency and redefines some relevant notions, building on Mill's Harm Principle and distinguishing in particular what I will call 'internal' and 'external' preferences; Sect. 4 explores some of the limits of the redefined Paretian approach; Sect. 5 concludes by summarizing the argument and signaling prospects for future research.[2]

2 Pareto Efficiency and Calabresi's Critique

In the standard understanding adopted here, Pareto efficiency concerns the satisfaction of individuals' preferences. The basic problem it responds to is the alleged impossibility of interpersonal comparisons of utility (Robbins 1938, Kaldor 1939, Hicks 1939), if utility cannot be traced back to a single objective scale (as Benthamite views wish instead). If it is impossible to compare the utility of Adam who eats an apple with the utility of Saul who eats a pear or reads a newspaper, it is because the satisfaction of the respective preferences is not susceptible of an evaluation and measurement in cardinal terms (one cannot say whether and by how much Adam's utility is greater than Saul's). One can speculate over the reasons for this. It may be for metaphysical reasons having to do with the constitution of human beings, or epistemic reasons concerning the limited knowledge we have of these phenomena, or technological reasons consisting in the lack of appropriate measurement tools. The fact is that attributing a cardinal value to the satisfaction of someone's preferences is at present impossible, and when that is done it is just arbitrary. Does this mean that we cannot compare and evaluate different allocations of goods and services? To this effect, Pareto's key idea was to consider the ordinal preferences of individuals (what they prefer over what) and rank allocations of goods and services in this perspective. Then, in a nutshell, an allocation is Pareto efficient when it increases the wellbeing of at least one individual (according to their own, ordinal preferences) without decreasing that of the others (again, according to their own,

[2] One link with the Italo-Iberoamerican context represented in this book lies in the fact that, for biographical reasons, both Calabresi and Pareto have had, and still have, a strong impact on the relevant discussion and scholarship. Focusing on such authors is therefore important to give an idea of the law-and-economics developments in that context.

ordinal preferences). Moving to a state of affairs that has a higher position in the ranking of an individual amounts to being better off for this individual, and moving to a state of affairs that is lower-ranked amounts to being worse off.

Going into more detail, Pareto efficiency can be conceptually decomposed into the notions of Pareto *superiority* and Pareto *optimality* (Coleman 1992, pp. 18–19), which consist respectively in this:

- a state of affairs S_2 is Pareto *superior* to another state S_1 if and only if no one is worse off in S_2 compared to S_1, and at least someone is better off in S_2 compared to S_1;
- a state of affairs S_o is Pareto *optimal* if and only if there is no state S_n such that S_n is Pareto superior to S_o.

Thus, in light of the ordinal preferences of the individuals involved, an allocation having the properties of S_2 is Pareto superior to an allocation like S_1, and an allocation like S_o (whose definition recursively exploits the Pareto superiority definition) is Pareto optimal. Let me stress this point: nothing in the Pareto framework requires a cardinal measurement of the utility that Adam or Saul derives from having some fruit or being given a certain resource, nor has it to do with the moral value of a certain allocation of resources assessed from an exogenous perspective. If Adam prefers apples over pears, and Saul is indifferent between them, then the allocation that gives an apple to Adam and a pear to Saul (S_2) is superior to the one that gives a pear to Adam and an apple to Saul (S_1). Likewise, if Adam prefers *aguardiente* over spring water, and Saul is indifferent, giving *aguardiente* to Adam and water to Saul is Pareto superior, notwithstanding the fact that liquor can worsen Adam's health. No exogenous moral criteria apply here, nor are paternalistic considerations relevant. Only preferences count. However, this does not mean that Pareto efficiency is devoid of moral value.

Morally speaking, one of the virtues of Pareto efficiency is the ingenious compromise it makes between altruism and selfishness. It is a sort of half-Kantian, half-Utilitarian compromise:[3] individuals can be selfish to the extent that their preferences do not harm others, just as the preferences of others cannot be imposed on the ones who do not entertain them. You can be made better off if the satisfaction of (some of) your preferences does not make someone else worse off, and, symmetrically, you cannot be made worse off because others would thereby be better off. This generates in fact a number of issues that must be put aside here. Some of them will be addressed below. For the moment, let us pause on the question of whether Pareto efficiency is of any interest to the jurist.

Can one evaluate legal allocations of economic resources along the lines of Pareto efficiency, namely with Pareto superiority and optimality? The Calabresian answer is skeptical, if not utterly negative, since passing the Pareto test for efficiency requires the unanimity of the 'votes' or preferences of the individuals

[3] Cf. in this respect Posner (1979). Among others, see also Nozick (1981), p. 494ff on 'deontology and teleology'.

involved. This seems unrealistic to obtain in contexts such as legislative ones, and by definition it is not obtained in judicial contexts when the claims of one party are accepted and those of the counterparty are rejected. Consider in particular a tort case, with damages awarded. The plaintiff will be better off, the defendant worse off. An outcome like this, which is legally normal, would be impossible under Pareto efficiency—because someone will be worse off. Still, Pareto efficiency makes sense of other legal contexts, such as contractual relationships—where all parties are better off unless some kind of contractual pathology, like duress, occurs—and it makes sense of legal arrangements where parties or members have a veto power (consider e.g. the U.N. Security Council). In short, if that is correct, Pareto efficiency has some explanatory and justificatory power in the legal domain but also has very serious limitations.

Calabresi's criticism dates back. In the seminal 1972 article co-authored with Douglas Melamed, *Property Rules, Liability Rules, and Inalienability: One View of the Cathedral*, it is noted on Coase's footing that in the absence of transaction costs the Pareto optimum will be achieved with any initial assignment of rights, and that, however, in our world characterized by transaction costs, externalities make it difficult to reach that point (Calabresi and Melamed 1972, pp. 1094–1096, 1103). Among the externalities and their consequences, 'moralisms' have a particular role; they are exemplified by the refusal that one can sell their kidney or that one can be willfully reduced to slavery (Calabresi and Melamed 1972, pp. 1112–1113). What Calabresi and Melamed call 'inalienability rules' prevent precisely this sort of transactions. For what matters here, moralisms generally aggravate the problem mentioned above, as they prevent the attainment of unanimity required to move from S_1 to S_2, or from S_n to S_o. In Paretian terms, the moralist who rejects the legitimacy of a kidney's sale will be worse off in the state of affairs in which someone can sell their kidney; therefore that moralist will not give their consent to this possibility. Notice that, at least in principle, the sale of a kidney will make the parties to the transaction better off, since the kidney-seller would be better off with the money than with the kidney, and the kidney-buyer would be better off with the kidney than with the money. The same applies, though less dramatically, to other transactions like the sale of alcohol, sex toys, or any other item that is charged with being central to immoral practices. And, vice versa, those who enjoy drinking alcohol and the like would be worse off in the world where alcohol is prohibited for the purpose of making the former moralists better off. All of this has a consequence that is not obvious at first sight. It should be observed that the result of opposing moralisms is a stalemate in which, due to the effect of crossed vetoes, the status quo paradoxically turns out to be the Pareto optimum, since it is impossible to change it without someone being worse off, or at least believing they are worse off. This fuels the objection that Pareto efficiency is biased in favor of the existing allocation of resources, whatever this is.

Calabresi's argument is elaborated on in the 1978 book written with Philip Bobbitt, *Tragic Choices*, where one can find the following claims, among others: (i) Pareto criteria are virtually useless, since a non-market allocation cannot be shown to be Pareto superior to a market one, nor, more importantly, can a market allocation be shown to be Pareto superior to a non-market one; (ii) Pareto criteria ignore distributive problems and their moral, political, and legal implications; (iii) to overcome some of those problems, efficiency can be understood as 'potential Pareto superiority with tolerable distributional effects' (Calabresi and Bobbitt 1978, p. 86). I will discuss potential Pareto superiority below; instead in this work I cannot deal with the issue of the conditions under which market allocations are superior to non-market ones, or vice versa; nor can I address here the issue of what is meant by 'tolerable' distributional effects. I limit myself to observing, again, that Pareto efficiency does not take into account the distribution of resources and favors their current distribution, ratifying the status quo and, paradoxically, the impossibility of changing it when people would like to but do not agree on the way to do it.

Calabresi insists on this line of argument in a 1991 critical essay specifically dedicated to Pareto efficiency and the Coasian approach, *The Pointlessness of Pareto: Carrying Coase Further*. In the presence of transaction costs, any society is always or will soon arrive at the Paretian optimum (Calabresi 1991, p. 1212)—especially, I would add, when 'moralisms' prevent certain changes and transform the status quo into the optimal state according to Pareto efficiency.[4] As a matter of fact, the Pareto test is a request for unanimity which is unrealistic to require in legal contexts (with the exception of transactions like contracts without negative externalities, I would say); therefore, the set of Pareto superior moves is basically 'void' and, as a consequence, the Pareto framework cannot be a normative criterion for the improvement of the status quo (Calabresi 1991, pp. 1215–1216).

In his 2016 book *The Future of Law and Economics*, Calabresi observes again that legal systems frequently take into account 'third-party moral costs', and reiterates the point that 'there are costs whose existence makes impossible reorganizations which, if they occurred, would make all people better off' (Calabresi 2016, pp. 22ff, 137).

Now, this line of argument is impeccable but Calabresi himself notes there is a way in which it could be circumvented. It is a way to escape its stringent conclusions. The idea goes like this: If we were to use a less demanding Pareto criterion (defining Pareto moves more specifically), we could solve the unanimity problem but we would introduce in the scheme some values that are not unanimously held (Calabresi 1991, pp. 1216–1217). This is precisely the idea on which I think we can still work.

But before developing such an argument in defense of Pareto, let us briefly indicate a few others. A first argument of a conceptual nature consists in saying that the Coase theorem is about the Pareto optimum, which therefore maintains a conceptual, if not normative, role. Why is that? Simply because the theorem implies it in postulating that without transaction costs individuals will bargain and allocate resources in the best economic way (Coase 1960; Coleman 1980, p. 230). The

[4] Compare the two points: the Pareto optimum will be reached in the *absence* of transaction costs because individuals will bargain and allocate resources in the best way (Coase 1960), but it will also be reached in the *presence* of transaction costs (and moralisms in particular) when these prevent people from reallocating resources and the actual distribution becomes Pareto optimal.

strength of this conceptual argument is limited. On the one hand, Calabresi does not deny that with no transaction costs the Pareto optimum will be achieved with any initial assignment of rights; this conceptual point is granted, but the normative role of the Pareto framework is impaired, on the other hand, by the obvious fact that the zero-transaction-costs world is a fictional one. Our own is a world with positive transaction costs, greater or lesser depending on the situation. If any, the normative value of the Pareto optimum would rather consist in being a sort of ideal limit that we are unable to reach but can approach to different extents. However, we must also consider that, by definition, the Pareto optimum is already achieved whenever it is impossible to change the status quo because someone would be worse off. All of that conspires to make Pareto efficiency 'pointless', to borrow Calabresi's wording.

A second argument consists in configuring a 'non-fanatical' Pareto efficiency test which replaces 'almost nobody' for 'nobody' and 'almost everyone' for 'everyone' (Posner 1980, p. 495). If so, there would be a less rigorous Pareto test which, for the move from S_1 to S_2 or the choice of S_2 instead of S_1, does not require that 'no one' is worse off but that 'almost no one' is worse off, and does not require the consent of 'everyone' but of 'almost everyone'. There is at least a modicum of reasonableness in this mitigation of the Paretian rigor, but there is also a problem of principle (Dworkin 1980, pp. 580–582): How to justify that someone's preferences are not taken into consideration? How to justify to this person that their preferences are given less value—or no value at all—compared to someone else's preferences? In order to move from 'everyone' to 'almost everyone' being better off, and from 'nobody' to 'almost nobody' being worse off, someone must be excluded from the picture. This person would be treated differently. Putting it with no euphemism, this person would be discriminated. So, how to reject this conclusion and justify that some preferences do not count as other preferences?

3 An Argument in Defense of Pareto Efficiency

The argument I would like to present here focuses precisely on the moral reasons for using a less demanding Pareto criterion. This is not to say that where 'almost everyone' agrees, those who do not agree must put their hearts at rest. It is to indicate a principled reason with which to define more specifically 'valid' preferences and acceptable moves from one state of affairs to another.

The starting point of the argument is John Stuart Mill's *Harm Principle*. This principle too is susceptible to being specified and understood in different ways. A number or issues depend upon this, especially upon the way 'harm' is read (Feinberg 1984). But let us try to understand the principle in its essential core, according to which we are permitted to interfere with the conduct of an individual only if the conduct of this individual harms other subjects.

> That principle is, that the sole end for which mankind are warranted, individually or collectively, in interfering with the liberty of action of any of their number, is self-protection. That the only purpose for which power can be rightfully exercised over any member of a

> civilized community, against his will, is to prevent harm to others. His own good, either physical or moral, is not a sufficient warrant. (Mill 1859, pp. 21–22)

The principle is anti-paternalistic. The own good of an individual is not a sufficient reason to interfere with their conduct. Mill deals with this in relation to forms of prohibition widespread in his time, and in particular he refers (1859, pp. 144, 177) to the criminalization by the law of certain forms of conduct, including gambling, drunkenness, fornication. Now, it should be observed that a violation of the Harm Principle—that is, prohibiting what does not harm others, and, even more so, criminalizing conduct that does not have harmful effects on others—is a *Pareto worsening*. It is so because banning something harmless worsens someone's position without improving that of others according to their respective preferences. Anyone who would like to engage in the conduct in question, given the prohibition, is in a worse situation than without the prohibition, while those who do not suffer any harm are not in a better position, since in any case they do not receive any benefit from the ban. Mill denounces these forms of prohibition and fears their perverse effects:

> there are, in our own day, gross usurpations upon the liberty of private life actually practiced, and still greater ones threatened with some expectation of success, and opinions propounded which assert an unlimited right in the public not only to prohibit by law everything which it thinks wrong, but, in order to get at what it thinks wrong, to prohibit a number of things which it admits to be innocent. (Mill 1859, p. 158)

If, therefore, it is correct to see a connection between the Harm Principle (or rather its violation) and Pareto efficiency (or rather Pareto inefficiency), we can articulate as follows the notions of Pareto *inferiority* and Pareto *worst* and subsequently relate them to the prohibition of harmless conduct:

- a state of affairs S_1 is Pareto *inferior* to another state S_2 if and only if no one is better off in S_1 compared to S_2, and at least someone is worse off in S_1 compared to S_2;
- a state of affairs S_w is Pareto *worst* if and only if there is no state S_n such that S_n is Pareto inferior to S_w.

A violation of the Harm Principle brings to an inferior Pareto state, it is a worsening in the allocation of resources including legal rights and duties. Harmless conduct being banned, no one is better off and someone is worse off.

The further step of the argument in defense of Pareto efficiency consists in drawing a distinction between *internal* and *external* preferences. Mill is again a source of inspiration. He notes that there are preferences concerning oneself and preferences concerning others, and he criticizes the latter from a moral point of view.

> There are many who consider as an injury to themselves any conduct which they have a distaste for, and resent it as an outrage to their feelings; as a religious bigot, when charged with disregarding the religious feelings of others, has been known to retort that they disregarded his feelings, by persisting in their abominable worship or creed. But there is no parity between the feeling of a person for his own opinion, and the feeling of another who is offended at his holding it; no more than between the feeling of a person for his own opinion, and the feeling to another who is offended at his holding it; no more than between the

> desire of a thief to take a purse, and the desire of the right owner to keep it. And a person's taste is as much his own peculiar concern as his opinion or his purse. (Mill 1859, pp. 150–151)

Economic theory draws a similar distinction in terms of self-regarding and other-regarding preferences. We can call preferences that concern oneself or one's own conduct 'self-regarding', or 'internal' for short, and those that concern others or their conduct 'other-regarding', or 'external' for short.[5] Prohibition is typically an expression of external preferences on top of internal ones, that is, the requirement that others too refrain from what we do not want to do or force ourselves not to do. As I will discuss below, there may be hard cases in this respect. There may be cases in which it is unclear whether the relevant preferences are to be classified as internal or external. This should not be taken, however, as an argument against the existence of clear cases of internal and external preferences (e.g., Adam wants to drink *aguardiente* instead of water, and you want him to drink water instead of *aguardiente*).

At this point, the argument in defense of Pareto efficiency can be outlined as consisting of five main steps:

1. a development of the Paretian logic to encompass Pareto inferior and worst states;
2. an analytical distinction between internal and external preferences (self-regarding and other-regarding);
3. the endorsement of the Harm Principle as a moral argument to limit 'valid' preferences to internal ones;
4. an understanding of the unanimity requirement as referred to internal preferences only, given that external preferences can generate Pareto inferior states of affairs;
5. the extension of the Harm Principle to other branches of law in addition to the criminal one.

By distinguishing internal from external preferences (although there will be doubtful cases and the distinction cannot be claimed to be crystal clear), Mill's Harm Principle can be invoked as a moral reason for excluding, from the preferences that validly count, at least some of the 'moralisms' pointed out by Calabresi: moral externalities should not make a difference insofar as they generate external preferences unsupported by the Harm Principle, i.e. preferences on what others should be or should do—more often *not* be or *not* do, as these preferences are expressed in the form of prohibitions—unsupported by harm considerations.

Note that some moralisms must be treated differently, though. One thing is the ban on drinking or oral sex; another is the ban on selling oneself as a slave. Insofar as practices like drinking and performing oral sex do not harm those who dislike them and disapprove of them, the Harm Principle makes it unjustified to ban those practices. The state of affairs in which drinking is prohibited is Pareto inferior

[5] An analogous distinction is found in Dworkin (1978), p. 234, as he distinguishes between 'personal' and 'external' preferences (in the context of a critique of utilitarianism which we pass over here). For a condensed version of the argument presented here, see Tuzet (2024).

because someone is worse off and no one is better off *according to their internal preferences*. Those who disapprove of drinking do not get any benefit from the prohibition, apart from the satisfaction of their external preferences. But if these do not count, such a moralism should not be endorsed and enforced by law. The case of the ban on voluntary enslavement is different: Mill (1859, p. 184) points out that, by selling themselves for a slave (assuming this act reflects a genuine desire and preference), the subject 'abdicates' their liberty, because they forgo any future use of it, beyond that single act. For Mill, this counts as a defeat of the very purpose which is a justification for allowing people to dispose of themselves—presumably, their wellbeing. What justifies this moralism from a Paretian viewpoint too is the fact that the subject, by 'abdicating' their liberty, deprives themselves of the possibility of autonomously satisfying any other internal preferences they might have. The ordinal logic of the Paretian approach is centered on the very possibility for individuals to determine and revise their preferences, which would become impossible in the enslavement scenario.[6]

Once that has been established, the test for Pareto efficiency can be reformulated by saying that the unanimity of the sole internal preferences is required: that is, the subjects involved must all agree that the choice of a certain state of affairs, or the move from one state to another, makes them better off or indifferent from the viewpoint of their own internal preferences, namely the preferences that they have about themselves and their conduct. This seems applicable not only to criminal law (whose sanctions particularly concerned Mill) but also to other branches of law and legal issues such as the conferral of civil rights. In this regard, the example of same-sex marriage is telling: whoever opposes it typically expresses an external preference, which in the Pareto perspective redefined here has no reason to be validly counted for the purposes of unanimity. The opponents of same-sex marriage derive no advantage for themselves from its prohibition, and are willing to impose a ban on other individuals who, as a result, would be worse off. Put into economic terms, there would be no benefits for the opponents of that and there would be costs for others.[7] Obviously, this is true if we disregard the benefits of seeing that one's external preferences are satisfied, together with the costs of seeing that they are not satisfied. This disregard is not morally outrageous, for some preferences are in tension with others, especially if one agrees on the fundamental value of liberty—and Calabresi is sensible to this Millian point (Tuzet 2019). Such tensions can be resolved through the Harm Principle and the protection of harmless conduct. The persons who do not have same-sex preferences for their own life are not forced to engage in such transactions nor have a duty to, where same-sex marriage is legal, and those having those preferences have also the right to proceed that way. This

[6] Whether the 'ultimate' value behind this is wellbeing or autonomy remains an open question. One option is to claim that autonomy is instrumental to wellbeing; another is to claim that autonomy is 'ultimate' in its own right. See, among others, Sunstein (2014).

[7] However, extending and enforcing rights has costs too. This is a usual rejoinder to the Millian argument. Then one should compare the relevant states of affairs (e.g. where same-sex marriage is permitted and where it is not) under a cost-benefit analysis.

amounts to Pareto improvements notwithstanding external preferences to the contrary.

We can thus *analytically redefine the notion of Pareto efficiency*:

- a state of affairs is Pareto *superior* to another if and only if someone is better off in the former compared to the latter (according to their internal preferences), without anyone being worse off (again, according to their internal preferences);
- a state of affairs is Pareto *optimal* if and only if it is impossible to change it in such a way as to make at least someone better off (according to their internal preferences) without making anyone worse off (again, according to their internal preferences).

And we can *redefine the Harm Principle applied to law* in this way:

- the law is not justified to interfere with someone's conduct for the purpose of enforcing someone else's external preferences unsupported by harm considerations.[8]

The example of same-sex marriage given above should be enough to illustrate the point. The state of affairs in which the prohibitionists win is a Pareto worsening, and the state of affairs in which they have won everything there is to win is a Pareto worst.

Let me also add that, from a legal perspective, Pareto superiority appears to be more important or more salient than Pareto optimality. The latter is more attractive to economists who wish to model and design the ideal allocation of resources given a set of assumptions; the former is more valuable to jurists who are committed to improving conditions in given contexts, step by step—in particular by extending rights. Piecemeal improvements resonate with Pareto superiority, whereas a grand reform is closer to the ideal of an optimal allocation of resources, including legal resources such as legal rights and duties. Superior states of affairs constitute a progress from, not necessarily a progress to.

4 The Argument's Weaknesses

It must be admitted that the argument presented above has some weaknesses. The first is a certain vagueness of the distinction between internal and external preferences. Surely there may be dubious and intermediate cases, with respect to which we can try to make the distinction more precise, with no illusion about the possibility of getting rid of the difficult cases once and for all. The world is too complex to perfectly fit our definitions.

---

[8] Note instead that when conduct is harmful but generates benefits for the agent the situation falls under the Kaldor-Hicks framework (see below, Sect. 4). The utilitarian calculus applied there raises serious concerns when the conduct is criminal. What if the rapist gets more benefits than the costs imposed on the victim?

A second weakness—related to the first but on a more radical point—is that the distinction itself becomes untenable if one considers that any human being has relationships with others and any preference has effects on others. Mill was well aware of the problem.

> The distinction here pointed out between the part of a person's life which concerns only himself, and that which concerns others, many persons will refuse to admit. How (it may be asked) can any part of the conduct of a member of society be a matter of indifference to the other members? No person is an entirely isolated being; it is impossible for a person to do anything seriously or permanently hurtful to himself, without mischief reaching at least to his near connexions, and often far beyond them. (Mill 1859, p. 143)

You can imagine in this respect Adam's wife, Eve, complaining about his drinking *aguardiente* because this not only will harm his health but also their life together, on top of the money spent to buy liquor. Is Eve's preference about Adam's drinking a merely external one? Responding in the affirmative would distort her argument, which is supported by harm considerations and concerns the bad effects of Adam's conduct for him *and for her*. It is different from the abstract reprimand by someone unrelated to Adam. And there is more, if to some degree the argument can be extended to the whole of society.[9] However, Mill points out (1859, pp. 146–147) that what we really disapprove of in such situations (or should disapprove of) is not the bad habit in itself but rather the lack of care for someone's relatives, or the fact that someone does not discharge their obligations in different respects (e.g. an unpaid debt because money was spent on alcohol). In these cases interference by morality or law is justified. In the other cases it is not:

> with regard to the merely contingent, or, as it may be called, constructive injury which a person causes to society, by conduct which neither violates any specific duty to the public, nor occasions perceptible hurt to any assignable individual except himself; the inconvenience is one which society can afford to bear, for the sake of the greater good of human freedom. (Mill 1859, p. 147)

The 'greater good of human freedom' justifies some such costs imposed on society. This seems to assume that some external preferences are supported by harm considerations (and therefore are not purely 'external').[10] A sensible cost-benefit analysis will dispose of them in the proper way.

A third weakness consists in the vulnerability of the argument with respect to the many situations in which the allocation of a good necessarily makes someone better off and someone else worse off according to the relevant internal preferences. It happens when a scarce resource, such as an organ for a transplant, must be assigned either to Adam or Saul. Then no Pareto improvement is possible even if redefined as above. (Paradoxically, again, the only justified option would be not to assign the good, and maintain the status quo as a Pareto optimum.) In such situations, help can

[9] 'I fully admit that the mischief which a person does to himself may seriously affect, both through their sympathies and their interests, those nearly connected with him and, in a minor degree, society at large.' (Mill 1859, p. 145).

[10] A different way to make the point is to claim that external preferences are indirect internal preferences, i.e. relative to the consequences of the conduct of others on us.

come from the efficiency of Kaldor-Hicks, which consists in making certain preferences prevail over others under given conditions (Coleman 1992, pp. 167–169).[11] We can define it like this:

- according to the Kaldor-Hicks test, S_2 is efficient compared to S_1 if and only if in S_2 the 'winners' can compensate the 'losers' in a way that no one is worse off compared to S_1 and at least someone is better off compared to S_1.

Hence, according to Kaldor-Hicks efficiency, resource allocation S_2 must be preferred to allocation S_1 when those who benefit from S_2 have a sufficiently large benefit to compensate those who bear costs, and still be better off given the net benefit. If compensation occurs in such a way that no one in S_2 is worse off compared to S_1 and at least someone is better off, then the move to S_2 is certainly efficient. But note that the Kaldor-Hicks test requires only that compensation *can occur* in such a way, not that it actually occurs. If it actually occurs, an efficient move according to the Kaldor-Hicks test becomes a Pareto superior move (provided that compensation itself does not have too high transaction costs). Thus the Kaldor-Hicks test is also seen as a criterion of potential Pareto superiority. In this sense, as we have seen, Calabresi and Bobbitt (1978, p. 86) refer to a 'potential Pareto superiority' test to which they associate 'tolerable distributional effects'. So it is correct to say that Pareto efficiency remains in the background as a conceptual resource to be integrated with the appropriate normative considerations. This turns out to have the same point of the first argument in defense of Pareto sketched above, there in reference to the Coase theorem, here to the Kaldor-Hicks test for efficiency: Pareto efficiency is not entirely 'pointless', for it remains in the background as a conceptual, if not normative, resource that makes sense of bargaining and reallocations *à la* Coase and of reallocations *à la* Kaldor-Hicks.

However, there is a crucial problem with using Kaldor-Hicks to rescue Pareto efficiency. Kaldor-Hicks efficiency requires a comparison of someone's benefits with someone else's costs. When the 'winners' gain more than the 'losers' lose, the move is deemed efficient. But this technique of cost-benefit analysis reintroduces a cardinal measurement of the utilities and disutilities of the subjects involved, in place of the Pareto ordinal logic. It reintroduces those interpersonal comparisons of utility that Pareto had tried to exclude from the picture by judging them impossible. The only counterargument I see here in defense of Pareto consists in claiming that Kaldor-Hicks potential compensation can be seen along the lines of ordinal rankings. If the 'winners' can make it the case that the 'losers' in S_2 are brought back to the same ranking level of S_1, and notwithstanding this the 'winners' in S_2 remain on a higher-ranked level, this state of affairs is Pareto superior and efficient.

Finally, it should be noted that in recent discussion fueled by behavioral economics (Sunstein 2014) the Harm Principle is criticized to the extent that individual preferences may not be in the best interests of their holders. This would justify a paternalistic intervention when individuals are not autonomously able to achieve the

[11] On Kaldor's and Hicks' contributions, respectively, see Torriti and Ikpe (2019), p. 407.

goals and wellbeing they wish for themselves. With such intervention they would be protected from their own errors and the costs thereof. This is a line of argument that cannot be examined here, but it should be noted that the possible divergence of wellbeing and preferences is a serious threat to the Pareto logic and the argument presented here, because it puts into doubt the fundamental assumption that wellbeing consists in the satisfaction of internal preferences.

5 Prospects for Future Research

In order to summarize the present work, let me repeat that Calabresi has developed a powerful critique of Pareto's efficiency. Among other things, he has shown that Pareto improvements require the unanimity of the relevant preferences (because they require, at least, that someone is better off and no one is worse off). I have tried to defend Pareto's test for efficiency with an argument built upon Mill's 'Harm Principle' and thanks to the analytical distinction between self-regarding and other-regarding preferences, which, for short, I have called 'internal' and 'external' preferences. If the core of Calabresi's critique is the unanimity condition required by Pareto's test, this requirement can be better satisfied by counting only internal preferences and justifying this with Mill's Principle. At the same time, I have pointed out some limits and weaknesses of the redefined Paretian approach, and offered considerations that reduce their critical impact. I have also suggested that, for jurists, Pareto superiority is more salient than Pareto optimality.

Now I wish to highlight some prospects for future research. One is the prospect of further analytical work to better clarify the distinction between internal and external preferences. This would also help adjudicate unclear cases and those where external preferences could be seen as indirect internal ones. Eve complains about Adam's drinking because it harms her too. The workers hired in the morning complain because those hired in the evening receive the same money (parable of the workers in the vineyard, Matthew 20: 1–16). When the right to vote is extended from men to women, a man protests that his vote now has lesser weight. When the right to marry is extended to same-sex couples, someone protests that this has costs in terms of social budget (e.g. for the social security and pension system in particular). Work is needed to capture the logic of these arguments, appreciate their distinctive features, and assess their strength.

Another prospect is work on how to implement in practice the distinction between internal and external preferences. How to implement the policy of disregarding external preferences unsupported by harm considerations? Conferring rights whose exercise does not harm others? This sounds correct but tautological. How to model constitutional design and legislation in this respect? Is constitutional review sufficient for this? Can we imagine a legislative process where external preferences do not count for voting purposes? The threat to the liberty of political opinion and action is significant.

Those are some of the issues that future research can address. In conclusion, to reiterate a point mentioned at the outset of this work, 'Law & Economics' is not only a technical discipline focused on mathematical formalizations and abstract modeling; it is also a way of dealing with the moral and political problems that legal and economic systems face.

References

Calabresi G (1991) The pointlessness of Pareto: carrying Coase further. Yale Law J 100:1211–1237
Calabresi G (2016) The future of law and economics. Essays in reform and recollection. Yale University Press, New Haven
Calabresi G, Bobbitt P (1978) Tragic choices. W.W. Norton & Company, New York
Calabresi G, Melamed D (1972) Property rules, liability rules, and inalienability: one view of the cathedral. Harv Law Rev 85:1089–1128
Coase RH (1960) The problem of social cost. J Law Econ 3:1–44
Coleman JL (1980) Efficiency, exchange, and auction: philosophic aspects of the economic approach to law. Calif Law Rev 68:221–249
Coleman JL (1992) Risks and wrongs. CUP, Cambridge (reprinted in 2003, OUP, Oxford)
Dworkin R (1978) Taking rights seriously. Harvard University Press, Cambridge
Dworkin R (1980) Why efficiency? Hofstra Law Rev 8:563–590
Feinberg J (1984) The moral limits of the criminal law. Vol. 1, Harm to others. OUP, Oxford
Hicks JR (1939) The foundations of welfare economics. Econ J 49:696–712
Kaldor N (1939) Welfare propositions of economics and interpersonal comparisons of utility. Econ J 49:549–552
Mill JS (1859) On liberty. Parker and Son, London
Nozick R (1981) Philosophical explanations. Harvard University Press, Cambridge
Posner R (1979) Utilitarianism, economics, and legal theory. J Leg Stud 8:103–140
Posner R (1980) The ethical and political basis of the efficiency norm in common law adjudication. Hofstra Law Rev 8:487–507
Robbins L (1938) Interpersonal comparisons of utility: a comment. Econ J 48:635–641
Singh R (2019) Economic efficiency. In: Marciano A, Ramello GB (eds) Encyclopedia of law and economics. Springer, New York, pp 637–640
Sunstein C (2014) Why nudge? The politics of libertarian paternalism. Yale University Press, New Haven
Torriti J, Ikpe E (2019) Cost-benefit analysis. In: Marciano A, Ramello GB (eds) Encyclopedia of law and economics. Springer, New York, pp 404–410
Tuzet G (2019) Calabresi and Mill: bilateralism, moral externalities and value pluralism. Global Jurist 19:1–8
Tuzet G (2024) Preferences, internal and external. In: Marciano A, Ramello GB (eds) Encyclopedia of law and economics. https://doi.org/10.1007/978-1-4614-7883-6_821-1

Applied L&E and Institutional Policy-Making

"Economist Legislators": The Use of Economic Analysis of Law in the Lawmaking Process

Roberta Simões Nascimento

Abstract The article investigates how the economic analysis of law (EAL) can be useful to legislators. It starts from the premise that legislators who choose to legislate make a rational choice. Reason, however, is not the postulate of the rationality of the legislator traditionally used in legal discourse. Legislation is assumed to involve a rational decision in which the expected costs and benefits of using legislation as a social conflict resolution mechanism are weighed. After a brief explanation of the main characteristics of the EAL, this methodology is used to understand the process of drafting legislation. Next, the EAL application exercise is carried out to explain the legislative choices regarding the textual formulations of the norms. In legislative technique, traditionally, it is read that laws must be clear, simple and easy for citizens to comply with. However, the use of EAL suggests other readings, showing in a special way that legislative choices depend on several parameters. The literature produced debating the degree of precision or specificity of the legislation is incorporated for the understanding of the activity of legislating with vague norms (*standards*), to the detriment of specific norms (rules). The methodology used is a literature review on the economic analysis of law itself. But the research is also descriptive and exploratory. Although it does not exhaust the theme, it seeks both to describe the connections between EAL and the elaboration of laws and to provide bases for further investigations, notably with regard to the use of legislative technique. The result goes in the sense that the improvement of the process of drafting laws generates a higher *ex ante cost* for legislators, but generates a reduction in *ex post costs* that more than compensates for the initial cost, as it provides savings in the face of all costs. overall benefits and costs incurred.

R. S. Nascimento (✉)
Universidade de Brasília, Faculdade de Direito, Brasília, Brazil

S. Zorzetto et al. (eds.), *Developments in Law and Economics in the Italo-Iberoamerican Context*, Economic Analysis of Law in European Legal Scholarship 21, https://doi.org/10.1007/978-3-032-03317-8_6

1 Introduction

In *That Which is Seen, and That Which is Not Seen*, Frédéric Bastiat (1801–1850) states that, in the economic sphere, an act, a habit, an institution, a law generate not only an effect, but a series of effects, of which only the first is immediate, as the others only appear later. This would allow you to differentiate between the visible effect and effects that are not visible. Still according to Bastiat, the bad economist focuses only on the effect *that is seen*, while the good economist takes into account both the effect that is seen and those *that must be foreseen*.

The relevance of Bastiat's idea persists and the same logic could serve to guide the reasoning of legislators in the legislative function. By legislating, it is understood the activity of elaborating norms (whether rules or vague norms), through which new legal commands are created. Legislating implies choosing, among the various possible options, the alternative that most matters in each case. As a consequence of the activity of legislating, there will be the creation, modification or extinction of legal norms, and, sometimes, the main one: the definition of an apparatus for its implementation or imposition in case of non-compliance.

Well then. To paraphrase Bastiat, the bad legislator would be the one who has not learned to discern between the effect *that is seen* and the effects *that are not seen* of the norms that he intends to see approved. In turn, the good legislator manages to see beyond the immediate favorable (or unfavorable in the short term) consequence, also discerning the disastrous subsequent consequences (or beneficial in the long term) of the laws passed by parliament.

In a very simplified way, the economic analysis of law (EAL) proposes precisely to answer what are the effects of legal rules on the decisions of agents—especially the addressees of laws, considering them in a broad sense to include public officials and judges responsible for its application and interpretation—as an analytical step prior to the decision on whether or not these effects are desirable from a social, economic, etc. perspective.

The EAL still seeks to gather instructions on how to design the legislation, public policies and institutions that will be the product of the laws so that they generate the right incentives, towards the aspired objectives. The approach serves to prevent problems related to "legislative failures", thus understood as laws that do not lend themselves to solving (or even worsen) the problems that gave rise to legislative intervention.

This explanation about the EAL, although brief, already denotes the potential of this tool if properly used by legislators. At the same time, the law-making activity itself can be explained through the lens of EAL. This is because legislation (as an activity) can also be seen as a "service" governed by the laws of supply and demand. In the same way, legislation (as a result) is assimilable to a "product", which is available to the market.

By this logic, it would be possible to state that the Legislative Power—and to some extent the Executive Power—fulfills the task of producing goods that characterize the offer, so that, within the concept of market, such institutions would correspond to the "sellers". On the other hand, there are the interest groups—the name under which the entire range of addressees of the laws can be gathered—which would correspond to the "buyers".

From the considerations about this "market" of laws and public policies—which ideally would work under a "monopoly" model, but, in practice, this is not confirmed, since it has been more and more frequent that interest groups seek their objectives by resorting to the judicial system, instead of looking for representative bodies–, there are other reflections on what are the incentives that legislators may have to dedicate themselves to the task of producing these "goods".

In this context, it starts from the premise that legislators who choose to legislate make a rational choice. It is assumed that there is a rational decision in which the expected costs and benefits of using legislation as a social conflict resolution mechanism are weighed.

The EAL approach can also yield ideas towards an ideal institutional design of the legislative process, shedding new light on how the procedural rules that discipline the *iter* of law formation can minimize the problems and costs related to this activity.

Traditionally, it is read that laws must be clear, simple and easy for citizens to comply with. However, the use of EAL suggests other readings, showing in a special way that legislative choices depend on several parameters. The literature produced debating the degree of precision or specificity of legislation is useful for understanding the activity of legislating with vague norms (standards). Specific norms (rules) are more costly to create, have less flexibility, and ideally would lower the cost of enforcement by judicial and administrative bodies.

However, the EAL serves to examine three strategic dimensions of legislation or, if you prefer, three critical variables between which legislators move: (1) the degree of specificity (or generality) of normative formulations, (2) the timing of *legislative* intervention and (3) the spatial scope of application of the created right. Legislators' choices on these three elements can maximize the cost or value of legislation.

From this perspective, the present work is dedicated to investigating the role of EAL in the process of drafting laws, starting with a review of the literature already produced on the subject—which is scarce and dispersed—, to then indicate how EAL can be useful to legislators. The methodology employed is the economic analysis of law itself. But the research is also descriptive and exploratory. Although it does not exhaust the theme, it seeks both to describe the possible connections between EAL and the elaboration of laws and to provide bases for further investigations, notably with regard to the use of legislative technique.

In order to achieve the objective, the work is divided as follows: the next item (Sect. 2) is dedicated to briefly explaining what the economic analysis of law (EAL) consists of; the subsequent item (Sect. 3) is concerned with presenting the activity of drafting legislation from the perspective of the EAL; next, there is an item (Sect. 4) to, using the EAL keys, make an approximation to the legislative technique used in choosing the textual formulations of the norms. Afterwards, an item (Sect. 5) devotes comments to the Brazilian case. Finally, a conclusion resumes the main points discussed in the text.

2 The Economic Analysis of Law (EAL)

The Economic Analysis of Law (EAL) is the field of knowledge whose main objective is to use the tools of economics—both theoretical foundations and empirical studies—with a view to expanding the understanding and scope of law, improving the development, application and evaluation of legal norms.[1] EAL is dedicated to the legal phenomenon especially with regard to real-world consequences. The economic approach serves to understand, explain and predict the factual implications of a given legal norm or its interpretation in the legal system. Seen in these terms, it is above all a method of investigation.

In the definition of Nicholas Mercuro and Steven G. Medema,[2] the approach can be defined as the application of economic theory—mainly microeconomics and the basic concepts of welfare economics—to examine the formation, structure, process and economic impact of law and legal institutions. These authors prefer the term "Law and Economics", but this is a minor controversy, since it does not change the essence or substance of their concerns.

Raquel Sztajn[3] synthesizes EAL as the mere application of the theory of rational choice to law—regardless of whether it is positive law, dealing with usages and customs, judicial decisions, etc.–, as a way of considering the rewards and punishments associated with legal norms, which are associated with institutions and economic rationality.

The discipline is not intended to provide definitive answers to legal problems, nor is it limited to the debate around efficiency.[4] As Bruno Meyerhof Salama explains, the profile is much more descriptive and explanatory of reality, in order to illuminate the implications of the different normative choices.[5] The theoretical body deals especially with the incentives generated by legal institutes. Sometimes, the aforementioned author refers to EAL as a "movement", which would have several "strands" (Chicago School, New Haven School, Austrian School, etc.), whose distinctions would require time and space that are not available here.

For the purposes of this work, it is sufficient to explain the two dimensions of EAL: the first, positive or descriptive, dealing with the real world of facts; and the second, normative or prescriptive, dedicated to the connections between the notions of justice, efficiency, wealth maximization and welfare maximization. Here, the first aspect is of particular interest.

The most famous works dedicated to EAL,[6] however, do not provide further details on the methodology of EAL. Based on models from other authors they cite,

---

[1] Gico Jr. (2016).

[2] Mercuro and Medema (2006), p. 1.

[3] Sztajn (2005), p. 82.

[4] Salama (2008).

[5] Salama (2008), p. 6.

[6] For example: Posner (2007); Cooter and Ulen (2014).

Mackaay and Rousseau[7] propose three levels of analysis, here subtly simplified and adapted to highlight what matters: (1) analysis of the effects of norms (abstaining from moral judgments); (2) the foundation of norms (explaining why certain norms exist); and (3) desirable norms (allowing you to decide which norms should exist).

The analysis is carried out in four stages: (1) to calculate the effects, it is necessary to establish the structure of incentives, for which, in turn, it is convenient to compare a certain norm with its opposite; (2) from the previous step, it is possible to contrast the different norms and assess which best meets the underlying objectives; (3) consideration of transaction costs, notably regarding the standard's potential to reduce them, considering the cost it creates, including relevant and undesirable secondary effects; and (4) after the conceptual analysis of the previous steps, the empirical analysis is carried out, testing the previously formulated hypothesis.

In the present work, the EAL is not applied with the methodological rigor that has just been explained, nor will any empirical study be carried out. The idea is much more to explain the fundamentals of the approach. The investigation, therefore, was carried out according to the more contemplative style and inclinations typical of the legal world.

In this sense, still as a methodology, EAL is based on some postulates, [8]for example: (1) that society's resources are scarce; (2) that every choice presupposes a *trade-off* or opportunity cost, consistent with the preferred alternative; (3) that agents are rational and act to maximize their well-being, weighing costs and benefits of possible courses of action; (4) as a consequence of the above, the postulate that agents respond to incentives, so that changes in the structure of incentives (read in legal rules) can lead to them changing their conduct; and (5) rational maximizing behavior leads agents to exchange until the costs associated with each exchange are equal to the benefits earned, that is, until equilibrium is reached.

Such basic assumptions of the EAL justify the undertaking of the EAL and, in a special way, its application to the elaboration of legal norms. In the words of Ivo Gico Jr.:[9]

> If people respond to incentives, then, from the point of view of a consequentialist ethics, the rules of our society must take into account the incentive structure of the affected agents and the possibility that they will change their behavior if these rules are changed. In particular, it must be taken into account that this change in conduct may generate undesirable or unforeseen effects. One of the functions of juseconomics is to help identify these possible effects.

---

[7] Mackaay and Rousseau (2020), p. 666 and later.

[8] Gico Jr. (2016), pp. 21–24.

[9] Gico Jr. (2016), p. 26. Originally: "Se pessoas respondem a incentivos, então, do ponto de vista de uma ética consequencialista, as regras de nossa sociedade devem levar em consideração a estrutura de incentivos dos agentes afetados e a possibilidade de que eles mudem de conduta caso essas regras sejam alteradas. Em especial, deve-se levar em consideração que essa mudança de conduta pode gerar efeitos indesejáveis ou não previstos. Uma das funções da juseconomia é auxiliar na identificação desses possíveis efeitos.".

The perspective of the EAL is also justified in a special way in the context of legal research in Brazil,[10] mainly due to the need for theoretical constructions aimed at *explaining* and *understanding* the process that leads to the approval of legislation, only, without necessarily adhering to a commitment to *solve* a problem or dogmatically systematize the field. There is a gap—or a "relative delay" to use Marcos Nobre's words—[11] in legal thinking regarding this type of research using EAL focused on the process of drafting laws in Brazil.[12] Although the present work is not going to fill this void, at least it intends to contribute by shedding more light on the area.

Furthermore, it seems necessary to better study the functioning of parliaments as the political institutions that they are. In Porto and Garoupa's explanation,[13] economic institutions and economic growth itself are determined by political institutions. Returning to the argument of Acemoglu, Johnson and Robinson,[14] the authors claim that there is a *hierarchy of institutions*, so that political institutions impact on economic institutions, and the results of this interaction affect economic growth. They suggest that "political institutions are more important than any other institutional set in a society".[15] Therefore, the best way to change economic outcomes would be through changing political institutions.

This reflection justifies the application of the EAL to the process of legislative decisions, as will be done below.

---

[10] Nobre (2003).

[11] The author explains that there are two main reasons for the delay: (1) the isolation of law in relation to other subjects in the human sciences; and (2) the confusion between professional practice and academic research. an overview about it, see Nobre (2003).

[12] The EAL has been more used in a juristocentric perspective or in specific branches of law, such as civil law (notably property law, civil liability, family), business, competition, tax, labor, insurance, criminal, environmental, etc. But almost nothing about the lawmaking process by legislators. Just look at the indexes of the main works on EAL. Perhaps this is precisely due to the *a contrario reading* of the reasons mentioned in the previous footnote: (1) it is almost impossible to account for the legislative process by looking only at the legal norms that govern it; and (2) there are few practical professionals who both effectively understand the subject and are involved in legal research. This diagnosis of few researches in Law and Economics on norms had already been pointed out by Arida (2005), pp. 60–73.

[13] Porto and Garoupa (2020), p. 37.

[14] Acemoglu et al. (2005), pp. 385–472.

[15] Porto and Garoupa (2020), p. 37.

3 The Drafting of Legislation (as an Activity) Seen by the EAL

Under the lens of EAL, it starts from the premise that the choice to "legislate" is a rational choice. This is not due to the postulate of the rationality of the legislator,[16] which functions more as a useful fiction for the legal system, given its various dogmatic consequences. The idea of a "rational legislator" is much more a construction aimed at justifying various argumentative schemes used by jurists, attributing them to the anthropomorphized figure of the legislator.[17] Legally, the postulate serves to interpret the legislation as if the legislator were rational, even though this is just a hypothesis in need of empirical confirmation. The EAL is not based on this postulate.

Differently, the starting point of EAL to conceive the activity of legislating as rational is in the concept of economic efficiency. In the traditional explanation, the market is not always able to promote efficiency. Therefore, the intervention of the State via regulation or legislation occurs to ensure the proper functioning of the economy. From this, the judgment of the norms inserted in the order is based on their effect on the allocation of resources.

Efficient in the Pareto sense[18] will be the norm that produces a state of affairs in which no other allocation of resources is capable of making someone better off without making someone else worse off. The efficiency in the Kaldor and Hicks criterion suggests that the norms should be designed in order to generate the maximum well-being for the greatest number of people.[19]

Given these assumptions, rules in general (whether legislation or regulation) designed without due care tend to generate more costs than benefits. Instead of resolving market failures, they end up introducing new distortions, the so-called government failures, generating even more problems than those they were intended to solve. There are other obstacles—also already mapped by the EAL literature—that prevent the legislation from fulfilling its role. It refers here in a special way to: (1) cases of capture of legislators by interest groups;[20] (2) flaws in the representation system that induce parliamentarians to vote against their voters' preferences;[21] and (3) lack of information regarding the economic effects of the standards in the process of being approved.

---

[16] About this legal perspective of the rational legislator, there is a lot written, for example, by all: Calvo García (1986), pp. 101–132; Ezquiaga (1994), pp. 69–98; Igartua Salaverria (1990), pp. 113–126.

[17] Something similar happens with the intention of the legislator. On the subject, check out: Nascimento (2021a), pp. 167–193.

[18] Gico Jr. (2016), p. 24. There are, however, other meanings of efficiency, as explained in: Porto (2019), pp. 25–50.

[19] It is important to differentiate efficiency from another concept, that is, effectiveness. Effectiveness concerns the ability to produce effects, while efficiency corresponds to the ability to generate the best result with the least amount of waste (errors or loss of resources).

[20] Olson (1971).

[21] Arrow (1970).

This last data means that, sometimes, it is speculative markets that produce more accurate forecasts. Robin Hason[22] sees the markets as a source of information, the operation of which implies, at the same time, a condition for a given public policy to be accepted or rejected. Simplifying the author's explanation, a lot, markets act as an aggregator of collective knowledge and may end up "vetoing" a certain legislative proposal if they understand that the measure will not improve well-being. This takes the form of a "bet", depending on the behavior (purchase or sale of financial assets or securities).

Naturally, this estimation of markets is distorted, as markets end up becoming the main mechanism through which policies are approved or not.

None of this, however, undermines the explanation that the activity of "legislating" is endowed with rationality. It is that, still from the perspective of the EAL, the legislation is the result of a rational decision also from another path.

The interest groups that seek parliamentarians, as well as the legislators themselves who decide to take forward the discussion of a legislative proposal, make a rational decision in which the expected costs and benefits of using this mechanism for resolving social conflict are weighed. Although intuitively, the actors try to estimate the probability of success, as well as the costs associated with parliamentary articulation so that the legislation comes out in the desired manner. It is assumed that the cost of seeking "legislation" is lower than the cost of trying another way to resolve the specific issue, for example, the alternative of regulation through regulatory agencies or litigation with the Judiciary.[23]

Without prejudice to the fact that the actors incur margins of error, the fact is that these estimates will determine, to a large extent, the process of legislative elaboration. As with any voluntary exchange, chances are that a legislative proposal will pass when the maximum utility of the bill desired by interest groups exceeds the minimum benefit acceptable to rational legislators. Rational legislators will pass legislation when the expected return from the providence is equal to or close to what interest groups are willing to bargain for. It is, to some extent, about rent-seeking.

In practice, this means the need for the content of the proposition to be able to reach the number of votes corresponding to the approval quorum, gathering the necessary consensus to defeat rival proposals. Adapting the explanation given by Black,[24] it can be said that those interested in approving the legislation will make a rational calculation, so that the content of the proposal contemplates the average preference of the parliamentarians who participate in the vote, regardless of the subject to be addressed.[25]

---

[22] Hanson (2013), pp. 151–178.

[23] This calculation depends on the interest group, the subject, the moment, etc. There will be situations in which it will be less costly for an interest group to achieve its objectives through the Judiciary or regulatory agencies.

[24] Black (1948), pp. 23–34.

[25] More detailed explanations on the literature of economic analysis of law applied to the process of drafting laws can be found in: Nascimento (2021b), pp. 297–349.

Applying Black's analogy to the legislative process, the approval of laws (in certain terms) reflects a point of intersection between demand and supply,[26] which in a market would be represented by the "price", which, in this case, of the legislative decision, considers the opinions or preferences of parliamentarians.

Given that the intensities of parliamentarians' preferences are not identical, as they vary according to the subject of the proposition under debate, the position of legislators can oscillate between stages of indifference, opposition and staunch defense. This is what causes the so-called *logrolling* or exchange of votes between parliamentarians. Upon entering parliament, legislators quickly learn that their vote is a valuable asset in the legislative process. As Buchanan and Tullock explain,[27] as the Legislative House (read, a certain fixed group of parliamentarians) will make several decisions throughout the legislature, and the individual vote in these collective decisions produces economic effects, this context provides opportunities for the creation of a "market". "This is because each participant comes to recognize the economic value of his own vote for others on certain issues and, in return, also recognizes the economic value for him of the votes of others on different issues."[28]

Although Buchanan and Tullock[29] adopt the perspective that the legislative process would be reduced to this "take-and-give-away", and that the strategic behavior of parliamentarians would revolve around the interests of the various groups committed to the approval of legislation, the authors clarify that there is no reason to envisage illegality, corruption or dishonesty in practice. Indeed, parliamentary negotiations are mutually beneficial to those involved. The reason for this is also given by Buchanan and Tullock themselves:[30] the welfare of an isolated parliamentarian tends to increase if he accepts a decision contrary to his individual wishes in an area where his preferences are weak, in exchange for a decision that be supportive in another area where your feelings are strongest.

Thus, "there is an advantage in *logrolling* until the marginal cost of voting in favor of something (with which one does not agree) is equal to the expected marginal benefits of the vote(s) secured in exchange for support for the issues that are in the voter's best interest.[31] Thus, the approval of legislation by parliaments can be understood as the result of a rational calculation by the agents who decide to cooperate with each other in order to allow reciprocal gains, even though the benefits and costs tend not to be distributed equally to the rest of the population of the population.[32]

---

[26] Black (1948), p. 28.

[27] Buchanan and Tullock (1993), p. 151.

[28] Nascimento (2021b), pp. 297–349.

[29] Buchanan and Tullock (1993), p. 173.

[30] Buchanan and Tullock (1993), p. 179.

[31] Nascimento (2021b), pp. 297–349.

[32] Therefore, Porto and Garoupa, for example, understand that *logrolling* would be a failure of the government, because "the representatives of the population end up voting not taking into account their voters, but due to negotiations with other political agents". See Porto and Garoupa (2020), p. 78.

In a scenario like this, the legislation will only not be approved if the estimates of the interested parties do not coincide at all. Hence the importance of everyone involved being able to predict (with as much precision as possible) what the effects of passing the legislation will be. In this simplified approach, in which it is assumed that those involved know in advance what their returns and losses are with the approval of a given legislative proposal, the tendency is to produce adjustments and improvements even during the process of drafting the legislation, since it is irrational that pass a law that generates more costs than gains.

It turns out that, in practice, this model could seem unrealistic, because to some extent there is always information asymmetry between the parties. More commonly, some actors have more or better information than others, which creates an imbalance of power during parliamentary discussions, and therefore this can sometimes lead to allocation problems. The theme will be resumed later, after the following topic on the possible relationship between EAL and legislative drafting techniques.

4 The Legislative Drafting Techniques Seen by the EAL

It is worth repeating the understanding that regulation in general—including the option to adopt legislation—[33] has among its objectives the reduction of transaction costs and mitigation of other market failures. Therefore, as already indicated, its effects may end up being less beneficial or even counterproductive if legal planning is poorly designed. The lack of planning of the norms implies direct and indirect costs that, in turn, generate misallocation of resources. Hence the importance of tools that increase the rationality of the decision-making process and reduce information asymmetry, such as the impact analysis.

In this sense, the legislative technical guidelines also play an important role, from which it can be read that the wording of norms must be: (1) clear, easy to understand and without room for ambiguities; (2) simple, concise, devoid of superfluous elements; and (3) accurate, so as not to leave room for doubt on the part of your recipients. To achieve this aim, style guides offer a series of recommendations for composition, grammar and language.[34] As a consequence of this perspective,

[33] Legislation and regulation are different concepts. There are similarities, differences and, especially in contemporary times, overlaps, although the fields of one and the other are not completely coincident, which is the main aspect to be highlighted. It is not the purpose of this work to draw an analytical map on the subject, which was addressed in footnote n° 22 by Nascimento (2021a), pp. 1–34. Another perspective on the subject is in Kosti et al. (2019), pp. 169–178.

[34] One of the classic guides is Dickerson (1954). But this kind of concern with linguistic formulation is strictly still present, for example, in the traditional *Thornton's Legislative Drafting*, whose updating has been in charge of Helen Xanthaki (2022). There are also: Butt (2013); Martineau and Salerno (2005); Neumann Jr. and Entrikin (2018). In Spanish, see: García-Escudero Márquez (2011); Navarro Atienza (2015). In Brazil, unfortunately, there are few of these manuals, worth mentioning only: Campos (1972).

imperfections in legislative drafting are usually considered contempt, neglect and carelessness of good legislative technique.

Such a view, however, does not adhere to the actual processes of writing legislation, which have their own characteristics, for example: they are highly variable and contextual, each proposition ends up having its own path; it is usually civil servants, lobbyists and professional drafters who draft laws rather than parliamentarians themselves; and although writers are familiar with style rules, they are not systematically integrated into the writing process for a variety of reasons,[35] including avoiding accountability and protecting their careers.[36] In summary, the legislative technique framework and its style guidelines, in isolation, do not account for real practices, so their approach can be integrated with the EAL to better explain what happens.

In the light of the EAL, the underlying reason for the recommendations on the wording of the rules would be basically the same as just seen before: excessively complex or poorly written rules are more difficult for agents to implement, generate legal uncertainty, which, in turn, turn, tend to erode economic efficiency. It turns out that there are other factors to be weighed besides the clarity, simplicity and precision seen above.

It is that the degree of accuracy of the provision or textual wording[37] of the standard has an impact on the primary behavior and costs associated with the administration of the standard.[38] That is to say, non-compliance with the principles of style may be justified by other reasons of practical necessity—for example, the impossibility of legislators being able to accurately foresee all the circumstances to which the legislation will be applicable—or in the service of fulfilling other objectives, along the lines of what will be explained below.[39]

---

[35] For further details on this discussion, see: Nascimento (2019a), pp. 17–44; Nourse and Schacter (2002).

[36] Hadfield (1994), p. 550.

[37] It is worth remembering that texts are not to be confused with norms. The normative texts are the documents prepared by the competent authorities to produce the sources of law in a given legal system. In turn, norms are the meanings extracted or reconstructed from normative texts through interpretation. A norm does not necessarily have a text or provision, as is the case, for example, with the principle of legal certainty or judicial impartiality. It may also happen that the same device can be extracted from different standards. Even with the dissociation between text and norm, the relevance of efforts aimed at well-designed texts that increase the degree of certainty and predictability persists. This is because provisions can be more or less vague or ambiguous, so as to carry different (and sometimes even contradictory) meanings. On the subject, see: Guastini (2011), pp. 133–156; Avila (2021), pp. 50–51.

[38] Diver (1983), pp. 65–109.

[39] The discussion about the vagueness of normative texts also relies on abundant literature produced in the field of legal theory. Unfortunately, for reasons of time and space, such an approach is outside the present investigation. However, it is necessary to register that the focus of the theory of law is also different, with concerns aimed at offering a conceptual map of vagueness, dissecting the different species, pointing out the problems that it entails for the rule of law (excessively vague norms create problems of discretion and compliance) and reflect on what are the human behaviors that simply cannot be regulated by precise rules. There are also writings highlighting other instru-

John D. Huber and Charles R. Shipan[40] explain that specific laws make it difficult for other political actors, especially bureaucracies, to adopt policies other than those preferred by legislative majorities. Specificity limits discretion, while vague norms give a broader role to other actors in policy making. These authors also indicate that the extent of legislation is an indicator of the efforts of legislation to control the implementation of public policies. Longer laws tend to impose more limits on the actions of other actors because they contain specific details that restrict bureaucrats in particular.

Robert C. Post also correlates the degree of vagueness and discretion.[41]

Such options can be translated as costs.[42] The legislative process works as a function with fixed and variable costs. A greater degree of legislation specificity generally increases the cost of enactment, which corresponds to a fixed cost, but requires lower implementation costs by agencies and courts, which represents a variable cost. The cost of creating specific norms (rules) is higher because they require the content of the norm to be determined in advance.[43, 44] Once enacted, all legislation has an implementation and adjudication cost that varies.

---

mental and strategic functions of vagueness, pointing in the sense that a vague rule is better than no rule at all or that vagueness may be necessary to guarantee flexibility in the application of the law, as well as for people's capacity for deliberation. For a deeper discussion on vagueness from the theory of law, see: Endicott (2000; 2011), pp. 14–30; Waldron (2011), pp. 58–82; Keil and Poscher (2016); Asgeirsson (2020); Lanius (2019, 2021), pp. 752–780.

[40] Huber and Shipan (2002), pp. 17–43.

[41] Post (1994), pp. 491–507. The author uses the following examples of formulations addressed to the traffic police:

(1) Regulate traffic as you see fit;
(2) Regulate traffic in order to avoid congestion;
(3) Regulate traffic to alternate between two minutes north/south movement and three minutes east/west movement.

Discretion decreases as vagueness decreases. For the author, vagueness conveys the opportunity for judicial control.

[42] Ehrlich and Posner (1974), pp. 257–286; Hadfield (1994), pp. 541–554.

[43] Kaplow (1992), pp. 557–629.

[44] Here is an example of a specific rule of the Brazilian Civil Code: "Art. 500. If, in the sale of a property, the price is stipulated per measure of extension, or if the respective area is determined, and this does not correspond, in any case, to the dimensions given, the buyer will have the right to demand the complement of the area, and, if this is not possible, to claim the termination of the contract or a proportional reduction in the price.

§ 1 It is presumed that the reference to the dimensions was simply enunciative, when the difference found does not exceed one-twentieth of the total area stated, with the buyer having the right to prove that, in such circumstances, he would not have carried out the transaction.

§ 2 If, instead of a lack, there is an excess, and the seller proves that he had reasons for ignoring the exact measurement of the area sold, it will be up to the buyer, at his choice, to top up the amount corresponding to the price or return the excess.

§ 3 There will be no addition to the area, nor return of excess, if the property is sold as a certain thing and itemized, with the reference to its dimensions only being enunciative, even if it is not expressly stated that the sale was ad *corpus*".

It is true that the application of standards implies the consideration of facts and circumstances of the concrete case,[45] which reduces the problems of over-inclusion and under-inclusion. But there is criticism that the use of standards deprives the substantive character of the norms, as it does not clearly inform the conduct to be followed by the addressees.[46] The adoption of vague norms implies a kind of *ex post* regulation.[47] Nevertheless, for the EAL, it can be said that the value of legislation is a function of precision.[48]

In a rules-dominated regime, more individuals become informed and are more likely to adjust their conduct to the precepts of legislation. Under a *standard* such as reasonableness, what is "reasonable" under the circumstances can vary widely. As Parisi and Fon (2009) explain, "The forward-looking and deterrent functions of law are thus more effective when laws are formulated as precise rules. This is another benefit of law's specificity".[49]

The ideal degree of specificity of legislation should be chosen in order to maximize the value of the law, considering the fixed cost of legislation and the variable cost of adjudication. Following this logic, the frequency with which the legislation will be applied is important to determine the ideal level of specificity.

If a standard is applied frequently, its variable costs of adjudication will tend to be higher than its enactment costs. In that case, choosing a rule will be less costly and more efficient. On the other hand, for legal matters that rarely arise and whose circumstances are varied, the elaboration of a rule that meets each relevant contingency would require a high fixed cost and would be a "waste", since most of these hypothetical circumstances would hardly arise in real cases. Thus, when the frequency of application of the norm is low, a standard is preferable.[50]

---

[45] Here is an example of a vague norm of the Civil Code: "Art. 113. Legal transactions must be interpreted in accordance with good faith and the customs of the place where they are concluded."

[46] In the second chapter of her doctoral thesis, Natasha Salinas is dedicated to exposing the legislative design strategies, presenting the discussion on the comparative advantages and limitations of rules vis a *vis* standards. As the author explains, the best strategy will depend on the evaluation of several variables and that it is not possible to determine *a priori* and in a resolute way which matters should be dealt with by one and the other. However, it also states that the excessive use of standards tends to make legislation ineffective, which compromises the implementation process. In addition, it gives other clues, for example: the need for adaptability of the subject indicates the use of standards, while prohibitive legal norms require a more accentuated level of assertiveness, recommending treatment by rules. The author's reconstruction of the debate between pages 64 and 107 is essential reading. For further details, see: Salinas (2012).

[47] "The choice of legislators to enact a precise norm or set of rules is implicitly also a choice between legislative and judicial norm-making." In the original: "The legislatures choice whether to enact a standard or a set of precise rules is implicitly also a choice between legislative and judicial rulemaking.". See Ehrlich and Posner (1974), p. 261.

[48] Parisi and Fon (2009), p. 11.

[49] In the original: "The forward-looking and deterrent functions of law are thus more effective when laws are formulated as precise rules. This is another benefit of law's specificity." See Parisi and Fon (2009), p. 12.

[50] Parisi and Fon (2009), p. 16.

Another factor to be considered when choosing the degree of specificity of the rules concerns the susceptibility of changes in the regulated environment. Specific rules are more prone to obsolescence.[51] In general, the more verbose a rule is, the more often it will need to be changed.[52] Hence, if volatility is expected at the regulated level, lower levels of specificity should be chosen.

In addition, the complexity of the reality on which one intends to intervene must be considered. Here the reasoning also becomes more complex. A more complex reality raises the legislative fixed cost, but also increases the adjudication cost. Therefore, an increase in legislative fixed cost tends to favor a lower degree of specificity (standards), while an increase in adjudication cost favors a greater degree of specificity (rules). The forces would seem to cancel each other out.

Hence, explain Parisi and Fon,[53] with an increase in the complexity of the regulated environment, a greater use of rules would be justified when legislative costs are lower than judicial costs. An increase in judicial human capital, on the other hand, would reduce[54] judicial costs and thus justify the use of looser legislation in response to an increase in the complexity of the regulated environment.

The quantity or quality of information available on the current or future circumstances of the subject to be regulated is also an element to be considered. When legislators have incomplete information about the issue to be regulated, they must adopt standards while waiting for information to emerge. As these emerge, they can increase the level of specificity. This is a useful way of dealing with uncertainty.

Louis Kaplow[55] introduces another factor to take into account: risk aversion, which in his analysis is associated with the cost of legal advice that citizens will resort to in order to guide their conduct. Rules suggest a lower cost in this regard compared to standards. More informed individuals tend to support less risks. By this logic, therefore, under standards individuals tend to be less informed, and may end up bearing more risks than would be socially desirable.

As it is already possible to perceive, legislators must weigh the costs and benefits of the specificity and complexity of the legislation. Such costs are of three orders: (1) costs related to the elaboration of specific norms; (2) costs related to enforcement or adjudication by regulatory agencies and courts and (3) costs related to compliance, in terms of advice and legal uncertainty for citizens.[56]

[51] Ehrlich and Posner (1974), pp. 257–286.

[52] Ehrlich and Posner (1974), p. 278.

[53] Parisi and Fon (2009), p. 21.

[54] Here it is important not to confuse with the complexity of the norms themselves. As Louis Kaplow explains, the greater complexity of the rules would allow for better control of behaviors. It turns out that more complex rules are more costly for individuals to understand and for courts to apply *ex post*. To understand the full argument, see: Kaplow (1995), pp. 150–163. The author still connects the degree of complexity as an element for the comparison between rules and standards, according to Kaplow (1992).

[55] Kaplow (1992), p. 571, 605.

[56] Shäfer (2002).

Everything that has been indicated so far also sheds light on historical trends in legislation, especially in the special areas of private law, which tend to rely on detailed and long-lasting codes.

Diver[57] uses a very didactic example to explain the issue, offering three models of verbal formulation:

- Model I: No person may fly a commercial airliner after their sixtieth birthday.
- Model II: No person may fly a commercial aircraft if he or she presents an unreasonable risk of accident.
- Model III: No person may fly a commercial aircraft if he falls into the following categories. (Tables follow with all combinations of values for numerous variables, including years and level of experience, hours of flight time logged, age, height, weight, blood pressure, flight speed, eyesight, and other vital signs that would disqualify a pilot more eligibility to fly an aircraft).

Next, Diver dedicates himself to reflecting on what is the most transparent textual formulation. In this case, the answer is easy: Model I, as everyone knows what "sixtieth" and "anniversary" means. The Model II concept of "unreasonable" is susceptible to a wide range of interpretations. Model II is shorter than Model III and requires a single judgment: the "reasonableness" of the risk. However, this judgment can be based on a set of subsidiary questions as numerous and complex as those included in the set of more explicit tables of Model III.

In the author's reflection, the assumption that Model II is more congruent than Model I is unreliable. In turn, to understand the ultimate objective of the legislator, Model II depends on the barely verifiable assumption that "unreasonable" connotes "economically inefficient".

Diver's exercise is useful to show that each of the normative formulations presents difficulties. The Model I can be applied mechanically, but without a doubt it will ground many pilots who should continue flying and allow some pilots who should remain on the ground to continue flying. Even if we admit that Model II is easy and faithful to the intentions of the legislators, it generates very different interpretations in concrete cases. Model III is commendably more objective and can even accurately discriminate between low and high risks. But this goal is achieved only at the cost of difficulty in application.

For Diver, trying to escape these tradeoffs with a fourth model seems futile. His reasoning moves forward starting with Model I (the "age 60" version). As the main flaw of this rule is its apparent inconsistency, one might try to smooth out its hard edges by allowing exceptions in particularly meritorious cases. For example, particularly robust sixty-year-olds could be allowed to continue flying. But this strategy only raises a new enigma: how to define the category of exempt pilots? Of course, there are many options, but all seem to suffer to one degree or another from problems of opacity ("fairly healthy"), inconsistency ("able to press 68 kg and run 8 km in 40 minutes"), or inaccessibility (model tables). III).

[57] Diver (1983), p. 69.

Likewise, based on the Model II standard of "unreasonable risk", its transparency could be increased by adding a list of components of "unreasonable risk", for example, "taking into account age, physical condition, mental acuity, skill and experience of the person". However, such lists add relatively little transparency when neither the meaning nor the relative weight of the listed elements is specified. The required specification, however, makes the pattern less congruent or accessible.

The example is didactic to explain that verbal formulations involve different combinations of transparency, accessibility and congruence. Tradeoffs are inevitable, although *not* all formulations are equally acceptable. For this reason, explains Diver, a normative criterion is needed to compare the formulations, given that the invocation of moral values such as justice, equity or community offers little hope. From there, the author dedicates himself to presenting what would be the costs and benefits of precision, for which he refers directly to his text.

Anyway, the most important idea is the following: rule-like normative formulations are typically more expensive to create than standards, while the latter are more expensive for individuals to interpret when they act, and for a judge to apply to a past conduct.[58] As much as it is recognized that rules and standards function as just two poles of a spectrum—that is, there are different intermediate levels of precision, complexity and clarity of norms—the EAL approach offers several explanations that need to be integrated into the literature aimed at understanding the activity of legislators.

5 The Brazilian Case

Having made the above points on the basis of thc literature, a brief comment is in order on the Brazilian reality regarding the drafting of legislation and how EAL can help in the corresponding analysis of this data. As has been explained, in general, tools aimed at rationalizing legislative decisions—such as impact analysis, for example—imply a higher *ex ante* cost for legislators. However, this simple analytical exercise already implies a reduction in *ex post* costs in global terms, which tends to provide savings in view of the benefits and all the global costs incurred.

At this point, it is important to emphasize that impact analysis, specifically, represents a typical EAL methodology, in that it helps legislators (and jurists in general) to better identify, predict and explain the social consequences of political choices associated with intended legislation. Impact analysis, therefore, is a methodological procedure that serves to support legislative decision-making. However, despite this, this tool has not been regularly adopted by the Brazilian National Congress.

In Brazil, the level of adherence to these institutional mechanisms is still low (if not zero) and, the way they have been designed in the country, there are many

[58] Kaplow (1992).

loopholes for them not to be carried out. For example, *Decreto n° 10.411/2020*—which regulated the regulatory impact analysis, and provides for its content, the minimum requirements to be examined, the cases in which it will be mandatory and the cases in which it may be waived—established that the impact analysis is not required for the edition of decrees or normative acts to be forwarded to the National Congress (art. 1°, § 3°). Nor is there any rule, even of a soft law nature, obliging parliament to carry out impact analyses before passing laws.

As a result, and given the way parliaments operate, there is also evidence that legislators are "optimistic" about the outcome of their decisions. An examination of legislative arguments reveals that parliamentarians invariably believe that legislative intervention is necessary in order to, if not solve, alleviate the social problem.[59] Laws are not passed on the grounds that they will "worsen" the legal system or bring undesirable costs. In fact, these are the typical arguments of the opposition,[60] which oppose the approval of proposals and which, if they prevail, imply the rejection rather than the approval of the law.

From this, it could be said that the vast majority of laws in Brazil are passed without reliable information to support them, under a bias of optimism or wishful thinking, a cognitive limitation that makes agents believe that they are exposed to lower risks of adverse events than other people. Especially after the planning stage of the regulation—in which the drafters must estimate the chances of negative events arising from the proposal—parliamentarians tend to overestimate the success brought about by the legislation.

In principle, this modus operandi for passing laws in Brazil can be interpreted as an agent-principal problem, along the lines of EAL. This is because legislators may not be totally transparent with their electorate, since passing laws (especially under the label that they will "improve" the status quo) is a win-win situation for parliamentarians. For this reason, it is not always possible to measure the true usefulness of legislation for the population.

Hence the importance of legislators clearly determining the problem to be solved, its causes and the objectives to be achieved with the legislative measure. This would be done through an impact analysis, which would also analyze the evidence produced. This document would play the role of correcting the "optimism" of the legislators and would guide the recipients (especially the bureaucracy and judges) to readjust their expectations. The measure also has the potential to encourage a higher level of adherence to the legislation, reducing future costs. The analysis is based on the assumption that compliance with the rule (in the terms in which it was approved) is feasible and that the means chosen are capable of achieving the desired ends.

As a result of not using EAL, it can be said that many laws are passed without an adequate study of their practical feasibility, resulting in ineffective rules or those that require extensive regulations to be applied. This scenario contributes to a

[59] Nascimento (2019b).

[60] Bentham (1990).

legislative system that is bureaucratic and often disconnected from the real needs of society, costly for economic agents, complex and unstable.

Another example from Brazil's regulatory quality policy concerns the provision in art. 18 of *Lei Complementar 95/1998*, which provides for the drafting, editing, amending and consolidating of laws. According to this provision: "Any formal inaccuracy in a rule drawn up through a regular legislative process does not constitute a valid excuse for non-compliance".[61] This means that non-compliance with the guidelines for good legislative technique or *drafting* (especially in terms of clarity, objectivity and systematization) does not result in defects that tarnish the validity of the rule produced. Coercion is lacking: there are no effective sanctions for bills that fail to comply with its guidelines; there is no unconstitutionality.

The normative provision in question denotes a certain backwardness in Brazilian regulatory policy, which not only gives very little enforcement to traditional legislative technique provisions—including the most basic ones, aimed at avoiding contradictions, overlaps and the constant need for corrective legislative changes—but has also failed to incorporate the most modern tools and insights produced by the literature in the field of EAL, as presented in this chapter, notably the theoretical advances with regard to legislative strategies for dealing with situations of uncertainty about the subject of legislation (for example, the advance of technology), for deciding the optimum timing of legislative intervention, for defining the appropriate degree of precision, detail or specificity of textual formulations, etc.

6 Conclusions

In his essay *The good legislator*, written in 1971, Norberto Bobbio (1909-2004) did not envision the ability to reason about the consequences of laws as one of the attributes to recognize a good legislator. In turn, when Frédéric Bastiat (1801–1850) wrote *That Which is Seen, and That Which is Not Seen,* he certainly did not aim at the figure of the legislator. But, after all the journey carried out in the present work, it is clear that the good legislator has something (in fact, a lot) of the good economist of Bastiat, who manages to see beyond the effect that is seen (the immediate consequence), *also predicting* the *foreseeable* effects (the long-term consequences) generated from laws passed by parliament.

It was seen that the economic analysis of law (EAL) is a useful research method for legislators—perhaps no other field of knowledge offers such broad and concrete support for understanding the legal phenomenon–, insofar as it presents tools that, if well employed, contribute to understanding, explaining and predicting the factual implications of a given legal norm, including the prediction of its possible interpretations in the legal system. Although it does not offer definitive solutions to legal

[61] Originally: "Art. 18. Eventual inexatidão formal de norma elaborada mediante processo legislativo regular não constitui escusa válida para o seu descumprimento".

problems, EAL, based on the premise that agents respond to incentives, deals with the indication of what incentives are generated by legal institutes, in this case, legal norms.

The use of the EAL is also justified in the context of legal research in Brazil, which requires more studies to *explain* and *understand* legal phenomena and, especially, areas such as the process that leads to the approval of legislation and the functioning of the Legislative Houses, as political institutions that are. Research focused on the process of drafting laws in Brazil using the EAL methodology to analyze the most internal aspects of the legislative process is still rare. From this data, the present work sought to present analytical tools that can be useful in the evaluation of legislative choices in concrete situations.

In this sense, it was explained that, under the lens of the EAL, choosing to "legislate" is a rational choice because State intervention via legislation occurs to ensure the smooth functioning of the economy, correct market failures and promote economic efficiency. In addition, it is assumed that the cost of the option of seeking "legislation" is lower than the cost of trying another way to resolve the specific issue, for example, the alternative of regulation through regulatory agencies or litigation with the Judiciary.

In turn, for rational legislators, the approval of legislation will occur when the expected return with the measure is equal to or close to what interest groups are willing to bargain (rent-seeking logic).

As another typical finding of economic analysis, the proposition has chances of being approved when it is able to reach the number of votes corresponding to the approval quorum. Thus, those interested in approving the legislation will make a rational calculation, so that the content of the proposal contemplates the average preference of the parliamentarians who will participate in the vote, regardless of the subject to be addressed.

But nothing is enough to guarantee the quality and effectiveness of legislation.

It is known that the lack of planning of norms implies direct and indirect costs that, in turn, generate misallocation of resources. The EAL literature also reveals other obstacles that prevent legislation from fulfilling its role. In addition, overly complex or poorly written rules are more difficult for agents to implement, create legal uncertainty, which, in turn, tend to erode economic efficiency.

In the eyes of the EAL, the legislative process was presented as a function with fixed and variable costs. A greater degree of legislation specificity generally increases the cost of enactment (a fixed cost) but requires lower implementation costs by agencies and courts (a variable cost).

The EAL was applied to reread the traditional logic of legislative technique, for which good norms are clear, simple and easy to comply with by citizens. The EAL makes explicit the role that vague norms play in the *design* of legislation, demonstrating that legislators need to consider more complex aspects. It remained clear that the legislative choices regarding the textual formulations of the norms depend on several parameters and that different situations justify the rationality of the legislation based on vague norms (standards).

From the literature, some criteria were provided to be considered to determine the ideal level of specificity: (1) the frequency with which the legislation will be applied; (2) the susceptibility of changes in the regulated environment; (3) the complexity of the reality on which the intention is to intervene; (4) the degree of uncertainty, the amount or quality of information available about the current or future circumstances of the subject to be regulated; and (5) risk aversion. The operation of each of these elements was dealt with in due course. The conclusion of the analysis goes in the sense that, sometimes, in some contexts, but not always, the law does not need to be defined in a specific way to enforce its fulfillment.

In general, the work provided an overview of the explanations and connections between the EAL and the process of drafting laws, as well as a map of possibilities for applying theoretical models that can serve as hypotheses to be verified in future empirical studies. Even so, regardless of the theoretical character, the result of the present research goes in the direction that the improvement of the law elaboration process generates a higher ex ante cost *for* the legislators, but generates an overall reduction of the global *ex post costs*, which tends to to provide savings in the face of benefits and all global costs incurred.

References

Arida P (2005) A pesquisa em Direito e em Economia: em torno da historicidade da norma. In: Direito & Economia: Análise Econômica do Direito e das Organizações, dir. Zylbersztajn, Decio; Sztajn, Rachel. Elsevier, Rio de Janeiro, pp 60–73

Bentham J (1990) Falacias políticas. Centro de Estudios Constitucionales, Madrid

Black D (1948) On the rationale of group decision-making. J Polit Econ 56(1):23–34

Buchanan JM, Tullock G (1993) El cálculo del consenso. Fundamentos lógicos de la democracia constitucional. Planeta-Agosniti, Barcelona

Diver C (1983) The optimal precision of administrative rules. Yale Law J 93(1):65–109

Ehrlich I, Posner RA (1974) An economic analysis of legal rulemaking. J Legal Stud 3(1):257–286

Gico Jr (2016) Introdução à Análise Econômica do Direito. In: O que é análise econômica do direito: uma introdução, dir. Ribeiro, Marcia Carla Pereira; Klein, Vinicius: Belo Horizonte: Forum, pp 17–26

Hadfield GK (1994) Weighing the value of vagueness: an economic perspective on precision in the law. Calif Law Rev 82(3):541–554

Huber JD, Shipan CR (2002) Deliberate discretion? The institutional foundations of bureaucratic autonomy. Cambridge University Press

Kaplow L (1992) Rules versus standards: an economic analysis. Duke Law J 42(3):557–629

Kaplow L (1995) A model of the optimal complexity of legal. J Law Econ Org 11(1):150–163

Mercuro N, Medema SG (2006) Economics and the law: from Posner to post-modernism and beyond. Princeton University Press, Princeton

Nascimento RS (2019a) Quem redige as leis? O desenho institucional da redação legislativa na experiência internacional e no Brasil. In: Poder Legislativo: Defesa institucional, representação judicial e assessoramento jurídico, dir. Pereira, Gabrielle Tatith, pp 17–44

Nascimento RS (2019b) Teoria da Legislação e Argumentação Legislativa: Brasil e Espanha em perspectiva comparada. Alteridade, Curitiba

Nascimento RS (2021a) O argumento da intenção do legislador: anotações teóricas sobre uso e significado. Revista de Informação Legislativa: RIL 58(232):167–193

Nascimento RS (2021b) Análise econômica do processo legislativo: a teoria da escolha pública, a racionalidade coletiva e o comportamento estratégico na política brasileira. In: Temas em direito e economia, dir. Pinheiro, Armando Castelar; Porto, Antônio José Maristrello; Sampaio, Patrícia Regina Pinheiro. Lumen Juris, Rio de Janeiro, pp 297–349
Nobre M (2003) Apontamentos sobre a pesquisa em Direito no Brasil. Revista Novos Estudos Cebrap 66:145–154
Nourse VF, Schacter JS (2002) The politics of legislative drafting: a congressional case study. New York Univ Law Rev 77(3):575–624
Parisi F, Fon V (2009) The economics of lawmaking. Oxford University Press, Oxford
Porto AJM (2019) Princípios de análise do direito e da economia. In: Direito e economia: diálogos, dir. Pinheiro, Armando Castelar; Porto, Antônio José Maristrello; Sampaio, Patrícia Regina Pinheiro, pp 25–50
Porto AM, Garoupa N (2020) Curso de Análise Econômica do Direito. Atlas, São Paulo
Post RC (1994) Reconceptualizing vagueness: legal rules and social orders. Calif Law Rev 82(3):491–507
Salama BM (2008) O que é pesquisa em direito e economia? Cadernos Direito GV 5(2):5–58
Salinas NSC (2012) Legislação e políticas públicas: a lei enquanto instrumento de ação governamental. Thesis (Doctorate) – Faculty of Law, University of São Paulo
Sztajn R (2005) Law and economics. In Direito & Economia: Análise Econômica do Direito e das Organizações, dir. Zylbersztajn, Decio; Sztajn, Rachel. Elsevier, Rio de Janeiro, pp 74–83
David, Lanius (2021) What Is the Value of Vagueness? Abstract Theoria 87(3) 752-780 10.1111/theo.v87.3 10.1111/theo.12313

Better Regulation, Cost-Benefit Analysis and Evidence Based Legal Design: A Critical Inquiry

Silvia Zorzetto

Abstract Policy makers are increasingly turning to behavioural economics to address complex policy challenges, such as improving education systems, increasing private savings, promoting energy and resource conservation, strengthening (cyber)security, combating climate change, and reducing corruption. This approach aims to implement evidence-based policies grounded in people's actual behaviours and cognitive processes. Emphasis is placed on the importance of context for responsible and effective decision-making. It is considered essential to empirically study a wide range of individual and collective factors, taking into account the social, psychological, and economic influences on people's thoughts and actions. This perspective is prevalent globally, as demonstrated by the activities of the World Bank and its Mind, Behaviour and Development Unit, the Organisation for Economic Cooperation and Development (OECD), and the Inter-American Development Bank. In the European context, the concept of Smart/Better Regulation has emerged as a mature product of this dominant trend and is gaining increasing importance. The objective of this chapter is to analyse the state of the art within the European context, with special consideration given to models derived from economic and organisational theory that have been applied to the so-called legislative cycle. The study aims to reflect on the communication methods employed in the context of Smart/Better Regulation and examines the symbolic, persuasive, and self-legitimising dimensions pursued institutionally through the innovative techniques of so-called legal design.

S. Zorzetto (✉)
Department of Law, University Telematica Pegaso, Naples, Italy
e-mail: silvia.zorzetto@unipegaso.it

S. Zorzetto et al. (eds.), *Developments in Law and Economics in the Italo-Iberoamerican Context*, Economic Analysis of Law in European Legal Scholarship 21, https://doi.org/10.1007/978-3-032-03317-8_7

1 Introduction: Legal Method and Methodological Hybridism

In the wide-ranging and complex debate on *legal method and methodology*,[1] the reflections and discussions have never ceased on the question of whether and to what extent lawyers[2] apply their own method or take methods from other disciplines as a model.

The fact that the legal method possesses its own specificity compared to any other may be regarded as a minimum common element in legal methodology. The question of these peculiarities, however, remains a contentious matter. In this regard, it is difficult to identify convergences, apart from the observation that differing concepts and conceptions of law also influence the understanding and definition of the legal method. Conversely, it is equally true that adherence to a particular concept or conception of method tout court influences one's approach to the legal world, both at the level of methodology and in terms of what the law is (or is presumed to be).

The notion that law as a subject depends upon the method by which it is approached is perhaps one of the few insights gleaned from contemporary social science. On the other hand, the degree of scientific intersubjectivity that may exist in relation to social phenomena historically and culturally characterised as valid law remains extraordinarily contested. The crux of the issue lies in the extent to which the method and the subject reciprocally shape and respond to each other.

It should be noted that lawyers can conceive of their own method and law in the abstract. Yet, despite ideal experiments and intellectual exercises, lawyers cannot avoid asking themselves what is common at the level of method and object, and what possesses general, albeit generic, efficacy within and for a political community. The recognition that law is not merely an abstract concept or an ideal object is but a first step towards understanding whether a legal method has its own particularities—whatever those may be among the many that are debated. Indeed, it must not be forgotten that, even if one accepts the existence of a legal method, its peculiarities are by no means uncontentious, even among lawyers themselves.

In any case, the assumption that the legal method has its own peculiarities does not necessarily imply that it is entirely distinct from others or that it is conditioned by one or more external methods. When one considers whether, and to what extent, lawyers employ their own method or adopt models and methods from other disciplines, the focus shifts from the specificity of the legal method to its autonomy or *autopoiesis*.[3]

---

[1] About the distinction between legal method and methodology see Vega (2018); Scarpelli (1956, 1971).

[2] The term lawyers is used here in its broadest sense to refer to all persons concerned with the practise and/or theory of law, such as judges, civil servants, solicitors, barristers, legal experts, legal scholars, legal theorists and philosophers, legal sociologists, legal anthropologists, etc.

[3] As is well known, the term originates from Maturana and Varela (1980). Despite some reinterpretations, this theory is not suitable for making simple analogies between the biological and the

By greatly simplifying, the *vexata quaestio* is whether a general feature of the legal method is its tendency to adopt methods from other disciplines and bodies of knowledge as models, combining them in original ways. In other words, one might figuratively ask whether the legal method possesses its own inherent substance or whether it is, instead, porous and permeable to methodological orientations and directions that have emerged throughout history for other purposes.

Of course, the question posed above encompasses a multiplicity of related issues, each necessarily and coincidentally interconnected with the others, yet whose answers do not follow derivatively or automatically from one another. Without claiming to be exhaustive, and without suggesting that the order of enumeration reflects logical priorities or hierarchies of importance, one might ask:

Do lawyers perceive the legal method as something inherent to the law, prioritising the law over the method, or as a kind of method tout court that prioritises the broader genus of method, of which law is merely a specification?

When we refer to the legal method, do we imply something scientific, and if so, in what sense of the term "science"?

Is the legal method—within the framework of the above questions—a scientific method? Specifically, does it share features with the methods of other sciences, or is it a product of jurisprudence that is distinct from any other form of scientific knowledge?

Do lawyers regard the legal method as something they create themselves, as something governed by general methodological principles, or as something regulated by the law itself?

Do lawyers develop their own methodology by modelling it on the method and object of law, or do they adopt methodologies from other sciences, which they take as their model?

Why do lawyers tend to look beyond the boundaries of law and legal method to other disciplines or areas of social reality when developing their own methodology?

What disciplines do lawyers turn to for guidance?

What models or methodologies inspire legal scholarship?

Do attitudes towards these questions vary among different categories of lawyers—such as legislators, judges, legal scholars, and theorists—or between lawyers and non-lawyers?

Is the legal method itself regarded as a model for other disciplines?

To further complicate the analysis, these questions can be approached from various perspectives: those of experts, practitioners of law, non-lawyers, methodologists, and others.

The history of legal method reveals that answers to these questions differ significantly depending on the philosophical framework, the historical period, and the legal context within which the analyses are conducted. Moreover, the answers shift

social world, and even less so between human artefacts and the technical world. On the contrary, it had an anti-reductionist intention, even in relation to the same biology and philosophy of biology: see Varela and Maturana (1972). I recall the concept of *autopoiesis* also because it is a precursor of the trend analysed in this contribution.

depending on whether the analyses are undertaken from a contemporary legal standpoint or a historical one.

They also vary based on whether the primary aim is to offer descriptive-explanatory insights or to develop methodological models. Finally, the responses are influenced by the fundamental and, ultimately, metaphysical assumptions regarding the nature of science and knowledge.[4]

In this chapter, it is not feasible to provide definitive answers to the previous questions. The scope of the analysis is far more limited and modest: it aims to present a compelling example of lawyers adopting approaches from other disciplines. The focus is on European Better or Smart Regulation (hereafter referred to as 'BeRg').

This example serves as a litmus test for exploring the interplay between legal cultures. The influence of the civil law tradition and Latin heritage is diminishing in comparison to the growing dominance of global American culture, which has profoundly shaped Western legal systems throughout the twentieth century. BeRg represents both a product and a driving force of this trend. BeRg illustrates how a legal culture, deeply rooted in centuries of tradition, is undergoing profound transformation under the influence of prevailing economic paradigms that permeate contemporary society.

This transformative moment is unfolding at a pace that challenges our capacity for full comprehension. The rapidity of this shift makes it increasingly difficult to adopt an external vantage point from which to observe and evaluate its implications. Nonetheless, I suggest that the inherent resilience of cultural traditions grants the European and Latin legal frameworks a distinct advantage in recognising this wave of change originating from the Global US-centric economic ideology. Like a wave traversing the Atlantic, this cultural shift affords its recipients a fleeting opportunity to anticipate its arrival. Yet, as the analysis will show, the wave has already made landfall. Over the relatively short period during which this analysis has been conducted (approximately the past 5 years), developments have progressed swiftly, moving from initial projects, launches, and prototypes to concrete plans in action. What once belonged to the realm of the future has already become part of history.

2 BES, BeRg and Nudging: A Suspicious Alliance Between Business, Politics, and Science

To understand this phenomenon and its complexity, it is essential to briefly describe the context within which BeRg emerged.

Since the last two decades of the nineteenth century, many governments around the world and international organizations have increasingly turned to behavioural economics ('BES') to improve their public policies. In many countries, including

[4] Kantorowicz and Patterson (1928).

the European Union, the overall goal is to develop more effective and efficient policies that can improve individuals' economic and social well-being.

As the World Bank's Mind, Behavior, and Development Unit recalls, some governments began systematically institutionalising the use of BES in public policy in the early 2010s.[5] International organisations such as the World Bank, the Organization for Economic Cooperation and Development (OECD), the Inter-American Development Bank (IDB) and the European Commission have supported this trend. In 2014, the OECD published 'Regulatory Policy and Behavioral Economics', which summarised the applications of BES to policy, with a focus on applications in regulatory policy.[6] The World Bank dedicated its annual flagship development report 2015 to behavioural science, providing a roadmap for in-depth analysis in developing countries and contexts.[7] In 2017, the OECD published 'Behavioral Insights and Public Policy: Lessons from Around the World,' which takes stock of interventions in different sectors around the world.[8] In September 2020, the World Bank published the second volume of its 'Behavioral Science Insights around the world'.[9] This second volume looks at 17 international organisations that systematically apply behavioural science and highlights more than 150 cases.[10] The aim of the initiative is overtly normative: this second report, like the first one from 2018, which presents 10 leading countries,[11] offers a vision, inspiration and lessons for other organisations making similar efforts.[12] The third volume is a product of its time (the 2019–2021 pandemic) and is therefore dedicated to the theme of global health: the pandemic emergency has trigged a spiral of regulation marked by BES-oriented approach and has acted as an accelerator in relation to the trend under analysis.[13]

The European BeRg is an important part of this legacy.[14]

---

[5] World Bank Group (2022) and (2025), https://www.worldbank.org/en/programs/embed.

[6] Lunn (2014).

[7] World Bank Group (2015).

[8] OECD (2017).

[9] Manning et al. (2020).

[10] Besides the World Bank Group, the institutions profiles belong to Deutsche Gesellschaft Für Internationale Zusammenarbeit Gmbh; European Commission; Foreign, Commonwealth & Development Office; Inter-American Development Bank; International Committee of the Red Cross; International Rescue Committee; OECD; Overseas Development Institute; Save the Children; United Nations System Organizations; United Nations Entity for Gender Equality and the Empowerment of Women; United Nations Development Programme; United Nations International Children's Fund; International Organization for Migration; World Health Organization; United States Agency For International Development.

[11] Afif et al. (2019). The report captures behavioural sciences phenomena in 10 countries, selected as innovators or early adopters in the field: Australia, Canada, Denmark, France, Germany, Netherlands, Peru, Singapore, the U.S., and the UK.

[12] Manning et al. (2020), p. 12.

[13] World Bank and the World Health Organization (2024).

[14] OECD (1995, 2022a); in addition, BeRg official website.

In 2016, the European Commission published the document Behavioural Insights Applied to Policy, which provides a summary of the BES policies and programmes in Europe;[15] on the other hand, the Interinstitutional Agreement on Better Law-Making was signed, which became a key moment for the institutionalisation of BES and BeReg within EU policies and thus also in the Member States. The objectives are to 'promote simplicity, clarity and consistency in the drafting of Union legislation and to promote the utmost transparency of the legislative process'; 'legislation should be comprehensible and clear, allow citizens, administrations and businesses to easily understand their rights and obligations, include appropriate reporting, monitoring and evaluation requirements, avoid overregulation and administrative burdens, and be practical to implement'.[16] As for multi-annual planning, there are three better regulatory tools: 'Impact assessments', 'Public and stakeholder consultation and feedback' and 'Ex-post evaluation of existing legislation'.[17]

For the 2017 European Commission's 'Communication Completing the Better Regulation Agenda: Better solutions for better results', the three key pillars of BeRg are: (i) 'Impact assessment: new proposals are accompanied by impact assessments which explore how policy goals can be achieved in the most efficient way without imposing unnecessary burdens'; (ii) 'Evaluate first: all revisions of existing legislation would assess opportunities to simplify and reduce unnecessary costs based on analyses and stakeholder inputs'; 'Stakeholder engagement: better regulation is underpinned by the active engagement of civil society, which invites inputs from stakeholders at all points in the policy cycle using a range of feedback tools and consultation activities'.[18]

According to the 2021–2023 Better Regulation Guidelines, BeRg 'is about creating legislation that achieves its objectives while being targeted, effective, easy to comply with and with the least burden possible'. The regulatory instruments aimed

---

[15] Sousa et al. (2016).

[16] OJ L 123, 12 May 2016, pp. 1–14; see 'I. COMMON COMMITMENTS AND OBJECTIVES'.

[17] OJ L 123, 12 May 2016, pp. 1–14; see 'III. TOOLS FOR BETTER LAW-MAKING': 'Impact assessments should cover the existence, scale and consequences of a problem and the question whether or not Union action is needed. They should map out alternative solutions and, where possible, potential short and long-term costs and benefits, assessing the economic, environmental and social impacts in an integrated and balanced way and using both qualitative and quantitative analyses. The principles of subsidiarity and proportionality should be fully respected, as should fundamental rights. Impact assessments should also address, whenever possible, the "cost of non-Europe" and the impact on competitiveness and the administrative burdens of the different options, having particular regard to SMEs ("Think Small First"), digital aspects and territorial impact. Impact assessments should be based on accurate, objective and complete information and should be proportionate as regards their scope and focus'; 'In the context of the legislative cycle, evaluations of existing legislation and policy, based on efficiency, effectiveness, relevance, coherence and value added, should provide the basis for impact assessments of options for further action. To support these processes, the three Institutions agree to, as appropriate, establish reporting, monitoring and evaluation requirements in legislation, while avoiding overregulation and administrative burdens, in particular on Member States. Where appropriate, such requirements can include measurable indicators as a basis on which to collect evidence of the effects of legislation on the ground.'

[18] EC (2017).

to get this goal are ‘comprehensive evaluations and fitness checks’, ‘impact assessments’, ‘input from stakeholders’, and ‘compliance promotion tools’.[19] BeRg is presented as an approach which shall be ‘comprehensive’, ‘coherent’, ‘proportionate’, ‘participative’, ‘evidence-based’, as well as based on ‘transparency’ and ‘learning from experience’.[20] The related ToolBox lists a number of key dimensions, including ‘high quality’, ‘strategic/forward-looking’, ‘participatory/open to stakeholder’s views’ and ‘respect for the principle of subsidiarity and proportionality’, but legislation should also be ‘comprehensive’, ‘coherent/conducted collectively’, ‘proportionate’, ‘transparent’, ‘independent’, ‘appropriately resourced and organized’ and ‘sustainable’.[21]

The European Commission’s Communication of 29 April 2021 ‘Better Lawmaking: joining forces to produce better laws’ states that in order to improve the overall quality of legislation and to ensure its clarity, readability and comprehensibility, better regulation should follow the principle of ‘one in, one out’, pursue the objectives of sustainable development and implement the principle of ‘do no significant harm’ as well as the principle of ‘digital by definition’.[22]

In this context, on 28 June 2022, the OECD published Better regulation practises across the European Union 2022, which, in order to promote measures that can improve people’s economic and social well-being, focuses on the introduction of instruments that guide alternative behaviours: non-authoritarian, non-coercive.[23]

BeReg thus falls on fertile ground and is linked to the other global phenomenon of nudging,[24] the so-called gentle push, which also emerged from the studies of BES.

As described by Richard Thaler and Cass R. Sunstein,[25] who are unanimously considered its fathers, nudging is an aspect of the architecture of decision-making that alters people’s behaviour in a predictable way without forbidding or preventing them from making a decision or substantially altering their economic incentives; to be considered a nudge, the intervention must be easy and cheap to avoid. To explain nudging, Thaler and Sunstein contrast two ideal types of individuals: Econs and Humans. The two have different attitudes towards predictability and incentive conditioning. Humans would typically make random or systematic mistakes and act/decide based on unreflective and intuitive responses, be conditioned by fashions and the variety of biases highlighted by BES. There is no exhaustive catalogue of nudges; some of them are:[26] (1) default rules; (2) simplification; (3) social norms; (4) tools that facilitate and simplify choice; (5) disclosure; (6) graphic or other warnings; (7) precommitment strategies; (8) reminder incentives; (9) prompts to

[19] EC (2021a, 2023a).

[20] EC (2021a, 2023a).

[21] EC (2023b).

[22] EC (2021b).

[23] OECD (2022b).

[24] Ferraro and Zorzetto (2019).

[25] Thaler and Sunstein (2009).

[26] Sunstein (2014).

implement intentions; (10) information about the nature and consequences of past choices.

It is therefore a highly diversified characterisation, which in practice can take on countless facets. That's also why nudges are sometimes associated with the broad category of so-called soft laws and, strictly speaking, smart law, regulation, or BeRg.

Nudges share certain features with BeRg and can be used as some kind of preliminary field experience for BeReg. It is integrated into the legislative process: it has its own metanormativity. That is part of the law as it stands. On the other hand, as the Alfred Nobel Prize Committee noted to illustrate Thaler's contribution, nudging helps gather evidence on which policies actually work as expected before they are implemented on a larger scale. Ideally, policies should be tested and evaluated in randomised field trials.[27] In this context, for example, many studies have highlighted several real-life situations where human intuitions and perceptions about values and attitudes to risk have had consequences, illustrating, among other things, the influence of the so-called endowment effect on individuals' perceptions of fairness/inequity.[28]

BeReg and Nudges are phenomena designed to facilitate compliance and to make better decisions, simpler, more citizen-centric, more transparent, more efficient, etc. It concerns the future technological development which pervades every aspect of life and policy. Literature and practise are full of implementations of BES in this regard: from visual design in the legislative process to high-tech devices such as ICTs used to improve surveillance and social control.[29] Technological advances are used to increase preparedness for emergencies and disasters or for daily life, e.g. by using healthier food; Do-It-Yourself ICTs (e.g. web platforms, wearable sensors, drones and open-source monitoring and mapping kits) are used to raise awareness and protect health and the environment, etc.[30]

On the other hand, BeRg and nudging are also victims of their success and the target of many critiques. We often witness a conflict of principles between those who present them as intelligent tools for improving life and society and those who stigmatise them as surreptitious means of manipulating behaviour in the name of a hypocritical paternalism or dirigisme of bureaucratic elites. This double vision, which oscillates between a nightmare for opponents and the noble dream of supporters, can well be summed up in the opposition Nudge vs. Sludge, i.e. Nudge for Good on the one hand and Nudge for Evil on the other.[31] As Thaler himself acknowledges, the architecture of decisions can be used for purposes that we do not consider 'benevolent', 'right' or 'better' for us.[32]

---

[27] Thaler (2017).

[28] Thaler (2015); a classical terms of reference is Kanheman et al. (1991).

[29] Boucher et al. (2018).

[30] Tallacchini and Biggeri (2014).

[31] Thaler (2018).

[32] Thaler (2018).

The above phenomena, including BeRg, are neither morally nor politically neutral, as the juxtaposition of nudge vs. Sludge and the debates about the purely symbolic or actual ameliorative effect of BeRg itself show.

This applies to any decision-making architecture (legal design) and the use of BES at both the public policy level and in the private sector. The other BES instruments, including BeReg and nudges, are neither inherently good nor bad; it depends on their specific content in each circumstance and on the moral principles and policy goals we want them to pursue.

3 The Experimental Case of EU Smart/Better Regulation

3.1 Why Does Smart/Better Regulation Deserve Attention?

The BeRg credit predominantly originates from the political and institutional sphere. As with the classical tripartite division of powers (legislative, executive, judicial), it is the executive that plays the pivotal role in this context. This is a crucial point, one that merits particular emphasis. BeRg permeates and shapes the policies and practices of public servants, while simultaneously being influenced by them. While the so-called jurisprudence—encompassing doctrine and the broader theory of lawyers and philosophers—appeared initially inert, it seems to be gradually becoming more receptive. This is especially true of doctrine, which has long engaged with the quality of regulation, even at the national level.

Although general doctrine, theory, and legal philosophy have not devoted much attention to it, BeRg is nonetheless a tangible and undeniable phenomenon, now firmly embedded in the present legal landscape. I contend that, within the framework of applicable EU law and the legislation of Member States, engaging with BeRg is not only useful but also indispensable. This holds true for both lawyers and non-lawyers alike—that is, for each and every one of us. BeRg is an omnipresent and pervasive phenomenon, characterising contemporary normative production at every level of so-called sources, both national and international, far exceeding the narrow competencies of the European Union.

Its power is vast, and its influence extends well beyond specialist domains, literature, and practice. Moreover, it is acutely relevant, impacting the current work of lawyers and every individual citizen, while also holding the potential to be influenced—albeit tentatively.

Thus, this analysis is not merely explanatory or reconstructive; it is also normative in its intent. It is, of course, not neutral. The aim is to subject BeRg to critical reflection, inviting lawyers engaged in jurisprudence to participate in this process. Criticism here does not imply ideological opposition or a denial of the system; rather, it represents an effort—if not to bridge the gap between intellectual and political reflection, as Norberto Bobbio lamented with profound disillusionment—at least to mediate between the two parallel tracks that seldom intersect: the history of ideas and the history of action.[33]

3.2 A Magic Formula?

What does Smart/Better Regulation mean? What sort of phenomena is this referring to?

As I said, the terms have been coined and developed over the last three decades within the OECD and the European Union (before the EEC), but there is still no single accepted definition. The formula is paraphrased and translated into the various natural languages, using expressions such as '*legiferare meglio*', '*legislar melhor*', 'buena regulación', 'mejora de la regulación', 'regulación inteligente o regulación eficiente', etc.[34]

All these words and concepts are filled with positive connotations. But we can debate the values, ideas and meanings they convey. On the one hand, they appear as a source of vision and inspiration. On the other hand, as the proof of substitution teaches,[35] it would be completely unhappy on a linguistic-pragmatic level to speak of the opposite: that is, of a bad, worse, foolish, unintelligent regulation, etc. Nobody can reasonably claim that a regulation or a statute is worse, unintelligent, ineffective, etc. Where the contrary does not make sense, pragmatism teaches us to be very careful and highlights the high degree of underdetermination of the BeRg formula.

It's important to note that the comparative term is typically hidden: better or superior, when compared to what? The answer is hidden, though it is clear: traditional legislation or (already existing) legislation. Alongside the formula, then, lies a clever and powerful rhetorical move.[36] In an unspoken way, a symbolic turn in the opposite direction is constructed.

---

[33] Bobbio (1975, 1993). This view is not universally accepted. The literature advocating a neutral approach to law and assigning a central role to functions is quite extensive: see e.g. Ehrenberg (2009).

[34] The BeRg is taken seriously and highly developed in particular in Spain: see Gobierno de España (2023) and ICE (2019). See also OECD (2022c), where BeRg is explained in connection with 'regulatory policy' and 'deregulation' as 'an explicit, dynamic and consistent "whole of government" policy to promote continuous improvements in the quality of rule-making»; it a set of tool that «enhance the [economic] performance, cost-effectiveness, or legal quality of regulation and formalities'. Many official documents do not provide any explicit definition. According to the 2017 EU Better Regulation Guidelines, '"Better regulation" means designing EU policies and laws so that they achieve their objectives at minimum cost. Better regulation is not about regulating or deregulating. It is a way of working to ensure that political decisions are prepared in an open, transparent manner, informed by the best available evidence and backed by the comprehensive involvement of stakeholders'.

[35] See Domaneschi and Penco (2017).

[36] In general, about the symbolic and expressive uses of legal concepts and discourses, it is a classic reference Posner (1998). In this book, see the chapter written by Ferraro.

BeRg presents itself in an attractive new light and involves the belief that the existing legislative process and legacy legislative outputs are comparatively worse. But what matters most is where that refreshment comes from and what food it provides. In fact, the phenomenon itself has been engendered and promoted by the very institutions that hold legislative and executive power. Even if no one notices it: the fact that better lawmaking is being promoted today is not an implicit recognition that what the same institutions did the day before was worse. We are not willing to admit any limits or liabilities. Rather, it is a powerful apparatus, fully engaged in improving its development, with maximum commitment and effort in terms of communication and economic resources.

Like a two-faced Janus, there is a stanza—which goes completely unnoticed—that looks to the past and acknowledges the poorer legislation and the negative judgement of the competent authorities on their own work. On the other hand, everyone is looking forward: BeRg is a manifesto of renewal in which the same authorities appear under a new and better disguise. Although the first stanza remains obscure, the second stanza is the subject of extensive communication activity, making use of the latest achievements of BES. Hence the ubiquitous use of images and expressions with a considerable number of redundancies that have a symbolic function.[37] From an immense production, a few examples from recent institutional communication are cited here in Figs. 1 and 2.

Verbal and nonverbal language are utilized with all their positive expressive possibilities to activate the emotional aspects of the recipients, as demonstrated by this small selection of examples. Verbal and non-verbal signs are skilfully used to complement each other, one reinforcing the message conveyed by the other. And all this in a context where associations with primitive, ordinary intuitions that override common sense and the more instinctive, emotional, unreflective aspects keep coming up.[38]

Metaphors are often used that are mainly related to nature or biology and the concept of construction (edification). The place where they are most prominent is the New European Bauhaus, which is the end point of the BeRg approach within the Green New Deal that lasted several decades (see Fig. 3).[39]

In the context in question, there is constant reference to values such as goodness, transparency, quality, clarity, simplicity, etc., which are capable of being fine or cold. When talking about good legislation—although it is an expression linked to the idea of goodness and the virtue of goodness—discourses are formulated that are positively oriented but do not adhere to a particular individual morality.[40] The good/

---

[37] Vimercati (2018) underlines the evocative-symbolic meaning of the term BeRg and, contrary to exaggerated sceptical tendencies, highlights the basic problem, namely what determines the goodness of a legislative, regulatory, etc. process or product.

[38] Baldi (2020).

[39] EU (2023) and https://new-european-bauhaus.europa.eu/index_en.

[40] Useful in relation to the expressive use of BeRg is Stevenson (1937).

Fig. 1 Overview of the EU's better regulation approach, illustrating the life cycle of legislation and the inclusive, participatory tools that support evidence-based policymaking. The figure shows how the European Union seeks to improve the quality and legitimacy of its laws by integrating all stages of the legislative cycle—from agenda-setting and impact assessment, through adoption and implementation, to evaluation and revision. The initiative "Better regulation: Joining forces to make better laws" emphasizes interinstitutional cooperation, stakeholder engagement, and transparency. The visual also highlights the "EU Have Your Say" platform, which enables citizens, businesses, and organizations to contribute feedback and suggestions throughout the legislative process, promoting democratic participation and responsiveness [Press release relating to the EC (2021b); Iconic representation of the legislative production cycle used on institutional websites and in official documents, e.g. in the Better Regulation Guidelines. See also the EU website https://commission.europa.eu/law/law-making-process/planning-and-proposing-law/better-regulation_en#have-your-say%2D%2Dshare-your-views-and-ideas; See https://commission.europa.eu/law/law-making-process/planning-and-proposing-law/better-regulation_en#have-your-say%2D%2Dshare-your-views-and-ideas and https://ec.europa.eu/info/law/better-regulation/; EC (2019a) and related Conference—Better regulation: taking stock to take it forward held on 29 April 2019 in Brussels; in addition, EC SW (2019b)]

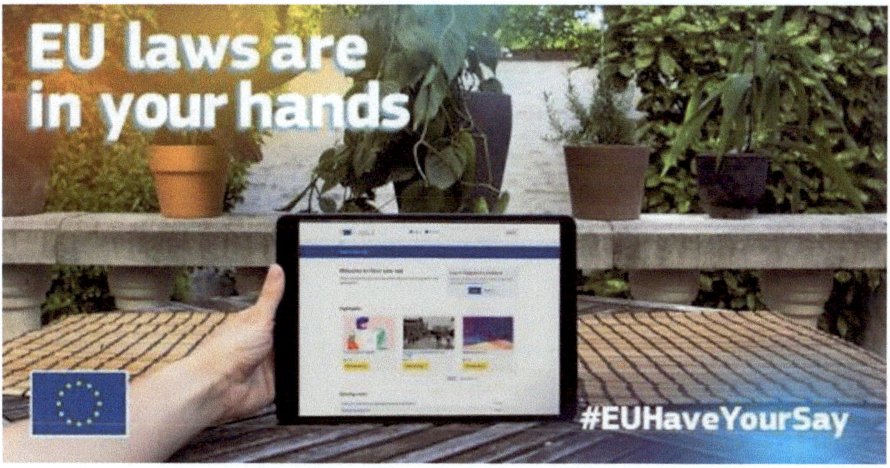

Fig. 1 (continued)

better is thus understood as a general positive evaluative concept based on an inclination or guidance towards general approval.[41]

Leaving individual morality aside, if we want to go deeper into the language game, wise or better are in any case expressions of the legitimacy of an institutional project and therefore reflect a precise choice of public ethics.

On the other hand, words do not always have a constitutive power in themselves: and the property of being truly wise, better, etc. does not depend only on the expressive use of language. It is a quality that—prosaically speaking—must be acquired in

[41] See Kovesi (1967), pp. 1–2.

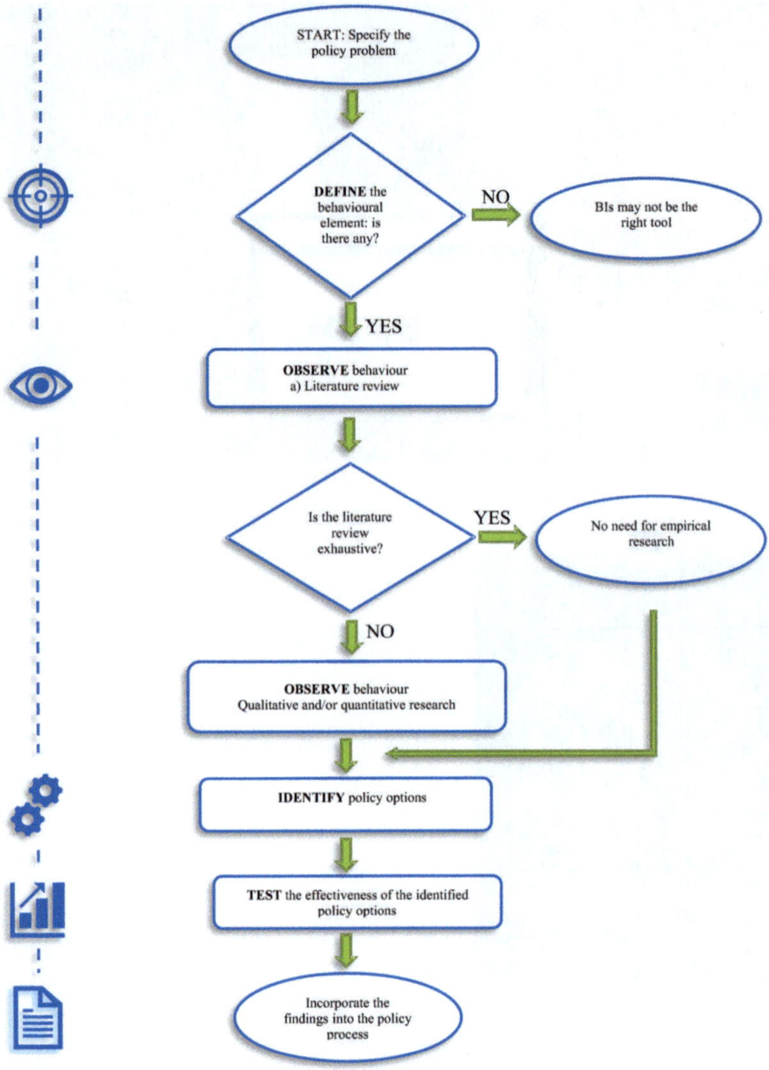

Fig. 2 Practical implementation steps for applying behavioural insights in policy design, summarised through the acronym DO IT (Define, Observe, Identify, Test). The figure illustrates a four-stage sequence guiding policymakers: (1) Define the behavioural issue to be addressed; (2) Observe how people behave and investigate the underlying drivers; (3) Identify and design suitable policy options to influence the behaviour; and (4) Test the effectiveness of the selected interventions. Each step is represented as a distinct box arranged in a logical flow, emphasizing iteration and evidence-based adaptation. This model is part of Tool #69, which explores emerging policy instruments such as behavioural insights and regulatory sandboxes in the context of better regulation practices [EC (2023a), p. 608]

Fig. 3 Logo of the New European Bauhaus price initiative, edition 2021, with the motto "Beautiful | Sustainable | Together". The composition integrates a tripartite horizontal layout of core values, emphasizing the project's commitment to aesthetics, environmental responsibility, and collective participation. The logo combines a typographic structure with stylized, child-like pencil drawings representing an urban and natural environment—trees, houses, and people at play—evoking a sense of childhood and the imaginative hope of a world seen through the eyes of future generations. Stylized light-blue clouds complete the image, reinforcing a tone of simplicity and aspiration [EU (2023) and related explanatory documents found at https://europa.eu/new-european-bauhaus/system/files_en?file=2021-01/New-European-Bauhaus-Explained.pdf]

practise. This is all the more true given the empirical-experimental approach that the model it takes.[42]

3.3 *'SMART': Looking Through the Spyglass*

As can be seen from the above examples and the many others used on a daily basis, the institutions and literature on BeRg are mainly concerned with objectives and outcomes, input-output, etc. A variety of principles with changing clusters of criteria are used to illustrate the phenomenon. All this takes place in a constant production of generated neologisms with a highly technical vocabulary and using an operational and management approach.

In this environment, BeRg proves to be a territory more suited to being traversed inch by inch in search of signs and signals (which are always more precarious, more or less divided and conventional) than to being understood in the abstract. In this respect, a revival of the so-called operational definitions[43] could be helpful to make some conceptual clarifications.

Like any other terms currently in vogue, such as that of artificial intelligence, BeRg is a good example of the fact that there is no permanent dictionary or encyclopaedia for highly complex phenomena characterised by very rapid, constant change. According to some estimates, the world will generate about one yottabyte (one

[42] The basis for better regulation is the idea of monitoring the process of regulation through annual surveys EC, the activity of the Regulatory Scrutiny Boards and their annual reports: see EC (2022, 2023c).

[43] See Alpert (1938); Dodd and Shanas (1943); Ennis (1964).

million trillion megabytes) of data per year by 2030 and 180 zettabytes by 2025. The rapid growth of the 'infosphere'[44] prompted the Paris General Conference on Weights and Measures in 2022 to introduce new prefixes for the International System of Units with immediate effect. The new prefixes, ronna and quetta, stand for 10^{27} and 10^{30} respectively. This is the first update since 1991, when zetta (10^{21}) and yotta (10^{24}) were introduced. It is estimated that 2012 was the year when the total amount of digitised data used worldwide exceeded one zettabyte, and in 2016, global internet traffic alone exceeded this amount. In such an environment, reflected at the semiotic level, even sortal or rhizome models seem inadequate and unlimited semiosis seems to be realised in action.[45]

From a semiotic point of view, BeRg can be a useful addition to understand both the narratives involved (in another era one would have spoken of ideologies) and the assumptions and the more philosophical and ultimately metaphysical implications.

From a language standpoint, smart/better-law-making is ambiguous and allusive. We are dealing with a powerful and sophisticated form of metaphor.[46]

A metaphor that not only expresses the full wonder of this figure that has captivated the curiosity of the human mind for millennia,[47] but also reflects an age in human history. In order to understand the underpinnings of BeRg, it is useful to step back, that is to remember the concept that preceded it and from which it emerged, namely the similar concept that is still almost synonymous or interchangeable today, namely Smart Regulation.

As we mentioned in the previous paragraph, smart can (better) be understood in its most immediate, ordinary meaning, which refers to qualities or characteristics that are also and especially inherent in a person. Thus, we speak of a smart person who has a neat, tidy and stylish appearance, or of an intelligent person who is able to think quickly and wisely in difficult situations; a smart person acts wisely and effectively.

SMART is a mnemonic acronym that stands for some criteria that are believed to lead to better results in project management.[48] The abbreviation usually stands for Specific, Measurable, Agreed, Realistic and Timed, but the exact terms derived from the initials vary both in the literature and in practise. For example, the 'S' can stand for 'Specific' or 'Stretching', 'Strategic', etc., as can the 'A' for 'Assignable', 'Appropriate' or 'Achievable', etc.; 'R' for 'Relevant', 'Reasonable', and so on. The idea is that these five criteria are fitting for scrutinizing the objectives in a performance management system. The theoretical rationale is teleological and comes tra-

---

[44] Floridi (2014).

[45] Eco (1984), pp. 109–111 distinguishes between dictionary and encyclopaedia, conceiving the latter as a semiotic postulate and regulative hypothesis, while being aware that the general system of sciences is a kind of labyrinth with a winding path that can wreck any encyclopaedic tree, classification or typology.

[46] The fact that many (other) metaphors are used to talk about BeRg is a consequence of the creative process triggered by BeRg, as a metaphor itself.

[47] We can recall the admirable Aristotelian spyglass: Tesauro (1663).

[48] The term was first proposed by Doran (1981).

ditionally from Peter Ferdinand Drucker's theory of Management by Objectives.[49] This theory, originally developed for corporations and business world, was then extended to individuals and societies.[50]

According to classic literature, it is not realistic to assume or seek to ensure that the above criteria and objectives are strictly quantified or objectively measurable. A smart approach is influenced by numerous evaluative factors. What matters is the combination of goals and related action plans. In the current digital era, the smart approach is about artificial intelligence systems and tools. The former would not exist if it were not for the latter. And the same BeRg is presented as SMART in its own nature.[51]

Given the above, the Smart/Better Regulation phrase expresses a trope or thematic jump from the animated to the inanimate, from the natural to the artificial. The current frontiers of regulation are at the planetary and European levels, as attested by the OECD: the green and digital transitions. It is also noteworthy how, through the converging lines of history, we find reflected the enduring metaphor that unites and merges the natural with the artificial.[52] It thus presents the characteristics of synesthesia and conjures up an oxymoronic image.[53] Various basic assumptions underpin the BeRg and its symbolic and expressive power. On the one hand, we assume that laws/regulations generally are essential for societies and humans as social animals, and that laws/regulations are established by and for humans. On the other hand, we suppose that laws and, more generally, normativity and law have a sort of double nature: natural and artificial. BeRg carries a combination of ideas that reconcile the animated with the natural and the artificial with the inanimate. This metaphor is constructed on two fundamental archetypal connections: the ideal Homo faber type and the archetypal connection between the soul and intellect.

In the words of Giabattista Vico, most expressions referring to inanimate things are connected with the transport of the human body and its parts.[54] As Umberto Eco noted, metaphor establishes an unprecedented relationship between two elements that triggers a reordering of knowledge and gives rise to new ontologies.[55] The

[49] Drucker (1964).

[50] Drucker (2003).

[51] The links to management theory are profound and widespread. A key example is the REFIT Program—an acronym for REgulatory FITness and Performance—and its associated platform, which ran from 2016 to 2019. The new Fit for Future Platform has been in operation since 2021. Connected to it is the Have Your Say: Simplify! portal cited above Also in 2021, RegHub 2.0 was launched: a network of regional hubs to monitor regulatory implementation and stakeholder engagement at regional and local levels. Following the 2016 Interinstitutional Agreement, the Task Force on Subsidiarity and Proportionality and on Doing Less More Efficiently was launched in 2017: EC (2018).

[52] OECD (2023, 2024).

[53] Neuwirth (2022).

[54] Vico (2007), p. 588.

[55] Eco (1980), pp. 191–236.

metaphor creates new entities in the philosophical sense, but also in the physical sense: it presents us with a part that, wherever it was deposited, was not before our eyes.[56]

This connection between BeRg and synaesthesia/oxymoron extends beyond the discursive or rhetorical-figurative dimension and the achievements of modern science. For example, if it is true that the discoveries of neurology explain synaesthesia (also) on a biological basis, taking into account sensory and perceptual capacities, then the BeRg metaphor has a much deeper meaning. It is a symbol or representation of a parable that starts from a conception of man as an animate being characterised by intellect (the anthropocentric, anthropologically based notion that man is the most intelligent of all animals recedes into the background) and arrives at a conception that allows for the opposite, in which intelligence is no longer the exclusive preserve of man but can be replicated in the inanimate through man-made artefacts.[57]

The BeRg thus constitutes a privileged position in the contemporary world. As Lakoff and Johnson remind us, old myths, rooted in good sense, envision a man as something distinct from the environment. The substratum is a largely objectivist concept that thinks in terms of functional success, the notion of knowledge as power and science as control over nature.[58]

4 Old and New Ideologies Between Renewed Empiricism and Functionalism

Each of the features outlined in the previous sections on BeRg warrants further scrutiny. The focus here is on a few aspects that are often overlooked. Beyond the appealing nomenclature and explicit declarations, BeRg addresses a classic issuc of legislation and legislators: namely, the quality of legislation.

This is the central concern that transcends the diverse descriptions found in official documents. The various qualities attributed to BeRg reformulate numerous attempts to clarify and answer the question of what constitutes "good" legislation. Upon comparison, certain recognitions appear to be almost universal. The first is the acknowledgment that legislation is a complex system, one that necessitates models grounded in a multitude of factors, components, and elements. Exemplifying these efforts are, for instance, dashboards designed to monitor the geopolitical, green, digital, social, economic, and health dimensions of resilience.[59] Moreover, BeRg

[56] Eco (1984), p. 164.

[57] Ansuátegui Roig (2020).

[58] Lakoff-Johnson (1980), p. 229.

[59] EC (2024, 2021c).

resembles the general tendency of bureaucracy to meta-regulate according to a recursive superstructure.[60]

Clearly, the use of buzzwords and references to a variety of techniques and concepts associated with ex ante or ex post monitoring and control has emerged in other contexts: from experimental scientific approaches applied to natural and environmental phenomena to those suited for modelling artificial processes at a high technological level. The use of diverse concepts and principles, characterised by their content and relationships in a series, assumes a serene and natural harmony as a prevailing trend.

In this context, however, it is not immediately clear what precisely constitutes the quality of legislation—whether it pertains to the process, the act, or the normative product itself. While it is easy to accept within the realm of jurisprudence and legal policy that quality in law is a desirable ideal, and that it is particularly appropriate to seek incremental improvements in any regulatory process or product (including legislation and laws more broadly), defining what quality entails and identifying what constitutes "better" is an extremely difficult task.

Clarity, readability, comprehensibility, transparency, simplicity, and proportionality—just a few of the components of BeRg—are neither inherent properties nor can they be reduced to empirical or factual elements. They are attributes that presuppose certain value hypotheses and involve pragmatic evaluations. Each of these terms depends on the context in which they are used, and their meanings vary depending on the object to which they refer (e.g., a procedure, a legal act, a rule, or a text), even before their possible interpretations are considered.

Particularly, clarity is the result of the interpretative process (which may include verbal or non-verbal linguistic elements or natural signs or meaningful elements such as human actions). Neither text, behaviour, nor action is inherently clear or imprecise. For instance, we speak metonymically of clear texts, speeches, gestures, and behaviours. Rather, it is the meanings ascribed to them that are (more or less) clear or unclear, depending on how we understand them and consider them (more or less accurately) in response to the relevant communicative goals within that particular context. What is clear to the sender may be entirely unclear to the recipient, and vice versa. That which is clear in one context and with one communicative objective may not be clear at all in another context or with another objective.

The concept of transparency is even more complex, particularly when referring to regulatory processes, actions, and products. It is more metaphorical than the concept of linguistic clarity. While clarity is associated with the metaphor of light—understood as the visible spectrum through which humans can perceive and ascribe meaning—transparency is rooted in a material or physical metaphor. Transparency refers to a body's ability to allow light to pass through it; an object or surface is transparent if one can see through it. In its true sense, therefore, no natural or linguistic sign (whether verbal, non-verbal, or contained in actions) is inherently

---

[60] Williamson's analysis and organisational theory continue to be very instructive in this regard: Williamson (1999) and Hayes and Wood (1995).

transparent or opaque. For clarity, it is true that a sign, when viewed from its material aspect, can be (more or less) transparent or opaque: for example, one may see through a thin smoke sign or a letter beneath a stroke of colour. However, when speaking of transparency in the context of standardisation, we mean something entirely different: behind the text, discourse, or actions, there are usually the goals, motives, or reasons that led to their adoption or specific interpretation and application in practice.

According to a prevailing leitmotif, BeRg signifies neither more nor less legislation. However, the use of more/less is fraught with ambiguity: gradations, as is well known, can be understood either qualitatively or quantitatively. This is yet another rhetorical device concealing the complex issue of redundancy. The matter could be quite extensive, considering the various factors at play. In brief, and at least as a starting point, linguistic redundancies in natural languages should be distinguished from those typical of legal discourse, as the latter are not isomorphic to the former. Furthermore, legislative and legal redundancy are not congruent concepts. Linguistic and normative/legal redundancies are not identical. An analysis should account for the different levels of (legal) discourse, the respective context, the standpoint adopted, the ethical-political goals chosen by the participants, and so forth.

This attention to semiotics is often neglected. The prevailing approach, in contrast, is functionalist and teleological, both in terms of the content of the prescription and its underlying assumptions. Developing the argument involves examining both the process and the product. The general pattern is one of legislation based on budgets (and associated constraints) and objectives, often mirroring business organisation models. The inherent functions of law are the primary focus of contemporary legal discourse. It is controversial what these functions are, as there is no unified understanding of the concept of function. Emphasising the functions of law does not imply adherence to a functionalist conception or the adoption of a functionalist approach. Conversely, adopting such a conception raises the question of what law is for, what functions or purposes it serves, and how and why. As is well known, functionalist thought and teleological thought are not identical; thus, equating function with purpose or telos is itself a contentious matter.

The general objectives of regulation (meta-) are often presented or explained as though they are self-evident (though one could argue whether, how, and to what extent they truly are). The basic model remains that of programming or planning.[61]

Each goal is articulated through the cadence of declamations, values, and normative (ethical-political) concepts, framed within a perspective of harmony, wherein the figure of the totipotent legislator lingers in the background.

Two pervasive metaphors dominate the discourse surrounding normative production: the biological and the constructive. These metaphors converge in a natural co-production, wherein, among other things, the natural and the artificial are seamlessly integrated. On one hand, one need only consider the legislative life cycle. The notion of a cycle, inspired by the success formula of the circular economy, extends

[61] Shapiro (2017) is a pioneer and advocate of this view.

its reach into the domain of law, even though the analogy to the physical law of classical mechanics—specifically the conservation of mass—remains an open question, deserving of scrutiny from both philosophical and epistemological perspectives. On the other hand, the metaphor of construction presents itself as inherently plastic, evoking the engineering-architectural model, with its focus on design, structure, and the intentionality of creation.[62] And the reassuring, hidden image of the common home.

This context reflects the convergence of various values, such as scientific evidence, simplification, co-determination, and other similar concepts, all of which underscore the prominence of the nudging ideology that underpins BeRg. Further borrowings from other models emerge in the methods of regulating production: toolbox, sandbox, experimental legislation, and so on.

The manifesto serves, in essence, as a form of propaganda at the symbolic level, framing the actions and documents within a broader context.[63] Its overt aim is to enhance political and legal legitimacy. Familiar marketing patterns, drawn from the media world, are employed to facilitate this. As advertising teaches us, there is little point in concealing the real purpose when recipients are aware that they are being exposed to commercials. Rather, the explicit articulation of the purpose enhances the effectiveness of the subconscious conditioning mechanisms operating behind the scenes.

Whether, from the perspective of the history of ideas, this phenomenon represents a particular model of economically oriented rationality or whether it is a manifestation of the behaviourally driven applied sciences is open to debate. Regardless of one's stance on this matter, BeRg undeniably marks the beginning of a broader phenomenon: the executive branch gains both normative and meta-normative spaces of power and, crucially, the self-legitimacy to assert itself within juridical-political systems.

While much of the speculation within jurisprudence focuses on the relationship between legislation and jurisprudence, a new chapter emerges in reflections on the rule of law, one that places particular emphasis on the third executive branch, as compared to the legislative and judicial branches.

5 Jurisprudential Considerations: Against Scepticism

John Stuart Mill has said that 'there is hardly any kind of intellectual work which so much needs to be done, not only by experienced and exercised minds, but by minds trained to the task through long and laborious study, as the business of making

[62] Example par excellence the #NewEuropeanBauhaus. Nudging plays an important role in the diffusion of this mainstream which is precisely based on the idea of the architecture of choice.

[63] Hallsworth (2023).

laws'.[64] However, as he detected, 'it must be acknowledged that a bureaucratic government has, in some important respects, greatly the advantage. It accumulates experience, acquires well-tried and well-considered traditional maxims, and makes provision for appropriate practical knowledge in those who have the actual conduct of affairs. But it is not equally favourable to individual energy of mind. The disease which afflicts bureaucratic governments, and which they usually die of, is routine. They perish by the immutability of their maxims; and, still more, by the universal law that whatever becomes a routine loses its vital principle, and having no longer a mind acting within it, goes on revolving mechanically though the work it is intended to do remains undone. A bureaucracy always tends to become a pedantocracy'.[65]

The literature surrounding BeRg generally aligns with the institutional frameworks or shares the predominant cultural context from which it originates. Contributions to this discourse are typically presented with a benevolent stance. In contrast, critics argue that it represents a harmful form of science serving policy agendas. Rather than fostering genuine debate, the subject has become embroiled in ideological skirmishes. Beyond the admiration and critique, this analysis acquires a deeper significance.

The particularity that makes BeRg especially compelling in this context pertains to the core of legal production. It engages with the quintessential subject of speculation within the philosophy of law. It is noteworthy that legal theorists and philosophers have largely overlooked this issue. Indeed, engaging with methodologies and approaches that differ so fundamentally from traditional legal thought proves undeniably challenging. However, at its best, BeRg represents a historical phase in the development of Western constitutional law.

BeRg is a phenomenon of meta-regulation and meta-legislation that began in the 1990s, initially within the OECD, and has since gained prominence over the last decade to 15 years. The recent post-pandemic resurgence of the European Union has further accelerated this process. BeRg advocates for the design of policies and laws that achieve their objectives with minimal cost. The core issue is not the regulation or deregulation per se, but rather the approach to policymaking that ensures decisions are crafted in an open, transparent manner, grounded in the best available data, and involve full stakeholder participation. This brings us back to the long-standing and unresolved question of the quality of legislation and how it can be improved. It is essential to clarify that the scope of these measures extends far beyond the quality of legislative texts, with the design of laws being only one component of this broader phenomenon.

While BeRg undoubtedly begins with the question of better legislation, it is not a theoretical answer—it is an administrative, bureaucratic response. This phenomenon is noteworthy because it exemplifies the increasing prevalence of methodological syncretism that influences both the legal method and its underlying methodology.

---

[64] Mill (2001), p. 64.

[65] Mill (2001), p. 74.

BeRg is both a political and institutional phenomenon. The executive and bureaucratic apparatus function as the engines within the classical tripartite division of powers (legislative, executive, and judicial). In this context, BeRg represents a metaregulatory policy and an integral element of existing law. My argument is that, whether we approve of it or not, we must acknowledge its presence. Above all, it is a pervasive phenomenon, characterizing regulatory production at all levels of the so-called sources of law—national and international—far beyond the competences traditionally ascribed to the European Union.

The power of BeRg is not only considerable but also extends far beyond the circle of specialists and the literature and practice from which it originates. Observing documents and images alone does not convey the full extent of its influence in contemporary legal realities.

A critical element of BeRg lies in its sophisticated communicative strategies, which incorporate the latest insights from cognitive and behavioral sciences. It extensively employs symbolic images, videos, words, and phrases, often with considerable redundancy. Both verbal and non-verbal language, imbued with positive connotations, is strategically used to activate the emotional responses of recipients. The discourse often draws on primitive intuitions, appealing to common sense and to the more instinctual, emotional, and unconscious aspects of human thought. Metaphors, frequently drawn from nature or biology, as well as the concept of construction, are pervasive in its rhetoric.

When we discuss better or smart regulation, we must recognize that these terms are far from neutral; they are laden with positive connotations. The use of terms such as "bad," "poor," or "foolish regulation" would be politically unwise, both linguistically and pragmatically.

BeRg presents itself as a dual-faced phenomenon, akin to Janus Bifrontius, with one aspect looking backward and the other looking toward the future. It serves as both a manifesto of renewal and a form of propaganda, positioning authorities in a new and more favorable light.

What, then, are the key features of BeRg? The fundamental elements are (a) forward planning, (b) impact assessment, including evaluation, fitness checks, quality control, and both ex-ante and ex-post or continuous monitoring, and (c) public engagement, involving stakeholder participation. These three pillars—the notion of law as purposeful practice, cost-benefit analysis in its broadest sense, and the problem of legitimacy—form the foundation of BeRg.

The idea of cost-benefit analysis, and the pursuit of a positive balance—more benefits than costs—is a hallmark of BeRg, as reflected in its definitions, documents, and initiatives over the decades. However, the actual substance of the analysis often remains opaque, as it forms part of a broader communication strategy and the ideal of a harmonious design underlying institutional foundations. This approach is more aligned with design principles borrowed from business administration, management, and process studies than with traditional economic analysis of law. The one-in-one-out approach and the concept of efficiency, often undefined, are particularly emblematic. Efficiency, in this context, refers not to mere quantity but to axiology, focusing on the values associated with equity.

In schematic terms, BeRg represents the tip of an iceberg, embodying a teleological-functionalist and systemic approach both at the process and product levels—applicable to both the content of legislation and its enactment. The general model mirrors that of legislation as a process of goal-setting, constrained by budgets and targets, similar to the operational models of business organizations.

Two metaphors dominate BeRg's discourse: that of biology and that of construction. These metaphors converge in a natural co-production, wherein the natural and artificial are seamlessly integrated. The life cycle of legislation, akin to the circular economy, is a key analogy. Philosophically and epistemologically, this raises questions regarding the classical law of mass conservation. BeRg also shares the ideology of nudging, as evidenced by its convergence of values such as scientific evidence, simplification, self-determination, and participation, although this influence often operates beneath the surface. The construction metaphor, borrowing from engineering and architecture, is particularly effective.

The overarching goal of BeRg is to enhance political and legal legitimacy. It adopts marketing models familiar to the media industry, relying on techniques akin to advertising. As advertising teaches, it is counterproductive to obscure the ultimate objective when the recipients of the message are aware that they are being targeted. Explicit disclosure facilitates the efficiency of subconscious retro-conditioning. The debate, however, centers on whether this phenomenon represents a particular, economically-driven model of rationality, and whether it is the result of applied behavioral science. Regardless of this, BeRg marks the beginning of a broader trend: the executive branch is expanding its normative and metanormative powers, as well as its self-legitimation processes. While much jurisprudential inquiry has focused on the relationship between legislation and judicial interpretation, a new chapter is unfolding in the consideration of the rule of law, in which the executive power assumes a more prominent role relative to the legislative and judicial branches.

Looking into the future, the words of the classics ring out. Mill's memento is still valid: 'Of the three varieties of mental excellence, intellectual, practical, and moral, there never could be any doubt in regard to the first two which side had the advantage. All intellectual superiority is the fruit of active effort. Enterprise, the desire to keep moving, to be trying and accomplishing new things for our own benefit or that of others, is the parent even of speculative, and much more of practical, talent. The intellectual culture compatible with the other type is of that feeble and vague description which belongs to a mind that stops at amusement, or at simple contemplation. The test of real and vigourous thinking, the thinking which ascertains truths instead of dreaming dreams, is successful application to practice. Where that purpose does not exist, to give definiteness, precision, and an intelligible meaning to thought, it generates nothing better than the mystical metaphysics of the Pythagoreans or the Vedas. With respect to practical improvement, the case is still more evident. The character that enhances human life is one that fights with natural powers and tendencies, not one that gives way to them. The self-benefiting qualities are all on the side of the active and energetic character: and the habits and conduct which promote the advantage of each individual member of the community must be at least a part of those which conduce most in the end to the advancement of the community as a whole'.[66]

References[67]

Afif Z, Islan WW, Calvo-Gonzalez O Dalton AG (2019) Behavioral science around the world: profiles of 10 countries. eMBeD Washington, D.C

Alpert H (1938) Operational definitions in sociology. Am Sociol Rev 3(6):855–861

Ansuátegui Roig FA (2020) Nuove tecnologie e spazio pubblico. In: Salardi S, Saporiti M (eds) Le tecnologie 'morali' emergenti e le sfide etico-giuridiche delle nuove soggettività, Emerging 'moral' technologies and the ethical-legal challenges of new subjectivities. Giappichelli, Torino, pp 22–41

Baldi B (2020) Persuasion we live by: symbols, metaphors and linguistic strategies. Quaderni di linguistica e Studi Orientali 6:337–382

Bobbio N (1975) Per una filosofia critica. Libri nuovi 7(1):3

Bobbio N (1993) Intellettuali non dinosauri. Le idee sopravviveranno alle ideologie. Brescia Oggi, 28 september 1993

Boucher P, Nascimento S, Tallacchini M (2018) Emerging ICT for citizens' Veillance: theoretical and practical insights. https://doi.org/10.1007/s11948-018-0039-z

Dodd SC, Shanas E (1943) Operational definitions operationally defined. Am J Sociol 48(4):482–491

Domaneschi F, Penco C (2017) Presupposizioni. APhEx p 15

Doran GT (1981) There is a S.M.A.R.T. way to write management's goals and objectives. Manage Rev 70(11):35–36

Drucker P (1964) Managing for results; economic tasks and risk-taking decisions. Harper & Row, New York

Drucker P (2003) A functioning society: selections from sixty-five years of writing on community, society, and polity. Taylor & Francis, New Brunswick

Eco U (1980) Metafora. In: Enciclopedia Einaudi, IX. Einaudi, Torino, pp 191–236

Eco U (1984) Semiotica e filosofia del linguaggio. Einaudi, Torino

Ehrenberg KM (2009) Defending the possibility of a neutral functional theory of law. Oxf J Leg Stud 29:91–113

Ennis RH (1964) Operational definitions. Am Educ Res J 1(3):183–201

European Commission (2017) Completing the Better Regulation Agenda: Better solutions for better results https://ec.europa.eu/info/sites/default/files/better-regulation-guidelines.pdf

European Commission (2018) Report 10 July 2018 https://ec.europa.eu/info/sites/default/files/report-task-force-subsidiarity-proportionality-and-doing-less-more-efficiently_it_0.pdf

European Commission (2019a) Better Regulation: taking stock and sustaining our commitment https://commission.europa.eu/law/law-making-process/planning-and-proposing-law/better-regulation/better-regulation-taking-stock-and-sustaining-our-commitment_en

European Commission (2019b) Commission Staff Working Document , Taking Stock of the Commission's Better Regulation Agenda https://eur-lex.europa.eu/legal-content/EN/TXT/?uri=CELEX%3A52019SC0156

European Commission (2021a) 'Better regulation' toolbox https://commission.europa.eu/law/law-making-process/planning-and-proposing-law/better-regulation/better-regulation-guidelines-and-toolbox_en

[66] Mill (2001), p. 41.

[67] All websites, and references available on web: accessed 19 January 2025.

European Commission (2021b) COM(2021) 219 final - Better regulation: Joining forces to make better laws https://eur-lex.europa.eu/legal-content/EN/TXT/?uri=celex:52021DC0219

European Commission (2021c) Resilience dashboards for the social and economic, green, digital, and geopolitical dimensions https://joint-research-centre.ec.europa.eu/scientific-activities-z/resilience/resilience-dashboards_en

European Commission (2022) The European Union's efforts to simplify legislation https://commission.europa.eu/publications/annual-burden-survey_en

European Commission (2023a) Better Regulation https://ec.europa.eu/info/law/better-regulation/

European Commission (2023b) 'Better regulation' toolbox https://commission.europa.eu/law/law-making-process/planning-and-proposing-law/better-regulation/better-regulation-guidelines-and-toolbox_en accessed 19 January 2025

European Commission (2023c) Regulatory Scrutiny Board https://commission.europa.eu/law/law-making-process/regulatory-scrutiny-board_en

European Commission (2024) Resilience Dashboards Update Spring 2024 https://commission.europa.eu/strategy-and-policy/strategic-foresight/2020-strategic-foresight-report/resilience-dashboards_en

European Union (2023) New European Bauhaus https://new-european-bauhaus.europa.eu/index_en and https://europa.eu/new-european-bauhaus/system/files_en?file=2021-01/New-European-Bauhaus-Explained.pdf

Ferraro F, Zorzetto S (2019) Legislation and nudging: towards a suitable definition. In: Oliver Lalana D (ed) Conceptions and misconceptions of legislation. Springer, Zaragoza, pp 107–132

Floridi L (2014) The fourth revolution: how the infosphere is reshaping human reality. OUP, Oxford

Gobierno de España. Ministerio de Asuntos Económicos y Transformación Digital (2023) Mejora de la Regulaciòn https://portal.mineco.gob.es/es-es/economiayempresa/unidadmercado/mejoraregulacion/Paginas/ART_CABECERA.aspx

Hallsworth M (2023) A manifesto for applying behavioural science. Nat Hum Behav 7:310–322. https://doi.org/10.1038/s41562-023-01555-3

Hayes K, Wood LL (1995) Utility maximizing bureaucrats: the bureaucrat's point of view. Public Choice 82:69–83. https://doi.org/10.1007/BF01047730

ICE, Revista De Economía 907 (2019). https://www.revistasice.com/index.php/ICE/article/view/6814

Kanheman D, Knestch JL, Thaler RH (1991) Anomalies: the endowment effect, loss aversion, and status quo bias. J Econ Persp 5(1):193–206

Kantorowicz HU, Patterson EW (1928) Legal science. A summary of its methodology. Columb Law Rev 28, 6:679–707

Kovesi J (1967) Moral notions. Routledge and Kegan Paul, London, pp 1–2

Lakoff G, Johnson M (1980) Metaphors we live by. University of Chicago Press, Chicago

Lunn P (2014) Regulatory policy and behavioural economics. OECD Publishing, Paris, https://doi.org/10.1787/9789264207851-en

Manning L, Dalton A G, Afif Z, Vakos R, Naru F (2020) Behavioral science around the world volume II: profiles of 17 international organizations. eMBeD, Washington DC

Maturana H R, Varela F (1980) Autopoiesis and cognition. The realization of the living. Reidel, Dordrecht

Mill JS (2001 [1861]) Representative Government, Batoche Books Limited, Kitchener

Neuwirth RJ (2022) Law, artificial intelligence, and synaesthesia, AI & Society https://doi.org/10.1007/s00146-022-01615-8

Organisation for Economic Co-operation and Development – OECD (1995) OECD Recommendation on Improving the Quality of Government Regulation. OECD Publishing, Paris

Organisation for Economic Co-operation and Development – OECD (2017) Behavioural insights and public policy: lessons from around the world. OECD Publishing, Paris, https://doi.org/10.1787/9789264270480-en

Organisation for Economic Co-operation and Development – OECD (2022a) Recommendation of the Council on Improving the Quality of Government Regulation. OECD Publishing, Paris, https://legalinstruments.oecd.org/public/doc/128/128.en.pdf

Organisation for Economic Co-operation and Development – OECD (2022b) Better regulation practices across the European Union. OECD Publishing, Paris, https://doi.org/10.1787/6e4b095d-en
Organisation for Economic Co-operation and Development – OECD (2022c) Better Regulation in Europe: an OECD assessment of regulatory capacity in the 15 original member states of the EU. https://www.oecd.org/gov/regulatory-policy/44952782.pdf
Organisation for Economic Co-operation and Development – OECD (2023) Better regulation for the green transition. OECD Public Governance Policy Papers, No. 40, OECD Publishing, Paris. https://doi.org/10.1787/c91a04bc-en
Organisation for Economic Co-operation and Development – OECD (2024) Regulatory experimentation: Moving ahead on the agile regulatory governance agenda. OECD Public Governance Policy Papers, No. 47, OECD Publishing, Paris. https://doi.org/10.1787/f193910c-en
Posner EA (1998) Symbols, signals, and social norms in politics and the law. J Legal Stud 27:765–797
Scarpelli U (1956) La natura della metodologia giuridica. Rivista internazionale di filosofia del diritto 33:247–255
Scarpelli U (1971) Il metodo giuridico. Rivista di diritto processuale 26:553–574
Shapiro SJ (2017) The planning theory of law. Yale Law School, Public Law Research Paper https://ssrn.com/abstract=2937990
Sousa LJ, Ciriolo E, Rafael Rodrigues Vieira De Almeida S, Troussard X (2016) Behavioural insights applied to policy - European Report. Publications Office of the European Union, Luxembourg
Stevenson CL (1937) The emotive meaning of ethical terms. Mind 46(181):14–31
Sunstein CR (2014) Nudging: a very short guide. J Consum Policy 37(4):583–588
Tallacchini M, Biggeri A (2014) La vigilanza dei cittadini sulla salute ambientale tra tecnologie digitali e genomica. Epidemiol Prev 38(5):292–301
Tesauro E (1663) Il cannocchiale aristotelico. O'sia, Idéa dell'arguta et ingeniosa elocutione, che serve à tutta l'Arte oratoria, lapidaria, et simbolica esaminata co' Principii del divino Aristotele. Paolo Baglioni, Venezia
Thaler R H (2015) Misbehaving. The making of behavioral economics. Norton & Company Inc, New York
Thaler R H (2017) Integrating Economics with psychology. The Committee for the Prize in Economic Sciences in Memory of Alfred Nobel. https://www.nobelprize.org/uploads/2018/06/advanced-economicsciences2017.pdf
Thaler RH (2018) Nudge, not sludge. Penguin, London, p 431
Thaler RH, Sunstein CR (2009) Nudge. Improving decisions about health, wealth and happiness. Penguin Books, London
Varela F, Maturana H (1972) Mechanism and biological explanation. Philos Sci 39(3):378–382
Vega J (2018) Legal philosophy as practical philosophy. Revus 34. https://doi.org/10.4000/revus.3859
Vico G (2007 [1744]) Principi di scienza nuova. Mondadori, Milano
Vimercati E (2018) Natura e strumenti della better regulation. Un contributo allo studio dell'integrazione tra i diversi livelli di governo. Giappichelli, Torino
Williamson OE (1999) Public and private bureaucracies: a transaction cost economics perspective. Int J Law Econ Org 15(1):306–342
World Bank and the World Health Organization (2024) Behavioral Science Around the World Volume III: Public Health. World Bank, Washington, DC. https://blogs.worldbank.org/en/health/How-Are-Governments-Integrating-Behavioral-Science-in-Public-Health
World Bank Group (2015) World Development Report 2015: Mind, Society, and Behavior
World Bank Group (2022) Mind, Behavior, and Development Unit Results Portfolio: Applying Behavioral Science to End Poverty and Enhance Equity. http://documents.worldbank.org/curated/en/688661608104181834/Mind-Behavior-and-Development-Unit-Results-Portfolio-Applying-Behavioral-Science-to-End-Poverty-and-Enhance-Equity
World Bank Group (2025). https://www.worldbank.org/en/programs/embed

Silvia Zorzetto Full professor of Legal Philosophy at the Department of Law, Pegaso Telematic University. Previously researcher and associate professor at the University of Milan, where she obtained her PhD. She has published books, articles and chapters on legal concepts, legal language, legal reasoning, economic analysis of law and "nudging". Her publications in English include: *Legislative Architecture and Nudges: Complementary Tools to Increase Legal Order Resilience?* (in *Exploring the Province of Legislation, Legisprudence*, eds. F. Ferraro and S. Zorzetto, 2022), *Rational, Reasonable and Nudged Man* (in *Theory and criticism of social regulation. Special Issue Economics, Law and Humanities: Homo-what?* (2019–2020); *Is economic analysis of law relevant in Italian case law? Some remarks about consequentialism and equity* (in *Law and Economics as Interdisciplinary Exchange: Philosophical, Methodological and Historical Perspectives*, eds. P. Cserne and M Małecka, Magdalena, 2020); *On impossibility in law* (in *Law and State. Classical Paradigms and Novel Proposals*, eds. L. Burazin, Đ. Gardasevic, and A. Sardo, 2015).

Nudge in Criminal Law

Behavioral Analysis Challenges to Traditional Justification of Punishment in Criminal Law Theories

Diego Moreno-Cruz

Abstract The objection advanced by Harel and Teichman (HT) to governments' reliance on "policy recommendations prescribed by behavioral theorists"—intended to induce compliance with penal rules and thereby prevent crime—can be read as raising twin concerns about the ethical permissibility and practical usefulness of what I call "criminal-nudging policies." This paper does not aim to provide an exhaustive definition of that type of public policy or to defend its legitimacy. Rather, it identifies the challenges these measures pose to traditional theories of criminal law—the framework on which HT's critique rests—and, given the ubiquity of nudging, recognizes behaviorally informed choice architecture as a non-optional parameter for criminal governance; the issue, then, is implementation rather than adoption: namely, how to use it effectively within legal and ethical constraints.

1 Introduction

In this paper, I will offer a set of theoretical reasons for justifying the use of "behavioral economics analysis of law" (BAL), i.e., a class of policy action that consists of the application of tools, tactics, and techniques that rely on findings from cognitive psychological experiments about how the human mental apparatus works. I will focus my analysis on a specific type of that class of policy action that could be named "criminal nudge policy", that is, a behaviorally informed action of the government intended to control people's criminal behavior by a self-conscious choice

A previous Spanish version of this paper was published in Moreno-Cruz (2018b), pp. 99–135.

D. Moreno-Cruz (✉)
Centro de Investigación en Filosofía y Derecho; Universidad Externado de Colombia, Bogotá, Colombia
e-mail: diego.moreno@uexternado.edu.co

S. Zorzetto et al. (eds.), *Developments in Law and Economics in the Italo-Iberoamerican Context*, Economic Analysis of Law in European Legal Scholarship 21, https://doi.org/10.1007/978-3-032-03317-8_8

of an architect about the "architecture choice" of people, that is, the design or shape of the context in which they choose to obey or disobey criminal rules.

For doing so, I object to Harel and Teichmann's (HT) purpose of curbing the widespread enthusiasm of governments to follow "policy prescriptions" formulated from BAL, which aims to lead people to obey penal rules and, hence, prevent crimes from occurring.[1]

They claim that a future success of BAL on criminal law and policy matters depends on the degree to which BAL's enthusiasts cope with the burden of justification created by each one of the following three problems: (1) BAL's assumptions about people's rationality and BAL's justification of criminal law and punishment are inconsistent with the assumptions and justifications of traditional criminal legal theories (*e.g.*, Duff's communicative theory); (2) the predictive force of BAL is compromised by the fact that, from a behavioral science explanation, BAL enthusiasts offer different, and sometimes contradictory, hypotheses about the (probable) outcomes of applying a specific nudge on criminal matters: in other words, there is an indeterminacy about the probable effects of applying this type of policy-instruments in criminal legal contexts; and (3) these instruments are useless if are not aligned with the non-consequentialist intuitional judgments, non-economic reasons and views of people about criminal punishment and policies related with some offences (e.g., fairness of criminal justice system).

I will try to overcome the problems raised by HT. First, I will identify some inaccurate statements on HT's reconstruction of BAL's methodology because they trade on a series of ambiguities. And I will suggest some clarifications to specify the subject matter of HT's argument, i.e., "criminal nudging policy". Even though the term "nudging" does not appear in their essay, their theoretical problems may be understood as ethical permissibility and practical usefulness concerns about applying nudges in criminal policy matters (Sect. 2).[2] Second, I will show that the second issue they raised, which I will call the "methodological problem", is not a problem for BAL but a general problem for social control through the law. I will offer reasons for overcoming the first and third issues HT raised, which I will call the "normative problem" (Sect. 3). To conclude, I will highlight some challenges to traditional criminal legal theories (Sect. 4).

[1] Harel and Teichman (2018), pp. 31–58.

[2] About the use of nudges by Colombia government's policies in financial decision-making, see Moreno-Cruz (2018), pp. 411–445; in healthy eating, private savings and investing decision-making, see Monroy (2017), pp. 211–247; about "behavioral public choice" objections to nudges in Administrative law, see Monroy (2023), pp. 469–509; for an analysis of constitutional (in)validity of using nudges in Chile, see Ponce de León Solís (2019): pp. 345–371.

2 BAL and Choice Architecture

HT reconstruct BAL's approach by confronting it with an Economic Analysis of Law (EAL). Both methods are intended to offer governments prescriptions or recommendations about controlling human behavior. However, HT's reconstruction of BAL is inaccurate in two points that require some clarification to avoid misunderstandings about the subject matter of the problems raised by HT.

(1) The first inaccurate statement of their reconstruction is that EAL assumes that people make their choices based on the costs and benefits of their actions, and that BAL, in contrast, considers that people's choices and actions are also influenced by their beliefs and preferences. In other words, HT claim that EAL does not consider people's beliefs and preferences for its policy recommendations.

However, both EAL and BAL assume instrumental or mean-to-a-end rationality of people in resolving decision problems and that they make their choices based on a cost-benefit analysis that would not be possible without considering that people form in their minds beliefs and preferences; both analytical approaches are based on a belief-preference model of instrumental reasoning of people underlying the traditional "rational decision theory" upon which both methods are built, each one in different ways. Let's see.

According to the rational decision theory, a decision problem is a set of alternative actions, outcomes, and circumstances. The assessments of probabilities (degrees of belief) to the relevant events of the world—that the agent believes might affect the results of the optional acts—and values (or preferences) to each one of the risky outcomes are both represented by numbers that jointly determine an estimate of utility for each of the optional courses of action under consideration.[3] The utility of each action is equivalent to the value assigned to the alternative outcomes attached to the optional action, weighted by its probability.[4] The outcome's value and circumstances' probabilities are subjective in that they reflect the preferences and beliefs of the agent, irrespective of (moral or factual) external reasons for believing and preferring it.[5]

EAL is based on expected utility theory as a logical theory "that prescribes how decisions should be made and as a description of how *Econs* make choices"[6]: to choose the act with the maximum estimated utility, that is, an action that produces an outcome which is at least as good as that of every other possible outcome.

BAL is built upon a cognitive theory of human decision-making intended to describe "how Humans make risky choices, without assuming anything about their rationality"[7]: a cognitive psychological theory about how people's instrumental rationality works. It shows that *Humans* depart systematically from the traditional

[3] Jeffrey (1985), p. 1.

[4] Kahneman (2011), p. 274.

[5] Jeffrey (1985), p. 1.

[6] Kahneman (2011), p. 270.

[7] Kahneman (2011), p. 271.

(economic) theory of rational decision in the two senses or uses that economists make of it: either as a normative theory of choice that offers a set of logic and axiomatic propositions for assessing values to outcomes and probabilities to world's circumstances correctly, to achieve what it already wants, prefer or value and as a descriptive theory of decision-making process of *Econs*.[8]

By relying on the description of Humans' decision-making, the cognitive theory offers a set of psychological propositions that explains why people choose systematically and then, predictably, to behave in an instrumentally incorrect way to maximize their utility in the eyes of an Econ. The systematic deviations that are identified from the normative axioms of the decision theory are called "biases", which are explained and predicted based on the identification of systematic application of "heuristics" in the decision-making process of people: mental shortcuts that reduce the complexity and costs related with the concentration and time required for gathering and evaluating information, that is, for fixing the set of alternatives actions and assigning both values to outcomes and probabilities to the circumstances of the world; or as merely affective reactions to the frame of the context in which they make choices and regardless of any conscious purpose of saving cognitive costs and time.[9] Those mental shortcuts usually produce a correct outcome; they work well. However, it is also true that they lead systematically and, hence, are predictable to people to commit errors (biases), that is, to form preferences and beliefs that lead them to choose an action that is inadequate for maximizing their utility: that is, an action that would be dismissed by the correct assessment of value and probabilities made by an *Econ*. Therefore, heuristics help explain and predict cognitive biases and, hence, people's behavior.

Cognitive theory is suitable for describing, explaining, and predicting human behavior. Still, it is not a normative theory for evaluating the available information and guiding people's behavior. It is also true that the decision theory indicates how to assess values and probabilities correctly. Still, it is neither suitable for describing nor guiding people's behavior.[10] Based on the explanations and predictions of cognitive psychological theory, BAL offers a set of policy prescriptions that are intended to correct or use cognitive biases of human beings to fulfill the normative goals of the legal system: that is, the reasons that justify why an act-type is subject to legal prohibitions (e.g., criminalization), obligations and permissions. BAL uses a descriptive theory for normative aims within an economic frame. So, BAL cannot be considered a theory but a set of policy prescriptions intended to make compelling law obedience and fulfill different legal system normative goals.

A central question of BAL has been how the normative goals of the legal system can be made to entwine with what is, or might be, known about human psychology. With this question in mind, BAL prescribes policies that rely on behavioral science insights. A set of explanations/predictions that complement or undermine what

[8] Kahneman (2011), p. 270.

[9] Tversky and Kahneman (1981), p. 458.

[10] Tversky and Kahneman (1981), p. 458.

EAL has done to answer this theoretical question.[11] BAL enthusiasts claim that policy prescriptions that rely on findings from cognitive psychology experiments are more accurate and reliable than policy prescriptions of EAL that are not behaviorally informed, that is, policies that do not consider how the background of people's minds —unintentional mental elements: affective reactions, capacities, abilities, habits, dispositions[12]—conditions and shape their behavior (in)dependently of deliberative intention, that is, policy-actions that do not take into account the mental background of people which is presupposed by acting intentionally in one and not in other possible way. The greater descriptive accuracy of human decision-making leads to more predictive reliability of human behavior and, hence, to greater effectiveness of policy actions in fulfilling normative goals.[13]

To sum up, both EAL and BAL are based on "rational decision theory" but in different ways. EAL is based on it as a normative theory about how an *Econ* decides how to behave. Behavioral economics is based on rational decision theory, with both descriptive and explanatory aims: to demonstrate and explain systematic deviations human decision-making from this theory. So, BAL is based on a cognitive theory that uses rational decision theory as a reference point for the correction of decision-making of Econs from which it is possible to identify cognitive biases and describe, explain, and predict human behavior. Therefore, EAL and BAL consider the beliefs and preferences of the decision-makers.[14]

(2) The second inaccurate statement of HT's reconstruction of BAL's methodology rests in their claim that according to BAL's enthusiasts, the policy-maker influences people's choices by changing "the ways the world seems to be without changing the way the world is". However, an essential claim of BAL's enthusiasts is, precisely, that "how we believe that the world is" is an outcome of a "choice architecture".[15] Let's see.

Each decision presupposes a "choice architecture", that is, "the background conditions for people's choices"[16]: a particular way in which the options, circumstances, and outcomes of decision problems are arrayed, framed, or structured; the shape, or design, of the context in which people choose one of the optional courses of action. So, "a choice architecture will nudge" people's behavior because people's beliefs and preferences about which action to perform depend on the choice architecture of the decision problem. Consequently, nudging is pervasive and ubiquitous,[17] whether

[11] Sunstein et al. (1998), pp. 2080–2081.

[12] Searle (2010), pp. 31–32.

[13] Jolls et al. (1998), pp. 1471–1550.

[14] For a more detail comparison of methodological differences between EAL and BAL, see Moreno-Cruz (2014), pp. 93–124.

[15] Thaler and Sunstein (2009), pp. 20–24, 56–57, 83–102; Sunstein (2016), chap. 2.

[16] Sunstein (2016), p. 22.

[17] Sunstein (2016), pp. 36–37, 76.

choice architecture is self-consciously designed or an outcome of an unconscious psychological process: "There is no getting away from this".[18]

So, it is reasonable to consider that "[l]aw creates some form of choice architecture",[19] which "attempted to shape both individuals' lives and the common culture" by both sanctions and (positive) incentives.[20]

However, a nudge is understood as a self-conscious intervention of policymakers in the mental activity of people that consists of slightly changing their choice architecture. It is intended to lead people to predictable and replicable reactions in their behavior and, therefore, to obtain socially beneficial outcomes. A minimum degree of interference that neither forbids any option —that is, that does not reduce the set of available options— nor imposes significant economic costs or unreasonable cognitive efforts on people for choosing to "opt-out" "cheaply and easily" of the nudge.[21] Accordingly, a nudge is an intentional exercise of power by the government[22] that is intended "to steer people in particular directions but also allow them to go their own way".[23] Therefore, nudges are different from a self-conscious and behaviorally informed policy-action of the government that changes the architecture choice of people by forbidding some option or by imposing significant economic incentives on them: e.g., "mandates, ban and incentives".[24] Nudge "is a policy intervention for redirecting an agent's choices by very slightly altering their choice conditions so that the interference is kept to a minimum".[25]

Governments may intentionally use their power to alter people's behavior in different decision-making contexts and, hence, to fulfill other social aims of legal systems through various nudges.

Some nudges steer people in the direction they want to go; others steer people in the direction architects wish them to. Some nudges are used to prevent people from harming themselves with their actions. Some others are used to prevent people from harming others.[26] Some nudges are intended to improve both social welfare and the self-regarding interests of decision-makers, while others are designed to achieve the former outcome rather than the latter[27]. Some nudges (e.g., labels, warnings, and reminders) counteract behavioral biases (*e.g.*, present bias and optimistic bias[28]),

---

[18] Waldron (2014).

[19] Sunstein (2016), p. 20; Sunstein (2018), p. 62.

[20] Green (2012), p. xxxii.

[21] Yeung (2012), pp. 122–148, 129; Thaler and Sunstein (2009), p. 9.

[22] Searle (2010), p. 155.

[23] Sunstein (2016), p. 21.

[24] Sunstein (2018), p. 65.

[25] However, nudge is an equivocal concept that is far from having a clear content-meaning: it is used in different and also contradictory senses, see Mongin and Cozic (2018), pp. 107–124.

[26] Sunstein (2016), p. 32.

[27] Yeung (2012), pp. 123–124.

[28] Sunstein (2018), p. 64: Present bias refers to people's tendency to give more weight to present desires than to long term beneficial outcomes. Optimistic bias refers to the tendency that our actions lead to outcomes that turn out better to us than bad outcomes that statistical data shows it

other nudges (*e.g.*, default rules) work because of the bias (e.g., inertia and procrastination), and others are intended to make easier to people to get wherever they want to go, regardless of any behavioral biases, for example, by disclosing relevant information to the decision-maker.[29]

Some of these nudges target people's deliberative capacities to make them actively or consciously choose a particular course of action based on the content-meaning of the data of the decision problem, *i.e.*, System 2 nudges. Nudges that are intended to inform or to educate people to choose better: e.g., labels, warnings, reminders, etc. Other nudges target the intuitive, irreflexive, automatic, cognitive mental activity of people to lead them to choose a particular course of action as an unconscious reaction to the stimuli produced in their mind by how the decision problem is framed, regardless of the content-meaning of its data; nudges that are not intended to inform or to educate, but either to counteract biases or to use an (unchangeable) heuristic to produce a desirable social outcome. In such cases, people behave in a certain way without realizing or being aware that their actions or abstentions to act are the result of the nudge's influence on their choices. Default rules are an example of this kind of nudge. Nudges that do not enhance human agency or active choosing of people, i.e., System 1 nudges.[30]

So, if it is true that the beliefs and preferences that people form in their minds are an outcome of a "choice architecture", therefore, HT's statement that BAL's enthusiasts advocate for prescriptions that manipulate people's choices could be understood as recommendations to lie to them about the data of decision's problems or about which the context of their choice is. Suppose this is the sense of their statement. In that case, therefore, it is something that, in the case of being true, would be a bad and reproachable attitude of policymakers, as would be the same for all the policy actions of governments based on a lie to make people obey the law. In this sense, this is an unquestionable ethical objection.[31]

However, using the architectural choice of people does not necessarily mean that the policy action would be a lie, neither when nudges are physical—nudges that work on illusion bias of people's perception, *e.g.*, painting stripes on roads to create the illusion (false belief) that the vehicle is speeding up for making drivers slow in zones (e.g. school zones) where there is a risk of causing harm to other users of the road—nor when nudges are psycho-physical—nudges that work on how a decision problem is framed—.[32]

---

is obtained with such an action. If I smoke is because I believe that bad things won't happen to me. Nudge counteract these biases by emphasizing the long-term risks of smoking.

[29] Sunstein (2018), p. 64.

[30] Sunstein (2016), pp. 122, 149–153. For a analytical reconstruction of the nudges and some objections about its use, see Moreno-Cruz (2018), pp. 411–445.

[31] Sunstein (2016), pp. 3, 60.

[32] Yeung (2012), pp. 132–133.

2.1 Criminal-Nudge-Policies

Criminal law is a coercive system that shapes the context of people's choices by forbidding them from choosing available options. Penal rules are "orders backed by threats" that are "[…] the expression of a wish that *others* should do or abstain from doing certain things". People with more weight reasons for disobeying the rules "[…] are provided with a motive for conformity in the sanction added to the rule".[33] So, penal rules are forms of choice architecture that are intended to be obeyed by appealing to the active-choosing-capacity of people for acting in the way that is desired for the architect, that is, the capacity of people to consider the rules as (moral or prudential) reasons for action.

Penal rules are coercive instruments of social control that "[…] express and channel social power"[34] through their content-meaning, that is, as reasons for action, and also through other forms that are independent of the content-meaning of the rules itself and that are used for steering people to obey them.

For a beneficial social outcome, the lawmaker can create a penal rule relying on behavioral sciences to use rules as behavioral informed tools for achieving legal aims. However, criminal rules are tools that alter people's behavior by forbidding a type-act and by imposing significant (des)incentives for (dis)obeying what the law requires to do or abstain from doing, that is, by committing a token-act of that type of criminal actions. Therefore, a penal rule is not a nudge in the strict sense; controlling people's behavior by orders backed by threats is not a token of the control type of nudging.

Even though it is possible to nudge people to lead them to obey penal rules by criminal-nudging, that is, a type of behaviorally informed action that is intended to alter people's behavior by appealing to the stimuli produced in their minds and that maintains freedom of people to choose to obey or to face with some degree of probability a punishment that the rule itself attached to its disobedience. These interventions in people's minds are self-conscious choices made by lawmakers through framing the criminal rule in some way or by policymakers by shaping the context in which people choose to obey or disobey a penal rule. Both are criminal nudges that are used to prevent crime from occurring, that is, interventions that use people's choice architecture to avoid them from harming others, and not the kind of nudges intended to prevent people from harming themselves with their actions.

On the one hand, people can be nudged to obey the law by appealing to their intuitive cognitive activity, that is, to the unconscious reactions of people to the stimuli produced by the shape or design of the legal rule itself, regardless of its content-meaning as a reason for action. For example, it has been shown that people react differently to normative sentences that express the same legal rule, that is, that have identical content meaning but are formulated or framed in different deontic modal terms: "You are prohibited from carrying out more than one of the following

[33] Hart (1961), pp. 39, 42.

[34] Green (2012), p. xxxii.

actions"; "You are permitted to carry out only one of the following actions". The first sentence, "You are prohibited", makes it easier for people to know what action is impermissible than the second sentence ", You are permitted.[35]

On the other hand, some criminal nudges exert their influence through techniques of social control that are not carried in the body of the rules: slightly changing some aspect of the choice architecture of the context of people's choice (to obey or to disobey a criminal rule) to lead them to conform to what the law requires them to do or abstain from doing.

Some nudges target the deliberative or active-choosing capacity of people. For example, public educations campaigns, propaganda, that are used to convey a message for making explicit the reasons that underlies the criminalization of a class of action, that is, why to disobey a criminal rule is considered morally wrong by society; to inform scrupulously statistical data about detections and convictions of some class of criminal actions, to counteract optimistic biases of people or to protect them against deception and manipulation produced by self-conscious choice architecture of private architects; that is, policy-nudges for counteracting private-nudges that are intended to lead people to commit crimes.

Some nudges work by appealing to the automatic cognitive activity of people, that is, for making people behave in a certain way as a reaction to the stimuli produced in their minds by how the problem of choice is presented to them, and independently of any reason for action. Some of these nudges use heuristics that people already follow to lead them to obey the law, for example, by reporting some event of detection and/or conviction of a crime to trigger the "availability heuristic" that leads people to predictable bias in judgments, that is, a nudge that works because of people over-estimate the rate and relevance of events relying on the ease of memory to retrieve instances of a class of events. An extended coverage in the media of these events prompts in people's minds the belief that instances of that event have occurred more times than those indicated by relevant statistical data or considerations. It is not by chance that authoritarian regimes worry so much about which events must be covered by the media and which events must not be reported.[36]

---

[35] "You are permitted to carry out only one of the following actions:

Take the apple or the orange, or both.

Take the pear or the orange, or both.

Are you permitted to take the orange?"

"You are prohibited from carrying out more than one of the following actions:

Take the apple or the orange, or both.

Take the pear or the orange, or both.

Are you permitted to take the orange?"

The logical answer to both problems is "no". If you take the orange, you are carrying two actions. People react differently if the problem is framed in terms of permission or prohibition, and people more easily react correctly to the second framing than the first one, based on mental models that people construct as mental representations of the content-meaning of those sentences. Those reactions show that people commit inferential errors in deontic reasoning, that is, "deontic illusions", Bucciarelli and Johnson-Laird (2005), pp. 183–188.

[36] Kahneman (2011), pp. 8, 59–70.

The nudges that BAL's enthusiasts prescribe may well be understood as a set of deontic sentences that are used as directives or technical rules to be followed in policymaking by governments, that is, rules that indicate "the *means* to be used for the sake of attaining a certain *end*"—e.g., how to use architecture choice for preventing crime from occurring—, and that presuppose an "anankastic proposition",[37] that is, the verification of an explanation and prediction of people behavior in particular contexts of choice that is based on behavioral findings from cognitive psychology's laboratory experiments. The reliability and accuracy of the technical rule, e.g., "if you, government, want to increment deterrence's rate, that is, prevent people from not paying taxes, then use samples of taxpayers selected at random at the beginning of the year," presuppose the anankastic proposition "if samples of taxpayers selected at random at the beginning of the year are (not) being used people's deterrence from not paying taxes will (not) become incremented".

3 Theoretical Problems About Criminal Nudges

HT argue that future success of BAL on criminal law and policy matters depends on the degree to which BAL's enthusiasts cope with the burden of justification created by three problems that can be reformulated as normative and methodological concerns about applying "criminal-nudging-policies" for preventing crime from occurring: (1) incongruence problem with the assumptions about people's rationality and criminal law justifications of traditional criminal normative legal theory; (2) methodological indeterminacy problem about the probable effects of applying a "nudge" in criminal legal contexts of choice; (3) to use criminal-nudges for preventing crime from occurring is not aligned with the non-consequentialist intuitional judgments, non-economic reasons and views of people about criminal punishment and policies related with some offences.

First, I will analyse (2), i.e., the methodological problem. Second, I will analyse problems (1) and (3): the first one has to do with the assumption about people's rationality for (dis)obeying the penal rules, and the second with the reasons that people, in general, have for believing that the policy-actions of the policymaker for controlling criminal people's behavior are (im)permissible, i.e., normative problem.

3.1 Methodological Problem

It is impossible to disagree with HT's claim that "What is required at this point is empirical research of *actual criminal behavior* that will corroborate, refute or refine the hypotheses set forth in the behavioral literature". However, what is questionable

[37] von Wright (1963), pp. 9–11; 101.

about their argument is their suggestion that this is an exclusive practical necessity of criminal policy recommendations as the criminal law field is unique. The methodological indeterminacy problem that TH points out concerns all kinds of public policy, so it could not be a challenge only for applying BAL for analyzing criminal policy matters. Instead, this problem requires the technical duty of paying attention to empirical explanations/predictions in decision-making and policy action and analyzing people's actions as if they were irrational.

On the other hand, if TH's claim that people have non-economic-reasons for justifying criminal control—that is, the third problem raised by them—relies on empirical hypotheses from cognitive psychology experiments, then it suffers from the same indeterminacy problem raised by them about the application of criminal-nudges. Therefore, the methodological problem does not challenge only BAL's policies. It is a problem that challenges the justification of any legal control and governmental administration of the law.

3.2 Normative Problem

Nudges are policy tools intended to (re)direct people to choose to follow the law either by appealing to their deliberative capacities for active choosing or by appealing to their unconscious and irreflexive psychological choosing process. In the latter case, people are unaware that their choice is an outcome of such intervention: a reaction to the stimuli that the intervention produces in their minds. Nudge is an exemplar of BAL policy prescriptions.

So, BAL enthusiasm for criminal nudging assumes the means-to-an-end rationality of people and presupposes an instrumental justification of criminal law.

On the one hand, when people face the problem of choosing between obeying or disobeying what the law requires them to do or abstain from doing, they choose the option that they judge to be, compared with the alternative option(s), an adequate means to achieve what they already want or prefer or value. To choose to disobey the law expresses the disposition of an individual to face the risk of suffering a punishment which is previously and scrupulously warned to her by the rule itself, relying on her subjective assessments of values to the alternative outcomes and probabilities to circumstances that condition the occurrence of each one of the risky outcomes.

On the other hand, criminal nudging is justified for promoting compliance with the law. A behaviorally informed policymaker knows that people use heuristics that produce predictable biases in judgments, that is, systematic errors in assessing values to outcomes and probabilities to the circumstances of the world; she also knows that choice architecture is helpful for counteracting, or using, behavioral bias in order to steer people to obey the law; she also knows that she can nudge people by persuasion—e.g. public educations campaigns—, that is, by making explicit the moral justification that underlies why a type of action is criminalized by the lawmaker and why it is justified to punish to those who choose to commit tokens of that type, therefore, by appealing to system 2, that is, to reasons for acting and to deliberative capacity of people's active choosing; she also knows that she can nudge people to conform with penal rules by appealing to system 1, that is, to their unconscious cognitive reactions to stimuli produced by the way in which decision problem is presented to them, and not by offering to them reasons for action, that is, people are unaware that they choose to obey the law by the influence that the nudge exerts in their choices.

Both are nudges that are intended to prevent crimes from occurring. Even though nudging for obtaining this purpose has constraints. These interventions in people's minds must be exerted without limiting or changing the options of choice that are available to them (i.e., to obey or to disobey) and without imposing significant (economic or cognitive) costs on choosers, that is, that choosers can easily and cheaply opt for choosing a different course of action (to disobey) from the action that is preferred by the architect (to obey).

TH argue that the criminal nudging policy that BAL enthusiasts advocate conflicts with both the agent's rationality assumption and justification of punishment of "traditional criminal law theories", more precisely, with traditional deontological theories of retribution and trial rational communication (1) and, also BAL's instrumental assumptions and justifications are inconsistent with non-consequentialist intuitional judgments, non-economic reasons and views of people about criminal punishment and policies (2).

(1) Criminal law is not about controlling human behavior and inducing people to conform to penal rules to prevent (or deter) crime from occurring; it is, instead, about persuading people to conform rationally to them (HT). That is, people deserve to be treated as rational human beings.

BAL perceives people as bad human beings: people (dis)obey the law based on the probability of being sanctioned, that is, motivated by rules that are back up by threats, and not by the reason that committing an act-token of the act-type that is criminalized by a penal rule is morally wrong. Criminal rules are moral reasons for action, and criminal law is justified for making people *follow* them as guides for their behavior; that is, rules are not created merely to be *observed* for prudential reasons. Therefore, from this approach, people's rationality is not an instrumental one—"it is not about which is the best action to promote their own interests"—but a morally informed rationality: people are perceived as human beings with the capacity of making autonomous choices based on what is "right and wrong, moral and immoral".[38]

This normative inconsistency problem is illustrated by confronting BAL with "Duff's theory of communication" (the "curial view"[39]).

The central purpose of criminal law is to call the suspect of offence to account in criminal courts. Trials are an opportunity to engage in a "rational discourse between

[38] Harel and Teichman (2018), p. 36.

[39] Edwards (2018).

the criminal and the state".[40] The trial is central in procedural criminal law proceedings and substantive criminal law.[41] Trials allow defendants to offer reasons for denying the accusation against them or pleading a defense.[42] The proceedings through which this rational communication is possible have an intrinsic value: to pass from the attribution of responsibility to the imposition of just-deserved punishment as an outcome of the moral rational discussion between the criminal and the state.[43]

The primary purpose of criminal law is not to impose a justified punishment but to determine if the suspected offender is responsible for her behavior and to punish her if she does not offer "adequate" excuses for what she did. Most importantly, the trial has the function of prompting the offender to recognize that she has committed a wrong and deserves to be punished for such behavior. Also, suppose it is the case that the excusing conditions are proved. In that case, a trial triggers the recognition in the rest of society that the defendant does not deserve to be punished for her behavior.[44] Therefore, the primary purpose of criminal law is fulfilled even if punishment is not imposed on the defendant as an outcome of the trial.[45]

The primary concern raised by HT for claiming such theoretical normative inconsistency is that, from traditional criminal law theory approaches, "criminal law is about clarifying rationally whether a wrong has been committed and in the appropriate cases triggering a recognition on the part of the offender that he has committed a wrong". The criminal is perceived "as a rational being who needs to be educated and transformed" and not as a gullible stimulus machine that is easily fooled and manipulated. So, "exploiting cognitive errors and irrational behavior" for preventing crime is a manipulative and fraudulent policy action that treats people like "automatons", that is, "as potentially dangerous beasts that ought to be controlled by exploiting their weaknesses".[46]

(2) Based on empirical backgrounds, HT's claim that BAL's instrumental assumptions and justifications are inconsistent with non-consequentialist intuitional judgments, non-economic reasons, and people's views about criminal punishment and policies. The empirical hypothesis works well for justifying the theoretical beliefs of the retributive punishment theories.

Suppose a token-act of the type of action forbidden by a general rule is committed. In that case, the offender deserves to suffer the legal consequence that the rule attached to the commission of acts of that type; that is, if events of rule violation occurred, it is justified to punish the guilty wrongdoer. Punishment is justified because the offender deserves to suffer for a guilty wrong committed by her—"the

[40] Harel and Teichman (2018), pp. 36–40.

[41] Edwards (2018).

[42] Edwards (2018).

[43] Duff (2012), pp. 145–168.

[44] Duff (2012), pp. 155 and ff.

[45] Duff (2012), p. 148.

[46] Harel and Teichman (2018), p. 38.

suffering must be proportionate to the wrongdoer's guilt"[47]—but it is not justified to inflict suffering to the wrongdoer neither for deterring people from committing token-acts of that type nor for incapacitating the offender from commits future crimes for the period that she will be, deprived from her liberty, in prison. The only reason for imposing punitive suffering on a criminal is that she deserves it. In other words, justified punishment must be imposed for desert reasons (the "punitive view"[48]).

Likewise, for other theories of retribution, the threat of punishment warned by penal rules expresses some normative moral meaning—*e.g.*, the community's disapproval of criminal's actions; those who commit a crime deserve to be punished—and then, penal rules are irreducible to merely be a negative incentive, or motive, for obeying the law.

This theoretical approach is consistent with empirical findings about non-economic people's views, non-consequentialist intuitions, and justification of criminal punishment. The size of the sanctions is independent of the probability of detection. Criminal punishment is not about deterring crime from occurring but inflicting justified desert suffering on wrongdoers, if and only if that punishment is attuned with people's moral intuitions about the fairness of the criminal legal system. If the criminal justice system deviates from what people's moral (non-consequentialist) intuitions about fairness are, then people have reasons for disobeying what criminal law requires from them; that is, the effectiveness of obedience to the law becomes diminished.

So, from this claim, it is possible to conclude that if penal rules and criminal control policies are not aligned with non-consequentialist intuitional judgments and views that people have about criminal punishment and policies (at least, related to some offences), then nudging is pointless to make a practical difference in human mental activity.

From deontological traditional criminal law theories of retribution and rational communication of trial, criminal nudging could be considered an impermissible and morally reproachable policy action. It is impermissible to use the imposition of suffering on a criminal as a policymaker's self-conscious architecture choice intended to deter others, and those who are who are punished, from committing crimes in the future.

3.2.1 A False Problem

The theoretical, normative inconsistency problem HT raises an ambiguity: they do not make a difference between the influence of the law exerted through penal rules as reasons for action and the tactics the government uses to make people obey penal rules (1). This problem is flawed in two senses: BAL and deontological legal

[47] Gardner (2008), p. xvi, note: 7.

[48] Edwards (2018).

criminal theories of retribution (and rational trial communication) are incomparable because each one of these analytical approaches is different and refers to various problems and functions of criminal law (2), and these functions are not inconsistent with each other; that is, instrumental justification of criminal punishment is consistent with a non-instrumental justification of just-desert-punishment imposition to the defendant as an outcome of the trial, as a mix theory of criminal law could accept, e.g., Hart's deontological theory of prevention (3).

(1) The normative problem raised by HT is ambiguous about the control of human action through rules and policy making: that is, this challenge to BAL's policies refers to different conceptions of the influence of the law in humans' mind: to make people obey the law through penal rules is different from making people obey the law through strategies or tactics of governmental administration of the law, that is, policy-tools that are different from the rules as reasons for action.

To obtain social outcomes that are "beneficial" in the light of one or more of the normative goals of the legal system, the law is intended to alter people's behavior predictably through the "medium" of the influence that legal rules exert on their minds.[49] This statement presupposes that for the law to be an effective tool, its obedience should be obtained through legal rules that people can follow as moral or prudential reasons for action. However, legal rules cannot be self-enforced. Then, in contexts of the choice of particular people, the law must be subjected to governmental administration. In other words, sometimes it is necessary to use policy instruments (techniques, tactics) that are different from the content-meaning of the legal rules—i.e., as prudential or moral reasons for action—for leading people to do or abstain from doing what the law requires from them.

Criminal nudging is precisely to apply policy tools of law administration, that is, a class of policy-action that refers to the intentional exercise of the social power of governments over people's psychological activity for attaining effective obedience to the law to prevent people from disobeying penal rules, by instruments that are different of the legal rules as reasons for action.

Therefore, the normative problem raised by HT is about obeying the penal rules as reasons for action—criminal law is about making people rationally conform to what penal rules require them to do or abstain from doing; people obey the law whether the reasons for obeying it are attuned with the intuitional views about the fairness of the criminal justice system—and not about the law-administration for making people obey the penal rules through means that are different from the rules itself, or from its underlying reasons (moral or prudential) for obeying it.

(2) Based on the explanations and predictions of cognitive psychological theory, BAL offers a set of policy prescriptions intended to correct or use cognitive biases of human beings. BAL uses a descriptive and psychological cognitive theory for normative aims within an economic frame. Then, BAL cannot be considered as a theory but as a set of policy prescriptions that is intended to make effective (legal) obedience to the law and, hence, to fulfill different normative goals of the legal

[49] Hart (1968), pp. 39, 44.

system, that is, the reasons that justify why a type-act is subject to legal prohibitions (e.g., criminalization), obligations and permissions. Therefore, it is not easy to talk about BAL as a theory, neither as a set of axioms for assessing values to outcomes and probabilities to circumstances correctly, nor as a set of moral values from which it is possible to know how to act in a particular situation and context of choice. Then, BAL differs from the theoretical character of traditional criminal legal theories as argued by HT.

On the other hand, the function of criminal law in Duff's theory is to call (even through coercion) the suspect of a criminal offence to account in criminal courts. This function has to do with the response of the law to the detection of the commission of a crime—"*a fait accompli*"—and then with the problem regarding whether the attribution of responsibility and the imposition of punishment to the suspected offender is justified. The criminal-nudging policy advocated by BAL, on the other hand, has to do with a different function of criminal law and punishment, i.e., to prevent criminal behavior from occurring.

The primary function of criminal law could not be to call suspected offenders to account in criminal trials and to punish them if they do not have a satisfactory answer, considering that they are excused for doing what they did. The functions of imposing deserved punishment and trial's opportunity to engage in rational discourse with a criminal presuppose that the function of preventing crime has failed in the first place. The former are expected functions that criminal law must fulfill—this is unquestionable—but only if criminal law does not fulfill the latter. That is, "the principal functions of the law as a means of social control are not to be seen in private litigation or prosecutions, which represent vital but still ancillary provisions for the system's failures. It is to be seen in the diverse ways in which the law is used to control, to guide, and to plan life out of court".[50]

The function of rational communication in criminal law trials cannot prevent people from committing a crime in advance, as the function of preventing crime is useless concerning whether it is justified to punish the defendant who offers reasons on trial for excusing her from what she already did. Also, the instrumental or prudential reasons that the wrongdoer had for believing and valuing with the highest utility the action she did do not work to justify or excuse her from being responsible for committing a wrong. E.g., "I did it because I believed that the probability of being detected was low and that the satisfaction of doing it was higher than the value that I assigned to being punished".

Whether it is accepted that the retributive claim (which is aligned with the intuitional judgments of people) that the primary function of criminal law and punishment is not to prevent crimes from occurring, it is also true that to prevent crime is an unintentional consequence of criminal law-making. When a lawmaker creates a penal rule that criminalizes a type of action, it is unreasonable to deny that the exercise of this normative power of criminalization is intended to alter people's behavior to make crimes go uncommitted; that is, the punishment has a looking-forward

[50] Hart (1961), p. 40.

function of avoiding criminal behavior of people. It is difficult to imagine that lawmakers' criminalization of some action does not usually aim to prevent people from causing harm to others by performing an action-token of that type of criminal act. It is a fact that cannot be denied by the just-desert theories of punishment. To impose punishment is not only justified for inflicting on the wrongdoer a deserved suffering. The imposition of suffering must be based, with or without, on instrumental reasons for avoiding future suffering, rather that on the suffering itself.[51]

Also, whether it is the retributive claim that to prevent crime must not be a reason for judges to impose a punishment—that is, to impose punitive suffering in a criminal for deterring others from committing a crime—to deter is an unavoidable effect, even though unintentional, of punishing a part of the criminal process. The same could be said about the incapacitation produced with punishment (e.g., with prison): it is not the outcome the punisher intends to obtain with its punishing action. Incapacitation prevents those who have been punished from committing future crimes, and it is possible that it also works to prevent others from misbehaving in such a way.

(3) There are also traditional criminal law theories that assume the mean-to-an-end rationality of people and claim that criminal law's function is to prevent people from committing criminal offences, *e.g.*, Hart's theory. Punitive measures impose a cost justified only by the countervailing benefit of reducing future criminal conduct. The number of uncommitted crimes would measure the success of the criminal law system.[52] Criminal punishment is justified because it helps discourage people from disobeying the law.

The reason that the rule by itself offers for being obeyed usually coincides with people's underlying moral or prudential reasons for obeying it, e.g., because they accept what the legal rules require, or to avoid the risk of being punished or to follow what others do, etc.[53]

The obedience of the law is a rule-following practice, and it is not an accidental or mere habitual pattern of behavior.[54] Then, it requires general obedience to the law, which they accept, because what a penal rule requires to do or abstain from is valuable, regardless of the consequent sanction attached to its disobedience, i.e., its legal effectiveness.[55] In this scenario, threats are irrelevant in the practical reasoning of people: there is no constraint on doing what someone wants to do.[56] The threat serves as a motive for obedience to penal rules, constraining only those who, without such motivation, would be inclined not to comply with the rule's requirements.

[51] Hart (1968), p. 160.

[52] Hart (1968), p. 47.

[53] Gardner (2008), p. xliii.

[54] Hart (1961).

[55] Gardner (2008), p. xliii.

[56] Searle (2010), p. 160.

A threat of punishment is a negative incentive for discouraging criminal behavior: if you choose misbehavior, then you face the risk of being punished. That is, you must "pay a cost". However, punishment is more than a mere negative incentive. Criminal rules have a normative meaning, that is, that criminal behavior is morally wrong,[57] and they are "meant to be taken seriously as a standard of behavior [...] Punishment is different from a mere tax on a course of conduct [...] the first involves, as the second does not, an offence or breach of duty in the form of a violation of a rule set up to guide the conduct of ordinary citizens".[58]

Disobedience of penal rules does not imply that rules are irrelevant in the practical reasoning of people but that they have internal reasons that weigh more than the reasons for rational conforming to what the rule prescribes to them. In other words, it is possible to consider that people obey a penal rule because they assign moral value to the outcome that is obtained for doing or abstaining from doing what the rule requires from them, that is, a value that they are personally concerned to maximize: e.g., do not commit theft maximize the moral value of respecting others property, or doing what the law requires because is required by the law. However, it is possible to consider that the reasons for maximizing this value are *pro tanto*, that is, defeasible reasons: to commit theft to maximize a different value that people are personally concerned most, e.g., to commit theft to buy an expensive medicament to save the life of a beloved relative. So, criminal rules are "[...] reasons for exercising choice in the direction of obedience, leaving to individuals to choose".[59] The criminal can weigh the cost which she assigns to obey the law against the satisfaction that could be obtained for disobeying it, weighted by the probability of not being detected and punished: "if the sanctions of the criminal law are applied, the pains of punishment will for each individual represent the price of some satisfaction obtained from the breach of the law".[60]

Dignity implies recognizing that everyone is a "choosing being"[61] that takes care of their concerns and is provided with instrumental reasoning to reach this purpose with their chosen action. Individuals who need to know what the courts will do and want to know exante the material consequences of their actions. People can predict "the incidence of the public force through the instrumentality of the courts" and, based on this prediction, choose prudently one of the alternative courses of action.[62] This instrumental account of people's rationality for obeying the law "[...] can sound like very cold, if not immoral attitude toward the criminal law, general obedience to which we regard as an essential part of a decent social order. But this attitude seems repellent only if we assume that all criminal laws are ones whose operation we approve. To be realistic we must also think of bad and repressive criminal laws;

[57] Sunstein (2016), p. 19.

[58] Hart (1968), p. 44; Hart (1961), p. 39.

[59] Hart (1968), p. 44.

[60] Hart (1968), p. 48.

[61] Hart (1968), p. 49.

[62] Holmes (1897).

in South Africa, Nazi Germany, Soviet Russia, and no doubt elsewhere, we might be thankful to have their badness mitigated by the fact that they fall only on those who have obtained a satisfaction form knowingly doing what they forbid".[63]

On the other hand, the communicative function of the criminal process and the preventive function of criminal nudging are not mutually exclusive. The functions of the criminal law including prevention, imposition of justified punishments, and provision of opportunities for rational communication in a criminal trial, are complementary and consistent in maximizing free choice and individual freedom within a coercive criminal system. Justified punishment presupposes a guilt relation between a wrong and wrongdoer; therefore, a distinction between innocent and guilty persons: to punish an innocent is immoral.[64] Even though unjustified punishment is an undesirable risky outcome, and its occurrence is an unavoidable bad outcome —that is, it must be accepted with some tolerable degree of probability (Hart, 1969)— the trial is an opportunity for verifying that excusing conditions are not present and then for imposing a justified punishment on the offender: "we look on excusing conditions as something that *protects* the individual against the claims of rest of society".[65]

So, the functions of imposing justified punishment and rational communication on trial are consistent with the assumption of instrumental rationality of people: they enhance the capacity of individuals to make more reliable predictions about the consequences of their own choices, that is, to behave intentionally in one way and not in another possible way. *e.g.*, the defendant is not liable to punishment if there are "excusing conditions" for considering that from her internal point of view, her action was unintentional, that is, on account of her mental condition, she must be excused, because it would be unjust to punish her for something that she did unintentionally.[66]

Both the prevention function and the (no) imposition of justified punishment as an outcome of a trial are complementary for maximizing free choice and individual freedom within the coercive framework of a criminal system.[67] Assuming that people (dis)obey what is required by criminal rules based on instrumental reasoning is consistent with the idea of the rule of law guiding human action through rules, that is, by reason. The criminal rules provide legal guidance by offering warnings about the imposition of punitive suffering to those who choose to commit a crime. So, criminal rules announce specific standards of behavior and the sanctions attached to deviation, leaving individuals to choose between obeying or paying.[68] Individuals can plan their own lives if they know how to behave so that criminal punishment

[63] Hart (1968), p. 47.
[64] Gardner (2008), p. xviii.
[65] Hart (1968), p. 44.
[66] Hart (1968), p. 47.
[67] Hart (1968), p. 47.
[68] Hart (1968), p. 44.

does not interfere in their lives: that is, the capacity to avoid breaking the law and, hence, criminal punishment.[69]

This does not mean that the law alters people's behavior only through goads. However, as a "choosing system" that guides people to behave in a particular way, and not in other possible ways: "We must cease to regard the law simply as a system of stimuli goading the individual".[70] Law is legally effective in a unique way that is irreducible to an effective goad. Law is legally effective because its rules guide people, that is, by offering authoritative rules as reasons for action. Law is legally effective if rules are followed, not merely observed, by people. It does not mean to reject the aspect of the goading effectiveness of the law, but that the law, to be effective, must be generally obeyed in legally effective terms and, exceptionally, merely observed by people.

Therefore, the rule of law is a means to different aims that cannot be maximized together: free choice and effectiveness of the law.[71] The freedom of people to obey or disobey the law can lead to widespread disobedience or obedience to rules for prudential reasons. Then, fulfilling the aim of enhancing people's freedom of choice can lead to diminished legal effectiveness of the law: rules can turn incrementally disobeyed or merely observed and not followed. Fulfilling the aim of enhancing the legal effectiveness of the law can lead to the value of free choice of people becoming irrelevant. If people obey the law by following the rule as a guide or as a non-prudential reason for action, disobeying the law is not an option.

Moreover, to enhance the effectiveness of the law through a system of stimuli that goads people to conform to criminal rules might produce the worst possible outcome, that is, to diminish the free choice of people and the legal effectiveness of the law: that is, to make that freedom of choice and to follow the rule turns to be not an option. On the one hand, by leading people to believe that they chose to obey a criminal rule either for prudential reasons (that is, that they are choosing to observe the law) or because they are accepting it as a guide, that is, that they are following it as an authoritative reason for acting. On the other hand, by leading people to be unaware that they are being causally conditioned to behave in a particular way and not in another optional way, that is, to be unconscious that they are reacting to the stimuli produced in their minds by a self-conscious choice architecture of the policymaker regardless of the content meaning of rules, that is, independently of (prudential or other kind of) reasons for acting as a rule requires.

However, the effectiveness of the law is not the only purpose of criminal law. More is at stake than incrementing the degree of efficacy of law. Then, it must be accepted that an aim might be sacrificed to fulfill another legal aim. Recognition of excusing conditions for not being liable is justified even if the efficacy of threats is diminished.[72]

[69] Hart (1968), p. 23.

[70] Hart (1968), pp. 40–44.

[71] Gardner (2008), pp. xli–xlii.

[72] Hart (1968), p. 44.

Therefore, this problem is related to a traditional theoretical disagreement regarding whether reasons for desert or prevention justify punishment.

So, the future of BAL is not the only one that depends on coping with this problem, but this normative issue would challenge the future of every criminal legal theory of prevention. However, such a claim seems unjustified, as it also would be unjustified to claim that the future of traditional theories of retribution (and Duff's rational communicative theory) depends on dealing with the normative inconsistency with preventive theories. Instead, the future of BAL in criminal law depends on fitting with traditional theories of prevention, which do not consider that whatever means to achieve the most prevention is justified, that is, that preventing offences has constraints in preventive terms, i.e., maximizing the freedom of people within a coercive system. Therefore, it is possible to justify prevention in non-consequentialist terms.

4 Conclusions

Behavioral sciences put into evidence the fact that every criminal rule presupposes an architectural choice. So, behavioral insights put policymakers in a difficult position. To know, or to be aware, that architecture choice is a government tool that affects people's behavior creates a burden of justification for policymakers: they must justify why they frame the decision problem in one way and not in another possible way; they must pay attention to what they choose and how to frame the decision problem. Additionally, they must justify why some information frames are preferred over others, considering both social advantages and costs. There is no way to escape from this fact. Then, whether criminal nudging is justified is not the question. The challenge is to apply criminal nudging in a permissible and helpful manner .

The application of BAL's policy instruments is justified if and only if it is used for "good", that is, policy actions that produce social maximization (or do not diminish) of liberty and protection of free choice of people in a coercive system. A criminal legal theory based on explanations and predictions that make clear that people's behavior is shaped by normative ideals that they consciously endorse (e.g., the Rule of Law), combined with psychological tendencies or unconscious processes that are made without any deliberative intention.[73] This purpose has justification in the objective of trying to overcome, in the measure of the possible, some challenges for (traditional) criminal law theories, from which the future success of these theories depends: that is, their capacity to adapt to what is, or might be, known about human psychology, that is, to the "[…] new beliefs about the human mind".[74]

[73] Shafir (2004), p. ix.

[74] Hart (1968), p. 3.

Nudging policies could be serviceable to maximize individual freedom by framing the decision problem for people so that they make free choices. Also, even if it is assumed that criminal law's primary function is to call suspected offenders to account in criminal courts, a nudge helps obtain that aim. The architecture choice for framing the decision problems of prosecutors, judges, and juries to maximize what Duff's theory values the most—establish a rational communication between the criminal and the state and pass from responsibility to justified punishment—seems permissible. Nudges could help reach the purpose of the function of accounting on the trial of the wrongdoer: to frame the context of choice of jurors, judges, lawyers, and people in general, to make them comply with the procedural rules by appealing to their cognitive and automatic mental process, and, hence, to establish a rational communication between the offender and the state. Question: Are these procedural nudges objectionable because policymakers treat them all as automatons?

Additionally, if nudging is ubiquitous, there are pro tanto reasons for permitting governments to deploy behaviorally informed tools to counter deceptive and manipulative architectural choices that instrumentalise individuals for the private ends of the architect. For example, drug-trafficking organizations in Colombia may mislead prospective drug couriers by understating the probability of detection at Bogotá's El Dorado International Airport; a behaviorally informed governmental counter-nudge that corrects such risk-perception errors and neutralizes the deceptive architecture would be permissible, subject to the legal and ethical constraints discussed above.

References

Bucciarelli M, Johnson-Laird P (2005) Naïve Deontics: a theory of meaning, representation, and reasoning. Cogn Psychol 50(2):159–193

de León P, Solís V (2019) El nudge, su aplicación en el derecho chileno y sus potenciales problemas de constitucionalidad. Revista Chilena de Derecho 46(2):345–371

Duff RA (2012) Responsibility and liability in criminal law. In: Kramer M, Grant C, Colburn B, Hatzistavrou A (eds) The legacy of H.L.A. Hart: legal, political, and moral philosophy. Oxford University Press, Oxford. Spanish Edition: Duff RA (2012) Responsabilidad y punibilidad en el derecho penal (trans: Orunesu C, Rodríguez J). Marcial Pons, Madrid, pp 145–168

Edwards J (2018) Theories of criminal law. In: The Stanford encyclopedia of philosophy. Stanford University. Available via https://plato.stanford.edu/archives/fall2018/entries/criminal-law/

Gardner J (2008) Introduction. In: Hart H (ed) Punishment and responsibility. Essays in the philosophy of law, 2nd edn. Oxford University Press, Oxford, 1968, pp xiii–liii

Green L (2012) Introduction In: Hart, HLA (1961) The concept of law, 3rd edn. Oxford University Press, Oxford, pp xv–lv

Harel A, Teichman D (2018) Análisis conductista del derecho penal y su aplicación: una amistosa revisión crítica. Discusiones 22(2):31–58

Hart HLA (1961) The concept of law, 3rd edn. Oxford University Press, Oxford

Hart HLA (1968) Punishment and responsibility. Essays in the philosophy of law, 2nd edn. Oxford University Press, Oxford

Holmes OW (1897) The path of the law. Harv Law Rev 8(10):457–478

Jeffrey R (1985) The logic of decision. University of Chicago Press, Chicago

Jolls C, Sunstein C, Thaler R (1998) A behavioral approach to law and economics. Stanford Law Rev 50:1471–1550
Kahneman D (2011) Thinking fast and slow. Penguin Books, London
Mongin P, Cozic M (2018) Rethinking nudge: not one but three concepts. Behav Public Policy 21(2):107–124
Monroy D (2017) Nudges y decisiones inconscientes: sesgo de statu quo y políticas públicas en Colombia. Desafíos 29(1):211–247
Monroy D (2023) La economía del comportamiento en la Administración pública: una introducción al *Behavioral Public Choice*. Balance y desafíos del Estado Regulador, supervisor, promotor y empresario. Universidad Externado de Colombia, Bogotá, pp 469–509
Moreno-Cruz D (2014) Three realistic strategies for explaining and predicting judicial decisions. In: Mathis K (ed) Law and economics in Europe. Foundations and applications. Springer, Dordrecht, pp 93–124
Moreno-Cruz D (2018a) Un punto de vista normativo acerca del Nudge financiero. In: Castaño D (ed) El derecho administrativo como idea y sus transformaciones contemporáneas. Universidad Externado de Colombia, Bogotá, pp 411–445
Moreno-Cruz D (2018b) La política criminal del Nudge. Algunos desafíos del Análisis Conductista a las teorías del Derecho Penal tradicionales. Discusiones 22(2):99–135
Searle J (2010) Making the social world. The structure of human civilization. Oxford University Press, Oxford
Shafir E (2004) Introduction and biography. In: Eldar S (ed) Tversky a preference, belief, and similarity. MIT Press, Cambridge, pp ix–xv
Sunstein C (2016) The ethics of influence. Government in the age of behavioral science. Cambridge University Press, New York
Sunstein C (2018) Misconceptions about nudges. J Behav Econ Policy 2(1):61–67
Sunstein C, Kahneman D, Schkade D (1998) Assessing punitive damages (with notes on cognition and valuation in law). Yale J 107:2071–2153
Thaler R, Sunstein C (2009) Nudge: improving decisions about health, wealth and happiness. Penguin Books, London
Tversky A, Kahneman D (1981) The framing of decisions and the psychology of choice. Science 211:453–458
Von Wright G (1963) Norm and action. A logical enquiry. Routledge and Kegan Paul, London
Waldron J (2014) It's all for your own good. The New York Review of Books Oct 9
Yeung K (2012) Nudge as fudge. Mod Law Rev 75(1):122–148

Criminal Law and Economic Analysis of Law. Is It Worth the Money?

Juan Antonio García Amado

Abstract Preventive theories of penalties presuppose a calculation of deterrent effectiveness. The economic analysis of law offers a methodology for the economic calculation of criminal justice effectiveness. In any case, an individual rational choice model that evaluates an offense as a benefit and the criminal part as a cost is presupposed. However, the economic analysis of law has become more complex when incorporating behavioral law and economic discoveries.

1 Economic Analysis of Criminal Law: A Matter of Method

The history of the Law and Economics (hereafter L&E) school, known as economic analysis of law, is well known and has been explained in several publications. I am not going to expand on this aspect, but I will only comment on some details of interest.

The first convenient action to do is to end misunderstandings and remove prejudices. The misunderstanding consists in believing that the L&E movement suggests that legal regulation must be examined only considering the economic cost perspective. It is not about simply looking at what regulations are more economically profitable for the State, companies, or legal persons in general or particular ones. And we must consider that the key term is not profitability, but *effectiveness* as we are about to examine. Economic profitability can be considered as one of the manifestations of *effectiveness*, especially of the economic type, but this economic profitability or effectiveness does not cover the concept of effectiveness that is part of the L&E's core. Therefore, economic effectiveness is one of the variables that are worth considering when designing public policies and crime policies. However, it is not the only key effective variable, I insist.

J. A. G. Amado (✉)
University of León, León, Spain
e-mail: jagara@unileon.es

S. Zorzetto et al. (eds.), *Developments in Law and Economics in the Italo-Iberoamerican Context*, Economic Analysis of Law in European Legal Scholarship 21, https://doi.org/10.1007/978-3-032-03317-8_9

Why does this school or movement is called *Economic* Analysis of Law? The answer to this question should help us clarify this initial and elemental aspect. It is called this way because of the method applied to legal analysis, which is a method coming from the economic analysis.[1] This idea is related to the rational choice theory assumed by economists as a starting point. In other words, the citizen who, as an economic individual, makes decisions in the market trying to maximize benefits, especially economic profits. The citizen that interacts in society and works as a legal individual also makes decisions trying to maximize certain benefits such as being freer, living better, having better wellness, enjoying certain pleasures or even being happier. Such benefits in some cases are translated to money, but in some other cases, it is difficult to do that conversion.[2]

L&E does not take the economic "values", but certain *methodological tools* from economics, specifically the rational choice theory, and other contributions such as the Game Theory. Therefore, we can say that L&E takes the model of *homo economicus* from the economic theory as a self-interested decision-maker who calculates and responds to incentives, and not as a caricature of the so-called compulsive egoist, or the implacable businessman.

Thus, we can mention two main ideas of L&E: human beings decide, trying to maximize their benefits or interests, in a very broad sense, not only the economic one. As a result, when deciding their actions, they respond to positive and negative stimuli; the law operates as a system of incentives for individuals, and as such it influences behaviors. Therefore, we must consider that those legal rules are not the result of chance, but respond to a *telos*, and they are explained through social objectives, and they deter or promote certain behaviors among citizens. It makes perfect sense that, among other parameters, important relevance is given to the analysis of legal regulations in terms of effectiveness from the viewpoint of their general adequacy to accomplish the objectives that explain them considering the perspective of their concrete consequences.

2 Effectiveness Conditions for Criminal Regulation

How does L&E approach Criminal Law? We must start by recalling something that plays a very visible role in the criminal field. Even though it is not exclusive to it, it is common to all branches of law. I am referring to the two types of fundamental legal decisions, such as the legal policy decisions that establish regulations and decide the contents of the corresponding regulations, and the decisions of the individuals to whom the regulations are addressed, decisions regarding obedience or disobedience to the norm.[3]

---

[1] In this regard, and also on the unavoidable need to differentiate between analysis of economic law and economic analysis of law, see Ortiz de Urbina (2004), p. 35.

[2] Alfaro Águila-Real (2007).

[3] Evidently, we could and should add decisions made by the judges and tribunals applying the laws in their cases.

Criminal policy decisions end as law legislation content. We all know that in the criminal field, symbolic legislation[4] is not scarce, and that legislators frequently prefer legitimizing themselves demagogically for electors to creating effective and efficient criminal legislation. However, we are going to leave these political-legislative anomalies aside and imagine a responsible legislator, who does not have punitive excesses and who intends that the criminal types are legitimized by their preventive effects and are, in this sense, effective to the greatest possible extent. If we add L&E presumptions to this ideal criminal legislator, the following data must be considered as conditioning aspects of the legislative activity in terms of crime:

(a) The main postulate of the deterrent efficiency of criminal law is that the individual's decision on whether or not to commit an offense is essentially conditioned by the relationship between two magnitudes: the severity of the penalty and the probability of its imposition. The probability of the imposition of the penalty depends on combining the probability that the criminal is discovered and arrested, the probability that he is prosecuted, and the probability that he is convicted.
(b) Consequently, the overall effectiveness of the criminal justice system and the fact that there are more or fewer offenses will depend on three types of political-legislative decisions.

The first one is about the number of economic resources allocated to law enforcement in charge of crime prevention and prosecution, and to the judiciary, which is responsible for the prosecution of offenders. We could also add public investment in the penitentiary system and the execution of penalties in general, which will also have an influence on the preventive efficiency of the criminal justice system.

The second one is about how the security system and the judiciary (and the penitentiary system) are managed with their more effective functioning.

The third one is about the decision on how many behaviors and which ones can and should be classified as criminally punishable. This is because, if the number of offenses that can be criminally prosecuted increases, either the public budget allocation for these purposes will be increased or the effectiveness of the police and judiciary will decrease proportionally to the increase in the number of offenses.

3 The *Homo Economicus* and Its Benefits

The L&E's core, in general terms and in its criminal application, is found within the individual rational choice, specifically in the presumed model of an individual rational choice model. At this point, there is unanimity in terms of doctrine when indicating that two phases must be differentiated in the L&E movement: the one related to the classical economic model and the one called behavioral economy or "behavioral law and economics" by many people.

[4] Vid. García Villegas (2018), pp. 19–37.

The first or original model of L&E is based on the *homo economicus* of the standard or neoclassical economics theory. According to this perspective, the human being decides and acts always trying to maximize his individual benefit in terms of well-being. For that reason, he weighs up costs and benefits and as a consequence, he responds to positive and negative stimuli. Within his perfect rationality and having these guidelines influencing his behavior, this person is predictable. A simple example is assuming that every rational human being prefers to be free and to be able to move without impediments, he also has strong feelings of well-being or is happier than when he is in prison. This individual would always prefer liberty to prison, and to have a shorter imprisonment than a longer one, thus, he will decide according to his preferences.

This *homo economicus* model is a construction of the economic theory and due to its ideal nature and as it is far from the human being's reality, it has been frequently criticized from diverse doctrinal and ideological parameters. What is more, there is still a great debate in economics and social sciences about how to measure individual benefits or which units can be used to measure individual benefits, which is the benefit that everyone is trying to continuously maximize.

If the individuals' behavior is predictable (each individual is influenced by the desire to maximize individual benefit), it is possible to redirect these individuals' benefit to a common pattern of measurement, and it can be measured not as a mere strictly subjective magnitude, but as a level of achieving an important common goal. The main patterns in contemporary debates for achieving that goal are well-being or happiness. However, those two patterns are really abstract and compatible with the fact that for everyone things or events that increase or decrease the feeling of well-being or happiness are different. Someone can experiment a really great feeling when reading a good book of literature or studying a treatise on physics, while others perhaps consider that those activities are very disgusting and do not find pleasure when doing them.

Personal scales can vary a lot. If you have to choose, would you prefer not to be hungry in prison or be hungry in liberty? Are you happier when having a good personal library or having a very potent and comfortable car? And if we talk about penalties, do you prefer to spend five years in prison for accumulating a big fortune by using criminal means and then enjoy all that money or keep your liberty all the time but not do have everything you illicitly obtained? Probably people would answer differently.

There have been attempts of converting such patterns to money or wealth, such as Richard Posner's attempt at a certain moment. Money gives us the opportunity of purchasing anything that can increase our feeling of well-being or that makes us happy, thus, the amount of money someone is willing to pay depends on his preferences and also on which things he is willing to pay more or less money if he had the money. Perhaps, the money pattern is useful for the distributive justice theory, considering that economic resources must be properly distributed to citizens and they can autonomously organize their life according to their preferences. However, when it is not about discerning the fair distribution of assets, but about being able to predict people's behaviors, this criterion is not useful. In the end, there are people who are happy living in poverty and people that consider that their well-being or happiness do not depend on how much wealth they have to satisfy their desires, but on other types of "spiritual" possibilities.

In any case, if social science seeks to predict behavior, the nature of this purpose is general or statistical. It is not a matter of knowing what someone will prefer when deciding his behavior according to his personal scale of benefit, but of finding out what general effects certain causes will have. Therefore, an economist can certainly anticipate that a high rise in the price of meat will cause a decrease in meat consumption and an increase in the demand for fish or other meat substitutes, considering that there are a certain number of vegetarians who are not directly affected by this situation in their consumption patterns. Likewise, the consequence of the fact that a type of behavior changes from not being punished to being punished with a five-year prison sentence is that many of those who chose to misbehave because they feel satisfaction or they benefit somehow, will stop doing it. However, there are some people that prefer to continue misbehaving and taking risks because they prefer to feel immediate pleasure in doing that action or they do not care about going to prison.

The penal theory implies these general preference scales, based on its more severe and less severe penalties classification, and assumes that the vast majority of individuals regret firstly the loss of their liberty and, secondly, the loss of money. That is why prison sentences are stipulated for the most serious offenses (having the idea of changing the commission of such offenses), and pecuniary penalties for the next less serious ones. Without this perspective, or if it were radically erroneous, the penal theory could not have preventive effects to justify penalties or preventive penal policies would absolutely fail.

Therefore, if the criminal lawyer opposes the figure of *homo economicus* used by economists and the followers of L&E, he will immediately have to face the question about the *homo penalis*. If it did not make sense for economists to build their economic forecasts based on the rational choice model of the *homo economicus* who tries to maximize his individual benefit, the criminal individual who is thought to prefer to maximize his liberty or his money would have no sense, and consequently, nor the dissuasive effect on the threat of a custodial or pecuniary penalty. As we know the ideal of the economic individual does not always correspond to the preferences of a real individual, besides there are those who continue to consume things that become more expensive, even if they will be completely ruined.[5] It is known

[5] As Íñigo Ortiz de Urbina expresses, "When using *homo economicus* the rational choice approach intends not to describe how individual human beings are, but to explain and/or describe social phenomena. For that, it operates using models that remove characteristics of reality to facilitate their treatment, and this is done in full awareness of idealizations". He adds that "The rational choice approach does not claim that all people are rational. The proponents of this type of model are fully aware that their model understood as a description of individual behavior, is false. However, at the same time, they think that such a model is useful in the analysis of human behavior" (Ortiz de Urbina 2004, p. 40).

that there are criminals who are not affected by the threat of punishment or it is even a stimulus for their risky behavior.

The criminal lawyer must choose any general rational choice model as a basis for preventive justification of the penalty or he will not have any other alternative than impose a penalty as a return for the bad action made by the offender and defend the fact that the retributive justice must be used when punishing for offenses, even if this punishment proves to lack dissuasive and preventive effects, I insist.

4 Is It Worth It?

We shall go back to the model of an ideal individual that calculates and maximizes individual benefits, which L&E assumes as general terms and also when applying the economic analysis method to criminal law.

L&E presupposes that criminal regulation is explained and legitimized for its effects on individual decisions. The *homo penalis or* individual that can be legally punished decides among alternatives of action depending on a calculation of consequences and according to the effects that it has in terms of benefit, well-being, or happiness when analyzing each action. This would happen in any field of life.

We shall start with this individual from the perspective of criminal law according to the L&E approaches. The action classified as criminal by penal law is only going to be executed by the individual whose personal benefit will increase and who thinks that executing this action will give him a benefit. I insist one more time that when talking about rational choice theory, we are referring to a benefit or advantage, it is not necessarily about an economic benefit or selling. If we are in the criminal field, it is obvious that crimes such as stealing, robbery, misappropriation, etc. are executed for an economic benefit, but it is also evident that not even these offenses must be executed only for an economic motive. It is also evident that most crimes are executed for a benefit different from the economic one. As a result, the offender when committing a crime responds to positive stimuli and is trying to increase his individual benefit.

At the same time, the threat of criminal punishment acts as a negative stimulus. Therefore, the individual compares the positive benefit of the criminal action and the negative part of the penalty. But the negative part calculated for the penalty by the individual is the result of the combination of two parameters: the severity of the penalty legally foreseen for that behavior and the probability of the imposition of such a penalty for that behavior. At the same time, the probability that the penalty will be applied to him depends on the combination of several probabilities: the probability that the criminal will be discovered and arrested, the probability that he will be prosecuted, and the probability that he will be convicted.[6]

[6] It should be mentioned that in certain situations, the probability that the imposed penalty will be effective once the offender is convicted.

Assuming that it is possible to quantify benefits and losses considering the aforementioned nuance, imagine that individual S considers choosing a behavior that he knows is punishable. The expected benefit is 5000. The maximum possible penalty for this crime would be 8000. But this penalty must be multiplied by the probability that will be imposed on S, as a result of the three or four variables already mentioned. Assuming that the probability established for this penalty is 50%, as a result of the accumulated experience of the police and criminal justice system functioning in general, and of what has been happening with this offense or with this kind of offense. In other words, we know that more or less, half of such criminal actions are not punished. Therefore, we would have:

$$8.000 \times 0.5 = 4.000$$

Therefore, if S finds that the benefit is higher than the punishment multiplied by the probability of its imposition, he will be more motivated to commit the crime than to avoid it. The penalty will have little deterrent effect. Logically, the deterrent effect will be even lower if the probability of criminal punishment is 20%, since:

$$8.000 \times 0.2 = 1.600.$$

In both cases and especially for that crime, Criminal Law will not be effective. It will be effective if the cost of the penalty multiplied by its probability is higher than the expected benefit of the crime. Supposing that, the benefit is 5000 and the "cost" of the penalty is 8000, the probability of punishment is 80%. Then:

$$8.000 \times 0.8 = 6.400.$$

The important lesson from this perspective is that, in order to increase the effectiveness of criminal regulation, we can play with any of these two variables: either the severity of the penalty or the probability of its imposition, as a result of the management of the security system and the judiciary.

For the moment, when stopping at this core and elemental item for managing Criminal Law in terms of L&E, we can make a few observations:

To begin with, these two (the severity of the penalty and the probability of its effective imposition) are not the only variables that can and normally will influence the individual's decision. That is why sometimes an additional general variable is left, as Íñigo Ortiz de Urbina[7] has explained so well: this additional variable can include influential factors in certain individuals, such as their temperament, their education, their socialization, the behavioral alternatives they have, the appropriate opportunity cost, etc.

Because of this additional general variable, each individual's decision and, consequently, his reaction to the threat of the penalty and the balance of costs and benefits between the criminal action and the penalty is not exactly foreseeable. However,

[7] Ortiz de Urbina (2004), pp. 52 and 55.

this element of the unpredictability of each individual's decision is compatible with certain general probability calculations. Since it is reasonable to predict that an increase in the price of meat will lead to a decrease in its consumption, it seems a reasonable general pattern to predict that an increase in penalties for a crime, or the effectiveness of its prosecution will increase the deterrent effect of the corresponding criminal regulation. If criminalists did not agree with this reasoning, it would not make sense to assign preventive effects to the criminal justice system as justification. And this applies not only to the criminal justice system but also to penalties in general. If drivers know that the fine for parking in a forbidden area of the city has increased from fifty to three hundred euros, and if we are also aware that the number of agents assigned to fine these infractions has increased, it is entirely predictable that the number of infractions will decrease significantly.

Another issue is whether it is right and reasonable to apply strictly mechanical reasoning in this field, considering that there is always an increase in the preventive or dissuasive effectiveness of the regulation for any offense when the penalty is increased, or that there will be limiting thresholds in all or some cases. And, it is similar when this effectiveness increase will always result from greater investment or better management of the security system and judiciary. The general intuition of L&E (and of crime prevention in general) may be true, but the most interesting thing for the theory and practice are the exceptions.

5 Is There a Punitive Conspiration?

The second observation: even admitting accurate exceptions to the general rule of effectiveness, as we have seen that L&E calculates it, it can be thought that this doctrine leads to a significant justification of excessive punishment, which is a good basis for the large increase in penalties for any offense, except in certain special cases. Such an increase will lead to greater preventive effectiveness and also to undoubted benefits for society. There are different manners to object to this as some L&E defendants have been doing.

It is worth mentioning that this risk of having a tendency to punishment is not exclusive to L&E but to any justification of penalty in terms of benefit or within a preventive approach, provided that any of those criminal law foundations have no levels of nuances or are not combined with any retributive justice excuse or even with the defense of certain minimum procedural guarantees, such as those that make it difficult to convict innocent people or those that hinder the indiscriminate extension of dangerous crimes or the punishment of certain individuals simply because of their potential dangerousness.

For L&E, the justification for the description of a criminal offense and punishment of certain actions is the collective social costs of such actions. The crime is one of them or should be because those actions described as a crime are actions that "impoverish" society and reduce the general or average level of well-being or happiness.

In this last item, we found a methodological peculiarity of L&E, related to its application to criminal law. On the one hand, it places at its center the *homo economicus* or the individual who decides rationally based on the calculation of the benefit from his alternatives of action. This individual will therefore choose between complying with the prohibitive regulation or violating it. On the other hand, for L&E, the criminal justice system is not justified for any individual or any individual's assets itself, not to protect the individual victim or to retribute the misconduct of the offender, but for macro-reasons and for social reasons, since the criminal justice system (and the Law in general) is configured as a tool of social engineering and is aimed at increasing the general balance of well-being or happiness as much as possible.

As a result of the above-mentioned, it is possible to understand the first possible argument against the accusation against L&E which says that it is a doctrine that supports uncontrolled punishment, justifying it for the sake of the greater effectiveness of criminal regulation. If the most important thing is not the prosecution of certain behaviors because of their immorality, injustice, or intrinsic evil, or their harmful nature for the specific victims, but having the best possible level of well-being or general happiness, we must consider that a criminal justice system, which includes punishments and limitations on liberty, not only increases well-being but also limits it. And there is a threshold, where the balance of a criminal justice system having more severe penalties is no longer positive, but negative. It is not difficult to think that in a society where even the smallest infraction would be severely punished and where the penalties for the most severe crimes would be extremely severe, there would certainly be great preventive effectiveness, but little well-being or happiness as a result of everyone's fear of its misuse. The *homo economicus* or the rational choice individual would calculate his actions, and the results of this calculation could be not to commit a crime. However, it would be a calculation resulting from a terror condition or great discomfort of the individual. It may make sense to mention that when passing this threshold, there is a decreasing marginal benefit from the increase of penalties aiming for well-being until arriving at a point where the additional increase of penalties is not only useless but harmful to the well-being of the group.

6 Commensurability

Third observation. It is very likely that any reader of the previous pages will have thought that everything rests on a chimera since it is assumed that the "benefit" of the offense, and the intensity of the penalty are measurable and commensurable. Naturally, this presumption can be discussed, but the objecting criminalist may be subjected to some objections that are not easy to solve.

Firstly, it is difficult to deny that, in our ordinary life, we make this type of assessment, comparative valuations, and weightings of alternatives. It is true that we almost never assign numerical magnitudes to alternatives, except when we make economic cost calculations with sufficient information on prices. When the night I went out with friends for dinner and my partner stayed at home, I consider whether I am going to come back at a reasonable hour or I am going to stay up until late having drinks with the last colleagues to leave, I assign certain importance to the possible anger of my partner and its effects on my life and my mood, on the one hand, and to the fact that I hope to have fun with my colleagues the rest of the night, on the other hand. Depending on the balance I will decide. That is why there is an important and definitive difference between deciding this manner or deciding to play heads or tails with the alternatives.

In addition, the principle of proportionality between the seriousness of the crime and the severity of the penalty, which is pleasing to criminal lawyers, loses support if a comparative consideration of both extremes is not possible; this comparison starts by attributing some degree or magnitude. We do that for example, when we say that the penalty for a certain offense is more severe or less severe than the one that corresponds to the seriousness of the offense. If it were claimed that such judgments lacked any support or the slightest rationality, the principle of proportionality in criminal law would be out of scene and we would have to disregard such a regulative idea.

It may be argued that when making such a balance of proportionality, it is assumed a pattern of measurement that is more related to some form of morality or to some form of value, which is very different from the criterion of costs and benefits for well-being according to L&E. There are two possible responses to this observation: the first one is the fact that it is not so evident that the same idea used by the L&E cannot be used as a guideline for the idea of criminal proportionality. The second one is that, as more than one distinguished representative of the L&E has emphasized, there is no theoretical incompatibility when it comes to complementing the L&E's analysis with important ideas of justice.

We shall return to the distinction that was mentioned previously, the distinction between the "calculations" of criminal policy and the "calculations" of the individual who is going to decide between different actions, one which involves committing a crime. In both cases, I believe it is not out of place to speak of a balance of costs and benefits. However, there is no reason to think that this calculation is or should be reducible to a purely economic or monetary calculation.

7 Calculations Made by Legislators and How They Do It

We shall begin with *criminal policy* decisions. Those related to whether or not to punish certain behavior. Criminal Law punishes behavior, not merely because it is or can be seen as immoral or reprehensible somehow, but to protect certain individuals or social assets. This protection can be done by punishing the action that damages this asset or, in certain cases, by punishing the endangerment of this asset. However, while in religion, a person who has bad thoughts can be considered to be sinning or behaving immorally, for criminal punishment the protected asset (life, property, etc.) is required to be damaged or endangered. The latter can happen as preparatory acts (if they are punishable) or attempts (for offenses in which an attempt is punishable), or because of the high risk to the protected asset caused by certain actions not directly aimed at damaging the protected asset. To sum up, we can say that Criminal Law is not about the qualification of the action itself, but that the behavior is penalty punished because of its actual or potential effects. We could call it the consequentialist element in Criminal Law.

If the unavoidable objective is always to protect a certain individual or social asset (life, property, peace or public order, certain institutions of the State, constitutional order, etc.), then speaking of costs as a basic component of criminal policy, both in the economic and non-economic sense, has a basis as well as the following items.

(i) In the first place, it is necessary to evaluate whether or not a certain generic behavior damages an asset considered worthy of such special protection. Previously, the assets susceptible to criminal protection must be cataloged, but we are going to take for granted that this catalog is already established or that we are talking about assets that deserve criminal protection without any doubt, such as life, physical integrity, or property.

How much is a person's life worth, in general, or on average?[8] Supposing we asked a hundred people to rate on a scale from 1 to 10, how serious they thought it was to kill someone intentionally without very strong reasons (such as legitimate self-defense or self-defense of a third party) to justify the homicide. Surely the magnitude of the scale would be the highest: between 8 and 10. If we ask a hundred people to rate the punishment for homicide on a scale of severity of penalties, also between one and ten, it is certain that they will assign very similar values to the aforementioned offenses. It is difficult to imagine that anyone would consider that a very serious crime deserves a minor penalty, for example. This is a kind of elementary intuition of retributive justice or the principle of criminal proportionality.

If we agree that this simple experiment is feasible and makes sense and that it could be executed for a large number of possible behaviors that are generally considered to be punishable or not punishable,[9] the most interesting theoretical issue will soon appear: where can we redirect these assessments, and *what unit or pattern of measurement underlies them*?

[8] The qualification "in general or on average" is important. If we ask ourselves how much Hitler's life is worth, or Stalin's or Pol Pot's or the life of any other tremendously bloodthirsty tyrant, for the purposes of deciding whether their life should be criminally protected, many of us would surely agree that it is worth nothing and that those who would kill them would not deserve punishment, but a reward, if anything.

[9] This would leave the problematic cases out, the highly controversial ones, those behaviors that have a great social disagreement as to whether they are reprehensible (and to what degree) or admissible. This would be the case, for example, of voluntary abortion, certain offenses related to the trafficking of certain drugs or certain expressions, such as blasphemy, or the formulation of certain opinions of a political nature (such as those in favor of a political group or a terrorist group, etc.).

If we say that this is a moral pattern entrenched in positive social morality, we are surely saying something that is as true as well as almost trivial. I have written before that it is difficult for any behavior that is not socially considered morally reprehensible to be an offense, at least in a democratic state. If we want to be more specific, the problem turns more complicated because of the very different nature of the protected asset depending on the type of offense. In this sense, offenses against life, property, or the public treasury, for example, have little in common. However, these diverse behaviors against such different assets are not incommensurable in practice or for the citizens.

Imagine another simple experiment. If we ask a hundred individuals whether they consider a homicide to be more serious (and, therefore, deserving a more severe penalty) or less serious (deserving a less severe penalty) than a tax fraud of twenty thousand euros, they will agree on the fact that the crime against life is more serious. It may seem that life and public money are incommensurable assets, but everyone compares them for this type of assessment purposes. In addition, even in very plural and pluralistic societies in terms of moral and political spheres, such as ours, the coincidences in the result of these comparisons are much wider than the discrepancies.

I am not trying to hypothesize the patterns that constitute these assessments that underlie and give meaning to any reasonable criminal policy. Surely an entire series of variables of very diverse patterns of judgment are combined in these assessments. We are interested in emphasizing that as a result of these patterns, no matter their nature, there are always assessments used to make judgments about the seriousness of certain behavior that is actually or potentially harmful to certain assets and about deserving a penalty that corresponds to the seriousness of the harmful behavior. Therefore, for analytical purposes, we shall call V the pattern or unit of value underlying as a result of these combinations.

The value of a criminally protected asset is measured in V. The seriousness of an offense against the protected asset is equivalent to the costs in V. Similarly, the damage that the penalty represents for the criminal is equivalent to the costs in V. For example, if a penalty is pecuniary, its cost is economic. If it is deprivation of liberty, its cost is partly intangible (loss of liberty during the time spent in prison plus loss of social consideration or stigma, etc.), but there may also be economic costs, especially in the form of loss of profit. Regarding the damage to the victim, it can be fundamentally intangible (such as offenses against honor) or it can be mostly economic, as in offenses against property. However, I mention it again, we are going to use the variable V to refer to costs, as an expressive unit of the surprising commensurability of these costs in social practice.

In the previous section, we referred to costs for the victim, when it is individualized, and for the perpetrator of the crime who is punished for it. However, Criminal Law entails other costs, which can be translated into money because the economic cost maintains the state apparatus of security and justice, the penitentiary system, and prison sentences; and the economic costs are also translatable to the costs of processing, in its various variants. In addition, offenses also have social costs, beyond the specific victims, which can be easily calculated in cash. Apart from that, depending on whether there are more or fewer offenses, citizens will be forced to take more or fewer precautions to anticipate[10] them on their own, or to mitigate their effects,[11] economically; such measures also involve costs.

However, it is not unreasonable to mention that from this social perspective, there are also intangible costs (c^i) for crimes, such as those affecting public tranquility, the confidence of citizens, their leisure, their life, and professional alternatives, etc.

The costs in V, from the victim and criminal perspective, in terms of social approach, can be seen as the addition of intangible costs plus economic costs (c^e).

Thus, the cost of a crime (c^d), in units of V, can be represented as follows:

$$c^d\left(V^d\right) = c^{i1} + c^{i2} \ldots + c^{in} + c^e$$

The same formula can be used for representing the penalty cost (c^p)

$$c^p\left(V^p\right) = c^{i1} + c^{i2} \ldots + c^{in} + c^e$$

This formula can be used to represent the crime costs for the victim (when individualized) and the crime costs for state society in general, as well as the penalty costs for the criminal and the prosecution costs, conviction, and execution of the penalty for society in general.

L&E proposes, in terms of criminal policy, that for any crime, its social costs should not be less than the social costs of the penalty. This means that the amount invested by the State to punish that criminal behavior is not more than the behavior's social costs. In other words, the crime must deserve the penalty, in terms of the amount of money that the penalty costs us socially, as compensation for punishing it.

However, we cannot stop dealing with an essential item. According to L&E, the reason for justifying the description of the behavior as a crime, with the assumed "expense", is precisely the social cost of such behavior. The objective of the penalty is not to make the offender pay the individual cost to the victim,[12] but the general deterrence: if the rate of such behavior decreases, the cost invested in it will decrease too. The more effective is Criminal Law, the more deterrent it is, and at a lower cost. A criminal justice system for offense D, that deters 90% is more effective than one that deters 80%. But one that deters 90% at a lower cost is more effective than one that does it at a higher cost.[13]

---

[10] Consider the example of purchasing alarms and security systems for homes, institutions or companies.

[11] The most obvious example is the purchase of insurance policies against theft, fire crime, etc.

[12] That, on the other hand, can be an important function of the law of torts.

[13] Note that, once we have accepted that the costs are not merely economic, but also include intangible costs (such as loss of freedom, social stigma, etc.), we have one more reason to claim that, for equal deterrence, a lesser penalty is more efficient. If a sentence of three years and a sentence

The State determines a large part of the deterrent efficiency for criminal regulation through a series of economic and management decisions that have to do especially with the police system and the justice system. Therefore, the more personnel and material resources the police have at their disposal, the more criminals can be found and brought before a judge, and, the better designed the criminal procedural system is, the more it will avoid the anti-preventive effect of many criminals escaping conviction.[14] The greater the investment (and better management) in these two systems, the greater the preventive effectiveness of criminal law is, but also the higher the economic costs are and, to some extent, the higher the intangible costs are. L&E tells us that at some point there has to be a balance, which the criminal policy of the states should ideally aspire to achieve.

I note herein the considerations on criminal policy from the L&E perspective, proposing the fundamental issue of whether there would be an incompatibility with the use of ideals and approaches of criminal theory and dogma among us, especially if they are, as usual, a markedly preventive theory and dogma. The fact of reducing the criminal analysis of L&E to its most elementary logic indicates that criminal policies that entail significant costs and are scarcely deterrent, or criminal regulations that are justified by the need to limit crimes and do not go together with the proper investment to make them effective and remain merely as symbolic criminal legislation have no sense. We should not punish anything that has no social costs (in the broad and comprehensive sense of the term) and the necessary means should be put in place to ensure that criminal regulation deters behaviors that have such costs, but always making sure that the cure is not worse than the disease and that the costs of criminal prosecution do not exceed the costs of the crime itself.

8 Is the *Homo Penalis* Rational and Unpredictable? The Revolution of Behavioral Law and Economics

In its first period, Criminal Law and Economics took the model of rational individuals of neoclassical economics as the basis for the possible forecast of the effectiveness of the criminal justice system. This individual, as we have already seen, decides his actions on the basis of a calculation of costs and profits and is always guided by the maximization of his individual benefit. In other words, he chooses the alternative that, according to his accounts, has the more reliable and accurate information, which will bring him a better balance. The penalty is always a loss opposing illicit benefits. And we have already seen that this loss is calculated by multiplying anything the penalty has taken away by the probability of its imposition.

---

of two years are equally dissuasive for crime D, it will be more efficient to impose a sentence of two years, as it saves economic costs and intangible costs.

[14] Or that innocent people suffer from it, which may also have a certain anti-preventive effect and, in any case, undermines an important part of the system's basis.

Of course, this ideal rational individual who pursues the maximization of his individual benefit is perfectly predictable in his decisions when he has all the relevant information and, consequently, he includes in his calculation such things as opportunity costs. So, in ideal conditions, the decisions of that individual are very foreseeable. If stealing 1000 euros from a neighbor has a penalty of 2000 euros and if the probability of being caught, prosecuted, and convicted is 30%, then, the loss is 600, so that the offense leaves a "benefit" of 400 and the criminal regulation that provides such a penalty for that theft[15] will not have a good deterrent effect.

The transition from traditional criminalistics (mainly of European origin) to the economic analysis of criminal law meant the transition from a theoretically preventive model, but not based on a model of a rational individual that would allow the calculation of the effectiveness of criminal regulations, to a criminal theory having such a model of rational choice and decision-maker in the forefront of its elaborations. However, after some decades, within the L&E movement, there was a big change that revolutionized such theory: *the presupposed rational individual, so exquisitely elaborated, seemed to be completely unreal.*

The attack from the inside came from a series of psychological[16] experiments that showed that real humans do not behave frequently as expected, in other words, as the rational individual: *homo economicus*. Therefore, to sum up, real individuals are not as cold or cerebral as him when managing information and, calculating, since they are subjected to a wide array of cognitive biases. What is more, they are not that selfish nor merely interested in individual benefit or in maximizing it, because they are frequently guided by a sense of altruism, justice, or fairness, which makes them not choose the most beneficial alternative, or at least not the better economic benefit.

Regarding the influence of cognitive biases, a series of experiments are continually indicating that certain conditions of our way of assimilating and remembering information mean that the effects of some stimuli on our decisions are not as expected. Thus, it seems to be demonstrated that when we live an experience in a certain time, we do not remember everything that happened to us during that time the same way. We remember more precisely or especially the first and final moments, and that is the main impression we have. If, for example, we go on a twenty-day trip during the summer vacation and we have extraordinary weather during all that period, except for the last two days because it rains non-stop, we will have the feeling that we had very bad luck because of the bad weather during that trip. Contrary to if it rains four days in the middle of the trip and then the weather changes to

[15] I am working with an extraordinarily simplified, almost caricatural model since I have only considered the cost of the real threat of punishment of this pecuniary penalty, a real threat that comes from multiplying the legally stipulated penalty by the probability of its effective imposition. But there can usually be other costs that should be included in this calculation, such as the cost of social stigmatization (when there is any) for being convicted as a thief among others.

[16] There are two wonderful and extraordinarily entertaining books that relate the genesis of these experiments and the personalities and reactions of some of their most important authors. These books are Kahnemann's (2011) and Thaler's (2015).

sunny. Or if after eighteen perfect days, the last two days are rainy, and the return flight is delayed for five hours. It would seem to us as if we had a terrible vacation.

If these experimental results are true, in order to have a deterrent effect on those who have already experienced a prison sentence and they do not commit this offense again, the feelings when entering prison and in the final moments would be more important than the duration of the sentence itself. This would question the old dogma that a custodial sentence is more deterrent when is longer.

Another very popular finding is that human beings tend to keep constant their levels of happiness or sense of well-being by adapting these feelings to changes in our fortunes and circumstances. We would think that a person who has a serious accident and has to stay forever in a wheelchair is going to be very unhappy for the rest of his life or less happy than he was before. Likewise, we believe that if someone wins the lottery and becomes a millionaire, he will be much happier from that moment. But experience shows that this is not the case and that happiness always tends to balance out for everyone after a little time depending on the person. In other words, the person who had the accident after a year will already feel very similar to how he used to feel before, and, it is similar for the lucky winner of the lottery.

Regarding the sense of justice as a motive for decisions, very interesting tests have also been executed. According to the neoclassical model of rational choice, we practically always tend to choose the most favorable alternative for us in terms of the balance of costs and benefits, and even more when that balance is monetary or easily translated into monetary terms. But certain key experiments show that this is far from being true and that our decisions, even the most evident economic ones, are strongly influenced by a certain sense of what is fair or morally abusive.

Considering the famous example of the "ultimatum game"[17]: two groups of randomly selected people are formed. They are put together in separate pairs. Within each pair, one is the proposer and the other one is the respondent. The game conditions are as follows: The proposer receives 100 euros and the respondent knows that the proposer has received it to play with him. Each proposer can offer the respondent the amount of money he wants to share from the 100 euros. The respondent can accept the amount of money or not, but each player only has a single chance. In other words, the proposer can make only one offer and the respondent can accept it or not, but he cannot haggle or make other proposals. If the respondent accepts the single offer of the proposer, each of them stays in the property forever with their corresponding amount of money: the responder will have the amount of money he accepted, and the proposer will keep the rest of the money. If the respondent rejects the offer, no one wins.

The question is: how much the *homo economicus* of the neoclassical economic theory assumed by the L&E as the rational choice model would offer and accept?

---

[17] I will tell the story by adapting the case that, among many others, is narrated by Thaler (2015, pp. 140ff.). Thaler says that this experiment was conducted by Daniel Kahneman, Jack L. Knetsch, and himself in the 1980s, but they later discovered that a similar experiment with the same results had been conducted by a team led by the German economist Werner Güth, and that it was this German team that gave it its enduring name, the "ultimatum game" (ibid., p. 141).

Thaler explains the undoubtedly expected result: "If we use the standard economic assumption that people are selfish and rational, the game theory has a clear prediction for this game. The proposer will offer the lowest possible amount (fifty cents) and the responder will accept; fifty cents is more than nothing.[18] However, the results did not confirm that hypothesis, but one of the authors of the experiment: one of the individuals' motives is a sense of justice or fairness, and they assume the high risk of losing everything if the offer seems unfair. These respondents prefer to punish the selfish proposers and make them also lose everything, even if they lose everything too. According to Thaler, the results show a strong tendency of respondents to reject any offer below 20% of the amount at the game.

Fairness motives also have a determinant influence on our economic decisions. This explains, for example, why there are many people who need to buy a pair of tennis shoes and are not willing to buy the cheapest tennis shoes on the market if they know that they are made by semi-slave children, so they pay a higher price for any other pair of tennis shoes. Or we can understand why not everyone keeps the extra money of the change when the taxi driver or waiter makes a mistake, that would be typical of the *homo economicus* who thinks only of himself and of maximizing his individual utility.

And how will this affect criminal law and the calculations about its effectiveness? If the vast majority of citizens are like the *homo economicus* of the neoclassical economics and of the first L&E, the criminal policy calculations that should bring an effective criminal law may presume that:

(a) Every potential criminal who analyses whether or not to perform criminal behavior will only consider the comparison between the expected benefit and the feared damage.[19] If the balance is positive for the crime, he will commit it.
(b) Any citizen who feels individually or collectively affected by an actual or potential offense will be in favor of the highest penalty for offenders, since, theoretically, this penalty will have minimal or no cost for him. Nevertheless, the deterrent effects for potential offenders will be higher if these costs are higher in terms of the penalty they will carry.

I have the firm conviction that there is no need to be a psychologist or an American economist to know that we do not feel or decide in that manner. If a hundred thousand Spanish were asked if they agreed that anyone stealing a mobile phone or a car stereo system had a 30-year prison penalty, we would unanimously say no. The answer would be also no if the question was about whether we would dare to rape a person we are very attracted to if there was a total and absolute guarantee that we would not be punished.

---

[18] Thaler (2015), p. 141.

[19] Obviously, the opportunity costs must also be considered. An individual knows that he can dedicate the next few months to finish preparing for getting a job that will bring him a certain profit or to commit a robbery he rightly expects to be very profitable calculating that the risk of being caught and convicted is minimal, based on good information.

The contribution of so-called "behavioral economics" to the economic theory through its experiments was the empirical basis for the crisis of the neoclassical *homo economicus*. The first generation of L&E considered the rational choice model as their model, which was also affected by a powerful variant called *"Behavioral Law and Economics"* or behavioral economic analysis of law. Has it been a revolutionary change that puts an end to the previous model of L&E or will it only result in a readaptation of a few theses and to more complex formulas that seemed simpler before?

These two opposing theses, the revolutionary and the integrative one, have been strongly confronted in terms of doctrine over the last three decades. I will not stop here on the arguments of one or the other, but I will mention only a couple of considerations in order to move toward the end of this work.

9 What Kind of Costs and Benefits Do We Choose?

In my humble opinion, behavioral economics removes forever from the economic and social sciences the idea that our "normal" and common rationality, as humans, only or very preferentially considers the economic, and monetary balance of our choices of action. Economic reasons have a strong influence on our decisions, and these reasons may lead us to prefer a better-paid job to a worse-paid one, between two jobs that satisfy us similarly; or to prefer to buy a house that costs less rather than one that costs more money if we have to choose between two that are basically comparable in terms of other elements that are important to us. But it also seems quite evident that we do not always (rather rarely) decide to marry the richest person, but we often prefer the house that costs us more money if it offers a better view of the landscape, or we also prefer the lower-paying job if it is the one that allows us to feel more personally fulfilled.

We have already mentioned that there have been very few L&E authors who have tried to put all costs in terms of money or in terms of the price of anything or the amount of money anyone would be willing to pay. We have also said that the array of stimuli or conditioning factors that hypothetically allow us to predict people's decisions include economic ones, but also others that we call intangibles. That is why we have previously called V the theoretical unit of measurement applied when deciding.

I consider that it is not incompatible with L&E to understand that the unit of value V is part of everything that we generally value as positive or negative in our lives. There will certainly be very few people who, when asked whether they would prefer to receive more money or less money, will answer truthfully that they would prefer less money because the less money the better. But it is likely that there will be a vast majority that when asked if they would like to receive, without any compensation on their part, a large amount of money as a result of a very violent robbery including deaths, will say not at all. Is it all because, incongruously, sometimes we appreciate money and sometimes we despise it? No, it is because money is not the only motivation that stimulates our behavior, but it competes with others of a very different nature. In more than four opportunities many will prefer to be economically damaged as long as their action is related to love, compassion, a sense of fairness, and similar feelings and impulses; or even hatred, envy, pride, vanity, or others of that kind.

Although it may sound tautological, we can say that in our decisions on how to behave, positive stimuli are those that contribute to improving our lives and negative stimuli are those that harm us. These favorable or unfavorable stimuli depend on the reference of the value patterns where we build our lives: wealth or money is one of them. The sense of justice, which allows everyone who lives according to it to feel better, the pride for achieving certain personal goals or for achieving higher goals than our competitors, etc. are part of the determining patterns for our decisions. Therefore, we cannot label criminal law as radically irrational or as completely surprising, because of its unpredictability: the decision of those who choose punishable behavior as a last resort to keep their self-esteem, even if the penalty is very severe and the probability of conviction is very high; or those who choose to obey the law even if they had the possibility of escaping from a life of misery at very low risk of high punishment cost.

To make it worse, another element that psychology has provided decisively in recent times has been confirming that when there is any type of risk, there is not only one type of rational individual but three types of people following their preferences: there would be people that love risk, some others that are indifferent to it and the ones that feel aversion to it. The ones who feel aversion to risk have a strong propensity to choose the less risky alternative, the ones who are indifferent to it will not be influenced by this factor when weighing up actions, and the ones who love risk will tend to choose the more adventurous one. Perhaps that is why there are people who love mountaineering and those who would not risk climbing a dangerous mountain at all, even if they are gifted in it. Perhaps that is the reason why some invest in the stock market and others, with identical capital, choose much safer investments with predictable results. Perhaps because of these reasons related to personality, some people divorce and get married again, while others do not want to live the bad things they already know.

This risk-tendency level affects also the basis of the economic analysis of criminal law. Penalty, as a risk that causes a criminal offense, will deter the ones who feel aversion to risk, will have no influence on the ones who are indifferent to it, and will serve as a stimulus for the ones who love it.

If human behaviors are in general unpredictable, because of the enormous number of variables that influence the decision on one's own actions, L&E loses ground and will lack any possible benefit as a pattern of criminal policy. No matter how many times we have said that effectiveness is a laudable objective of such a policy, it is completely impossible to predict citizens' future behaviors based on the expected responses to criminal incentives, thus, the method and rambling approaches of L&E would serve absolutely no purpose. Therefore, claiming that criminal law must be effective would be as vain and gratuitous as claiming that it must be lyrical, sustainable, or comforting, which is empty verbiage and a concession to expressive fashions.

Eppur si muove, most of the time, we act predictably, although there may be occasional exceptions. Our behavior is predictable and it is possible to be influenced. For example, in the consumption area, there is advertising, and a discipline such as marketing is developed. Apparently, any of us is capable of predicting with little margin of error the future decisions of our acquaintances, as long as we have sufficient and true information about them and their circumstances. And if you ask me if there will be fewer drivers in cities who double park where it is forbidden, knowing the fine for this has increased from 50 to 200 euros, and knowing that the police have received the order to make a special effort to punish these offenses, I will answer that there will be fewer infractions; and I will be right[20] about this. We do not make mistakes so often; however, sometimes we have made them.

In my opinion, it is not unreasonable to combine two statements. The first one is that the previous model, the one about the *homo economicus* of neoclassical economics, and about the first L&E is not very accurate because it hardly corresponds to a real individual who decides what to do and whether or not to engage in the punishable behavior. Thus, as a guide to criminal policy, I can say that it can lead to error or disproportion.[21] The second one is that, in spite of everything, the basic approach of L&E is improved with the inputs of behavioral economics and therefore oriented towards constructing more realistic models of rational choice, and more realistic models of the standard individual who, in real social life, make decisions considering his behavioral alternatives.

Certainly, if the model of the *homo economicus* who thinks only of benefits and damages calculated in terms of wealth were real and not so far from the real people we deal with, the predictive capacity would be very high because the variables of that basic equation are very manageable. There are only two variables: the severity of the penalty and the probability of its application. But this model is barely realistic because we are learning with certitude in the theory we study what people already knew, which is a lot of content and variables that have an influence on them, and therefore, things and calculations are not so simple.

However, this does not disqualify or dismiss the method that L&E brings to criminal law and criminal policy for being useless. It indicates that we must escape from simplifications and automatisms and that criminal policies must be built on more complex formulas covering more variables than those that actually operate,[22]

[20] Provided, of course, that information on other possible determining factors is not missing. If the question is about such behaviors in a city where the minimum wage is twenty thousand euros per month, the situation would change and it would be expected that the change in the rate of such offenses would be non-existent or nil.

[21] Since it is foreseen that, with an equal probability of conviction, a higher penalty is always more dissuasive than a lower penalty.

[22] According to Nuno Garoupa: "behavioral analysis is not an alternative approach, but rather is about providing classical law and economics with insights from actual human behavior, improving the quality of predictions or prescriptions about the law. One of the objections to rational choice is that it yields inaccurate predictions. But it does not follow that people's behavior is random, unpredictable, or rule-free. On the contrary, the behavioral approach aims at qualifying such choices by understanding behavior and decision" (Garoupa 2003, p. 6).

considering our individual psychology and the social influences to which our choices are subjected.[23] It may seem complicated, and surely it is, but if it is possible to make moderately accurate predictions about voting, consumer behavior, accident rates resulting from certain road law reforms, etc., why should criminal law be oblivious to these predictions or reluctant to a criminal policy that gives them a high priority?

References

Alfaro Águila-Real J (2007) Los juristas -españoles- y el análisis económico del derecho. InDret, 417

García Villegas M (2018) The powers of law. A comparative analysis of sociopolitical legal studies. Cambridge University Press, Cambridge

Garoupa N (2003) Behavioral economic analysis of crime: a critical review. Eur J Law Econ 15:5–15. https://doi.org/10.1023/A:1021152523137

Kahnemann D (2011) Thinking, fast and slow. Straus and Giroux

Ortiz de Urbina I (2004) Análisis económico del derecho y política criminal. Revista de Derecho penal y Criminología, segunda época 2:31–73.

Thaler RH (2015) Misbehaving. The making of behavioral economics. W.W. Norton & Company, New York

[23] A very clear and almost trivial example of this: where behavior is deeply rooted and is socially not frowned upon, it will almost useless to punish it for preventive purposes, even with high penalties. We can think of some ideological or religiously motivated crimes, but I prefer to quote the case of corruption in our Latin American countries, where everyone asks for a recommendation in secret as soon as they can and where it is considered to be a heartless thing not to give favorable treatment in the public administration to relatives, friends, lovers, and co-religionists.

The Contributions of a Credit View of Money (and Heterodox Economics) to a Better Understanding of the Monetary System

Gissella Alejandra López Rivera

Abstract This chapter aims to show how an alternative theoretical account of the economy may provide conceptual tools to understand the function of the monetary system and allow us to think about new forms of institutional designs facing new regulatory challenges. The first part explains the credit view by contrasting it with the commodity view of money to defend the thesis that the monetary phenomenon is not a natural nor a simple functional kind but an institutional artifact. In the second part, by explaining the nature of new phenomena such as cryptocurrencies, the analysis explains how the heterodox view of money performs better than its rival orthodox view in explaining the nature of a monetary system. The third and concluding part comments on some legal frameworks stated by some countries and the challenges our legal systems face from the legal necessity of recognizing these 'innovative disruptions'.

1 Introduction

In 1905, the German economist Georg F. Knapp opened his seminal monography, *The State Theory of Money,* with the sentence, '[money] only is a creature of law. A theory of money must therefore deal with legal history'. Knapp proposed the

This chapter has been writen with the support Fondecyt of Initiation N° 11241368: Desafíos dogmáticos de las criptomonedas y otros medios de pago digitales: propuestas para el derecho privado y público chileno. I owe special gratitude to Diego Montecinos for his feedback on various aspects of the paper.

G. A. L. Rivera (✉)
Facultad de Derecho, Universidad Diego Portales, Santiago, Chile

Facultad de Derecho, Universidad de Chile, Santiago, Chile
e-mail: gissella.lopez@udp.cl

S. Zorzetto et al. (eds.), *Developments in Law and Economics in the Italo-Iberoamerican Context*, Economic Analysis of Law in European Legal Scholarship 21, https://doi.org/10.1007/978-3-032-03317-8_10

revolutionary idea that money has *validity* (*Geltung*), property 'which is not bound to its [pieces of money] material content'.[1]

Contemporarily with Knapp, the British diplomat and economist Alfred Mitchell-Innes published in 1913 and 1914 in *The Banking Law Journal* the papers 'What is Money' and 'The Credit Theory of Money.' Under certain premises, he objected to Adam Smith's classical view of money (and Menger's, I would add), who sees money as a commodity with a value that emerged to overcome bartering. Mitchell-Innes declared that money has no relation to its physical support, and that the exchange of commodities has always been done by assuming promises to pay. In this account, the monetary unit of account is the primary concept for understanding money.

Both lines of thinking are known as the 'credit view of money' and have greatly influenced the heterodox view of economics. *A Treatise on Money,* published by Keynes in 1930, made an explicit reference to Knapp's work. Explaining that when the State 'enforces the payment of the thing which corresponds to the name or description in the contract' and 'in addition, it claims the right to determine and declare what thing corresponds to the name, and to vary its declaration from time to time':

> It is when this stage in the evolution of money has been reached that Knapp's chartalism—the doctrine that money is peculiarly a creation of the State—is fully realised.[2]

Nowadays, economists Mosler, Wray, and Kelton defend the credit view of money.[3] From this account, money is an instrument of debt recognition or a promise to pay in the future ('IOU') made by an issuing entity, such as the State (public issuer) or banks (private issuers).

This article aims to show how an alternative theoretical account of the economy, as referred to above, may provide conceptual tools to understand the function of the monetary system and allow us to think about new forms of institutional designs facing new regulatory challenges.

The first part of this chapter explains the credit view by contrasting it with the commodity view of money to defend the thesis that the monetary phenomenon is not a natural nor a simple functional kind but an institutional artifact. Following the American philosophers Dipert and Thomasson, I propose that the monetary system has author, user agents, concrete and abstract tool properties in a functional sense, and tool-communicating properties in a semiotic sense. Following that characterization, I will explain how the different sub-artifacts of the monetary system realize the classical functions of money, and that the imposition and recognition of a collective status to them by collective intentionality, known as status function *à la* Searle,[4] are necessary but not sufficient conditions for the emergence and maintenance of a monetary system.

---

[1] Knapp (1924), pp. 24–25, 31.

[2] Keynes (1930), p. 4.

[3] See Mosler (2013), Wray (2015), Kelton (2020).

[4] Searle (2010).

In the second part, by explaining the nature of new phenomena such as cryptocurrencies, I will demonstrate how the heterodox view of money performs better than its rival orthodox view in explaining the nature of a monetary system. On one hand, by means of the philosophical analytic tools and the lens of the credit view of money, I will clarify the ontological status of these phenomena and, in a mapping exercise, conceptually locate them in the legal monetary system. On the other hand, old and traditional private law concepts, as '*ius in personam*' or '*ius in rem*', 'claims', 'debts' or 'payment of debt', will be necessary to understand the ontology and legal nature of this new and disruptive phenomenon.

In the third and concluding part, I will briefly comment on some legal frameworks stated by some countries and the challenges our legal systems face from the legal necessity of recognizing these 'innovative disruptions'.

2 Money Is an Institutional Artifact

2.1 A Brief Philosophical Approach to the Ontology of Money: Two Theories in Dispute

According to the entry 'Philosophy of Money and Finance' of the Stanford Encyclopedia of Philosophy, the clarification of the ontological status of money is provided by two theories: the commodity theory, which corresponds to a classical or orthodox view of economics, and the credit theory or claim theory, related to a heterodox view of economics.[5] In Schumpeter's words, these are the only two monetary theories that deserve to be considered.[6]

The first view was assumed by Adam Smith and followed by Jevons, Menger, and Von Misses,[7] among others. It characterizes money as a commodity given in exchange for another commodity, a tool that people use after a natural state of the

[5] De Bruin Boudewijn et al. (2020), pp. 3–4.

[6] Schumpeter (1917–1918), p. 649.

[7] Smith (1776), Jevons (1875), Menger (1982), Von Mises (1912). Please note, that Marx must be included as a classical author regarding its money nature conception (as a commodity). Ingham explains "Marx's *analytical* positions is similar that of classical economics. […] In company with all commodity theorist, Marx failed to consider money as abstract value, defined by a money of account and sustained by its ow social relations of production." cfr. Ingham (2004), p. 62. Marx points out "[a]s soon as it had won a monopoly of this position in the expression of value for the world of commodities, it became the money commodity, and only then, when it had already become the money commodity, did form D become distinct from form C, and the general form of value come to be transformed into the money form. "Marx (1976), p. 163, adding "[t]he commodity which functions as a measure of value and therefore also as the medium of circulation, either in its own body or through a representative, is money. Gold (or silver) is therefore money. It functions as money, on the one hand, when it has to appear in person as gold. It is then the money commodity, neither merely ideal, as when it is the measure of value, nor capable of being represented, as when it is the medium of circulation.", Marx (1976), p. 227.

economy based on barter. Besides, Menger postulates that money is not born by convention or law but spontaneously in the face of the high costs of barter precisely because of the problem of double coincidence.[8] Smith describes this problem in this way: for merchant A to exchange his merchandise, M_1, he needs to find someone else, merchant B, who owns some other merchandise, M_2, and who would like to exchange M_2 for M_1.[9] Menger explains that there would have been a single commodity that, exhibiting the property of being *saleableness*, may be able to be traded at a lower price and in a reasonable time (*Absatzfahigkeit* in Menger's original writing). This commodity came to be accepted as the general medium of exchange, reducing transaction costs.[10]

This theory 'traces money to a purely commodity origin and discovers the principle regulating purchasing power in supply and demand, in marginal utility, or in the production costs of the money-stuff'.[11] In general terms, the classical approach posits that money (i) has as its primary function to serve as a medium of exchange, (ii) is a commodity, and (iii) is neutral in the economy, not affecting production or economic traffic, since it is only representative of the existence of value in goods and services.[12] Metallism is a now an abandoned derivation of the commodity view, which assumes that money is money insofar it is minted in a particular metal so that tokens money have their intrinsic value bound to the metal content. Over time, the idea of the metallic value of money was abandoned. Classical economists gave prominence to the approaches offered by Fisher's quantitative theory of money—The Purchasing Power of Money, 1911—revived by Friedmann in the 1970s.[13] It could be assumed that a metallist understanding of money was abandoned in 1971 with Nixon's declaration of the dollar-gold's inconvertibility. That historical event, nevertheless, confirmed that the intrinsic value of the pieces of money was never the reason that they granted them the status of means of payment.

However, the contemporary rcconceptualization of money mentioned, i.e., the commodity view, has been unable to explain how money is an essential condition for the existence of a market economy, and why economic agents would have chosen some assets as money.[14] Moreover, there are abundant evidence and arguments provided by various and diverse social science disciplines which deny the historical plausibility of the commodity view. Metaphorically, Randall Wray calls the world where the barter as a market system existed the 'Never-Never Land'.[15] He assumes that the explanatory priority of the origin and subsequent functioning of the money

[8] Menger (1982), pp. 15–16.

[9] Smith (1776), pp. 15–16.

[10] Menger (1982), pp. 20–21.

[11] Ellis (1937), p. 4.

[12] Ingham (2004); Rahmatian (2020), p. 3.

[13] See Ingham (2004), pp. 20–22, 28–33.

[14] Orleán quoted in Dodd (2014), p. 19.

[15] Wray (2000), p. 42.

system is the creation by any authority of a 'money unit of account'.[16] The anthropologist Caroline Humphrey points out that 'barter was indeed very rare as a system dominating primitive economies',[17] and explains the difference between money (payment) and barter (interchange) in the following terms:

> The key point about money is that, whatever functions it may have, the payee is able to perform them by virtue of the payment but can only do so by making a further payment. [...] Barter, on the other hand, entails no further transaction. It is, in principle, a one-off affair, because the objects exchanged are mainly objects for use.[18]

Grierson proposed in 1978 that money had emerged as a mechanism of criminal compensation under the assumption that a society cannot function if violent behaviour is highly prevalent.[19] Money and monetary valuation would not be exclusive to a market economy but to pre-market societies that generated a scale of valuation of personal damages, as the 'Wergeld'—which would have also given the name to the object 'money' in German, 'Geld'. The operation of the *Wergeld*, as a compensation rate (scale), functioned as a standard of damage value and would have prevented bloodshed under the law of retaliation. The scale distinguished the type of victim, the damage caused, and how that damage was inflicted, allowing the payment of fixed compensation for crimes.[20]

Others criticize the classic theory of money for its weak institutionalist explanation of the monetary phenomenon,[21] considering that the provision of money in an economy would require a certain degree of control, among other reasons, due to the high complexity of its operation and the consequent creation (or in conjunction with) of other institutions by the monetary phenomenon, which shows the need for an institutional framework that allows its operation.[22]

The point is that all States currently operate with fiat money, which means that it has no asset backing and no intrinsic value, and, in this line, the credit approach grants a better explanation of money.[23] The credit view emerged at the beginning of the twentieth century from the theoretical proposals of the German economist Georg Friedrich Knapp in 1905, and British economist and diplomat Alfred Mitchell-Innes in 1913. The chartalist and the claim accounts—branches of this theory—identify money as a social and legal phenomenon based on an underlying credit and debit relationship between the issuer of money and its holder, assuming that the existence of a fixed unit of account is the core of any explanation of the monetary theory.

16 Wray (2000), p. 43 ff.

17 Humphrey (1985), p. 50.

18 Humphrey (1985), p. 51.

19 Grierson (1978), p. 2.

20 Grierson (1978), pp. 12–13.

21 Goodhart (1989), p. 24.

22 Crump (2010), p. 1.

23 Keynes (1930), p. 4.

Following Keynes, '[f]iat money only appears when the State goes further and abandons the objective standard'.[24]

The opening of *The State Theory of Money* assumes that money needs the law to emerge and function, and at that level, the action of the State is also required. In brief terms, Knapp proposes that money appears in a nation when the State (i) establishes a unit of monetary account, (ii) chooses an object as a means of payment (money), calls it the same as the unit of account and declares it as a valid means of payment, and (iii) accepts to receive that object as a means of payment of its credits.[25] That object becomes a generally accepted means of payment and is used in trade between private parties and between private parties and the State.

Related to the distinction between barter and monetary payment made by Humphrey, the credit theory of money proposed by Mitchell-Innes is based on the idea 'that a sale and purchase is the exchange of a commodity for a credit.' Mitchell-Innes adds:

> the value of credit or money does not depend on the value of any metal or metals but on the right which the creditor acquires to 'payment', that is to say, to satisfaction for the credit and on the obligation of the debtor to 'pay' his debt, and conversely on the right of the debtor to release himself from his debt by the tender of an equivalent debt owed by the creditor, and the obligation of the creditor to accept this tender in satisfaction of his credit.[26]

The 'unit of monetary account', like the dollar and euro, is not the coin. It is not a concrete object but a quantifier that enables us to express and measure the value of goods, formulate and enter into monetary obligations and clear them in the future. It is an instrument of account, such as kilometres and miles, and its selection is arbitrary, like grammar rules.[27]

The concept of the unit of account transforms the monetary system into a nominalist one, a feature that Knapp calls '*lytric*'. This term was taken by Knapp from the Greek «λύτρον» (*lytron*) which meant the payment made for a ransom, signifying the idea that the paid amount liberates the debtor. We express the value of commodities in a *lytric* way when such value is not expressed in another commodity but in a unit of value.[28] The unit of account allows us to omit the value of the medium of exchange when we interchange two commodities. The unit of account has not been fixed in a 'technical' way—as in the fabrication of coins—but in a historical one.[29] An example of historical fixation is the irrevocable conversion rates between the euro and national currencies. For example, the conversion rule declared that '1 euro is equivalent to 40.3399 Deutsche mark' or '1 euro is equivalent to 1936.27

---

[24] Keynes (1930), p. 10.

[25] Knapp (1924), p. 102.

[26] Mitchell-Innes (1914), p. 152.

[27] Wittgenstein (1974), para 133.

[28] Knapp opposed the *lytric value* of a commodity to the *authylic value* of a commodity. We can explain the lytric value using the Marx example: "[l]et us take two commodities, such as a coat and 10 yards of linen, and let the value of the first be twice the value of the second, so that, if 10 yards of linen = *W*, the coat = *2W*", Marx (1976), p. 132.

[29] Knapp (1924), pp. 10–11.

Italian lire'.[30] That means that the ability of the new means of payment, i.e., the euro, to serve as a generally accepted means of payment depends on that legal declaration made by the EU Council on December 31, 1998.

This rule shows that the modern monetary system works continuously, allowing the debts and means of payment to be *lytric*. The so-called '*compensatory* means of payment'—that preceded the lytric means of payment—function as a means of payment by delivering tokens, which must be counted, weighed, or measured to determine payment conformity. In a modern (*lytric*) monetary system, the means of payment are governed by the Nominalism principle. For example, the former debt incurred in lire must be paid in the new unit of account, the euro, after it started to be in force. In a lytric means of payment system, the 'nominal' condition of any debt is shown by the fact that the payable units of account then in force must be calculated about the earlier unit as the conversion rule declared. So, Knapp said that '[t]he State, therefore, conceives lytric debts not as 'real debts' in the material for payment which was in use when the debt was incurred but as nominal debts repayable in the material in use at the time of repayment'.[31]

About this historical fixation of the unit of account, Keynes characterized that as *continuous*, saying that:

> Thus there can be no real breach in the continuity of descent in the pedigree of the money of account, except by a catastrophe in which all existing contracts are simultaneously wiped out.[32]

Another feature of the monetary system observed by the credit view of money is that it always underlies a credit relationship. Money is a social relation of credit and debt, and using Simmel's classic statement, '[m]oney is only a claim against society',[33] Ingham says:

> the possessor of money is owed goods. But money also represents a claim or credit against the issuer – monarch, state, bank and so on. Money has to be 'issued'. And something can only be issued as money, if it is capable of cancelling any debt incurred by the issuer.[34]

In other words, any modern monetary system is always subject to an underlying credit relationship, which means that its users, as holders of tokens of money, have claims to others and are subject to the invocation by others of counterclaims. The claim is eventual: it is updated only when the central clearing office asserts against that holder the claim of another—a counterclaim for the former. At that time, the holder can invoke her claim—now in the act—by delivering currency to comply with her obligation.[35]

---

[30] https://www.ecb.europa.eu/press/pr/date/1998/html/pr981231_2.en.html, Accessed March 11, 2023.

[31] Knapp (1924), pp. 15–16.

[32] Keynes (1930), pp. 4–5.

[33] Simmel (2004), p. 176.

[34] Ingham (2004), p. 25.

[35] Knapp (1924), p. 154.

The holder of money issued by the State or private entities has the power to deliver the holding token money as a means of payment to the issuer of such money or against another member of the community of payments formed by the corresponding issuer. And *vice versa*, the rest of the holders of instances of money have against others, as a counterclaim, the power to insist on payment with the delivery of that token money. In any payment community, money issuers occupy the Hohfeldian positions of rights or claims, power, duty, and liability in time.[36] The play of money claims and counterclaims requires an independent third party that receives and registers the lytric claims and clears the credits and debits, fixing the final balances from time to time and conclusively extinguishing debts with settlements.[37]

2.2 *Money as an Institutional Artifact*

Simmel identified money as

> the purest form of the tool, in the category mentioned above [as intensified means]; it is an institution through which the individual concentrates his activity and possessions to attain goals that he could not attain directly. [...] The nature and effectiveness of money is not to be found simply in the coin that I hold in my hand; its qualities are invested in the social organizations and the suprasubjective norms that make this coin a tool of endlessly diverse and extensive uses despite its material limitations, its insignificance and rigidity.[38]

Simmel rightly describes money as a tool that is not intelligibly isolated. In contemporary language, money is an institutional artifact. As a complex piece, money is part of a picture composed of other elements inserted within the declaration of rules, practices, and conventions that construct the social reality.[39]

Chartalism has the virtue of understanding how money works in a community which is not anchored to a metal or other commodity. It develops not just an economic theory but a legal theory of money. However, its explanation must be complemented by theoretical concepts developed by the social ontology and philosophy of artifacts to give us an overview of the emergence and maintenance of the monetary phenomenon in any society.

I will argue that money is an institutional artifact with a twofold constitutional base. On the one hand, money needs a central authority that rules the system's operation after the declarations that constitute the unit of account and the objects that will count as tokens to release debts. On the other hand, money is a social

---

[36] Hohfeld (1920), p. 65.

[37] Knapp (1924), p. 152; López (2024), p. 135.

[38] Simmel (2004), p. 210.

[39] Searle (2010); López (2024).

phenomenon that realizes its monetary functions through the recognition and treatment of money by an intended audience with collective intentionality.[40]

I call the first set of conditions the 'state-based conditions' that are necessary but insufficient to create and operate the monetary system. In turn, I call the second set of conditions the 'social-based conditions' and consist of recognizing the state declarations by a community.

Rather than its creation, the problem of the cash is its acceptance.[41] Following Searle, the money tokens will perform the functions not solely by their physical structure but by the treatment given in commerce by a community with collective intentionality.[42] Both conditions are individually necessary and jointly sufficient in any monetary system.

An artifact, following Dipert, is a tool that intentionally signals or communicates that it is a tool. Any artifact has tool-communicating and tool properties. The tool-communicating properties allow the users' community to recognize the particular properties that will enable the agent to achieve her goals in the artefactual object. They 'are made with the intention to bring about a belief in another agent'.[43]

Money is a public artifact; that is, it does 'not depend merely on the individual intentions of their makers; they also depend on public norms',[44] in the way 'that members of *public* artifact kinds must be intended to be *recognizable* as artifacts of that kind by a certain *intended audience*'.[45] Public artifacts require '*to be treated, used, or regarded* in some ways rather than others'.[46] They are normative objects, grounded in "constitutive norms' of treatment [...]',[47] objects that realize their function only if they are used by certain people, in a certain way, in specific contexts, etc. To count as public artifacts, they must exhibit 'an *intended feature*, essential to membership in the kind [public artifact], that they are subject to those norms'.[48] In legal terms, money as a public artifact is a legal artifact, too, and law grants money most of its properties.

On the one hand, tool properties are those that allow money to serve its functions in any market. I distinguish first-order and second-order of tool properties. The first-order properties serve money's abstract and concrete functions. While the abstract function of money consists of the possibility to express the value of things, services, and patrimony using the unit of account, allowing us to formulate debts, the concrete function of money is to fulfil the payment of debts by delivering money tokens. The second-order properties are the functions of a store of value and a subsidiary

[40] Searle (2010).

[41] Minsky (2008), p. 79.

[42] Searle (2010) 1995.

[43] Dipert (1993), p. 102.

[44] Thomasson (2014), p. 47.

[45] Thomasson (2014), p. 50.

[46] Thomasson (2014), p. 52.

[47] Thomasson (2014), p. 52.

[48] Thomasson (2014), p. 52.

means of enforcing any obligations, including debts. The first and second-order properties are possible by the complementary properties of monetary systems: nominalism and fungibility.

On the other hand, tool-communicating properties show us the concrete and abstract function that money may realize, performing a semiotic function. Again, in Simmel's words

> [a]s a visible object, money is the substance that embodies abstract economic value, in a similar fashion to the sound of words which is an acoustic-physiological occurrence but has significance for us only through the representation that it bears or symbolized.[49]

The explanation above allows us to understand money as a normative artifact or, in social ontology terms, an *institutional artifact*.[50] That money is an institutional artifact implies that it is created for both a constitutive rule and the successful following of constitutive and regulatory rules. Successful recognition and its use as money by the particular audience determine its use as money, bringing things full circle. Its users' regulative rules must cover aspects such as how that artifact should be used, for what purpose, by whom, and in under what context or circumstance. In other words, a series of constitutive and regulative rules allow the existence and regulate the different spheres of creation and use, respectively, of public artifacts within a community.[51] In Ludwig terms:

> Since a rule-governed social transaction is an essentially intentional joint action type, for anything to play the role in question, it must be used intentionally by the participants as the object mentioned in the constitutive rule governing the action type.[52]

3 The Legal Nature of Cryptocurrencies

3.1 Some Conceptual Clarifications

I will argue that cryptocurrencies are not (still) money and will hardly become money in the future unless the States decide to treat them as such. To explain this statement, it is necessary to introduce the chartalist distinction between *valuta* and *accessory* money and to take note of a fundamental conceptual clarification.

Assuming that money is a proclaimed means of payment of general acceptance expressed in the current unit of account, accepted by the State, and that is not and does not represent any asset, the individually necessary and jointly sufficient conditions for something to count as *valuta money* are the followings:

---

[49] Simmel (2004), p. 118.

[50] See López (2024), chapter I.

[51] See Thomasson (2014), pp. 52–55; Searle (2010), pp. 9.10.

[52] Ludwig (2017), pp. 113–114.

(a) it must be compulsory money, i.e., it must be accepted in payment by private persons, whether paid by another private person or by the State,
(b) it must be definitive, that is, inconvertible, so that with its delivery, the process of payment is concluded for the payee, for the payer and the issuer of the money, and
(c) the money is both compulsory and definitive, and the State keeps such money ready to pay with it, having the power to oblige its citizens to accept it.

On the other hand, *accessory money* is the chartal means of payment that lacks, at least, some of the conditions a, b, or c.[53] An easy way to check the *valutaeness* of money within a given national territory is if the citizens of the related country can buy the corresponding tokens. Those tokens are accessory money if citizens can buy them (or need to buy them). On the contrary, regarding valuta money, citizens can obtain such tokens by working, selling goods and services, or receiving them from the State through payments or aids delivered by the latter. From the characterization of the kinds of money referred to, it can be inferred that in chartalism, money is not characterized according to whether the State has issued it as a necessary condition. Also, it does not need to be legal tender to count as money. The truth of this assertion can be proved by resorting to Bank notes.

As Gouge wrote in 1833, the Bank notes were the following:

> *simple evidences of debt* due by the Bank. [...] For the promissory notes of the Banks, the Banks *receive* interest. [...] Bank notes are never paid.
>
> Payment of them in the aggregate is never demanded because what could be got in payments would, for most purposes of domestic trade, serve no better purpose than Bank notes themselves.[54]

In its origins, the Bank notes were issued by commercial banks with the promise to convert them to metal or state money. Generally, the State declared that it would receive them in payment of its credits and used them to pay its credits, always at par value —exhibiting its nominal character. However, in periods of economic crisis or war, the State declared the notes unconvertible. The Bank notes were accessory money: they were used as a general and facultative means of payment, were tokens issued under a unit of account and not asset-backed—in Chile, banks had to issue them against 30% of its capital— but under the promise to convert them in other asset and accepted by the State in payment. But when the inconvertibility was declared, they became valuta money. The State accepted them, used them, and kept them ready to pay its debts.[55]

A noteworthy point to understand the view defended in this work is the relation between the expressions 'money' and 'means of payment'. Many misunderstandings in monetary theory conceptualization come from the lack of separation between

---

[53] Knapp (1924), pp. 95–105.

[54] Gouge (1833), p. 54. See Desan (2015).

[55] Knapp (1924), pp. 132–134, 139. For the Chilean case, see Ossa (1993), pp. 3–6, and López (2023).

both concepts. Classical authors assumed the assimilation; Samuelson says, '[w]hat is money? Money is anything that serves as a commonly accepted medium of exchange'. However, the fact that they are not synonyms does not mean there is no relation between them: both expressions are in a genus (means of payment) to species (money) relationship. Assuming that both terms refer to the same object implies the collapse of the concept of money. For example, when we say, 'a box of cigarettes is money,' because, in some war camps, cigarette boxes were used to interchange commodities between prisoners, we trivialize the concept of 'money.' The box of cigarettes is simply an object exchanged for another object, constituting the referred transaction as a barter and not a sale. An economy based on barters is not a monetary system—maybe not an economy at all—and if the barter succeeds in a monetary system, what has probably happened there is that the State has lost its power, or the community is facing a political crisis.[56]

Suppose we separate both terms, assuming the genus-to-species relationship is correct. In that case, we can make distinctions that would have a legal theoretical yield. For example, clarifying that bank deposits, which economic theory calls 'bank money' or 'money in the abstract sense', are not money but a personal right operated under a unit of account. With this characterization, we can conclude that bank money is an *ius* (a claim), which is governed by the rules of the irregular deposit contract and some special rules of banking law and not by property law. This characterization makes it possible to understand why the clients of any bank do not have ownership over the monetary tokens deposited, making it impossible to vindicate them. The clients have a mere *ius in personam* over a sum of money, not an *ius in rem.* A bank deposit creates a debt from the bank to the client. The deposit does not create money; the deposit made by the client will only transfer the ownership of the deposited signs of money in the bank's current account to the bank.

Following F. A. Mann, lawyers should not give in to economists. He says that:[57]

> As a rule, however, the economist's view that everything is money that functions as money is unacceptable to lawyers. Bank accounts, for instance, are debts, not money, and deposit accounts are not even debts payable on demand. Similarly, bills of exchange are not money; on the contrary, they require the drawee to pay 'a sum certain in money'. Debts are contracted in terms of money, not in terms of bank accounts or bills. In the absence of the creditor's consent, [...] debts cannot be discharged otherwise than by the payment of what the law considers as money, namely legal tender. [...] Money is not the same as credit. Nor is the law of money identical with the law of credit. Nor does the fact that 'bank money' largely functions as money prove that in law it necessarily and invariably is money.

With this first conceptual distinction, it is possible to make progress in identifying the legal status of cryptocurrency and new digital means of payment without admitting that they are money.

Therefore, the fact that some means of payment are not money does not mean they are irrelevant to the monetary system. The chartalism distinction between *chartal* and *giro* means of payment will be helpful to understand this point. The giro

[56] See Lerner (1947), p. 313; Wray (1998).

[57] Mann (1992), pp. 5–6.

means of payment, for example, checks drawing, electronic transfer of money, credit, and charge cards use, does not consist of delivering *something* to the creditor. On the contrary, its operation consists of creating complex legal relationships between the debtor, creditor, issuer, and institutions that manage each giro's means of payment. The indicated operation implies the debts' payments through the creation, assignment, and setting of sums of money credits expressed in the current monetary unit of account.[58]

Knapp observes that '[i]n a pay-group every transferable right to dispose of units of value is means of payment if the holder can by transfer set up in the central office a counterclaim which is at any rate eventual', adding that in the giro payment, the creditor does not accept a thing but a 'legal method'.[59] Specifically, the payment made to the debt's creditor implies her acceptance of the acquisition of a right in person, the object of which is the promise of a future payment. The conditions that make this legal method an effective means of payment is that the unit of account has a conceptual, logical priority in the monetary system. So, as Knapp says, it is possible to abolish money without abolishing the debts if we retain and operate the giro systems. That is so because the essential characteristic of the system is the expression of debts in units of account—they are lytric debts.[60]

3.2 *The Moneyness of Cryptocurrencies*

3.2.1 Are Cryptocurrencies Money?[61]

For this point, I will use the literature on Bitcoin because it is possible to find refined and massive studies, unlike other cryptocurrencies. Leaving aside those who accept the monetary condition of cryptocurrencies,[62] most authors either affirm or deny their monetary condition, appealing to the concept of money as a *functional kind.* The mainstream monetary literature assumes that what counts as money is that which fulfils the economic functions that Jevons proposed in 1875, namely, medium of (inter)exchange, unit of account, and store of value.[63] Legal authors such as Ascarelli, Nussbaum, Proctor, Schmidt, Staudinger, Fox, and Papadopoulos, have observed the relevance of a functionalist approach in the monetary theory.[64] In the same vein, sociologists such as Ingham, Dodd, or Bjerg,[65] economists such as

[58] López (2024).

[59] Knapp (1924), pp. 155–156.

[60] Knapp (1924), p. 156.

[61] López (2023).

[62] See Glass (2017), p. 486, Grinberg (2012), p. 60, Girasa (2018), p. 8, and Geva (2016), p. 283.

[63] Jevons (1875), pp. 13–14.

[64] Ascarelli (1928), p. 48; Nussbaum (1937), p. 867; Proctor (2012), Schmidt (1983), pp. 23–24; Von Staudinger (2016), Fox (2008), § 1.19, Papadopoulos (2009), p. 953.

[65] Ingham (2004), Dodd (2014), p. 8; Bjerg (2016).

Schumpeter[66] and authorities as the Bank of England or the IRS,[67] have also made their contributions on this matter. Moreover, some classical economists, such as Samuelson, assume that money is simply a medium of exchange.[68]

Those who assume that Bitcoin is money and *mutatis mutandis* (at least) fiat cryptocurrencies understand that they fulfil one or more of the mentioned functions, albeit defectively. Hence, Bitcoin serves as a medium of exchange and unit of account, even though the ability to serve as a store of value is defectively realized in attention to their price volatility. This volatility mainly affects *fiat cryptocurrencies* as opposed to what happens with *stablecoins* because of their financial structure.[69] The exchange function can be performed competitively given its virtuality, low costs, speed, and anonymity. It serves as a standard of value because it operates under an autonomous monetary unit of account (e.g., *bitcoin* and *satoshi*), making it possible to express value in that unit.[70]

Bjerg describes Bitcoin adequately: it operates as an independent currency, and its relevant feature is that it does so without being based on gold, without generating debt, and without a State.[71] Rahmatian points out that Bitcoin is 'the most important example of a private digital currency', but adds that 'it is not money [currency] as normally understood'[72] because none of the three monetary functions already referred to are well fulfilled.

In contrast, arguments to deny the money status of cryptocurrencies appeal to their condition as speculative assets,[73] assuming that their high volatility price prevents them from functioning as a standard of value,[74] and for those who understand[75] and empirically prove[76] that, ultimately, Bitcoin does not perform any of the monetary functions satisfactorily, being, in short, a *para-money* currency, transmitting economic value and not being money.[77]

From a functionalist conception of money, cryptocurrencies count as a means of payment, even though their general acceptance must be tested empirically and based on conventional standards. However, in general terms, such currencies are of low acceptance in commercial stores and operate on the margins of the banking system, facts that make them less massive. This solely fact can serve to deny their monetary condition, but it is convenient to review the performance of other functions. First, its

66 Schumpeter (2014).

67 Ali et al., (2014), p. 279; IRS, 2014: S. 2ª.

68 Samuelson and Nordhaus (2010), p. 458.

69 See Kim (2022).

70 Vardi (2016), p. 60.

71 Bjerg (2016), p. 68.

72 Rahmatian (2020), p. 100.

73 Kirkby (2018), p. 536; Seetharaman et al. (2017), p. 238.

74 Yermack (2015), Barroilhet (2019).

75 Hanley (2013).

76 Evans (2014), pp. 9–10.

77 Papadopoulos (2015), pp. 155–156.

price is highly volatile and has dropped sharply over between 2022 and 2023: on March 28, 2022, the price of Bitcoin was US$ 47,100, and on March 5, 2023, it was US$ 22,464, which is less than half of its price. Last year, the difference between semesters was high: on January 15th, 2024, the Bitcoin price was UD$ 41,715; on June 8th, 2024, it was 53,991; and on January 10th, 2025, it was 92,494.[78] Second, its unit of value function is performed defectively because it is still associated with State currencies such as the US dollar. The volatility of its price in the stock market makes the valuation of other goods in such cryptocurrencies unstable, without serving 'as a reference price for other goods due to its volatility'.[79]

Using chartalist tools, cryptocurrencies, specifically fiat ones such as Bitcoin, are closely like money: they are not backed in an asset or in the issuer's equity. However, they count as accepted means of payment, operate against an autonomous monetary unit of account receiving their instances the same unit of account denomination, and have no use value.

Why have they not yet achieved the status of money? Firstly, they are not generally accepted as means of payment on ordinary interchanges; secondly, they lack a credit relation, which is the fundamental feature of modern money. Following Jansen, '[w]here the contemporary money is self-referential, Bitcoins refer to nothing as they are created and pre-distributed as transactions without a source'.[80] The fiat cryptocurrencies issuers do not assume any obligation to the users of such currencies: issuers do not have the duty to accept them back later, do not give any guarantee to the owners of instances in case of system collapse, and do not promise to convert the currency to another currency or asset.

Finally, if someone assumes that the underlying credit and debit relationship is not a necessary condition to generate a monetary system, it would be necessary to review the money's status of cryptocurrencies. Under some conceptions of monetary system, if cryptocurrency tokens became generally accepted as a means of payment, the cryptocurrencies would be considered a kind of money. If in the future these currencies are generally accepted, it will become mandatory to be received by the creditor, will be inconvertible into another asset, and will be held and used by the State to pay its debts, cryptocurrencies will exhibit the condition of valuta money—in the relevant economy—but if any of the mentioned conditions are lacking, cryptocurrencies will be considered accessory money.

3.2.2 Are Cryptocurrencies a Kind of Means of Payment?

Cryptocurrencies are indeed a means of payment. They allow the acquisition of goods and services against the transfer of an asset that exhibits the character of lytric, according to the explanation given above. However, the conclusion as to whether cryptocurrencies count as a means of giro payment is not easy to determine.

[78] https://coinmarketcap.com/es/currencies/bitcoin/.

[79] Barroilhet (2019), p. 48.

[80] Jansen (2013), p. 17.

In one sense, their operation does not presuppose a credit relationship between the issuer and the user; on the contrary, as already mentioned, the issuer does not assume any obligation with the users, though they assume the risk in holding such tokens. Yet, from another point of view, the system's operation has similarities with the form and object of operation of the giro system. In Knapp's terms, the last is a legal method and does not operate based on the delivery of something.[81]

Thus, the order to transfer a certain number of bitcoins, for example, to another member of the payment community, is carried out in favour of the receiver by crediting a new register in his account balance consisting of adding an amount of bitcoins. In other words, an *ius in personam* is assigned from one user to another after the acceptance of other miners—who must resolve a complicated mathematical problem to add the transaction to the blockchain. Likewise, compensation, which is at the heart of a giro means of payment, cannot be invoked due to restrictions inherent to the design of the Bitcoin system.

Because of the way cryptocurrencies operate as means of payment, they shall be assumed as *sui generis* means of payment, which will generate the need for further regulation, as shown in the following section.

4 A Brief Reflection of the Regulation and the Legal Challenges of the 'Innovative Disruptions' Payment Systems

The regulation of electronic or digital means of payment, i.e., including giro systems and, especially, the so-called 'virtual currencies', has been ambivalent. Some regulations treat them as a means of payment, others as financial assets considering their high speculative risk, and others as cash.

The European Union regulation is a sample of the *mercurial* condition of the word 'money', explained above. According to Directive 2014/65/EU of the European Parliament and the Council (MiFID II), some crypto-money are considered 'financial instruments', because they qualify as instruments 'specified in Section C of Annex I, including such instruments issued by means of distributed ledger technology' (Article 4(1)(15)). With this wording, tokens that are fully decentralized applications without an intermediary, such as Bitcoins, are considered financial instruments exempted from the scope of the recent Regulation (EU) 2023/1114 of the European Parliament and of the Council of 31 May 2023 on markets in crypto-assets, known as 'MICA'. The mentioned exception has been declared in Recital 22 and in Article 2(2)(a) of MiCA; the last article sets forth that the regulation does not apply to crypto-assets qualified as financial instruments. However,

[81] See Nussbaum (1937), p. 867.

partially decentralized applications remain within the scope of Titles III and IV of MICA.[82]

On the other hand, some virtual currencies are defined as 'electronic money' and are ruled by Directive 2009/110 of the European Parliament and of the Council. Electronic money 'means electronically, including magnetically, stored monetary value as represented by a claim on the issuer, which is issued on receipt of funds for the purpose of making payment transactions as defined in point 5 of Article 4 of Directive 2007/64/EC, and which is accepted by a natural or legal person other than the electronic money issuer'. It is not under the scope of MICA, but if it is considered an 'electronic money token', according to MICA definition, titles II and III of MICA shall apply, unless otherwise stated in Title IV of MICA related to e-money token (Article 48 (3)).

On the other hand, on May 31, 2023, Regulation 2023/1114 (MICA) regulate 'the undertakings that are engaged in the issuance, offer to the public and admission to trading of crypto-assets or that provide services related to crypto-assets in the Union' (Article 2(1)). By 'crypto-asset', MICA understands 'digital representation of a value or of a right that is able to be transferred and stored electronically using distributed ledger technology or similar technology' (Article 3(1)5). Article 2 distinguishes three kinds of crypto-assets under the scope of the regulation: (i) 'asset-referenced token', known as 'ART', defined as 'means a type of crypto-asset that is not an electronic money token and that purports to maintain a stable value by referencing another value or right or a combination thereof, including one or more official currencies' (Article 3(1)6); (ii) 'electronic money token' or 'e-money token', 'ERT', that is a 'type of crypto-asset that purports to maintain a stable value by referencing the value of one official currency' (Article 3(1)7), and (iii) other crypto-asset, than asset-referenced tokens or e-money tokens' (Title II), such as 'utility token' (Article 3(1)9). It is worth noting that MICA scope is the stable digital tokens, i.e., coins (EMT) and other representations of value (ART) that aim to maintain stable value in relation to one asset or a set of assets, like legal tender coins or a commodity. So, Bitcoin is not within the scope of the law because it has not been defined as electronic money or EMT.

The Regulation 2024/1624 of the European Parliament and of the Council of May 31, 2024, on the prevention of the use of the financial system for the purposes of money laundering or terrorist financing ('AML'), is consisted with the institutional ecosystem digital representation of financial and monetary assets created by the European Union. It assumes the definitions of 'crypto-asset' and 'electronic money' of MICA and MiFiD, respectively, in order to prevent its use to launder money. However, by a practical need, AML expands its scope to any 'fund' or 'property', defined as 'means assets of any kind, whether corporeal or incorporeal, movable or immovable, tangible or intangible, and legal documents or instruments in any form, including electronic or digital, evidencing title to, or an interest in, such assets' by Article 2(2) Directive 2018/1673. According to AML, totally

[82] See Zetzsche and Sinnig (2024), pp. 6, 21–22; Revolidis (2025) pp. 168–169.

decentralized tokens such as Bitcoin will be within the European Union's regulation to prevent money laundering.

Finally, by Regulation 2022/858, the Euro Zone has adopted a pilot legal framework for the decentralized registration technology used in the crypto markets—known by the acronym 'DLT'—which allows cryptocurrencies to operate. Under this Regulation, the European Union is trying to take up, pursue, and supervise the decentralized registration technology prudentially, granting and withdrawing specific permissions to operate DLT market infrastructures (Article 1). The objective is 'to allow for innovation and experimentation in a sound regulatory environment while preserving investor protection, market integrity, and financial stability' (recital 23). The weak spot of the pilot Regulation is that it admits to trading or recording on a DLT market infrastructure only shares, bonds, and units in collective investment undertakings that benefit from the execution-only exemption under Directive 2014/65/EU. Finally, currently under discussion is the proposal of the Parliament and the Counsel for a regulation of the markets in crypto assets, published on September 29, 2020. The proposal aims to 'cover crypto-assets falling outside existing EU financial services legislation, as well as e-money tokens'. The proposal sets forth that the objectives or regulations are to (i) grant legal certainty; (ii) support innovation; (iii) grant consumer and investor protection and create market integrity, and (iv) ensure financial stability.

The monetary authority of Singapore has rightly summarized the risks that regulation of the new means of payment must face: money laundering and terrorism financing, protection of the user, interoperability of the payment instruments considering a so-called fragmented landscape, and the technology risk.[83] Japan was the first country to accept virtual currencies as a means of payment, but it did not consider them legal tender.[84] Singapore adopted cryptocurrencies as a legal means of payment in 2019 but did not assimilate them into money. The Payment Services Act 2019 (No. 2 of 2019) of Singapore[85] defines a 'digital payment token' as 'any digital representation of value (other than an excluded digital representation of value) that —(a) is expressed as a unit; (b) is not denominated in any currency, and is not pegged by its issuer to any currency; (c) is, or is intended to be, a medium of exchange accepted by the public, or a section of the public, as payment for goods or services or for the discharge of a debt; (d) can be transferred, stored or traded electronically; and (e) satisfies such other characteristics as the Authority may prescribe'. However, the digital payment token is excluded from the concept of 'money'; it includes e-money but excludes any digital payment token and any excluded digital representation of value (Part 1.2).

---

[83] https://www.mas.gov.sg/-/media/MAS/FAQ/PS-Act-Infographic.pdf?la=en&hash=2FB2519F0C369FFFD6D2BEF6367E9A136399BA65.

[84] Payment Services Act (Act No. 59 of 2009), see https://www.japaneselawtranslation.go.jp/en.

[85] See https://www.mas.gov.sg/regulation/acts/payment-services-act. Accessed March 19 2023.

In 2021, El Salvador declared Bitcoin a legal tender currency through the Bitcoin Act.[86] Nevertheless, it is difficult to analyze their results due to the limited reliable information that can be obtained. Finally, the Central African Republic, following El Salvador, adopted Bitcoin in April 2022 as an official currency alongside its local currency, the CFA franc.[87]

The Chilean Central Bank has stated that means of payment are indispensable for the proper functioning of the economy, contributing to implementing monetary policy, ensuring the circulation of money. This relevance explains that several institutions are focused on regulating and implementing improvements to the means of payment systems by including digital solutions. The Chilean Central Bank has self-imposed an 'Agenda on Digital Means of Payment',[88] considering it a necessary element to boost the reactivation and financial inclusion, and a fundamental task in its strategic plan. This work resulted in the document titled *First Report: Preliminary Evaluation*. The Chilean Central Bank highlights its interest in analysing changes in the payment systems 'and developing a medium/long-term agenda to anticipate new challenges and strengthen the payment system for the country'.[89] The statements of entities such as the World Bank prove the transversality of this concern.

While the Chilean Central Bank is studying the necessity, convenience, and ways of issuing Chilean pesos in digital support, from March 2023, Chilean law assumed the existence of this phenomenon through Act No. 21,252 of 2023. The Act recognizes some part of the so-called in the literature 'stablecoins': cryptocurrencies based on national or foreign money (including in these the documents payable in foreign currency or basket of them). It describes them as 'digital, electronic or computerized representations, registered using systems that use distributed registry technologies or other analogous ones, of units whose value is directly determined and backed by money' already referred to. For their operation, control, and effects in Chile, the Act grants competence to the Chilean Central Bank to determine the minimum standards and conditions to be set by the operators and issuers by a general rule not yet issued.

These new state-of-the-art innovations, such as private digital currencies, challenge a model based on state monopoly more than any other means of payment, as they operate without the need for the State. The issuance of state money as an expression of sovereignty is not only translated into the State printing of papers containing images, signatures, and seals that remind us of the existence and power of the issuer but also constitutes the very idea of a modern state. The issuance of money 'became a regular attribute of the modern Nation State: an independent country issued its own standardized currency, which was legal tender within its territory and the States authenticated and protected the issuance of its money'.[90]

---

[86] Diario Oficial, El Salvador, https://www.diariooficial.gob.sv/.

[87] Kedem (2022), p. 48.

[88] Banco Central de Chile (2022).

[89] Banco Central de Chile (2021).

[90] Carruthers and Arslan (2019), para 4.2.

It will be fundamental, then, to address the money system as a legal institution constitutive of the market and of a national economy from a new perspective and to reconstruct the State's competence in the monetary system if the market wants to survive in an orderly and safe manner.

References

Ascarelli, T (1928) La Moneta. Considerazione di Dritto Privatto. Cedam, Padova

Banco Central de Chile (2021) Prioridades para la agenda de pagos del Banco Central de Chile. In: Presentación ante la Comisión de Hacienda del Senado, Comisión de Hacienda del Senado, 27 de septiembre de 2021 https://www.bcentral.cl/documents/33528/133214/mmc27092021_senado.pdf/34dcd590-304a-a3d1-6aac-15b37af3d634?t=1632759778523

Banco Central de Chile (2022) Emisión de una moneda digital de banco central en Chile: Primer Informe. https://www.bcentral.cl/web/banco-central/areas/observatorio-tecnologico/exploracion-de-monedas-digitales-de-banco-central

Barroilhet A (2019) Criptomonedas, economía y derecho. Revista Chilena de Derecho y Tecnología 8:29–67

Bjerg O (2016) How is bitcoin money? Theory Cult Soc 33(1):53–72

Carruthers B, Arslan M (2019) Sovereignty, law, and money: new developments. Ann Rev Law Soc Sci 4(1–4):18

Crump T (2010) The phenomenon of money. Routledge & Kegan Paul, London

De Bruin Boudewijn HL, O'Neill M, Sandberg J (2020) Philosophy of Money and Finance. In: Zalta EN (ed) The Stanford Encyclopedia of Philosophy. https://plato.stanford.edu/archives/win2020/entries/money-finance/

Desan C (2015) Making money. Coin, currency, and the coming of capitalism. OUP, New York

Diario Oficial El Salvador, https://www.diariooficial.gob.sv/

Dipert R (1993) Artifacts, art works, and agency. Temple University Press, Philadelphia

Dipert R (2005) Some issues in the theory of artifacts: defining 'artifact' and related notions. Monist 78(2):119–135

Dodd N (2014) The social life of money. Princeton University Press, Princeton

Ellis HS (1937) German monetary theory 1905–1933. Harvard University Press, Cambridge

Evan D (2014) Economic aspects of Bitcoin and other decentralized public-ledger currency platforms. Coase-Sandor Institute for Law and Economics Working Paper 685:1–21

Fox D (2008) Property rights in money. OUP, Oxford

Geva B (2016) Mobile payments and bitcoin: concluding reflections on the digital upheaval in payments. In: Gimigliano G (ed) Bitcoin and Mobile payments. Constructing a European Union Framework. Palgrave Macmillan, London, pp 271–287

Grinberg, R (2012) Bitcoin: An innovative alternative digital currency. Hastings Science and Technology Law Journal, 4: 159–208

Girasa R (2018) Regulation of cryptocurrencies and Blockchain technologies. National and International Perspectives. Palgrave Macmillan, Switzerland

Glass J (2017) What is digital currency. IDEA: J Franklin Pierce Center Intellect Prop 57(3):455–518

Goodhart CAE (1989) Money, information and uncertainty, 2nd edn. Macmillan Education Ltd., Hamsphire-London

Gouge WM (1968 [1833]) A short history of paper money and banking in the United States. To which is prefixed an inquiry into the principles of the system. August M. Kelley Publishers, New York

Grierson P (1978) The origins of money. Res Econ Anthropol 1:1–35

Hanley B (2013) The false premises and promises of bitcoin. Discussion Paper: 1–30 https://arxiv.org/abs/1312.2048

Hohfeld W. N (1920) Fundamental legal conceptions as applied in judicial reasoning: and other legal essays. In: Walter Wheeler Cook (ed) Yale University Press, New Haven
Humphrey C (1985) Barter and economic disintegration. Man New Ser 20(1):48–72
Ingham G (2004) The nature of money. Polity
Jansen M (2013) Bitcoin: the political 'virtual' of an intangible material currency. Int J Commun Curr Res 17(A):8–18
Jevons S (1875 [1896]) Money and the mechanism of exchange. D. Appleton and Company, New York
Kedem S (2022) Central African Republic adopts Bitcoin as legal tender. Afr Bus 494:48–49
Kelton S (2020) The deficit myth: modern monetary theory and the birth of the people's economy. PublicAffairs, Nueva York
Keynes JM (1930 [2013]) A treatise on money. The collected writings of John Maynard Keynes, V, The pure theory of money. Cambridge Univesity Press, Cambridge
Kim SR (2022) How the cryptocurrency market is connected to the financial market. https://ssrn.com/abstract=4106815
Kirkby, R (2018) Cryptocurrencies and digital fiat currencies. The Australian Economic Review, 51 (4): 527–539
Knapp GF (1924) [2003] The state theory of money. Lucas and Bonar. Macmillan & Co., London
Lerner A (1947) Money as a creature of the state. Am Econ Rev 37(2):312–317
London Internal Revenue Service (2014) Notice 2014-21. https://www.irs.gov/pub/irs-drop/n-14-21.pdf. Accessed 29 Feb 2023
López G (2021) Sobre la 'litricidad' y la 'unidad de cuenta dineraria': dos conceptos claves de la teoría cartalista del dinero. In: Cruz Hidalgo E, Parejo Moruno M, Rangel Preciado J (eds) Elementos para un Green New Deal: finanzas, cuidados y educación para una Economía social. Universidad de Extremadura, Cáceres, pp 59–74
López G (2023) ¿Es el *Bitcoin* dinero?: Un análisis de su condición dineraria desde la teoría crediticia del dinero. Revista Chilena De Derecho Y Tecnología 12:1–36. https://doi.org/10.5354/0719-2584.2023.69921
López G (2024) El dinero y las obligaciones de dinero. Marcial Pons, Barcelona, Buenos Aires
Ludwig K (2017) From plural to institutional agency. Collective Action II. OUP, Oxford
Mann FA (1992) The legal aspect of money, 5th edn. Clarendon Press, Oxford
Marx K (1976) Capital. A critique of the political economy, I, 4th edn. (trans: Fowkes B, Fernbach D) Penguin Books, Aylesbury
Menger C (1982 [2009]) On the origins of money. Ludwig von Mises Institute, Auburn
Ministry of Justice, Japan, https://www.japaneselawtranslation.go.jp/en
Minsky H (2008) Stabilizing an unstable economy. McGraw-Hill, New York
Mitchell-Innes A (1913) What is money? Bank Law J 30: 377–408
Mitchell-Innes A (1914) The credit theory of money. Bank Law J 31:151–168
Monetary Authority of Singapore, Payment Services Act 2019 https://www.mas.gov.sg/regulation/acts/payment-services-act
Monetary Authority of Singapore, A Guide to the new Payment Services Act 2019 https://www.mas.gov.sg/-/media/MAS/FAQ/PS-Act-Infographic.pdf?la=en&hash=2FB2519F0C369FFFD6D2BEF6367E9A136399BA65
Mosler W (2013) Soft currency economics II: what everyone thinks they know about monetary policy is wrong, 2nd edn. CreateSpace Independent Publishing Platform
Nussbaum A (1937) Basic monetary conceptions in law. Mich Law Rev 35(6):865–907
Ossa F (1993) La creación del Banco Central de Chile en 1925: antecedentes previos y los primeros años de operación. Estudios de Economía 20(1):69–101
Papadopoulos G (2009) Between rules and power: money as an institution sanctioned by political authority. J Econ Iss XLIII 4:951–969
Papadopoulos G (2015) Blockchain and digital payments: an institutionalist analysis of cryptocurrencies. In: Kuo Chuen DL (ed) Handbook of digital currency. Bitcoin, innovation, financial instruments, and big data. Academic Press, Singapore, pp 153–172

Proctor C (2012) Mann on the legal aspect of money. OUP, Oxford
Rahmatian A (2020) Credit and creed: a critical legal theory of money. Routledge, Oxon, New York
Revolidis I (2025) Boosting digital finance and the digital single market? An overview of the rules on the offering of crypto-assets according to the markets in crypto-assets regulation. In: Mifsud I, Sammut I (eds) The EU internal market in the next decade – quo vadis? Brill Publishers, Netherlands
Samuelson P, Nordhaus W (2010) Economics, 19th edn. McGraw-Hill, New York
Schmidt, K (1983) Geldrecht: Geld, Zins und Währung im deutschen Recht. J. Schweitzer Verlag KG Walter de Gruyter & Co., Berlin
Schumpeter J (1917/18) Das Sozialprodukt und die Rechenpfennige: Glossen und Beiträge zur Geldtheorie von heute. Archiv für Sozialwissenschaft und Sozialpolitik: 672–715
Searle J (2010) Making the social world. Oxford University Press, New York
Seetharaman A, Saravanan AS, Patwa N, Mehta J (2017) Impact of bitcoin as a world currency. Account Financ Res 6(2):230–246
Simmel G (2004) The philosophy of money. In: Frisby D (ed) (trans: Bottomore T, Frisby D). Routledge, London
Smith A (2007 [1776]) The wealth of nations. Harriman House Ltd., Hampshire
Thomasson A (2014) Public artifacts, intentions, and norms. In: Fransen M, Kroes P, Reydon T, Vermaas P (eds) Artefact kinds: ontology and the Humean-made world. Springer International Publishing, Cham
Vardi N (2016) Bit by bit: assessing the legal nature of virtual currencies. In: Gimigliano G (ed) Bitcoin and mobile payments. Constructing a European Union framework. Palgrave Macmillan, London, pp 55–72
Von Mises L (1912 [1981]) The theory of money and credit, H. E. Batson (tra). Liberty Fund, Indianapolis
Von Staudinger J (2016) Kommentar zum Bürgelichen Gesetzbuch mit Einführungsgesetz und Nebengesetzen Buch 2 Recht der Schuldverhältnisse §§ 244-248, PrKG (Geldrecht). Seiller – de Gruyter, Berlin
Wittgenstein L (1974) Philosophical Grammar. In: Rhees R (ed) (trans: Kenny A). Basil Blackwell, Oxford
Wray R (1998) Understanding modern money. Edward Elgar Publishing, Inc, Northampton
Wray R (2000) Modern money. In: Smithin J (ed) What is money? Routledge, London, pp 42–66
Wray R (2015) Modern money theory, 2nd edn. Palgrave Macmillan, Cham
Yermack D (2015) Is bitcoin a real currency? An economic appraisal. In: Kuo Chuen DL (ed) Handbook of digital currency. Bitcoin, innovation, financial instruments, and big data. Academic, Singapore, pp 31–43
Zetzsche D, Sinnig J (2024) The EU approach to regulating digital currencies. Law Contemp Probl 87(2) https://ssrn.com/abstract=4707830 or. https://doi.org/10.2139/ssrn.4707830

Collateral Estoppel in the Brazilian Civil Procedure: A Law and Economics Approach

Luiz Guilherme Marinoni and Vinícius Klein

Abstract This paper addresses the problem of the prohibition of relitigation over issues (collateral estoppel) through the lens of Law and Economics. The article applies the tools and concepts of Law and Economics to the issue of collateral estoppel, aiming to assess how it can impact legal security and effectiveness of adjudication.

1 Introduction

The new Brazilian Civil Procedure Code, which went into effect in March 2016, extended the *res judicata* to incidental issues. In that way, the Code diverged from the usual *civil law* notion of *res judicata*, present until then in Brazilian law.

The problem of the prohibition of relitigation over issues already decided along the procedure does not matter just for the parties, who obviously do not need more than one opportunity to argue over one single issue. Such a prohibition is inherent to the authority of State decisions.

The current paper addresses this civil procedure question through the lens of Law and Economics applied to Civil Procedure and its impacts on the efficiency of the Judiciary in Brazil. In that perspective, the need for a mechanism in civil procedure that prevents repeated litigation of the same issue is rooted in the goal of the juridical system to achieve social pacification and legal security. In addition, Law and Development (L&D) tools are important to enlighten the relation between the relevance of the adjudicatory function of the Judiciary in society.[1] L&E applied to

[1] Trebilcock and Prado (2014), pp. 45–62; Klein (2015a), pp. 32–64.

L. G. Marinoni (✉) · V. Klein
Federal University of Paraná, Curitiba, Brazil
e-mail: guilherme@marinoni.adv.br

S. Zorzetto et al. (eds.), *Developments in Law and Economics in the Italo-Iberoamerican Context*, Economic Analysis of Law in European Legal Scholarship 21, https://doi.org/10.1007/978-3-032-03317-8_11

Civil Legal Procedure will be used to allow a broader view on investment in legal capital is an important feature of economic and social development,[2] especially in the case of developing countries such as Brazil. Predictability and the correctness of solutions to legal disputes is an important asset and the lack of legal security is usually pointed out as an institutional factor that reduces development.[3] The adequate application of the legal rules and commitments in general is extremely relevant in building market institutions and inclusive institutions[4] even though institutional change is a challenging and difficult process.[5] In the case of Brazil access to an adequate solution of legal disputes is a fundamental right grounded in the constitution, so achieving it in an efficient way is a condition for economic social development. However, the reality of Brazil is a Judiciary Tragedy, with a significant backlog of processes and a high cost to society.[6]

In that context, the institute of collateral estoppel and the different models of collateral estoppel[7] must be assessed and evaluated in comparison with the *res judicata* from civil law countries such as Brazil.[8] After all, a correct design of the collateral estoppel can contribute to better law enforcement and higher legal certainty, reducing frivolous litigation.[9] On the other hand, the simple legal transplant of a foreign legal institute is not an effective solution.[10]

To achieve this task the present article will present the institute of collateral estoppel in the first section, showing both the institute in Brazilian Civil Procedure from a dogmatic point of view and in a comparative view with the United States' treatment of the *res judicata* applied to incidental issues. In the next section, the tools and concepts of Law and Economics will be presented and applied to the issue of collateral estoppel, aiming to assess how the implementation of res judicata in incidental questions can impact legal security and effectiveness of adjudication in Brazil. The third section will use the previous debate to present the question of institutional change and design in the Brazilian Judiciary and the impacts on economic development of the adoption of collateral estoppel.

[2] Schwartz and Tullock (1975), pp. 75–82.

[3] North (1990), pp. 107–117; Battesini and North (2019), pp. 85–94.

[4] Acemoglu and Robinson (2012), pp. 45–95.

[5] Krasinski and Klein (2016), pp. 157–162.

[6] Yeung and Azevedo (2011), pp. 343–356; Gico (2020), pp. 33–41.

[7] Spurr (1991), pp. 47–61.

[8] Marinoni (2019), pp. 343–358.

[9] Polinsky and Rubinfeld (1993), pp. 397–435.

[10] Berkowitz et al. (2003), pp. 163–204.

2 Collateral Estoppel in Brazilian Civil Law Procedure

The Brazilian institute of "*coisa julgada*" can be traced back to the roman law *res judicata* as other civil law countries. According to article 503, 1st paragraph of the Brazilian Civil Procedure Code, the *res judicata* befalls the "resolution of an incidental issue, explicitly and incidentally decided in the lawsuit, if: (i) the judgment upon the merits depends on that resolution; (ii) it has been submitted to a previous and effective adversarial proceeding, not occurring when there is a default judgment; (iii) the court has jurisdiction over the matter and the person to solve it as if it were a principal issue".

In the former Civil Procedure Code, the incidental declaratory judgment action was the only option for those who intended to have the incidental issue definitively judged. The new Code abandoned the *civil law* tradition's usual systemization of the *res judicata*. In tow of U.S. law, there were established criteria that must be met to create *res judicata* over an issue. Thus, it is the judge's duty to define whether (i) the issue has been properly decided, (ii) there has been a previous and adequate opportunity to litigate, (iii) the claim depended on a decision regarding the issue, and (iv) the court that decided on the incidental issue had jurisdiction to decide on it if it were the principal issue. When *res judicata* is argued in a following lawsuit, those criteria must have been met to prohibit the relitigation of the question.

Article 472 of the revoked Brazilian Civil Procedure Code of 1973 set out that "the judgment creates *res judicata* between the parties to whom it is given, *not benefiting neither harming third parties* (…)". Article 472 went far beyond the Italian Civil Code's article 2909, stating the impossibility of the *res judicata* to benefit third parties.

Article 472, of the 1973 Code, has details that would awe even the most enthusiastic of mutuality rule defenders, a rule that is nowadays important only as to the *history* of the U.S. *common law*. The rule of article 472 kept Brazilian courts and jurisprudence from thinking about the possibility of third parties invoking *res judicata* for their own benefit.

Notwithstanding, it must be said that the Italian Civil Code's article 2909 did not hold Michele Taruffo back from arguing that that rule did not deny the possibility of the third-party invoking *res judicata* in his or her own benefit and against the original party. According to Taruffo, article 2909—even though it was thorough in establishing those who would fall under the effects of *res judicata*—did not exclude the possibility of others profiting from the beneficial effects of *res judicata*, which would mean that the third party, even though he or she is not directly bound to the *res judicata* that arose between the parties, could make use of the beneficial *res judicata* in an action in which it litigates against a former party.[11]

Anyhow, the 2015 Brazilian Code, in due time, made it clear that *res judicata* just must not harm third parties, indicating, thus, that it certainly can benefit them (art. 506 of the Brazilian Civil Procedure Code of 2015, "CPC" from now on). It must be

[11] Tarrufo (1972), p. 297; Pugliese (1969), p. 25.

underlined that, according to the new Civil Procedure Code, the *res judicata* affects issues that were discussed, decided upon, and that were needed to decide on the claims (art. 503, CPC), being unable to affect a third party just when it might harm him or her (art. 506, CPC).

In other words, the Brazilian procedural statutes now encompass the essence of *res judicata*, which must not lose its efficacy against one who argued and lost, as otherwise, it would lose its authority and would not provide legal certainty, besides not contributing to the effectiveness of justice distribution nor the efficiency of the management of public affairs.

The *res judicata*, when it falls over an *issue*, has a potentiality for subjective use that is much greater than the potentiality of the *res judicata* that is circumscribed to a *claim*. That is important for the comprehension of the *res judicata* for benefit of third parties.

Usually, the *res judicata* circumscribed to the judgment of the claim is of interest solely to the parties. But it is worthwhile to notice that the *res judicata* over a claim might interest third parties when it refers to an issue decided *principaliter*, that, later on, could be decided *incidenter tantum* in another litigation. As an example, if the claim is one of declaration of (in)validity of a patent's registration, the *res judicata* that falls over the claim regards the patent's declaration of (in)validity. Thus, if the claim is denied, the *res judicata* might be argued by any third party over whom befalls an action of prohibitory injunction, started by the same plaintiff, based on the patent that has already been declared invalid. In this example, the *res judicata* will be argued to stop a favorable decision for the claim and, thus, the prohibitory injunction. It must be remembered that the *res judicata* is violated when there is nonobservance of *res judicata* produced over a requirement on which depends either the granting or the denial of relief for the right.[12]

But on the hypothesis of a lawsuit, based on a patent, which aims to inhibit the production of a given product, the judgment for denial of the prohibitory injunction, based on the premise that the patent's registration is invalid, is of interest to the defendant only, who must not be bothered anymore as he or she makes the product. Third parties may only have interest on the *res judicata* that fell over the issue of invalidity of the patent's registration. In that way, if another lawsuit, offered by the same plaintiff, is once more based on the patent, the new defendant—a third party as to what concerns the first lawsuit, in which the patent has been declared invalid—may argue the *res judicata* (over the issue) in their own benefit.

In the example of an accident with a few victims, the judgment granting the claim, rendered in the first action for damages, may create *res judicata* over the claim for the payment of damages and over the issues as to the liability for the harmful fact. In this scenario, the sole *res judicata* that may be of interest to the other victims is the one that falls over the liability issue; never the *res judicata* over the condemnation to pay. The latter concerns just the prevailing party, who is the one to whom the compensation was granted.

---

[12] Pisani (1994), p. 535.

Since the third parties may be directly involved in the issue and, thus, have a solid interest in its solution, their interest in the *res judicata* originates in the decision of the incidental issue above all else. The decision on an issue often is of concern to third parties. It is correct, then, to state that allowing the *res judicata* over issues makes one notice, as an obvious consequence, the need for it to be extended for the benefit of third parties. It must be underlined that the non-mutual *collateral estoppel* is a kind of following step of the American *collateral estoppel*, or, to put it best, it is the expected and nearly natural development of the *collateral estoppel* previously restricted to the parties.

The restriction of the *res judicata* to the claim has a relation of cause and effect to the restriction of the *res judicata* to the parties only. If the *res judicata* regards just the adverse parties, what (usually) matters to them becomes immutable, which is the judgment of the claims. To the third parties (usually) matters the issue, which is to say that, when the judgment of the issue becomes immutable, it stands clear that the *res judicata* concerns and may benefit those who did not take part in the lawsuit.

Before the 1940s, the prevailing rule in the United States was a rule called "mutuality". That rule said that a party might argue *collateral estoppel* against another just when both had taken part in the action in which the *collateral estoppel* was created. X might only argue *res judicata* over an issue against Y when this last one could—in the hypothesis of an inverse judgment—argue *res judicata* against X. Thus, only those who might be harmed by the *res judicata* could invoke it for their own benefit.

That rule, based on a notion of proportionality, restricted the *res judicata* to the parties, in a fashion similar to *civil law* rule. If the *collateral estoppel* can only be argued by those whom it can also be used against, the *res judicata* is obviously restricted to the parties. In Triplett v. Lowell,[13] it was ruled in that exact sense, creating the famous precedent that was eventually overruled in Blonder-Tongue,[14] when the United States Supreme Court accepted the non-mutual *defensive collateral estoppel*, which is to say the possibility that the defendant, without having taken part in the lawsuit that originated the *collateral estoppel*, might argue it against the losing party. In Triplett, judged in 1936, it was stated that the rules of the *common law* could not prohibit the rediscussion of a patent's validity because that same patent had been declared invalid in a lawsuit *against a different defendant.*[15]

The mutuality rule was reaffirmed by the 1942 *Restatement of Judgments,*[16] which said that one who was not a party to the lawsuit in which the judgment was rendered could not be harmed by, but neither could claim any benefits from a decision upon any issue that was taken in the action.[17]

[13] Triplett v. Lowell, 297 U.S. 638 (1936).

[14] Blonder-Tongue v. University of Illinois Foundation, 402 U.S. 313 (1971).

[15] Triplett v. Lowell, 297 U.S. 638 (1936).

[16] Vestal (1981), p. 464.

[17] "a person who is not a party or privy to a party to an action in which a valid judgment ... is rendered ... is not bound by *or entitled to claim the benefits* of an adjudication upon any matter decided in the action" (§ 93, Restatement of Judgments, 1942).

Before that, however, the Courts were manifesting themselves in the opposite way to the rule, establishing exceptions to the rule of mutuality. That happened in cases in which, after a vehicle driver's irresponsible behavior was recognized in a judicial decision, the losing claimant would sue the vehicle's proprietor in a new action. In such a situation, recognized by US jurisprudence as exemplary in the overcoming of the mutuality rule's history, the proprietor was granted—he who was a defendant in the second lawsuit—the faculty of invoking *collateral estoppel* to stop the claimant from discussing again the issue of their fault, which was already decided upon in the first case.[18]

Notwithstanding, the first—and, nowadays, notorious—decision that questioned the validity of the rule, without simply intending to establish an exception, was rendered by the Supreme Court of California in 1942, in the trial of Bernhard v. Bank of America.[19] It was stated that the problem resided in not perceiving that the criteria for allowing and prohibiting the invocation of *collateral estoppel* could not be taken in equal terms. The non-perception of the distinction between both criteria is the one thing that could justify the prohibition for the third party to invoke *res judicata* in his or her favor, as there would be no logical reason for demanding that only those who were parties to the lawsuit in which the decision was rendered could benefit from the *res judicata*.[20]

The Supreme Court of the United States stated the validity of the invocation of *collateral estoppel* by third parties on two occasions: in Blonder-Tongue v. University of Illinois Foundation,[21] judged in 1971, and in Parklane v. Shore,[22] judged in 1979. Even though the first decision dealt with non-mutual *defensive collateral estoppel* and the second one dealt with non-mutual *offensive collateral estoppel*, what truly matters is that, in both cases, the need for the Courts to abandon the mutuality rule was made clear.

In Blonder-Tongue, the Supreme Court partially revoked Triplett—the precedent that established, in 1936, the impossibility that a losing party might argue once more a patent that had already been declared invalid against another adversary—, *stating that the main issue involved in the argument would be the logic behind conceding more than one opportunity for someone to argue a same issue, demanding another decision from the Judiciary*. The Supreme Court then declared that granting someone multiple opportunities for discussion of the same issue *constitutes an attack on the public administration logic and disregards the evils that litigiousness inflicts on the economy and on private matters.*[23]

[18] Note, Res judicata – mutuality of estoppel and privity rules in automobile negligence field, New York University Law Quarterly Review, n. 18, 1941, p. 565 e ss.

[19] Bernhard v. Bank of America Nat (1942).

[20] Scott (1942), Currie (1957).

[21] Blonder-Tongue v. University of Illinois Foundation, 402 U.S. 313 (1971).

[22] Parklane v. Shore, 439 U.S. 322 (1979).

[23] Blonder-Tongue v. University of Illinois Foundation, 402 U.S. 313 (1971).

In Parklane v. Shore, the Supreme Court made a point of explaining the reason behind the mutuality rule, to show it then to have been overcome. In that way, the Court restated that, based on the assumption that it would be unfair to allow someone to invoke *res judicata* when that same person is not subjected to it, the losing party was being allowed to litigate once more against new adversaries an issue that had already been decided upon. But soon afterward it was noticed that was the result of confusion prevailing over the conception of the mutuality rule, which made it harder to notice the distinction between the position of the party that litigated and lost and the position of the party that had no opportunity to discuss. Not to eliminate this confusion—removing the mutuality rule from the stage—would imply continuing to regard the unfavorable decision to the party as a *"non-decision"* or as a permit for the party to freely reargue the same issue as many times as it found convenient.[24]

With that situation in mind, it must be asked why American Law managed to notice and overcome something that in most *civil law* countries still is a doctrine, a dogma. The *civil law* has procedural statutes that bind the *res judicata* to the parties, which draws oxygen from jurisprudence, not allowing it to think freely and adequately on the subject. May it be reminded that US Law managed to break free from the mutuality rule or the binding of the *res judicata* to the parties largely because of the efforts of a legal opinion that recognized the true meaning of the *res judicata* upon an issue (*collateral estoppel*) and especially because of the efforts of a Judiciary keen on the importance of legal certainty and efficiency in the administration of justice.

There is no doubt that *civil law* jurists could not define the meaning of "*res judicata* for all" since they always made a connection between the *res judicata*'s essence and its subjective efficacy. The discussion could not move beyond the question of the *res judicata*'s efficacy for those who are the holders of the right that is being decided in a situation that depends on the right being decided or on the *res judicata*. More than that would be unnecessary for those who are bound by a rule that says that the *res judicata* falls upon the parties or those who can be considered equals to the parties.[25]

The *res judicata*, beyond having a meaning that goes far beyond the parties, constitutes a procedural technique that above all intends to safeguard legal certainty, preventing modification and discussion once more of what the judge decided. The *res judicata* does not constitute something that stems exclusively and necessarily from the judgment of the claims, nor does it concern just the parties present at the lawsuit.

As background, it should be considered that since the *res judicata* was seen as a kind of shield against those who intend to disregard the judgment, it was thought that it needed to protect no one else besides the parties and a few thirds of others

[24] Parklane v. Shore, 439 U.S. 322 (1979). See Shapiro (2001), p. 48; Issacharoff (2009), p. 160; Friedenthal et al. (2009), p. 1310.

[25] Tarrufo (1972), pp. 293–294.

who were bound to them through substantial law. It must not be forgotten, in the first place, that the *res judicata* is inherent to the Rule of Law and should be, thus, used to prevent discussion again of matters already settled by the State.

Besides, when the *res judicata* affects just the parties, one is denying the due State-issued penalty to the losing party. The penalty that should arise from the *res judicata* is the prohibition of relitigation over what has already been decided, against the former party or whomever else. It is curious, to say the least, to state that the losing party is not allowed to litigate just with those whom they have already discussed with. That statement would be solid if the State's distribution of justice logic could base itself on the principle that his specific adversary defeats the losing party and not because they are judicially declared to have no grounds. One who loses in a lawsuit is declared to have no rights; they are not simply declared to have lost in face of a winner. If the decision, despite having been issued in a lawsuit between A and B, says that A has no grounds, it obviously should be valid in all lawsuits in which A claims again to be right, regardless of A saying that against C, D, or anyone else.

Finally, if a judicial decision reveals the State's understanding of an issue that regards many, there is no reason for one to infer that such an understanding should be valid only in the lawsuit in which the decision is issued as if it were addressed just to the winning party. The idea that the *res judicata* serves parties and, especially, the winning party, hid from view the true recipients of the *res judicata*. There is no serious reason for one to pretend that the res judicata, as an expression of the protection of legal certainty, could protect just the parties, as if all those who depend on a decision for the judicial relief of their rights should be indifferent to the res judicata that benefits them.

The *res judicata*, at a first glance, can benefit all, even though it cannot ever harm those who did not participate in the lawsuit. But, if its harmful effects are denied at a constitutional level, insofar as no one can be harmed by a judgment issued in a lawsuit in which that same person could not participate in an adversarial procedure, its beneficial efficacy can be or not be limited or can even have its concrete application deferred to the judge by the lawmaker, always according to its choice of a due process of law, adequate to the protection of rights.

Explaining it further: the *res judicata* can always be invoked, in abstract or in potential, by those who can legitimately benefit from it. Nevertheless, as the *res judicata* is a technique bound to serve constitutional values, legal certainty in particular, the lawmaker can be awed by the freedom to litigate and restrict the *res judicata* to the parties without falling into unconstitutionality. This is not, though, doubtlessly, the best option, since it does not just ignore the protection of reliability in the State's decisions, but above all else, it ignores the need for coherency in the distribution of the law.[26]

The truth is that the *res judicata*, to benefit a third party outside the lawsuit, depends precisely on the prerequisites outlined in article 503 of the Brazilian Code of Civil Procedure (CPC), clearly inspired in § 27 of the *Restatement (Second) of*

[26] Marinoni (2019), pp. 343–358.

Judgments. The circumstance that the Code searched for its inspiration in US law justifies, even more, a notion of *res judicata* unchained of its subjective efficacy.[27]

The only times when the *res judicata* upon an issue is not created and, then, cannot be transferred to another lawsuit, be it between the same parties or between a third party and the losing party, when the issue was not discussed due to default (article 503, § 1st, II, CPC), could not be duly discussed due to some restriction to the adversarial principle (article 503, § 2nd, CPC), was not (adequately) decided (article 503, § 1st, CPC), did not constitute a necessary prerequisite to the judgment of the claims (article 503, § 1st, I, CPC) or when the judge that issued the decision had no jurisdiction, due to the matter being judged or the people present in the lawsuit, to issue a judgment on it as a principal claim (article 503, § 1st, III, CPC).

This reasoning it is also supported by a Law and Economics and Law and Development approach that will be explored in the next section.

3 Effectiveness of Legal Decisions and Legal Security in the Economic Analysis of Civil Law Procedure

The pivotal relevance of the adjuratory function in economics, which involves the resolution of disputes and the enforcement of legal decisions, is hardly questioned in economic theory or in the Law and Development literature. Economic theory and the Law and Economic Development literature recognize the importance of formal institutions, such as the legal system, in facilitating economic growth and development. However, there is an ongoing divergence on the role of formal institutions in comparison to informal ones, and on the relative importance of the institutional factor.

The relevance of institutions to economic development is not an novelty, but different concepts have been used to produce different frameworks for the analysis of institutions. For instance, both Original Institutionalists as John Commons and New Institutionalists as Douglas North recognized the critical role of institutions in shaping economic behavior and promoting economic development, but with different concept of institutions.

In Douglas North's view, institutions are constraints, either formal or informal, that shape human behavior and interactions. Formal institutions include as governments and legal systems since they are connected to the State and informal ones are not written, such as societal customs.[28] Both formal and informal institutions can be enforced through a variety of mechanisms, including legal sanctions. In his view, societies with strong and effective institutions are more likely to experience economic growth and development, while those with weak or ineffective institutions may struggle to achieve sustained economic progress. One of the key points in that

---

[27] Carpi (1974), p. 347.

[28] North (1990), p. 17.

reasoning is the reduction of uncertainty trough institutions. In the same approach, but in a more recent construction, institutions were classified as inclusive—enhancing access to markets and individual choice—and beneficial to economic development or extractive—focusing on wealth transfer from one societal group to another—and detrimental to economic development.[29]

On the other side John Commons defined institutions as: *collective action in control, liberation, and expansion of individual action.*[30] In this proposition the expansion of individual action through collective norms must be highlighted. So, collective action is viewed as necessary and beneficial to enhance individual action, not just a constraint.

A common point with New Institutional Economics definition is the fact that reducing uncertainty and coordinating individual action is necessary and beneficial to economic development. After all, if a formal institution such as the law is effective economic agents can anticipate the behavior according to the law and, therefore, make economic decisions with less uncertainty. If the institutional framework is effective and incentivizes a behavior that produces entrepreneurship, innovation and social wealth economic development will be more likely.

The Law and Economics approach uses this starting point to put emphasis on the role of the enforcement of contracts and property rights as a condition and an adequate infrastructure for economic transactions, in which a well-performed adjuratory function can provide the necessary infrastructure for a vibrant and productive economy.[31] After all, low levels of uncertainty and low costs of enforcement for economic transactions are critical in an economy coordinated by the market mechanism and a consequence of a well-performed adjuratory function.

Another relevant point is that uncertainty even when assessed by individuals aggregates costs to economic decision. For instance, imagine that a company wants to write a long-term contract with a supplier and needs to reach an agreement regarding the current price and the formula that will to adjustment the price every year. In a country where there is institutional stability it is possible to use a general inflation and/or a specific index of sectorial costs made by official sources. But, in these of the absence of an reliable index the company will have to create an specific index for the price adjustment, that will add costs to the transaction and depending on the surplus the transactions generates will make the transaction impossible. Also, if the risk of non-compliance with the contract is high and courts fail to enforce the deal the same transaction maybe does not happen for the excessive uncertainty.

With an adequate institutional matrix there is less uncertainty, generating a reduction on costs of the function of the economy and a better performance.[32] The

[29] Acemoglu and Robinson (2012), pp. 80–81.

[30] Commons (1931), p. 648.

[31] Coase (1960), pp. 13–15.

[32] Williamson (1996), p. 2.

Judiciary has a fundamental role in that context and must guarantee public and private bargains to make possible the function of market and modern societies.[33]

The relevance of predicable law enforcement for economic development is also presented in social theory by Max Weber's analysis of the capitalist system. According to the German sociologist and philosopher, the concept of legal rationality highlights the importance of predictable law enforcement and the rule of law for economic development.[34] For him, this legal rationality is a key element of the modern capitalist system, because it provides a stable and predictable framework for economic activity, allowing the economic actors to make decisions with confidence, knowing that legal disputes will be resolved fairly and efficiently.

In law theory, the primary function of law includes producing social peace and coordinating social behavior through adjudication, besides preventing undesirable behavior, and proving infrastructure for private arrangements and redistributions of goods.[35] So, the legal system should provide a fair and impartial forum for resolving disputes, by operating one of the adjudications' functions to use the judicial system to help manage the social peace and reduce the likelihood of violent or disruptive conflicts. After all, an effective legal system is a reliable guide for future actions and for the formation of legitimate expectations of behavior.

The legal system must be also predicable since as present before one of the most relevant benefits of its existence for economic development is to reduce uncertainty. The idea of predictability can be traced back to the Rule of Law and to the fundamental right of legal certainty.[36] Legal certainty can be defined as the property of legal system to allow individuals the ability to make plans.[37] To allow that the level of predictability must be superior to a threshold that allow individuals to in an effective manner anticipate the legal consequences of their actions. So legal certainty and predictability are connected concepts. So, legal certainty understood as an adequate level of predictability of law is fundamental for the Rule of Law since to obey the law is necessary to understand what the law demands from individuals. Adjudication is not the only source of legal certainty, for instance is the need for accessible language in legal norms so they can be observed in a maximum level.[38]

But if the adjudication function does not work properly legal security and predictability will be damaged. Another way to approach is to say that Law in the Books—the legal norms in legislative and executive acts—can differ from Law in Action—how legal norms really operate when enforced in real cases—, but a significant divergence is not good to legal certainty.[39] After all, an individual reading a

---

33 Gico (2013), p. 459.

34 Weber (1978), p. 139.

35 Raz (2009), pp. 162–179.

36 For an approach on the traditional and a more account of the role of predictability in legal systems see: Popelier (2017), p. 33.

37 Wardhaugh (2020), p. 3.

38 Popelier (2017), pp. 29–54.

39 For a classical analysis see: Pound (1910), pp. 12–36.

legal norm should not have reasonable expectations being disregard by how that legal norm operates when enforced.

In a Law and Economics perspective it is important to highlight that a legal norm must be able to coordinate behavior and reduce uncertainty making economic decisions easier and less costly.[40] The complex of society and the principle of the division of labor in capitalism makes necessary that people bargain for services that they do not know to execute in the market. For these bargains to be successful and the price system operate it is essential a level of predictability regarding rights and the legal infrastructure in general. In this context, a high level of legal predictability generates legal security, providing the parties greater confidence and certainty to enter contracts, and promoting economic growth and development.

This need for a predictable decision by the Judiciary must be accompanied by low levels of judicial error so that parties can rely on for their economic decisions. There is a trade-off between correctness of a decision and legal security that is recognized in legal literature.[41] After all, changing a precedent for minor corrections could damaged legal security and produce less benefit than expected.

The institutional matrix that provides legal security and predictability represents society's legal capital that relates to the cycle of litigation. An adequate level of legal capital makes agents capable of predicting a result in a conflict (when A happens, B will probably be the result). An institutional matrix with an adequate level of legal capital allows long-term planning, better risk allocation, discourages certain opportunistic behaviors,[42] and in the last analysis, the cooperation between agents.

The formation of legal capital is not entirely allocated to the Judiciary since the production of well-designed legal norms is the main responsibility of the Legislative and more recently the Executive. Therefore, if a legal norm is excessively ambiguous or problematic to be enforced the reduction of legal capital is not due to the Judiciary.

When there is legal insecurity and agents have different expectations about the law in action the Judiciary is more frequently called to provide a solution. This makes litigation numbers rise and the Judiciary gets busier, so the production of judicial decisions is bigger, and should provide more precedents that are reliable. Then, litigation diminishes since expectations about the content of the norm in action start to converge. In that case, litigation goes down until a new trend of divergent expectations appears.[43]

Nevertheless, the problem in a more concrete reality is that a rise in litigation does not necessarily produces a rise in better and more reliable precedents. It is possible to have a rise in the number of decisions, but they do not produce a clear understanding of the norm in action and fail to guide society's expectations, so they

---

[40] For a analysis of the coordination function of law see: Hadfield and Weingast (2012), pp. 471–514.

[41] Aley (2015), pp. 441–451.

[42] Williamson sees opportunistic behavior as "self-interest seeking with guile" (Williamson 1996, p. 56).

[43] Gico (2013), pp. 448–449.

do not converge. Also, the rise in litigation can generate a rise in the time of judgment or in the number of judicial errors.

This feature of the judicial decision-giving rise to an adequate judicial precedent is a case of an externality since the societal benefits of a good precedent that increases legal capital by improving legal predictability and security are not retained by the litigants.[44]

In the past years, Brazil has been doing this, since the rising number of disputes in the Judiciary are not a source of adequate and reliable precedents, the country has implemented various measures aiming to improve the judicial system's efficiency and reliability. Particularly, in the judicial backlog, one main measure was the creation and usage of the National Justice Council (CNJ), this entity is responsible for promoting the judiciary's effectiveness and ensuring the observance of judicial ethics and standards.

By promoting effectiveness and ensuring ethical and standard compliance, the CNJ incentivizes judges and court officials to work more efficiently and follow proper procedures, all of this represents a structure of incentives to the Judiciary.

The functioning of the Judiciary when parties must resort to the court to resolve their disputes produces costs not only regarding the legal fees and expenses of litigation but also the time and effort spent on preparing and presenting evidence, attending court hearings, and complying with court orders. In parallel, there are costs related to the amount spent on creating and maintaining the CNJ and the costs of training judges and court officials to comply with new standards and regulations, additionally, there may be unintended consequences or unforeseen challenges that arise from implementing these measures, which may also result in additional transactional costs.

In the Law and Economics literature there are four assumptions around litigation and legal certainty: "i) litigation results in the creation of precedents, which help clarify uncertain laws; settlement does not produce precedents; ii) uncertainty in the law supports litigation because it makes parties more likely to have different expectations concerning the outcome of the adjudication and thus less likely to settle out of court; iii) litigation costs borne by the parties in a controversy affect their propensity to go to trial, instead of settling out in court: higher costs reduce the rate of litigation, while lower costs foster litigation; and iv) the legislature may vary the amount of resources invested in reducing the degree of uncertainty while promulgation new laws or amending existing ones".[45]

Economic Analysis of Law literature canonical approach to judicial efficiency is the maximization of the decision's quality or, at least, minimization of the judicial error. However, to maximize the decision's quality[46] (better decisions or less error), there are some things to keep in consideration, like resources (material, human, and

[44] Gico (2013), p. 456.

[45] Dari Mattiacci and Deffains (2007), p. 633.

[46] There is a difference between a legal approach that usually focus on the quality of decisions but an efficiency analysis must consider also other factors such as time and costs of a decision. See Yeung and Azevedo (2011), pp. 343–356.

time). On the other hand, to increase speediness, quality can diminish. For quality to rise, a long decision time is expected, and this influences efficiency. Efficiency must be measured including the speediness in the calculus, as well as quality. That's why "efficiency and quality must walk hand-in-hand[47]".

But all of this also brings costs that influence the quality of the decision. Those costs are, for example, the information itself, the obligation, the enforcement, the performance, the metering, and the knowledge costs.[48] Those costs also represent the costs to keep the Judiciary branch going. All of these represent a trade-off with the decision's quality.

There's also a cost whenever there's the possibility to discuss once more the incidental matters that were not covered by *res judicata,* beyond the usual costs of judicial procedures, or the costs of discussing again those questions incidentally.

Inefficiency comes at hand. Basically, it is frequent in Brazilian courts, and this is attributed to two factors: a shortage of material and human resources and procedure law.[49] It's also said that there are several reasons to explain overcapacity at courts and the relatable inefficiency, for instance: lack of resources, complex procedure, lawyers and judges' incentives, litigation culture, low investment in legal security, and so on.[50]

In a Law and Economics approach applied to Civil Procedure the central goal is to design a process that minimize social costs of the adjudicatory function,[51] that are the sum of administrative costs and error costs. The cost of the Judiciary is an administrative cost and an efficiency approach to the management of the Judiciary is needed to improve it and the cost of judicial error are a function of the quality of legal procedure and judges. So, a new investment in the Judiciary is efficient is this perspective if it reduces the social costs of adjuration: it can be by reducing administrative costs (for instance investment in information technology) or legal error (for instance a new civil law procedure that corrects judicial error). To be efficient the investment must cost less than the benefit. So, if a new procedure adds costs to legal process, it must reduce legal error in a amount that is greater than the cost to implement it. Investments in legal capital are not exclusively on the Judiciary, for instance an investment by the Legislative on more easily enforced rules or a personal investment of a judgment in legal knowledge can reduce administrative and error costs. So, the civil procedure design can contribute to legal capital also by creating incentives for the agents to make personal investments and decisions that can impact the cycle of litigation and the reduction of the social costs of adjudication.

This framework will be applied to the question of the res judicata in the section.

---

[47] Yeung and Azevedo (2011), p. 346.

[48] Gico (2013), pp. 444–448.

[49] Yeung and Azevedo (2011), p. 344.

[50] Gico (2019), p. 2.

[51] Cooter and Ulen (2016), pp. 384–386.

4 *Res Judicata*, Collateral Stoppel and Institutional Development in Brazil

So, in the case of collateral stoppel besides the compatibility with the Brazilian Civil Procedure Code as explained before its implementation can be analyzed through a law and economics approach. In this case the implementation of collateral stoppel should be analyzed by the impact on the capacity of uncertainty reduction by formal institutions, on the administrative and error costs of decisions and on the incentives of the agents to contribute to the legal capital.

The first point is question of uncertainty. New institutes and rules, especially if transplanted, can bring legal insecurity, since it is hard to anticipate how they will function in action.[52] Then, when there is this transplant and the country applies a rule that was created under other circumstances, in a foreign socioeconomic order, the interpretation itself can differ and the application of this law can also be different and bring other effects that were not the expected. That's why rules from other countries must be studied, adapted, and not only imported. So, it is possible that in the beginning at least parties can have difficulties in estimate the expected result. Moreover, it's important to remember that the insecurity from low legal capital also rises private costs and enhance opportunistic behavior.[53] In the case of collateral stoppel the need for an adaption period relates to persons involved in the adjudicatory function and to the legal system as well. The good function of the collateral stoppel outside Brazil presupposes a working system of precedents and effectiveness of the res judicata in preventing new demands on the same question.

On the other side, the reduction of conflicting decisions is an important contribution from collateral stoppel to reduce uncertainty. After all, the expansion of the res judicata will impose a heavy burden on the possibility of different decisions in each case and can contribute to legal predictability. When correct decisions are made and res judicata prevails, there's a minoring in conflicting decisions and minimization of judicial errors with less administrative costs. This minimizes the social costs of adjudication, as well the quality of the infrastructure law offers to private transactions, since the chance of opportunistic behavior is reduced.

In this sense, a correct judicial decision is not made just in the interest of the parties but as a public good that has important positive externalities. The costs of producing legal decisions are administrative costs that societies have already paid. So, letting the State be exposed to relitigation just because the losing party is litigating against another adversary is denying authority to what has already been decided. It is transforming the State's ruling into an "opinion", stimulating the losing party to litigate against anyone else. In fact, it is pretending that the decision issued by a court is worth just to solve the winning party's problem, not the correct enforcement and interpretation of the law. In the Law and Economics approach incurring in the

[52] Berkowitz et al. (2003), p. 167. The authors define the transplant effect happens for those who "received their formal legal order from other countries", as transplants.

[53] Gico (2013), p. 456.

costs of making a new decision and not applying a precedent should take place only if there is a need to correct an error in a decision and not because the parties are different.

If a legal decision should be trustworthy and respected, that civil procedure might not be designed in such a way as to give the judge the possibility of deciding multiple times over the same issue for the same party. If a decision can change, after having declared something fundamental to the protection of the rights of many, those same people cannot have any legitimate expectations of the government authorities created to protect those rights. The legal procedure must not be designed to rediscuss something that has been decided for the simple fact that the losing party is facing someone else in a different legal dispute. After all, the Judiciary and the adjudicatory function produces a public good to society when settling a legal dispute, not a private good that allows repeated litigation the number of times as a litigant wants. The protection of citizens' trust in legal decisions and legal certainty must prevail against an individual desire to litigate the same question several times.

It must be reminded that if the patent is declared invalid in the inhibitory injunction filed by A against B, there is no rationality in allowing that A may file an injunction against C based on the same patent. As it is obvious, C is also a recipient of the *res judicata* created upon the validity of the patent, insofar as A is saying that C has breached the patent. The *res judicata* is as important to those who may be said to be infringing the patent as to the litigant whose arguments were concretely recognized in the lawsuit in which the patent was declared to be invalid. It should be noted that, when one excludes third parties from the scope of the protection of *res judicata*, one is opting for an irrational and undue restriction of the protection of certainty to B. Then, B only, and no one else, would be able to keep A from litigating again based on the patent already declared to be invalid, making all other adversaries of A vulnerable to the harmful effects of unbridled litigation.

All adversaries of A should be recipients of the res judicata that made the patent invalid for the simple fact that the decision of invalidity does not regard just the winning party but regards all—in this case specifically those who are adversaries to the party claiming to be the patent's owner. If one opted for the restriction of the res judicata to A and B, denying the possibility of being invoked by third parties, the justification would be that just those who took part in an adversarial procedure, arguing and proving, could make use of the res judicata, understanding then the res judicata more as an achievement of the party than as a mechanism in defense of legal certainty.

The *res judicata* is, above all, a requisite intended to protect the authority of legal decision and, therefore State coercion power. So, it must not be modified or rediscussed just for the private interest of the losing litigant. Since it is an attribute intended to grant authority to judicial decisions, the *res judicata*, besides being essential to the structuring of the Rule of Law, can be invoked by all those who, in a judicial procedure, have a legitimate interest in preventing discussion anew of what has already been decided.

To put it differently, even though the *res judicata* is created in a procedure between A and B, it is evocable against the one who argued and then lost by anyone that might legitimately benefit from it. It is this, and not another, the meaning that must be extracted from the saying that the *res judicata*, in despise of being established for A and B, is valid before all. The *res judicata* is not valid before all just because it should be respected by all. If it were like that, there would not even be a reasonable motivation in losing time phrasing things this or that way. The *res judicata* is valid before all when all those who legitimately can invoke it before the one that was declared to have no grounds can argue it.[54]

In this context it is important to reinforce that in the case of a new lawsuit about the same issue with a new decision will not annulate or correct the first one. After all, a new decision in a different dispute does not necessarily focus on correcting the first one, it is just a new decision with divergent understanding about the same issue.

The Law and Economics lens can help to understand the nature of legal decisions and precedents. A legal decision in a civil procedure framework is not necessarily a binding precedent, but at least in the in Law and Economics approach it is possible to say that in some extent every decision has at least the potential to integrate the legitimate expectation of the parties since a similar case should be decided with the same interpretation of the legal rule as demanded by the Rule of Law. So legal rules have the potential to affect not just the behavior of the litigants in the transaction that was decided by a legal decision but also in other similar transactions and also in similar transactions that happen with other individuals. Of course, a binding precedent from the Supreme Court form instance will have more strength to be incorporated in the expectations of individuals, but a decision from a lower court in an almost identical or similar case that is in the knowledge of an individual can and should also guide his behavior. In economic theory this can be understood as positive externalities since the ability to coordinate behavior and reduce uncertainty to formal and legal institutions such as the Judiciary benefits the society and not just the litigants on the dispute that initiated the legal process.

The concept of externalities has a long history in economic theory and has the feature of a residual concept, since it relates to what is external of markets.[55] Also, that can be traced to the idea of external economies or diseconomies from Alfred Marshal.[56] A more contemporary conception is the idea of externality as a missing market stated by Kenneth Arrow that can be stated as an unpriced effect that impacts the utility or the production function of an agent.[57] So, in the case of legal decisions the benefits a good judicial decision that coordinates effectively and in a desirable direction the behavior of agents in society does not impact the utility of litigants or the production function of the Judiciary. On the side, a decision that contradicts an older one without a proper reasoning and reduces legal certainty and predictability produces negative externalities. In that context it is necessary to create mechanism

[54] Marinoni (2022), pp. 179–206.

[55] Lagueux (2010), pp. 957–973.

[56] Marshal (1890).

[57] The original definition can be found in Arrow, Kenneth (1969), pp. 59–73. For an analysis of the relevance of the definition proposed by Arrow, see Berta (2017), pp. 287–318.

that enhance the chance of legal decisions become good precedents in the coordination aspect and avoid legal decisions that reduce the validity or do not enhance the pipeline of legal precedents. A legal decision that contradicts another decision and can do that because of the lack of the collateral estoppel is mainly going to produce negative externalities in this framework and therefore should not incentivized.

Another approach is to see that precedents are public goods. A public good is a non-excludable and non-rivalrous good, meaning that a decision cannot be easily restricted to a certain individual or group.[58] Decisions are made by the court and are available to the public and it becomes part of the legal capital of a society. The decision affects the individuals, the parties involved, but also has effects on society as already pointed out. So, when legal decisions influence the public, the society, yet made for individuals, it may be considered as a public good. Legal decisions—and legal rules—can produce unintended consequences, that's why judges and lawmakers need to take accountability and be committed to high level decisions or a high investment in legal capital. Law is also discussed as non-rival once the consumption of law by one does not reduce the utility or the availability of consumption by another.[59]

A private good, in other hand, are goods that are both excludable and rivalrous. It can be owned and used exclusively by individuals, and their use by one person reduces their availability for others.[60] As such, it is tempting to view a judicial decision as a private good, since it is specific to those parties and not easily shared with others. However, this view overlooks the broader impact that the decision may have on society.

Judicial decisions in general and precedents cannot only be treated as a private good, once they have a significant impact on society as a whole and it is important to recognize that it has potential to create positive externalities.[61] Legal decisions and precedents establish legal rules that affect the future cases of the same or similar matter and the development of the law. Also, inconsistent precedents can destroy the value of a precedent system structure and create unwanted effects.[62] When judges promulgate vague standards, they allow each party to have a chance in a new dispute. If precedents are correctly set, in prior, this chance can be diminished. In general, literature has accepted law as a public good,[63] and this knowledge is important for understanding the behavior of adjudicative systems.

A final thought is that a high number of cases does not equals to better or more precedents that can effectivity coordinate behavior. After all, the Judiciary has limitations in the number of high-quality decisions and efficiency since there is a need

[58] Cooter and Ulen (2016), p. 40.

[59] Gico (2020), p. 650.

[60] One easy example of a private good in the law world is a patent, that grants the owner exclusive rights to use and profit from an invention.

[61] Marinoni (2009), pp. 82–89.

[62] Posner and Landes (1979), p. 239.

[63] Gico (2020), p. 646.

of bigger resources and administrative costs if the access to Judiciary is cheap and a lot of decisions must be made at the same time. This risk of inconsistences and the long time to produce a decision undermine the quality of the precedents system and the predictability and certainty of the legal order and reduce legal capital.

Considering that decisions and precedents are public goods and, the legal certainty is enhanced when lower courts follow precedents set by higher courts, collateral stoppel helps this cycle of litigation diminishes. This, in sum, contributes to the idea that legal certainty and correct legal decisions build up a legal capital that is strong, predictable, consistent, and effective. That's why correct decisions have public good interest, with positive externalities, as they contribute to the stability and legitimacy of the legal system, promote confidence in the rule of law, and ultimately benefit society.

The possibility of a new decision that can be different can reduce the incentives for the parties to behave cooperate with the quality of the legal decision. Legal capital can be the result of private investment for judges and parties as well as the State. So, in the case of parties that invest in evidence gathering and make efforts in contribute with technical expertise during the legal process the chances of having better decisions are higher. On the other side with the production of evidence and the instruction of the legal process is poorly made the chances of wrong decisions are higher.

In that setting it is possible that a litigant adopts an opportunistic behavior and keep new litigation about the same subject with a pressure on administrative costs of the Judiciary. This can lead to a waste of resources, time, and money: for the litigants, the judicial system and society.

The final issue is the impact on the quality of the decision and the correction of judicial error in the first decision, since it will be easier to produce a new decision correcting the new one.

In that regard the lack of incentives to have a high-quality decision since it will not become a precedent is problematic and can have the effect of producing conflicting low-quality decisions. This can result in a lack of coherence in the legal system, making it unpredictable and ultimately undermining public trust in the legal system. Moreover, inconsistent, and conflicting decisions can also lead to inefficiencies and unnecessary litigation, as parties may be uncertain about their legal rights and obligations.

Therefore, it is crucial for the legal system to incentivize the production of high-quality decisions at all levels of the judiciary, whether they have the potential to become precedents. This can be achieved through various means, such as providing judges with appropriate resources, training, and support, encouraging open and transparent decision-making processes, and promoting a culture of accountability and professionalism within the Judiciary. But also, by design procedure rules that produce incentives for cooperation between the parties and the judges.

On the other side, if the decision to be taken is going to be very costly to change there is an incentive for the judge and the litigants to invest resources in the production of high-quality decisions. This is because such decisions are less likely to be overturned, which can be costly, time-consuming, and uncertain.

In cases where the stakes are high, litigants may hire skilled and experienced lawyers, provide more comprehensive evidence, and make more compelling arguments to convince the judge of their case, which arise the costs of litigation and perpetuate the cycle. Similarly, judges may be more cautious, diligent, and thorough in their analysis, research, and reasoning. See that the cost of changing a decision is not the only factor that affects the production of high-quality decisions: the judge's expertise, workload, bias, and motivation, as well as the litigants' resources, strategy, and behavior, can also play a significant role in determining the quality of the decision. Therefore, a comprehensive approach is needed to ensure that the incentives for producing high-quality decisions are aligned with the public good, creating a strong legal capital.

Therefore, establishing precedents may be an efficient way to resolve similar cases in the future, as it provides a clear and predictable framework for judges and lawyers to follow. Also, can lead to a reduction in the cost of new litigation by helping parties to understand the likely outcome of a case and can lead to a settlement or early resolution, thereby reducing the cost and time of litigation, preventing, or reducing the re-litigation cycle or even the opportunistic agents.

However, collateral stoppel can have different impact on each type of jurisdiction, that's why each legal system in each one of the countries must be consider. For instance, in legal system that have a stricter rule of precedent, such as United States, *collateral stoppel* can have a different effect than in countries where legal precedents are not binding or not embedded in the legal culture.

The key point here is to understand the trade-off between the efficiency promoted by the precedents and the risks of judicial errors in the first established decision. This is because the decision may be based on limited information or understanding of the issue at hand and may not fully consider all relevant factors or potential consequences, in this way, it is important to analyze also the establish mechanisms in the legal system for review and reconsider legal decisions in the case of error. As already mentioned, there is a cost in changing legal decision and usually legal systems create rigid rules for that.

Therefore, a correct design of collateral estoppel can contribute to better law enforcement and higher legal security. Nevertheless, this need to be done correctly, otherwise, the costs and all the effects that come together can be very negative to the judicial system and to legal security.

5 Conclusion

The Brazilian Civil Procedure Code of 2015 made possible the incorporation of the *collateral stoppel* (*res judicata* over the issue) and this movement is also good as a tool to enhance legal capital and improve the contribution of the adjudicatory function of the Judiciary to the economic and social development of Brazil.

The acceptance of the *res judicata* over the issue makes it much easier to perceive that the decision of the issue concerns also third parties (art. 506, CPC). The *res judicata* should be seen as a procedural technique that aims to safeguard legal certainty, prevent modification and discussion of what the judge decided, and protect the due State-issued penalty to the losing party. It should not be limited to keeping the losing party from relitigating against those they have already litigated against, but rather prohibit re-litigation over what has already been decided, against the former party or anyone else.

In other hand, Law and Economics approach put emphasis on contracts enforcement, and in adequate infrastructure for economic transactions. Considering this, remember that institutions, that can shape interactions and human behavior, such as governments and legal systems, play an important role in *collateral stoppel.*

Economic implications of legal rules and procedures must be a topic of study. By analyzing, for example, the costs and benefits of the extension of the *collateral stoppel*, legal systems can be designed more effectively, promoting predictability and legal security. There's also costs involved in judicial error, that may allow rediscussing of an issue that was wrongly decided. Administrative costs, as well judicial costs also need to be considered.

Considering all that, a predictable decision by the Judiciary must have low levels of error, so parties can rely on them for their economic decisions. High levels of legal predictability generate legal security, and all of this forms the legal capital. A strong legal capital can attract foreign investments, promote economic growth in general, so it's necessary for every nation.

However, the risk of importing external legal institutes into local legal systems carries the risk of unintended consequences, unforeseen costs, and wrong effects in the Law application. This also effects the quality of the legal capital. *Collateral stoppel*, when wrongly applied, can allow opportunistic behavior, when some litigants aim to rediscuss third-party issues or even prolong the judicial battle for no reason. That's why the imposition of costs on parties that engage in frivolous litigation can be a way to discourage this kind of behavior.

Nevertheless, the correct *res judicata* application can prevent this kind of behavior. When designing the legal system and redesigning it with importations, policymakers must consider the economic effects of that design. Moreover, *collateral stoppel* and the Law and Economics approach can promote, together, efficiency and predictability, creating moreover strong legal capital.

References

Acemoglu D, Robinson JA (2012) Why nations fail: the origins of power, prosperity and poverty. Crown Business, New York

Aley R (2015) Legal certainty and correctness. Ratio Juris 28(4):441–451

Battesini E, North D (2019) In: Klein V, Becue SMF (eds) Análise Econômica do Direito: Principais Autores e Estudos de Caso. Editora Crv, Curitiba

Berkowitz D, Pistor K, Richard J (2003) The Transplant Effect. The American Journal of Comparative Law 51(1): 163–204

Berta N (2017) On the definition of externality as a missing market. Eur J Hist Econ Thought 24(2):287–318
Carpi F (1974) L'efficacia 'Ultra Partes' della Sentenza Civile. Giuffrè, Milano
Coase RH (1960) The problem of social cost. J Law Econ 3:13–15
Commons J (1931) Institutional Economics. The American Economic Review 21(4): 648–657
Cooter R, Ulen T (2016) Law and economics, 6th edn. Addison-Wesley, Boston
Currie B (1957) Mutuality of collateral estoppel: limits of the Bernhard doctrine. Stanford Law Rev v:9
Dari Mattiacci G, Deffains B (2007) Uncertainty of law and the legal process. J Inst Theor Econ 163(4):627–656
Friedenthal JH, Miller AR, Sexton JE, Hershkoff H (2009) Civil procedure – cases and materials. West, St. Paul, p 1310
Gico I Jr (2013) O Capital Jurídico e o Ciclo de Litigância. Revista Direito GV 9(2):435–464
Gico IT (2019) Bem-Estar Social E O Conceito De Eficiência (Social Welfare and the Concept of Efficiency). Faculdade de Direito Centro Universitário de Brasília – UniCeuB Brasília – 2019, Working Paper
Gico I Jr (2020) Análise Econômica do Processo Civil. Editora Foco, Indaiatuba
Hadfield GK, Weingast BR (2012) What Is Law? A Coordination Model of the Characteristics of Legal Order. Journal of Legal Analysis 4(2): 471–514
Issacharoff S (2009) Civil procedure. Foundation Press, New York, p 160
Kenneth J (1969) The organization of economic activity: issues pertinent to the choice of market versus nonmarket allocation. In: The analysis and evaluation of public expenditures: the PPB system, Vol. 1. Congress of the United States, pp 59–73
Klein, V. (2015a) A Economia Dos Contratos: Uma Análise Microeconômica, Curitiba, Editora Crv
Klein V (2015b) Os Contratos Empresariais de Longo Prazo: Uma Análise a Partir da Argumentação Judicial. Editora Lumen Juris, Rio de Janeiro
Krasinski R, Klein V (2016) Instituições e Mudança Institucional. In: Ribeiro MCP, Domingues VH, Klein V (eds) Análise Econômica do Direito: Justiça e Desenvolvimento. Editora Crv, Curitiba
Lagueux M (2010) The residual character of externalities. Eur J Hist Econ Thought 17(4):957–973
Landes W, Posner R (1979) Adjudication as a private good. Thc Journal of Legal Studies 8(2): 235–284
Marinoni LG. (2009) Why does the civil law disregard precedents – a justification in a modern historical perspective. New York
Marinoni LG (2019) Res judicata over issues and third parties. ZZPInt - Zeitschrift für Zivilprozess International: Jahrbuch des Internationalen Zivilprozessrechts 24:343–358
Marinoni LG (2022) Coisa Julgada Sobre Questão, 3rd edn. Revista dos Tribunais, São Paulo
Marshal A (1890) Principles of economics. Macmillan, London
North DC (1990) Institutions, institutional change and economic performance. Cambridge University Press, New York
Pisani AP (1994) Lezioni di Diritto Processuale Civile. Jovene, Napoli
Polinsky AM, Rubinfeld DL (1993) Sanctioning frivolous suits: an economic analysis. Georgetown Law J 82:397–435
Popelier P (2017) Legal certainty and the European courts: accessibility and legitimate expectations as standards of reasonableness. In: Fenwick M, Siems M, Wrbka S (eds) The shifting meaning of legal certainty in comparative and transnational law. Hart Publishing, Oxford, pp 29–54
Pound R (1910) Law in books and law in action. Am Law Rev 44(1):12–36
Pugliese G, (1969) Giudicato. Enciclopedia Del Diritto, XVIII, n. 25
Raz J (2009) The authority of law: essays in law and morality, 2nd edn. Clarendon Press, Oxford
Schwartz WF, Tullock G (1975) The costs of a legal system. J Legal Stud 4(1):75–82
Scott A (1942) Collateral estoppel by judgment. Harv Law Rev 56

Shapiro D (2001) Preclusion in civil actions. Foundation Press, New York, p 48
Spurr SJ (1991) An economic analysis of collateral estoppel. Int Rev Law Econ 11(1):47–61
Tarrufo M (1972) Collateral Estoppel e Giudicato Sulle Questioni – n. II, Rivista di Diritto Processuale, 1972
Trebilcock MJ, Prado MM (2014) Advanced introduction to law and development. Edward Elgar, Cheltenham
Triplett v. Lowell, Supreme Court of The United States, 297 U.S. 638, 1936
Vestal AD (1981) The restatement (second) of judgments: a modest dissent. Cornell Law Rev 66
Wardhaugh B (2020) Competition, effects and predictability: rule of law and the economic approach to competition. Hart Publishing, Oxford, p 3
Weber M (1978) Economy and society: an outline of interpretive sociology, vol 2. University of California Press, Berkeley, p 139
Williamson OE (1996) The mechanisms of governance. Oxford University Press, New York
Yeung LL, Azevedo PF (2011) Measuring efficiency of Brazilian courts with data envelopment analysis (Dea). IMA J Manag Math 22(4):343–356

Italo-Iberoamerican Experiences of EAL

The Importance of the Economic Analysis of Law (EAL): Some Thoughts for Colombia, Chile, and Ecuador

Ruben Mendez Reategui

Abstract As a result of the juxtaposition juridical vs legal institutions institution, the chapter deals with the institutional framework and discusses whether their strength (legal and normative security) or weakness (progressive and/or radical affectation of the social rule of law) for countries such as Colombia, Chile, and Ecuador constitute identifiable dependent variables placed in harmon. The Chapter examines therefore the institutional framework of Colombia, Chile, and Ecuador, considering the following issues: (a) the limitation of political power, (b) the general interest, (c) social justice as a result of the prevalence of law and order, (d) an equitable relationship between efficiency and social efficacy, and (b) the approach to a scenario of multidimensional well being that is sustainable and sustainable over time.

This chapter is related to CONVERGENCIA Research Group (UA) and to ANID CIN 2025 - Proyecto: Centro de Investigación para el estudio de derechos de los habitantes de Chile sobre las aguas y su mejora legislativa y regulatoria sostenible.

R. M. Reategui (✉)
Research Institute (IID) and the Faculty of Law of the Universidad Autonoma de Chile (UA), Providencia, Chile
e-mail: ruben.mendez@uautonoma.cl

S. Zorzetto et al. (eds.), *Developments in Law and Economics in the Italo-Iberoamerican Context*, Economic Analysis of Law in European Legal Scholarship 21, https://doi.org/10.1007/978-3-032-03317-8_12

1 Introduction

Juridical institutions are not *per se* the equivalent of *legal institutions*.[1] The former, in a broad sense, refers to those normative constructions, which may or may not be an expression of rationality and constructivism and are grouped in turn as *formal and informal rules of the game*, being—in addition—juxtaposed by a broad group of authors who originally come from and/or who, being jurists, are influenced to a greater or lesser degree by political science, sociology, international relations, and economic theory.[2]

As a result of this juxtaposition we will come to know them as an *institutional framework* and this concept, in turn, will be used as an overture to raise discussions in terms of whether their *strength* (legal and normative security) or *weakness* (progressive and/or radical affectation of the social rule of law) for countries such as Colombia, Chile, and Ecuador constitute identifiable dependent variables placed in harmony and, (a) the limitation of political power, (b) the general interest, (c) social justice as a result of the prevalence of law and order, (d) an equitable relationship between efficiency and social efficacy, and (b) the approach to a scenario of multidimensional well being that is sustainable and sustainable over time.[3]

On the other hand, if we accept that *juridical institutions* transcend those areas which, in Law and, *in strictu sensu*, we presume to be legal and which must be approached through all the sources of law, a term used in allusion to Savigny's hydraulic metaphor—which has proved fortunate over time-; on the other hand, *legal institutions* would properly constitute a form of manifestation and materialization of *positive law*, understood in a simplified way as legislation. This consideration is also relevant and opportune if we intend to develop a theoretical reflection on tools such as the Economic Analysis of Law (EAL) and its academic-scientific impact on the study of the institutional framework of Colombia, Chile, and Ecuador, which is the central theme and justification of this chapter.

2 What Do We Mean by EAL in this Chapter?

In Colombia, Chile, and Ecuador, EAL is still symbolized as a legal movement, which appeared in Anglo-Saxon countries based on some advances in neo-institutional economic thought, especially between 1930 and 1970, if we consider the publication of seminal articles such as *The Nature of the Firm* and the Problem of Social Cost by Ronald H. Coase or *The Cost of Accidents* by Guido Calabresi. In short, we can state that in these countries EAL is approached as a methodological

[1] Rules (e.g., laws and regulations) to a divergent and yet ever-changing social reality.

[2] Juridical and legal systems or orders.

[3] Finally, this mixture of parameters has been baptized under the seductive name of *institutional quality*, which is affected by the problem of statistical endogeneity.

approach that, being part of Legal Science or an applied extension of Economic Science,[4] resorts to economics and its analytical and theoretical-conceptual arsenal to study problems linked to (legal) institutional design.

Among the main "economic" concepts used are property rights, which can be understood as the ability to decide on goods and/or services, i.e. rights within the legal and juridical market, transaction costs or market costs or price mechanism, marginal returns on the actions of market agents, structures for the governance of interpersonal relationships (e.g. corporate models and contractual designs), efficiency under different definitions, among others.[5]

2.1 EAL as a Research Program

Likewise, in Colombia, Chile, and Ecuador, as in the other countries of the Latin American region, when characterizing EAL, some of the following aspects stand out, which may be nuanced depending on the author or the specific thematic and/or conceptual review carried out:

(a) It is argued in a generalist way that EAL involves the application or use—for the most part—of theories and methods from classical microeconomics to study the institutional framework. It is based on the *Maximisation-Market-Efficiency* triad (under a Social Cost-Benefit perspective). Furthermore, it is accepted that it allows establishing that law and legal practice should be built on economic principles as a standard (Lozano Rodríguez 2016). Thus, the participation of juridical institutions, legal institutions, and the conduct of their operators (civil servants and other relevant counterparts) must be integrated into the economics of social behavior and rational choice.

(b) Moreover, EAL is perceived as a set of messianic postulates that tend to pursue the optimization or use of resources in a world of scarcity, providing economic arguments to strengthen, modify or perfect the a priori or ex-post normative

[4] There is a latent discussion that presents EAL as an independent discipline, i.e., as ius-economics or as the result of a theoretical and applied symbiosis between both areas of human knowledge.

[5] From an epistemological and gnoseological perspective, EAL re-evaluates the use of economic tools to evaluate the functioning of legal and juridical institutions, that is, to understand their functional aspects more rigorously. Also, through cost-benefit analysis (CBA) and cost-effectiveness analysis (CEA), EAL facilitates the calculation of the impact that the rules of the game (laws, regulations, or judicial decisions) will have on the behavior (incentives and perverse incentives) of individuals and society in terms of *social performance*. EAL allows one to appreciate how a goal for society (e.g., harmony and/or peaceful coexistence in a framework of respect for others) can be achieved in different ways with divergent individual and/or societal costs. Even though EAL can be recognized as a "non-legal" discipline on how economics is linked to law. It is recognized that in a world of scarce resources and unlimited human desires and/or needs, Law is transcendent if it allows the desired social goals to be achieved by fulfilling criteria such as the lowest possible cost, sacrifice and/or loss, and that, therefore, that there will be very different goals given our historical context (short-, medium- and long-term temporality).

design (laws and regulations) whose central element for many would-be economic efficiencies (Cachanosky 2006, p. 5).

(c) In Colombia, Chile, and Ecuador, the postulate that EAL is based on the theoretical consideration that it is not possible to only characterize legal institutions in an abstract sense (traditional dogmatics) and that it is necessary to link their construction with their function and social impact (e.g. economic aspects and effects) is commonly adhered to Bullard Gonzalez (2006), Trujillo Cabrera (2012) and others. Furthermore, it makes it possible to establish that law and legal practice must be constructed based on economic principles as a standard. Thus, the participation of juridical institutions, legal institutions, and the conduct of their operators (civil servants) must be integrated into the economics of social behavior and rational choice.

(d) In Colombia, Chile, and Ecuador, positions are taken on EAL. These positions are dominated by those that promote social objectives such as, for example, the search to reduce the cost of diluting the economic damages resulting from human activities (e.g. the case of accidents and tort liability) and even the legal-economic doctrine in these countries argues, for example, that the cost of these damages should be integrated into the cost of providing a certain good or service and the risk. Furthermore, when studying EAL in Colombia, Chile, and Ecuador, as in other jurisdictions, it is also necessary to consider the presence of positions that opt for a possible criterion of analysis.[6]

2.2 *On Positive Law and the EAL*

Positive law understood as a synonym of written text subject to the logical principle of noncontradiction, is the "dominant" one in the Roman-Germanic legal tradition or Civil Law, to which the legal institutions of the Colombian, Chilean, and Ecuadorian jurisdictions belong and which was constructed and taught—firstly—in these experiences thinking of a simplified design that was capable of responding to the need to extend protection to the binomial formed by the notions of personal rights (subjects of law) and real rights (objects of law). In this order of ideas, positive law has been the prevailing concern of those academics interested in promoting and carrying out an EAL exercise focused on some aspect of the legal and juridical institutions of the aforementioned countries (Lozano Rodríguez 2016; (Villanueva Andrade 2018).

[6] For example, if we consider the problems related to non-contractual liability, we will argue that the latter should be constructed by incorporating a logic that inherently reflects on proposals such as (a) *Primary costs*, which for Trazegnies De (1995) involve reducing the number and severity of accidents, achieved through *general prevention* or the market method and specific prevention or the collective action method; (b) *Secondary costs or* those that affect neither the number of accidents nor their severity, but the social costs (SC) derived from them; and finally (c) *Tertiary costs* which are those concerning the management of accidents, whose objective is to reduce primary and secondary costs.

3 On Legal and Regulatory Transplant

Similarly, in the countries under review in this chapter, legal institutions have been integrated, even though they reflect divergent cultural models, transplanted from structured societies with advanced transitional economies (Mendez Reategui 2014) and this has led to a *perverse legacy* that been discussed through the gradual—and not necessarily persistent—introduction of EAL as a mechanism, tool and implicit justification for the implementation of processes such as cost-benefit analysis (CBA), regulatory impact analysis (RIA), regulatory reform, regulation through contractual networks, a comprehensive vision of the elimination of legal (bureaucratic) barriers, among others.

It is therefore important to establish that, although there are opposing opinions on the dogmatic differences in terms of how, why, and for what purpose substantive rules of law should be formulated and/or adopted, the use of EAL is not a recurrent discussion and/or latent debate in the academia of Colombia, Chile, and Ecuador. Therefore, other aspects and topics prevail as unpeaceful scenarios that have stumbled the interest of jurists in those countries. This can be verified if we *survey* existing contributions and concerns about concepts that can be deconstructed from EAL (understood as a synonym for *iuseconomics*) such as procedural economics and the costs of the public justice system.

Although in these countries there remains a certain disenchantment with the dogmatic characterization of the concepts and institutes of law, the majority of Colombian, Chilean, and Ecuadorian academics have preferred to maintain their preference for univocal and dogmatic-traditional or, to a large extent, similar regimes for the formulation, implementation, interpretation, and application of legal and juridical institutions. And although the indicators of institutional quality in these countries describe and facilitate the estimation that to date it is evident that in Colombia, Chile, and Ecuador there is a significant rate of *accumulated residual institutional loss,* in part derived from the preponderance of nineteenth-century dogmatism and legal transplant (Mendez Reategui 2020a, b), which in successive waves has been received since independence.[7]

However, despite the problems involved in making the transition from a transitional legal and juridical development such as the one that has characterized the countries in question, the law in these countries has sought the prevalence of efficient, effective and efficient legal and juridical institutions (Lescano Galeas et al. 2016), and in the event of finding some that are not, it has proceeded, through the tool of institutional reform, to eliminate or replace them to avoid perverse effects on society and market economic agents (individuals, families, and companies). However, this imperfect process of "continuous improvement" has not—necessarily—been grounded in the EAL. That is to say, at this point, we can conjecture that

[7] Therefore, behind this scenario lies the need for tools that allow the introduction of an *effective improvement of processes* involving the management and administration of juridical rules, and legal and justice circumstances.

EAL has been and is a valuable tool for carrying out abstract analytical exercises or for inspiring academic proposals or reasoning exercises at the undergraduate and postgraduate levels, rather than an indubitable material foundation promoting major transformations that bring us closer to scenarios of justice and equity.

A random example of change without the impact of EAL are those institutes of private law such as smart contracts, whose relevance and prominence have been approximated, with real transcendence and impact in our region, from other movements such as Law and New Technologies and Legal Tech. We are facing a scenario in which human needs and the effects of commercial practice have been the pivots of this "new" legal institution which, in addition, competitively has proved to be the most efficient for numerous factual scenarios of digital intermediation. In short, it is the conditions of a disruptive social context that have influenced the conduct of the market and its economic agents in Colombia, Chile, and Ecuador and not academic foundations, formulated from EAL or other perspectives that conceptually and haphazardly incorporate terms of widespread use throughout economic theory such as, for example, transaction costs.

In this order of ideas, we can conclude that the use of economic terminology by legislation or regulation is not a sufficient condition to assert that the EAL and other tools formulated from applied microeconomics have had a tangible impact in Colombia, Chile, and Ecuador, influencing the Colombian, Chilean or Ecuadorian legislator and/or those who have the "responsibility" to intervene in the commercial dynamics as relevant doctrinal sources of law; Nor has the EAL inspired or influenced in a transcendental way the criticism through public opinion, the explicit derogation or the tacit alteration—*default*—of other legal and juridical institutions, by the ordinary citizen, as is the case of the antichresis versus the mortgage.

A scenario of legal change, instituted by the will of the legislator or another spontaneous or factual change resulting from individual action, in the system of rules of the game are not the only examples of the limited incidence of the EAL in the regulatory spectrum of Colombia, Chile, and Ecuador. Certainly, in a complex world, the human *ratio*, often expressed through the will of the legislator, has managed to develop other mechanisms as a result of the commitment of administrative entities when regulating or positioning regulatory policies. Perhaps, having said that the administration is one of the few areas where results have been obtained that are, in a way, more transcendent if our attention is focused on the incidence of EAL as a useful, appreciable, or unavoidable tool for forging socially proactive change.[8]

[8] In Colombia, Chile, and Ecuador, the dogmatic of the EAL holds that in case of observing errors to correct in the traffic of the free market of the economy, it must aim to amend through sanctioning procedures, likewise, if there are factors that reach efficiency in the market, it must be the law that establishes the conditions in which it can effectively be reached; seeking its action to bring equilibrium to the market. To fulfill the primary objectives of the *general interest, common good,* and *social peace, the law* must ensure reliable and ethical exchange concerning the use of goods and productive factors. It is then up to the law to guarantee the security and freedom of the market and to correct discordant or adverse scenarios through the coercive mechanism or rational collective action. Given the above, the dogmatics of EAL in the countries are not far removed from partisan considerations, and perhaps this is the fact that has influenced its instrumental and theoretical-conceptual transcendence (Trujillo Cabrera 2012).

At present, we consider that this study, concerned with reflecting on the transcendence of the EAL in Colombia, Chile, and Ecuador, is justified and assists us in thinking about regulatory policies as a valid space in which the EAL gained importance, inspiring technocrats and their proposals. In line with the first, second, and third-generation reforms and the guidelines obtained from the Washington Consensus, they raised them under the banner of economic efficiency and progress in terms of material well-being. The suggestion of the EAL in these regulatory policies is evident both in the Latin American literature that distanced itself from the OECD recommendations and in the literature that embraced them, since in both cases Better Regulation was promoted as a valid tool to introduce a regulatory counter-narrative if we consider the standards under which the Administration was governed in the mid-1990s. The common objective, therefore, was expressed through actions focused on the generation of clear regulations, the establishment of simplified procedures and services, as well as the implementation of entities within the Administration that, through a proactive behavior towards the administered, would result in effective collaborators to obtain the greatest possible value from *collective action. However,* as time went by, the initial impact of the EAL dissipated, giving way to discussions based on other areas of applied economics such as insurgent and irreverent interpretations of the Theory of Regulation and/or technocratic approaches ascribed to mainstream economics used for the treatment of market failures.

In synthesis, EAL can be understood in its splendor as a movement that in Latin America leveraged the design of public policies, the efficient use of available resources within the state apparatus, and, in a Paretian sense, the optimal functioning of economic activities of production, consumption, and savings. In other words, human action is expressed through acts of commerce, industrial processes, the generation of services, and, consequently, the material human development of society (private and public sectors).

4 Considerations from the Input of the Main EAL "Partners"

EAL is a movement that has shared tools of analysis and economic naturalism applicable to processes of rational and/or quasi-rational choice or bounded rationality, in other words, to decision-making in a context of structural constraint originating from the legal apparatus. However, as a movement, it is not univocal and, on the contrary, it must be conceived as a way of perceiving the contextual interference of legal and juridical institutions. Also, it is important that, in this chapter, we argue for and resort to the identification of some of the main precursors and referents of EAL, which implies that we should mention academics of British and North American origin.

We caution that this selection may also be judged to be discretionary, and thus to have incurred the possibility of excluding several of the most important representatives of the movement. Because of this risk, we have constructed our selection in alphabetical order and according to a chronological criterion and the fact of having received (a) a distinctive recognition such as the Nobel Prize in Economics, (b) having been listed as a leading representative by the specialized academia and/or (c) having been mentioned and/or considered in the nomination process.

4.1 Kenneth J. Arrow

As is well known, Professor Arrow was born in the USA in 1921. He received the 1972 Nobel Prize in Economics jointly with the British economist John R. Hicks, for his decisive contribution to the development of macroeconomics through his contributions to the Theory of General Equilibrium and the Theory of Welfare. He studied at City College and Columbia University. Among Arrow's foundational contributions at the academic and scientific level, his revolutionary use of the *symbolic logic notation system* stands out, with which he was able to analyze the *problem of the transitivity of social preferences.* Let us recall *Arrow*'s so-called *Impossibility Theorem.* Through this contribution, it has been established that there is no democratic mode of voting through which a transitive and rational social choice can be achieved. This has generated a wide debate in public economics and political science since making stable and unambiguous decisions in the realm of social choice would require us to resort to a mechanism of government established in a one-man dictatorship or to reduce the possibilities of choice to two. Looked at in this way, we can argue that Arrow's contribution is extensive to the social sciences in general, and therefore cannot be defined as a development specific to the EAL movement. Nor is it viable to argue that it has had a transcendence in the EAL when it was presented as a discursive solution to the problems of governance that have affected Colombia and Ecuador in particular. Or that it would have been considered when proposing the legal, economic, political, and social rules of governance for one of the most stable economies in the region, such as Chile.

4.2 Gary S. Becker

Born in 1930 in the US and died in 2014, Professor Becker received the Nobel Prize in Economics in 1992 for having extended the domain of microeconomic analysis to a broad field of human behavior and interaction, including non-market behavior. He studied at Princeton and Chicago. Professor of Economics at Columbia (1960–1970) and at the University of Chicago. Becker is credited with being the main representative of the imperialism of economic science (Becker 1968), that is, of using the theoretical instruments of economics to explore and conquer new territories. In his doctoral thesis, he analyzed the reasons for racial and sexual discrimination in employment. In "Crime and Punishment" he analyzes the rationality of the criminal by calculating the probabilities of the benefits and costs of crime. It remains to be said that Becker's contributions must also be characterized as transversal to economics and the social sciences and that they can't be exclusively alienated by EAL, whether this is understood as a movement or even as an analytical tool. In addition, Becker and his ideas can—mainly—be understood as a relevant doctrine with an impact that transcended university classrooms and the influence of any intellectual movement, and which were used to design or outline models of legal-economic governance in general.

4.3 James M. Buchanan

Professor James McGill Buchanan was born in the USA in 1919 and died in 2013. He was awarded the Nobel Prize in Economics. He is the leading representative of the mainstream *Public Choice Theory*. Through his proposals, Professor Buchanan succeeded in linking Political Economy with Political Science and, indeed, he provided the latter with a methodology. Among his most notable proposals, we can mention the study of politics by not considering it in terms of effect distribution as a primary purpose or objective, but on the contrary, by explaining that it should not allude to the *set of strategies* (public policies). In other words, politics revolves around a complex process of choosing the rules of the game that set a standard in terms of exchange and distribution. Buchanan is also considered the father of the research program known as Constitutional Political Economy. Through this program, he looks beyond how decisions are made within the amalgam of rules in force and focus on how these rules of the game are accepted, as well as measuring aspects such as their relative efficacy.

In the case of Buchanan, it can also be argued that, like Arrow's contribution, his ideas are extensive to the social sciences in general, and that they never led to the institutionalization of a movement such as Public Choice (understood as "EAL plus Political Science") in Colombia, Chile, and Ecuador. This author indeed inspires legal doctrine that advocates a minarchist approach to constitutional design, but his influence and impact do not allow us to argue that EAL influenced, through Buchanan and/or vice versa, the constitutional reform movements that brought some countries such as Chile closer to a more permeable design in the face of private property and the market economy.

4.4 Guido Calabresi

Professor Calabresi was born on 18 October 1932 and is an internationally renowned jurist who became Dean of Yale Law School. He has been a professor since 1959 and serves as Sterling Professor Emeritus. He is a senior judge of the United States

Court of Appeals for the Second Circuit. He is widely regarded, along with Coase, Posner, and Manne, as one of the founders of EAL. His contributions also include the foundational article co-written with Melamed in 1972 entitled *Property Rules, Liability Rules, and Inalienability: One View of the Cathedral.* That said, we can also argue that Calabresi is perhaps one of the doctrinaires with the best reception of his contributions and ideas in Latin America. However, the degree of permeability differs greatly in each country, being important in Colombia and Chile among those academics and university professors whose area of interest is Patrimonial Civil Law (real, obligations, contracts, and tort liability) and Commercial Law. However, Professor Calabresi's influence as a doctrinarian has been very scarce in other countries such as Ecuador, which is verifiable without carrying out necessarily robust research in a methodological sense and simply by visiting the bibliographic repositories of the main universities in that country.[9]

4.5 Ronald H. Coase

Professor Ronald H. Coase was born in the UK in 1910 and remained active as a lecturer at the University of Chicago even after he passed his 100th birthday (he died in 2013). He received the Nobel Prize in Economics in 1991 for his "finding" and "clarification" of the meaning and relevance of transaction costs (costs of using the market) and property rights for the institutional amalgamation or set of rules of the game and/or behavioral constraints in permanent interaction and the functioning of the market process. Formally, it is credited with the birth of EAL, although it is also treated as such by representatives of the new institutional economics and modern accounting and organizational theory.

His 1960 article entitled *The Problem of Social Cost* is perhaps the most cited text in economic literature. It is noteworthy, as recognized by *mainstream* economics, that his seminal proposal was introduced in the 1937 article *The Nature of the Firm*. In this contribution, Coase presented the widespread idea in modern economics that there is no *free lunch* since any price allocation system or mechanism carries an implicit cost (opportunity and/potential sacrifice) and that, therefore, economic evaluation of rules, modes of association and organization for organizational production and exchange, and payment and/or transfer mechanisms are feasible. That said, we can argue that Coase's case is different from that of the other social scientists mentioned in this survey. He is a doctrinaire who brought Economics closer to Law and has allowed some sophisticated advances and this scenario makes it possible to argue that his ideas have been transcendent in explaining the limits of regulation and setting objectives for legislation and regulations. However, it is also true that Coase's work cannot be subsumed by EAL as a movement and that many times,

[9] Profiling the suggested search through key terms such as "dissertations+calabresi" and/or "books+calabresi".

it is his ideas incorporated into *mainstream* economics and not as a specialized expression of applied economics, which have helped economists and lawyers to reflect on the short, medium and long term effects and consequences of regulations concerned with the protection of subjective rights.

4.6 John R. Commons

Rescuing the contribution of Roemer (1994), we can argue that several of the main contributions that the EAL incorporates from the theoretical *corpus of* economics have been derivations constructed by a group of authors grouped through the American institutionalist economics movement (succeeded by the new institutional economics and neo-institutional economics). In this order, one of its main representatives was Professor Commons, born in the USA in 1862, who was a professor of economics at numerous prestigious institutions of higher learning such as Indiana University, Syracuse University, and Wisconsin University. He also served as president of the American Economic Association (AEA), the most important and influential economic association in the world. Certainly, his relevance is manifest in historical and academic terms. Although his concern for the role of the state, his ideas on the necessary synthesis between classical political economy, law and ethics, labor legislation (re-evaluating health and safety conditions), the reformulation of unemployment insurance, and the analysis of social security (retirement) programs are highly noteworthy, it is not possible to assert—first—that he has been an author with great and direct influence in the countries analyzed in this chapter, nor—second—that he has had a tangible and/or measurable impact on how public and regulatory policies have been structured in those countries.

4.7 Henry G. Manne

Professor Manne was born in the US in 1928 and taught at multiple universities such as Wisconsin, George Washington, Rochester, Stanford University, Miami, Emory, George Mason, Chicago, and Northwestern. Although for the international academy, Manne was a pioneer in the application of applied economic principles to the study of corporations and corporate law, it may be puzzling that he is a little-known author in Colombia and Chile and almost ignored in Ecuador (Villanueva Andrade 2018). However, this does not detract him in any way and he should be considered as one of the founding fathers of EAL. His foundational contribution includes the article *Mergers and the Market for Corporate Control* (1965), which should be credited with opening up the field of corporate law to economic analysis and is a forerunner of what is known as the *efficient market hypothesis.*[10] Likewise, his book *Insider Trading and the Stock Market* (1966) was the first academic work to challenge the logic of insider trading laws and remain the most influential book on the subject today.

4.8 Douglass C. North

Born in the USA in 1920 and died in 2015, Professor North received the Nobel Prize in Economics in 1993 jointly with the economist Robert W. Fogel. This recognition was awarded for having revitalized economic history research by applying a combination of economic theory and quantitative methods (now known as *cliometrics*), which allowed a reformulation of the explanations hitherto in force and focused on analyzing the economic process (change) and institutional evolution or constraints on human behavior. North was also known for being critical of those approaches that sought to explain economic growth by overestimating the role of industrialization (Mendez Reategui and Alosilla Díaz 2015). Finally, we must characterize him as an author who is widely known to economists in Colombia, Chile, and Ecuador. However, he is rarely approached as a theoretical progenitor of EAL in those countries. Moreover, his ideas represent an important barometer and signaling mechanism that allows us to sustain the thesis that EAL has had little influence in Colombia, Chile, and Ecuador beyond the university classroom. This, although it does not undermine the intellectual and cognitive importance of the movement, forces us to rethink the actions that the doctrinaire members of the Latin American EAL movement must take to position (Ecuador) and/or consolidate (Colombia and Chile) their discourse outside the "enlightened and learned elites".

4.9 Elinor Ostrom

Born in 1933, Professor Ostrom[11] was the first woman to be awarded the Nobel Prize in Economics in 2009. She studied at the University of California at Los Angeles and served as President of the American Political Science Association (1996–1997). He has held various academic positions at the University of California at Los Angeles, Indiana University, and Arizona State University. His most recognized contribution revolves around the governance of shared resources or *common goods*. Therefore, his interest focused on aspects such as explaining why human beings interact to maintain long-term production levels of common resources. Also, he was concerned with understanding how different societies developed mecha-

[10] For which economist Eugene Fama was awarded the Nobel Prize in 2013.

[11] Died in 2012.

nisms such as communal practices through which they managed to preserve common resources and avoid the degradation of their environment.

Regarding the reception of Ostrom's work, it should be emphasized that it has gained recognition not as a manifestation of EAL. On the contrary, her link with this movement is not an aspect that is commonly highlighted by academics in Colombia, Chile, and Ecuador. Likewise, of the three countries, Ostrom's contributions have been very well received at the university level in Ecuador, where she is used as a bulwark to identify the problems associated with the de facto governance of the commons and is used as an input to justify a state that must become actively involved even as a "regulator" of the formalization of intersubjective relations and actively protecting the interests of minorities or vulnerable groups.

4.10 Richard A. Posner

Born in the USA in 1939, Judge Posner has been a professor at the University of Chicago since 1969. Posner has researched the application of classical microeconomics to various fields of law such as *antitrust* law, the regulation of commercial contracts, and the judicial system (Posner 1972). For Posner, the factual transcendence of the rules and their effectiveness (in the American Common Law system) is safeguarded by the fact that judges act to promote—as the north of the legal system—*social efficiency* and the gradual consolidation of complex processes such as the *maximization of wealth.* Then, he resorts to cost-benefit analysis to highlight the incidence of the *administrative costs* of the system versus the *costs of error* and other scenarios that arise from the praxis of legal operators. Like Calabresi and Coase, his work constitutes authoritative doctrine for legal economists in Colombia and Chile. However, he is an author whose voice has not been heard in Ecuador, either at a theoretical or applied level. On the contrary, it can be argued that having been characterized as a conservative or "right-wing" academic, he has generated the rejection of Ecuadorian academia in the legal, political, and legal-economic spheres, as these are akin to more progressive approaches such as those disseminated by authors like Cass Sunstein, Hugo Mattei, Duncan Kennedy, among others.

4.11 Oliver E. Williamson

Born in 1932, Professor Williamson[12] was a leading theorist and presenter of the new institutional economics. He was for many years an academic at the University of California at Berkeley. A recipient of the Nobel Prize in Economics, he is responsible for the concept of *governance mechanisms* to refer to systems for controlling

[12] Died in 2020.

the risk associated with any transaction. Although his main fields of research are the economics of institutions, organizational strategy, bureaucracy, politics, and transaction costs, he is not a recurrent author cited by academia focused on EAL in Colombia, Chile, and Ecuador. On the contrary, it is mostly received in economics and business administration departments. As has been the case with the scientific contribution of most of the authors reviewed, Williamson is not a distinguished author in the development of Latin American EAL. Finally, it would seem that this place should be given to the contributions of Coase and, to a lesser extent, Calabresi, especially in the case of Ecuador, with the Colombian and Chilean academia specializing in EAL being much more receptive and interested in the theoretical and conceptual contributions of the other authors on the list.

5 EAL in Colombia, Chile, and Ecuador Observed from the Different Branches of Law

In law schools in Colombia, Chile, and Ecuador, traditionally and in a pedagogical sense, it is usually explained that the main branches of legal science are:

(a) private law, consisting of:

   i. Civil law (including real law, civil contracts, obligations, legal acts and business, and private international law, among others); and
   ii. Commercial law (including other areas such as stock exchange, bankruptcy, banking, transport, contemporary contracting, regulatory, intellectual property, among others).

(b) Public law consisting mainly of:

   i. Procedural Law;
   ii. Constitutional Law;
   iii. Administrative Law;
   iv. Criminal law (among others).

(c) Social Law mainly composed of:

   i. labor law; and
   ii. Family Law.

Although this may seem extremely introductory, it is relevant in that the Social Sciences, their sub-disciplines, and derivations in any country in the world require a convenient prior location and contextualization for subsequent disquisition and analysis. This is certainly not alien to the legal realities of Colombia, Chile, and Ecuador. In Colombia, Chile, Ecuador, and other countries in the region and the world, what is understood by EAL if not the branches of law and their derivations? From the above, it would appear that no Latin American jurisdiction makes the mistake of assuming that EAL represents a branch of legal science.[13] However, a complementary survey of the available literature will allow us to identify that in Colombia, Chile, and Ecuador there is still confusion—perhaps due to the terminological similarity—between EAL and Economic Law (an expression of public property law). This type of impression can even be detected immediately in Ecuador, where more than a few authors assume conceptual synonymy (Villanueva Andrade 2018).[14] This, although superficial and quasi-anecdotal, needs to be corrected and explained in the classroom, because, as authors such as Alfredo Bullard, among others, explain, it constitutes confusing EAL, which is a method, or even an additional tool for the study of legal science and institutional processes, with one of the areas of disaggregation inherent to the law (Torres López 1987; Roemer 1994).[15]

6 How the Critical Considerations of the EAL Are Perceived

To date, in conjunction with the scrutiny carried out in Colombia, Chile, and Ecuador, numerous direct and indirect criticisms have been made of the EAL as a theoretical and applied approach. Among them, we will highlight the following, as we consider them to be a topic for discussion or of interest to the doctrinaires of the countries under study in this chapter:

(a) The use of the methodological and conceptual tools of economic science contributes to Law, which in turn also implies a loss of autonomy—as authors inspired by Hans Kelsen assume—by requiring other areas of knowledge (Bullard González 2006). Certainly, for a large part of the legal literature in Colombia, Chile, and Ecuador, the above implies a valid consideration, that is, an objection that has not been assumed or overcome by a large part of dogmatics.
(b) A second critical approach to EAL (which is often discussed in Colombia and Chile, and unnoticed as part of this movement in Ecuador) is the supposed contradiction between the *efficiency* paradigm, i.e. the relationship between the utility and/or total benefits of a situation X compared to the total costs of that

[13] In all Latin American jurisdictions, following the postulates of classical microeconomics, EAL is presented from two visions or approaches: (a) the normative and (b) the positive. The first revolves around the *"should be"* and aims to prescribe what the design of the institutions or rules of the game should be to achieve their objective (to be efficient, maximizing, etc.). The second is descriptive, i.e., it anticipates results and consequences in terms of incentives, alignment, or misalignment of behavior, among other aspects relevant to the cohesion, development, and evolution of the institutional framework.

[14] However, it should be clarified that apart from this aspect, the methodologies, approaches, approximations, and/or methods taught in law schools in Colombia, Chile, and Ecuador are not classified - in any case - as branches of law *per se*, nor are other methodological approaches such as exegetic, dogmatic, functionalist or even comparative or comparative law.

[15] It is maintained that, despite the many years that have passed since its symbolic foundation, the EAL is less accepted in Latin America than in the Anglo-Saxon world (Bullard González 2003).

situation; and *equity,* understood as the distribution of income or revenue among individuals in a society. Based on this consideration, an action would be efficient when it increases the utility or total benefits of X and decreases the total costs of a situation. On the other hand, an action would be equitable when it reduces the difference between the utility and/or benefits distributed among the members of a specific social fabric (Mattei and Pardolesi 1991).[16]

(c) The recurrent use in EAL of the a priori "rational conduct", is understood as a "tuitive" weighing by an individual of the utility and costs that his or her action brings him or her in committing an action. This consideration of rationality is very reticent among jurists and experts from other fields of knowledge who express their concern about the dehumanization of the individual and the mathematization and monetization of his or her conduct (to the detriment of abstract notions such as *free will* and reasonableness in the human *psyche*).[17]

7 Conclusions

This chapter presented the EAL as a theoretical instrument and potential input that to date is still of little significance in Colombia, Chile, and Ecuador if we try to identify it as a component (parameter) within a rational and articulated process proper to the expression of holistic public policies that a modern state (or grouping of these) should consider.[18]

It also highlighted its potential importance as a tool for welfare societies such as ours, when critically evaluating their legal and juridical institutions to enable inclusive social development, i.e. one that considers the population and its needs. This is so, as the value of respect for human life is undeniable and this also implies that the scarce resources of the social fabric are allocated to their most valuable (collective and private) uses.

Thus, discursively in Colombia, Chile, and Ecuador, it is argued that EAL seeks to contribute to the improvement of the design of the legal institutions (laws and regulations) that govern us to make them more efficient, proactive, productive, and beneficial.

---

[16] To this must be added the discussion still in force in Colombia and Chile regarding the restrictive, mechanistic, and scarcely real character of the hypotheses that can be incorporated in the models built under the rule of abstraction and *ceteris paribus,* typical of expressions of applied microeconomics such as the EAL. This is to the extent that both guiding conditions of modeling in economics cannot accommodate the full range of variables that condition the effectiveness and efficiency of legal and juridical institutions. This must be considered in conjunction with the problem of *endogeneity* inherent to the analysis and scientific method applied in the different fields of the social sciences.

[17] It is worth noting that despite the use of alternative models such as *homo agens* or the individual who acts in search of new opportunities and is not blinded by present-time utility or *bounded rationality,* the indicated criticism persists.

[18] This has been the case in EU countries, in particular the Netherlands, Belgium, Germany, and Italy.

Therefore, EAL, as a discipline, would provide an opportunity for the academic world interested in good living and social justice to interact within a framework where the state intervenes in the evolution of society through *social regulation* and *economic regulation*. The reader is also exposed to a critical judgment on the importance that should be given to the economic rationale to identify the rationality of a legislative, judicial, and/or regulatory decision. Furthermore, EAL plays a key role in facilitating *ex-ante* and *ex-post* evaluation in these highly complex areas.

Also as a tool, EAL can improve the process of normative production and the actions of the operators responsible for its application, and this is equally understood (but with different degrees of assimilation) by academia in Colombia, Chile, and Ecuador. Therefore, and in line with a recurring idea of Professor Calabresi, the above is relevant because the law will only have real effects on social change if it contributes to society's objectives at the lowest possible cost, i.e. avoiding wasted efforts in the public and private spheres.

Certainly, from the survey conducted, it is argued that in Colombia, Chile, and Ecuador, EAL transfers premises that can be classified as a behaviorist, above all to the approaches derived from the integration of psychology and experimentation, and implies a transfer from the individual to the collective. Therefore, and despite the criticisms against utilitarianism in social sciences that are also brought up in these countries, it entails assuming that *social efficiency is* linked to meta-juridical aspects such as maximizing the interest of the greatest number of individuals in a complex scenario that must incorporate—dissimilar—conditions to this tool for the study and design of the rules that govern social groups (e.g. quality of a democracy, degree of tolerance in the face of scenarios of inequality, among others).

Ultimately, this chapter aimed to provide a theoretical reflection and a general description of some previous (necessary) aspects for a better understanding of the impact attributable to the economic analysis of law in Colombia, Chile, and Ecuador as a valid instrument of analysis to promote reforms of the State and in the State (government) and in processes related to the strength and quality of the institutional framework, which contributes to scenarios such as economic and social innovation, the need for interpersonal trust in the economy, the productivity of the social fabric and the technical and economic efficiency in favor of general welfare. This aspect, which could be derived from the explicit use of EAL, will be presented as a scale. Alike, this outline will begin with a selection of the main representatives (precursors and proponents) of EAL, arguing whether there is a tangible transcendence of the *core of* its scientific contribution at the academic level, continuing with an explanation of its relevance and its type of use in Colombia, Chile, and Ecuador, and will end by pointing out some of the recent criticisms that have been formulated in opposition to the use of the economic methodology in law. However, it should be noted that we do not intend to carry out an extensive review and analysis of the underlying links between EAL and other areas and instruments such as regulatory reform, as this is a subject that we have dealt with conceptually before (Sumar Albujar et al. 2018; Mendez Reategui and Sumar 2021) and that in the future will be the specific focus of other documentary pieces.

References

Becker G (1968) Crime and punishment: an economic approach. J Polit Econ 76:169–217
Bullard González A (2006) Derecho y Economía. El análisis económico de las instituciones legales. Editorial Palestra, Lima, Peru
Cachanosky JC (2006) Economics, law and economic analysis of law. Retrieved from http://www.hacer.org/pdf/Cachanosky00.pdf
Calabresi G, Melamed D (1972) Property rules, liability rules and inalienability: one view of the cathedral. Harv Law Rev 8(6)
Coase RH (1960) The problem of social cost. J Law Econ 3:1–44
de Trazegnies GF (1995) La Responsabilidad Extracontractual, 5th edn. Fondo Editorial de la PUCP, Lima, Peru
Lescano Galeas NV, Mena Mena MC, Mendez Reategui R (2016) Eficacia, eficiencia y efectividad en la resolución de conflictos transigibles de niñez y adolescencia en el Ecuador. Revista de Derecho UNED, No 8
Lozano Rodríguez E (2016) Teoría y puesta en práctica del Análisis Económico del Derecho Colombiano. Editorial Ediciones UNIANDES
Mattei U, Pardolesi R (1991) Law and economics in civil law countries: a comparative approach. Int Rev Law Econ 11:265–275
Mendez Reategui R (2014) Structured, transitional, and unstructured civil societies an institutional approach. Market Proc Eur J Polit Econ 11(2)
Mendez Reategui R (2020a) Institutional competitiveness and bureaucratic barriers. In: 1st international seminar on law and economics (12 Nov.). Federal University of Bahia and Association of Federal Judges of Brazil (AJUFE)
Mendez Reategui R (2020b) Some critical considerations on applied law and economics. In: VII National Fair of Economic Analysis of Law and Economic Regulation (11, 12 and 13 Nov.). Externado University of Colombia
Mendez Reategui R, Alosilla Díaz R (2015) New economic history, institutions, and new institutional history: a brief retrospection. Laissez-Faire, 43
Mendez Reategui R, Sumar O (2021) Rule of law versus soft rule of law. UNED. Revista de Derecho Político 109:373–400
Posner R (1972) Economic analysis of law, 1st edn. Little Brown, Boston
Roemer, A. (1994). Introducción al Análisis Económico del Derecho. Fondo de Cultura Económica, Mexico City, Mexico
Sumar Albujar O, Mendez Reategui R, Vogel D, Calle Causol JP, Solís G, Francisco J, Ochoa FJ, Mendoza, Del Mastro Puccio F, Flores Borda G (2018) Regulatory improvement and multidisciplinary approaches. PUCE Publications Centre, Quito, Ecuador
Torres López J (1987) Análisis Económico del Derecho: Panorama Doctrinal. Tecnos, Madrid, Spain
Trujillo Cabrera J (2012) Análisis Económico del Derecho colombiano. Editorial: Dictus Publishing, Bogotá, Colombia
Villanueva Andrade M (2018) Aplicación del Análisis Económico del Derecho en las Ciencias Jurídicas. Editorial Grupo Compas, (Estudios para Ecuador)

Rise and Peak of Peruvian Law and Economics

José Enrique Sotomayor Trelles

Abstract The chapter provides an overview of the introduction and development of the Law and Economics (L&E) approach in Peru. To this end, it outlines a periodization of its evolution based on four major phases: the initial attempts, the boiling period, the peak, and the subsequent stabilization. Criticisms directed at Peruvian proponents of L&E are then presented and analyzed. This analysis closely follows a book authored by Castillo Freyre and Vásquez Kunze, which stands as the most systematic critical examination of Peruvian L&E to date. Finally, the chapter offers a balance of perspectives and identifies future directions for the approach's development.

1 Introduction

This paper examines the development of the Law and Economics (L&E) movement in Peru. The analysis is structured along two main axes: a historical reconstruction of the phases of this intellectual movement; and an exposition and evaluation of some of the criticisms and debates that have emerged in the Peruvian legal literature.

The Peruvian case is particularly interesting because the peak of the Law and Economics movement coincided with a period of aggressive neoliberalization of the economy and legal institutions during Alberto Fujimori's government. This alignment was by further influenced discussions surrounding the drafting of the 1993 Peruvian Constitution, which subsequently led to the establishment of a renewed institutional infrastructure, including antitrust agencies and new market regulators.

In this context, it is evident that the movement found fertile ground to flourish, beginning in the late 1980s but mainly during the 1990s. The next section provides a detailed periodization of the development of Law and Economics in Peru.

J. E. S. Trelles (✉)
Pontifical Catholic University of Peru, Lima, Peru
e-mail: enrique.sotomayor@pucp.pe

S. Zorzetto et al. (eds.), *Developments in Law and Economics in the Italo-Iberoamerican Context*, Economic Analysis of Law in European Legal Scholarship 21, https://doi.org/10.1007/978-3-032-03317-8_13

2 Stages of Law and Economics Development in Peru

The bibliography that offers a critical assessment of the development of the Law and Economics movement in Peru remains scarce and preliminary.[1] Nevertheless, the impact of this approach since the late 1980s has been remarkable in areas such as civil law, competition, and antitrust law.[2]

The following timeline in Table 1 illustrates the evolution of the movement, using the reconstruction offered by Bullard as a starting point.[3]

We have identified four phases of development of the Peruvian L&E movement: (i) first manifestations (second half of the 1980s), (ii) boiling period (early 1990s), (iii) peak (second half of the 1990s and first half of the 2000s), and (iv) stabilization and slight decline, from the second half of the 2000s to the present.

In its early stages, the literature on L&E was introduced through studies conducted by economists and lawyers affiliated with the Institute for Liberty and Democracy (ILD). Two academic figures are key to understand this initial wave: the economist Hernando de Soto and the lawyer Enrique Ghersi. The work of this think tank focused on analyzing the factors contributing to informality in Peru and addressing issues of ownership, particularly the problem of property titles.

As Bullard notes, in this initial phase, few people associated the ILD's work with the L&E movement that had been developing in U.S. universities since the second half of the twentieth century. It was not until a group of young lawyers, returning from postgraduate studies at U.S. universities, that the movement began to be associated with a research program.[4]

During what we have called the boiling period, a notable group of young lawyers, freshly returned from postgraduate studies abroad, began teaching courses mainly related to patrimonial civil law. Among these professors, Alfredo Bullard stands out as a central figure. Trained at Yale University, Bullard began teaching the introductory course on civil law for first-semester law students at the Pontifical Catholic University of Peru (PUCP) even before completing his graduate studies.[5] His prominence soon grew, and he eventually led the first L&E course in the country. This course was established with the support of the then-Dean of the Faculty of Law at the PUCP, Jorge Avendaño, a distinguished civil lawyer.[6]

The conditions were favorable: during his first term as dean, Avendaño had championed a functionalist approach to law. He had also facilitated a partnership with the University of Wisconsin, which significantly influenced the methodology

[1] Even though there are two recent attempts of systematization in Marciani et al. (2020) and Núñez del Prado (2023).

[2] According to Bullard's opinion (2019, p. 61), Peru is the Latin American country where the Law and Economics approach has achieved the greatest progress, acceptance, and impact.

[3] Bullard (2019), p. 61.

[4] Bullard (2019), p. 63.

[5] León (2013), p. 134.

[6] See Bullard (2004), pp. 73 ff.; León (2013), p. 135.

Table 1 Law and Economics Movement Development in Peru (from 1980 to present day)

Period	Key figures	Topics of interest	Bibliographic sample	Institutional context
First attempts (second half of the 1980s)[a]	Grouped around the Institute for Liberty and Democracy (ILD), led by Hernando de Soto and Enrique Ghersi.	Analysis of informality, over-regulation, property rights and the impact of the system of titularities.	*El otro sendero: la revolución informal* by De Soto et al. (1986).	Creation of the popular mortgage, by Legislative Decree No. 495 of November 1988.
Boiling period (early 1990s)	Lawyers who pursued graduate studies at universities in the United States, such as Yale, Chicago, Harvard, and Virginia. Some examples: Alfredo Bullard, Fernando Cantuarias, Beatriz Boza, José Antonio Payet and José Daniel Amado.	Patrimonial civil law, in areas such as property, contracts and civil liability. Also subjects as competition and antitrust, regulatory law and consumer protection.	*El costo de la legalidad: una aproximación a la falta de legitimidad del Derecho* by Ghersi (1991); *Un mundo sin propiedad* by Bullard (1991); "*¡Al fondo hay sitio!*" *¿Puede el Teorema de Coase explicarnos el problema del transporte público?* by Bullard (1992); *La Ley Antimonopolio: ¿por qué y cómo aplicarla?* by Fernández-Baca (1992); *Retracto: Réquiem de un Derecho "económico y social"* by Cantuarias (1992); *Responsabilidad civil y eficiencia económica: "matrimonio por conveniencia"* by Falla (1992); *La legislación antimonopólica y el mito del Muro de Berlín* by Bullard (1994).	Approval of the Law for the Development in Private Investment (Ley Marco para el Crecimiento de la Inversión Privada), given by Legislative Decree No. 757 of 1991. Creation of the National Institute for the Defense of Free Competition and the Protection of Intellectual Property (Indecopi), by Legal Decree No. 25868 of November 1992. Creation of the National Superintendence of Sanitation Services (Sunass), by Legal Decree No. 25965 of December 1992. Creation of the Supervisory Agency for Private Investment in Telecommunications (Osiptel), by Legislative Decree No. 702 of July 1991 (although it began operating in January 1994).

(continued)

Table 1 (continued)

Period	Key figures	Topics of interest	Bibliographic sample	Institutional context
Peak (from the second half of the 1990s to the mid-2000s)	Students of professors who brought L&E to Peru (several of them also pursued postgraduate studies in the USA and UK). Examples: José Juan Haro, Eduardo Sotelo, Carlos Patrón Salinas, Huáscar Ezcurra, Alejandro Falla, Freddy Escobar Rozas and Enrique Pasquel.	The interests and issues are mainly the same as in the previous period, but with an added emphasis on regulatory issues, corporate and bankruptcy law, competition law, telecommunications, intellectual property and consumer protection. Likewise, there is criticism of the justice administration system, and the defense of alternative dispute resolution mechanisms, such as arbitration. Finally, there is some interest in discussing the philosophical and political foundations of L&E.	*Introducción al análisis costo-beneficio de las normas* by Ortiz de Zevallos and Guerra García (1998); *Privaticemos la insolvencia* by Ezcurra (2002); *Derecho y Economía* by Bullard (2003); *¿Quién dijo que en Salem hubo brujas? La privatización del servicio de justicia: rompiendo el mito de la justicia estatal* by Bayly and Pasquel (2003); *La falaz leyenda de Robin Hood. Los dilemas económicos y filosóficos de la redistribución de la riqueza* by Pasquel and Solís (2003); *¿Es el análisis económico del derecho una herramienta válida de interpretación del derecho positivo?* by Escobar Rozas and Hernando (2006).	Creation of the Commission (today an Agency) for the Formalization of Informal Property (Cofopri), by Legislative Decree No. 803, Law for the Promotion of Access to Formal Property of 1996. Creation of the Energy and Mining Investment Supervisory Agency (initially Osinerg, today Osinergmin), by Law No. 26734 of December 1996. Creation of the Supervisory Agency for Investment in Transportation Infrastructure for Public Use (Ositran), by Law No. 26917 of January 1998. Enactment of the General Administrative Procedure Law, Law No. 27444 (in force since October 2001).

Stabilization and slight decline (from the second half of the 2000s to present day)	Students of foreign and Peruvian L&E scholars. Examples: Christian Chávez, César Higa, Renzo Saavedra, Gustavo Miro-Quesada, Guillermo Flores Borda, Eduardo Melgar, Gustavo Rodríguez y Óscar Súmar.	The interests are varied, although a decline in the treatment of civil law issues has been identified. On the other hand, applications of L&E began to appear in areas such as environmental, constitutional, and criminal law. Finally, a significant number of works have been optimistic about new lines of research such as Behavioral Law & Economics, or analyses based on game theory.	*Paradojas en la regulación de la publicidad en el Perú* by Súmar and Avellaneda (2010); *Análisis económico y comparado del Derecho privado* by Saavedra (2017); *Deconstruyendo al homo economicus: una revisión conductual de un paradigma del law and economics* by Saavedra (2011); *Análisis psicológico del Derecho* by Bullard and De la Jara (eds.), (2018); *Economía y Constitución: las libertades económicas en la jurisprudencia del tribunal constitucional* by Súmar and Iñiguez (2017); *El consumidor en su isla: una visión alternativa del sistema de protección al consumidor* by Rodríguez García (2013); *¿Un error lo comete cualquiera? Implicancias de los errores de condena sobre el nivel de disuasión en los procedimientos administrativos sancionadores* by Melgar (2014).	Subscription of free trade agreements between Peru and several countries (with the United States in 2006, and entered into force in February 2009; with China, in April 2009; with the European Union, signed in June 2012; among others). Currently, after signing the *Programa País* in 2014, Peru seeks to join the Organization for Economic Cooperation and Development (OECD) by 2021 (the accession process finally began in early 2022, upon invitation from the OECD). To do so, it must comply with a series of conditions regarding competitiveness, tax collection, regulatory quality, reduction of inequality, among others. Approval of Legislative Decree No. 1310 of January 2017, which adopts administrative simplification measures, and includes the obligation (for Executive Branch entities) to perform Regulatory Quality Analysis of administrative procedures.

Note: Own elaboration, taking as reference Bullard (2019), pp. 61–84

[a]It is possible to distinguish between the precursors of L&E in Peru, on the one hand, and the development of the movement itself, on the other. This distinction is analogous to the one proposed by Manuel Atienza in various works for theories of legal argumentation (see, e.g., Atienza 2016). If so, in addition to Hernando de Soto and Enrique Ghersi, other significant figures associated with the economic liberalization and deregulation that the country experienced in the first half of the 1990s should be mentioned. These figures include: Carlos Boloña, Minister of Economy between 1991 and 1993; Felipe Ortiz de Zevallos, a founder of Grupo Apoyo; and Augusto Álvarez Rodrich, a member of Grupo Apoyo, vice-president of Osiptel during Fujimori's administration, and co-author of *Principios de empresas estatales y privatización* (1992). Although these individuals primarily come from economics, their ideas were introduced during the arrival of L&E ideas in Peru and had a significant influence on the first generations of Peruvian jus-economists. I am grateful to César Higa for the insights he provided during an enlightening conversation, which significantly contributed to the development of this footnote

of teaching Law at the PUCP. From 1968 onward, Wisconsin was a hub for the Law & Society movement, which was gaining traction.[7] It was, therefore no surprise that during his second term as dean (1987–1993), Avendaño welcomed interdisciplinary approaches that bridged law with the social sciences.

As Bullard observed:

> [...] it should come as no surprise that the same Dean who, nearly thirty years ago, expressed the need to train lawyers in tools that would allow them to build bridges between the formal structure of law and reality is the same dean who incorporated the teaching of L&E not only at the Catholic University [PUCP], but also at Peruvian universities [...].[8]

This second phase of development includes several "classic" works of Peruvian Law and Economics. As noted in Table 1, most of these works focused on civil property law—particularly property, contract law, and civil liability——as well as competition law and regulation. The primary focus of analysis was the critique of legal institutions deemed inefficient or those that increased transaction costs. It is also worth noting the fresh and agile rhetoric employed by the young jus-economists, which contrasted with the weightiness of traditional doctrinal references. The context was favorable, as the country was transitioning towards a free market economy, symbolized by the spirited banner of the newly enacted Fujimori's Constitution of 1993.

At its peak, the Peruvian L&E movement found niches in law journals, universities, and institutions. Among these, the journal *Thēmis* became a key platform, serving as both a repository for translations of established authors and a space for the emerging voices of Peruvian L&E. It is no exaggeration to say that such a surge of bibliographical activity, all tied to a single research program, has rarely been witnessed in a Peruvian law journal. However, it is important to note the significant disparity the in quality of the texts appearing in its pages during this period. Contributions ranged from insightful critiques of doctrinal approaches to less polished works by enthusiasts of the approach. The now common practice of peer review was still far from being implemented in Peruvian law journals at the time.

During this period, Peruvian L&E also found a home in academia. While the Faculty of Law at the PUCPwas never "taken over" by the jus-economists, it served as a base. Other institutions, such as the Faculty of Law at the University of Lima and the newly established (in 1994) Peruvian University of Applied Sciences (UPC), also welcomed professors who taught from an L&E approach.

At the UPC, the leadership of Fernando Cantuarias was instrumental in consolidating the movement within its classrooms. The university's publishing house translated and published works such as *El análisis económico del Derecho y la Escuela de Chicago* by Posner[9] and *¿Por qué hay que cambiar el Código Civil?* by Cantuarias.[10] These compilations included contributions from the E&A approach,

[7] Ramos Núñez and Cuadros (2019), pp. 142–150.

[8] Bullard (2004), pp. 89–90.

[9] Posner (2002).

[10] Cantuarias (2001).

with the former by U.S. authors and the latter by Peruvian authors. In the 2000s, the UPC's contribution to the movement was joined by those of a new player: the Law School at the Universidad del Pacífico (UP), one of the institutions that has had the greatest influence on the management of the country's economy.

Since 1992, when the National Institute for the Defense of Competition and Protection of Intellectual Property (Indecopi) was established, regulatory bodies, as well as competition and consumer protection agencies, have become institutional niches for jus-economists. Topics such as regulation and contract law provided ideal avenues to apply the insights of economic theory. These were learned either from national professors returning from postgraduate studies abroad or directly from the world's leading L&E scholars. A "gringo invasion" was spreading like a catchy fad among an important sector of new jurists. However, as León cautiously notes, the movement has remained largely confined to the capital. Outside Lima, the influence of L&A) appears to have been minimal.[11]

Today, the L&E program is a well-established approach within Peruvian legal doctrine. Its survival beyond being a mere trend indicates its continued relevance and utility in analyzing various legal institutions and phenomena. Nevertheless, the quantity of bibliographical production has declined, and theoretical development has largely remained anchored in classical references such as Coase, Calabresi, Becker, and Posner. Likewise, newer trends—such as the theory of legal argumentation and neoconstitutionalism—have been gaining ground in Peruvian academia.

For Peruvian L&E to achieve a qualitative leap and continue contributing novel ideas and approaches to the study of law in the country, it must deepen its use of economic tools and empirical analysis. More rigorous training in economics, econometrics, and statistics, as well as interdisciplinary work, seem imperative for this to be the case. Likewise, the ideological alliance of L&E with neoliberalism has sparked a series of criticisms revealing that many of the arguments presented by Peruvian L&E as self-evident actually concealed biased views on the roles of legal systems and markets.[12] Similarly, the supposed asepsis on issues concerning the justice and fairness in institutions was frequently replaced by contentious—and often poorly informed—diatribes. This last point is not about adding stronger conceptual tools from economics but rather about conducting a more thorough and detailed study of the philosophical-political, ethical, and even epistemological foundations of the movement. This constitutes a critical agenda for a new generation of jus-economists, from whom more thoughtful and better-substantiated contributions are anticipated.

Parallel to this agenda, some emerging legal economists have shown interest in the impact of technology and the management of large datasets on markets and law, as well as in integrating advances in neuroscience and cognitive-behavioral psychology into legal analysis.[13] Additionally, a third group has been interested in

[11] León (2013), pp. 141–142.

[12] Merino (2008, 2016).

[13] Saavedra (2011); Bullard and De la Jara (2018).

developing approaches rooted in game theory, extending beyond the interaction models traditionally employed in the economic analysis of competition.[14] All these issues require, once again, a more cautious rhetoric than that exhibited by the classical proponents of Peruvian L&E. If undertaken responsibly, these efforts should yield methodologically better-founded works that are also more cautious in their conclusions.

3 Minefield: Criticisms to Peruvian Law and Economics

In Peru, the development of L&E faced significant resistance. It is nevertheless important to recognize that, much of this criticism stemmed from misunderstandings of the movement's core theses. The often belligerent, and at times superficial, rhetoric of Peruvian L&E during the 1990s and early 2000s provoked strong, and occasionally exaggerated, reactions from critics. As Bullard notes, "[s]ome 'schizophrenics'"—as he calls the approach's critics—"reacted aggressively and vehemently, using strong epithets against L&E."[15] A second group dismissed the movement with disinterest and disdain, treating it as a fleeting trend. In this environment, a good deal of nostalgia for traditional approaches inevitably became a key element of the resistance.[16]

This section examines the criticisms of L&E in Peru in two sections: (i) an analysis of the five types of criticism identified by Bullard, and (ii) a reconstruction of the most systematic critical project articulated against the L&E thesis in Peru, as presented by Castillo Freyre and Vásquez Kunze.[17]

3.1 *On Bullard's Typology of Criticism to Law and Economics*

In a useful categorization of the types of criticisms—or "types of schizophrenia", as he calls them—of L&E in Peru, Bullard[18] groups them into five broad types:

[14] Flores Borda (2011, 2014).

[15] Bullard (2002), p. 29.

[16] For example: "When our generation studied law [...], civil law reigned supreme. Civil Law ruled in the most illustrious chairs of the various courses on the subject, taught by those who, in turn, were the best professors that any university in Peru could boast" (Castillo Freyre and Vásquez Kunze 2004, p. 17).

[17] Castillo Freyre and Vásquez Kunze (2004), p. 17.

[18] Bullard (2002, 2006).

3.1.1 Type I

Criticism of the first type is made by those who believe that L&E is an inapplicable method or approach in a country with a Romano-Germanic tradition such as Peru, where jurisprudence and precedents are not as important as in common law. In its most extreme form, this criticism portrays L&E as a form of intellectual imperialism. Bullard groups this family of criticisms under the label of "la invasión gringa" (the *gringo* invasion). In its most rudimentary form, the critique is easily dismissed. As Bullard explains:

> That it was in the United States that this line of thought developed has only meant that the most common examples cited in L&E textbooks refer to U.S. jurisprudence or norms. But the conceptual tools can be used, without losing any of their analytical capacity, to any other form of legal system.[19]

Regarding Bullard's response, it could be noted that, while it is true that, methodologically, L&E can be applied to the analysis of various legal systems and traditions, a significant part of its original approach was centered on uncovering the economic rationality of judicial decisions in common law. This observation leads to the following conclusion: as a method—assuming it is defined as the application of economic theory to analyze the rationality and effects of legal institutions, decisions, and rules—L&E is indeed applicable to a variety of legal systems and traditions. However, as an intellectual movement, L&E emerged with a markedly jurisprudential orientation, in which economic analysts sought to identify or infer the implicit economic logic underlying judicial decisions.

3.1.2 Type II

Criticism of the second type is made by those who consider that L&E is the product of some ideologically driven brotherhood aimed at convincing people of the benefits of a virtually unrestricted free market and of the harmfulness of state intervention. Bullard groups this family of criticisms under the label "the neoliberal invasion".

Bullard responds to this criticism by reiterating that, in essence, L&E is simply a method advocating the incorporation of economic theory and methodology into the analysis of legal institutions, and that this can be done from within the broad ideological diversity found in economic theory itself. In short, L&E could be approached from orthodox, liberal, Marxist, Keynesian, Austrian, or other economic perspectives.[20] A good example of an academic defender of L&E who is far from neoliberal theses, according to Bullard, is Guido Calabresi. Furthermore, L&E has often been employed to justify an active state role in areas such as regulation or consumer protection. So much for Bullard's response.

---

[19] Bullard (2006), p. 94.

[20] Bullard (2006), p. 94; see, also, Sotomayor (2016).

The issue with this response lies in Bullard's ambiguous use of the term "L&E" in two distinct senses: first, as an intellectual movement with identifiable figures located within a specific historical and academic context (what we might call the "academic sociology perspective"), and, second, as a method or approach advocating the application of economic theory and methods to legal analysis (what we might call the "method perspective").

In the first sense, Bullard's observation would be—at least partially—wrong, while in the second sense, it is accurate. Indeed, as a method, L&E can be used by jus-economists of any political ideology. However, as an academic movement—particularly in its Chicago variant—it was developed within a perspective that aligns closely with what we would today identify as a neoliberal agenda. The example of Calabresi is illustrative here. He represents what could be called the Yale School of Law and Economics, as opposed to the Chicago variant which has exerted a dominant influence on Peruvian jus-economists. The Chicago School, rooted in the work of Henry Simons and Aaron Director, extends to authors such as Richard Posner.[21]

Thus, this second criticism is not merely "schizophrenia", as Bullard suggests, but rather a valid observation about the ideological orientation of Peruvian jus-economists. Bullard himself ultimately concedes this point, acknowledging that:

> [I]t cannot be denied that L&E, in the Peruvian historical experience, has served to support liberalization and privatization proposals. Many of the Peruvian academics involved in L&E advocate ideas of freedom and less state presence.[22]

Of course, none of this invalidates the method itself. However, this underscores the need to clarify Bullard's ambiguous response to the critique. Failing to do so risks perpetuating the very "confusion of the tool with the ideology" that he himself denounces.

3.1.3 Type III

Criticism of the third type is made by those who argue that the existence of legal institutions must be preserved and protected, viewing L&E as a threat to their survival—likening it to "unicorn poachers".[23] In response to this criticism, Bullard points out that L&E does not aim to eliminate conceptual categories but rather to shift the perspective in which these categories are understood. The idea is to stop thinking of legal concepts and institutions having a life of their own, and to recognize that their value is instrumental and "lies in their capacity to allow us to regulate human conduct in an adequate manner".[24] This position, according to Bullard, represents a realist view of law. Bullard's stance here aligns with legal realism and

[21] Teles (2008); Chiassoni (2013).

[22] Bullard (2006), p. 95.

[23] Bullard (2006), p. 96.

[24] Bullard (2006), pp. 96–97.

maintains a minimalist ontological framework in which only that which has a physical manifestation is considered "real".

A comment on Bullard's response to this critique: although the author does not delve deeply into the analysis of legal and social ontology, this issue is quite complex, and his critique could be viewed through the lens of theorists such as John Searle.[25] Searle offers a complex social ontology that acknowledges the "reality" of institutional and conceptual phenomena (through constitutive rules). However, criticizing Bullard from this angle might not be entirely fair, as his focus is more on the utility or functionality of legal concepts rather than on their ontological status. This focus on functionality rather than the fetishization of legal concepts was already present in the Scandinavian realist tradition, such as in Alf Ross's *Tû-tû*.[26]

3.1.4 Type IV

Criticism of the fourth type is made by those who argue that L&E proposes an unrealistic oversimplification of reality. Such oversimplification would, stem from the use of stylized models that rest on implausible assumptions. Bullard's response to this criticism is twofold.

First, he points out that legal dogmatics also relies on conceptual models, but unlike L&E, these models lack connections to reality. Thus, these models are unjustified frameworks that cannot even qualify as simplifications. Second, Bullard emphasizes that models are designed to explain a specific aspect of reality and, from there, to advance predictions. They are not designed to imitate reality in all its subtleties. This is exemplified by the assumption of rationality among economic agents, central to many models, about which Bullard states that "a relatively small number of rational beings is sufficient for the predictive model to be useful".[27]

This response is presented in rather general terms, which makes it difficult to assess. Bullard uses a classic microeconomic example—the relationship between price and demand—to illustrate the utility of such models. The basic prediction is that higher prices lead to lower demand and that, for the same price, consumers prefer the product with better characteristics.

Over time, more localized assumptions have emerged, in which the rationality premise is not only unrealistic but also generates poor predictions of economic behavior. Simply put, models relying on the rationality assumption fail in these scenarios. This criticism has opened the door to the E&A through a behavioral approach ("Behavioral Law & Economics"). This analysis builds on the discoveries and contributions of psychologists such as Daniel Kahneman and Amos Tversy,[28]

---

[25] Searle (2010), Chap. 5.

[26] Ross (2004).

[27] Bullard (2006), p. 98.

[28] Kahneman and Tversy (2000).

and has been advocated by authors such as Cass Sunstein, Richard Thaler, and Christine Jolls,[29] among many others.

3.1.5 Type V

Criticism of the fifth type is made by those who argue that L&E substitutes the value of justice with that of efficiency. While a more refined version of this criticism can be found in Dworkin's[30] objections to the proposals of Calabresi and Posner, the variant analyzed by Bullard is rather rudimentary. Bullard acknowledges that utilitarian tendencies are characteristic of some variants of L&E but insists that extending this critique to the whole movement is unfair. To counter this, he draws on Calabresi's argument that efficiency itself carries a valuational content: "[w]hile it is said that L&E may be trying to replace justice with efficiency, such a position loses sight of the fact that in a world where resources are scarce, waste is unjust".[31] Bullard further argues that the waste of resources—whether resulting from poor legal decisions or improper allocations of entitlements—leads to social loss, less available wealth, and, indirectly, greater poverty.

From Bullard's point of view, there are two further considerations: (i) the criterion of justice—unlike efficiency—is difficult to define and always subject to dispute; and (ii) even if one remains skeptical about efficiency, it is crucial to know how much justice costs. In this sense, "[t]o make apparently fair decisions in the context of the scarcity that the real world presents us with, is to assume justice with responsibility".[32]

The discussion on the normative value of wealth maximization centers around whether it constitutes an end in itself or is merely a means to other ends.[33] A major flaw in the normative defenses of L&E, according to Bullard, is that they lack a coherent theory of justice, except for the outline proposed by Calabresi. Additionally, in their emphasis on wealth maximization, L&E theories seem to overlook that human flourishing is not achieved by the mere accumulation of aggregate wealth but by ensuring the equitable distribution of rights, freedoms, and capabilities. In such a framework, attaining higher levels of wealth without achieving more equitable societies is, in itself, both useless and potentially harmful. This gap has been addressed in part through the capabilities approach advanced by authors such as Amartya Sen and Martha Nussbaum.[34]

In addition to questioning the instrumental or ultimate value of wealth maximization, another concern arises from the fact that most analyses within L&E adopt a

---

[29] Sunstein et al. (1998).

[30] Dworkin (1980).

[31] Bullard (2006), p. 100.

[32] Bullard (2006), p. 101.

[33] Driesen and Malloy (2017), p. 302.

[34] See Sen and Nussbaum (1993) for an extensive bibliography on the subject.

Kaldor-Hicks-type efficiency criterion. This criterion suggests that efficiency and wealth maximization may go hand in hand with significant levels of inequality. The justification for this inequality occurs when the gains of the winners exceed the losses of losers.[35] Thus, the operation of the Kaldor-Hicks criterion shows that L&E requires more than mere efficiency as a criterion for evaluating legal institutions and rules.

While Bullard's reconstruction of the criticisms of L&E in Peru is somewhat uncharitable, it provides a useful cognitive map of both the impact of the movement and the orientation of its critics. This is important in a country like Peru, where many critiques of the L&E approach never appeared in the form of articles or books but were articulated in university classrooms and informal conversations. In the next section, we examine the most thorough and structured critique of L&E within Peruvian legal doctrine.

3.2 A Response to Peruvian Law and Economics from Traditional Legal Dogmatics

The primary arena of confrontation for Peruvian L&E was civil law, where a significant battle occurred between the enthusiasts of L&E and the supporters of the more traditional legal dogmatics. In a detailed account of the legal institutions in civil law that L&E questioned and criticized, Castillo Freyre and Vásquez Kunze highlight areas such as property law, hardship and gross disparity (*excesiva onerosidad de la prestación*), injury and lesion, the covenants of non-alienation, minimum lease terms, prohibition of succession agreements, retraction, maximum interest rates, and fault as a factor of attribution in civil liability, among others.[36]

Felipe Osterling, in the preface to what is perhaps the only book entirely devoted to critiquing Peruvian L&E,[37] invokes perspectives from scholars like Posner and Coase, viewed through Hayek's lens. Hayek's From the latter's standpoint, the primary purpose of law is not efficiency but the optimization of individual rights and liberties. This criticism intersects with the question of whether efficiency is an instrumental or final value content.

However, rather than dismissing L&E as a research and teaching method for law altogether, Osterling just underscores the need for a basic legal training. This, he argues, would provide students with a solid foundation for a more informed criticism: "[i]f the law student is given a traditional civil law training, he will later have a solid basis to criticize, with full mastery, the Code that has formed him".[38]

[35] Driesen and Malloy (2017), p. 302.

[36] Castillo Freyre and Vásquez Kunze (2004), p. 19.

[37] Castillo Freyre and Vásquez Kunze (2004).

[38] Osterling Parodi (2004), p. 14.

From our point of view, the main criticisms proposed by Castillo Freyre and Vásquez Kunze can be grouped into eight key themes, outlined as follows:

3.2.1 Criticism 1: The Colonization of Economics

In this line criticism, L&E would advocate for a sort of colonization of the economy over law, by attempting to establish economic criteria as the foundation for legal validity. They argue that this notion is not new, as the Marxist theory of law had already proposed similar ideas. In response to this, Castillo Freyre and Vásquez Kunze defend the scientific rigor of law in the Kelsenian tradition.[39]

This first criticism is nevertheless flawed, as few, if any, serious proponents of L&E argue for replacing the criterion of legal validity with economic criteria. Rather, economics offers jus-economists a framework for evaluating the quality of regulation, but it does not function as a test of legal pedigree or validity.

3.2.2 Criticism 2: The Methodological Oversight

The fourth chapter of the book by Castillo Freyre and Vásquez Kunze is dedicated to critiquing L&E's analysis of property, and it begins by highlighting the movement's lack of attention to methodological issues that the movement has exhibited in Peru:

> While in the United States the academic community has made an effort to [test their hypotheses with a methodology] in each of the specific cases criticized—that is, in each of the legal institutions economically analyzed—in Peru, most of the followers of this economic trend with legal dalliances have avoided the difficult path of evidence to reach the goal of conclusion in a somersault.[40]

The first important point to clarify here is that L&E can operate at two levels of research, which roughly correspond to the descriptive (positive) and normative levels in economics.

In one of L&E research levels, a set of economic concepts and theories is applied to analyze the potential effects of a given regulatory body. A statement corresponding to this level of research might be framed as follows: "According to economic theory X, the effects that legislation Y could have on Z are A, B, …, N". It is crucial to note here that, in this level, the researcher does not necessarily know whether these effects have actually occurred or are currently taking place.[41]

The second research level involves empirically measuring and identifying the effects of a legislative body using certain variables. This research then uses economic theory to explain the observed results. The disciplines that primarily assist in

[39] Castillo Freyre and Vásquez Kunze (2004), pp. 29–38.

[40] Castillo Freyre and Vásquez Kunze (2004), pp. 67–68.

[41] See Grant (2018), Chap. 6; Parisi (2005).

this type of work are statistics and econometrics. The corresponding statement might read: "According to the analysis of data obtained through empirical methods L, it seems that legislation Y is producing effects A, B, …, N, which can be explained by theory X".

Now, regarding the critique by Castillo Freyre and Vásquez Kunze, it seems to be valid primarily about the second level of L&E research in Peru. Indeed, it has been a common pattern among the first and second generations of Peruvian jus-economists to overlook empirical testing of their claims. A more difficult question to address is, however, whether Peruvian L&E has been negligent in terms of theoretical and methodological rigor at the level of economic theory research. This question is difficult to answer because, although concepts like "transaction costs", "efficiency criteria", "externalities", "public goods", among others, are often mentioned, their use is sometimes generic, imprecise, or oversimplified.

Despite these concerns, in recent years, works that are better supported both theoretically and methodologically have begun to appear.[42] These works incorporate the analysis of empirical data analyzed using statistical and econometric methods.[43] It is still too early to claim that an empirical turn has taken place in Peruvian L&E, but these developments offer some reason for optimism. Additionally, the annual conferences of L&E, such as those hosted by the Latin American and Iberian Association of Law and Economics (ALACDE), now feature a category for empirical research in L&E (The Edgardo Buscaglia ALACDE Award for Empirical Research in Law and Economics).

3.2.3 Criticism 3: The (Relative) Practical Irrelevance

In Chapter 4 their book, Castillo Freyre and Vásquez Kunze also argue that criticisms of L&E in Peru have focused on a limited set of legal institutions found in norms of the Peruvian Civil Code, many of which are not particularly important in practice:

> What we wonder is what is the sense of making a picturesque and anecdotal question the axis of a criticism of all civil law, presenting a non-existent academic and social problem, because the objects of criticism have no gravitation in the national legal environment.[44]

This criticism overlooks the fact that, beyond the economic repercussion of the legal institutions in question, what is actually being evaluated is the merit of the criticisms themselves. Therefore, it is not relevant whether such institutions are incidentally employed by legal practitioners, but whether criticisms against them make economic sense. However, the authors are partially correct when they claim that one cannot extrapolate a critique of the entire body of civil law from the critique of a few inefficient legal institutions. In argumentative terms, this would be a fallacy of

[42] See, for example, Flores Borda (2011, 2014), in the case of game theory.

[43] See, for example, Melgar (2014).

[44] Castillo Freyre and Vásquez Kunze (2004), p. 69.

composition, wrongly assuming that the inefficiency of some elements of civil law implies the uselessness of all (or a large part of) of civil law institutions. If the rhetoric of the Peruvian L&E has hinted at such an attitude, greater humility is indeed desirable.

3.2.4 Criticism 4: The Illusion of Robinson Crusoe

In Daniel Defoe's classic adventure novel, Robinson Crusoe stranded on a deserted island, initially believes that he is the sole inhabitant. This illusion of solitude generates, among other things, the irrelevance of a freedom coordination system, since there are no other people with whom to do it. To a large extent, Crusoe can act as he pleases (or, at least until he meets Friday). Why is this story relevant to our reconstruction of the criticism of Peruvian L&E? Well, some defenders of the movement have questioned the "relativity" of property rights within the Peruvian legal system, as these rights are subject to limits. Specifically, they point that relativity lies in provisions such as Article 923 of the Civil Code, which stipulates that property rights must be exercised in harmony with social interest and within the limits set by law.

In response to these concerns from Peruvian jus-economists, Castillo Freyre and Vásquez Kunze argue that limits on property rights are grounded in the fact that human beings live in communities, and thus, absolute rights cannot exist. Even so, the representatives of Peruvian L&E acknowledge that a legitimate limit on the property rights arises when it affects the rights of third parties.[45] The core of the criticism, then, is ideological: supporters of Peruvian L&E view the concept of a "social civil code" as a contradiction in terms. They assert that:

> A social civil code, that is, a Code of Social Private Law, is a contradiction in terms, it is the denial of its own function. It is a norm that is oriented to setting limits on autonomy instead of promoting it. It is a norm that dilutes the private in an abstract collective where the private loses all its essence. A social civil code cannot be civil and social at the same time.[46]

As Castillo Freyre and Vásquez Kunze point out, Bullard's primary concern seems to be rooted in the constitutional concept of expropriation.[47] However, they argue that the expropriations carried out during the Revolutionary Government of the Armed Forces (1968–1980) under Juan Velasco Alvarado were better understood as tyrannical political overreach rather than as legal actions facilitated by the laws then in force.

In short, according to Castillo Freyre and Vásquez Kunze:

> [I]t has been demonstrated that it has been necessary for economic analysts of law to justify their criticism of Article 923 of the Civil Code, to invoke a ghost: the ghost of retrograde

[45] Castillo Freyre and Vásquez Kunze (2004), p. 72.

[46] Bullard (2006), p. 138.

[47] Castillo Freyre and Vásquez Kunze (2004), p. 74.

> concepts which are horrible and dangerous, that and which represent a sword of Damocles hanging over the development of the economy and private investment in Peru.[48]

Thus, the Peruvian L&E's suspicion of the supposed relativity of property rights is due to an ideological illusion or deceit: one that (i) leads them to embrace the illusion of Crusoe, and (ii) fosters a fear for acts that, in any case, reflect excesses of politics over law.

3.2.5 Criticism 5: The Crystal Ball Illusion and the Sanctity of Contracts

Chapter 5 of Castillo Freyre's and Vásquez Kunze's book tackles the L&E's critique of certain civil law institutions related to unforeseen circumstances that may arise during contractual performance, such as hardship. Authors such as Carlos Patrón Salinas argue that, strictly speaking, there are no truly unpredictable events, only events that are foreseeable at a very high cost.[49] Consequently, according to Bullard, the standard for predictability should be tied to the costs of foreseeing specific contingencies in a contract, with the equilibrium being what could be called an "optimal contract".[50]

Building on a point made by Hayek, Castillo Freyre and Vásquez Kunze argue that the illusion of predictability only holds in a world of omniscient gods, far from reality. They argue:

> If we start from the certainty of the imperfection of human knowledge, we will get very far soon—and without difficulty—to conclude that very little can be foreseen, regardless of the time available to us and the cost of such an effort. Both, time and cost, are, as can be seen, pretexts to justify, precisely, the economic impossibility of "foreseeing everything".[51]

For this reason, the hardship is based on the fact that, in reality, unforeseen circumstances can arise that the parties could not have reasonably anticipated. To illustrate their point, Castillo Freyre and Vásquez Kunze reference a case from the Paris Court of Cassation: the case of engineer Capronne, who had contracted to build irrigation canals during the Franco-Prussian War (1870–1871). Due to the war, the cost of the service became prohibitively expensive. The case, decided by the Paris Court of Cassation, is cited to show how the nineteenth-century doctrine of the inviolability of contracts was relativized. The authors argue that L&E's defense of unrestricted contractual autonomy is an anachronistic remnant from a perspective that—within the context of continental civil law—has long been outdated.[52]

The criticism here is not only directed at the notion that unforeseen circumstances can occur, but also at the fact that the solution proposed by the Peruvian L&E relies on the thesis of almost unrestricted and indefeasible inviolability of

---

[48] Castillo Freyre and Vásquez Kunze (2004), p. 77.

[49] Patrón Salinas (2001), p. 151.

[50] Castillo Freyre and Vásquez Kunze (2004), p. 83.

[51] Castillo Freyre and Vásquez Kunze (2004), p. 84.

[52] Castillo Freyre and Vásquez Kunze (2004), pp. 88–89.

contracts. This point is revisited in Chapter 7 of the book, where the critique focuses on L&E's criticism against prohibiting the disposal or encumbrance of assets in contractual agreements.[53]

3.2.6 Criticism 6: The Problem of Opportunists

Chapter 6 of deals with the problem of regulating injury (*lesión*) the under Peruvian Civil Code. Here the critique focuses, first, on the theory of value that L&E adopts in its analysis of injury. L&E adopts the marginalist and subjective theory of value, according to which:

> All valuation is subjective and, therefore, two different people can assign different values to exactly the same good according to their own preferences, without budgetary limitations and depending on the circumstances in which the transaction occurs.[54]

From the of Castillo Freyre and Vásquez Kunze's point of view, this theory of value remains relevant in economics. Moreover, they argue that law can rely on an artificial objectification of value, which then becomes the sole parameter of justice:

> Any price is deemed fair by the law then [...] because, given the case, the law has established it arbitrarily for situations involving a conflict over price between the contracting parties.[55]

In the Peruvian case, the market becomes the objective parameter for determining the values involved. However, the civil code imposes a threshold greater than two thirds, based on one party's use of the other party's pressing need (Art. 1447 C.C.), for the action of injury to proceed. This creates a difficult standard to meet and places significant obstacles to filing such an action. This begin the case, Castillo Freyre and Vásquez Kunze wonder, why this provision is maintained in the legal system if it is so rarely used in practice. They suggest that its persistence is because:

> The law considers inadmissible the mere possibility that abuse of others is permitted under its rule, and it suspects that it is under the assumptions legislated in Article 1447 of the Civil Code that this abuse could have produced.[56]

Thus, the injury provision is largely symbolic: although rarely used, it sends a message that the legal system does not tolerate the exploitation of a state of necessity.

The central normative question raised by the authors is whether this defense amounts to a form of legal perfectionism, coercively imposing the virtue of the Good Samaritan through the law. While the practical irrelevance of the injury provision mitigates the strength of the criticism, it remains important to consider that, even in cases where one party is in a state of necessity, the decision to engage in a transaction was formally free. This line of reasoning leads us to the next critique.

[53] Castillo Freyre and Vásquez Kunze (2004), p. 106.
[54] Castillo Freyre and Vásquez Kunze (2004), p. 95.
[55] Castillo Freyre and Vásquez Kunze (2004), p. 96.
[56] Castillo Freyre and Vásquez Kunze (2004), p. 98.

3.2.7 Criticism 7: The Ignorance of Social Structures

In Chapter 7 of their book, Castillo Freyre and Vásquez Kunze offer a robust and well-supported criticism against one of the theses of Peruvian L&E with implications for family environment. Specifically, the criticism focuses on the handling of matrimonial assets when one spouse disposes of them without the knowledge and authorization of the other. Peruvian jus-economists argue that the spouse who suffers from the fraudulent transaction should bear responsibility for it—essentially, no penalty should be applied for such a transaction. The reasoning behind this thesis is straightforward: the spouse who is the victim of fraud is precisely the one best positioned person to foresee and prevent the fraudulent act.

However, Castillo Freyre and Vásquez Kunze counter that this argument overlooks a critical social reality in Peru and other Latin American countries: the spouse who bears the risks of such fraud is almost always the woman. They note:

> To nobody is a secret, and much less for those who exercise the professional practice of law, than in our country, the vast majority of spouses defrauded in the patrimony of social assets by those who at the time vowed to honor and respect them until death parted their ways are women.[57]

Given this, the authors argue that such a situation would result in a form of discrimination:

> Because by discriminating the risk and charging it to one of the spouses, who in more than 90% of cases are women, trusting in the good faith of the other, what is being proposed—de facto—is the discrimination of women and their patrimony from the protection of the law.[58]

This criticism runs deeper, as it reflects a broader concern with the lack of attention paid by Peruvian L&E to the social structures in which legal relations occur. And here the echo of the Lochner period of the United States Supreme Court resonates in a variety of ways. Just as contracts can only perceived as free from coercion when thought of in the abstract—ignoring the asymmetries of social relations and power—so too can one believe that the spouse defrauded by the mismanagement of marital assets must pay "the piper". This perspective, however, disregards the persistent and rigid division in Peru between the public-masculine sphere and feminine domestic space.[59] This divide is crucial in this context, as it disproportionately causes women to be the victims of such deceptions.

3.2.8 Criticism 8: The False Enemy

In the final critique addressed in Castillo Freyre and Vásquez Kunze's book, they turn to the issue of non-contractual civil liability. This issue is addressed in Chapter 12 begins with a review of the main functions of a civil liability system, as understood by L&E: (i) a dissuasive function, aimed at deterring undesirable behaviors;

[57] Castillo Freyre and Vásquez Kunze (2004), p. 131.

[58] Castillo Freyre and Vásquez Kunze (2004), p. 132.

[59] Sotomayor (2019).

(ii) a compensatory function, ensuring effective compensation for damages caused by fault of others; and (iii) the function of reducing system administration costs.[60] In Peru, the non-contractual civil liability system is based on two core principles: (1) those who indemnify are to blame for the damage; and (2) there must be causality between the event and the damage produced.[61] According to some jus-economists, the current non-contractual civil liability system is inefficient because judges tend to under-indemnify victims, and behaviors are not sufficiently discouraged.

In response, Castillo Freyre and Vásquez Kunze argue that the relevant provisions of the Civil Code are not the source of the practical distortion in the system. They contend that the issue lies not with the legal framework itself but with how it is applied in practice. In other words, the problem is a classic case of the false cause fallacy[62]:

> There, it is not our civil liability system that fails to send a clear and transparent message to society, prescribing how it wants individuals to behave (Article 1969) and how it wants to compensate the victims (articles 1985 and 1988), but that the Judiciary is to blame for the anxiety and disappointment of those who come authorized by the Code in search of a fair compensation and are mocked in their right.[63]

Furthermore, L&E advocates for a model of social diffusion of risk through insurance systems.[64] While this may be beneficial in some cases, Castillo Freyre and Vásquez Kunze note that it also introduces new problems. Specifically, insurance systems can encourage reckless behavior, create incentives for individuals to falsely allege damage, and ultimately result in inadequate compensation for the victims.[65] In short, L&E's response to the practical shortcomings of the Peruvian civil liability system is partial and incomplete.

3.2.9 Synthesis

To conclude this review of some of the criticisms directed at the Peruvian L&E movement by Castillo Freyre and Vásquez Kunze, it is useful to synthesize the main points in the form of key slogans. These are the following:

(a) L&E represents an attempt to colonize the methodological and scientific purity of law with an alien discipline, namely economics.
(b) This attempt is nevertheless somewhat clumsy, marked by a lack of methodological refinement and a reluctance to empirically test theoretical predictions.
(c) Likewise, L&E intends to infer a total crisis in civil law institutions based on a limited analysis of provisions with relatively little practical significance.

---

[60] Castillo Freyre and Vásquez Kunze (2004), pp. 167–168.

[61] Castillo Freyre and Vásquez Kunze (2004), p. 168.

[62] Castillo Freyre and Vásquez Kunze (2004), p. 169.

[63] Castillo Freyre and Vásquez Kunze (2004), p. 170.

[64] See De Trazegnies (2001), pp. 28 ff.

[65] Castillo Freyre and Vásquez Kunze (2004), pp. 172–173.

(d) It also ideologically assumes extreme positions on issues such as the inviolability and sanctity of contracts, and nearly unrestricted limits on property rights.
(e) Furthermore, it adopts an amoral stance in relation to law, judging institutions with a foundation that is, to some extent, perfectionist.
(f) Finally, L&E often theorizes in a vacuum, without considering the social structures in which market relations evolve in a country like Peru.

These points offer fertile ground for future discussions on the limitations and potential perspectives of the L&E movement in Peru.

So far, we have sought to provide a broad and comprehensive overview of the development of L&E in Peru. This work is essential for forming a well-balanced judgment of both the virtues and flaws of this approach to legal analysis, and it was, certainly, a necessary task within the specialized academic context.

4 Conclusion

This chapter aimed to provide a comprehensive overview of the development of the L&E in Peru, while evaluating some of the central criticisms levied against it. The L&E movement has had a profound influence in Peru, especially during the 1990s, when the country underwent significant economic reforms with the adoption of the 1993 Constitution. This period also saw the creation of a regulatory institutional apparatus, with many lawyers influenced by L&E theories and ideas. However, the movement's influence has not been matched by the theoretical and methodological sophistication that would support it.

In this sense, the Peruvian L&E movement is currently experiencing a moment of stagnation. This stagnation is due to two primary factors: the need to (a) move beyond a neoliberal approach to economic issues and (b) to incorporate more methodologically rigorous empirical analysis. These are the major challenges the movement faces in order to solidify its position in the academic landscape.

References

Álvarez Rodrich A (1992) Principios de empresas estatales y privatización. Universidad del Pacífico, Lima
Atienza M (2016) Las razones del derecho. Teorías de la argumentación jurídica. Palestra, Lima
Bayly A, Pasquel E (2003) ¿Quién dijo que en Salem hubo brujas? La privatización del servicio de justicia: rompiendo el mito de la justicia estatal. Thēmis 46:315–336
Bullard A (1991) Un mundo sin propiedad. Derecho PUCP 45:131–157
Bullard A (1992) "¡Al fondo hay sitio!" ¿Puede el teorema de Coase explicarnos el problema del transporte público? Thēmis 21:93–100
Bullard A (1994) La legislación antimonopólica y el mito del muro de Berlín. Thēmis 30:243–260
Bullard A (2002) Esquizofrenia jurídica. El impacto del análisis económico del derecho en el Perú. Thēmis 44:17–35

Bullard A (2003) Derecho y economía. El análisis económico de las instituciones legales. Palestra, Lima
Bullard A (2004) ¿Qué tan buen economista es Jorge Avendaño? In: De Blaunde J, Bullard A, Pizarro L, Soto CA (eds) Homenaje a Jorge Avendaño, vol 1. PUCP, Lima, pp 73–108. https://doi.org/10.18800/9789972426452
Bullard A (2006) Derecho y economía. El análisis económico de las instituciones legales, 2nd edn. Palestra, Lima
Bullard A (2019) Análisis económico del derecho. PUCP, Lima
Bullard A, De la Jara JM (eds) (2018) Análisis psicológico del derecho. Thēmis, Lima
Cantuarias F (1992) Retracto: réquiem de un derecho "económico y social." Thēmis 24:61–68
Cantuarias F (ed) (2001) ¿Por qué hay que cambiar el Código Civil? UPC, Lima
Castillo Freyre M, Vásquez Kunze R (2004) Analizando el análisis: autopsia del análisis económico del derecho por el derecho civil. PUCP, Lima
Chiassoni P (2013) El análisis económico del derecho. Palestra, Lima
De Soto H, Ghersi E, Ghibellini M (1986) El otro sendero: la revolución informal. ILD, Lima
De Trazegnies F (2001) La responsabilidad extracontractual, vol II, 7th edn. PUCP, Lima
Driesen D, Malloy RP (2017) Critiques of law and economics. In: Parisi F (ed) The Oxford handbook of law and economics, vol 1, Methodology and concepts. Oxford University Press, Oxford, pp 300–319
Dworkin R (1980) Why efficiency? – A response to professors Calabresi and Posner. Hofstra Law Rev 8(3):563–590
Escobar Rozas F, Hernando Nieto E (2006) ¿Es el análisis económico del derecho una herramienta válida de interpretación del derecho positivo? Thēmis 52:341–354
Ezcurra H (2002) Privaticemos la insolvencia. Ius et. Veritas 12(24):198–210
Falla A (1992) Responsabilidad civil y eficiencia económica: "matrimonio por conveniencia.". Thēmis 24:81–91
Fernández-Baca J (1992) La ley antimonopolio: ¿por qué y cómo aplicarla? Thēmis 21:87–91
Flores Borda G (2011) Game theory and the law: the "legal-rules-acceptability theorem" (a rational for non-compliance with legal rules). Derecho & Sociedad 36:301–314
Flores Borda G (2014) Game theory and the law: rule interactive interpretation. Revista de Actualidad Mercantil:53–58
Ghersi E (1991) El costo de la legalidad: una aproximación a la falta de legitimidad del derecho. Thēmis 19:5–14
Grant D (2018) Methods of economic research. Craftsmanship and credibility in applied microeconomics. Springer, Cham. https://doi.org/10.1007/978-3-030-01734-7
Kahneman D, Tversky A (eds) (2000) Choices, values, and frames. Cambridge University Press, Cambridge
León L (2013) El efímero encanto de "nuestro" law and economics. Ius et Veritas 47:132–151
Marciani B, Sotomayor JE, Cornejo L (2020) Justicia, derecho y mercado: una investigación sobre el análisis económico del derecho en el Perú. CICAJ-PUCP, Lima
Melgar E (2014) ¿Un error lo comete cualquiera? Implicancias de los errores de condena sobre el nivel de disuasión en los procedimientos administrativos sancionadores. Revista de Derecho Administrativo 14:447–498
Merino R (2008) ¿Recepción o resistencia? Americanización y análisis económico del derecho en el Perú. Cardozo Electr Law Bull 14:69–133
Merino R (2016) Justicia social y economía en la teoría del derecho. Palestra, Lima
Núñez del Prado F (2023) La historia del análisis económico del derecho en el Perú. Advocatus 43:17–35. https://doi.org/10.26439/advocatus2023.n043.6410
Ortiz de Zevallos G, Guerra García G (1998) Introducción al análisis costo-beneficio de las normas. Instituto Apoyo, Lima
Osterling Parodi F (2004) Prólogo. In: Castillo Freyre M, Vásquez Kunze R, Analizando el análisis: autopsia del análisis económico del derecho por el derecho civil. PUCP, Lima, pp 11–16

Parisi F (2005) Positive, normative and functional schools in law and economics. In: Backhaus J (ed) The Elgar companion to law and economics, 2nd edn. Edward Elgar, Cheltenham, pp 58–73

Pasquel E, Solís G (2003) La falaz leyenda de Robin Hood. Los dilemas económicos y filosóficos de la redistribución de la riqueza. Ius et Veritas 13(26):310–327

Patrón Salinas C (2001) ¿Mentiras verdaderas?: reflexiones en torno de la regulación del derecho contractual. In: Cantuarias F (ed) ¿Por qué hay que cambiar el Código Civil? Universidad Peruana de Ciencias Aplicadas, Lima, pp 131–153

Posner EA (ed) (2002) El análisis económico del derecho y la Escuela de Chicago: lecturas en honor de Ronald Coase. UPC, Lima

Ramos Núñez C, Cuadros H (2019) Crónicas de claustro: cien años de historia de la Facultad de Derecho de la PUCP. Facultad de Derecho de la PUCP, Lima

Rodríguez García G (2013) El consumidor en su isla: una visión alternativa del sistema de protección al consumidor. Universidad del Pacífico, Lima

Ross A (2004) Tû-Tû. Quartier Latin, São Paulo

Saavedra R (2011) Deconstruyendo al homo economicus: una revisión conductual de un paradigma del law and economics. Ius et Veritas 21(42):54–85

Saavedra R (2017) Análisis económico y comparado del derecho privado. Fogueras, Lima

Searle J (2010) Making the social world. The structure of human civilization. Oxford University Press, Oxford. https://doi.org/10.1093/acprof:osobl/9780195396171.001.0001

Sen A, Nussbaum M (eds) (1993) The quality of life. Oxford University Press, Oxford https://doi.org/10.1093/0198287976.001.0001

Sotomayor JE (2016) Calabresi sobre el futuro del movimiento law & economics (I): el análisis económico del derecho y el law & economics. Enfoque Derecho https://web.archive.org/web/20200923031551/https://www.enfoquederecho.com/2016/06/29/calabresi-sobre-el-futuro-del-movimiento-law-economics-i-el-analisis-economico-del-derecho-y-el-law-economics

Sotomayor JE (2019) La teoría de la reproducción social como marco conceptual para comprender derechos en el ámbito doméstico: el caso del Plan Nacional de Derechos Humanos 2018–2021. Revista del Ministerio de Justicia y Derechos Humanos 4:213–231

Súmar O, Avellaneda J (2010) Paradojas en la regulación de la publicidad en el Perú. Universidad del Pacífico, Lima

Súmar O, Iñiguez E (2017) Economía y constitución: las libertades económicas en la jurisprudencia del tribunal constitucional. Thēmis, Lima

Sunstein C, Thaler R, Jolls C (1998) A behavioral approach to law and economics. Stanford Law Rev 50:1471–1550

Teles S (2008) The rise of the conservative legal movement. Princeton University Press, Princeton

Understanding the Origins of Economic Analysis of Law in Mexico

Maria Susana Dávalos Torres

Abstract The Economic Analysis of Law (EAL) in Mexico emerged in the 1980s amid economic crises and the deregulation of the economy. Founded in the 1940s to educate economists devoid of Marxist, Keynesian, or interventionist ideologies, and having thrived during the 1980s, the Instituto Tecnológico Autónomo de México (ITAM) created a conducive environment for EAL. Conversely, many other universities, especially public institutions such as the Universidad Nacional Autónoma de México (UNAM), disregarded or scorned it.

The essay provides a historical overview of the origins and challenges faced by EAL in Mexico, highlighting its historical political economy and its impact on higher education. It delves into the political economy of Mexico during the twentieth century, demonstrating how socialism and liberalism influenced higher education programs, especially those at UNAM and ITAM. The paper provides a brief description of the involvement of several federal government entities in the creation of EAL studies and the function of the federal judiciary in resolving cases that utilize EAL.

The findings of this text are inconclusive yet provide a significant contribution to future research on this subject.

1 Introduction

Economic Analysis of Law (EAL) emerged in Mexico during the 1980s, a decade of deep economic crises and the start of the liberalization of the Mexican economy. The Department of Law at the Instituto Tecnológico Autónomo de México (ITAM) first introduced EAL, and ITAM's scholars and graduates not only adopted and advanced it, but many other universities overlooked and even despised it.

M. S. D. Torres (✉)
Instituto de Investigaciones Jurídicas, Universidad Nacional Autónoma de México (UNAM), Mexico City, Mexico
e-mail: sdavalos@unam.mx

S. Zorzetto et al. (eds.), *Developments in Law and Economics in the Italo-Iberoamerican Context*, Economic Analysis of Law in European Legal Scholarship 21, https://doi.org/10.1007/978-3-032-03317-8_14

The purpose of this text is to make a historical account of the origins and barriers to the development of EAL in Mexico, for which purpose the article focuses to a large extent in the history of political economy in Mexico and its effects in higher education.

This text aims to provide a historical account of the origins and barriers to the development of EAL in Mexico, primarily focusing on the history of political economy in Mexico and its impact on higher education. The first part outlines the current state of EAL in Mexico, revealing that its growth has been restricted and localized. The second part explores the history of political economy in Mexico during the twentieth century, showing that there are two approaches that have shaped higher education programs, namely, liberalism and socialism. These approaches have shaped higher education institutions and their programs, particularly those of Universidad Nacional Autónoma de México (UNAM) and Instituto Tecnológico Autónomo de México (ITAM), which have been instrumental in producing the highest-ranking public servants responsible for designing public policies over the past 30 years. For this reason, the text examines the history of such universities in relation to EAL.

The final section offers a brief review of the functions of certain federal government agencies in the production of EAL studies, as well as the role of the federal judiciary in adjudicating matters through the application of EAL.

The results of this text are not conclusive, but they serve as a valuable contribution to future research.

2 The Emergence of EAL and Its Current Status in Mexico

Considering that Andrés Roemer was the inaugural Mexican author to write a book on the EAL, it is imperative to take his perspective into account when examining the antecedents of this movement in Mexico. Andrés Roemer asserts that the EAL was introduced in Mexico in 1983[1]; however, he did not furnish a specific rationale for this occurrence. Nevertheless, in a distinct text, Roemer suggests that he was the catalyst for the movement in Mexico. Roemer observes that he identified a vibrant, intellectually stimulating, and essential domain at ITAM, characterized by the significant interplay among philosophy, law, and economics. This discovery originated from Dr. Arturo Fernández's Microeconomics course focused on non-market activities, in which he held the position of adjunct professor and contributed as an assistant in the domain of microeconomic analysis pertaining to legal science. Roemer additionally instructed courses in economic theory and jurisprudence at the National Autonomous University of Mexico (UNAM) and the Escuela Libre de Derecho.

[1] See Roemer and Valadés (2000), p. 273.

Indeed, Roemer's undergraduate thesis at both universities concentrated on EAL in the context of property rights and regulation.[2]

In 1994, Roemer published his book, "Introducción al Análisis Económico del Derecho." This text influenced key Mexican legal scholars to write about this topic. However, the excitement surrounding EAL in the legal field was fleeting. Roemer identifies several reasons for this, including the formalistic nature of legal knowledge in Mexico and the closer affiliations Mexican scholars have with their continental European counterparts, particularly Spanish, Italian, and French scholars, rather than with American scholars who have significantly influenced this discipline. He notes that an additional reason is the heightened engagement of Mexican legal scholars in the political arena; they also serve as members of the judiciary, within the executive branch, in Congress, and alongside senior bureaucratic officials.[3]

Recently, Rafael Ramírez Villaescusa has recognized additional issues impeding the progress of AEL in our nation, specifically: (a) language, (b) mathematics, (c) "inherited legal traditionalism," (d) Kantian tradition, and (e) the dominance of Marxist and Keynesian doctrines in colleges.[4]

Regarding language, Ramírez Villaescusa elucidates that texts pertaining to the Economic Analysis of Law are predominantly composed in English, a language that is not essential for the study or practice of law.[5] English has emerged as the lingua franca for Comparative Law, and scholarly research in this domain has proliferated as a result of globalization.[6] However, only a limited segment of the population in Mexico is proficient in speaking and writing in English. In this context, data from the National Institute of Statistics and Geography in Mexico (INEGI) indicates that, in 2014, there were over 10 million individuals aged 18 and older who communicated in a language other than Spanish. Among this demographic, only 5.5 million were proficient in English, representing a mere 6.8% of the total population surveyed, which amounted to 80 million individuals.[7]

---

[2] Roemer (1997), p. 72.

[3] Roemer and Valadés (2000), pp. 262 and 263.

[4] See Ramírez Villaescusa (2015), p. 221.

[5] Idem.

[6] *See* Örücü (2004), pp. 1 and 35, and Siems (2007).

[7] INEGI yearly reports on the standards of living as seen by individuals, referred to as Self-Reported Well-Being (BIARE in Spanish); the report and its variables adhere to the OECD Guidelines on Measuring Subjective Well-Being.

Ramirez Villaescusa similarly observed that the findings align with those reported in other nations across Latin America.[8] Similarly, according to a report by Consulta Mitofsky conducted in 2013, José Raúl Rodríguez Jiménez and his colleagues emphasize that merely 11.6% of Mexicans are proficient in a language other than Spanish, predominantly English. Notably, 38% of this demographic comprises individuals holding a college or university degree.[9] The authors also discovered that, according to the English Level Index, Mexico was ranked 40th out of 70 countries in 2015.[10]

In addressing the challenges associated with the advancement of AEL in Mexico, Ramírez Villaescusa also claims that legal research within the country is predominantly endogamous. This insularity has permitted legal scholars to concentrate primarily on local issues and, in his opinion, to engage in conservative analyses, thereby diminishing the necessity to adopt diverse methodological approaches. No supporting data is presented to substantiate this assertion; nonetheless, it is a recognized fact that the predominant emphasis of the majority of legal articles and publications pertains to local or domestic statutes and precedents. This is primarily due to the fact that the intended audience for such texts is also local or domestic in nature. A similar phenomenon occurs within the realm of legal education.[11] In this context, Mathias Siems posits that "[i]n most countries legal education is focused on preparing students for legal practice with the result that legal academics frequently see their task as 'stamp collecting': primarily providing an accurate and coherent description of the law as it is applied domestically".[12]

Regarding Mathematics, Ramírez Villaescusa contends that there exists a prevailing animosity towards this discipline within legal educational institutions.[13] Mathematics has been removed from the curricula of nearly all law programs at public universities in Mexico. It is important to note that Mexican legal scholars are often perceived as lacking proficiency in quantitative methods, as these methods necessitate mathematical reasoning.[14]

Quantitative methodologies serve as a crucial instrument within the field of the Sociology of Law. This discipline seeks to identify the underlying causes that give rise to legal norms and the subsequent social effects they engender. This endeavor necessitates empirical research that employs social science methodologies, encompassing both quantitative and qualitative techniques, including surveys, in-depth interviews, and direct or experimental observation, among others.[15]

---

[8] See Charles-Leija and Torres García (2022) p. 171.

[9] See Rodríguez Jiménez et al. (2018), pp. 215–232.

[10] Idem.

[11] Ramírez Villaescusa (2015).

[12] Siems and Mathias (2007), p. 4.

[13] Ramírez Villaescusa (2015) and Ahumada Lobo and Butler Silva (2009).

[14] See Roemer and Valadés (2000), p. 265.

[15] See Fix-Fierro et al. (2018), pp. 262–263.

It is important to acknowledge that the Sociology of Law is a relatively recent discipline in Mexico. As explained by Alberto Abad, since the latter half of the twentieth century, there have been educators who imparted legal theories from a sociological standpoint, exemplified by Luis Recasens Siches.[16] By the conclusion of the twentieth century, the Sociology of Law was incorporated into the curriculum of one of the nation's foremost law schools, thereby fostering a generation of distinguished law professors, including Luis Molina Piñeiro and Jorge Moreno Collado.[17] This development subsequently catalyzed research in the intersection of law and society, conducted by scholars such as Marcos Kaplan, Emilio Ordoñez Cifuentes, and Óscar Correas.[18] However, it was not until the commencement of this century that Héctor Fix-Fierro, in his capacity as the Director of Advanced Legal Studies and Dean of the Institute of Legal Research at UNAM, significantly strengthened and systematized the Sociology of Law, particularly in the training of graduate students in this discipline and the conduct of empirical research.[19] It is noteworthy to highlight that Diego Valadés, in his capacity as the previous Director of the Institute of Legal Research at UNAM, initiated a program focused on empirical legal research, which was led precisely by Héctor Fix Fierro.[20] Unfortunately, due to the absence of mandatory courses in quantitative and qualitative methodologies in the majority of law institutions,[21] it has become an increasingly common trend of recruiting trained professionals in Sociology and Political Science to undertake a significant portion of the empirical research within legal academia.[22]

---

[16] *See* Suárez Ávila (2015), p. 448.

[17] The Law School at UNAM is the oldest in the nation, with the highest enrollment and the greatest number of faculty, and it is undoubtedly the most influential in the region.

[18] See Suárez Ávila (2015), p. 450.

[19] Idem.

[20] Informe de actividades del Doctor Diego Valadés, correspondiente a septiembre de 2003- agosto de 2004. Boletín mexicano de derecho comparado, 28(111), 476–572.

[21] Lawyers do not inherently necessitate quantitative and qualitative methodologies in their daily practices, nor do they consider these as obligatory courses. Rafael Díaz Vázquez and Walter Gerardo Valencia Jiménez observed that the prevalence of empirical legal work is rising daily, alongside the enthusiasm of researchers and mentors to engage in such endeavors; nonetheless, challenges persist in executing empirical research, including time constraints for both faculty and students, insufficient resources, and concerns regarding personal safety. See Díaz Vázquez and Valencia Jiménez (2020), pp. 131 and 132.

[22] This symptom is peculiar to the designated location. Legal scholars lack expertise in empirical research; hence, specialists from other fields, such sociologists, economists, and psychologists, undertake this work. The participation of these professionals in legal academics has notably improved empirical research, however it also raises specific concerns. As per Del Pozo and colleagues:

> Un factor no intrínseco a la materia en sí que ha estimulado el enfoque empírico en las facultades de Derecho han sido los ingresos que las universidades han podido obtener por este medio. En diversos países las universidades se han visto impulsadas a buscar fondos más allá de su subvención principal del gobierno. La investigación empírica, por ejemplo, en el ámbito de la justicia penal, ha resultado atractiva para los posibles patrocinadores- incluidos los departamentos gubernamentales- y las universidades han considerado que les

An additional barrier to the reception of EAL in Mexico identified by Ramírez Villaescusa is the traditionalism transmitted by doctrinal legal scholarship. This assertion is grounded in an article authored by Héctor Fix-Fierro and Sergio López Ayllón, in which they assert that legal education in Mexico is predominantly traditional, relying heavily on theoretical-legal frameworks from the nineteenth century. Furthermore, the majority of law professors do not remain current in their field, resulting in a lack of familiarity with contemporary pedagogical methodologies.[23] Roemer observed a similar phenomenon, remarking that "[j]uridical formalism in Mexico prioritizes definitions over the objectives of legal provisions."[24] Jorge Vázquez Robles has recently contended that the curricula of law schools are structured to encompass a substantial volume of descriptive content, which predominantly promotes learning that relies on short-term memory retention.[25]

Recent advancements in human rights, along with significant occurrences such as the COVID-19 pandemic, are influencing the substance and methodologies of legal education. In light of these changes, Luis Fernando Pérez Hurtado and Hedilberto Rivera Villegas have observed that constitutional amendments pertaining to criminal law and human rights in our country have significantly influenced the evolution of legal education over the past decade. This has necessitated that law schools integrate new subjects and extracurricular activities designed to equip students with the necessary competencies for professional practice. Particularly, topics pertaining to oral litigation, techniques, and alternative dispute resolution mechanisms have been integrated into the curriculum. Furthermore, students have been actively encouraged to engage in internships, moot court competitions, and public legal clinics. Furthermore, the COVID-19 pandemic accelerated the integration of

---

> interesa mantener a los investigadores empíricos que son capaces de generar esos ingresos. Además, dado que la auditoría y el control externos de las actividades académicas han cobrado cada vez más importancia en el empeño por hacer que estas instituciones rindan cuentas públicamente, la capacidad de llevar a cabo investigaciones empíricas a gran escala ha pasado a considerarse uno de los distintivos de una facultad de derecho diversa y académicamente vibrante.
>
> …[E]sta evolución ha ido de la mano de la incorporación de personas que no son abogados a las facultades de Derecho, y también de la colaboración más allá de las fronteras disciplinarias e institucionales. De hecho, es sorprendente el número de investigadores empíricos destacados en el ámbito del derecho que tienen una formación en otras disciplinas. Algunos se licenciaron en humanidades, pero la mayoría se formó en alguna de las ciencias sociales. Probablemente, sea justo decir que no ha habido una visión intelectual coherente subyacente a esta contratación y colaboración. Más bien, ha tendido a ser fortuita y casual, reflejando tal vez el hecho de que los académicos trabajan en la misma institución o una convergencia fortuita de intereses.

Del Pozo Franco et al. (2022), pp. 169 and 170.

[23] *See* Fix Fierro and López Ayllón (2002), p. 102.

[24] Roemer and Valadés (2000), p. 265.

[25] Vázquez Robles (2016), p. 163.

technological tools within legal education in this nation, resulting in the adoption of active teaching methodologies that promote student engagement during class sessions.[26] Notwithstanding these developments, the status of empirical research methods instruction within the field of law remains unchanged, as these occurrences have not influenced the methodologies employed in legal research.

In relation to Kantian philosophy and its cultural impact, Ramírez Villaescusa claims that Kelsen's legal theory has permeated the legal culture within our nation, thereby complicating the integration of utilitarian perspectives into legal education.[27] It is crucial to keep in mind that, as articulated by Dulce Granja Castro, the influence of Kantian philosophy on Mexican intellectuals, educators, and philosophers can be traced back to the nineteenth century.[28] Marxism, nonetheless, has exerted a significant influence over Mexican politics, economy, and culture throughout the majority of the twentieth century. Numerous public universities demonstrate that Marxism remains influential,[29] despite its impact on the employment rates of their graduates by both private enterprises and government entities, particularly over the past three decades marked by the implementation of various neoliberal policies.[30]

The dismissal of mathematical reasoning is not confined solely to law institutions. Owen Eli Ceballos Mina and Carlos Alberto Duque García have demonstrated a notable deficiency in enthusiasm, and even a pronounced aversion, towards Econometrics and Statistics, as well as the utilization of specialized statistical software within Economics departments, particularly at public universities. It has been observed that students tend to ascribe to Econometrics an almost mystical quality, perceiving it as an omnipotent discipline reserved exclusively for specific methodologies that align with conservative political ideologies. This perception renders the subject either discreditable or excessively complex to master.[31]

These findings elucidate, to a certain extent, the origins of the Economic Analysis of Law in Mexico and the manner in which students and scholars at ITAM were able

---

[26] Pérez Hurtado and Rivera Villegas point out that the COVID-19 pandemic highlighted the lack of technological resources and limitations in the pedagogical training of teachers in many universities, as well as the unequal access to technological resources by students. See Pérez Hurtado and Rivera Villegas (2022), pp. 12–17.

[27] See Ramírez Villaescusa (2015), p. 224.

[28] Granja Castro (2010), p. 10.

[29] For more information about curricula of Economics Departments at UNAM and ITAM see Loria Díaz (2002), pp. 44–50; also, Anaya Díaz who describes the curricula of the Economic Department at UNAM from 1929 to 1975, showing that in1929 there was a subject on socialist doctrines, Anaya Díaz (1980), and Negrete (2021).

[30] *See* Ahumada Lobo and Butler Silva (2009), p. 10.

[31] *See* Ceballos Mina and Duque García (2023), p. 66.

to embrace it. ITAM is a distinguished private university recognized for its comprehensive undergraduate program in Economics, with a particular emphasis on Econometrics, which is esteemed as one of the foremost programs in Mexico and Latin America.[32] Moreover, the university's Law program includes coursework in Microeconomics, Macroeconomics, and the Economic Analysis of Law.[33]

3 The Background to the EAL in Mexico: UNAM and ITAM, the Mirror of Two Distinct Approaches of Political Economy

For the purposes of better explaining the origins of EAL in Mexico it is necessary to make an account of the founding of ITAM, in contrast to UNAM, within the economic and political history of Mexico in the twentieth century.[34]

Luis Montes de Oca, who held the position of manager of the Bank of Mexico during the presidency of Lázaro Cárdenas (who served from December 1, 1934, to November 30, 1940), asserted that ITAM was established to cultivate economists who were not swayed by Marxist, Keynesian, or interventionist economic ideologies, which were prevalent at UNAM.[35] Comprehending the economic and political context of this statement necessitates an understanding of the era subsequent to the Mexican Revolution of 1910. This revolution originated in opposition to the dictatorship of Porfirio Diaz, whose regime persisted for more than three decades.

[32] According to QS World University Rankings by Subject 2024: Economics & Econometrics, it is the second best in Mexico and the sixth best in Latin America. https://www.topuniversities.com/university-subject-rankings/economics-econometrics?region=Latin%20America w https://www.topuniversities.com/university-subject-rankings/economics-econometrics?region=Latin%20America&countries=mx.

[33] See ITAM, Plan de estudios de la Licenciatura en Derecho (2024), https://carreras.itam.mx/licenciatura-derecho/.

[34] Due to their significant contributions to the development of public policy and the training of intellectuals and public officials, both institutions have shaped our nation's trajectory during the past three decades. According to Axel Sánchez: "El rumbo de México lo definen egresados de la Universidad Nacional Autónoma de México (UNAM y el Instituto Tecnológico Autónomo de México (ITAM), las instituciones que han educado casi a la mitad de los funcionarios que hoy toman las decisiones del país". Sánchez (2015a). and García Ugarte (2017), p. 26. In a different text, this author emphasizes that graduates of Tecnológico de Monterrey along with UNAM and ITAM are responsible for overseeing the biggest businesses in Mexico; in particular, their graduates serve as the CFOs of 45% of the companies listed on the Mexican Stock Exchange (Bolsa Mexicana de Valores, BMV). See Sánchez (2015b).

[35] According to García Ugarte, since it was well known that the UNAM School of Economics had done everything in its power to prepare students with economic theory for a professional life that opposed liberalism and private property, the objective is to prepare economists who were not influenced by the Marxist, Keynesian, and interventionist trends of the UNAM School of Economics. See García Ugarte (2017), p. 208.

3.1 The Porfiriato

The phrase "peace, order, and progress" encapsulates the Porfiriato, a period known for its development of science and technology infrastructure and institutions, economic growth, and political stability,[36] albeit at the expense of democracy and socioeconomic equality.[37]

This regime gave a preeminent place to science, technology, and the arts, thereby elevating education as well. The administration implemented modern pedagogical

---

[36] Porfirio Díaz did not directly come up with the motto; rather, it is said that when the train stopped at Ciudad Juárez, Chihuahua, on its way to Texas, the locals greeted him with flowers and placards that said "paz, orden y progreso". See. Tovar y de Teresa (2015), p. 101. Apart from the anecdotes, Diaz's government was undoubtedly impacted by the theories of Auguste Comte, a French philosopher. See Zea (1968), p. 39. For engineers, architects, and other university-educated individuals in particular, French culture was a reference to Mexican society at the time. Porfirio Díaz's Secretary of Home Affairs, Manuel Romero Rubio, made sure to surround himself with educated individuals; they would be referred to as "los científicos". See Valenzuela Aguilera (2012), p. 10. Those who shared positivist views were not limited to such public personnel. In fact, positivism was quickly embraced by Mexican society. Comte's views were introduced by Gabino Barreda. During one of the several invasions of Mexico, Gabino Barreda stayed in France and had the chance to enroll in a course on Comte's philosophy. On September 16, 1867, this speech was given in Oaxaca. Aspe Armella (2020), p. 390. Benito Juárez was so pleased by the speech that he asked Barreda to join the committee that was drafting a plan for public education. Ortega Esquivel (2010), p. 119.

Comte's theories had a significant impact on Mexican culture at the time. Leopoldo Zea, a prominent Mexican author, discussed Auguste Comte's influence on Mexican culture, particularly regarding the bourgeoisie that emerged post-French Revolution. This socioeconomic elite gained political power but faced ongoing challenges from other factions seeking influence. These groups adopted the same revolutionary ideals—liberty, equality, and fraternity—that the bourgeoisie had previously used to overthrow the aristocracy and clergy. As a result, the bourgeoisie found themselves in a precarious position, needing to discredit the very philosophy that had facilitated their rise. To maintain their power, they required a counter-revolutionary philosophy focused on order, while avoiding complacency with the status quo. Zea's analysis highlights the complexities of power dynamics and the ongoing struggle for influence within Mexican society during this transformative period. See Zea (1968), pp. 39–41.

According to Comte, order is always the prerequisite for progress in the new philosophy, and progress is also the necessary result of order. As the basis or fate, equilibrium and progress are inextricably linked. Comte, August (1934), p. 39. For more on the relationship between politics and science in Comte's thought, *see* Grange (2000).

[37] Porfirio Díaz despised "electoral processes and legislative-parliamentary institutions" because of his own bad political experiences. When Díaz ran for president in 1867 and 1871, he faced up against Benito Juárez, who served five terms as president—three by operation of law and two by election. García Diego (2010), p. 210. It should also be considered that Porfirio Díaz came to power after decades of internal struggles and foreign invasions, so during his first constitutional term from 1884 to 1888, Díaz aimed to eliminate political parties, viewing them as sources of unrest and threats to peace. He sought to end the influence of conservatives and former supporters of Juárez and Lerdo by positioning himself as a mediator in national affairs. This approach helped reduce dissent and paved the way for the Porfirio era, characterized by his long-term, uncontested leadership. He governed with an authoritative demeanor, likened to that of the "Eternal Father," overseeing the nation's progress without competition. See Iturribarria (1960), pp. 243 y 244.

approaches, established institutions for teacher training, and founded schools dedicated to the arts and crafts for the workforce. The Escuela Nacional Preparatoria received a significant impetus as part of the initiatives aimed at fostering economic growth. The regime exhibited a notable interest in higher education. In 1881, Justo Sierra, a distinguished historian, philosopher, and legislator, advocated for the establishment of the Universidad Nacional de México. This institution is recognized as the successor to the Real y Pontificia Universidad de México, which was established in 1551 and subsequently dissolved in 1834 by Valentín Gómez Farías, a liberal president. In 1910, Porfirio Díaz formally inaugurated the university in conjunction with the centennial celebrations of Mexico's independence. Unfortunately, the progress in education was characterized by qualitative improvements rather than quantitative enhancements.[38]

Science became a tool for the governmental initiative in this period. Gabino Barreda's address, entitled "Oración Cívica," served as a profound source of inspiration for an entire generation. Barreda is considered as one of the foremost Mexican intellectuals of the nineteenth century. In this address, he contended that the principles of science are inextricably intertwined with the progression of politics. He asserted that the failure of science to adequately integrate political considerations within its framework had had a profound impact on the political landscape of that period.[39] Although the speech occurred in 1867, the concepts and contributions of well-educated individuals significantly influenced the administration of Porfirio Díaz. A notable instance of this is José Yves Limantour, who held the position of Secretary of Finance for nearly two decades. He emerged as a significant figure in economic affairs due to his pivotal role in extricating the nation from bankruptcy. Furthermore, following 1894, the country reported a surplus of ten million pesos, which was credited to the financial acumen demonstrated by the Secretary of Finance.[40]

Following nearly a century of economic stagnation attributed to internal conflict and foreign invasions,[41] the administration of Porfirio Díaz successfully attained sustained economic growth,[42] particularly in the sectors of manufacturing and services, both in absolute and relative terms.[43] However, this growth was attained to the advantage of a select group of Mexican landowners and foreign industrialists, at the expense of the dispossessed, particularly the indigenous population.

To be brief, the economy during the Porfiriato was characterized by: (a) agricultural production in the hands of owners of huge extensions of land, who also benefited from the enslaved labor of the local population and, on many occasions, of

[38] For more about education during this period. See Bazant (1993).

[39] Aspe Armella (2020), p. 390.

[40] Iturribarria (1960), p. 246.

[41] Rosenzwieg (1965), p. 405.

[42] GDP was projected to be 2.1% per year, which was remarkable at the time, even when compared to the US and the UK. See Kehoe and Meza (2013).

[43] Rosenzwieg (1965), p. 405.

native peoples uprooted from their places of origin,[44] (b) industrial production in the hands of foreigners who benefited from the labor exploitation of workers, men, women and children,[45] (c) the exploitation of natural resources through foreign companies, being mining and oil extraction the most relevant activities,[46] (d) the construction of infrastructure with foreign capital, being the railroad lines that cross the country from south to north to the United States, the most relevant work of the time,[47] (e) the consolidation of a regional banking system that was mainly in charge of issuing currency and granting credit, as well as the establishment of the first modern banks with foreign capital directed to the national public,[48] and (f) a thriving stock exchange that channeled resources from abroad to the industrial and commercial activities of the country.[49]

3.2 *The Revolution of 1910 and the Subsequent Reconstruction Governments*

The political, economic, and social grievances of the populace, coupled with the anarchist and socialist ideologies espoused by its proponents, ignited the Mexican Revolution,[50] ultimately culminating in the Constitution of 1917. With the exception of Article 3, which mandated the provision of free basic education; Article 27, which mandated the redistribution of extensive landholdings, the establishment of new settlements, and the allocation of land and water resources to these communities; and Article 123, which guaranteed a minimum wage and established a maximum workday, the Constitution adhered to liberal principles, drawing its foundation from the Constitution of 1857.[51]

The Mexican Revolution adversely impacted the nation's economy. Between the years 1910 and 1921, the population experienced a decline from 15.2 million to 14.3 million. This decrease can be attributed to various factors, including fatalities resulting from armed conflict, deaths caused by famine, and the impact of the Spanish flu

[44] See Katz (1974), pp. 1–47; López-Córdova (2012), pp. 187–209; Turner (1909).

[45] See Meyer (1971), pp. 1–137; Nava (1992), pp. 157–176; Gómez Galvarriato Freer (2003), pp. 773–804.

[46] See Velasco (2007), pp. 64–69.

[47] See Ceceña Gámez (2014), p. 52.

[48] For more information about regional banking see Cerutti and Marichal (2003). For more information about nationwide banking see Ludlow and Marichal (1998), pp. 7–30.

[49] Moreno Lázaro (2017), pp. 98–139; Cardero García (1976), pp. 359–387.

[50] The Flores Magón brothers, anarcho-socialist thinkers, were the ideologists of the revolution and their ideas were embodied in the key articles of the 1917 Constitution. Their main ideas were expressed in the Manifesto of September 23, 1911 https://archivos.juridicas.unam.mx/www/bjv/libros/6/2625/54.pdf.

[51] Original text of the 1917 Constitution, published in the Diario Oficial de la Federación on February 5, 1917.

pandemic. Manufacturing output experienced a decline. Certain segments of the train and its tracks were subjected to dynamite explosions and utilized for military purposes, thereby obstructing the transportation of products. Two-thirds of the banking institutions were closed. Each warlord issued his own currency, resulting in hyperinflation and a pervasive lack of trust, as these currencies were unsupported by any tangible assets and ceased to be in circulation upon the warlord's downfall.[52] To facilitate economic recovery, it was imperative to reinstate the gold standard,[53] promote industrial development—particularly in the manufacturing sector—utilizing both domestic and foreign resources,[54] and to establish institutions, notably the Bank of Mexico, due to its crucial influence in economic matters.[55]

The first Banking Convention took place during the presidency of Plutarco Elías Calles.[56] The Secretary of Finance, Alberto Pani, chaired a commission comprising government officials, financiers, and business leaders.[57] Manuel Gómez Morin, Fernando de la Fuente,[58] and Elías S.A. de Lima,[59] collectively referred to as "the three musketeers,"[60] participated in a commission tasked with drafting the inaugural statute dedicated to banking law, known as the Ley de Instituciones de Crédito y

[52] See Moreno-Brid and Ros (2009), pp. 71 and 72.

[53] Ibid. pp. 74–77.

[54] See Zebadúa (1994).

[55] Gómez Galvarriato (2019), p. 225. Banco de México supported the founding of the Banking School in 1929 due to the demand for experts in banking and business problems. Ibid. p. 237.

[56] It was held from February 2 to 29, 1924. Turrent Díaz (2015a), p. 120.

[57] Alberto Pani served under Lázaro Cárdenas as Secretary of Industry, Commerce, and Labor, Álvaro Obregón as Secretary of Foreign Affairs and Finance, and Plutarco Elías Calles as Secretary of Finance. In order to solidify Banco de México as a central bank and give it the authority to oversee monetary policy, he helped restructure the Mexican banking sector and public finances. For more about Pani, see Pani (1943); also, Flores Torres (2009).

[58] A lawyer named Fernando de la Fuente had been connected to Calles and Obregón since the 1910 Revolution. Gómez Morin was approached by De la Fuente to join the Military Commission as a consulting attorney; there "[e]l ministro Pani, al advertir la capacidad técnica del abogado consultor, le ofreció inmediatamente encargos de mayor trascendencia, llevándolo hasta la encumbrada posición de 'filósofo detrás del trono' que Gómez Morin ocupó durante su gestión". Turrent Díaz (2015b), p. 124.

[59] When Elías S.A. de Lima, a politician and banker from New York, was named director of the Banco Mexicano de Comercio e Industria in 1910, he was able to interact with Mexican governmental staff. During the revolution, the bank had challenges, but Elías was able to secure Elías S.A. de Lima was a New York banker and politician, who arrived in Mexico in 1910 when he was appointed director of the *Banco Mexicano de Comercio e Industria*, a position that allowed him to meet Mexican public servants. The bank experienced difficulties during the revolution, but Elías managed to obtain the government's favor with the different governments that Mexico was going through, including lending money to Huerta's government and helping it import weapons from Japan, joining the Monetary Commission, investing in the Loan Fund for Irrigation and Agriculture Works, and adding León de la Barra to its council. Elías was asked to contribute to the creation of public policies for the Reconstruction governments following the end of the Revolution. Gómez Galvarriato (2019), pp. 229–232.

[60] Turrent Díaz (2015a), p. 121.

Establecimientos Bancarios, as well as the foundational act for the establishment of a central bank, recognized as the Banco de México.

In 1925, the central bank came into existence.[61] The board of directors has appointed Manuel Gómez Morin to the position of chair.[62] Gómez Morin was among the most prominent Mexican legal practitioners and political figures of his era. He obtained his law degree from UNAM. In his capacity as both a student and a professor, he gained considerable recognition for advocating for the autonomy of UNAM and for defending it against governmental encroachments. Gómez Morín played a pivotal role in the formulation of economic institutions and public policies, owing to his familiarity with the United States central banking system. In 1920, the Mexican government appointed him to negotiate the oil dispute with American investors and address the issue of foreign debt, subsequently residing in New York. In 1921, he enrolled at Columbia University to acquire knowledge in finance and to understand the operations of the Federal Reserve System.[63]

Under the stewardship of Gómez Morín, the central bank endeavored to function autonomously from the federal government to safeguard monetary policy from political interference; however, this objective proved unattainable. In 1926, the output of hydrocarbons and precious metals experienced a decline, precipitating a recession that ultimately culminated in default.[64] The Reconstruction administrations compelled the central bank to extend loans without adequate collateral[65] and, in some instances, to provide financing for political campaigns.[66]

In 1929, Gómez Morín tendered his resignation from the central bank due to the Mante case, in which the government compelled Banco de México to extend a loan to the sugar company "El Mante" without adequate collateral. This situation was further complicated by the fact that president Calles had a personal financial interest in the matter.[67]

The crisis of 1929 resulted in a significant devaluation of the peso, attributable to a 64% reduction in exports.[68] In response, a monetary law was enacted on July 25, 1931, which revoked the Banco de México's authority over currency and exchange operations and instituted a regulatory framework for the management of the exchange rate. Luis Aboites and Engracia Loyo provide a succinct summary of the economic situation: Mexico, like other nations relying on exporting minerals, agricultural, and livestock products, experienced significant economic detriment due to the global economic depression. Foreign trade decreased by nearly 50%, leading to a decline in government revenues. Miners in the northern region suffered job losses

[61] Act that creates the Bank of Mexico, August 31 of 1925.

[62] *See* Tamayo y Salmorán (2004), p. 267.

[63] Turrent Díaz (2015b), p. 123.

[64] Ibid., pp. 148 and 149.

[65] Ibid., p. 193.

[66] Ibid. p. 241.

[67] See Méndez Medina (2015).

[68] Brando and Nodari (2020), p. 121.

due to company cessation. Railroad employees also lost jobs. In Yucatán, the decline in henequen prices caused unemployment and social tensions. By 1932, over 350,000 laborers, 6% of the economically active population, were unemployed. Additionally, 300,000 migrants, mainly Mexicans, were compelled to leave the United States.[69]

The Ley Orgánica del Banco de México, promulgated in 1932, instituted a novel regulatory framework for the central bank and came into effect on April 12, 1932. The legislation mandated that the central bank cease its operations as a commercial banking entity in order to strengthen its role as a central bank. The crisis of 1929 instigated a shortage of currency, which led to the enactment of legislation aimed at deregulating the issuance of banknotes by the central bank, establishing a floating exchange rate system, and authorizing the acquisition of gold at market prices to augment reserves. The economic circumstances surrounding the crisis of 1929, coupled with Calles' efforts to reestablish his authority, precipitated a period of political upheaval that ultimately facilitated General Lázaro Cárdenas' ascension to leadership.

3.3 *Lázaro Cárdenas*

As previously noted, the Revolution of 1910 and the Constitution of 1917 introduced significant advancements in the realms of education, labor rights, and the regulation of private property. However, the pivotal transition from liberalism to socialism did not occur until Lázaro Cárdenas assumed the presidency of Mexico.[70]

Lázaro Cárdenas' administration was characterized by: (1) the largest redistribution of agricultural land in the history of the country, (2) the investment in infrastructure, which included the construction of three large dams, the distribution of clean water, building a network of sewer pipes, and the labor foundation of the largest electricity company owned by the government, Comisión Federal de Electricidad, (3) granting farm credit, (4) the creation of the second largest public university in the country, *Instituto Politécnico Nacional*, (5) the creation of the

---

[69] Aboites and Loyo (2010), p. 229.

[70] To learn more about how post-revolution governments still rely on foreign capital to explore minerals and oil, see Haynes (1991), pp. 225–251. Only a limited number of scholars, such as Carlos Iliades in his book Una Historia Intelectual (2018), have recognized that Mexico has intermittently embraced a socialist regime that imposes limitations on private property and private contracts. This acknowledgment is noteworthy, particularly given that market interventionism has fluctuated throughout the twentieth century, ranging from virtually imperceptible to pervasive. Scholars who advocate for extensive government intervention while neglecting to recognize the implementation of socialism in Mexico characterize the nation's economy as a mixed economic system, or modelo desarrollista. They highlight instances of industrialization and economic growth, frequently omitting the critical fact that these developments were predominantly driven by foreign direct investment. For an examination of the impact of foreign investment on the economic development of Mexico, please refer to the work of Wasserman (2015).

Partido de la Revolución Mexicana (PNR) which was integrated by representatives of labor, peasant, popular and military sectors; and (6) the creation of the Confederación de Trabajadores de Mexico (CTM).

In 1937, Cádernas issued a directive to expropriate the assets of foreign enterprises conducting operations within the nation. As a result, the Mexican peso depreciated from 3.60 to 4.99 pesos per dollar.[71] The reports from the central bank in 1938 indicate that the decline commenced at the conclusion of 1937 and continued throughout 1938, resulting in a reduction in the value of exports. Consequent to the oil conflict, there was a significant increase in bank withdrawals accompanied by the implementation of lending restrictions.[72]

The trajectory of the Mexican economy, however, experienced a notable transformation in 1939, as the country became a focal point for investment that had relocated from Europe in reaction to the outbreak of World War II. The Annual Report of Banco de México for the year 1940 provided the following information: The Bank of Mexico returned the country's currency to its previous exchange rate in the second part of the year with the intention of using surplus funds to raise living standards and productivity. This strategy avoided harm to exports, which would have decreased if the currency had experienced further revaluation, and supported the equilibrium of the balance of payments. The central bank predicted that it would probably increase for a while if some of this money stayed in the country and was invested over the long term, mostly in industrial endeavors. Nonetheless, since more investment would raise wages and consumption, this suggested that the economy was improving. Prices might drop again only once additional things became available as a result of these investments, unless a fresh round of investments temporarily stopped this from happening.[73]

Historically, there exist two distinct perspectives regarding Lázaro Cárdenas and his policies: one faction critiques them as populist, while the other advocates for them as *desarrollista* in nature. The statement "achieving monetary stability is not Mexico's problem. Mexico's economic challenge lies in increasing both national income and per capita income, with the ultimate goal of achieving a more equitable distribution of wealth", illustrate the dispute between these two perspectives. This statement was made by Suárez, who held the position of Secretary of Finance during the presidency of Lázaro Cárdenas, in response to Alberto Pani, who previously occupied the same role during the administrations of Álvaro Obregón and Plutarco Elías Calles and had expressed criticism of Cárdenas's policies.[74]

This episode serves as a poignant reminder of the historical fluctuations in public policies in Mexico, which have frequently oscillated between extremities of liberalism and socialism. These oscillations have often compromised democratic

---

[71] Banco de México (1938), p. 12.

[72] See Ibid., p. 11.

[73] See Banco de México (1941), p. 12 y 13. https://www.banxico.org.mx/publicaciones-y-prensa/informes-anuales/%7BD3A4FB22-814F-68AF-1198-0DE25D1CDEEE%7D.pdf.

[74] Martín (2019).

principles and had detrimental effects on marginalized communities. The primary challenge for policymakers resides in attaining a state of equilibrium between monetary stability and equality. On the one hand, monetary stability is crucial for maintaining the value of the currency, which, in turn, alleviates the rise in living expenses. However, the equitable distribution of resources and the provision of equal opportunities for access to prosperity are essential for promoting economic development.

Following Lázaro Cárdenas's inauguration, he sought to revise the Constitution to incorporate socialist principles into the educational policies characteristic of the Cardenismo period. The proposed amendment explicitly excluded all religious doctrines and mandated that the State would furnish an education characterized by socialist principles. Moreover, it sought to address fanaticism and prejudice. To accomplish this objective, educational institutions were required to design their curricula and activities in a manner that cultivated in young individuals a rational and accurate comprehension of the universe and social existence.[75] Lázaro Cárdenas appointed Ignacio García Téllez to hold the position of Secretary of Education, a decision made 1 month following Gómez Morín's resignation as Chancellor of the National Autonomous University of Mexico (UNAM).

To comprehend the origins of ITAM, it is critical to devote some attention to to the conflict that prompted Gómez Morín's resignation. Gómez Morin held the position of professor of legal theory and constitutional law at the Law School of the National Autonomous University of Mexico (UNAM). In 1933, Gómez Morin was appointed as the chancellor following a protracted effort to extricate the institution from governmental and political interference, as well as to counter attempts to integrate Marxist ideology into its educational and research programs. According to Tamayo and Salmorán, in October 1933, following the strike sparked by the announcement that the National University would adopt a Marxist orientation in its research and teaching, and following the departure of the two main sponsors of that purported reform, Rector Roberto Medellín and Lombardo Toledano, Director of the Preparatoria, from the university, the Constituent Assembly of the University, led by Antonio Caso, elected Gómez Morin as interim rector. A few days later, the new University Council formally elected him to the post.[76]

The appointment of Gómez Morin did not resolve the conflict with the government, which applied pressure to engage in the Marxist education initiative through budgetary cuts. Gómez Morín consistently championed university autonomy; yet, he ultimately submitted his resignation in 1934.[77]

---

[75] Ammendment to the Constitution of 1917, issued on December 13 of 1934: "La educación que imparta el Estado será socialista, y además de excluir toda doctrina religiosa combatirá el fanatismo y los prejuicios, para lo cual la escuela organizará sus enseñanzas y actividades en forma que permita crear en la juventud un concepto racional y exacto del universo y de la vida social."

[76] See Tamayo y Salmorán (2004), pp. 267 y 268.

[77] In his capacity as chancellor, Gómez Morín asserted that the university ought not to function as an echo chamber for prevailing political ideologies in the fowolling terms: "El trabajo universitario no puede ser concebido como coro mecánico de pensamiento político dominante en cada momento…, no apegado servilmente a los hechos del momento ni a la voluntad política triun-

This was hardly the final instance in which Gómez Morín contested the administration. He was pivotal in establishing the Partido Acción Nacional (PAN), a political party aimed at challenging the supremacy of the Partido de la Revolución Institucional (PRI), which ruled Mexico for 70 years. In 1938, Lázaro Cárdenas founded the Partido de la Revolución Mexicana (PRM), based on the core ideals of its predecessor, the Partido de la Revolución Nacional (PNR). In this context, Raúl Baillères[78] considered the creation of an educational institution for economists with a curriculum focused on Classical Economics.[79]

UNAM began an Economics program in 1929, shortly following a time marked by economic hardship, a political crisis exacerbated by the Cristero War, and the killing of former president Álvaro Obregón during his reelection campaign. The Economics curriculum was integrated into the law school and supported by Jesús Silva Herzog, who shown a positive disposition towards Marxism (Ávila Díaz 1985). He collaborated with Antonio Esparza de Monteros, Daniel Cosío Villegas, and others in developing the curriculum.[80]

According to Alfonso Anaya Díaz, the curriculum was designed with a social focus and intended to equip individuals for positions in public administration, private sector, or labor unions.[81] In 1935, the program was formally established as an educational institution, named the Escuela Nacional de Economía.

It is significant to note that Narciso Bassols held the position of chancellor during the inception of this program. He was one of the most esteemed intellectuals and public servants of his time. During the presidency of Abelardo Rodriguez, he served as both the Secretary of Education and the Secretary of the Interior. Subsequently, he was appointed as the ambassador to the United Kingdom by Lázaro Cárdenas. Narciso Bassols exhibited a proclivity towards socialist ideals. Sheldon B. Liss delineates his characterization in the following manner:

> Constant analysis of the inequalities of Mexico's class system led him, by 1932, to a socialist orientation, but far from scientific Marxism. Bassols used Marxist phraseology in his speech and writings, but ignored the dialectical method as Minister of Education. After leaving the post, he studied Mar's thoughts in depth and became consumed by them. By 1937, when he wrote the prologue to the Spanish edition of John Strachey's Theory and Practice of Socialism, Bassols displayed a remarkable grasp of Marxist theory, called what

fante…", with reference to socialista theories associated with the Revolution. Ibid. Following to Gómez Morin's tenure, Fernando Ocaranza was designated as Chancellor of UNAM; however, he encountered analogous challenges to those faced by Gómez Morin. Ocaranza tendered his resignation in 1935. As a result of the divergences between Rector Ocaranza and President Lázaro Cárdenas concerning the potential University's role to oversee secondary education, coupled with economic constraints, numerous internal disputes, and the support the rector had extended to factions opposing Tomás Garrido Canabal—and, by extension, President Cárdenas. This led to the election of Luis Chico Goerne, who would preside over the institution for over 3 years.Contreras Pérez (2004), p. 177.

[78] See Romero Sotelo (2019).

[79] García Ugarte (2017), p. 119.

[80] López de la Parra (2014), p. 67; Márquez (2004)

[81] Anaya Díaz (1980), p. 110.

exists in capitalist society as "false democracy", and saw liberty as an illusion for ninety-five percent of the population of capitalist countries.[82]

4 ITAM as an Alternative to UNAM

In this political setting, Baillères,[83] a prominent Mexican financier, met with fellow financiers Salvador Ugarte, Mario Domínguez, and Ernesto Amezcua. This group of financiers gained notoriety as the Grupo BUDA, an acronym based on their surnames, which later established the Asociación Mexicana de Cultura, A.C. This organization was instrumental in founding ITAM, initially referred to as the Instituto Tecnológico de México (ITM), in 1946.[84] This proposal garnered backing from UNAM professors, notably Eduardo García Máynez,[85] the first dean, and Gómez Morin, along with former public servants like Luis Montes de Oca.[86] Montes de Oca had a pivotal role in familiarizing ITAM with the Austrian School of Economics by facilitating communication between Ludwig von Mises and Friedrich Hayek and subsequently linking Mises with Baillères.[87]

Montes de Oca served as Secretary of Finance during the final year of Plutarco Elías Calles' administration, as well as throughout the tenures of Pascual Ortiz Rubio and Emilio Portes Gil. In this capacity, he implemented the tenets of classical economics. Ironically, Lázaro Cárdenas, a proponent of socialism, appointed Montes de Oca as the director of the central bank.[88] The decision is elucidated by the Mexican economy's dependence on foreign credit, notwithstanding the prevailing nationalism and the expropriation of assets belonging to foreign enterprises. Cárdenas required an individual such as Montes de Oca, who had established a network of both domestic and international connections during his tenure as Secretary of Finance. Certain scholars contend that Cárdenas perceived Montes de Oca as a man of integrity, possessing the requisite experience and expertise to fulfill the role of chair of the central bank, independent of any additional considerations.[89]

---

[82] Liss (1991), pp. 363 and 364.

[83] Raúl Baillères was the founder of Crédito Minero, S.A., Crédito Hipotecario, S.A. and Crédito Afianzador, S.A.; president of the Mexican Bankers Association from 1941 to 1942, shareholder of Cervecería Moctezuma, S.A., Palacio de Hierro, S.A., Manantiales Peñafiel, S.A., Metalúrgica Mexicana Peroles, S.A. and Compañía Fresnillo, S.A., Metalúrgica Mexicana Peroles, S.A. and Compañía Fresnillo, S.A. See ITAM, https://www.itam.mx/sites/all/themes/coursat/semblanza/raulballeres.pdf.

[84] *Ibid.*

[85] *See* García Ugarte (2017), p. 128.

[86] *See* Ceremonia Conmemorativa de los 50 años del Instituto Tecnológico Autónomo de México. https://www.itam.mx/documentos-itam/50aniversario.pdf.

[87] *See* García Ugarte (2017), p. 122.

[88] *See* Romero Sotelo (2019), p. 70.

[89] See Anaya Merchant (2020), p. 328; and Suárez Dávila (2003), p. 343.

Montes de Oca tendered his resignation from the central bank at the conclusion of Cárdenas' administration, owing to his disagreements with both the president and the Secretary of Finance, Eduardo Suárez.[90]

Regarding Montes de Oca, it remains unclear why, despite being a staunch advocate of classical economics, he agreed to serve as the chair of the central bank in an administration that implemented socialist policies. Nonetheless, Montes de Oca developed a friendship with Cárdenas during Cárdenas's tenure as the governor of Michoacán, which may provide a reasonable explanation for their association.[91]

Reflecting on the history of ITAM, the institution experienced significant growth by the conclusion of the 1960s and throughout the 1970s, following a prolonged period of financial challenges that jeopardized its continued existence. Throughout these decades, ITM started the sponsorship of its graduates to pursue studies at international universities, with a particular emphasis on graduate programs in Economics at the University of Chicago, where they had the opportunity to engage with Milton Friedman and Gary S. Becker. These graduates would return to serve as professors at ITM or as public servants under the Secretary of Finance. This relates to the case of Francisco Gil Díaz, who held the position of Dean of the Economics Department at ITAM following his return to the country after earning both a Master's and a Ph.D. in Economics from the University of Chicago. Subsequently, he became a member of the central bank's staff during the presidency of Ernesto Zedillo and served as the Secretary of Finance under the administration of Vicente Fox.[92]

The 1980s represented a significant era in the consolidation of ITM, attributable not only to its graduates undertaking advanced studies overseas but also to the administration of President Miguel de la Madrid, which resulted in the institution's rebranding from Instituto Tecnológico de México (ITM)to its current designation, Instituto Tecnológico Autónomo de México (ITAM).[93] Graduates of ITAM commenced assuming prominent roles within the Secretariat of Finance,[94] exemplified

[90] Eduardo Suárez recounts the opposition of Luis Montes de Oca as director of Banco de México to authorize a loan that exceeded the limits allowed by law. He explains:

> Suárez did not hesitate when faced with the dilemma posed by Mr. Luis Montes de Oca of either complying with the Law of Banco de México or assuming, as Secretary of Finance, the political responsibility of a "special credit", that was the euphemism used to avoid calling it an "illegal credit", which would allow giving resources to Banco Ejidal. Thus was born the famous "overdraft", which was made public at the Bank's Assembly held in February 1938. The amount of this "special credit" was a little less than 90 million pesos, a considerable figure in the Mexico of that time when the budget approved by the Chamber of Deputies for 1937 was a little more than 460 million pesos. The "overdraft" caused, in addition to Palacios Macedo's resignation from the Bank's Board, the departure of another of his dearest companions and friends: Don Manuel Gómez Morin.

Ibid, p. 38.

[91] Idem.

[92] See García Ugarte (2017), p. 412.

[93] Ibid.,p. 399. ITM was given autonomy in 1963; nevertheless, it was not permitted to change its name to reflect its independent status, unlike UNAM.

[94] Petricioli also served as the head of the Mexican Banking Association, the National Banking and Securities Commission from 1976 to 182, and Banco de México's first officer.

by Gustavo Petricioli during the administration of Miguel de la Madrid and Pedro Aspe under the administration of Carlos Salinas de Gortari.

In the course of this decade, Arturo Fernandez, who served as a professor and the Dean of the División Académica de Economía, Derecho y Ciencias Sociales at ITAM, encountered Andrés Roemer, who was then a student pursuing a major in economics,[95] at the same institution. Arturo Fernandez earned a Doctorate in Economics from the University of Chicago, where he studied under the esteemed scholars Milton Friedman, Theodore Schultz, Gary S. Becker, and Robert Lucas. At this juncture, Fernández acquainted Roemer with the Chicago School of Economics.[96]

Andrés Roemer had a pivotal role in the implementation and promotion of EAL in Mexico, especially beyond the confines of the Economics departments within Mexican universities. Roemer received a law degree from UNAM and a degree in economics from ITAM, both in 1989.[97] He earned a Master's degree in Public Administration from Harvard University in 1991 and subsequently obtained a Ph.D. in Public Policy from the University of California, Berkeley, in 1994. He taught economics and public policy at ITAM from 1987 to 2000, at Centro de Investigación y Docencia Económicas (CIDE) from 1997 to 1999, and at the Instituto Nacional de Administracion Pública (INAP) from 1996 to 2000.[98]

Roemer authored the 1994 book Introducción al Análisis Económico del Derecho, the first in Mexico to explain EAL. The objective of this book was to familiarize the reader with the theory of Law and Economics.[99] The author contends that Law and Economics constitutes the most substantial advancement in the legal sector in the last half-century.[100] The book seeks to outline diverse methodologies within the discipline, encompassing the Chicago School, neoinstitutionalism, public choice theory, legal critical studies, alongside other continental schools and Latin American perspectives that examine the interplay between the economy and law.[101]

Roemer is the author of additional works on the subject, including El Juego de la Negociación, published in 199; and Economía y Derecho: Políticas Públicas del Agua, published in 1997, co-authored with Esteban Moctezuma Barragán. Por un Gobierno Eficaz. El Servicio Civil de Carrera: Un Sistema Integral de Profesionalización, Evaluación y Desempeño de los Servidores Públicos in México, 1999; Law and Economics: A Literature Review, with a preface by Richard

[95] Arturo Fernandez had previously worked for the Secretariat of Finance as a public servant. See Currículum Vitae del Rector, Doctor Arturo Fernández Pérez. https://www.itam.mx/es/1/paginas/curriculum-vitae-del-rector.

[96] García Ugarte (2017), p. 417.

[97] See Roemer, "Testimonios sobre la filosofía del Derecho Contemporáneo en México-Andrés Roemer", op. cit.

[98] See Currículum de Andrés Roemer, Comisión Nacional de Derechos Humanos, Junio de 2010, https://www.cndh.org.mx/sites/all/doc/Transparencia/19/AndresRoemer.pdf.

[99] See Roemer (1994), p. 3.

[100] Idem.

[101] Fernández (1994). Prefacio. Roemer A. Intorudccion al Analisis Economico. Fondo de Cultura Económica, Mexico.

A. Posner. Posner, in the year 2000; Economía del Crimen, 2000; Enigmas and Paradigms: An Exploration between Art and Public Policy, 2003; Felicidad: Un enfoque de Derecho y Economía, 2005; Terrorism and organized crime. Un enfoque de Derecho y Economía, in 2006. It is important to note that, with the exception of the initial book on AEL and the compilations, the majority of his authored works, are primarily intended for dissemination rather than scholarly inquiry.

Roemer is an active figure in various organizations dedicated to the advancement and examination of Law and Economics (AED). He served as the founding president of the Mexican Academy of Law and Economics (AMDE), established in 1995,[102] as well as the Latin American Association of Law and Economics (ALADE), which was founded in 1994.[103] Both organizations aim to promote the study of AED. Roemer is additionally a member of the American Association of Public Policy Analysis and Management, the European Association of Law and Economics, and the American Law and Economics Association.[104]

ITAM consolidated throughout the decades of the 1980s and 1990s. It underwent expansion and underwent an administrative reorganization. In connection with EAL, Víctor Blanco, who was the Dean of the Department of Law at that time, extended an invitation to José Ramón Cossío to become a member of the faculty at ITAM, specifically as a professor of constitutional law. In 1995, Cossío succeeded Blanco as the Director of the Department of Law and as the Head of the Academic Department. He was appointed as a Justice to the Supreme Court of Justice of the Nation in 2003.[105] In his capacity as Director of the Law School and Head of the Department, he successfully initiated a program that facilitated the placement of law graduates in various esteemed positions within Secretaries of State, including the Ministry of Health, the Ministry of Agrarian Reform, and the Ministry of Foreign Affairs. Additionally, this program extended to autonomous constitutional entities such as the Federal Electoral Institute and the Bank of Mexico. Traditionally, ITAM graduates from the Economics Department joined the Secretary of Finance and the central bank, while graduates from UNAM held positions at the other Secretaries of State. Throughout his tenure, he extended invitations to ministers of the Supreme Court of Justice, as well as to political figures such as Santiago Creel and Felipe Calderón, the former president of Mexico, to serve as instructors.[106]

---

[102] In addition to Miguel de la Madrid Hurtado (President of Mexico from 1982 to 1987) and Arturo Manuel Fernández Pérez, Roemer also had the backing of Robert Cooter and Albert Fishlow, who were both professors at UC Berkeley, where Andrés Roemer earned his PhD in Public Policy (1994). See Roemer and Valadés (2000), p. 264.

[103] This association changed its name in 1995 to the Latin American and Caribbean Association of Law and Economics (ALACDE) and in 2014 became the Latin American and Iberian Association of Law and Economics (ALACDE).

[104] 116 Andrés Roemer's Curriculum Vitae, National Human Rights Commission, June 2010, https://www.cndh.org.mx/sites/all/doc/Transparencia/19/AndresRoemer.pdf.

[105] García Ugarte (2017), pp. 426–427.

[106] Ibid., p. 35.

José Ramón Cossío is widely recognized as one of the leading legal scholars in contemporary Mexico, having made substantial contributions to the field through a critical examination of EAL. He graduated from the Universidad de Colima, and received a Master's degree in Constitutional Law and Political Science from the Centro de Estudios Constitucionales de Madrid; he obtained a Master's degree in Law from UNAM, and a Doctor of Laws degree from Universidad Complutense de Madrid.[107] Additionally, Rodolfo Vázquez, a distinguished Mexican legal philosopher and professor at ITAM, authored a critical review of Roemer's book, which has emerged as a significant contribution to critical studies on AED in Mexico.[108]

In addition to Roemer, Vázquez and Cossío, there exists a limited number of Mexican authors who have addressed EAL from a legal standpoint. Among these individuals, some are alumni of ITAM, while others have pursued advanced legal degrees in the United States or Spain,[109] where AEL has witnessed significant progress not only within academic circles but also in judicial practice and legal policy.

5 Federal Government Agencies and the Judiciary

Numerous other texts, especially those pertaining to banking, the stock market, monetary policy, labor markets, antitrust, and taxation, integrate economic theory and encompass legal issues. Nonetheless, these texts are composed by economists. Federal authorities and agencies such as Banco de México, the Comisión Federal de Competencia Económica, and the Comisión Nacional de Mejora Regulatoria,

[107] Curriculum vitae of José Ramón Cossío Díaz, SCJN, 2018, https://www.supremacorte.gob.mx/sites/default/files/ministro/curriculum/cvjrcd20180731.pdf.

[108] Vázquez (2016), pp. 143–152.

[109] For example, José Diego Valadés in collaboration with Roemer, Law and Economics in Mexico (1999); Adriana García García and Dirk Zavala Rubach, Derecho y economía (2009); Rafael Ramírez Villaescusa, Algunas reflexiones en torno a la enseñanza del análisis económico del derecho en las Universidades Públicas Mexicanas; Benjamín Ruíz García, Epistemología del Análisis Económico del Derecho: Un trazo de las pretensions teóricas (2017). There are other texts written by Mexican legal scholars that refer to efficiency, market competition, and regulation, such as: Competencia económica. Aspectos jurídicos y económicos by Francisco González de Cossio in collaboration with Richard A. Posner and Dennis W. Carlton (2005); Guía de las decisions del PJF en materia de competencia económica: Cómo genera una cultura de la competencia by Ana Elena Fierro and Adriana García (2008); Las imperfecciones del mercado como justificación para la intervención del Estado by Solange Maqueo (2009);Análisis Económico del Derecho by María Solange Maqueo in collaboration with Juan Javier del Granado (2012); Corporate Vei Piercing: A Proposal for Mexico by Susana Dávalos; Regulación y evolución de organismos reguladores en telecomunicaciones: El caso de México y Francia by Jorge E. Culebro M. and Christian González Laporte (2013); The Rejection of Executory Contracts: A Comparative Economic Analysis by Susana Dávalos (2018); La responsabilidad civil extracontractual desde la perspectiva del análisis económico del derecho y la economía del comportamiento by María Solange Maqueo Ramírez (2020); La ineficiencia de los jueces familiares de la Ciudad de México by Jorge Rúa (2020).

predominantly staffed by economists, strongly promote for the dissemination of research grounded in economic analysis.

A division of the Mexican Central Bank focuses on economic research. This agency manages the gathering, processing, and enhancement of data related to Mexico's key economic and financial indicators. Consequently, the central bank's economists not only produce reports on financial and monetary policy matters but also compose research papers, often integrating EAL.The Comisión Federal de Competencia Económica (COFECE) is responsible for preventing and rectifying market barriers to free competition; thus, it deters and penalizes monopolistic practices. COFECE's economists also produce papers and research publications, many of which utilize EAL. The Comisión Nacional de Mejora Regulatoria (CONAMER) is a federal institution that assesses and examines regulations to guarantee that their social benefits exceed their costs.[110] The agency's predecessor, Comisión Federal de Mejora Regulatoria, published manuals to assess regulation and create the appropriate technique for quantifying the costs and benefits of regulation.[111]

Judicial rulings, especially regarding telecommunications and antitrust matters, have also employed EAL. This is illustrated by the rulings of Jean Claude Tron Petit in the Coca-Cola System case in 2003[112] and the Aristegui case in 2015.[113]

6 Concluding Remarks

The political context of the twentieth and twenty-first centuries is crucial to comprehending EAL in Mexico. EAL in our country has encountered numerous challenges, making it difficult to envision a promising future for its development.

Regrettably, in the wake of the global proliferation of the #MeToo movement, a significant number of individuals who have experienced harassment and sexual assault publicly accused prominent figures in Mexico in 2019. This encompassed faculty members from both public and private universities, several of whom are or have been public servants. The offenders exhibited a spectrum of ideological

---

[110] See Ley de Mejora Regulatoria, published in the Official Gazette of the Federation on May 18, 2018, Mexico, art. 7.

[111] For example, see COFEMER, Anexo Técnico Metodologías de Evaluación de Impacto Regulatorio, December 11, 2017. https://www.gob.mx/conamer/documentos/anexo-tecnico-metodologias-de-la-evaluacion-de-impacto-regulatorio.

It is important to note that this agency has not conducted regulatory impact analyses in recent years. For instance, in 2019, "The costs and benefits of the majority of the ordinances were unknown because only 13.1% of the regulatory proposals that were issued last year, at the federal level, had a Regulatory Impact Analysis (AIR)." Only 132 of the 1066 regulatory proposals that were issued in 2019 received analysis, according to the National Commission for Regulatory Improvement (Conamer) report. This means that the consequences of the regulations cannot be assessed. Gascón (2020).

[112] See Tron Petit and Martínez Jiménez (2012), pp. 237–269.

[113] See Tron Petit et al. (2016), pp. 323–378.

orientations, encompassing individuals with the most liberal viewpoints to those with the most conservative inclinations, including ardent advocates of free-market principles as well as individuals committed to communist ideologies.[114] Such denunciations included EAL scholars.[115]

Additionally, the prevalence of inequality has precipitated the resurgence of leftist movements within the region, thereby revitalizing Marxist policies. Furthermore, the present administration exhibits a tendency towards autocratic governance, which has significantly influenced the educational landscape.[116] For example, the federal government's developed materials for primary and secondary education, scheduled for distribution at the commencement of the 2004 academic year, exhibit a substantial reduction in mathematical content and exclude universal literature, among other deficiencies.[117]

This piece of work does not constitute a definitive study. Conversely, we need to delve deeper into the analysis of EAL in Mexico to validate the claims stated in this text. Specific inquiries on perceptions and attitudes toward capitalism and socialism, along with the view of mathematical reasoning in Mexico across various educational tiers and sectors, require both quantitative and qualitative research. Evaluating the perception of EAL among Mexican legal scholars is also essential. Mexican legal scholars frequently categorize EAL within the Sociology of Law, employing it as a pragmatic tool for analyzing legal norms; yet, they regard it as ineffective in promoting justice. Paradoxically, EAL is not on the radar of legal sociologists—at least in our country—as they collect and analyze data without the aid of economic analysis. Similarly, individuals who perceive EAL solely as a pragmatic instrument neglect methodological frameworks such as neoinstitutionalism and behavioral economics, thereby exhibiting a disinterest in broadening their comprehension of EAL beyond the viewpoints presented by Posner. They also neglect to acknowledge the beneficial applications of EAL in domains such as taxation, finance, and antitrust regulation. It is imperative to conduct both quantitative and qualitative studies to substantiate these assertions.

---

[114] *See* "Estudiantes de mas de 20 universidades de México denuncian a sus acosadores", *Expansión Política*, Viernes 13 de marzo de 2020. https://politica.expansion.mx/sociedad/2020/03/13/estudiantes-de-universidades-de-mexico-denuncian-a-acosadores Also see "El ITAM no corrió a Salmerón por motivos ideológicos, responden a AMLO", El Universal, 27 de enero de 2022. https://www.eluniversal.com.mx/cultura/el-itam-no-corrio-salmeron-por-motivos-ideologicos-responden-amlo/.

[115] "Libro 'El Roedor' expone 20 años de abusos de escritor mexicano Andrés Roemer", The San Diego Union Tribune en Español, February 18, 2022. https://www.sandiegouniontribune.com/en-espanol/noticias/mexico/articulo/2022-02-18/libro-el-roedor-expone-20-anos-de-abusos-de-escritor-mexicano-andres-roemer.

[116] For more about the history of autocracy in Mexico, see Hernández Rodríguez (2023), pp. 5–40.

[117] See Soriano, Rodrigo, "López Obrador responde a los críticos de los libros de texto: 'Ni siquiera los han leído'", El País, 3 de agosto de 2023. https://elpais.com/mexico/2023-08-03/lopez-obrador-sobre-los-criticos-a-los-libros-de-texto-ni-siquiera-los-han-leido.html.

References

Aboites L, Loyo E (2010) La construcción del nuevo Estado, 1920-1945. In García EV et al. Historia General de México Ilustrada: Volumen II. 1st, edición conmemorativa ed., El Colegio de Mexico, 2010. JSTOR, https://doi.org/10.2307/j.ctv47wf77. Accessed 14 Jan 2025

Ahumada Lobo I and Butler Silva F (2009) La enseñanza de la Economía en México, Research Department Working Papers, Inter-American Development Bank, 672. https://doi.org/10.18235/0011873

Anaya Díaz A (1980) La Facultad de Economía. Investigación Económica 39(151)

Anaya Merchant L (2020) Luis Montes de Oca (1894-1958). El renovador, el hacendista, el banquero y la familia revolucionaria, UAEM-CICSER, México

Aspe Armella V (2020) Los dilemas políticos de las transformaciones de México: una aproximación filosófica. Tópicos, México 58: 375–410. https://doi.org/10.21555/top.v0i58.1157

Ávila Díaz A (1985) In Memoriam Jesús Silva Herzog. Investigación Económica 44(174):215–229

Baillères R (2024) Semblanza. Instituto Tecnológico Autónomo de México, https://www.itam.mx/sites/all/themes/coursat/semblanza/raulballeres.pdf

Banco de México (1941) Informe Anual. 1940. Décima Novena Asamblea General Ordinaria de Accionistas. https://www.banxico.org.mx/publicaciones-y-prensa/informes-anuales/%7BD3A4FB22-814F-68AF-1198-0DE25D1CDEEE%7D.pdf

Banco de México IA (1938) Décima séptima Asamblea General Ordinaria de Accionistas, México (1939). https://www.banxico.org.mx/publicaciones-y-prensa/informes-anuales/%7B0DC84FCF-AC4C-D0C1-6F89-678BDB46E9E5%7D.pdf

Bazant M (1993) Historia de la Educación durante el Porfiriato, El Colegio de México

Brando CA, Nodari G (2020) Políticas bancarias durante la gran depresión: Colombia y México, 1929-1937. Análisis Político 33(100):118–145. https://doi.org/10.15446/anpol.v33n100.93364

Cardero García ME (1976) Evolución financiera de México: Porfiriato y Revolución. Rev Mex Sociol 38(2):359–387

Ceballos Mina OE, Duque García CA (2023) Econometría en los programas de economía: mitos y barreras de enseñanza-aprendizaje. Revista Nicolaita De Estudios Económicos 17(1):65–82. https://doi.org/10.33110/rnee.v17i1.335

Ceceña Gámez JL (2014) La Penetración Extranjera y los Grupos de Poder Económico en el México Porfirista. Problemas Del Desarrollo. Revista Latinoamericana de. Economia 1(1):49–88. https://doi.org/10.22201/iiec.20078951e.1969.1.44534

Cerutti M, Marichal C (eds) (2003) La banca regional en México (1870)-1930), Fondo de Cultura Económica, Mexico

Charles-Leija H & Torres García AJ (2022) English proficiency and salary in Mexico. Análisis Económico, 37(94), 167–180

COFEMER (2017) Anexo Técnico Metodologías de Evaluación de Impacto Regulatorio, Dec 11. https://www.gob.mx/conamer/documentos/anexo-tecnico-metodologias-de-la-evaluacion-de-impacto-regulatorio

Comte A (1934) Discurso sobre el espíritu positivo, translated by Julián Marías, Alianza Editorial, Madrid (2017)

Contreras Pérez G (2004) La Universidad: nacional y autónoma. Perfiles educativos 26(105–106):173–179

Del Pozo Franco PE et al (2022) La política social y la investigación empírica en derecho. Revista Universidad y Sociedad, Universidad Científica de Cienfuegos 14(3)

Díaz Vázquez RF, Valencia Jiménez WG (2020) Una Introducción a las Investigaciones Empíricas en Derecho: Estudio de Caso. Verba Iuris 44(186):215. https://doi.org/10.18041/0121-3474/verbaiuris.44.6877

El Universal (2022) El ITAM no corrió a Salmerón por motivos ideológicos, responden a AMLO, J 27. https://www.eluniversal.com.mx/cultura/el-itam-no-corrio-salmeron-por-motivos-ideologicos-responden-amlo/

Fix Fierro H, López Ayllón S (2002) Cambio jurídico y autonomía del derecho: un modelo de la transición jurídica en México. In: Serna de la Garza JM, Caballero JA (2002) Estado de derecho y transición jurídica, IIJ-UNAM, México
Fix-Fierro H et al (2018) Manual de sociología del derecho. Dieciséis lecciones introductorias, IIJ-UNAM-FCE, México
Flores Magón R et al (1911) Manifiesto del 23 de septiembre de 1911. https://archivos.juridicas.unam.mx/www/bjv/libros/6/2625/54.pdf
Flores Torres O (2009) Autoexilio, revolución y arte. El caso del mexicano Alberto J. Pani, 1913-132, XXII Jornadas Interescuelas/Departamentos De Historia. Departamento de Historia, Facultad de Humanidades Y Centro Regional Universitario Bariloche, Universidad Nacional del Comahue, San Carlos Bariloche, Argentina. https://cdsa.aacademica.org/000-008/1125.pdf
Galván M (2020) Estudiantes de más de 20 universidades de México denuncian a sus acosadores", Expansión Política, Mar 3 (2020). https://politica.expansion.mx/sociedad/2020/03/13/estudiantes-de-universidades-de-mexico-denuncian-a-acosadores
García Diego J (2010) El Porfiriato (1876–1911). In Von Wobeser, Gisela, Historia de México, FCE-SEP
García Ugarte ME (2017) Tiempo y Memoria. Historia del ITAM (1946-2016) México
Gascón V (2020) Descuida Gobierno impacto regulatorio, El Norte, 3 Nov.
Gómez Galvarriato A (2019) La etapa inicial del banco central: creación, consolidación y crisis. In: Ludlow L, Romero Sotelo ME (eds) El banco de México a través de sus constructores 1917–2017. IIH-UNAM, México, pp 1925–1932
Gómez Galvarriato Freer A (2003) Industrialización, empresas y trabajadores industriales, del porfiriato a la Revolución: la nueva historiografía. Historia Mexicana LII(3), 773–804
Grange J (2000) Auguste Comte. La politique et la science, Odile Jacob, Paris
Granja Castro DM (2010) Kant en el México del siglo XX: recepción e influencia de su filosofía. Signos Históricos 12(23):08–61
Haynes KA (1991) Dependency, Postimperialism, and the Mexican revolution: an historiographic review. Mexican Studies/Estudios Mexicanos 7(2):225–251. https://doi.org/10.2307/1052065
Hernández Rodríguez R (2023) El autoritarismo presidencial en México. Entre la tradición y la necesidad. Foro Internacional 63(1 (251)):5–40
Iliades C (2018) Una historia intelectual. Taurus, México
ITAM (1996) Ceremonia Conmemorativa de los 50 años del Instituto Tecnológico Autónomo de México, Oct 21 (1996). https://www.itam.mx/documentos-itam/50aniversario.pdf
Iturribarria JF (1960) Limantour y la caída de Porfirio Díaz. Hist Mex 10(2):243–281
Katz F (1974) Labor conditions on haciendas in Porfirian Mexico: some trends and tendencies. Hisp Am Hist Rev 54(1):1–47. https://doi.org/10.2307/2512838
Kehoe T, Meza F (2013) Crecimiento rápido seguido de estancamiento: México (1950-2010). El trimestre económico 80(318):237–280
Liss SB (1991) Marxist thinkers in Mexico: each to his own revolution. In Camp RA et al (eds) Los intelectuales y el poder en México: memorias de la VI Conferencia de Historiadores Mexicanos y Estadounidenses = Intellectuals and power in Mexico (1st ed., Vol. 75, pp. 359–376). El Colegio de Mexico. https://doi.org/10.2307/j.ctv513805.22
López de la Parra M (2014) La UNAM y la Facultad de Economía en la historia de México. Economía Informa 386:64–76
López-Córdova D (2012) Peonage and slave labor in Mexico during the Porfirian age. Review (Fernand Braudel Center) 35(3/4):187–209
Lora E, Ñopo H (2009) La formación de los economistas en América Latina. Revista de análisis económico 24(2):65–93
Loria Díaz E (2002) Mundo cambiante, currícula rígida. Diez años después Economía Informa 310:44–50
Ludlow L, Marichal C (eds) (1998) (1998) La banca en México La banca en México. Instituto Mora/El Colegio de México/El Colegio de Michoacán/IIH-UNAM, México

Márquez G (2004) Daniel Cosío Villegas, sus años como economista. El Trimestre Económico 71(284):877–907. https://www.eltrimestreeconomico.com.mx/index.php/te/article/view/2504
Martín S (2019) El debate de la política económica cardenista: una perspectiva contemporánea. América Latina en la historia económica 26(1). https://doi.org/10.18232/alhe.916
Mathias S (2007) The end of comparative law. J Comp Law 133(2)
Méndez Medina DE (2015) En los bordes de la corrupción: análisis de la conformación, funcionamiento y expropiación de la Compañía Azucarera del Mante (1930-1939). Región y sociedad 27(62):209–248
Meyer J (1971) Los obreros en la revolución mexicana: Los 'batallones rojos'. Hist Mex 21(1):1–37
Moreno Lázaro J (2017) La Bolsa de Valores de México durante el porfiriato y la revolución, 1885–1934. America Latina en la historia económica 24(1):98–139. https://doi.org/10.18232/alhe.v24i1.729
Moreno-Brid JC, Ros J (2009) Development and growth in the Mexican economy. A historical perspective. Oxford University Press
Nava G. et al (1992), Jornales y jornaleros en la minería porfiriana. In La Economía Mexicana: (Siglos XIX-XX), 1st ed., 4:157–76. El Colegio de Mexico, 1992. https://doi.org/10.2307/j.ctv5138v7.
Negrete R (2021) Los días dorados del marxismo en la Facultad de Economía de la UNAM, Nexos. https://redaccion.nexos.com.mx/los-dias-dorados-del-marxismo-en-la-facultad-de-economia-de-la-unam/
Ortega Esquivel A (2010) Gabino Barreda, el positivismo y a filosofía de la historia mexicana. Revista de Hispanismo Filosófico 15:117–127
Örücü E (2004) The enigma of comparative law. Variations on a Theme for the Twenty-first Century, Springer, Dodrecht
Pani AJ (1943) APUNTES AUTOBIOGRÁFICOS. Senado de la República, México
Pérez Hurtado and Rivera Villegas (2022) Panorama de la educación jurídica mexicana. Revista Pedagogía Universitaria y Didáctica del Derecho 9(2):1–24
Ramírez Villaescusa R (2015) Algunas reflexiones en torno a la enseñanza del análisis económico del derecho en las Universidades Públicas Mexicanas 13(16):215–231
Rodríguez Jiménez JR et al (2018) Estudiantes universitarios y lenguas extranjeras: Características de los estudiantes en la Universidad de Sonora. Reencuentro Análisis de Problemas Universitarios 29(75):215–232
Roemer A (1994) Introducción Al Análisis Económico Del Derecho. Fondo de Cultura Económica, Mexico
Roemer A (1997) Testimonios sobre la filosofía del Derecho Contemporáneo en México-Andrés Roemer, Isonomía. Revista de Teoría y Filosofía del Derecho 7:72–76
Roemer A, Valadés JD (2000) Law and economics in Mexico. In: Bouckaert B, Gerrit DG (eds) Encyclopedia of law and economics. Edward Elgar, Cheltenham
Romero Sotelo MA (2019) Los secretarios de Hacienda a debate. Alberto J Pani contra Luis Montes de Oca, Eduardo Suárez y Ramón Beteta, EconomíaUNAM 16(48):66–97
Rosenzwieg F (1965) El desarrollo económico de México de 1877 a 1911. El Trimestre Económico 32(127(3)):405–454
San Diego Union Tribune (2022) Libro 'El Roedor' expone 20 años de abusos de escritor mexicano Andrés Roemer, Feb 18. https://www.sandiegouniontribune.com/en-espanol/noticias/mexico/articulo/2022-02-18/libro-el-roedor-expone-20-anos-de-abusos-de-escritor-mexicano-andres-roemer
Sánchez A (2015a) Egresados del Tec, ITAM y UNAM administran 45% de empresas de BMV. El Financiero. https://www.elfinanciero.com.mx/empresas/egresados-del-tec-itam-y-unam-administran-45-de-empresas-de-bmv/
Sánchez A (2015b) Egresados de la UNAM y el ITAM, con las riendas del gobierno mexicano. El Financiero https://www.elfinanciero.com.mx/empresas/egresados-de-la-unam-y-el-itam-con-las-riendas-del-gobierno-mexicano/

Siems, Mathias, (2007) The End of Comparative Law, Working Papers, Centre for Business Research, University of Cambridge, https://EconPapers.repec.org/RePEc:cbr:cbrwps:wp340, p. 4.
Soriano R (2023) López Obrador responde a los críticos de los libros de texto: 'Ni siquiera los han leído'". El País. https://elpais.com/mexico/2023-08-03/lopez-obrador-sobre-los-criticos-a-los-libros-de-texto-ni-siquiera-los-han-leido.html
Suárez Ávila AA (2015) La sociología del derecho en el Instituto de Investigaciones Jurídicas de la UNAM. In: Bernal B et al (eds) Testimonios y remembranzas acerca del Instituto de Investigaciones Jurídicas. 75 años, IIJ-UNAM, México
Suárez Dávila F (2003) Bosquejo Biográfico. In Eduardo Suárez. Comentarios y recuerdos (1926-1946), Senado de la República, México (2003). https://micrositios.senado.gob.mx/BMO/files/historiaX.pdf
Tamayo y Salmorán R (2004) Gómez Morín (En la encrucijada de la autonomía universitaria). Revista de la Facultad de Derecho de México 54(242), México (2004)
Tovar y de Teresa R (2015) De la paz al olvido. Porfirio Díaz y el final de un mundo, Penguin Random House, Mexico
Tron Petit JC, Martínez Jiménez A (2012) El caso Big Cola. Revista de Derecho Privado 1(1). https://doi.org/10.22201/iij.24487902e.2012.1.8970
Tron Petit JC et al (2016, 2016) Derechos de las audiencias y las obligaciones del IFT de garantizarlos (Caso Aristegui). Revista del Centro de Estudios Constitucionales 2(3)
Turner JK (1909) México bárbaro, Colección Sepan Cuantos, Ed. Porrúa, México (2023).
Turrent Díaz E (2015a) Historia del Banco de México. Banco de México, Mexico
Turrent Díaz E (2015b) Las reformas monetarias de 1931 y 1932 en México: críticas e incomprensión. Am Lat Hist Econ 22(2):50–70
Valenzuela Aguilera A (2012) Racionalidad y poder. Las élites en la Ciudad de México, 1876-1940. Iberoamericana 11(47):9–27
Vázquez R (2016) Comentarios sobre algunos supuestos filosóficos del análisis económico del derecho, Isonomía. Revista de Teoría y Filosofía del Derecho 5:143–152
Vázquez Robles J (2016) La cultura jurídica básica como herramienta en la educación jurídica. In: Nieto Cáceres E (ed) Pasos hacia una revolución en la enseñanza del derecho en el sistema romano-germánico. IIJ-UNAM, México
Velasco C et al (2007) Minerales industriales en el porfiriato. Artes México, Issue 86:64–69
Wasserman M (2015) Pesos and politics. Business, elites, foreigner and government in Mexico, 1854–1940. Stanford University Press
Zea L (1968) El positivismo en México: Nacimiento, apogeo y decadencia, Fondo de Cultura Económica, Mexico
Zebadúa E (1994) banqueros y revolucionarios: la soberanía financiera de México, El Colegio de México, Fideicomiso de las Américas, Fondo de Cultura Económica, Mexico

The Stages of the "Italian Style" in Law and Economics. Origins, Evolutions and Latest Developments

Carlo Vittorio Giabardo

Abstract This Chapter summarizes and critically discusses the key stages of the "Law & Economics" scholarship in Italy. It aims to provide a comprehensive panorama of the trajectory L&E has followed in Italy over the last 60 years. This Chapter is structured into three conceptual parts: origins (1960–1970), evolutions (1970–2000) and latest developments (2000 -). After contrasting the L&E approach with the traditional legal method that dominated in Italy and Europe before the 1960s, the analysis touches upon the contribution of Pietro Trimarchi—unanimously regarded as the father of Italian L&E. It then elucidates the consolidation of L&E, particularly in the field of tort law (driven, among other factors, by the influence of Guido Calabresi), and the emergence of the "Social" moment in the Italian academia, between the 1970s and 1980s, with particular reference to property rights and the concept of commons. Finally, the Chapter considers contemporary critical perspectives (such as the "Comparative Law & Economics" project), explores the latest lines of research, outside the traditional domain of Private Law, and briefly describes the innovative trends and themes gaining prominence (such as Behavioural L&E). Methodologically, this Chapter situates each period within its specific historical and ideological background and considers the work and impact of prominent Italian legal scholars who have contributed most to this field.

C. V. Giabardo (✉)
Department of Law, University of Turin, Torino, Italy
e-mail: carlovittorio.giabardo@unito.it

S. Zorzetto et al. (eds.), *Developments in Law and Economics in the Italo-Iberoamerican Context*, Economic Analysis of Law in European Legal Scholarship 21, https://doi.org/10.1007/978-3-032-03317-8_15

1 Introduction. "Italian Exceptionalism" and "Italian Style" of Law & Economics: Law & Economics as a Comparative Law Discipline

Italy stands as an exception within the civil law tradition when it comes to Law & Economics (L&E).[1] In this field, Italian academia occupies a central place among civil law countries, and it was one of the first jurisdictions (if not *the* first, in our tradition) to introduce the L&E methodology during the 1960s, initially focusing on the study of private law rules—and especially of tort law. This occurred independently of the parallel evolutions taking place at that same time in the United States.

In the decades that followed, Italy maintained a keen interest in the L&E approach, establishing an enduring dialogue with American scholars (often facilitated through translated works) and developing in original ways many of the key themes that were discussed overseas.[2] Since 1999, a dedicated law review—*Mercato, concorrenza, regole* ("Market, Competition, and Rules")—has provided a forum for scholarly contributions in this field.[3] In 2005, the *Società Italiana di Diritto ed Economia* (Italian Society of Law & Economics) was founded and it organizes every year an important conference featuring both international and national speakers. Today, L&E is a well-established and dynamic academic discipline, with many Italian law schools offering dedicated courses on the subject.

The current Italian L&E landscape includes a wide variety of perspectives and voices (descriptive vs. normative, traditional vs. critical, conservative vs. progressive, mainstream vs. innovative, theoretical vs. empirical, etc.) as well as diverse academic backgrounds (Law, Economy, Philosophy of Law, Public Policies, Psychology, etc.). The interest in the method grew exponentially over the last 20 years, extending beyond the traditional domain of private law (such as in Criminal and Public law). Emerging topics of inquiry include the critique of the rational choice model, the study of cognitive biases and fallacies in decision-making, the application of "nudges" in public policy, the exploration of legislative rationality (*Legisprudence*), and the development of new forms of "smart regulations".[4] However, Private Law has been, since the inception of L&E—and continues to be, at least to a certain extent—an elected area for research in Italy.

---

[1] In this article, I will use the expression *Law & Economics* as a synonym for *Economic Analysis of Law*, even if I am aware that there is a different nuance in the meanings. In the phrase *Economic Analysis of Law*, Law is the (passive) object of study, with the Economy serving as the lens through which the law is analyzed. In *Law & Economics*, instead, the two areas of knowledge stand as equally important in the equation. *See*, for this distinction, Calabresi (2016).

[2] Specifically, on the Italian tradition of L&E, see Pardolesi and Bellantuono (2015); Caroccia and Pardolesi (2014); Pardolesi (1992); León (1991). For a key example of the cultural proximity between Italian and American scholars, in Italian, Cooter et al. (2006).

[3] Edited by *Il Mulino* (Bologna).

[4] *See infra*, Ch. 5.1. E.g., Ferraro and Zorzetto (2022); Zorzetto and Ferraro (2019); Zorzetto and Esposito (2015).

As a general observation, certain defining features can be identified in what might be termed the "Italian style" of L&E. The most important one is that, in Italy, L&E is characterized by a visible and strong comparative perspective. Indeed, historically, the majority of Italian L&E scholars have emerged from the field of Comparative Law, a discipline that has been particularly robust and internationally influential—mainly thanks to the activities of the three giants of the twentieth-century Italian comparative legal studies: Gino Gorla, Mauro Cappelletti, and Rodolfo Sacco. Italian L&E proponents were not, in the main, economists nor legal philosophers by training (although, of course, many exceptions exist, especially in recent years).

We might wonder why this has been the case. One possible explanation for why L&E developed in Italy within the borders of Comparative Law is that scholars accustomed to thinking about law *comparatively* have always been resistant to formalism and traditional accounts. As a result, comparative lawyers were likely among the first to recognize the dramatic changes occurring in legal methodology during the 1960s and to embrace this new, radically anti-formalistic perspective.

Also, generally speaking, L&E claimed to provide a shared and uncontroversial language—the common language of microeconomics—able to overcome the differences between legal cultures. By its nature L&E is transnational and transcultural, and quite reluctant to consider customary particularities and cultural specificities (a point that has been critiqued, as we shall see). This potential capacity of L&E to lead to an international consensus around how legal institutions or judicial decisions should be designed, reached and enforced—a sort of common core—might also have played a role in generating the enthusiasm of those comparative lawyers who sought to harmonize and uniformize different legal orders to foster market efficiency (as it has emblematically occurred within the European Union).

However, the "Italian style" of L&E has never been so *extremist* in its ends. Instead, its strong comparative orientation has given it a distinctly multi- and interdisciplinary character. Historical and cultural analyses are integral to this style. For this reason, it would be fair to say that Italian L&E literature demonstrates more awareness of the cultural foundations of the whole L&E project and is, therefore, more conscious of the inherent limitations of it. This has resulted, to speak in very broad terms, to a less radical and more nuanced attitude, distinguished by a more "humanistic" tone compared to its American counterpart.

Also, it is important to stress that the success of L&E has not been confined to legal academy, but it has influenced numerous jurisprudential and legislative changes.[5] It has also fostered political debates on pressing social topics, too, as it has happened in relation to the public discussion around "commons" that took place, in Italy, in recent years.

All this is something that should not be taken for granted. Indeed, civilian jurisdictions have been less likely to shift from a traditional approach to a

[5] On the reception of L&E by Italian courts and judges, see Pardolesi and Tassone (2003, 2005); Zorzetto (2017, 2019c); Villa (2015).

non-formalistic, non-dogmatic one in studying the law. In France, for instance, L&E developed much later, struggled to gain academic recognition and it still does not occupy the same importance as it does nowadays in Italy.[6] In Spain, too, L&E is still not extremely popular among positive law professors (those who primarily engage with positive law disciplines). L&E courses are usually offered within the area of Philosophy of Law, rather than Private or other discipline of law: legal theorists, not private lawyers, are its main proponents, creating a significant division within the Spanish legal academy.

Considering all this, it is possible to speak of an "*Italian exceptionalism*".

The reasons for the difficulty of the L&E method in penetrating our traditions are not easy to figure out. Some even argue that civil law legal systems are *by origin* less predisposed to economic rationality and capitalism and more hesitant to adapt their laws to the demands of the economy. Hence their minor success in terms of economic performance and general income, compared to common law orders—this is the highly-questionable *Legal Origins Theory.*[7] Another, and more convincing, explanation for the difficulty of civil law systems in widely accepting and using L&E as an analytical tool might have something to do with the presence, in continental Europe, since the beginnings of the nineteenth century, of *codes*—that is books designed to encompass and systematize the entirety of legal knowledge within a specific domain (most notably, private law).[8] As a concept, the code was intended to represent both the beginning (the *alpha*) and the end (the *omega*) of a legal field. Perhaps for this reason, civilian legal scholars (and judges as well) tended less, so to say, to *venture* beyond the borders of codes in studying, interpreting and applying the law, or in reasoning about rules and consequences. It seems that this factor had played a significant role in shaping the *mentalité* of law professors and decision-makers belonging to the civil law family. However, this reconstruction fails to account for why in England, which is the common law country *par excellence*, L&E has not been particularly successful, at least initially, either: which leads us to embrace the idea that there is no inherent connection between L&E and common law legal culture.[9]

---

[6] Harnay (2015) speaks of "French indifference", at least until the mid-1990s (123, "*In the 1980s, EAL was still a terra incognita for French academics. Foreign advances in the field were simply ignored, there were no publications by French authors in the field and French scholars did not refer to works published either in the US or in other European countries*").

[7] It is not possible to deepen this complex issue here. *See* La Porta et al. (2008). However, for a critique, Mattei and Pardolesi (1991).

[8] The idea of the code is indeed much more complex to describe than it might seem. A code is not simply a book. It is, rather, a "mythical concept", tied to the rise of national states and to the reduction of "law" (intended as "*diritto, Recht, droit*") to "legislation" (intended as "*legge, Gesetz, loi*"). The code is therefore a cultural product that informed deeply the ways of understanding law in the civil law world. See Grossi (2001). In English, Graziadei and Zhang (2023). It is quite common to underline, however, that over the past decades the ideological model that sustained the creation and the success of codes is itself in deep crisis; Irti (1979, 1999) refers to this phenomenon as "*the age of decodification*".

[9] Caroccia, Pardolesi (2014), p. 199.

Anyway, it is certain that Italy began quite soon to develop a particular awareness of the economic implications of private law rules. However, it would be certainly an exaggeration to claim that this awareness has been, or even now is, prevailing in the legal curricula of law schools. The early success of L&E was more attributable to the vision of specific legal scholars belonging to specific schools of law, rather than a widespread and shared phenomenon. For that, any examination of the L&E landscape in Italy must include specific references to the scholars who contributed to its development.

2 From Traditional Legal Thought...

In this paragraph, I wish to particularly emphasize the paradigm shift brought about by the Economic Analysis of Law, comparing this method with the classical and traditional approach—still predominantly in use today in the curricula of Italian law schools.

The roots of the L&E perspective in Italy trace back to the early 1960s. At that time, the traditional approach to legal institutions still dominated in continental Europe—although signs of its weakening were beginning to emerge. The community of law professors—referred to as the "doctrine" (*la doctrine* in French,[10] *la dottrina* in Italian[11])—used to focus on private law bodies of rules (above all, on its three main components: contract law and obligations, tort law, property law) mainly by studying them in isolation from considerations outside the legal domain strictly considered. There was little external view on legal institutions. Legal rules were essentially treated like geometric forms that were meant to be studied in their "purity." That was the powerful and long-lasting legacy of Kelsen's legal positivism as a pure theory of law (*Reine Rechtslehre*), as elaborated and refined from the early 1930s onwards. As its name tells, Kelsen's theory sought to make the study of positive law independent (i.e., pure) from non-legal expertise (economics, sociology and social sciences, history, political philosophy, morality, ethics, ideology, politics, etc.).[12] The idea was that law, *qua* science, should stand on its own.

That attitude has largely been foreign to common lawyers.[13] As applied by European law professors, especially in Germany and Italy, the approach became

[10] On *la doctrine* as the community of law professors and their written production, with special reference to France, see Jestaz and Jamin (1998).

[11] On the traditional features of *la dottrina* in Italy, see Merryman (1965). The German term *Juristenrecht* has a slight twist in the meaning.

[12] See, in English, Kelsen (1941), p. 44: "*It is called "pure" because it seeks to preclude from the cognition of positive law all elements foreign thereto. The limits of this subject and its cognition must be clearly fixed in two directions: the specific science of law, the discipline usually called jurisprudence, must be distinguished from the philosophy of justice, on the one hand, and from sociology, or cognition of social reality, on the other*".

[13] This claim should be nuanced; see, recently, Graziadei (2019a, 2019b).

known as "legal dogmatics" or "legal systematics" (in Italian: *dogmatica giuridica* and *sistematica giuridica*[14]; in German: *Rechtsdogmatik* and *Rechtssystematik*). These expressions capture well the fact that legal rules were viewed as abstract *dogmas* (that is, something that cannot be discussed or evaluated, but has to be taken and studied as it is) and as components of a larger, and surely fictional, "system"—i.e., technically speaking, a structurally coherent, ideally exhaustive, gapless and closed normative order.[15]

As John Merryman—the great American scholar, one of the most acute external observers of the Italian legal thought—summed up:

> The theoretical structure (…) consists of general concepts and institutions of a high order of abstraction, arranged and interrelated in a systematic way. The components of the structure and the relationship between them (…) are strictly legal, and indeed it is believed that their purity (…) would be destroyed by the introduction of non-legal elements. Consideration of other than legal factors would be unscientific.

And he went on stressing the "abstractness" of the Italian legal thought:

> (…) in two senses: First, it is insulated against the intrusion both of social facts and value judgments; sociology on the one hand, and philosophy, on the other, are foreign to it. Second, it is not so much concerned with the solution of concrete problems and with the facts of actual cases as with the development and elaboration of the scientific structure.

Although somewhat naïve, this picture might be considered quite accurate and reflects the state of Italian (and European more largely) legal scholarship in the first half of the twentieth century.

So, for example, classical private law scholars were not concerned whether the rules governing contract law (e.g., the remedies following a breach of contract) were just, or efficient, or socially desirable, or functional to the finalities they were expected to reach, or if they fitted a certain ideology: all these questions would imply an involvement with non-legal elements (such as the definitions of "justice" or of "efficiency" or the study of the concrete social consequences and implications deriving from the application of the rules during a certain period of time and in certain places, or given certain circumstances, etc.) that lay outside the legitimate purposes of the science of law *as* science.[16] Instead, the work of legal scientists traditionally focused either on describing what a norm objectively stated—an approach epitomized by the so-called "exegesis school" (*École de l'Exégèse*), which

---

[14] From a very critical perspective, Guastini (1991).

[15] "*(…) attention was not paid primarily to social and economic problems but to the law itself. (…) The thing studied was the law to the exclusion of other materials*", Merryman (1965), pp. 44–45. For many references on this method, although through a slightly different periodization, in relation to the "first globalization" of law (i.e., *Classic Legal Thought*), see Du. Kennedy (2001).

[16] "*The attitude is that the law is a self-contained discipline or phenomenon that can be understood and perfected by a systematic study. It is summed up in the phrase "legal science", which carries with it the assumption that such study is a natural science in the same way that the study of other natural phenomena—say biology or physics—is a science. The work of legal scholar is like the work of other scientists*", Merryman (1965), p. 45.

was highly influential in France[17]—or on classifying and elaborating upon legal norms to construct increasingly general concepts capable of encompassing more specific ones.

In both cases, the realm of reality—the actual, outer world and its concrete mechanisms—was left outside the door. Paolo Grossi, a prominent Italian legal historian, well described the paradigmatic shift in the Italian legal thought following the forceful entry of the "reality" (the "material facts") into legal discourse, connecting it with the issue of "factuality" and the "effectiveness of the law" (*fattualità, effettività del diritto*).[18]

2.1 ... *To the Rise of the Law & Economics Movement. The 1960s*

From the early 1960s to date, L&E has brought fresh air to the study of law. In the United States, that change was anticipated and facilitated by the advent of American Legal Realism and Pragmatism—jurisprudential movements that opposed Llewellyn's Legal Formalism. In particular, Legal Realism paved the way to the proliferation of the various "*Law Ands*" (Law & Literature, Law & Society, Law & Critics, Law & Feminism, Law & Race, and the like), whose popularity, nowadays, in American law schools, is indisputable.[19] What all these trends share in common is that they *dethroned* law from its empyrean position and looked at it from external standpoints.

In Europe, too, with the L&E approach, legal norms ceased to be seen in their purity—merely as geometric figures whose lengths legal scholars should measure, or as pieces of a larger puzzle to be arranged elegantly in various way—and began to be studied as incentives, or disincentives, for human action (albeit initially considering an idealized, perfectly rational individual). Law stopped being understood just as a *text* (as it had been within the civil law mentality) and started to be studied as a concrete *force* capable of influencing human action. In simpler terms: in L&E, law is considered a system of prices and sanctions, of costs and benefits.[20] Indeed, what matters in the L&E framework is the practical capacity of legal rules to effectively influence behaviors and achieve their expected social consequences. So, L&E was at the time disruptive for one simple reason: it shifted the focus of legal study from the abstract world of concepts to the concrete functioning of society.

As observed before, the standard, traditional, dogmatic study of law was rigorously non-instrumental. On the contrary, L&E is consequentialist (or utilitarian) at

---

[17] Halpérin (2017).

[18] Grossi (2016), spec. Cap. II, *Sulla odierna fattualità del diritto* (*On the Current Factuality of Law*). See also Benedetti (2017).

[19] Galanter (1997).

[20] Cooter (1984).

its core. All L&E is about the consequences of a certain normative intervention, assessed in light of efficiency.

The differences between L&E schools lie rather in how the notion of efficiency is conceptualized: (a) if merely "*as a means*"—that is, simply intended as the capacity to reach the socially desired outcome, whatever it is, without waste, that is, with fewer costs, more rapidly, more effectively, etc. (so-called normative, Yale-style, *Calabresian* approach); or (b) if understood "*as an end*" in itself—that is, as the ultimate goal to be pursued by the legal order in its entirety (here efficiency is conceived as a "wealth-maximization" command: so-called positive, Chicago-style, *Posnerian* approach).[21]

However, in both cases, L&E analysis is inherently pragmatic and empirical by nature. In this regard, we can say that L&E is deeply *anti-Kelsenian*, inimical to, and incompatible with, his purist view of the task of jurists.

3 The Origins of Law & Economics in Italy. The Contribution of Pietro Trimarchi

The introduction of L&E in Italy was first and foremost due to the pioneering work of Pietro Trimarchi (1934 -), who is considered unanimously to be the founding father of Italian L&E.[22] Trimarchi is a prominent figure of Italian Private Law. He has been a Full Professor of Private Law since 1966 and then Emeritus Professor at the State University of Milan. He is the author of a famous textbook on Private Law (first edition: 1973) and an internationally recognized scholar in the field of L&E (he is an Honorary Member—Lifetime Achievement Award, 2005—of the European Association of Law and Economics, *EALE*). During his career, he participated in the legislative committees for the reforms of Italian law on product liability, company law and arbitration law.[23] He contributed academically to many areas of private law, such as its foundational concepts (especially causation), tort law, unjust enrichment, contract law, competition law, punitive damages, etc., always with an economic and non-dogmatic perspective. In 2020, the University of Trento Law School honored his path with a full Congress dedicated to him.

In 1961, while a Professor at the University of Urbino, he published an innovative monograph in defense of strict liability, an under-researched topic in Italy back

[21] For a more general discourse, Giabardo (2021).

[22] Of course, this claim is conventional. The relation between Economy and Law has been explored before, historically, even though in a different way and as a part of legal philosophy; *see*, e.g., Del Vecchio (1954). On these roots, see the very interesting essay by Lanneau (2015).

[23] On the figure of Pietro Trimarchi in the Italian L&E movement, *see*, recently, Bellantuono and Izzo (2022a); *see* also Frezza and Parisi (2005) and Parisi (2007). Trimarchi is the only one Italian included in the *Elgar Companion of Law & Economics* (positioned between George Stigler and Thorstein Veblen).

then: *Rischio e responsabilità oggettiva* (1961).[24] We can fairly say his book marks the starting point of L&E scholarship, in its modern meaning, in Italy. It is worth noting that the publication of Trimarchi's volume is (almost) contextual to the publication of Guido Calabresi's article *Some Thoughts on Risk Distribution and the Law of Torts* (1961), written independently, and Ronald Coase's essay *The problem of social cost* (1961).[25] These two contributions are conventionally regarded as marking the birth of L&E as an autonomous academic discipline in the United States.

In that seminal book, Trimarchi sought to assess whether, and to what extent, a general principle of strict liability for risks caused by enterprises existed—or should exist—in the Italian private law architecture. While such a principle was, at least rhetorically, denied by the Italian Civil code (which contains only particular and specific provisions on strict liability), the law in action—*diritto vivente*, "the living law"—of the time appeared to accept, at least partially, the principle of strict liability of the entrepreneur regarding enterprise risks.[26]

In his descriptive and normative analysis, Trimarchi embarked on a consequences-oriented reasoning on the functions of strict liability of entrepreneurs for business risks. He considered especially the French and the English common law traditions—hence the profound comparative dimension of his work—which were more inclined to respond to the practical needs posed by the advent of industrialized societies and economic production. In the end, Trimarchi argued that in certain situations there is an economic justification to impose civil liability even when the damage is caused faultlessly, insofar as this helps to minimize social costs (that is, by incentivizing enterprises to adopt optimal levels of precaution).

Methodologically, the study of private law institutions was in his book linked to the workings of the economy and political choices, rejecting the traditional, dogmatic method. That approach represented an authentic change in the study of tort law doctrines.

4 The Evolutions. The "Tort Law & Economics" Explosion

Although part of the Italian legal academia was, at that time, skeptical about that novel approach, in the following years interest in L&E rapidly expanded.

---

[24] Trimarchi (1961).

[25] Coase (1991).

[26] "This work - writes Trimarchi in the first page of his book - aims to ascertain whether and to what extent a principle of strict liability for enterprise risk is realized within the Italian legal system. It is true that such a principle is officially and authoritatively denied in the report by the Minister of Justice accompanying the Civil Code, and it is frequently rejected in the reasoning of the judgments of the Court of Cassation. However, if we look beyond formulas and declarations of principle and examine the law "in action", we must acknowledge that, at least to some extent, the entrepreneur is subjected to strict liability for the risks associated with their business activity". (my transl.), Trimarchi (1961), at p. 1.

The 1970s and the 1980s are the years of the Italian L&E explosion (although, at that time, only within Private Law). The studies published during that time marked and influenced the lines of investigations for the following decades.

The 1970s and the 1980s are the golden decades for L&E in the United States, too. In 1970, Guido Calabresi, Professor at Yale Law School, published his brilliant book *The Costs of Accidents. A Legal and Economic Analysis*, one of the most foundational advancements in the field, ever.[27] Pietro Trimarchi wrote a review of the original version.[28] Calabresi's contribution was then translated into Italian in 1975 by three comparative law professors at the University of Florence: Anna de Vita, Vincenzo Varano, and Vincenzo Vigoriti.[29] In 2015, that first edition was reprinted, with a new presentation by Enrico Al Mureden. Stefano Rodotà (1933–2017)—as we will see, a key figure in Italian L&E scholarship—wrote the foreword to the first Italian edition, and Antonio Gambaro wrote a review of the first Italian translation.[30]

It is important to note that between Guido Calabresi (who was born and raised in Milan before moving to the United States at the age of three) and the Italian universities the relationship has always been very entrenched, not only academically, but also at a personal level. His contributions are essential to understand Italian tort law and his ideas have shaped past and present developments of Italian debates. Nearly all of Calabresi's works have been translated (certainly the most important ones) and thoroughly discussed, and they all had a major influence on the trajectories of Italian scholarship.[31] He also contributed to many Italian collective books, seminars, presentations and classes. He received six degrees *honoris causa* from different Italian law schools (the first one being awarded by the University of Turin, in 1982, at the initiative of Professors Rodolfo Sacco and Norberto Bobbio) and lately he was awarded a PhD *ad honorem* from the University of Rome "La Sapienza" (10 May 2018).

Due to the deep influence of Guido Calabresi, it is no surprise therefore that tort law was—and to a certain extent still is—at the center of the reflections on L&E in Italy. The economic perspective in tort law is so pervasive that it is nearly impossible today to study the rules on damages and responsibility in Italy without referencing their economic and behavioural perspective. The L&E perspective of tort law has been particularly influential in courts, and in particular in the jurisprudence of the Italian Supreme Court. In fact, in the Italian Civil code there are only a few general provisions on extracontractual liability, which have not undergone significant changes since 1942. The activity and creativity of judges ensured that the architecture of Italian tort law kept pace with the social, technological and economic

---

[27] Calabresi (1970). As known, in that book, among many others influential ideas, Calabresi argued that tort law is not about *avoiding* damages, but rather *minimizing* their social cost, ensuring thereby the effective functioning of society. This perspective positioned tort law as both a social and public concern.

[28] Trimarchi (1971).

[29] De Vita et al. (1975).

[30] Gambaro (1975).

[31] Recently, Bellantuono and Izzo (2022b).

innovations that have occurred since. It would not be exaggerated to say that, in Italy, tort law is in the main a product of judicial law-making.

Without claiming to be exhaustive, among the legal scholars—all comparative private lawyers by training—who have contributed most to tort law, it is worth mentioning Guido Alpa (a disciple of Stefano Rodotà), who dedicated many works not only to the law of accidents and product liability, but also to the general method of L&E and its coordinates[32]; Pier Giuseppe Monateri, who contributed especially to the comparative dimension of tort law,[33] and Giulio Ponzanelli, who specializes in comparative tort law, personal injuries, insurance law and punitive damages.[34] All these streams of inquiry are very vital nowadays, too.

Of course, in those decades, other tracks of investigation in L&E outside the sphere of tort law originated, too: Property Law (see *infra*), Contract Law, in all its facets (notably, Roberto Pardolesi, who studied in Chicago, contributed to antitrust and consumer law[35]), Unjust Enrichment and Restitutions (Paolo Gallo[36]), the Law of Trust and Fiduciary Law and Law & Globalization (Michele Graziadei[37]), and Industrial and Commercial law (Francesco Denozza[38]).

4.1 *Law & Economics and* "The Social". *The Case of Property Law*

During the 1960s and 1970s, many Western countries underwent a process of radical change in their ideological backgrounds. It is what Duncan Kennedy, in his famous periodization of legal thought, dubbed "The Social" (1900–1968), that is, in his words, a particular *legal consciousness*—contraposed to the previous one called "Classical Legal Thought"—characterized by the preeminence of ideas such as social justice, social function, solidarity, welfare, and by a deep and shared desire for reforms.[39] In that epoch, many classical liberal notions of private and contract law that were central in earlier L&E analysis—such as freedom of contract, private autonomy, will theory, etc.—were submitted to critique.

In Italy, too, during the 1970s, legal scholars began to get more acquainted with public policies and the social impact of rules and became more engaged in political

[32] *Ex multis*, Alpa (1975, 1987, 2017).

[33] *Ex multis*, Monateri (1995).

[34] *Ex multis*, Ponzanelli (1992).

[35] *See*, e.g., Cucinotta et al. (2002).

[36] In English, Gallo (1992); *see* also Gallo (1998).

[37] Graziadei (2022, 2017, 2015, 2014).

[38] In general, Denozza (2002).

[39] Duncan Kennedy (2001) provides the following definition of "legal consciousness": "(...) a conceptual vocabulary, organizational schemes, modes of reasoning, and characteristic arguments (...) I will refer repeatedly to the consciousness, understood as a vocabulary of concepts and typical arguments, as a *langue*, or language (...)".

change.[40] Many legal studies that were published during that decade used Marxist categories and a Marxist vocabulary in order to interpret social and legal reality.[41] Over the following years, the leftist political movement (in the broader sense of the word) of Critical Legal Studies—championed, in the United States, by Duncan Kennedy—had a certain impact on part of the Italian academy. The notion of "social function" was at the center of those kinds of studies in almost all the areas of private law, and also in civil justice, family law, and labor law.[42]

In that political context, property law was an important part of the L&E analysis. The interest of Italian scholars in property law—studied through non-dogmatic lenses—was quite recent. Stefano Rodota's early work *Note critiche in tema di proprietà* (1960)[43] had a noticeable influence in shaping the future juridical and social discussions. In that quite extensive essay, Rodotà sought to explore the "historicity", and thus contingency, of the category of property and its inevitable connection with political questions. His reconstruction of the "*social function*" of private property—as explicitly recognized by art. 42 of the Italian Constitution—opened up an entire school of thought that went on questioning the traditional distinction between the "private" and the "public" in all private law institutions. Rodotà's perspective was genuinely critical. The scope of his investigation was not to elucidate how to allocate, and then protect, legal entitlements in order to reach an efficient use of resources (like it would have later been in the well-known study by Calabresi and Melamed[44]), but rather to unmask and debunk the claimed *naturalness* of property rights and read them in the light of constitutional and collective values of social justice.[45]

Property law has since then become a major field of L&E scholarship, explored through comparative eyes by other private lawyers, with different positions. Among them, Antonio Gambaro (Emeritus Professor of Comparative Private Law at the State University of Milan, co-author of an important monograph on comparative property law between France, Italy and Germany[46]) and, along the same path traced by Rodotà, Maria Rosaria Marella[47] and Ugo Mattei. In particular, Mattei, in many past and recent works, sought to reconsider the ideological structure of traditional private property, highlighting its historical and political links to the classical liberal paradigm and envisioning new forms of common rights on goods. In fact, the study

[40] In the Italian scholarship, on the methodological revolution of the 1970s in many areas of legal education, *see* Nivarra (2008).

[41] From an historical and backward-looking viewpoint, Barcellona (2000). See also, for an important instance of that moment in the study of civil procedural institutions, Chiarloni (1975, reprinted, 2023).

[42] Macario, Miletti (2017); Barcellona (1997).

[43] Rodotà (1960).

[44] Calabresi and Melamed (1972).

[45] *See* Marini (2019), in an article that explores more at large the contributions of Rodotà.

[46] Candian et al. (1992); Gambaro (1996).

[47] E.g., Marella (2012, 2014).

of "commons" is an entirely new stream of L&E research that is still well alive in present days.[48]

The academic and socioeconomic discussion around the various forms of properties was not alien to political activism, either. Between 2007 and 2008, the so-called "*Rodotà Committee*" (*Commissione sui beni pubblici, Committee on Public Goods*) was created within the Italian Ministry of Justice. It consisted of a panel of legal experts called to elaborate the reform of public goods in the Italian civil code. Mattei himself was part of that Committee. Some years later Mattei also animated the Italian referendum against the privatization of water service (in 2011), which resulted in the victory of those who supported water as a common good.

Other fields of discussion connected to the issue of "commons" are now environmental and ecology law,[49] the law of the cities and urban contexts,[50] and the legal and social dimensions of the occupation of public spaces.

5 Latest Developments. Critical Comparative Law & Economics

One of the most debated and recent lines of research within the Italian (but not only Italian) L&E scholarship is the "Comparative Law & Economics" project. Oversimplifying: this project—advanced since the early 2000s—aims to make visible the ideological underpinnings of the L&E enterprise as applied to different realities, as well as its often unspoken political claims.[51] This critical reflection is wider in scope than *micro* L&E (L&E that focuses on specific law institutions) and questions the movement at its foundations. According to this, L&E—a methodology born and raised in the cultural *milieu* of the United States—would hide a hegemonic side. What this movement seeks to do is thus to debunk the pretense of scientific objectivism and political neutrality (or *innocence*) of L&E by showing how it promotes a neoliberal agenda, made up of cyclical waves of privatization and assaults on national welfare states. In this view, L&E becomes an ideological tool linked to global and financial institutions (such as the World Bank, the International Monetary Fund, the World Trade Organization, but also non-profit organizations, transnational corporations, the tech industry, and the like) that aim to impose a new legal order based on global capitalism. Within this framework, legal rules are treated as commodities, that is as entities that can be exchanged, exported, or imported like any other good. This would lead to an "americanization" of law, especially for

---

[48] E.g., Mattei et al. (2023).

[49] Mattei and Quarta (2019).

[50] Mattei and Quarta (2015).

[51] *See*, e.g., Mattei and Monti (2001); Mattei (1994). On this project, generally, Caterina (2012), Eisenberg and Ramello (2016); Vargas Weil (2011). Also, Ajani (2001).

countries of the Global South and those that do not belong to the Western Legal Tradition.[52]

In Mattei's words:

> The distinctive American flavour of traditional law and Economics leaves open a fundamental question that Comparative Law and Economics attempts to tackle: what is the legitimacy of a scholarly paradigm when applied outside the cultural context in which it has been developed (…)? What are the political implications of using L&E outside of the cultural environment in which it has developed? (…) In other words: Is the diffusion of L&E outside of the political context of the US an episode of hegemonic diffusion of US law or are we in front of a new legal order (…)?

The absence of opposition, or even critical debates, on this matter in Europe should thus be regarded:

> with worry particularly because the traditional grand theory of L&E has been successfully received and implemented by the new almighty producers of global law, the international institutions of global governance, both private and public (…). the traditional L&E scholar is at high risk of being transformed in an ideological weapon of hegemony (…)

More generally, these concerns were part of a larger debate pointing out at the pretense of L&E to measure the laws and legal systems by ranking them according to a set of economic indicators of performance (as exemplified by the now-paused "Doing Business Reports" of the World Bank). This operation—it is said—might risk ignoring the role of other, and perhaps overriding, values besides efficiency, which it would nonetheless be important to consider, instead, such as justice, equality, culture, history, etc.[53]

5.1 New Directions and New Methodologies in Italy

Despite its critics, L&E is now by and large an accepted and fully recognized tool of analysis in Italy. In recent years, L&E has attracted the attention of legal philosophers, too—especially of those linked to the analytical tradition—who gave this field of inquiry a rigorous foundation and a robust theoretical basis. Objects of research here include the philosophical premises of L&E—that is, as seen, essentially American Legal Realism and Pragmatism—and what reasoning in terms of weighting between costs and benefits tells us about the nature of rules.[54]

One of the major changes in the Italian scenario of L&E over the past two decades is probably its expansion outside the traditional domain of Private Law. It is a fact that L&E methodology has now permeated some previously neglected areas

[52] Mattei (1994).

[53] On the pretense to measure the law, in the Italian scholarship, see Gambaro (2012); Denozza (2012). In the specific context of civil justice, critically, Caponi (2018). More generally, from a critical comparative law standpoint, Glenn (2001).

[54] Chiassoni (1991, 1992, 2013, 2016); Canale (2013); Tuzet (2017, 2018).

of law—often following past and current discussions that originated mostly overseas. It is not possible here to delve into each of these areas.

Suffice it to provide an overview of the current situation.

First, Criminal Law and Criminology. The fact that the Criminal L&E is a *latecomer* in Italian scholarship (let us say, from the late 1990s onwards) is quite surprising, given that probably the very first international figure of the economic analysis of crimes and criminal sanctions is the Italian philosopher Cesare Beccaria (1738–1794). In fact, his well-known *Trattato dei delitti e delle pene*, 1764 (*An Essay on Crime and Punishment*) openly inspired the early works of Gary Becker (1930–2014, Nobel Laureate in Economic Sciences in 1992) on the rationality of criminals and the optimal level of the State response. Becker is rightly considered the initiator of Criminal L&E in its modern sense and his research lies at the base of this research in Italy, too.[55]

Second, Public and Constitutional Law and Public Administration, along the path of the Public Choice Theory (that is, the investigation, using the tools of the Rational Choice model, of the dynamics between citizens and political-institutional agents).[56]

Third, an unfortunately underexplored—yet potentially extremely rich—area of research for L&E is Civil Procedure and Dispute Resolution. Exceptions in this area are represented by topics such as Class and Collective Actions,[57] Evidence Law,[58] Access to Justice,[59] and Litigation Costs and Funding.[60] However, it should be noted that procedural topics are often treated from a L&E perspective also by economists, in Economics departments, rather than by civil procedural law scholars, who are, generally speaking, more tied to positive law, codes, and traditional legal dogmatics—although this is beginning to change.

Other growing and interdisciplinary fields of law in Italy that are dealt with micro- (but also macro-) economic tools—fields that could not be adequately studied with traditional instruments—include, in a non-exhaustive list: EU governance, environmental and food regulation, carbon market and climate change, corporate social responsibility, data governance and privacy, labor market and job regulations,[61] corporate governance, financial markets, corruption law, artificial intelligence and

[55] Becker (1968). In the Italian Criminal Law doctrine, e.g., Paliero (2006), Pesce (2011). In the L&E one, Ramello and Marciano (2018).

[56] *See* Napolitano and Abrescia (2009).

[57] E.g., Giussani (1996). In the Economics literature, e.g., Cassone and Ramello (2011), Ramello (2019); Cenini et al. (2011); Ramello (2019).

[58] Pi et al. (2020), Guerra et al. (2018).

[59] Segatti (2024, 2016).

[60] D'Alessandro (2019); Poncibò and D'Alessandro (2021).

[61] Ichino (2001).

machine responsibility,[62] migration, legal aspect of sharing economy, housing law,[63] and more.

Lastly, it is important to point out that Italian L&E is not just expanding its traditional reach, but it is revolutionizing its own dominant paradigms and finalities, too.

In this, Behavioural L&E is now a significant, although still emerging, part of L&E in Italy. As known, this approach examines the limitations of human reason by drawing on the discoveries from cognitive sciences, psychology in particular. It includes the role of emotions and feelings in decision-making and seeks to deconstruct, thus, the classical rational choice model on which the functioning of the market was theoretically based (it is the critique to the so-called *homo oeconomicus*, the perfectly informed and perfectly calculative individual).[64]

The research on these topics has surely been pushed by numerous soft law instruments supported by international institutions and the European Union. Many of them are seeking to encourage new forms of "better" or "smarter" regulations for an entire range of diverse and sensible political issues that require large-scale collective behavioural shifts (such as, e.g., environmental protection and climate change, sustainability, public health policies). Law- and policy-makers are therefore the primary audience for all these studies. A typical form of new regulation is the strategic use of non-authoritative and non-binding instruments, called "nudges".[65] These seek to guide behaviour by subtly pushing agents towards the desired (more efficient) outcome, without the imposition of a proper sanction; instead, the undesired outcome is made less accessible and less efficient to reach, fostering spontaneous compliance.

All these lines of research, with all their shades and variations, are tremendously promising and there is no doubt that they will represent an increasingly significant part of the Italian L&E context, which is now more open than ever to expanding beyond the realm of law strictly considered.

References

Ajani G (2001) Legal change and economic performance. Glob Jurist Adv 1(1):1–12. https://doi.org/10.2202/1535-1661.1016

Alpa G (1975) Responsabilità del produttore e tutela del consumatore. Giuffrè, Milano

Alpa G (1987) Interpretazione economica del diritto (Economic Analysis of Law). Novissimo Digesto Italiano, *appendice* IV, UTET, Torino, pp 315–324

Alpa G (2017) Stefano Rodotà, innovatore del metodo giuridico. Politica del diritto 3:495–498

[62] Calabresi and Al Mureden (2021), Guerra et al. (2022).

[63] Sardo et al. (2024). See also the European Research Council Project: "*HABITAT: How European Big Cities and Legal Systems Trigger Urban Inequality*", won by A. Sardo, at the University of Genoa School of Law.

[64] Vella (2023).

[65] Bombelli (2019); Zorzetto (2019b).

Barcellona M (1997) L'«idea del sociale» nella teoria del diritto privato: il caso italiano (ma non solo). Riv Trimest Dirit Proced Civ 51(3):717–733

Barcellona M (2000) La scienza giuridica italiana ed il marxismo, prima e dopo «l'uso alternativo del diritto». Rivista critica di diritto privato 18(4):715–739

Becker GS (1968) Crime and punishment: an economic approach. J Polit Econ 76(2):169–217

Bellantuono G, Izzo U (eds) (2022a) Il contributo di Piero Trimarchi all'analisi economica del diritto. Atti del Convegno 16–18 dicembre 2020, Università di Trento, Quaderni della Facoltà di Giurisprudenza 56, Trento. https://iris.unitn.it/handle/11572/333138

Bellantuono G, Izzo U (eds) (2022b) Il rapporto tra diritto, economia e altri saperi: la rivincita del diritto. Atti della Lectio Magistralis di Guido Calabresi in occasione della chiusura dell'anno accademico del Dottorato in Studi Giuridici Comparati ed Europei. Facoltà di Giurisprudenza. Trento, 24 ottobre 2019, Quaderni della Facoltà di Giurisprudenza 55, Trento. https://iris.unitn.it/handle/11572/333104

Benedetti G (2017) "Ritorno al diritto" ed ermeneutica dell'effettività. Riv Trimest Dirit Proced Civ 72(2):763–781

Bombelli G (2019) Processi decisionali e categorie giuridiche: tra razionalità "classica" e spunti dal *nudging*. Teoria e critica della regolazione sociale 18:25–40

Calabresi G (1970) The costs of accidents: a legal and economic analysis. Yale University Press, New Haven

Calabresi G (1975) Costo degli incidenti e responsabilità civile. Analisi economico-giuridica. (translation by De Vita A, Varano V, Vigoriti V). Giuffrè, Milano; original work published in 1970)

Calabresi G (2016) The future of law and economics: essays in reform and recollection. Yale University Press, New Haven

Calabresi G, Al Mureden E (2021) Driveless cars. Intelligenza artificiale e futuro della mobilità. Il Mulino, Bologna

Calabresi G, Melamed D (1972) Property rules, liability rules, and inalienability: one view of the cathedral. Harv Law Rev 85(6):1089–1128

Canale D (2013) Forme e usi della Law and Economics. Ars interpretandi 18(2):27–42

Candian A, Gambaro A, Pozzo B (1992) Property, Propriété, Eigentum. Corso di diritto privato comparato. Cedam, Padova

Caponi R (2018) "Doing business" as a purpose of civil justice? The impact of World Bank doing business indicators on the reforms of civil justice. In: Althammer C, Roth H (eds) Instrumentalisierung von Zivilprozessen. Mohr Siebeck, Tübingen, pp 79–91

Caroccia F, Pardolesi R (2014) Analisi economica del diritto: "the Italian job". Foro italiano 137(9):193–214

Cassone A, Ramello GB (2011) The simple economics of class action: private provision of club and public goods. Eur J Law Econ 32:205–224. https://doi.org/10.1007/s10657-011-9254-7

Caterina R (2012) Comparative law and economics. In: Smits JM (ed) Elgar Encyclopedia of comparative law. Edward Elgar Publishing, Cheltenham and Northampton, pp 191–197

Cenini M, Luppi B, Parisi F (2011) Incentive effects of class actions and punitive damages under alternative procedural regimes. Eur J Law Econ 32:229–240. https://doi.org/10.1007/s10657-011-9241-z

Chiarloni S (2023) Introduzione allo studio del diritto processuale civile. Collana "La memoria del diritto", XIII, TrE-Press, Università degli Studi Roma Tre, Dipartimento di Giurisprudenza, Roma (original work published in 1975). https://romatrepress.uniroma3.it/wp-content/uploads/2023/05/intr-schi.pdf

Chiassoni P (1991) L'analisi economica del diritto negli Stati Uniti: formalismo o realismo? Quadrimestre:128–179

Chiassoni P (1992) Law and economics. L'analisi economica del diritto negli Stati Uniti. Giappichelli, Torino

Chiassoni P (2013) Modelli economici e scienza del diritto: considerazioni introduttive. Ars interpretandi, Rivista di ermeneutica giuridica 2:7–26

Chiassoni P (2016) La terra promessa del professor Calabresi. Contratto e impresa 32:608–615
Coase RH (1991) The problem of social cost. J Law Econ:1–44
Cooter R (1984) Prices and sanctions. Columbia Law Rev 84:1523–1560. https://doi.org/10.2307/1122472
Cooter R, Mattei U, Monateri P, Pardolesi R, Ullen T (2006) Il mercato delle regole. Analisi economica del diritto civile. Il Mulino, Bologna
Cucinotta A, Pardolesi R, Van den Bergh R (eds) (2002) Post-Chicago developments in antitrust law. Edward Elgar, Cheltenham, Northampton
D'Alessandro E (ed) (2019) Perspectives on third party funding in Italy. Ledizioni, LediPublishing, Milano
Del Vecchio G (1954) Diritto ed Economia. Studium, Roma
Denozza F (2002) Norme efficienti. L'analisi economica delle regole giuridiche. Giuffrè, Milano
Denozza F (2012) È possibile una misurazione delle prestazioni dei sistemi giuridici? Annuario di diritto comparato e di studi legislativi, 73–80
Eisenberg T, Ramello GB (eds) (2016) Comparative law and economics. Edward Elgar Publishing, Cheltenham and Northampton
Ferraro F, Zorzetto S (eds) (2022) Exploring the province of legislation. Theoretical and practical perspectives in Legisprudence, Legisprudence library, vol 9. Springer, Cham. https://doi.org/10.1007/978-3-030-87262-5
Frezza G, Parisi F (2005) Pietro Trimarchi (1934 -). In: Backhaus JG (ed) Elgar companion to law and economics, 2nd edn. Edward Elgar Publishing, Cheltenham and Northampton, pp 709–726
Galanter M (1997) The path of the law ands. Wis Law Rev:375–386
Gallo P (1992) Unjust enrichment: a comparative analysis. Am J Comp Law 40:431–465
Gallo P (1998) Analisi economica del diritto. Giappichelli, Torino
Gambaro A (1975) Costo degli incidenti e responsabilità civile. Responsabilità civile e previdenza: 375–385
Gambaro A (1996) L'analisi economica e la ricerca della logica proprietaria. Rivista critica di diritto privato: 235–244
Gambaro A (2012) Misurare il diritto? Annuario di diritto comparato e di studi legislativi 21: 17–47
Giabardo CV (2021) Efficiency as a means and as an end: some thoughts on happiness, wealth and justice in the legal economic debate. In: Almanza D, Pereira M (eds) A economia comportamental aplicada ao direito: estudos sobre racionalidade, políticas públicas e leis. Íthala, Curitiba, pp 57–74
Giussani A (1996) Studi sulle class actions. Cedam, Padova
Glenn HP (2001) Are legal traditions incommensurable? Am J Comp Law 49(1):133–145
Graziadei M (2014) Virtue and utility: fiduciary law in civil law and common law jurisdictions. In: Gold AS, Miller PB (eds) Philosophical foundations of fiduciary law. Oxford University Press, Oxford, pp 287–301. https://doi.org/10.1093/acprof:oso/9780198701729.003.0015
Graziadei M (2015) The many voices of the law in a globalised world: legal monism, legal pluralism, and the new tasks of comparative law. Annuario di diritto comparato e di studi legislativi, pp 485–502
Graziadei M (2017) Dentro le dinamiche della globalizzazione: questioni di riconoscimento e di giustizia distributiva. Annuario di diritto comparato e di studi legislativi, pp 306–323
Graziadei M (2019a) Not on the other side of the channel! Review of Rechtsdogmatik in England. Rechtsgeschichte. Journal of the Max Planck Institute for European Legal History. http://rg.rg.mpg.de/en/article_id/1294
Graziadei M (2019b) A bridge to cross. Legal education, the civil lawyers and the common law: an Italian perspective. In: Saucier J, Campos H (eds) Viajes y fronteras de la enseñanza del derecho comparado. Pontificia Universidad Católica del Perú, Lima, pp 73–91
Graziadei M (2022) La proprietà fiduciaria, la proprietà nell'interesse altrui, e i trust. Un itinerario. Trusts, pp. 26–47
Graziadei M, Zhang L (2023) On civil codes: a twenty-first century perspective. In: Graziadei M, Zhang L (eds) The making of the civil codes. Ius Gentium: comparative perspectives on law and justice. Springer, Singapore, p 104. https://doi.org/10.1007/978-981-19-4993-7_1

Grossi P (2001) Mitologie giuridiche della modernità. Giuffrè, Milano

Grossi P (2016) Ritorno al diritto. Laterza, Bari

Guastini (1991) Dogmatica giuridica. Digesto delle discipline civilistiche VII. Utet Giuridica, Torino

Guerra A, Luppi B, Parisi F (2018) Standards of proof and civil litigation: a game-theoretic analysis, the B.E. J Theor Econ 19(1):1–19. https://doi.org/10.1515/bejte-2017-0005

Guerra A, Parisi F, Pi D (2022) Liability for robots I: legal challenges. J Inst Econ 18(3):331–343. https://doi.org/10.1017/S1744137421000825

Halpérin JL (2017) L'École de l'exégèse. In: Sellers M, Kirste S (eds) Encyclopedia of the philosophy of law and social philosophy. Springer, Dordrecht. https://doi.org/10.1007/978-94-007-6730-0_339-1

Harnay S (2015) A short history of economic analysis of law in France 1980–2014. Preliminary milestones. History of economic ideas. Law and Economics in 20th-century Europe: History and Methodology 23(3):121–146

Ichino P (2001) Il dialogo tra economia e diritto del lavoro. Rivista italiana di diritto del lavoro 20(2):165–201

Irti N (1979) L'età della decodificazione. Giuffrè, Milano

Irti N (1999) L'età della codificazione, vent'anni dopo. Giuffrè, Milano

Jestaz P, Jamin C (1998) The entity of French doctrine: some thoughts on the community of French legal writers. Leg Stud 18(4):415–437

Kelsen H (1941) The pure theory of law and analytical jurisprudence. Harv Law Rev 55(1):44–70

Kennedy D (2001) Three globalizations of law and legal thought: 1850-2000. In: Trubek M, Santos A (eds) The new law and economic development: a critical appraisal. Cambridge University Press, Cambridge, pp 19–73

La Porta R, Lopez-de-Silanes F, Shleifer A (2008) The economic consequences of legal origins. J Econ Lit 46(2):285–332. https://scholar.harvard.edu/files/shleifer/files/consequences_jel_final.pdf

Lanneau R (2015) To what extent did European legal theory pave the way for an economic analysis of law? Insights from Kelsen, Hart and Del Vecchio. History of economic ideas. Law Econ 20th-Century Europe: Hist Methodol 23(3):195–224. https://www.jstor.org/stable/43924295

León L (1991) El análisis económico del derecho civil en Italia. Un inventario histórico-bibliográfico mínimo Themis 42:317–335

Macario F, Miletti MN (eds) (2017) La funzione sociale nel diritto privato tra XX e XXI secolo. , TrE-Press, Università degli Studi Roma Tre, Dipartimento di Giurisprudenza, Roma

Marella MR (2012) Oltre il pubblico e il privato. Per un diritto dei beni comuni. Ombre Corte, Verona

Marella MR (2014) La funzione sociale oltre la proprietà. Progetto EuroNomade. http://www.euronomade.info/?p=2114

Marini G (2019) Trasformare la critica: l'eredità di Stefano Rodotà (in margine a "Vivere la democrazia"). Rivista critica del diritto privato 37(4):615–643

Mattei U (1994) Efficiency in legal transplants: an essay in comparative law and economics. Int Rev Law Econ 14(1):3–19. https://doi.org/10.1016/0144-8188(94)90032-9

Mattei U, Monti A (2001) Comparative law & Economics: borrowing and resistance. Glob Jurist Front 1(2):1–24. https://doi.org/10.2202/1535-1653.1038

Mattei U, Pardolesi R (1991) Law and economics in civil law countries: a comparative approach. Int Rev Law Econ 11:265–275. https://doi.org/10.1016/0144-8188(91)90004-W

Mattei U, Quarta A (2015) Right to the city or urban communing? Thoughts on the generative transformation of property law. Ital Law J 1(2):303–327

Mattei U, Quarta A (2019) The turning point in private law. Ecology, technology and the commons. Edward Elgar Publishing, Cheltenham and Northampton

Mattei U, Quarta A, Valguarnera F, Fisher RJ (eds) (2023) Property meeting the challenge of the commons (conference proceedings). Ius Comparatum, Global studies in comparative law 59. Springer, Cham. https://doi.org/10.1007/978-3-031-25218-1

Merryman JH (1965) The Italian style I: doctrine. Stanford Law Rev 18:39–65

Monateri PG (1995) Risultati e regole. (Un'analisi giuridica dell'analisi economica del diritto). Rivista Critica del Diritto Privato, pp 605–619
Napolitano G, Abrescia M (2009) Analisi economica del diritto pubblico. Teorie, applicazioni e limiti. Il Mulino, Bologna
Nivarra L (ed) (2008) Gli anni Settanta del diritto privato. Atti del Convegno 7–8 luglio 2006, Università di Palermo, Facoltà di Giurisprudenza 11. Giuffrè, Milano
Paliero CE (2006) L'economia della pena (un work in progress). Riv Ital Dirit Proced Penal:1336–1401
Pardolesi R (1992) Law & economics in Italy. In: Bouckaert, De Geest (eds) Bibliography of law and economics 2(1):592–595
Pardolesi R, Bellantuono G (2015) Law & Economics in Italy. Some thoughts about the academic and judicial reception of EAL. Law Econ 20th-Century Eur Hist Methodol 23(3):89–119
Pardolesi R, Tassone B (2003) I giudici e l'analisi economica del diritto privato. Il Mulino, Bologna
Pardolesi R, Tassone B (2005) I giudici e l'analisi economica del diritto privato due anni dopo. Mercato concorrenza regole VII(3):579–600
Parisi F (2007) Laudatio: Pietro Trimarchi. Rev Law Econ 3(1):3–9. https://doi.org/10.2202/1555-5879.1123
Pesce F (2011) Alle radici di un difficile binomio: analisi economica e diritto penale. L'indice penale: 29–68
Pi D, Parisi F, Luppi B (2020) Quantifying reasonable doubt. Rutgers Univ Law Rev 72:455–508
Poncibò C, D'Alessandro E (2021) State of play of the EU private litigation funding landscape and the current EU rules applicable to private litigation funding, EPRS - European Parliamentary Research Service, https://www.europarl.europa.eu/RegData/etudes/STUD/2021/662612/EPRS_STU(2021)662612_EN.pdf
Ponzanelli G (1992) La responsabilità civile. Profili di diritto comparato. Il Mulino, Bologna
Ramello GB (2019) Class action and aggregate litigations. In: Marciano A, Ramello GB (eds) Encyclopedia of law and economics. Springer, pp 226–232. https://doi.org/10.1007/978-1-4614-7753-2_553
Ramello GB, Marciano A (2018) Cesare Beccaria: Back to the future of law and economics. Eur J Law Econ 46:271–274
Rodotà (1960) Note critiche in tema di proprietà. Riv Trimest Dirit Proced Civ:1252–1341
Sardo A et al (2024) The judicial response to rent controls in Europe: protecting property rights against state's intervention? Eur J Law Econ 58:221–281. https://doi.org/10.1007/s10657-024-09820-0
Segatti M (2016) A capabilities approach to access to justice. Unfulfilled promises, and promising strategies in the US and in Europe. Teoria Politica 6:335–359
Segatti M (2024) Equal access to justice. On the duty to pause, cool down, and listen. Springer (Law and Philosophy Library, vol. 145), Cham. https://doi.org/10.1007/978-3-031-52939-9
Trimarchi P (1961) Rischio e responsabilità oggettiva. Giuffrè, Milano
Trimarchi P (1971) Economia e diritto nel sistema della responsabilità civile. Politica del diritto 11(3):353
Tuzet G (2017) Note critiche sui rapporti tra diritto ed economia. In: Bernardini MG, Giolo O (eds) Le teorie critiche del diritto. Pacini, Pisa, pp 273–294
Tuzet G (2018) L'analisi economica come argomentazione giuridica. Teoria Jurídica Contemporanea 3(2):97–122. https://doi.org/10.21875/tjc.v3i2.21920
Vargas Weil E (2011) Map and territory in comparative law and economics. Glob J Comp Law 11(1):1–35. https://doi.org/10.1163/2211906X-11010001
Vella F (2023) Diritto ed economia comportamentale. Il Mulino, Bologna
Villa G (2015) Le idee di Guido Calabresi e la giurisprudenza italiana. In: L'analisi economica del diritto a quarant'anni dall'edizione italiana di Costo degli incidenti e responsabilità civile. Notizie di Politeia Rivista di etica e scelte pubbliche 31(4):93–101

Zorzetto S (2017) Some remarks about economic analysis of law in the Italian case law: consequentialism or equity in the legal reasoning? Rivista internazionale di filosofia del diritto 94:31–51

Zorzetto S (2019b) Rational, reasonable and nudged man. Teoria e critica della regolazione sociale 19:73–94. https://doi.org/10.7413/19705476005

Zorzetto S (2019c) Is economic analysis of law relevant in Italian case law? Some remarks about consequentialism and equity. In: Cserne P, Małecka M (eds) Law and economics as interdisciplinary exchange. Routledge, London, pp 158–188

Zorzetto S, Esposito F (2015) The rational and the reasonable. Brief notes about a topos of the Law and Economics in juristic style. In: Manzin M, Puppo F, Tomasi S (eds) Further steps towards a pluralistic approach. Studies on argumentation and legal philosophy. Quaderni della facoltà di giurisprudenza, 10, Università degli Studi di Trento, Trento, pp 81–106

Zorzetto S, Ferraro F (2019) Legislation and nudging. Towards a suitable definition. In: Oliver-Lalana D (ed) Conceptions and misconceptions of legislation. Legisprudence library 5. Springer, Cham, pp 107–129

Carlo Vittorio Giabardo is qualified as an Associate Professor in the sector of Civil Procedural Law and serves as a Senior Researcher in Civil Procedural Law at the Department of Law of the University of Turin. He co-teaches the course Climate Change Litigation. He was a Professor of Law at the Law Department of the Pontifical Catholic University of Peru, having previously been a Postdoctoral Researcher in Legal Theory at the University of Girona School of Law. In both institutions he taught Law and Economics. His main research areas include national and comparative civil procedural law, climate change litigation, and the economic analysis of law and procedure.

Law and Economics in Portugal: An Overview of the Last 20 Years

Raquel Franco

Abstract This chapter presents an overview on the evolution of the field of law and economics in Portugal for the past twenty years, as well as an examination of its current situation. Though the topic is still far away from standardized knowledge, or speech, within the relevant communities, some evolution has occurred within academia, the courts, and the public administration. The road ahead is still long, but might not be that winding.

1 Introduction

In the work that follows, the use of the expression "law and economics" instead of "economic analysis of law" is a purely esthetical choice, though well acquainted with the distinction put forward by GEOFFREY MILLER, that is not subscribed in these lines (no problem with law being, *sometimes*, a passive subject of economics).

> The term "law and economics" privileges the contribution of economics. The activity is done by economics, which is mentioned first; law is a passive subject. In the case of "law and economics" in contrast, the disciplines are described as equal partners, with a slight preference to law if any hierarchy is to be inferred. These linguistic differences mirror matters of substance. The "law and economics" is the use of economic principles and reasoning to understand legal materials. It is a branch of economics. Law comes into the picture as an object of study. Just as macroeconomics looks at matter such as employment, growth and productivity, "law and economics" looks at legal rules and institutions and seeks to analyze them from an economic point of view. "Law and economics", on the other hand, is a genuine partnership of two disciplines, each with something in contribute. Economics adds the

R. Franco, PhD (✉)
Faculty of Law, University of Lisbon, Lisbon, Portugal
e-mail: raquelfranco@fd.ulisboa.pt

S. Zorzetto et al. (eds.), *Developments in Law and Economics in the Italo-Iberoamerican Context*, Economic Analysis of Law in European Legal Scholarship 21, https://doi.org/10.1007/978-3-032-03317-8_16

> insights of economic science; law adds the understanding of complex institutions, politics and social policies.[1]

Aside from the esthetical appeal, the use of 'law and economics' instead of 'economic analysis of law does fit well with the distinction put forward more recently by Guido Calabresi. In his words:

> What I call Economic Analysis of Law uses economic theory to analyze the legal world. It examines that world from the standpoint of economic theory and, as a result of that examination, confirms, casts doubt upon, and often seeks reform of legal reality. In effect, it acts as an Archimedean place to stand and upon which to place a lever, a lever that permits the scholar, when appropriate, to argue for change in that legal reality. In its most aggressive and reformist mode, having looked at the world from the standpoint of economic theory, if it finds that the legal world does not fi t, it proclaims that world to be "irrational."
>
> What I call Law and Economics instead begins with an agnostic acceptance of the world as it is, as the lawyer describes it to be. It then looks to whether economic theory can explain that world, that reality. And if it cannot, rather than automatically dismissing that world as irrational, it asks two questions. The first is, are the legal scholars who are describing the legal reality looking at the world as it really is? Or is there something in their way of seeing the world that has led them to mischaracterize that reality?
>
> If, however, even a more comprehensive view of legal reality discloses rules and practices that economic theory cannot explain, Law and Economics asks the second question. Can economic theory be amplified, can it be made broader or more subtle (without thereby losing those characteristics that give it coherence and make it as powerful as it is) so that it can explain why the real world of law is as it is? If such a more nuanced theory can do this, Law and Economics then proposes that this expanded economic theory be used more broadly. It suggests that the changes imposed on economic theory to make it capable of explaining a specific legal reality be made part of economic theory generally.[2]

The evolution of law and economics from its early days in mid-twentieth century, hand in hand with the Chicago School of Economics strain of thought, foundationalist as it was, and even a little immodest in its idiosyncrasy, until the present, more flexible view represented in Calabresi's sneak peek at the future, has not been captured in Portugal. The shortage of academic debate, resulting from the negligence with which, in general, university has looked at this area, together with a Portuguese tradition that is not very receptive to interdisciplinarity, have defined the path of law and economics in Portugal as a short and very linear line.

For most of those who refer to law and economics and who work in the field, the project still identifies with the notion put forward by Nuno Garoupa: law and economics, also known as economic analysis of law, studies the answer to two fundamental questions: *(a)* a positive question, related to the impact of laws and regulations on the behaviour of individuals; and *(b)* a normative question, related to the relative advantages of norms in terms of efficiency and gains in social welfare.[3]

---

[1] See Miller (2011), pp. 459–460.

[2] See Calabresi (2016), pp. 2–4.

[3] See Garoupa (2005), p. 23.

Let's see what goes by law and economics in Portugal. Our work focuses mainly on the evolution contained in the last twenty years: even if not extremely productive, they show something more than the previous twenty.

2 Now and Then: What Has Evolved in the Last 20 Years of Law and Economics in Portugal

Twenty years ago in Portugal, law and economics was something like a niche field pertaining only to a few scholars teaching at some of the Portuguese Law Faculties. Legal education was still very traditional and that prevented *curricula* from changing for extended periods of time. Even though law and economics basic concepts were well known between those scholars, its major contributions were not yet disseminated among students and practitioners as there was a lack of scientific work in the field—although some important exceptions should be noted.[4]

The scenario began changing with the increase of interest on the topic, particularly from the part of academics working in fields with greater contact with economic science, such as competition, tax, and financial law, as well as those teaching economics in law faculties. The number of scientific contributions related to law and economics and the research work in the field improved, as did the *curricula* of the main public and private faculties of law—perhaps in response to a growing interest from the side of students, both at the undergraduate and graduate levels. Courts also began acknowledging the field, although mostly in terms of theoretical background and in most cases to criticize it (and not always very accurately).

Notwithstanding this gradual change in the outlook of the discipline for the past decades, some factors still prevent it from general dissemination and acceptance. One is surely the poor communication between the field of law and other scientific fields related to law and economics, such as economics and management, if one is thinking of traditional law and economics, as well as psychology, the neurosciences, anthropology, biology, just to name some, if one is thinking of behavioral law and economics. The other one is conservatism, which translates into a very traditional approach to the teaching of law and to the exercise of legal professions in general. Another aspect that has slowed down the development of law and economics in Portugal is the lack of investment in its teaching at undergraduate level, which is responsible for the creation of a giant barrier to entry in the discipline.[5]

Notwithstanding the slow pace at which the discipline has been developing in Portugal, it is possible to signal some areas of development, whether at the level of scientific production, court decisions, or even in the very penetration of economic language in regulatory texts—showing at least some acknowledgment of its significance and prominence.

---

[4] See Moura e Silva (2000b), p. 313.

[5] See Araújo (2008a), p. 21.

3 Academia

3.1 Law and Economics in Undergraduate and Graduate Courses

The subject is still very scarcely found in university teaching in Portugal, both in law courses and in economics courses. In Law courses, economics in general is an area that does not go into great depth, typically taught in two semesters of introductory notions of micro and macroeconomics, together with one or two semesters of international economic relations or simply international economics. In Economics courses, there is sometimes a discipline of foundations of law in the first year, and then elective disciplines of Business Law and European Law in the following years.

At the Faculty of Law of the University of Lisbon, where around 500 students enter *per* year,[6] at the undergraduate degree course, there is no teaching of this subject at undergraduate level. At the post-graduate level, it is taught on the master's degree course in Law and Legal Science, specialization in Legal Economics, which has a subject on law and economics. On the Masters in Law and Legal Practice and on Law and Legal Practice in the European Union, students can chose a subject on Behavioral Economics and Law. The Masters in Law and Management does not have a subject on law and economics or any other similar subject. In terms of Doctoral Courses, there is a research seminar on law and economics in the Legal and Economic Sciences Course, specialization in Law and Economics.[7]

At the Faculty of Law of the University of Coimbra, where around 400 students enter the undergraduate course, *per* years,[8] there is no teaching of the subject at undergraduate, master's, or doctoral level.[9]

At the Faculty of Law of the University of Porto, where around 180 students usually enter the undergraduate course,[10] there is no teaching of the subject at undergraduate, master's or doctoral level.[11]

At the Law Faculty of the Universidade Nova de Lisboa, where around 100 students enter each year the undergraduate course,[12] the subject of "Law and

---

[6] Data available at https://www.dges.gov.pt/guias/indcurso.asp?curso=9078.

[7] Information regarding the courses taught at Faculty of Law of the University of Lisbon can be found here: https://www.fd.ulisboa.pt/cursos/.

[8] Data available at https://www.dges.gov.pt/guias/indcurso.asp?curso=9078.

[9] Information regarding courses taught at the Faculty of Law of the University of Coimbra can be found here: https://www.uc.pt/en/fduc/options-for-study/.

[10] Data available at https://www.dges.gov.pt/guias/indcurso.asp?curso=9078.

[11] Information regarding courses taught at the Faculty of Law of the University of Lisbon can be found here: https://sigarra.up.pt/fdup/pt/cur_geral.cur_inicio.

[12] Data available at https://www.dges.gov.pt/guias/indcurso.asp?curso=9078.

Economics" is an optional subject in the 3rd and 4th years. However, it is not taught at master's or doctoral level.[13]

As for Undergraduate courses in Economics, the Lisbon School of Economics and Management Bachelor in Economics has a first year discipline on the Foundations of Law, but no law and economics. In master's courses, there is no specific mention to law and economics. The scenario is the same at Nova School of Business and Economics, with no specific mention to law and economics.[14,15]

The undergraduate student's lack of preparation is probably an inhibiting factor in the attendance of the subject in post-graduate education, either in master's degrees or doctorates as well as throughout professional life.[16] Interdisciplinarity is still a mirage in university teaching in Portugal, which influences the persistence of an enormous disconnection between areas of scientific knowledge in our country. Not only is there no tradition in this sense, but also the creation of links and forms of joint work and research between different areas is still often viewed with a resistant and reluctant eye. If this interdisciplinarity is not promoted at university level, it appears with greater difficulty further on in the practical application of knowledge that occurs throughout professional life.[17]

3.2 Scientific Research

Sinde Monteiro's vision on law and economics, expressed more than 40 years ago, still carries its influence over traditional legal thought. In an article published back in 1981, after considering several methodological questions regarding the place of law and economics in the context of the 'science of law' (jurisprudence), he concluded that law and economics could usefully constitute an auxiliary science of law, but not science of law itself.[18] This is still a very present idea in most of Portuguese legal academic thought, still akin to the idea of self-sufficiency of

[13] Information regarding courses taught at the Nova School of Law can be found here: https://novalaw.unl.pt/#.

[14] Information regarding the Lisbon School of Economics and Management can be found here: https://www.iseg.ulisboa.pt/study/undergraduate/economics#programme-details.

[15] Information regarding the Nova School of Business and Economics Program can be found here: https://www.novasbe.unl.pt/en/programs/bachelors/economics/program.

[16] See Araújo (2008a), p. 21.

[17] See Patrício (2017), p. 21.

[18] See Monteiro (1981), p. 57.

law—apart from scholars dedicated to law and economics and to a few that are more sympathetic to the topic.[19]

In 1992, Sousa Franco would offer a different view,[20] emphasizing the role of law and economics in contributing with a framework for the analysis of content and purpose in legal rules, thus making it possible to bring together law and its practice, though warning against a certain materialistic and individualistic tendency stemming from the field. In that year, law and economics was announced with some pomp by the legal magazine Sub Judice, in an issue that brought together national and international authors in contributions on the subject, namely the one by Sousa Franco mentioned above.

After these more doubtful initial steps, the 2000s would prove to be a more fruitful decade as regards scientific research in the area of law and economics in Portugal, with some names assuming prominent positions. This is the case of Fernando Araújo,[21] Paula Vaz Freire,[22] Miguel Moura e Silva,[23] Rute Saraiva[24] e Miguel Patrício,[25] from the University of Lisbon Faculty of Law, Nuno Garoupa, now a Professor of Law at the George Mason University—Antonin Scalia Law School, but who was previously a Professor at the Universidade Nova de Lisboa, both at the Law and at the Economics Faculties,[26] and Vasco Rodrigues, from Católica Porto Business School.[27] Outside academia, but still a strong contributor to the development of law in economics in Portugal, Judge João Ramos de Sousa is also a proficient contributor to the field, in courts as well as in scientific research.[28]

Outside this niche of strong contributors to the field, law and economics is still mostly estranged from scientific research and academia in general. A strong confusion persists in legal thinking, where economics, in general, and law and economics, as a *subspecies*, are still seen as technocratic, *short-sided-mathematical-and-mostly--dedicated-to-accounting* topics. Law and economics is too often considered as a vehicle for the subjugation of "natural" values such as justice and the dignity of the

[19] For example, Paulo Mota Pinto, refers to the "economization of law" as a reduction in the scope of goals to be pursued by law in which distributional problems would be necessarily cast aside. The author also sustains that law and economics endorses a methodological as well as anthropological individualism and also a vision of the individual which is mainly dominated by a kind of utilitarian rationality in which law is only an instrument to attain the goals of maximization. See Pinto (2008), p. 60.

[20] See Sousa Franco (1992), p. 143.

[21] See Araújo (2000, 2001, 2002, 2005, 2007a, b, 2008a, b).

[22] See Freire (2015, 2020, 2021).

[23] See Moura e Silva (2000a, b).

[24] See Saraiva (2014, 2016, 2017). The author focuses mainly on behavioral economics.

[25] See Patrício (2005, 2015, 2017).

[26] See Garoupa (2003a, b, 2008, 2014a, b, 2017).

[27] See Rodrigues (2007).

[28] See Sousa (1992a, b, c, 2003).

human person,[29,30] a deep-routed prejudice that certainly contributes to shaping up misjudgments from the part of potential students, investigators and applicators of law.

4 Court Decisions

The use of law and economics by Portuguese courts is very limited. In most of the cases, it consists only of generic—and critical—references to the discipline, without any practical use of it on the grounds of the Court's decision. There is one very rare exception in the Lisbon Court of Appeal, which will be detailed below.

4.1 Constitutional Court

In the Constitutional Court case-law we found merely two references to law and economics. The first one, in a 1996 decision,[31] concerned a situation of simulation of a sports employment contract and the discussion was about a conflict regarding the amount of compensation when the contract was terminated. The Court, in a single paragraph, refers to law and economics in the following terms:

> The situation ultimately demonstrates one of the basic hypotheses of the economic theory used by the "law and economics": people act rationally selfishly; they pursue their interests selfishly by acting rationally, that is, by taking decisions which, given knowledge of the end, the means at their disposal and the environment in which they act, are predictable, what

[29] Pointing out to the fact that the common objections to law and economics in Portugal are too often a result of plain ignorance about the significance of assumptions and goals of the discipline see Garoupa (2006), p. 102. The author also stresses that "the concept of economic efficiency is unfortunately often misunderstood. Economic efficiency means maximum benefit (private or social) at a given cost (private or social), or minimum cost for a given benefit, that is, the best legislative option in terms of maximum social welfare", also clarifying that "the benefits and costs to be taken into account in a rigorous analysis are not limited to monetary benefits and costs." (pp. 86–87). See also Araújo (2005), pp. 910–911, in which the author sustains that "subscribing to a perspective that, being peculiar to the "law and economics" current, seems to us, nevertheless, eminently defensible in the widest of modern views on Law and Politics, which is that the efficiency value exhausts, in the current open and pluralist societies, much of what is consensually demanded of justice. (...) Moreover, we have no difficulty in accepting one of Richard Posner's basic theses—despite the blunt and polemical intent always present in it—that all waste can be considered immoral in a world of scarce resources, and that it is precisely for this reason that many legal solutions end up promoting efficiency (even when they are not consciously aimed at it): is that in many of the options they enshrine there is no other "materiality" than that of repressing conducts whose only devaluation consists in entailing waste of resources.

[30] For example, Menezes Cordeiro criticizes law and economics for the "associality" of its pragmatist and realistic background. See Cordeiro (2005), pp. 135–136.

[31] Case 929/96, 10.07.1996.

is called "methodological individualism" or, to use the English expression, the "REMM hypothesis" (resourceful, evaluating, maximising man: v.Hans-Bernd Schäfer/Claus Ott, Manual de Análisis Económico del Derecho Civil, Madrid 1991, p.61 e ss.).

The Court's aim seems to have been simply to borrow the assumption of rationality used by economic science to characterize the conduct of a player and his club in a simulated contracts case. The Court does not go beyond a very superficial and uncritical reference to rationality in the context of law and economics, which seems to serve only the purpose of conferring a scientific seal of approval to its characterization of the conduct of the agents in the case. On the one hand, it does not deepen the behavioral model used by law and economics in any interesting way, on the other hand, it does not analyze it critically and, finally, the issue does not seem to acquire decisive relevance in the context of the Judgment.

Now, if in the previous Judgement the reference to law and economics is elusive, it is even less relevant in a decision dated 2002,[32] in which reference to the topic does not even appear in the Court's decision, but only in an explanation of vote issued by one of the judges of the panel, who expresses doubts about the lack of proportionality in the application of specific tributes called "taxas", which, in her opinion, should be analyzed from the point of view of «*the economic analysis of the law and with criteria of justice in the economic area*». It seems that the reference is mainly intended to emphasize the need to consider criteria of an economic nature when analyzing the principle of proportionality, rather than to refer to concepts specifically addressed by law and economics as an autonomous discipline.

4.2 Supreme Court of Justice

As for the Supreme Court of Justice, the highest body in the hierarchy of ordinary courts, there are several references to law and economics, the first in 2013 and then four others in 2014, always with the same content.[33] In all these cases, the Court pondered the issue of the concrete measure of a penalty, and in all of them it uses the same segment to refer to the proportionality of the penalty in relation to the offending conduct and the legal good at stake: "*legal certainty and security may be at stake when there is a wide margin of latitude in the penalty to be applied, leading to indeterminacy. Resorting to the principle of proportionality, a penalty cannot be applied that is greater than what the seriousness of the conduct merits or what is required to protect the legal good*". In a footnote to this statement there then appears the reference to law and economics: "*Using law and economics one cannot apply an excessive price to obtain an inferior benefit: if what is at stake is freedom, one can-*

[32] Case 115/02, 12.03.2002.

[33] Case 339/09.0GDSTS-A.S1, 06.02.2014; case 2610/06.3TBALM.S1, 10.09.2014; case 273/07.8PCGDM.S2 03.12.2014; case 1744/11.7JAPRT.P1, 21.05.2014; case 286/11.5JAFAR.SL, 25.05.2013.

not consider penalties that are disproportionate to the seriousness of the behavior. In fact, it is not only necessary to weigh the degree of freedom that is achieved through the criminal sanction and the benefit that is obtained from it, but also the different interventions of the criminal law itself. Here the first thing that must be considered is whether the intervention of criminal law is within the parameters suitable for the protection of the legal good."

In a more recent Judgment, dated 2019,[34] in a case of *culpa in contrahendo* in the context of negotiations of a credit agreement, the Court makes an almost empty reference to law and economics:

> Through pre-contractual liability the well-founded confidence of each party that the other will conduct the negotiations in good faith is directly protected (…). It should be pointed out, however, that the teleological basis of this discipline goes beyond the mere consideration of the particular interests at stake. The concern to defend the social values of security and the ease of legal commerce stands out particularly clearly. It is not unheard of for postulates from law and economics to be adduced.

4.3 Courts of Appeal

The Courts of Appeal of the common jurisdiction have the largest number of rulings with reference to law and economics.

4.3.1 Coimbra Court of Appeal

The Coimbra Court of Appeal, in a 2005[35] Judgment analyzing the liability of a concessionaire in a traffic accident caused by a dog, examines the extent of the concessionaire's liability and refers, in a footnote, as follows:

> IV - In the plan of legal policy, it seems right, even from the point of view of law and economics, the aggravation of the liability status of the one who dominates the source of danger" (Prof. Sinde Monteiro, in RLJ 131°, 112, 1st col.) Let us also return to the Judgement of the Supreme Court of 22nd June 2004: "The appearance of a large dog on the carriageway of a motorway is a recognised danger for those travelling on it. It is Brisa's responsibility to avoid this (and other) sources of danger, this abnormality. The motorist cannot be held responsible for proving Brisa's negligence or the origin of the dog because it was not his fault, nor does he have effective management, de facto power over the motorway (as a whole, including fences, access ramps and rest and service areas).
>
> V - Only the "duly verified case of force majeure" exonerates the debtor (the concessionaire) from its obligation to guarantee circulation in safe conditions (art. 799, no. 1 of the CC) and, in the event of non-performance, from the duty to repair the damage caused" (points IV and V of the respective summary).

---

[34] Case 2758/15.3T8BCL.G1.S1, 11.04.2019.

[35] Case 152/05, 12.04.2005.

In 2007,[36] the Court was deciding a case on the scope of damages, in particular whether the winning party's lawyer's fees should be paid by the losing party. At one point it makes the following assessment:

> This aspect (possible reimbursement to the winning party of his lawyer's fees) receives disparate treatment in different legal orders. In fact, in Comparative Law, two main orientations are recognized in this matter: the so-called "American rule" and the so-called "English rule"[23]. In the first of these, lawyer's fees are considered (outside the framework equivalent to our legal aid) to be a tolerable economic cost for most people and, as such, not recoverable through the compensation in which the losing party is condemned, except in situations in which a Law (or a contract) orders that this cost be charged to the losing party[24]. In the second situation - the English rule, also referred to as the "loser pays" rule - the losing party is responsible for the amount of the winning party's attorney's fees. This system, which is the one of English Law and is prevalent in Continental Systems, such as ours, is in turn divided into the group in which the "recovery" of that cost is made directly through a claim for damages (which is what happens in England[25], outside the framework of the so-called "legal aid") or is included in the compensation that is ("officially"[26]) due to the winning party. The Portuguese system, through the aforementioned figure of the procuradoria, belongs to the latter group: inclusion of that cost in the taxation of the action and imputation of that cost to the winning party.

The reference to law and economics appears in a footnote to the analysis of the American system: "*As is the case in the United States in the case of actions brought against the State under the 1980 Act called the Equal Access to Justice Act (see Black's Law Dictionary, 6th ed., St. Paul Minnesota, 1990, p. 536). It should be noted that the practice of American Courts, admits exceptions to this system: "[t]he traditional "American rule" is that attorney fees are not awardable to the winning party (i.e. each litigant must pay his own attorney fees) unless statutorily or contractually authorized; however exceptions exist in that award may be made to successful party if the opponent has acted in bad faith [...]" (...).* The Court then adds that the *"the rationality of the American rule tends to be explained, using Law and economics, based on the idea that the opposite rule would discourage people from going to court, by anticipating that increased "transaction cost" consisting of the payment of the opposing party's lawyer's fees (...)."*

In the very same year,[37] in a case of error in buying a used car, the Court refers to law and economics at length: "*the statement that there was a relevant error-vice in the purchase of the vehicle is correct, adequately expressing the formation of the Appellant's will in relation to the purchase of that vehicle. In any case, deepening the relevance of such understanding - that is, of the understanding that had as a consequence the annulability of the deal due to an error concerning the qualities of the object, as these were signalled by the contracting parties at the time of the conclusion of the contract -, we intend to add to the reasoning another line of argument, proper of the so-called law and economics (...). Law and economics, an interesting interdisciplinary topic, with its main foundation in Economic Science over the last*

[36] Case 667/05.3TBGRD.C1, 13.03.2007 The Court would use the same line of argument in 2014 – case 2791/07.9TBFIG.C1.

[37] Case 53/2001.C1, 23.01.2007.

decades, consists of analysing legal rules, institutions and behaviours as restrictions to the free behaviour of economic agents or acts of creation and management of collective goods, whose provision obeys its own rules [...]"The Court then quotes George Akerlof, particularly *"The Market For "Lemons": Quality Uncertainty And The Market Mechanism"* and two Portuguese papers concerning the topic.

In 2009,[38] in a case on paternity investigation, the Court followed the path of the Constitutional Court back in 1996, referring to the behavioral fundamentals of law and economics, like the rational selfishness and the methodological individualism of *homo oeconomicus*: "*The safest thing, finally, when we think of the motives that move each human being, is to stick to the theory of 'law and economics' when it views us all, at the outset, as 'rational egoists'.* In a footnote, the Court adds the following: "*Economic science has always recognized the "methodological individualism" of homo oeconomicus, even speaking, in this respect, of "rationally selfish" behavior. (...)"*

4.3.2 Porto Court of Appeal

As for Porto Court of Appeal, the first reference we found to law and economics dates back to 2017.[39] In a case of conflicts in the fruition of horizontal property rights, the Court critically refers to law and economics in the following terms:

> Dismissing for the moment law and economics stream of legal thought, according to which legal processes, rather than securing rights, should produce the most efficient allocation of resources and which sees human beings as rational utility maximisers" (...) It will always be problematic to claim that law and economics can assume normative functions, since it is not given to the economist to say what goals a society should pursue, or what norms it should adopt. This is because the establishment of purposes, in democratic societies, is a matter always open to dialogic interaction among citizens.
>
> And we must agree that the main social function of law is to prevent conflicts, since the greatest challenge today is not how to live but how to live together. In this way we also have to evaluate the effectiveness of measures to prevent and remove dissension.
>
> Law as a social science is constituted by the set of norms that aim to discipline the behaviour of the individual in society and, to that extent, promote peaceful coexistence.

In 2021,[40] the Court seems to be more open to weighing up the issue in the light of law and economics:

> In fact, from the point of view of the "Law and economics", currently in vogue, in the "ratio" of the ends of the penalty, the only penalty that will have normative validity is the one that makes sense in the economy of the options and utilities valid for society and for the subject, which will be of great benefit in the field of special prevention, since the recovery

[38] Case 1000/06.2TBCNT.C1, 23.06.2009; the same comment appears in the decision on case 2791/07.9TBFIG.C1, dated 25.02.2014.

[39] Case 13721/16.7T8PRT.P1, 27.04.2017.

[40] Case 6928/17.1T9VNG.P1, 14.04.2021.

> of each citizen will be of great interest to him or her and to society as a whole. King D. João II already had an early vision of these theses when, as Garcia de Resende tells us in his chronicle, he gave guidance to the judges of the Superior Courts to avoid applying the death penalty "because a man is very hard to create". Transposing this view to the current legal system, instead of the death penalty, we are obviously dealing with sentences of long duration.

That same year,[41] the Court would use law and economics in a case in which the suspension of execution of a penalty was at stake. The court went a little further than before by quoting the following segment of a paper from Nunes Pires Salpico (The operationality of private enforcement of competition law: deterrence, class actions, and third-party litigation funding" in Revista de Concorrência e Regulação, Lisbon, No. 45 (2021), pp. 104-141): "In fact, the practice of illicit conducts will continue to occur as long as it remains advantageous for the agents, therefore, the best mode of prevention consists in decreasing the incentives, particularly by increasing their costs, in order to suppress the alleged advantage of the illicit."

The following year, also in a case concerning the determination of a penalty, the Court made the same quotation and added the following[42]: *"under this vision, the effects and efficacy of penalties are weighed and measured according to the agent's conditioning, his degree of social and professional integration, his risk factors, gauging his interests that go from his human condition to his personality, going through his habits, whose prognosis of the ends of the penalty cannot dispense with the field of utilities and associated costs. It should be noted that Law and economics is not associated with intimidation (negative general prevention). Rather, the virtualities of this conception allow for a very realistic assessment of the risks involved in the agent and the adequacy of the penalty to the degree of guilt, particularly in the aspects that arise connected with the requirements of special prevention. It cannot be ignored that many defendants with various criminal records reveal risk factors that persist, and the judge cannot ignore these risks when considering the sentence".*

4.3.3 Lisbon Court of Appeal

The Lisbon Court of Appeal is the most fruitful of the Courts of Appeal in using the tools provided by law and economics. This is, to our knowledge, due essentially to the contributions of Judge João Ramos de Sousa who, in various judgements for which he has been *rapporteur*, has applied contributions from law and economics to the legal solution of the specific case, in matters as diverse as the economic analysis of litigation, general contractual clauses, contract law in general, company law, burden of proof, insurance contracts, compensation calculations, parental responsibility regulation, extra-contractual civil liability, civil liability for medical treatment, civil liability for traffic accidents and good faith.

---

[41] Case 1738/15.3PAVNG.P1, 10.11.2021.

[42] Case 319/21.7KRMTS.P1, 22.06.2022.

In 2011,[43] the Court examines the contributions of economic analysis in matters of insolvency law. After describing the successive amendments introduced to the Portuguese insolvency regime as basically enhancers of economic efficiency, by promoting company recovery schemes and the creation of solutions that would allow, in the least bureaucratic way possible, to satisfy the interests of creditors in insolvency proceedings, the Court further explains that "*The insolvency regime must be viewed in the light of Coase's theorem and the theory of the firm. Measures which appear to favour the insolvent, such as the cancellation of the insolvent's debts, are a lesser evil compared to a legal regime which would inevitably lead to the legal and economic liquidation of the insolvent, inducing a chain of insolvencies and the consequent upheaval of the banking system, with very high social costs*". And he ends up by saying that, like all innovations not inspired by Roman Law, there are aspects of the insolvency regime which are alien to traditional legal thought. But it has an unassailable economic rationality and sooner or later "*it will end up being accepted as the way of thinking of jurists in Portugal.*"

In 2012,[44] in a case involving a neighbourhood negative externality (noise caused by the operation of a hotel's air conditioning and swimming pool), the Court analyses the situation from the point of view of the tools provided by law and economics, explaining what externalities, transaction costs and property rights are and then applying these concepts in deciding the case. The Court considers at a certain point that "*The whole procedure, not only procedural, but above all procedural, means very high transaction costs for the parties, who only now have the opportunity to have their rights defined.*" On the other hand, the ruling ponders the following: "*The Hotel plays a key role in the tourism of S.... Its guests and the village in general get benefits from this tourist activity. But the neighbours bear costs arising from the Hotel's air conditioning system and the operation of the swimming pool. Should we close the hotel? That would be absurd. The easiest way to solve these externalities would be to make the owners of the Hotel buy the right to make noise from the neighbours. How would that be done? By buying or expropriating (...) the building next to the Hotel, in order to install support services for the development. As the law does not establish this possibility, the Hotel owners installed the air conditioning system and the swimming pool pumps, and now must eliminate the noise they cause and compensate the nuisance caused. But all of these are huge transaction costs that translate into a delay in the resolution of the case in court.*" Finally, the court considers that the main question put forward by the case is "*the question of correcting the system of justice that intervenes in conflict situations*" and, in that respect, that "*law and economics is not just any theory of law: it is first and foremost a critical practice of law*". "*An investment made in 2000 is not defined in 2012 because the law does not provide a clear and rapid solution to property conflicts. It is this "problem" that is under consideration here: Hic Rhodus, hic salta!*"

[43] Case 1719/10.3TBALQ-D.L1-1, 06.12.2011.

[44] Case 160/04.1TBSSB.L1-1, 18.09.2012.

Still in 2012,[45] in a case on parental responsibility, the Court alludes to the contributions of Robert Mnookin and L. Kornhaser against the principle of the "best interests of the child". Thus: "*Mnookin (1973), Mnookin (1975) and then Mnookin/Kornhauser (1979), followed by Jon Elster himself (1989) have argued that the principle of the best interests of the child is an indeterminate principle. That is: there is no objective reason why we should conclude what the best interests of the child are. Because the best interests of the child, in practice, are nothing more than the interests of the parent disguised as the best interests of the child. The child's interest is that the parents do not fight over it, or that they are not in conflict independently of it, and this interest the court can never impose on the parents. So, in defining the best interest of the child, the judge always ends up making choices of his or her own preference... which he or she assigns superiorly to the child. (…) As with adults, the child's interest is a legal fiction constructed in court, which may not be the actual preference of the person concerned. As in so many other cases, legislative thinking constructs here a legal fiction that has a rhetorical function in the judicial narrative. That is: it serves to persuade the audience to which the judge is addressing (the lawyers, the judicial inspector, the higher court) of the correctness of his decision.*" Bringing up the argument is, by itself, a breakthrough facing traditional jurisprudence.

Also in 2012,[46] the Court again used the principle of good faith to decide a case about general contract law. Starting from the informational asymmetry between the parties, and considering that a violation of the principle of good faith might be at stake when such asymmetry is exploited, the Court considered that *"Imposing on the parties to use the utmost sincerity in providing information to the counterparty - in particular by not disguising the defects of the situation -, is thus a general principle of contract law, to avoid asymmetry of information and the consequent imbalance of benefits."* The case at hand involved a contract between a banking institution and its clients by which the bank imposed the rounding up of the interest rate, without its customers being able to immediately perceive the future economic consequences of such provision: as a result of this upward rounding they would end up losing the advantages of a promised low interest rate, a practice that the court considered to be *"compensatory for the Bank but clearly prejudicial to the final consumer"*. The Court concluded that the said clauses *"generate a disproportionate imbalance to the detriment of the contracting party, translated into an economic loss for the latter and, on the other hand, an exclusive benefit for the Defendant, who reaps the increased interest rate"* and that this imbalance translated *"into a withholding of information at the time of signing the contract and a gross violation of the principle of good faith, which must always govern the conclusion of these banking contracts"*, thus verifying a *"situation of asymmetric information which the law does not permit"*, for which reason it considered that the aforementioned general contractual clauses were *"obviously prohibited"*.

[45] Case 1900/05.7TBSXL-E.L1-1, 22.05.2012.

[46] Case 2839/08.0YXLSB.L1-1, 27.03.2012.

In the following year,[47] in a case of non-contractual civil liability for vehicle collision, the Court examined the economic efficiency of the legislation intended to distribute and reduce the risk of losses resulting from accidents, directing its critical appraisal not only to the system of civil liability for risk but above all to insurance law. The Court pointed out that "*insurance law has, from the very beginning of law and economics, been the target of fierce criticism for economic inefficiency, because it contributes to increasing the risk of accidents, in particular the risk of traffic accidents, by the sense of immunity it gives to insured persons and goods, even at the cost of excesses and ever higher insurance premiums. This turns insurance law into a great business for insurers, but does not create a general situation of greater security in society*." The Court further addresses the issue from the point of view of public choice theory, noting that "*The road traffic accident liability regime is closely intertwined with insurance law and the insurance business, which acts as a pressure group, seeking to influence liability and insurance legislation - in order to increase its sources of income, at the expense of the premiums and other economic transfers it receives from the policyholders who sustain it. Here, as in other areas of social life, policyholders are an inorganic plurality of people with few means to influence legislation, whereas the so-called 'insurance industry' is strongly centralised and organised to assert its particular interests vis-à-vis the Government and Parliament*." Finally, the Court also considers that "*law and economics lays bare a fundamental vice in the traditional conception of civil liability, a vice that urgently needs to be corrected, insofar as it removes responsibility from the legislative, executive and judicial powers for intervention in reducing collective problems*"—referring to the social cost of traffic accidents.

In 2014,[48] the Court examined the system of civil liability for road accidents. In the case at hand, the Court considered that the motorway concessionaire had the burden of proof of compliance with its safety obligations and that, although the applicable legal regime did not create objective liability for the concessionaire in case of accidents on motorways, it made it so difficult to rebut this presumption of fault of the concessionaire that one could speak of a regime of "*quasi-objective liability or almost risk liability*", the court ruled that the concessionaire was liable and that its insurer would have to provide compensation to the victims, adding that "*compensation for these accidents represents, after all, a relatively small expense in these losses, which are usually transferred from the motorist to the motorway concessionaire, and from the latter to the insurer*." Seeking a justification for a legal regime which is apparently so adverse to the concessionaire and its insurer, the Court then turns to an economic analysis of urban planning law and, within this, road law. Using Calabresi's studies, the Court identifies three main methods of risk distribution from the point of view of their ability to influence the frequency and severity of road accidents: (i) risk-spreading, (ii) deep-pocket and (iii) deterrence: "*Risk-spreading, or diffusion of risk, results from generous social security schemes,*

[47] Case 1721/11.8TVLSB.L1-1, 26.02.2013.

[48] Case 6185/08.0TBVFX.L1-1, 27.05.2014.

which make society at large bear the costs of accidents: and thus no one is prompted to take serious measures to prevent them. One way of spreading risk is by making companies responsible: by making them responsible for the damage caused by accidents, drivers feel exempt from the need to prevent them. Deep-pocketedness consists in making those who are best able to bear the losses bear them. This is therefore a method of redistributing income, such as social security contributions. Deterrence, or dissuasion, consists of making the losses fall on the activities that cause the accidents. This method seeks to decide which activity causes accidents and then lets the market determine whether these activities justify the social cost of compensating for the resulting losses. Thus, accident costs are treated as one of the costs incurred by the driver who has an accident, a driver who has to balance the benefits of using a particular type of car against its costs, such as workshop, fuel and possible accidents." The Court then went on to state that the system adopted by the Portuguese law, "*which, to a large extent, makes concessionaires liable for accidents on motorways, holding them almost always responsible for accidents occurring on motorways, but allowing them to transfer the respective liability to an insurer, is, in the end, a system of risk-spreading but disguised as deep-pocket. After all, it is not the concessionaire who bears the risk, but the insurer, and this explains the zeal with which F, called to action, came here to defend the position of B. But, in essence, it is not the concessionaire, and not even the insurer, who socially bears the losses of accidents on motorways, it is society as a whole, that is, the citizens who pay their taxes and in particular the insured who pay the insurance premiums.*"

In 2015,[49] in a case on interest rate swaps, which had become famous in the context of the subprime crisis, the Court uses public choice theory to make the point that "*faced with the capture of legislators by economic and financial power, the Court, as the regulator of society, intervenes to establish rules that restore the conditions of negotiating equality, for example, between an insurer and the owner of a car, between a telecommunications operator and its customers, between a bank and a company seeking to obtain financing.*"

That same year,[50] in a case involving the invalidity of general contractual clauses, the Court again turned to law and economics to refer to the critical analysis carried out in that context using the tools of game theory. It starts by contrasting traditional legal theory, mainly concerned with aspects of equality and balance between the parties from an essentially abstract point of view, with law and economics, the latter focusing more on concrete aspects of the factual relationship established between the contractual subjects, where differences in both economic and bargaining power emerge as well as the related transaction costs. The Court ends up deciding, in line with this regime, that a certain clause should be considered unwritten because it was not adequately communicated and negotiated between the parties. Law and economics is used as explanatory support for the regime of general contractual clauses, explaining its raison d'être and reinforcing the reasons why it is important, when

[49] Case 540/11.6TVLSB.L2-1, 28.04.2015.

[50] Case 766/14.0TVLSB.L1-1, 03.03.2015.

faced with this type of clause, to offer special protection to the weaker party in the contract.[51]

That same year,[52] the Court delivered a judgment with extensive reference to law and economics in the context of contract theory, largely like the one referred to in the previous judgment, but with an additional glimpse on good faith: "*In law and economics, the principle of good faith is approached from the point of view of asymmetric information theory. Information is asymmetric when in a negotiation one party has more or better information than the other: this creates an imbalance of bargaining power, which may lead to a situation of market failure. (…) In asymmetric information, at least one of the parties does not have all possible information about the circumstances in which it is negotiating. This situation is particularly critical where one party deliberately conceals those circumstances from the other, or deliberately or even fraudulently misrepresents them. In insurance fraud, the margin between civil intent and criminal intent can become blurred.*" Further on, the Court turns to an economic analysis of the franchise contract. "*From the point of view of law and economics, to invest is to incur immediate costs in expectation of future benefits. Seen in this light, investments, and the contracts in which they are formalised, occur everywhere in the capitalist mode of development (…) But contracts are not always a leap in the dark: they are not so when the investing entrepreneur has reasonable knowledge of his situation and above all the conditions of the market in which he is going to invest. In this case, the investment is defined as what in game theory is called a complete information move. (…) The franchisor has reasonable knowledge of the market and has working methods which he makes available to the franchisee. (…) In a world where entrepreneurs are subject to transaction costs (Coase, 1937), the franchise contract avoids heavy charges for the franchisee*

[51] "*The development of modern capitalist production has created mass production systems. As A.W.Katz (1998,3:502) notes, just as fixed costs and economies of scale lead manufacturers to develop standardized products in the industrial sector, so the same constraints lead service providers to develop standardized contracts to be signed by their customers. Under a simple slogan: take it or leave it.*

In a competitive market, those interested in contracting a service have contractual alternatives available to them. But what happens is that we are often in a market with little or no competition, oligopolistic or even monopolistic, where the customer has no real alternative choice of supplier. There are also situations of asymmetric information that further call into question the already fragile conditions for contract negotiation.

This second loss of market efficiency results from the asymmetric information of suppliers and customers: suppliers know perfectly well the quality of the goods and services they supply, but customers are only vaguely aware of it (this phenomenon was described by Akerloff, 1970, as the market for lemons, the market of "barrettes"). Finally, a third loss of efficiency results from the bargaining power of the supplier, who imposes unfair terms in standard contracts.

Then the State, as regulator of society, intervenes to establish norms that restore the conditions of negotiating equality that is possible, for example, between an insurance company and the owner of a car, between a telecommunications operator and its customers, between a bank and a company seeking to obtain financing. If the supplier is a large company, it will certainly have a legal department to prepare certain standard contracts for it and include terms which are always identical, establishing the legal situation in its favour: these are the general contractual terms."

[52] Case 1300/12.2TVLSB.L1-1, 01.12.2015.

with the definition of the business model, market research and knowledge of customers. The franchisor also escapes the risks of investment and control expenses of a network of agencies located far from the company's headquarters and controls the competition in each area of action of the franchisees, preventing unfair competition; if the business model he proposes is original and has conditions for great expansion in the market, he acts as a supplier in a monopoly regime. Hence the expansion of the first type of franchise: it corresponds to the success of the modern mode of capitalist development (…)

Transaction cost analysis shows that contractual clauses that in traditional contracts would be considered illegitimate have important implications for economic efficiency in franchise contracts - Klein 1995. Therefore, the US courts soon came to adopt a liberal criterion in matters of termination of these contracts."

Further on, the Court also uses law and economics to examine long-term contracts, describing them as more complex contracts, more prone to gaps and, consequently, to greater conflicts between the parties. "*The legal and economic reality of long-term contracts has radically changed the way parties and courts view the notion of contract. The classic notion of the contract saw it as a relationship between abstract legal persons, in which the fundamental issue was to guarantee the equality of positions; law and economics takes account of the insufficiency of this traditional paradigm when contracts are drawn up for durations of ten or twenty years (…) thus, the courts are obliged to intervene in order to solve any problems, under penalty of the system's economic inefficiency. And also, the parties feel the need to establish expeditious procedures to resolve doubts and conflicts that will arise during the time the contract is executed: for example, arbitration, recourse to an arbitration tribunal. This solution is very common in franchise contracts.*"

In 2016,[53] in a judgment on the nullity of a first instance decision, the Court refers at length to law and economics, introducing it to the reader from its beginnings, presenting Coase's Theorem and outlining the theses that follow from it. He then goes on to talk about the economic analysis of litigation, contrasting the way in which traditional legal theory viewed conflict with the more modern vision stemming from economic analysis: "*traditional legal theory viewed conflicts between individuals as a matter of applying the law, established by an abstract legislator, and olimpically applied by the Court in a logic of legal syllogism. It ignored conflicts between individuals, relegating them to an area of knowledge outside legal science, the domain of so-called judicial sociology. It presumed the equality of the parties in the legal relationship.*

But law and economics recognises and starts from the problem of the inequality of the parties and the power relations that this inequality necessarily generates. Law and economics focus its concerns on the economic efficiency aspect of the legal system and the legislation with which it operates; the aspect of the balance between the parties remains but is now reinforced from the point of view of economic reality,

[53] Case 2904/06.8TVLSB.L1-1, 16.02.2016.

relative transaction costs and the bargaining strength (bargaining power) of each contracting party.

Law and economics, in terms of the litigation process, shifts the question from the measures to be taken in relation to the behaviour of individuals to the measures to be taken in relation to the functioning of the justice system itself, which is called upon to intervene in conflict situations.

This critical analysis is based on considerations of the microeconomic theory of externalities, economies of scale and public goods. To the unpleasant surprise of classical dogmatics, legal analysis thus becomes a chapter of microeconomic analysis.

Above all, a requirement of the law and economics is the elimination of economically inefficient legal regimes. Here, the traditional conception of the legal relationship proves to be economically inefficient because it does not contain a mechanism that sufficiently dissuades the practice of illicit acts, but rather rewards the practice of these illicit acts by the economically stronger party. It is therefore necessary to restore the balance of legal situations.

This raises the question not only of repairing the particular situation, the conflict that is brought before the court, but above all of correcting the justice system that intervenes in conflict situations. Law and economics, then, is not just any theory of law: it is first and foremost a critical practice of law.

The law and economics and of the judicial process shows that litigation obeys criteria of rationality (Miguel Patrício 2005:*13). The so-called judicial process is itself a strategic game that develops according to the logic of game theory (Sousa* 2003:*388). This is usually studied in the discipline of applied mathematics called operational research.*

A strategic game is a trial in which the fate of one or several people is decided according to the strategy of the prosecution and the strategy of the defence, which they adopt towards each other (…).

From the point of view of game theory, it can be said that in the trial each one of the antagonists presents to the judge the proposal of reconstruction of the past that supposes to assure him the maximum gains and/or the minimum losses. The purpose of the trial, as a rhetorical game and a process of literary creation, is to establish, according to certain heuristic rules, an official, definitive version of the legal narrative. Once this is defined, the conditions are created for the judge to determine the gains and losses of each antagonist (…)."

In 2017,[54] in a Judgment on insurance contracts, the Court states that "*the primary concern of law and economics is to eliminate economically inefficient legal regimes*" and then critically depicts the statutory civil liability provision of Portuguese civil law, considering that it proves to be "*in many areas economically inefficient because it does not contain a sufficiently deterrent mechanism to the commission of torts*."

[54] Case 25093/13.7T2SNT.L1-1, 17.10.2017.

In 2017,[55] the Court was called upon to decide a case of civil liability for medical treatment, finding that such system of civil liability for medical treatment needed to be corrected in the light of the consideration of primarily objective liability, as shown by law and economics and the legislative experience of the most economically advanced countries. The Court emphasized that the health services market is not competitive, and that the patient has no real alternatives to choose from. Additionally, the Court considered that there are situations of asymmetric information that unbalance the conditions of negotiation of contracts: the supplier ends up imposing on the client the contractual conditions only he understands. He then continued to say that the medical liability system, *i.e.* a fault-based system of responsibility, only makes sense if its raison d'être is to impose a cost on doctors which is a deterrent to malpractice and an incentive to professional care. On the other hand, if the focus is to compensate patients who are victims of diagnostic and therapeutic errors, then a fault-based medical liability system will be inefficient because it will induce the dragging out of liability procedures and, consequently, the delay in compensating victims. The accused doctor may have an interest in dragging out the discussion and the insurance company, which will have its own litigation team, certainly will have an interest in doing so: the later it pays, the better, and the management of the process will represent a marginal cost increase. The system is particularly inefficient because it does not favor agreement between the parties, but rather litigation. It is also a system that favors the most economically powerful patient-consumer, who will more easily bear the costs (including the opportunity cost) of a system that is slow in defining responsibilities and allocating compensation.

Alluding to the specific case, the Court explained that this was precisely what happened: "*the energy with which the defendant doctors and the insurer defended themselves against the action. After all, it is not a question of compensating the plaintiff, it is a question of defending the prestige of the clinic or hospital and the doctors who did everything they could to cure her; and if the diagnosis and the subsequent therapeutic strategy adopted did not work, this was only due to factors independent of that diagnosis and therapy. Therefore, future patients can rest assured: they will consider their treatment at the clinic or hospital, whether public or private, to be well paid. From this point of view, the plaintiff's compensation is of totally secondary importance.*"

Going even further, the Court explains that the system of civil liability does, indeed, have a merit: that of signaling to patients the good and the bad medical services providers. If it were possible to have an administrative method of monitoring medical quality, such as a system of regular accreditation, the information which this would give patients would enable them to make informed choices. However, the Court acknowledges, "the medical profession is extremely averse to control by its professional colleagues. And the Medical Associations (in all countries with governing bodies elected exclusively by the doctors themselves without intervention by

[55] Case 1447/12.5TVLSB.L1-1, 26.04.2017.

the citizens, as if they were trade unions) are accused of covering up for them rather than controlling them."

The Court clarifies, finally, that these are the reasons why other countries, such as Sweden and New Zealand, have adopted alternative ways of resolving these conflicts: solutions in which civil liability is based primarily on risk, and in which fault plays an insignificant role.

The Court eventually decided in favour of the patient, considering that medical responsibility did not disappear as a result of signing a document with an exclusion of responsibility clause in which the doctor only guaranteed to do the best he/she could within the *legis artis*, without being able to guarantee the success of the operation.

4.4 Supreme Administrative Court

As for the Supreme Administrative Court, the highest body in the hierarchy of the courts of administrative and tax jurisdiction, we found no record of references to law and economics. The same applies to the Guimarães Court of Appeal, the Évora Court of Appeal and the Northern Administrative Central Court.

4.5 Courts of Appeal Within the Administrative and Tax Jurisdiction

Within the administrative and tax jurisdiction, we found references only by the Southern Central Administrative Court, in judgments of 2014, 2016 and 2018. In 2014,[56] the Court starts a trend which it will use, with adaptations, in several other judgments. After the opening statement and before beginning the operative part of the judgment, the Court states the following:

> The other procedural steps having been completed, it is now important to consider and decide in conference. We will bear in mind the following: (i) the primacy of the material democratic and social State of Law, in a context of a political and economic life submitted to the Common Good and to the supreme and equal Dignity of each person; (ii) the ethical-legal values from the point of view of our Fundamental Law and the principles or structural maxims in force, such as those of Juridicity, Equality and Proportionality.(…)" In a footnote, the Court refers to law and economics as follows: "All social coexistence and all social institutions are conditioned by Material Justice and the Equal Dignity of every Human Being (a value underlined and developed by I. KANT in the still essential "Critique of Practical Reason" of 1788, or in the simpler version, "Fundamentation of the Metaphysics of Customs", of 1785), which implies equality of rights and duties for all and also equality of opportunities for all people (cf. J. RAWLS, Uma Teoria da Justiça, 2nd ed.)

---

[56] Case 11434/14, 06.11.2014; Case 11427/14, 11.09.2014; Case 11020/14, 25.09.2014; Case 11043/14, 25.09. 2014.

In 2016, the trend continues, albeit with some fine-tuning of the discourse.[57] Before deciding, the Court states the following: "To decide, this high court has our Constitution omnipresent as the synthesis of the prevailing ideva-alue of Law, whose political model is of an ethical-humanistic nature and whose social-economic model is that of the social market economy supported by Law (models that are separate from the so-called "law and economics" of American origin, but close to a cultural nature of public power). (…)"

In 2018, a very similar reference is found as the Court states that[58]: "*We have omnipresent that: a) democracy is not "only" a government consented by the people, in which the latter has little or difficult access to information about public activities; b) democratic political power should not be submitted to economic power and financial power, national or international; c) the Constitution does not allow for a functionalist vision of Law, as it is the case of the North-American neoliberal and efficientist theory of the so-called "law and economics", started in 1960 with the theorem of R. H. Coase. The Constitution, which is concretised especially by administrative law, comprises a structural vision, such as Kelsen's or Bobbio's (…) and even a systemic perspective such as Luhmann's (…)*". Highly debatable, to say the least.

5 Legislation

Finally, there are some signs of a greater awareness of the advantages of using economic instruments in normative production in some legislative instruments created over the last years. Though one cannot say that law and economics is employed as a tool in areas such as policy making, legislative drafting or law reform—far from that—there are some important baby steps worth mentioning.

On the one hand, there are some examples of mandatory use of cost benefit analysis now in force: the Administrative Procedural Code, revised in 2015, which since then contains a provision regarding administrative regulations stating that "*regulations shall be adopted on the basis of a project, accompanied by a reasoned justification note, which shall include the weighting of the costs and benefits of the measures designed.*" Secondly, the Public Procurement Code, approved in 2008, provides that, in cases of contracts above € 5.000.000,00, or, in the case of partnerships for innovation, of contracts above € 2.500.000,00., the decision to contract shall be justified based on a cost-benefit analysis.

On the other hand, some important steps have been made concerning regulatory impact evaluation. In 2017, the government approved a model of *ex ante* evaluation to identify, measure and estimate costs (financial, transaction, opportunity costs) derived from legislation approved by the government with a view to ponder simpler

[57] Case 12705/15, 19.05.2016.

[58] Case 353/17.1BESNT, 31.01.2018.

alternatives and to rationally enhance overall efficiency. The model has, since then, been subject to some changes aimed at enhancing the scope of legislative evaluation, following a path of sophistication and diversification necessary to reinforce its application in a standardized way. To implement and coordinate the application of the program of impact assessment, the government created a technical unit to coordinate it (UTAIL), which also represented Portugal in international *fora* concerning the topic of better regulation. In 2021, UTAIL was integrated in PlanAPP—the Competence Centre for Planning, Policy and Foresight in Public Administration—but maintaining its previous role. In a country which was not used to doing cost-benefit analysis within the public administration, with all the barriers that represents, whether practical or cultural, the implementation of this model of *ex ante* and, in particular cases, *ex post*, evaluation is a significant change—for the better.

6 Conclusions

Although some evolution has occurred along the past twenty years, law and economics is still far from current knowledge and speech within the relevant communities in Portugal, be it academia, the courts, or public administration. There is a shortage of academic debate and teaching of the subject and consequently very little use of economic thinking within the field of law. There are, however, some indicators of change, mostly stemming from the growing interest in the field on the part of both scholars and students. Courts are still very far from standardized acknowledgement of the field—with very few exceptions—but the same is not true in the legislative and executive branches of the State, where there are some important signs of greater awareness to the advantages of using economic instruments in both the creation and application of law.

References

Araújo F (2000) A Retórica da Economia. Os Desafios de McCloskey. In AA.VV., Estudos em Homenagem ao Professor Doutor Pedro Soares Martinez, I, Almedina, Coimbra, pp 193–272

Araújo, F (2001) Adam Smith. O Conceito Mecanicista de Liberdade

Araújo F (2002), O Problema Económico do Controlo das Rendas no Arrendamento para Habitação. In Cordeiro, A.M., L.M. Leitão & J.C. Gomes (orgs.), Estudos em homenagem ao Professor Doutor Inocêncio Galvão Telles, Vol. III – Direito do Arrendamento Urbano, Almedina, Coimbra, pp 177–236

Araújo F (2005) Da Tutela Negativa da Confiança ao «Paradoxo da Indemnização»: Uma Análise Económica dos Contratos. In Miranda J, Pinheiro LL, Vicente DM (orgs.), Estudos em Memória do Professor Doutor António Marques dos Santos, II, Almedina, Coimbra, pp 441–583

Araújo F (2007a) Teoria Económica do Contrato. Almedina, Coimbra

Araújo F (2007b) A Eficiência do «Anti-Seguro» e da «Responsabilidade Decrescente»: Uma Análise Económica dos Contratos – II. In Cunha, P.P. (org.) Estudos em Homenagem ao Professor Doutor António de Sousa Franco, Almedina, Coimbra, pp 905–1004

Araújo F (2008a) Análise Económica do Direito. Programa e Guia de Estudo, Almedina, Coimbra
Araújo F (2008b) A Tragédia dos Baldios e dos Anti-Baldios. O Problema Económico do Nível Óptimo de Apropriação. Almedina, Coimbra
Calabresi G (2016) The future of law and economics. essays in reform and recollection. Yale University Press, New Haven, London
Cordeiro AM (2005) Tratado de Direito Civil Português, I – Parte Geral, Tomo I. 3rd edn. Almedina, Coimbra
Franco AS (1992) Análise Económica do Direito: Exercício Intelectual ou Fonte de Ensinamento? Sub Judice 2:63–70
Freire PV (2015) Análise Económica dos Programas de Clemência no Direito da Concorrência. RJLB 1:191–203
Freire PV (2020) Contrato de Seguro e Eficiência Económica. In Ricardo Lupion; Fernando Araujo (Orgs.) Direito, Tecnologia e Empreendedorismo. Uma Visão Luso-Brasileira, Editora Fi, Porto Alegre, pp. 558–578
Freire PV (2021) Análise Económica do Mercado de Trabalho: Breves Notas. Revista Internacional de Direito do Trabalho 1(1):1203–1217
Garoupa N (2003a) Optimal law enforcement when victims are rational players. Econ Gov 2:231–242
Garoupa N (2003b) Crime and social norms. Portuguese Econ J 2:131–144
Garoupa N (2005) Análise Económica do Direito. Legislação: Cadernos de Ciência e Legislação 22:23–37
Garoupa N (2006) Limites ideológicos e morais à avaliação económica da legislação. Cadernos de Ciência de Legislação 42/43:83–102
Garoupa N (2008) Providing a framework for reforming the legal profession: insights from the European experience. Eur Bus Org Law Rev (EBOR) 9(3):463–495
Garoupa N (2014a) Globalization and deregulation of legal services. Int Rev Law Econ 38:77–86
Garoupa N (2014b) Economic theory of criminal behavior. Encyclopedia of Criminology and Criminal Justice. Springer, New York
Garoupa N (2017) Explaining the standard of proof in criminal law: a new insight. Supreme Court Econ Rev 25(1):111–122
Miller GP (2011) Law and economics versus law and economics. ABI Law Rev 19(2011):459–460
Monteiro JS (1981) Análise Económica do Direito. Boletim da Faculdade de Direito da Universidade de Coimbra 57:247–251
Moura e Silva M (2000a) EC Competition Law and the Market for Exclusionary Rights. In AA.VV. (2000) Estudos Jurídicos e Económicos em Homenagem ao Professor João Lumbrales, Faculdade de Direito da Universidade de Lisboa - Coimbra Editora, Coimbra, pp 815–852
Moura e Silva M (2000b) Law and economics in Portugal. In BOUCKAERT, Boudewijn; DE GEEST, Gerrit, (orgs.) Encyclopedia of law and economics, Vol. I, Edward Elgar, Cheltenham, pp. 313-317
Patrício M (2005) Análise Económica da Litigância, Almedina, Coimbra
Patrício M (2015) Análise Económica das Formas Alternativas de Arbitragem. RLBJ 1(5):1161–1188
Patrício M (2017) Análise Económica da Responsabilidade Civil Médica. Lisbon Law Editions, AAFDL Editora, Lisboa
Pinto PM (2008) Sobre a alegada "Superação" do Direito pela análise económica (ilustrada com a análise das medidas da indemnização contratual). In Nunes AJA, Coutinho JNM. O direito e o futuro – o futuro do direito. Almedina, Coimbra, pp 169–211
Rodrigues V (2007) Análise Económica do Direito. Uma introdução. Almedina, Coimbra
Saraiva R (2014) Behavioural economics insights for international environmental law. In: Sancin V, Kovič Dine M (eds) International environmental law: contemporary concerns and challenges in 2014. GV Založba, Ljubljana
Saraiva R (2016) Academic Fraud at Hogwarts – behavioural law and economics: lessons for 'Muggles' of all ages. In: Mathis K, Tor A (eds) Nudging – possibilities, limitations and

applications in european law and economics. Law and economics in European Legal Scholarship, vol. III, chap. 17. Springer, Cham, pp 343–374
Saraiva R (2017) Behavioural and evolutionary approach to the law and economics of cap-and-trade. In: Mathis K, Huber B (eds) Environmental law and economics. Law and economics in European Legal Scholarship, vol 4. Springer, Cham, pp 405–435
Sousa JR (1992a) Ejan Mackaay, La Règle Juridique Observée par le Prisme de L'Economiste - Book Review. Sub Judice 2:44–46
Sousa JR (1992b) Frank Easterbrook, criminal procedure as a market system – Book Review. Sub Judice 2:47–49
Sousa JR (1992c) James Buchanan, politics without romance - Book Review. Sub Judice 2:50–52
Sousa JR (2003) Julgamento sem Romance: Processo Penal, Literatura Jurídica e Teoria dos Jogos. Revista Portuguesa de Ciência Criminal 13(3):387–416

Raquel Franco is Guest Assistant Professor at the Faculty of Law of the University of Lisbon where she currently teaches several economic disciplines. With a PhD in behavioural economics and public policies, that is her main topic of research. In addition to teaching and research, she is also a lawyer and an arbitrator.

MIX
Papier aus verantwortungsvollen Quellen
Paper from responsible sources
FSC® C105338
FSC
www.fsc.org

If you have any concerns about our products,
you can contact us on
ProductSafety@springernature.com

In case Publisher is established outside the EU,
the EU authorized representative is:
Springer Nature Customer Service Center GmbH
Europaplatz 3, 69115 Heidelberg, Germany

Printed by Libri Plureos GmbH
in Hamburg, Germany